Web Activities

The following Web Activities are available on the Companion Website:

Language in Mind

An Introduction to
Psycholinguistics

Language in Mind
An Introduction to Psycholinguistics

JULIE SEDIVY *University of Calgary*

 SINAUER ASSOCIATES, INC. • Publishers • Sunderland, Massachusetts • USA

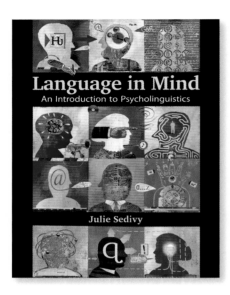

About the Cover Artist

Bruno Mallart is a talented European artist whose work has appeared in many of the world's premier publications, including *The New York Times*, *The Wall Street Journal*, and the *New Scientist*, to name a few. A freelance illustrator since 1986, Mallart first worked for several children's book publishers and advertising agencies using a classic, realistic watercolor and ink style. Later he began working in a more imaginative way, inventing a unique mix of drawing, painting, and collage. His work speaks of a surrealistic and absurd world that engages the viewer's imagination and sense of fun.

Despite the recurring use of the brain in his art, Mallart's background is not scientific (though both his parents were neurobiologists). He uses the brain as a symbol for abstract concepts such as intelligence, thinking, feeling, ideas, and, as seen here, human language and communication. His abstract representations beautifully illustrate the topics of *Language in Mind*; his work is seen not only on the book's cover, but in the distinctive chapter-opening images and as "icons" marking the book's various features. To see more of Bruno Mallart's art, please visit his website: www.brunomallart.com.

Language in Mind: An Introduction to Psycholinguistics

Copyright © 2014 by Sinauer Associates, Inc. All rights reserved.

This book may not be reproduced in whole or in part without permission from the Publisher. Address inquiries and orders to:

Sinauer Associates, Inc., 23 Plumtree Road PO Box 407, Sunderland, MA 01375 U.S.A.

Inquiries: publish@sinauer.com

Orders: orders@sinauer.com

FAX: 413-549-1118

www.sinauer.com

Library of Congress Cataloging-in-Publication Data
Sedivy, Julie.
    Language in mind : an introduction to psycholinguistics / Julie Sedivy --
First Edition.
        pages cm
    Includes index.
    ISBN 978-0-87893-598-7
1. Psycholinguistics. 2. Cognition. I. Title.
    BF455.S3134 2014
    401'.9--dc23   2014002893

Printed in China

5 4 3 2 1

For My Students

Brief Contents

Contents

CHAPTER 4
Learning Sound Patterns 105

CHAPTER 5
Learning Words 145

CHAPTER 6
Learning the Structure of Sentences 185

CHAPTER 7
Word Recognition 233

CHAPTER 8
Understanding Sentence Structure and Meaning 279

CHAPTER 12
Language Diversity 471

Note to Instructors

As psycholinguists, we get to study and teach some of the most riveting material in the scientific world. One of our greatest desires is surely that our students will come to have an inkling of why it is that this material is so endlessly absorbing, and what it can reveal about fundamental aspects of ourselves and how we interact with each other. That desire certainly provided the impetus for this textbook.

As I see it, a textbook should be a starting point—an opening conversation that provokes curiosity, and a map for what to explore next. This book is intended to be accessible to students with no prior background in linguistics or psycholinguistics. For some psychology students, it may accompany the only course about language they will ever take. What should such students get out of a course in psycholinguistics? With any luck, they'll acquire an ability to be intelligently analytical about the linguistic waters in which they will swim daily for the rest of their lives; an appreciation for some of the questions that preoccupy researchers who work in this young, rapidly changing field; and enough background to be able to maintain an ongoing interest in significant new developments in the field. Some students, of course, will wind up exploring the literature at close range, perhaps even participating in it as researchers. These students can benefit from an introductory textbook that lays out some of the important debates, integrates insights from its various subdisciplines, and points to the many threads of research that have yet to be unraveled.

Throughout this book, I've tried to encourage students to connect psycholinguistic theories and findings to observations about everyday language phenomena. In choosing the material for the text, I've been less concerned with giving students a snapshot of the latest "greatest hits" in research than with providing an overall conceptual framework for why it is that researchers care about the questions that they've chosen to pursue. My goal has been to make it as easy as possible for students to approach the primary literature on their own. (In my own classes, I've used each chapter as a preamble to journal articles that are subsequently assigned as readings.) I've tried to place an emphasis not just on what psycholinguists know (or think they know), but on how they've come to know it. Experimental methods are described at length, and numerous figures throughout the book lay out the procedural details, example stimuli, and results from some of the experiments discussed in the chapters. I've also tried to give students a balanced view of the diverging perspectives and opinions within the field (even though, naturally, I subscribe to my own favorite theories), and a realistic sense of the limits to our current knowledge.

And if, along the way, students happen to develop the notion that this stuff is really, really cool—well, I would not mind that one bit.

Thanks!

I hope that everyone understands that on the cover of this book, where it says "Julie Sedivy," this is shorthand for "Julie Sedivy and throngs of smart, insightful people who cared enough about this book to spend some portion of their brief lives bringing it into the world."

I'm indebted to the numerous scholars who generously took time from their chronically overworked lives to read and comment on parts of this book. Their involvement has improved the book enormously. (Naturally, I'm to blame for any remaining shortcomings of the book, which the reader is warmly encouraged to point out to me so I can fix them in any subsequent editions.) Heartfelt thanks to the following reviewers:

Erin Ament, The College of William and Mary

Janet Andrews, Vassar College

Stephanie Archer, University of Warwick

Jennifer Arnold, University of North Carolina, Chapel Hill

Julie Boland, University of Michigan

Craig Chambers, University of Toronto

Morten Christiansen, Cornell University

Suzanne Curtin, University of Calgary

Delphine Dahan, University of Pennsylvania

Thomas Farmer, Univerity of Iowa

Vic Ferreira, University of California, San Diego

Alex Fine, University of Rochester

W. Tecumseh Fitch, University of Vienna

Carol Fowler, University of Connecticut, Emeritus

Silvia Gennari, University of York

LouAnn Gerken, University of Arizona

Richard Gerrig, State Univerity of New York, Stony Brook

Ted Gibson, M.I.T.

Matt Goldrick, Northwestern University

Zenzi Griffin, University of Texas, Austin

Greg Hickok, University of California, Irvine

Carla Hudson Kam, University of British Columbia

Kiwako Ito, Ohio State University

T. Florian Jaeger, University of Rochester

Michael Kaschak, Florida State University

Heidi Lorimor, Bucknell University

Max Louwers, University of Memphis

Maryellen MacDonald, University of Wisconsin, Madison

Jim Magnuson, University of Connecticut

Utako Minai, University of Kansas

Emily Myers, Univerity of Connecticut

Janet Nicol, University of Arizona

Lisa Pearl, University of California, Irvine

Hannah Rohde, University of Edinburgh

Chehalis Strapp, Western Oregon University

Margaret Thomas, Boston College

John Trueswell, University of Pennsylvania

Katherine White, University of Waterloo

Eiling Yee, University of Connecticut

A special thanks to Jennifer Arnold and Jan Andrews for taking this book out for a spin in the classroom in its earlier versions, to their students and my own at the University of Calgary for providing valuable comments.

In today's publishing climate, it's become common to question whether book publishers contribute much in the way of "added value" to a book. The question is warranted in some cases—but most definitely not in this one. The editorial team at Sinauer Associates has been an utter joy to work with from the very first day, showing a single-minded devotion to producing the best book we possibly could. My collaborators at Sinauer have provided skills and expertise that are far, far outside of my domain, and lavished attention on the smallest details of the book. Thanks to: Sydney Carroll, who shared the vision for this book, and kept its fires stoked; Carol Wigg, who, as production editor, knows everything; Lou Doucette, who spotted the hanging threads and varnished up the prose; Jefferson Johnson, who designed exactly the kind of book I would have wanted to design, if only I had the talent; Elizabeth Morales, David McIntyre, and Chris Small for their intelligent attention to the visual elements of the book; Sharon Hughes for indexing under time pressure, a task that strikes me as terrifying. Thanks also to Graig Donini, now long gone from Sinauer, who first persuaded me to tackle a textbook on psycholinguistics. The project has been far more time-consuming and rewarding than I was led to believe, and I've been reminded at every step of the way what a deeply creative act it is to teach.

Deep appreciation to all the students who've come through my classrooms and offices at Brown University and the University of Calgary: for your curiosity, candid questions, and mild or strident objections; for wondering what this stuff was good for; for your questions; for rising to the occasion; and for occasionally emailing me years later to tell me what you learned in one my classes.

Every author inevitably closes by giving thanks to partners and family members. There's a reason for that. A real reason, I mean, not a ceremonial one. Very few projects of this scale can be brought to completion without the loving encouragement and bottomless accommodation of the people closest to you. To my daughter Katharine Sedivy-Haley, now on her way to becoming an independent scientist in her own right: thanks for the many discussions about science, Isaac Asimov, and teaching and learning. Thanks to my son, Ben Haley, whose insights about his own experiences as a student provided the bass line for this book. And to my husband Ian Graham: thanks for understanding completely why it was I was writing this book, even though it deprived me of many, many hours of your sweet company. This weekend, honey, I'm coming out skiing with you. And yes, we can finally have your parents over for dinner.

JULIE SEDIVY

Media & Supplements to Accompany
Language in Mind An Introduction to Psycholinguistics

eBook

Language in Mind is available as an eBook, in several different formats. Please visit the Sinauer Associates website at www.sinauer.com for more information.

For the Student
Companion Website
(sites.sinauer.com/languageinmind)

The *Language in Mind* Companion Website provides students with a range of activities, study tools, and coverage of additional topics, all free of charge and requiring no access code. The site includes the following resources:

- Web Activities
- Additional "Language at Large" Modules
- Web Essays
- Flashcards & Key Terms
- Chapter Outlines
- Further Readings
- Web Links

(See the inside front cover for additional details.)

For the Instructor

(Instructor resources are available to adopting instructors online. Registration is required. Please contact your Sinauer Associates representative to request access.)

Instructor's Resource Library

The *Language in Mind* Instructor's Resource Library includes all of the textbook's figures and tables a variety of formats, making it easy for instructors to incorporate visual resources into their lecture presentations and other course materials. Figures and tables are provided in both JPEG (high- and low-resolution versions) and PowerPoint formats, all optimized for in-class use.

1 Science, Language, and the Science of Language

Before you read any further, stand up, hold this book at about waist height, and drop it. Just do it. (Well, if you're reading this on an electronic device, maybe you should reach for the nearest unbreakable object and drop it instead.)

Now that you've retrieved your book and found your place in it once more, your first assignment is to explain why it fell down when you dropped it. Sure, sure, it's gravity—Isaac Newton and falling apples, etc.

Your next assignment is to explain: How do you know it's gravity that makes things fall down? What's the evidence that makes you confident that gravity is better than other possible explanations—for example, you might think of the Earth as a kind of magnet that attracts objects of a wide range of materials. Chances are you find it much easier to produce the right answer than to explain why it's the right answer. It's possible, too, that throughout your scientific education you were more often evaluated on your ability to remember the right answer than on being able to recreate the scientific process that led people there. And I have to admit that there's a certain efficiency to this approach: there's a wheel, learn what it is, use it, don't reinvent it.

The trouble with the "learn it, use it" approach is that science hardly ever has "the" right answers. Science is full of ideas, some of which stand an extremely good chance of being right, and some of which are long shots but the best we've got at the moment. The status of these ideas shifts around a fair bit (which partly explains why textbooks have to be revised every couple of years). If you have a good sense of the body of evidence that backs up an idea (or can identify the gaps in the evidence), it becomes much easier to tell where a certain idea falls on the spectrum of likelihood that it's right.

This was a point made by scientist and author Isaac Asimov in his well-known essay "The Relativity of Wrong" (**Box 1.1**). In this 1988 essay, Asimov challenged an English student who wrote to accuse him of scientific arrogance. The letter-writer pointed out that, throughout history, scientists have believed that they understood the universe, only to be proven wrong later. Hence, concluded Asimov's correspondent, the only reliable thing one could say about scientific knowledge is that it's bound to be wrong.

To this, Asimov countered that what matters isn't knowing whether an idea is right or wrong, but having a sense of which ideas might be more wrong than others. He used the flat-Earth theory as an example of how scientific theories develop. In ancient times, the notion that the Earth was flat wasn't a stupid or illogical one—it was the idea that happened to be most consistent with the available body of knowledge. Eventually, people like Aristotle and others observed things that didn't quite mesh with the flat-Earth theory. They noticed that certain stars disappear from view when you travel north, and certain others disappear if you travel south. They saw that Earth's shadow during a lunar eclipse is always round, and that the sun casts shadows of different lengths at different latitudes. In short, the available body of evidence had expanded. The flat-Earth theory was no longer the best fit to the observations, causing it to be abandoned in favor of the notion that the Earth is a sphere. As it turned out, when even more evidence was considered, this theory too had to be abandoned: the Earth is *not* exactly a sphere, but an oblate spheroid, a sphere that's been squished toward the center at the North and South Poles.

As Asimov put it, "when people thought the Earth was flat, they were wrong. When people thought the Earth was spherical, they were wrong. But if *you* think that thinking that the Earth is spherical is *just as wrong* as thinking the Earth

BOX 1.1
Wrong or insightful?
Isaac Asimov on testing students' knowledge

"Young children learn spelling and arithmetic, for instance, and here we tumble into apparent absolutes.

How do you spell "sugar?" Answer: s-u-g-a-r. That is right. Anything else is wrong.

How much is 2 + 2? The answer is 4. That is right. Anything else is wrong.

Having exact answers, and having absolute rights and wrongs, minimizes the necessity of thinking, and that pleases both students and teachers. For that reason, students and teachers alike prefer short-answer tests to essay tests; multiple-choice over blank short-answer tests; and true-false tests over multiple-choice.

But short-answer tests are, to my way of thinking, useless as a measure of the student's understanding of a subject. They are merely a test of the efficiency of his ability to memorize.

You can see what I mean as soon as you admit that right and wrong are relative.

How do you spell "sugar?" Suppose Alice spells it p-q-z-z-f and Genevieve spells it s-h-u-g-e-r. Both are wrong, but is there any doubt that Alice is wronger than Genevieve? For that matter, I think it is possible to argue that Genevieve's spelling is superior to the "right" one.

Or suppose you spell "sugar": s-u-c-r-o-s-e, or $C_{12}H_{22}O_{11}$. Strictly speaking, you are wrong each time, but you're displaying a certain knowledge of the subject beyond conventional spelling.

Suppose then the test question was: how many different ways can you spell "sugar?" Justify each.

Naturally, the student would have to do a lot of thinking and, in the end, exhibit how much or how little he knows. The teacher would also have to do a lot of thinking in the attempt to evaluate how much or how little the student knows. Both, I imagine, would be outraged."

From Isaac Asimov (1988). The relativity of wrong. In *The relativity of wrong: Essays on science.* New York: Doubleday. Used with permission.

is flat, then your view is wronger than both of them put together." Without the distinction that one is more wrong than the other, for example, you could be left with the belief that, for all we know, in 50 years, scientists will "discover" that the oblate spheroid theory was wrong after all, and the Earth is cubical, or in the shape of a doughnut. (In actual fact, the oblate spheroid theory *is* wrong: the Earth is very, very slightly pear-shaped, with the South Pole being squished toward the center just a bit more than the North Pole. Still, not a cube.)

Asimov's point about scientific progression and the graded "rightness" of ideas seems fairly obvious in the context of a well-known example like the flat-Earth theory. But unfortunately, the way in which people often talk about science can blot out the subtleties inherent in the scientific process. In many important discussions, people *do* behave as if they think of scientific ideas as being right or wrong in an absolute sense. For example, you've probably heard people express frustration upon reading a study that contradicts earlier health tips they've heard; a common reaction to this frustration is to vow to ignore *any* advice based on scientific studies, on the grounds that scientists are constantly "changing their minds." And when people talk about evolution as "just a theory" (and hence not something we need to "believe"), or object that the science of climate change "isn't settled," they're also failing to think about the *degree* to which these scientific ideas approach "rightness." Naturally, being able to identify whether an idea is very likely to be wrong or very likely to be right calls for a much more sophisticated body of scientific knowledge than simply having memorized what the supposedly right answer is. But ultimately, the ability to evaluate the rightness of an idea leaves you with a great deal more power than does merely accepting an idea's rightness.

I have a 3-year-old niece who is definitely on to something. Like many preschoolers, her usual response to things you tell her is to ask a question. But in her case, the question is almost always the same: whether you've told her that eating her carrots will make her healthy or that the sun is many, many miles away, she demands, "How do you know?" She makes a great scientific companion—in her presence, you can't help but realize where it is that your understanding of the world is at its shallowest. (Conversations with her have a way of sending me off on an extended Google search.) One can only hope that by the time she hits college or university, she hasn't abandoned that question in favor of another one, commonly heard from students: Which theory is the right one?

1.1 What Do Scientists Know about Language?

In studying the language sciences, it's especially useful to approach the field with the "how do you know?" mindset rather than one that asks which theory is right. The field is an exceptionally young one, and the truth is that its collection of facts and conclusions that can be taken to be nearly unshakable is really very small. (The same is also true of most of the sciences of the mind and brain in general.) In fact, scientific disagreements can run so deep that language researchers are often at odds about fundamentals—not only might they disagree on which theory best fits the evidence, they may argue about what kind of cloth a theory should be cut from. Or on very basic aspects of how evidence should be gathered in the first place. Or even the *range* of evidence that a particular theory should be responsible for covering. It's a little bit as if we were still in an age when no one really knew what made books or rocks fall to the ground—when gravity was a new and exciting idea, but was only one among many. It needed to be tested against other theories, and we were still trying to figure out what the best techniques might be to gather data that would decide among the competing explanations. New experimental methods and new theoretical approaches crop up every year.

All this means that language science is at a fairly unstable point in its brief history, and that seismic shifts in ideas regularly reshape its intellectual landscape. But this is what makes the field so alluring to many of the researchers in it—the potential to play a key role in reshaping how people think scientifically about language is very, very real. A sizable amount of what we "know" about language stands a very good chance of being wrong. Many of the findings and conclusions in this book may well be overturned within a few years (so you might make a habit of visiting the book's companion website to check for some important updates). Don't be surprised if at some point, your instructor bursts out in vehement disagreement with some of the material presented here, or with the way in which I've framed an idea. In an intellectual climate like this, it becomes all the more important to take a "how do you know?" stance. Getting in the habit of asking this question will give you a much better sense of which ideas are likely to endure, as well as how to think about new ideas that pop up in the landscape.

The question also brings you into the heart of some of the most fascinating aspects of the scientific process. Scientific truths don't lie around in the open, waiting for researchers to stub their toes on them. Often the path from evidence to explanation is excruciatingly indirect, requiring a circuitous chain of assumptions. Sometimes it calls for precise and technologically sophisticated methods of measurement. This is why wrong ideas often persist for long periods of time, and it's also why scientists can expend endless amounts of energy in arguing about whether a certain method is valid or appropriate, or what exactly can and can't be concluded from that method.

In language research, many of the *Eureka!* moments represent not discoveries, but useful insights into how to begin answering a certain question. Language is a peculiar subject matter. The study of chemistry or physics, for example, is about phenomena that have an independent existence outside of ourselves. But language is an object that springs from our very own minds. We can have conscious thoughts about how we use or learn language, and this can give us the illusion that the best way to understand language is through these deliberate observations. But how do you intuit your way to answering questions like these:

- When we understand language, are we using the same kind of thinking as we do when we listen to music or solve mathematical equations?

- Is your understanding of the word *blue* exactly the same as my understanding of it?

- What does a baby know about language before it can speak?

- Why is it that sometimes, in the process of retrieving a word from memory, you can draw a complete blank, only to have the word pop into your mind half an hour later?

- What does it mean if you accidentally call your current partner by the name of your former one? (You and your partner might disagree on what this means.)

- What exactly makes some sentences in this book confusing while others are easy to understand?

To get at the answers to any of these questions, you have to be able to probe beneath conscious intuition. This requires acrobatic feats of imagination, not only in imagining possible alternative explanations, but also in devising ways to go about testing them. In this book, I've tried to put the spotlight not just on the conclusions that language researches have drawn, but also on the methods they've used to get there. As in all sciences, methods range from crude to clever to stunningly elegant, and to pass by them with just a cursory glance would be to miss some of the greatest challenges and pleasures of the study of language.

1.2 Why Bother?

At this point, you might be thinking, "Fine, if so little is truly known about how language works in the mind, sign me up for some other course, and I'll check back when language researchers have things worked out a bit better." But before you go, let me suggest a couple of reasons why it might be worth your while to study **psycholinguistics**, such as it is.

Here's one reason: Despite the fact that much of the current scientific knowledge of language is riddled with degrees of uncertainty and could well turn out to be wrong, it's not nearly as likely to be wrong as the many pronouncements that people often make about language without *really* knowing much, if anything, about it (see **Table 1.1**). The very fact that we can have intuitions about language—never mind that many of these are easily contradicted by closer, more systematic observation—appears to mislead people into believing that these intuitions are scientific truths. Aside from those who *have* formally studied the language sciences, or have spent a great deal of time thinking analytically about language, almost no one knows the basics of how language works, or has the slightest idea what might be involved in learning and using it. It's simply not something that is part of our collective common knowledge at this point in time.

psycholinguistics The psychology of language; the study of the psychological and neurobiological factors involved in the perception, production, and acquisition of language.

TABLE 1.1 Some things people say about language (that are almost certainly wrong)

You can learn language by watching television.

People whose language has no word for a concept have trouble thinking about that concept.

English is the hardest language to learn.

Texting is making kids illiterate.

Some languages are more logical/expressive/romantic than others.

People speak in foreign accents because their mouth muscles aren't used to making the right sounds.

Some languages are spoken more quickly than others.

Saying *um* or *er* is a sign of an inarticulate speaker.

Failure to enunciate all your speech sounds is due to laziness.

Sentences written in the passive voice are a sign of poor writing.

Swearing profusely is a sign of a poor vocabulary.

Deaf people should learn to speak and lip-read in spoken language before they learn sign language, or it will interfere with learning a real language.

Speech errors reveal your innermost thoughts.

You can't learn language by watching television.

Try this: ask your mother, or your brother, or your boyfriend, or your girl-friend, "How can you understand what I'm saying right now?" Many people happily go through their entire lives without ever asking or answering a question like this, but if pressed, they might answer something like, "I recognize the words you're using." Fine, but how do they even know *which* bunches of the sounds you're emitting go together to form words, since there are no silences between words? And once they've figured that out, *how* do they recognize the words? What do "word memories" look like, and is there a certain order in which people sort through their mental dictionaries to find a match to the sounds you're emitting? Moreover, understanding language involves more than just recognizing the words, or people would have no trouble with the phrase *words I you're the using recognize.* Obviously, they're responding to the right order of words as well. So, what *is* the right order of words in a sentence— not just for this one, but more generally? How do people know what the right order is, and how did they learn to tell whether a sentence they've never heard before in their lives has its words strung together in the "proper" order?

Most people have a decent sense of how they digest their food, but the common knowledge of many educated people today does not contain the right equipment to begin answering a question as basic as, "How can you understand what I'm saying?" Imagine how it must have been for people, before awareness of gravity became part of common knowledge, for people to be asked, "Why does a rock fall to the ground?" A typical answer might have been, "It just does." Most people probably never thought to ask themselves why. Many might have stared and stammered—much as they do now when asked about how language works. So, by studying the psychology of language, you're entering a world of new questions and of new ways of thinking that isn't visible to most people. You'll be privy to discussions of ideas before they've become the officially received "right answers" that everyone knows. You might find this all so stimulating that you eventually wind up being a language researcher yourself. But the vast majority of readers of this textbook won't. Which brings me to the second reason to study psycholinguistics.

There are few subjects you can study that will have such a broad and deep impact on your daily life as the study of language. While you're unlikely to ever become a professional language researcher, you're *extremely* likely to use language in your daily life. Inevitably, you'll find yourself asking questions like these:

- How can I write this report so that it's easier to understand?
- What kind of language should I use in order to be persuasive?
- If I sit my kid in front of the TV for an hour a day, will this help her to learn language?
- Why do my students seem incapable of using apostrophes correctly?
- How can I make my poem more interesting?
- Should I bother trying to learn a second language in my thirties?
- Why is this automated voice system so infuriating?

Even a basic understanding of how language works in the mind will provide you with the tools to approach these and many, many other questions in an intelligent way.

Unfortunately, those of us who are deeply immersed in studying language don't always take the time to talk about how our accumulated body of knowledge might provide a payoff for daily users of language. This would be a poor textbook indeed if it didn't help you answer the questions about language that will crop up throughout your life. Ultimately, whether or not you become a professional psycholinguist, you should feel well equipped to be an amateur language scientist. And to do that, you need much more than "answers" to questions that researchers have thought to ask. One of the goals of this book is to give you the conceptual framework to address the questions that *you* will think to ask.

Throughout this book, you'll find many activities and exercises that are designed to immerse you in the scientific process of understanding language. The more deeply you engage in these, the more you'll internalize a way of thinking about language that will be very useful to you when faced with new questions and evidence. And throughout the book, you'll find discussions that link what can sometimes be very abstract ideas about language to real linguistic phenomena out in the world. Many more such connections can be made, and the more you learn about how language works, the more you'll be able to generate new insights and questions about the language you see and hear all around you.

GO TO
sites.sinauer.com/languageinmind

for **web activities, further readings, research updates, new essays,** and other features

2 Origins of Human Language

As far as we know, no other species on Earth has language; only humans talk. Sure, many animals communicate with each other in subtle and intricate ways. But we're the only ones who gossip, take seminars, interview celebrities, convene board meetings, recite poems, negotiate treaties, conduct marriage ceremonies, hold criminal trials—all activities where just about the only thing going on is talking.

Fine, we also do many other things that our fellow Earth-creatures don't. We play chess and soccer, sing the blues, go paragliding, design bridges, paint portraits, drive cars, and plant gardens, to name just a few. What makes language so special? Here's the thing: language is deeply distinct from these other activities for the simple reason that *all humans do it*. There is no known society of *Homo sapiens*, past or present, in which people don't talk to each other, though there are many societies where no one plays chess or designs bridges. And all individuals *within* any given human society talk, though again, many people don't play chess or design bridges, for reasons of choice or aptitude.

So, language is one of the few things about us that appears to be a true defining trait of what it means to be human—so much so that it seems it *must* be part of our very DNA. In fact, language has often been described as an innate instinct, something that we are inherently programmed to do. This **nativist view** is presented in Steven Pinker's book *The Language Instinct* (1994). In its strongest version, the nativist position says that not only do our genes program us to have a capacity for language, we're genetically programmed for the thing itself—its general structures, the building blocks that go into it, the mental process of acquiring it, and so on. One way to express this way of thinking is to say that as children, we don't so much *learn* language (the way we learn chess or

nativist view The view that not only are humans genetically programmed to have a general capacity for language, particular aspects of language ability are also genetically specified.

anti-nativist view The view that the ability of humans to learn language is not the result of a genetically programmed "language template," but is an aspect (or by-product) of our extensive cognitive abilities, including general abilities of learning and memory.

piano-playing) as *grow* language based on a genetic blueprint, much as birds grow wings, elephants grow trunks, and female humans grow breasts. This view of language as a genetically specified mental "organ," or as a preprogrammed instinct, captures why it is that language is not only common to all humans but also is unique to humans—no "language genes," no talking.

But many language researchers see it differently. The **anti-nativist view** is that language is not a specialized "organ," but a magnificent by-product of our impressive cognitive abilities. Humans alone learn language, not because we inherit a preprogrammed language template, but because we are the superlearners of the animal kingdom. What separates us from other animals is that our brains have evolved to become the equivalent of swift, powerful supercomputers in comparison with our fellow creatures, who are stuck with more rudimentary technology. Current computers can do qualitatively different things that older models could never aspire to accomplish. This supercomputer theory is one explanation for why we have language while squirrels and chimpanzees don't.

But what about the fact that language is universal among humans, unlike chess or trombone-playing (accomplishments which, though uniquely human, are hardly universal)? Daniel Everett, a linguist who takes a firm anti-nativist position, puts it this way in his book *Language: The Cultural Tool* (2012): Maybe language is more like a tool invented by human beings than an organ that's genetically programmed to grow. What makes language universal is that it's an incredibly *useful* tool for solving certain problems that all humans have—foremost among them being how to efficiently transmit information to each other. Everett compares language to arrows. Arrows are nearly universal among hunter-gatherer societies, but few people would say that humans are genetically programmed to make arrows *specifically*. More likely, making arrows is just part of our general tool-making, problem-solving competence. Bows and arrows can be found in so many different societies because at some point, people who didn't grow their own protein had to figure out a way to catch protein that ran faster than they did. Since it was well within the bounds of human intelligence to solve this problem, humans inevitably did—just as, Everett argues, humans inevitably came to speak with each other as a way of achieving certain pressing goals.

The question of how we came to have language is a huge and fascinating one. If you're hoping that the mystery will be solved by the end of this chapter, you'll be sorely disappointed. It's a question that has no agreed-upon answer among language scientists and, as you'll see, there's a range of subtle and complex views among scientists beyond the two extreme positions I've just presented.

In truth, the various fields that make up the language sciences are not yet even in a position to be able to resolve the debate. To get there, we first need to answer questions like: What *is* language? What do all human languages have in common? What's involved in learning it? What physical and mental machinery is needed to successfully speak, be understood, and understand someone else who's speaking? What's the role of genes in shaping any of the above behaviors? Without doing a lot of detailed legwork to get a handle on all of these smaller pieces of the puzzle, any attempts to answer the larger question about the origins of language can only amount to something like a happy hour discussion—heated and entertaining, but ultimately not that convincing one way or the other. In fact, in 1866, the Linguistic Society of Paris decreed that no papers about the origins of language were allowed to be presented at its conferences. It might seem ludicrous that an academic society would banish an entire topic from discussion. But the decision was essentially a way of saying, "We'll get nowhere talking about language origins until we learn more about language itself, so go learn something about language."

A hundred and fifty years later, we now know quite a bit more about language, and by the end of this book, you'll have a sense of the broad outlines of this body of knowledge. For now, we're in a position to lay out at least a bit of what might be involved in answering the question of why people speak.

2.1 Why Us?

The "language" of bees

Let's start by asking what it is about our language use that's different from what animals do when they communicate. Is it different down to its fundamental core, or is it just a more sophisticated version of what animals are capable of? An interesting starting point might be the "dance language" of honeybees, as identified by Karl von Frisch (1967).

When a worker bee finds a good source of flower nectar at some distance from her hive, she returns home to communicate its whereabouts to her fellow workers by performing a patterned waggle dance (see **Figure 2.1**). During this dance, she repetitively traces a specific path while shaking her body. The elements of this dance communicate at least three things:

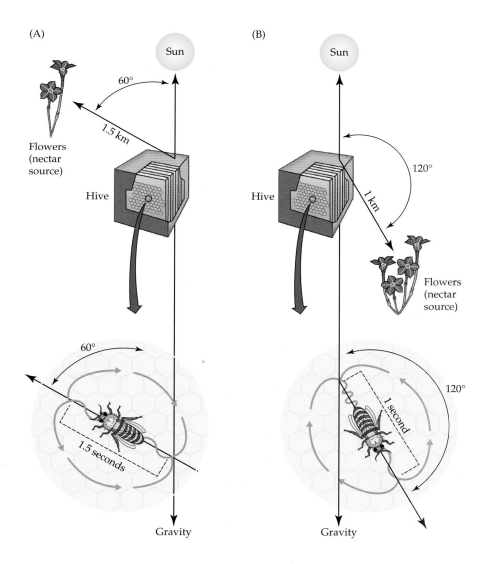

Figure 2.1 The waggle dance of honeybees is used by a returning worker bee to communicate the location and quality of a food source. The worker dances on the surface of the comb to convey information about the direction and distance of the food source, as shown in the examples here. (A) The nectar source is approximately 1.5 km from the hive flying at the indicated angle to the sun. (B) The nectar source is closer and the dance is shorter; in this case the flowers will be found by flying away from the sun. The energy in the bee's waggles (orange curves along the line of the dance) is in proportion to the perceived quality of the find.

1. *The direction in which the nectar source is located.* If the bee moves up toward the top of the hive, this indicates that the nectar source can be found by heading straight toward the sun. The angle of deviation away from a straight vertical path shows the direction relative to the sun.

2. *The distance to the source.* The longer the bee dances along the path from an initial starting point before returning to re-trace the path again, the farther away the source is.

3. *The quality of the source.* If the bee has hit the nectar jackpot, she shakes with great vigor, whereas a lesser source of nectar elicits a more lethargic body wiggle.

Different bee species have different variations on this dance (for example, they might vary in how long they dance along a directional path in order to indicate a distance of 200 meters). It seems that bees have innate knowledge of their own particular dance "dialect," and bees introduced into a hive populated by another species will dance in the manner of their genetic ancestors, not in the style of the adopted hive (though there's some intriguing evidence that bees can learn to *interpret* foreign dialects of other bees; see Fu et al., 2008).

In some striking ways, the honeybee dance is similar to what we do in human language, which is presumably why von Frisch used the term *language* to describe it. The dance uses body movements to represent something in the real world, just as a map or a set of directions does. Human language also critically relies on symbolic representation to get off the ground—for us, it's usually sequences of sounds made in the mouth (for example, "eat fruit"), rather than waggling body movements, that serve as the symbolic units that map onto things, actions, and events in the world. And, in both human languages and bee dances, a smaller number of communicative elements can be independently varied and combined to create a large number of messages—where bees can combine different intensities of wiggling with different angles and durations of the dance path, we can piece together different phrases to similar effect: "Go three miles northwest and you'll find a pretty good Chinese restaurant"; or "There are some amazing raspberry bushes about thirty feet to your left."

Honeybee communicative behavior shows that a complex behavior capable of transmitting information about the real world can be encoded in the genes and innately specified, presumably through an evolutionary process. Like us, honeybees are highly cooperative and benefit from being able to communicate with each other. But bees are hardly among our closest genetic relatives, so it's worth asking just how similar their communicative behavior is to ours. Along with the parallels I've just mentioned, there are also major differences.

Most importantly, bee communication operates within much more rigid parameters than human language. The elements in the dance, while symbolic in some sense, are still closely bound to the information that's being communicated. The angle of the dance path describes the angle of the food source to the sun; the duration of the dance describes the distance to the food source. But in human language, there's usually a purely arbitrary or accidental relationship between the communicative elements (that is, words and phrases) and the things they describe; the word *fruit*, for example, is not any more inherently fruit-like than the word *leg*. In this sense, what bees do is less like using words and more like drawing maps with their bodies. A map does involve symbolic representation, but the forms it uses are constrained by the information it conveys. In a map, there's always some transparent, non-arbitrary way in which the spatial relations in the symbolic image relate to the real world. No one makes maps in which, for example, all objects colored red—regardless of where they're placed in the image—are actually found in the northeast quadrant of the real-world

BOX 2.1
Hockett's design features of human language

1. **Vocal-auditory channel** Language is produced in the vocal tract and transmitted as sound; it's perceived through the auditory channel.

2. **Broadcast transmission and directional reception** Language can be heard from many directions, but it is perceived as coming from one particular location.

3. **Rapid fading** The sound produced by speech fades quickly.

4. **Interchangeability** A user of a language can send and receive the same message.

5. **Total feedback** Senders of a message can hear and internalize the message they've sent.

6. **Specialization** The production of the sounds of language serves no purpose other than to communicate.

7. **Semanticity** There are fixed associations between units of language and aspects of the world.

8. **Arbitrariness** The meaningful associations between language and the world are arbitrary.

9. **Discreteness** The units of language are separate and distinct from one another rather than being part of a continuous whole.

10. **Displacement** Language can be used to communicate about things that are not present in time and/or space.

11. **Productivity** Language can be used to say things that have never been said before, and yet are understandable to the receiver.

12. **Traditional transmission** The specific language that's adopted by the user has to be learned by exposure to other users of that language; its precise details are not available through genetic transmission.

13. **Duality of patterning** Many meaningful units (words) are made by the combination of a small number of elements (sounds) into various sequences. For example, pat, tap, and apt use the same sound elements combined in different ways to make different word units. In this way, tens of thousands of words can be created from several dozen sounds.

14. **Prevarication** Language can deliberately be used to make false statements.

15. **Reflexiveness** Language can be used to refer or describe itself.

16. **Learnability** Users of one language can learn to use another, different language.

Adapted from Hockett, 1960, and Hockett & Altmann, 1968.

---

space being described, while the color yellow is used to signal objects in the southwest quadrant, regardless of where they appear in the image.

Another severe limitation of bee dances is that bees only "talk" about one thing: where to find food (or water) sources. Human language, on the other hand, can be recruited to talk about an almost infinite variety of topics for a wide range of purposes, from giving directions, to making requests, to expressing sympathy, to issuing a promise, and so on. Finally, human language involves a complexity of structure that's just not there in the bees' dance language.

To help frame the discussion about how much overlap there is between animal communication systems and human language, the well-known linguist Charles Hockett listed a set of "design features" that he argued are common to all human languages. The full list of **Hockett's design features** is given in **Box 2.1**; you may find it useful to refer back to this list as the course progresses. Even though some of the features are open to challenge, they provide a useful starting point for fleshing out what human language looks like.

Primate vocalizations

If we look at primates—much closer to us genetically than bees—a survey of their vocal communication shows a pretty limited repertoire. Monkeys and apes do make meaningful vocal sounds, but they don't make very many, and

Hockett's design features A set of characteristics proposed by linguist Charles Hockett to be universally shared by all human languages. Some (but not all) of the features are also found in various animal communication systems.

the ones they use seem to be limited to very specific purposes. Strikingly absent are many of the features described by Hockett that allow for inventiveness, or the capacity to re-use elements in an open-ended way to communicate a varied assortment of messages.

For example, vervet monkeys produce a set of alarm calls to warn each other of nearby predators, with three distinct calls used to signal whether the predator is a leopard, an eagle, or a snake (as found by Seyfarth, Cheney, and Marler, 1980). Vervets within earshot of these calls behave differently depending on the specific call: they run into trees if they hear the leopard call, look up if they hear the eagle call, and peer around in the grass when they hear the snake alarm. These calls do exhibit Hockett's feature of *semanticity*, as well as an *arbitrariness* in the relationship between the signals and the meaning they transmit. But they clearly lack Hockett's feature of *displacement*, since the calls are only used to warn about a clear and present danger and not, for example, to suggest to a fellow vervet that an eagle *might* be hidden in that tree branch up there, or to remind a fellow vervet that this was the place where we saw a snake the other day. There's also no evidence of *duality of patterning*, in which each call would be made by combining similar units together in different ways. And vervets certainly don't show any signs of *productivity* in their language, in which the calls are adapted to communicate new messages that have never been heard before but that can be easily understood by the hearer vervets. In fact, vervets don't even seem to have the capacity to *learn* to make the various alarm calls; the sounds of the alarm calls are fixed from birth and are instinctively linked to certain categories of predators, though baby vervets do have to learn, for example, that the eagle alarm shouldn't be made in response to a pigeon overhead. So, they come by these calls not through the process of *cultural transmission*, which is how humans learn words (no French child is born knowing that *chien* is the sound you make when you see a dog), but by being genetically wired to make specific sounds that are associated with specific meanings.

WEB ACTIVITY 2.1

Considering animal communication
In this activity, you'll be asked to consider a variety of situations that showcase the communicative behavior of animals. How do Hockett's design features of language apply to these behaviors?

This last point has some very interesting implications. Throughout the animal world, it seems that the exact shape of a communicative message often has a strong genetic component. If we want to say that humans are genetically wired for language, then that genetic programming is going to have to be much more fluid and adaptable than that of other animals, allowing humans to learn a variety of different languages through exposure. Instead of being programmed for a specific language, we're born with the capacity to learn any language. This very fact might look like overwhelming support for the anti-nativist view, which says that language is simply an outgrowth of our general ability to learn complex things. But not necessarily. The position of nativists is more subtle than simply arguing that we're born with knowledge of a specific language. Rather, the claim is that there are common structural ingredients to all human languages, and that it's these basic building blocks of language that we're all born with, whether we use them to learn French or Sanskrit. More on this later.

One striking aspect of primate vocalizations is the fact that monkeys and apes show much greater flexibility and capacity for learning when it comes to *interpreting* signals than in producing them. (A thorough discussion of this asymmetry can be found in a paper by primatologists Robert Seyfarth and Dorothy Cheney, 2010.) Oddly enough, even though vervets are born knowing which sounds to make in the presence of various predators, they don't seem to be born with a solid understanding of the meanings of these alarms, at least as far as we can tell from their responses to the calls. It takes young vervets several months before they start showing the adult-like responses of looking up, searching in the grass, and so on. Early on, they respond to the alarm calls simply by running to their mothers, or reacting in some other way that doesn't show that they know that an eagle call, for example, is used to warn specifically about bird-like predators. Over time, though, their ability to extend their understanding of new calls to new situations exceeds their adaptability in producing calls. For instance, vervets can learn to understand the meanings of alarm calls of other species, as well as the calls of their predators—again, even though they never learn to *produce* the calls of other species.

Seyfarth and Cheney suggest that the information that primates can pull out from the communicative signals they hear can be very subtle. An especially intriguing example comes from an experiment involving the call behavior of baboons. Baboons, as it happens, have a very strict status hierarchy within their groups, and it's not unusual for a higher-status baboon to try to intimidate a lower-status baboon by issuing a threat-grunt, to which the lower-ranking animal usually responds with a scream. The vocalizations of individual baboons are distinctive enough that they're easily recognized by all members of the group. For the purpose of the study, the researchers created a set of auditory stimuli in which they cut and spliced together prerecorded threat-grunts and screams from various baboons within the group. The sounds were reassembled so that sometimes the threat-call of a baboon was followed by a scream from another baboon higher up in the status hierarchy. This is a situation that overhearing baboons would be very unlikely to ever hear in nature. Yet they reacted to this unusual pairing of sounds with surprise, which seems to show that the baboons had inferred from the sequence of sounds that a lower-status animal was trying to intimidate a higher-status animal—and understood that this was a bizarre state of affairs.

It may seem strange that animals' ability to understand something about the world based on a communicative sound is so much more impressive than their ability to *convey* something about the world by creating a sound. But this asymmetry seems rampant within the animal kingdom. Many dog owners are intimately familiar with this fact. It's not hard to get your dog to recognize and respond to dozens of verbal commands. It's getting your dog to talk back to you that's more difficult. Any account of the evolution of language will have to grapple with the fact that speaking and understanding are not necessarily just the mirror image of each other.

Can language be taught to apes?

As you've seen, when left to themselves in the wild, non-human primates don't indulge in much language-like vocalization. This would suggest that the linguistic capabilities of humans and other primates are markedly different. Still, a non-nativist might object and argue that looking at what monkeys and apes do among themselves, without the benefit of any exposure to real language, doesn't really provide a realistic picture of what they *can* learn about language. After all, when we evaluate human infants' capacity for language, we don't normally separate them from competent language users—in other words, adults— and see what they come up with on their own. Suppose language really is more like a tool than a biological organ, with each generation of humans benefiting from the knowledge of the previous generation. In that case, in order to see whether primates are truly capable of attaining language, we need to see what they can learn when they're allowed to have many rich interactions with individuals who have already solved the problem of language.

This line of thinking has led to a number of studies that have looked at how apes communicate, not with other non-linguistic apes, but with their more verbose human relatives. In these studies, research scientists and their assistants have raised young apes (i.e., chimpanzees, bonobos, orangutans, and gorillas) among humans in a language-rich environment. Some of the studies have included intensive formal teaching sessions, with a heavy emphasis on rewarding and shaping communicative behavior, while other researchers have raised the apes much as one would a human child, letting them learn language through observation and interaction. Such studies often raise tricky methodological challenges, as discussed in **Method 2.1**. For example, what kind of evidence is needed in order to conclude that apes know the meaning of a word in the sense that humans understand that word? Nevertheless, a number of interesting findings have come from this body of work (a brief summary can be found in a review article by Kathleen Gibson, 2012).

First, environment matters: there's no doubt that the communicative behavior of apes raised in human environments starts to look a lot more human-like than that of apes in the wild. For example, a number of apes of several different species have mastered hundreds of words or arbitrary symbols. They spontaneously use these symbols to communicate a variety of different functions, not just to request objects or food that they want, but also to comment on the world around them. They also refer to objects that are not physically present at the time, showing evidence of Hockett's feature of *displacement*, which was conspicuously absent from the wild vervets' alarm calls. They can even use their symbolic skills to lie—for instance, one chimp was found to regularly blame the messes she made on others. Perhaps even more impressively, all of the species studied have shown at least some suggestion of another of Hockett's features, **productivity**—that is, of using the symbols they know in new combinations to communicate ideas for which they don't already have symbols. For example, Koko, a gorilla, created the combination "finger bracelet" to refer to a ring; Washoe, a chimpanzee, called a Brazil nut a "rock berry." Sequences of verbs and nouns often come to be used by apes in somewhat systematic sequences, suggesting that the order of combination isn't random.

As in the wild, trained apes show that they can master comprehension skills much more readily than they achieve the production of language-like units. In particular, it quickly became obvious that trying to teach apes to use vocal sounds to represent meanings wasn't getting anywhere. Apes, it turns out, have extremely limited control over their vocalizations and simply can't articulate different-sounding words. But the trained apes were able to build up a sizable vocabulary when signed language was substituted for spoken language, or when researchers adopted custom-made artificial "languages" using visual symbols arranged in systematic structures. This raises the very interesting question of how closely the evolution of language is specifically tied to the evolution of speech, an issue we will probe in more detail in Section 2.4.

But even with non-vocal languages, the apes were able to handle much more complexity in their understanding of language than in their production of it. They rarely produced more than two or three symbols strung together, but several apes were able to understand commands like "make the doggie bite the snake," and they could distinguish that from "make the snake bite the doggie." They could also follow commands that involved moving objects to or from specific locations. Sarah, a chimpanzee, could reportedly even understand "if/then" statements.

Looking at this collection of results, it becomes apparent that with the benefit of human teachers, ape communication takes a great leap toward human language—human-reared apes don't just acquire more words or symbols than they do in the wild, they also show that they can master a number of Hock-

productivity The ability to use known symbols or linguistic units in new combinations to communicate ideas.

 METHOD 2.1

Minding the gap between behavior and knowledge

If a chimpanzee produces the sign for *banana* and appears satisfied when you retrieve one from the kitchen and give it to her, does this mean the chimp knows that the sign is a symbol for the *idea* of banana and is using it as you and I would use the word? It's certainly tempting to think so, but the careful researcher will make sure not to overinterpret the data and jump to conclusions about sophisticated cognitive abilities when the same behavior could potentially be explained by much less impressive abilities.

Since chimpanzees look and act so much like us in so many ways, it's tempting to conclude that when they behave like us, it's because they *think* like us. But suppose instead of interacting with a chimp you were observing a pigeon that had learned to peck on keys of different colors in order to get food rewards. How willing would you be to conclude that the pigeon is treating the colored keys as symbols that are equivalent to words? My guess is, not very. Instead, it seems easy enough to explain the pigeon's behavior by saying that it's learned to associate the action of pecking a particular key with getting a certain reward. This is a far cry from saying that the bird is using its action as a symbol that imparts a certain thought into the mind of the human seeing it, intending that this implanted thought might encourage the human to hand over food. In linking behavior to cognition, researchers need to be able to suspend the presumption of a certain kind of intelligence and to treat chimps and pigeons in exactly the same way. In both cases, they need to ask: What evidence do we need to have in order to be convinced that the animal is using a word in the same way that a human does? And how do we rule out other explanations of the behavior that are based on much simpler cognitive machinery than that of humans?

Sue Savage-Rumbaugh is one of the leading scientists in the study of primate language capabilities. In 1980, she and her colleagues wrote a paper cautioning researchers against making overly enthusiastic claims when studying the linguistic capabilities of apes. They worried about several possible methodological flaws. One of these was a tendency to overattribute human-like cognition to simple behaviors, as discussed in the paragraph above. They argued that in order to have evidence that an ape is using a sign or symbol referentially, you need to be able to show that the animal not only produces the sign in order to achieve a specific result, but also shows evidence of understanding it—for example, that it can pick out the right object for a word in a complex situation that involves choosing from among many possibilities. You also need to be able to show that the ape can produce the word in a wide variety of situations, not just to bring about a specific result. Moreover, you need to look at *all* the instances in which the ape uses a particular sign. It's not enough to see that *sometimes* the chimp uses the sign in a sensible way; if the same chimp also uses the sign in situations where it seems inappropriate or not meaningful, it lessens the confidence that the chimp truly knows the meaning of that sign.

Savage-Rumbaugh and her colleagues also worried about the possibility that researchers might unknowingly provide cues that nudge the ape to produce a sign that seems sensible given the context. Imagine a possible scenario in which a chimpanzee can produce a set of signs that might be appropriate in a certain context—for example, signs that result in getting food. If the chimp doesn't really know the meanings of any of these individual signs, it might start sloppily producing some approximate hand movements while watching the researcher's face. The researcher might inadvertently communicate approval or disapproval, thereby steering the chimp's signing behavior in the right direction. In order to be able to fairly evaluate what a chimp knows, the researcher has to set up rigorous testing situations in which the possibility of such cues has been eliminated.

Savage-Rumbaugh and her colleagues ultimately concluded that apes *are* able to learn to use symbols in a language-like way. But their remarks about good methodological practices apply to any aspect of language research with primates—including the young human variety, as we'll see in upcoming chapters.

ett's design features that are completely absent from their naturalistic behavior. This is very revealing, because it helps to answer the question of when some of these features of human language—or rather, the *capability* for these features— might have evolved.

Figure 2.2 The evolutionary history of hominids. The term *hominids* refers to the group consisting of all modern and extinct great apes (including humans and their more immediate ancestors). This evolutionary tree illustrates the common ancestral history and approximate times of divergence of *hominins* (including modern humans and the now-extinct Neanderthals) from the other great apes. Note that a number of extinct hominin species are not represented here.

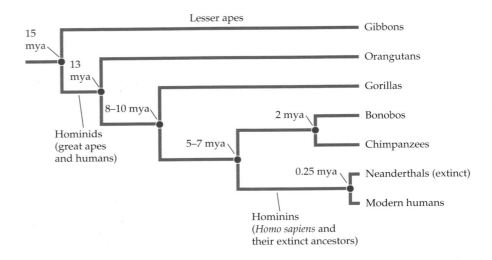

evolutionary adaptation A genetically transmitted trait that gives its bearers an advantage—specifically, it helps those with the trait to stay alive long enough to reproduce and/or to have many offspring.

Biologists estimate that humans, chimpanzees, and bonobos shared a common ancestor between 5 and 7 million years ago. The last common ancestor with gorillas probably occurred between 8 and 10 million years ago, and the shared ancestor with orangutans even earlier than that (see **Figure 2.2**). Evidence about *when* the features of human language evolved helps to answer questions about whether they evolved specifically because these features support language.

Among nativists, the most common view is that humans have some innate capabilities for language that evolved as adaptations. **Evolutionary adaptations** are genetically transmitted traits that give their bearers an advantage—specifically, an adaptive trait helps individuals with that trait to stay alive long enough to reproduce and/or to have many offspring. The gene for the advantageous trait spreads throughout a population, as over time members of the species with that trait will out-survive and out-reproduce the members without that trait. But not all adaptations that help us to use language necessarily came about *because* they gave our ancestors a communicative edge over their peers. Think about it like this: humans have hands that are capable of playing the piano, given instruction and practice. But that doesn't mean that our hands evolved as they did because playing the piano gave our ancestors an advantage over non-piano-playing humans. Presumably, our nimble fingers came about as a result of various adaptations, but the advantages these adaptations provided had nothing to do with playing the piano. Rather, they were the result of the general benefits of having dexterous hands that could easily manipulate a variety of objects. Once in possession of enhanced manual agility, however, humans discovered that hands can be put to many wonderful uses that don't necessarily help us survive into adulthood or breed successfully.

The piano-playing analogy may help to make sense of the question, "If language-related capabilities evolved long before humans diverged from other apes, then why do only humans make use of them in their natural environments?" That is, if apes are capable of amassing bulky vocabularies and using them creatively, why are they such linguistic underachievers in the wild? The contrast between their communicative potential and their lack of spontaneous language in the wild suggests that certain cognitive skills that are required to master language—at least, those skills that are within the mental grasp of apes—didn't necessarily evolve *for* language. Left to their own devices, apes don't appear to use these skills for the purpose of communicating with each other. But when the cultural environment calls for it, these skills can be recruited in the service of language—much as in the right cultural context, humans can use their hands to play the piano. This state of affairs poses a challenge to the "language-as-organ" view.

Nevertheless, it's entirely possible that the skills that support language fall into two categories: (1) those that are necessary to get language off the ground but aren't really specific to language; and (2) traits that evolved particularly because they make language more powerful and efficient. It may be that we share the skills in the first category with our primate relatives, but that only humans began to use those skills for the purpose of communication. Once this happened, there may have been selective pressure on other traits that provided an additional boost to the expressive capacity of language—and it's these later skills that are both language-specific and uniquely human.

It seems, then, that when we talk about language evolution, it doesn't make sense to treat language as an all-or-nothing phenomenon. Language may well involve a number of very different cognitive skills, with different evolutionary trajectories and different relationships to other, non-linguistic abilities.

Throughout this book, you'll get a much more intimate sense of the different cognitive skills that go into human language knowledge and use. As a first step, this chapter will start by breaking things down into three very general categories of language-related abilities: the ability to understand communicative intent, a grasp of linguistic structure, and the ability to control voice and/or gesture.

2.2 The Social Underpinnings of Language

Understanding the communicative urge

Imagine this scene from long ago: an early hominid is sitting at the mouth of his cave with his female companion when a loud roar tears through the night air. He nods soberly and says, "Leopard." This is a word that he's just invented to refer to that animal. In fact, it's the first word that's passed between them, as our male character is one of language's very earliest adopters. It's a break-through: from here on, the couple can use the word to report leopard sightings to each other, or to warn their children about the dangerous predator. But none of this can happen unless the female can clue in to the fact that the sounds in *leopard* were intentionally formed to communicate an idea—and were not due to a sneeze or a cough, or some random set of sounds. What's more, she has to be able to connect these intentional and communicative sounds with what's going on around her, and make a reasonable guess about what her companion is most likely to be trying to convey.

From your perspective as a modern human, all of this may seem pretty obvious, requiring no special abilities. But it's far from straightforward, as revealed by some very surprising tests that chimpanzees fail at miserably, despite their substantial intellectual gifts. For example, try this next time you meet a chimp: Show the animal a piece of food, and then put it in one of two opaque containers. Shuffle the two containers around so as to make it hard to tell where it's hidden. Now stop, and point to the container with the food. The chimpanzee will likely choose randomly between the two containers, totally oblivious to the very helpful clue you've been kind enough to provide. This is exactly what Michael Tomasello (2006) and his colleagues found when they used a similar test with chimpanzees. Their primate subjects ignored the conspicuous hint even though the experimenters went out of their way to establish that the "helper" who pointed had indeed proven herself to be helpful on earlier occasions by tilting the containers so that the chimp could see which container had the food (information that the chimps had no trouble seizing upon).

Chimpanzees' failure to follow the pointing cue is startling because chimps are very smart, perfectly capable of making subtle inferences in similar situations. For example, if an experimenter puts food in one of two containers and then shakes one of them but the shaken container produces no rattling sound, the chimpanzee knows to choose the other one (Call, 2004). Or, consider this variation: Brian Hare and Michael Tomasello (2004) set up a competitive situation between chimpanzees and a human experimenter, with both human and chimp trying to retrieve food from buckets. If the human extended her arm toward a bucket but couldn't touch it because she had to stick her hand through a hole that didn't allow her to reach far enough, the chimpanzees were able to infer that this was the bucket that must contain the food, and reached for it. Why can chimpanzees make *this* inference, which involves figuring out the human's intended—but thwarted—goal, but not be able to understand pointing? Tomasello and his colleagues argued that, whereas chimpanzees can often understand the intentions and goals—and even the knowledge states—of other primates, what they can't do is understand that pointing involves an *intention to communicate*. In other words, they don't get that the pointing behavior is something that's done not just for the purpose of satisfying the pointer's goal, but to help the chimpanzee satisfy *its* goal (see **Box 2.2**).

BOX 2.2
Dogs versus chimps: A pointed difference

Perhaps you were surprised to learn that chimpanzees don't understand pointing. Maybe you even thought, "That's impossible—even my dog understands that." Now, everyone knows that dog owners are prone to inflate their pets' intelligence in their own minds, but in this case, you'd be right. Dogs *do* understand pointing, as confirmed by studies using the same hidden food test that chimpanzees fail. Apparently, dogs respond to pointing even when the experimenter walks toward the wrong food container but points in the opposite direction at the right container.

In an interesting article, Brian Hare and Michael Tomasello (2005) describe a number of situations in which dogs outperform chimps on tests of social cognition—for example, dogs but not chimps are more likely to stay away from forbidden food when a nearby human's eyes are open than when they're closed. But it's not that dogs are smarter than chimps overall—dogs fail certain tests that chimps pass with flying colors. For example, chimps are more likely to pull on a string that's connected to food than one that's not, showing that they can understand simple cause-effect relationships; but dogs perform dismally on this test. So, the two species show an interesting inversion: dogs are better than chimps on tests having to do with social cognition, whereas chimps are better on tests that probe their understanding of the physical world.

Is the social intelligence of dogs due to good dog-rearing practices by humans? Apparently not. Puppies do well on the pointing test at a very young age, whether or not they've had much contact with humans. This suggests that the behavior has a genetic basis and isn't just the result of socialization. A second reasonable hypothesis is that complex social skills have evolved in dogs as a result of their pack structure in the wild. But the interesting thing is that domestic dogs are *better* than human-raised wolves at using social cues to find food, even though wolves perform at least as well as dogs on non-social problem-solving tests. So, the social skills of dogs do seem to have a hereditary basis, but *these skills appear to have evolved specifically in canines that have contact with humans*, during the process of domestication.

Added evidence for this conclusion comes from intriguing experiments with foxes. In 1959, Siberian scientists began an experimental breeding program in which they selected individual foxes that showed an inclination to approach humans without fear or aggression. Decades later, Brian Hare collaborated with these scientists to test foxes from this experimental population on their ability to use social cues (Hare et al., 2005). The "tame" foxes performed better on these tests than foxes of the same species that had not been part of this special breeding program—in fact, they did as well as puppies born to domestic dogs. In other words, selection for the general trait of seeking out human company seems to have resulted in human-like social skills.

To some researchers, it's exactly this ability to understand communicative intentions that represents the "magic moment" in the evolution of language, when our ancestors' evolutionary paths veered off from those of other great apes, and their cognitive skills and motivational drives came to be refined, either specifically for the purpose of communication, or more generally to support complex social coordination.

Some language scientists have argued that a rich communication system is built on a foundation of advanced skills in social cognition, and that among humans these skills evolved in a super-accelerated way, far outpacing other gains we made in overall intelligence and working memory capacity. To test this claim, Esther Hermann and her colleagues (2007) compared the cognitive abilities of adult chimpanzees, adult orangutans, and human toddlers aged two and a half. All of these primates were given a battery of tests evaluating two kinds of cognitive skills: those needed for understanding the physical world, and those for understanding the social world. For example, a test item in the physical world category might involve discriminating between a smaller and a larger quantity of some desirable reward, or locating the reward after it had been moved, or using a stick to retrieve an out-of-reach reward. The socially oriented test items looked for accomplishments like solving a problem by imitating someone else's solution, following a person's eye gaze to find a reward, or using or interpreting communicative gestures to locate a reward. The researchers found that in demonstrating their mastery over the physical world, the human toddlers and adult chimpanzees were about even with each other, and slightly ahead of the adult orangutans. But when it came to the social test items, the young humans left their fellow primates in the dust (with chimps and orangutans showing similar performance).

There's quite a bit of additional evidence showing that even very young humans behave in ways that are quite different from how other primates act in similar situations. For example, apes don't seem to be inclined to communicate with other apes for the purpose of helping the *others* achieve a goal, when there's nothing obvious in it for themselves. But little humans almost feel compelled to. In one study by Ulf Lizskowski and colleagues (2008), 12-month-olds who hadn't yet begun to talk watched while an adult sat at a table stapling papers without involving the child in any way. At one point, the adult left the room, then another person came in, moved the stapler from the table to a nearby shelf, and left. A little later, the first adult came back, looked around, and made quizzical gestures to the child. In response, most of the children pointed to the stapler in its new location. Apparently, this is very un-ape-like behavior; according to Michael Tomasello (2006), apes never point with each other, and when they do "point" to communicate with humans (usually without extending the index finger), it's because they want the human to fetch or hand them something that's out of their reach.

Skills for a complex social world

So, humans are inclined to share information with one another whereas other primates seem not to have discovered the vast benefits of doing so. What's preventing our evolutionary cousins from cooperating in this way? One possibility is that they're simply less motivated to engage in deeply social behavior than we humans are. Among mammals, we as a species are very unusual in the amount of importance we place on social behavior. For example, chimpanzees are considerably less altruistic than humans when it comes to sharing food, and they don't seem to care that much about norms of reciprocity or fairness. When children are in a situation where one child is dividing up treats to share and extends an offer that is much smaller than the share he's claimed for himself, the other child is apt to reject the offer, preferring to give it up in order to make the point that the meager amount is an affront to fairness. A chimp will take what it can get (Tomasello, 2009).

In fact, when you think about the daily life of most humans in comparison to a day in the life of a chimpanzee, it becomes apparent that our human experiences are shaped very profoundly by a layer of social reality, while a chimpanzee may be more grounded in the physical realities of its environment. In his book *Why We Cooperate* (2009), Michael Tomasello points out how different the human experience of shopping is from the chimpanzee's experience of foraging for food:

> Let us suppose a scenario as follows. We enter a store, pick up a few items, stand in line at the checkout, hand the clerk a credit card to pay, take our items, and leave. This could be described in chimpanzee terms fairly simply as going somewhere, fetching objects, and returning from whence one came. But humans understand shopping, more or less explicitly, on a whole other level, on the level of institutional reality. First, entering the store subjects me to a whole set of rights and obligations: I have the right to purchase items for the posted price, and the obligation not to steal or destroy items, because they are the property of the store owner. Second, I can expect the items to be safe to eat because the government has a department that ensures this; if a good proves unsafe, I can sue someone. Third, money has a whole institutional structure behind it that everyone trusts so much that they hand goods over for this special paper, or even for electronic marks somewhere from my credit card. Fourth, I stand in line in deference to widely held norms, and if I try to jump the line people will rebuke me, I will feel guilty, and my reputation as a nice person will suffer. I could go on listing, practically indefinitely, all of the institutional realities inhibiting the public sphere, realities that foraging chimpanzees presumably do not experience at all.

Put in these terms, it becomes obvious that in order to successfully navigate through the human world, we need to have a level of social aptitude that chimpanzees manage without.

At some level, the same socially oriented leanings that drive humans to "invent" things like laws and money also make it possible for them to communicate through language. Language, law, and currency all require people to buy into an artificial system that exists only because everyone agrees to abide by it. Think about it: unlike vervets with their alarm calls, we're not genetically programmed to produce specific sounds triggered by specific aspects of our environment. Nor do our words have any natural connection to the world, in the way that honeybee dance language does. Our words are quite literally figments of human imagination, and they have meaning only because we all agree to use the same word for the same thing.

But it may not just be an issue of general social motivation that's keeping our primate relatives from creating languages or laws of their own. It's possible that they also lack a specific cognitive ingredient that would allow them to engage in complex social coordination. In order to do something as basic as make a smart guess about what another person's voluntary mouth noises might be intended to mean, humans needed to have the capacity for **joint attention**: the awareness between two (or more) individuals that they are both paying attention to the same thing. Again, this doesn't seem especially difficult, but

joint attention The awareness between two or more individuals that they are paying attention to the same thing.

Tomasello and his colleagues have argued that, to any reliable extent, this capacity is found *only* in humans. Chimps can easily track the gaze of a human or another ape to check out what's holding the interest of the other; they can also keep track of what the others know or have seen. In other words, chimps can know what others know. But there's no clear evidence that they participate in situations where Chimp A knows that Chimp B knows that Chimp A is staring at the same thing. Presumably, this is exactly the kind of attunement that our ancestors sitting by their caves would have needed to have in order to agree on a word for the concept of leopard.

It turns out that joint attention skills are very much in evidence in extremely young humans. Toward the end of their first year (on average), babies unambiguously direct other people's attention to objects by pointing, often with elaborate vocalization. Months prior to this, they often respond appropriately when others try to direct their attention by pointing or getting them to look at something specific. It's especially relevant that success with language seems to be closely linked to the degree to which children get a handle on joint attention. For example, Michael Morales and his colleagues (2000) tracked a group of children from 6 to 30 months of age. The researchers tested how often individual babies responded to their parents' attempts to engage them in joint attention, beginning at 6 months of age; they then evaluated the size of the children's vocabularies at 30 months and found that the more responsive the babies were at 6 months, the larger their vocabularies were later on. Another study by Cristina Colonnesi and her colleagues (2010) documented evidence of a connection between children's pointing behaviors and the emergence of language skills. Interestingly, the connection was apparent for *declarative* pointing—that is, pointing for the purpose of "commenting" on an object—but not for *imperative* pointing to direct someone to do something. This is intriguing because when apes do communicate with humans, they seem to do much less commenting and much more directing of actions than human children do, even early in their communication. Both are very clearly *communicative* acts, and yet they may have different implications for linguistic sophistication.

It's increasingly apparent, then, that being able to take part in complex social activities that rely on mutual coordination is closely tied to the emergence of language. Researchers like Michael Tomasello have argued that there is a sharp distinction between humans and other apes when it comes to these abilities. But there's controversy over just how sharp this distinction is. It's also not obvious whether these abilities are all genetically determined or whether skills such as joint attention also result from socialization. What should we make, for example, of the fact that apes raised by humans are able to engage in much more sophisticated communication than apes raised by non-humans? Furthermore, we don't have a tremendous amount of detailed data about apes' capabilities for social cognition. Much research has focused on the limitations of non-human primates, but newer studies often show surprisingly good social abilities. For instance, many scientists used to think that chimpanzees weren't able to represent the mental states of others, but it now appears that they're better at it than had been thought (see **Method 2.2**; Call & Tomasello, 2010).

But whether or not the rich social skills of humans reveal a uniquely human adaptation, and whether or not these adaptations occurred largely to support communication (or more generally to support complex social activity), there are other skills that we need in order to be able to command the full expressive power of language. These other skills, in turn, may or may not be rooted in uniquely human adaptations for language, a theme we'll take up in the coming section.

 METHOD 2.2

Exploring what primates can't (or won't) do

Discussions about the evolution of language rely heavily on comparative studies, in which the abilities of different species are evaluated against each other in targeted experiments. These comparisons usually involve designing a test that seems appropriate for all of the species being studied, then applying the same test to members of all the species. The performance of the test subjects is then presumed to reveal something about their cognitive abilities.

But, as any schoolteacher knows, test results don't always tell the whole story when it comes to assessing a student's abilities or knowledge. Some students are highly intelligent but simply don't care, and so their test results are mediocre. Other students become anxious in test situations and freeze up, unable to fully access their knowledge. Test results for all of these students will underestimate what they know or are capable of doing. It's worth keeping this in mind when it comes to using performance on experimental tests as a way to gauge the abilities of various species.

Suppose we're trying to compare a human 2-year-old to an adult chimpanzee. Can we assume that the same test given to both will be an equally good measure of the targeted skills of each? Not necessarily. For instance, the very fact that a *human* experimenter is in charge might have very different effects on the two subjects. The child might be more motivated than the chimp to perform well for the human. The chimp might be more anxious than the child in the presence of a human.

Eliminating these potential problems isn't always possible—after all, we can't readily train a chimp to administer an experiment. But some potential problems can be avoided by paying close attention to the design of the experiments. Specifically, in testing to see whether primates have a particular skill, it makes sense to ask in what situations that skill would be useful to them in the wild. These are the situations in which we'd expect that they'd be motivated to use the relevant skill, and be less disoriented by the experimental setup. This strategy has led researchers to conclude that some past experiments have underestimated the social cognition of chimpanzees.

For example, in one study (Povinelli & Eddy, 1996), chimpanzees appeared to be unable to imagine the visual experience of another individual. The test involved putting a chimpanzee subject in the presence of two humans with food placed between them. One of the humans had a bucket over his head, and hence couldn't see the chimp. The experimenters were interested in learning whether the chimps would choose to beg for food from the human who could see them. Interestingly, their study subjects begged randomly from either human, as if oblivious to the fact that the person wearing the bucket was temporarily blind.

But a number of researchers have argued that, in the wild, a chimpanzee's social understanding is most useful in competitive situations than cooperative ones. A later study (Bräuer et al., 2007) built its experimental design around this premise. In the competitive setup, a lower-ranking chimpanzee competed with a higher-ranking chimpanzee for food. Two pieces of food were present, one of which could be seen by both chimps but the other of which was hidden from the higher-ranking chimp by a barrier. More often than not, the subordinate chimp decided to go for the food that the dominant chimp couldn't see.

The moral of the story seems to be, if you want to find out what a chimp is thinking, you have to think like a chimp as you set up your study.

2.3 The Structure of Language

Combining units

Being able to settle on arbitrary symbols as stand-ins for meaning is just one part of the language puzzle. There's another very important aspect to language, and it's all about the art of combination.

Combining smaller elements to make larger linguistic units takes place at two levels. The first level deals with making words from sounds. In principle, we *could* choose to communicate with each other by creating completely different sounds as symbols for our intended meanings—a high-pitched yowl might mean "arm," a guttural purr might mean "broccoli," a yodel might mean "smile," and so on. In fact, this is very much how vervets use sound for their alarm calls. But at some point, we might find we'd exhausted our ability to invent new sounds but still had meanings we wanted to express. To get around this limitation, we can take a different approach to making words: simply recruit a relatively small number of sounds, and combine them in new and interesting ways. For example, if we take just ten different sounds to create words made up of five sounds each without repeating any of the sounds within a word, we can end up with a collection of more than 30,000 words. This nifty trick illustrates Hockett's notion of *duality of patterning*, in which a small number of units that don't convey meanings on their own can be used to create a very large number of meaningful symbols. In spoken language, we can take a few meaningless units like sounds (notice, for example, that there are no specific meanings associated with the sounds of the letters *p*, *a*, and *t*) and combine them into a number of meaningful words. Needless to say, it's a sensible approach if you're trying to build a beefy vocabulary.

But the combinatorial tricks don't end there. There may be times when we'd like to communicate something more complex than just the concepts of leopard or broccoli. We may want to convey, for instance, that Johnny kicked Freddy in the shin really hard, or that Simon promised to bake Jennifer a cake for her birthday. What are the options open to us? Well, we could invent a different word for every complex idea, so a sequence of sounds like *beflo* would communicate the first of these complex ideas, and another—say, *gromi*—would communicate the second. But that means that we'd need a truly enormous vocabulary, essentially containing a separate word for each idea we might ever want to communicate. Learning such a vocabulary would be difficult or impossible—at some point in the learning process, everyone using the language would need to have the opportunity to figure out what *beflo* and *gromi* meant. This means that as a language learner, you'd have to find yourself in situations (probably more than once) in which it was clear that the speaker wanted to communicate the specific complex idea that *gromi* was supposed to encode. If such a situation happened to *never* arise, you'd be out of luck as far as learning that particular word.

A more efficient solution would be to combine *meaningful* elements (such as separate words) to make other, larger meaningful elements. Even better would be to combine them in such a way that the meaning of the complex idea could be easily understood from the way in which the words are combined—so that rather than simply tossing together words like *Jennifer, birthday, promised, bake, Simon,* and *cake,* and leaving the hearer to figure out how they relate to each other, it would be good to have some structured way of assembling sentences out of their component parts that would make their meanings clear from their structure. This added element of predictability of meaning requires a **syntax**—or a set of "rules"—about how to combine meaningful units together in systematic ways so that their meanings can be transparent. (For example, once we have a syntax in place, we can easily differentiate between the meanings of *Simon promised Jennifer to bake a birthday cake* and *Jennifer promised Simon to bake a birthday cake.*) Once we've added this second level into our communication system, not only have we removed the need to learn and memorize separate words for complex ideas, but we've also introduced the possibility of combining the existing elements of our language to talk about ideas that have never before been expressed by anyone.

Structured patterns

It should be obvious that the possibility of combining elements in these two ways gives language an enormous amount of expressive power. But it also has

syntax In a given language, the set of "rules" that specify how linguistic elements are put together so that their meaning can be clearly understood.

some interesting consequences. Now, anyone learning a language has to be able to learn its underlying structural patterns. And since, for the most part, human children don't seem to learn their native language by having their parents or teachers explicitly teach them the rules of language (the way, for example, they learn the rules of arithmetic), they have to somehow intuit the structures on their own, simply by hearing many examples of different sentences. You might think of language learning as being a lot like the process of reverse engineering a computer program: Suppose you wanted to replicate some software, but you didn't have access to the code. You could try to deduce what the underlying code looked like by analyzing how the program behaved under different conditions. Needless to say, the more complicated the program, the more time you'd need to spend testing what it did.

In case you're tempted to think that language is a fairly simple program, I invite you to spend a few hours trying to characterize the structure of your own native tongue (and see **Box 2.3**). The syntactic structures of human languages involve a lot more than just basic word orders. Once you start looking up close, the rules of language require some extremely subtle and detailed knowledge. For example, how come you can say:

Who did the hired assassin kill the mayor for?

meaning "Who wanted the mayor dead?" But you can't say:

Who did the hired assassin kill the mayor and?

intending to mean "Aside from the mayor, who else did the hired assassin kill?" Or, consider these two sentences:

Naheed is eager to please.
Naheed is easy to please.

These two sentences look almost identical, so why does the first involve Naheed pleasing someone else, while the second involves someone else pleasing Naheed? Or, how is it that sometimes the same sentence can have two very different meanings? As in:

Smoking is more dangerous for women than men.

meaning either that smoking is more dangerous for women than it is for men, or that smoking is even more hazardous than men are for women.

It's not only in the area of syntax that kids have to acquire specific knowledge about how units can be put together. This is the case for sound combinations as well. Languages don't allow sounds to be combined in just any sequence whatsoever. There are constraints. For instance, take the sounds that we normally associate with the letters *r, p, m, s, t,* and *o.* If there were no restrictions on sequencing, these could be combined in ways such as *mprots, stromp, spormt, tromps, rpmsto, tormps, torpsm, ospmtr,* and many others. But not all of these "sound" equally good as words, and if you and your classmates were to rank them from best- to worst-sounding, the list would be far from random.

Here's another bit of knowledge that English speakers have somehow picked up: even though they're represented by the same letter, the last sound in *fats* is different from the last sound in *fads* (the latter actually sounds like the way we usually say the letter *z*). This is part of a general pattern in English, a pattern that's clearly been internalized by its learners: if I were to ask any adult native speaker of English exactly how to pronounce the newly invented word *gebs*, it's almost certain that I'd get the "z" sound rather than the "s" sound.

WEB ACTIVITY 2.2

Finding structure in language
In this activity, you'll put yourself in the shoes of a language learner, and you'll try to find some of the patterns inherent in the structure of English and other languages.

BOX 2.3
The recursive power of syntax

Among the most impressive linguistic accomplishments of human-reared apes is their ability to combine signs in new ways (often producing them in some regular order) and their ability to distinguish the meanings of sentences based solely on how the words are combined. We might conclude from this that apes "get" the idea of syntactic structure, and that the only difference between apes and humans when it comes to combinatorial structure is that we can produce and understand longer, more complicated sentences than they can. But we'd be leaping to unwarranted conclusions. In Method 2.1, you were cautioned against the temptation to overinterpret the data, and to consider the possibility that two species behaving in similar ways at times doesn't mean that the behaviors are driven by the same underlying cognitive apparatus. This applies to evaluating apes' syntactic abilities just as well as it does to their symbolic powers.

Let's suppose that a chimp regularly produces neatly ordered sequences of signs that combine action signs with person/chimp signs. For example:

Washoe tickle. Lana eat. Sue give. Dog growl.

These look a lot like perfectly well-behaved (if minimalist) sentences of English that even a linguistics professor might sometimes utter:

John stinks. Bianca jogs. Students complain.

But this doesn't mean that the system of rules that has generated these sentences looks the same for the chimp and the linguistics professor. All of these sentences *could* be generated by a rule that says:

Symbol for person/chimp/animal doing the action + action

But let's suppose that the professor, in addition to making simple sentences like the ones above, is also capable of producing sentences like these:

John's brother stinks.

Bianca and Leila jog.

Students who are too lazy to do the readings complain.

In fact, our professor can probably even say things like:

John's brother's dog stinks.

Bianca and the girl who lives next door to John's brother jog.

Students who are too lazy to do the readings but want to get an A anyway complain.

Clearly, these sentences can't be produced by the simple rule that is perfectly sufficient to capture the chimp's combinations. It's not just a matter of stringing more words together, or even of having a larger number of rules that allow words to be strung together in a greater variety of ways. It's that the rules have to be different *in kind* from the one I proposed as sufficient for describing the chimp's combinations. For the professor, the linguistic units that get combined with the action words can't just be symbols corresponding to people/chimps/animals, etc. They have to be much more abstract objects—like, whatever it is that you might call the grouping *Bianca and the girl who lives next door to John's brother* or *students who are too lazy to do the readings but want to get an A anyway*. These abstract objects have to in turn be composed of other abstract objects such as *the girl who lives next door to John's brother*—which, by the way, also has to be an abstract object, composed of combinations such as *John's brother*. And so on. Rules that operate at this level of abstraction are called **recursive** because they allow linguistic objects of the same kind (for example, *John's brother*) to be nested within other linguistic objects of the same kind (*the girl who lives next door to John's brother*)—notice, for example, that either of these phrases by itself can be combined with an action word, which is a hint that they are the same kind of phrase.

Rules that work to combine not just words, but higher-order groupings of words, take the language to a whole new level. Whereas word-combining rules allow language users to put together existing words in ways they haven't seen before, rules that allow recursion literally allow users to produce an *infinite* array of meanings because small, abstract units can always be combined with others to make larger abstract units, which can always be combined with others to make larger abstract units, which can always be combined… you get the picture.

Although apes can manage a small number of word-combining rules, recursive rules appear to be beyond their cognitive reach, leading a number of researchers (e.g., Hauser, Chomsky & Fitch, 2002) to suggest that the property of recursion is part of a uniquely human set of skills for language.

---

recursion "Nesting" of related clauses or other linguistic units within each other.

So there's structure inherent at the level of sound as well as syntax, and all of this has to somehow be learned by new speakers of a language. In many cases, it's hard to imagine exactly *how* a child might learn it without being taught—and with such efficiency to boot. For many scholars of the nativist persuasion, a child's almost miraculous acquisition of language is one of the reasons to suspect that the whole learning process must be guided by some innate knowledge.

One of the leading nativists, Noam Chomsky (1986), has suggested that the problem of learning language structure is similar to a demonstration found in one of Plato's classic dialogues. (The ancient Greek philosopher Plato used "dialogues" written as scenarios in which his teacher Socrates verbally dueled with others as a way of expounding on various philosophical ideas.) In the relevant dialogue, Socrates is arguing that knowledge can't be taught, but only *recollected*, reflecting his belief that a person's soul has existed prior to the current lifetime and arrives in the current life with all of its preexisting knowledge. To demonstrate this, Socrates asks an uneducated slave boy a series of questions that reveals the boy's knowledge of the Pythagorean theorem, despite the fact that the boy could not possibly have been taught it.

Chomsky applied the term "Plato's problem" to any situation in which there's an apparent gap between experience and knowledge, and suggested that language was such a case. Children seem to know many things about language that they've never been taught—for instance, while a parent might utter a sentence like "What did you hit Billy for?" she's unlikely to continue by pointing out, "Oh, by the way, notice that you can't say *Who did you hit Billy and?*" Yet have you ever heard a child make a mistake like this?

Moreover, Chomsky argued that children have an uncanny ability to home in on exactly the right generalizations and patterns about their language, correctly chosen from among the vast array of logical possibilities. In fact, he's argued that children arrive at the right structures even in situations where it's extremely unlikely that they've even *heard* enough linguistic input to be able to choose from among the various possible ways to structure that input. In reverse-engineering terms, they seem to know something about the underlying language program that they couldn't have had an opportunity to test. It's as if they are ruling out some types of structures as impossible right from the beginning of the learning process. Therefore, they must have some prior innate knowledge of linguistic structure.

Are we programmed for language structure?

If we do have some innate knowledge of linguistic structure, what does this knowledge look like? It's obvious that, unlike vervets with their alarm calls, or bees with their dances, humans aren't born programmed for specific languages, since all humans easily learn the language that's spoken around them, regardless of their genetic heritage. Instead of being born with a preconception of a specific human language, Chomsky has argued, humans are prepackaged with knowledge of the kinds of structures that make up human languages. As it turns out, when you look at all the ways in which languages could possibly combine elements, there are some kinds of combinations that don't ever seem to occur. Some patterns are more inherently "natural" than others. The argument is that, though different languages vary quite a bit, the shape of any given human language is constrained by certain universal principles or tendencies. So, what the child is born with is not a specific grammar that corresponds to any one particular language, but rather a **universal grammar**, which specifies the bounds of human language in general. This universal grammar manifests itself as a predisposition to learn certain kinds of structure and not others.

universal grammar An innately understood system of combining linguistic units that constrains the structural patterns of all human languages.

If the idea that we could be genetically programmed to learn certain kinds of language patterns more easily than others strikes you as weird, it might help to consider some analogous examples from the animal kingdom. James Gould and Peter Marler (1987) have pointed out that there's plenty of evidence from a broad variety of species where animals show interesting learning biases. For example, rats apparently have trouble associating visual and auditory cues with foods that make them sick, even though they easily link smell-related cues with bad food. They also have no trouble learning to press a bar to get food but don't easily learn to press a bar to avoid an electric shock; they can learn to jump to avoid a shock but can't seem to get it through their heads to jump to get food. Pigeons also show evidence of learning biases: they easily learn to associate sounds but not color with danger, whereas the reverse is true for food, in which case they'll ignore sound but pay attention to color. So, among other animals, there seems to be evidence that not all information is equal for all purposes, and that creatures sometimes harbor useful prejudices, favoring certain kinds of information over others (for instance, for rats, which are nocturnal animals, smell is more useful as a cue about food than color, so it would be adaptive to favor scent cues over color).

Proposing a universal grammar as a general, overarching idea is one thing, but making systematic progress in listing what's in it is quite another. There's no general agreement among language scientists about what an innate set of biases for structure might look like. Perhaps this is not really surprising, because to make a convincing case that a specific piece of knowledge is innate, that it's unique to humans, and furthermore, that it evolved as an adaptation *for language*, quite a few empirical hurdles would need to be jumped. Over the last few decades, claims about an innate universal grammar have met with resistance on several fronts.

First of all, many researchers have argued that nativists have underestimated the amount and quality of the linguistic input that kids are exposed to and, especially, that they've lowballed children's ability to learn about structure on the basis of that input. As you'll see in upcoming chapters, extremely young children are able to grasp quite a lot of information about structure by relying on very robust learning machinery. This reduces the need to propose some preexisting knowledge or learning biases.

Second, some of the knowledge that at first seemed to be very language specific has been found to have a basis in more general perception or cognition, applying to non-linguistic information as well.

Third, some of the knowledge that was thought to be language-specific has been found to be available to other animals, not just humans. This and the more general applicability of the knowledge make it less likely that the knowledge has become hardwired specifically because it is needed for language.

Fourth, earlier claims about universal patterns have been tested against more data from a wider set of human languages, and some researchers now argue that human languages are not as similar to each other as may have been believed. In many cases, apparent universals still show up as very strong tendencies, but the existence of even one or a couple of outliers—languages that seem to be learned just fine by children who are confronted with them—raises questions about how hardwired such "universals" can be. In light of these exceptions, it becomes harder to make the case that language similarities arise from a genetically constrained universal grammar. Maybe they come instead from very strong constraints on how human cognition works, constraints that tend to mold language in particular ways, but that can be overridden.

Finally, researchers have become more and more sophisticated at explaining how certain common patterns across languages might arise from the fact

Engineering the perfect language

In all likelihood, the earliest users of languages never sat down to deliberately invent a system of communication in the way that humans invented Morse code or even the system of writing that we use to visually express our spoken languages. More likely, people intuitively fumbled around for the most natural-seeming way to express themselves, and language as we now know it was the eventual result. And the result *is* impressive. The combinatorial properties of human languages make them enormously powerful as communicative systems. By combining sounds into words and then words into sentences, we can create tens of thousands of meaningful symbols that can be combined in potentially infinite ways, all within the bounds of human ability to learn, use, and understand. An elegant solution indeed. But can it be improved upon?

It's interesting that when modern humans have turned their deliberate attention to language, they've often concluded that naturally occurring language is messy and poorly constructed. Many have pointed out its maddening irregularities and lapses of logic. For example, why in the world do we have the nicely behaved singular/plural forms *dog/dogs, book/books, lamp/lamps*, and *toe/toes* on the one hand—but then have *foot/feet, child/children, bacterium/bacteria, fungus/fungi*, and *sheep/sheep*? Why is language shot through with ambiguity and unpredictability, allowing us to talk about noses running and feet smelling? And why do we use the same word (*head*) for such different concepts in phrases like *head of hair, head of the class, head of the nail, head table, head him off at the pass*?

In a fascinating survey of invented languages throughout history, Arika Okrent (2010) described the various ways in which humans have sought to improve on the unruly languages they were made to learn. Many of these languages, such as Esperanto, were designed with the intention of creating tidier, more predictable, and less ambiguous systems. But unlike Esperanto, which was based heavily on European languages, some invented languages reject even the most basic properties of natural languages in their quest for linguistic perfection.

For example, in the 1600s, John Wilkins, an English philosopher and ambitious scholar, famously proposed a universal language because he was displeased with the fact that words arbitrarily stand in for concepts. In a more enlightened language, he felt, the words themselves should *illuminate* the meanings of the concepts. He set about creating an elaborate categorization of thousands of concepts, taking large categories such as "beasts" and subdividing them down into smaller categories so that each concept fit into an enormous hierarchically organized system. He assigned specific sounds to the various categories and subcategories, which were then systematically combined to form words. The end result is that the sounds of the words themselves don't just arbitrarily pick out a concept; instead, they provide very specific information about exactly where in the hierarchical structure the concept happens to fall. For example, the sounds for the concept of dog were transcribed by Wilkins as *Zita*, where *Zi* corresponds to the category of "beasts," *t* corresponds to the "oblong-headed" subcategory, and *a* corresponds to a sub-subcategory meaning "bigger kind."

Wilkins's project was a sincere effort to create a new universal language that would communicate meaning with admirable transparency, and he held high hopes that it might eventually be used for the international dissemination of scientific results. And many very educated people praised his system as a gorgeous piece of linguistic engineering. But notice that the Wilkins creation dispenses with Hockett's feature of *duality of patterning*, which requires that meaningful units (words) are formed by combining together a number of inherently meaningless units (sounds). Wilkins used intrinsically meaning*ful* sounds as the building blocks for his words, seeing this as an enormously desirable improvement.

But the fact that languages around the world *don't* look like this raises some interesting questions: Why not? And do languages that are based on duality of patterning somehow fit together better with human brains than languages that don't, no matter how logically the latter might be constructed? As far as I know, nobody ever tried to teach Wilkins's language to children as their native tongue, so we have no way of knowing whether it was learnable by young human minds. But surely, to anyone tempted to build the ideal linguistic system, learnability would have to be a serious design consideration.

that all languages are trying to solve certain communicative problems. We can come back to our much simpler analogy of the seeming universality of arrows. Arrows, presumably invented independently by a great many human groups, tend to have certain striking similarities—they have a sharp point at the front end and something to stabilize the back end; they tend to be similar lengths, etc. But these properties simply reflect the optimal solutions for the problem at hand. Language is far more complex than arrows, and it's hard to see *intuitively* how the specific shape of languages might have arisen as a result of the nature of the communicative problems that they solve—namely, how to express a great many ideas in ways that don't overly tax the human cognitive system. But an increasing amount of thinking and hypothesis testing is being done to develop ideas on this front.

2.4 The Evolution of Speech

The ability to speak: Humans versus the other primates

In the previous sections, we explored two separate skills that contribute to human language: (1) the ability to use and understand intentional symbols to communicate meanings, perhaps made possible by complex social coordination skills; and (2) the ability to combine linguistic units to express a great variety of complex meanings. In this section, we consider a third attribute: a finely tuned delivery system through which the linguistic signal is transmitted.

To many, it seems intuitively obvious that speech is central to human language. Hockett believed human language to be inherently dependent on the vocal-auditory tract, and listed this as the very first of his universal design features. And, just as humans seem to differ markedly from the great apes when it comes to symbols and structure, we also seem to be unique among primates in controlling the capacity for speech—or, more generally, for making and controlling a large variety of subtly distinct vocal noises. In an early and revealing experiment, Keith and Cathy Hayes (1951) raised a young female chimpanzee named Viki in their home, socializing her as they would a young child. Despite heroic efforts to get her to speak, Viki was eventually able to utter only four indistinct words: *mama, papa, up,* and *cup.* To understand why humans can easily make a range of speechlike sounds while great apes can't, it makes sense to start with an overview of how these sounds are made.

Most human speech sounds are produced by pushing air out of our lungs and through the vocal folds in our larynx. The vocal folds are commonly called the "vocal *cords,*" but this is a misnomer. Vocal sounds are definitely not made by "plucking" cord-like tissue to make it vibrate, but by passing air through the vocal folds, which act like flaps and vibrate as the air is pushed up. (The concept is a bit like that of making vibrating noises through the mouth of a balloon where air is let out of it.) The vibrations of the vocal folds create vocal sound—you can do this even without opening your mouth, when you making a humming sound. But to make different speech sounds, you need to control the shape of your mouth, lips, and tongue as the air passes through the vocal tract. To see this, try resting a lollipop on your tongue while uttering the vowels in the words *bad, bed,* and *bead*—the lollipop stick moves progressively higher with each vowel, reflecting how high in your mouth the tongue is. In addition to tongue height, you can also change the shape of a vowel by varying how much you round your lips (for instance, try saying *bead,* but round your lips like you do when you make the sound "w"), or by varying whether the tongue is extended forward in the mouth or pulled back. To make the full range of consonants and

Figure 2.3 Comparison of the vocal anatomy of chimpanzees (which is similar to that of the other non-human great apes) and humans. Their lowered larynx and down-curving tongue allow humans to make a much wider variety of sounds than other primates. Humans also differ from other primates in the lack of air sacs (blue) in the throat; the precise consequences of this anatomical difference are not known. (After Fitch, 2000.)

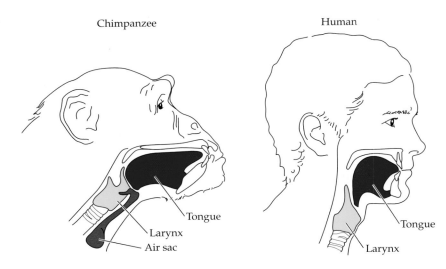

Chimpanzee

Human

Tongue
Larynx
Air sac

Tongue
Larynx

vowels, you have to coordinate the shape and movement of your tongue, lips, and vocal folds with millisecond-level timing.

A comparative glance at the vocal apparatus of humans versus the great apes reveals some striking differences. Looking at **Figure 2.3**, you can see that the human larynx rests much lower in the vocal tract than that of chimpanzees. This creates a roomier mouth in which the tongue can move around and make acoustically distinct sounds. We also have a very broad tongue that curves downward toward the throat. Chimpanzees, whose tongues rest flat in their long and narrow oral cavity, have more trouble producing sounds like the vowels in *bead* or *boo*.

The distinct shape of our vocal tract comes at a tremendous cost: for the great apes, the height of the larynx means that they can breathe and swallow at the same time. We can't, and so quite a few human beings die as a result of choking on their food or drink. It's implausible that this potentially lethal trait would have evolved if it didn't confer a benefit great enough to outweigh the risk. Some researchers have argued that speech is precisely such a benefit, and that (genetically speaking) our species accepted some risk of choking as a fair trade for talking (Lieberman et al., 1969). Still, the link between speech and a lowered larynx is not clear. Many animals can and do actively lower their larynx during vocalization, possibly as a way to exaggerate how large they sound to other animals (see, e.g., Fitch, 2010).

In any case, having the right anatomy for speech is only part of the story. Somewhere in the evolutionary line between chimpanzees and us, our ancestors also had to learn to gain control over whatever articulatory equipment they had. As an analogy, if someone gives you a guitar, that doesn't make you a guitar player (even if it's a really terrific guitar). You still have to develop the ability to play it. And there's reason to believe that, aside from any physical constraints they might have, non-human primates are surprisingly lacking in talent when it comes to manipulating sound. More specifically, they appear to have almost no ability to *learn* to make new vocal sounds—clearly a key component of being able to acquire a spoken language.

As we saw in Section 2.1, most primates come into the world with a relatively fixed and largely innate set of vocalizations. The sounds they produce are only very slightly affected by their environment. Michael Owren and his colleagues (1993) looked at what happened when two infant rhesus macaques were "switched at birth" with two Japanese macaques and each pair was raised by the other species. One revelation of this cross-fostering experiment was that the adopted animals sounded much more like their biological parents than their adoptive ones—obviously a very different situation than what happens with adoptive human infants (see **Box 2.4**).

The failure of primates to learn to produce a variety of vocal sounds is all the more mysterious when you consider that there are many species of birds— genetically *very* distant from us—who have superb vocal imitation skills. Songbirds learn to reproduce extremely complex sequences of sounds, and if not exposed to the songs of adults of their species, they never get it right as adults, showing that much of their vocal prowess is learned and not directly programmed into their genes (Catchpole & Slater, 1995). Many birds such as ravens or mockingbirds easily mimic sounds not naturally found among their species—for instance, the sounds of crickets or car alarms. And parrots are

BOX 2.4
Practice makes perfect:
The "babbling" stage of human infancy

Non-human primates are essentially born with their entire vocal repertoire, skimpy though it is. Human children, however, are certainly not born talking, or even born making anything close to intelligible speech sounds. They take years to learn to make them properly, so even after children have learned hundreds or thousands of words, they still cutely mispronounce them. Some sounds seem to be harder to learn than others—so words like *red* or *yellow* might sound like *wed* or *wewo* coming from the mouth of a toddler. All of this lends further support to the idea that there's a sharp distinction between human speech sounds and the primates' unlearned vocalizations, which need no practice.

Human babies go through an important stage in their vocal learning beginning at about five to seven months of age, when they start to experiment with their vocal instrument, sometimes spending long sessions just repeating certain sounds over and over. Language scientists use the highly technical term *babbling* to describe this behavior. Babies aren't necessarily trying to communicate anything by making these sounds; they babble even in the privacy of their own cribs or while playing by themselves. Very early babbling often involves simple repeated syllables like *baba* or *dodo*, and there tends to be a progression from a smaller set of early sounds to others that make a later appearance. The sounds of the *a* in *cat* and those of the consonants *b, m, d*, and *p* tend to be among the earliest sounds. (Want to guess why so many languages make heavy use of these sounds in the words for the concepts of mother and father—*mama, papa, daddy, abba*, etc.? I personally suspect parental

vanity is at play.) Later on, babies string together more-varied sequences of sounds (for example, *badogubu*), and eventually they may produce what sound like convincing "sentences," if only they contained recognizable words.

The purpose of babbling seems to be to practice the complicated motions needed to make speech sounds, and to match up these motions with the sounds that babies hear in the language around them. Infants appear to babble no matter what language environment they're in, but the sounds they make are clearly related to their linguistic input, so the babbling of Korean babies sounds more Korean than that of babies in English-speaking families. In fact, babbling is so flexible that both deaf and hearing babies who are exposed mainly to a signed language rather than a spoken one "babble" manually, practicing with their hands instead of their mouths. This suggests that an important aspect of babbling is its *imitative* function.

The babbling stage underscores just how much skill is involved in learning to use the vocal apparatus to make speech sounds with the consistency that language requires. When we talk about how "effortlessly" language emerges in children, it's worth keeping in mind the number of hours they log, just learning how to get the sounds right. It's also noteworthy that no one needs to cajole kids to put in these hours of practice, the way parents do with other skills like piano playing or arithmetic. If you've ever watched a babbling baby in action, it's usually obvious that she's having fun doing it, regardless of the cognitive effort it takes. This too speaks to an inherent drive to acquire essential communication skills.

affective pathway Sound production (vocalizations) arising from states of arousal, emotion, and motivation. Affective sound production is innate, doesn't require learning, and is generally inflexible.

cognitive pathway Controlled, highly malleable sound production that requires extensive auditory learning and practice. Includes human language sounds and some birdsong.

even able to faithfully reproduce human speech sounds—a feat that is far beyond the capabilities of the great apes—despite the fact that the vocal apparatus of parrots is quite unlike our own. This suggests that the particular vocal instrument an animal is born with is less important than the animal's skills at willfully coaxing a large variety of sounds from it.

Sophisticated vocal learning is increasingly being found in other non-primate species. For example, seals, dolphins, and whales are all excellent vocal learners, able to imitate a variety of novel sounds, and there are even reports that they can mimic human speech (e.g., Ralls et al., 1985; Ridgway et al., 2012). Recently, researchers have found that an Asian elephant is able to imitate aspects of human speech (Stooger et al., 2012). As evolution researcher Tecumseh Fitch (2000) puts it, "when it comes to accomplished vocal imitation, humans are members of a strangely disjoint group that includes birds and aquatic animals, but excludes our nearest relatives, the apes and other primates."

Why are other primates so unequipped to produce speech sounds? Several researchers (e.g., Jürgens et al., 1982; Owren et al., 2011) have argued that not all vocalizations made by humans or other animals are routed through the same neural pathways. They've pointed out that both humans and other primates make vocalizations that come from an **affective pathway**—that is, these sounds have to do with states of arousal, emotion, and motivation. The sounds that are made via this pathway are largely inborn, don't require learning, and aren't especially flexible. Among humans, the noises that crying babies make would fall into this category, as would the exclamations of surprise, fear, or amusement that we all emit. Notice that, while languages have different words for the concept of a dog, laughter means the same thing the world over, and no one ever needs to learn how to cry out in pain when they accidentally pound their thumb with a hammer. Non-human primates seem to be, for the most part, limited to vocalizations that are made by the affective pathway, and the alarm calls of animals such as the vervets are most likely of this innate and inflexible affective kind.

But humans (and some other animals, including songbirds and aquatic mammals) can also make vocal sounds via a **cognitive pathway**. These sounds usually involve a great deal of auditory learning before they can be reliably produced, take practice, and are highly malleable. Language sounds (unlike giggles or cries of terror) are the result of the cognitive pathway and are, under this view, different from ape vocalizations not just in variety and complexity, but in their fundamental nature.

Language without speech

It would appear, then, that perhaps the sharpest discontinuity between human and non-human primates lies in the ability to produce the speech signal by which linguistic meaning is usually conveyed. But here, the evolutionary story has a very interesting twist: as it turns out, Hockett was wrong, and human languages *aren't* universally spoken. It's true that speech is the default mode along which to transmit language—in every known society whose members have normal hearing, people communicate by shaping the noises that come out of their mouths. But when humans are deprived of their usual auditory powers, they can readily adapt language and produce it by means of gesture instead of speech. *Language*, as it turns out, is not at all the same thing as *speech*, and can exist independently of it. Far from being a form of pantomime, signed languages produced by deaf and hearing people alike have all the characteristics of fully fledged languages. This includes a level of "sound-like" structure where basic gestural elements are combined in various ways to form new words, and a level of complex syntactic structure that includes recursion (see Box 2.3). In fact, as far as language researchers can tell, there are no fundamental differences at all between spoken and signed languages and the ways in which they're learned, used, and understood by human beings. For the purpose of this book, just about all of the ideas that we explore about the psychology of language will apply equally well to signed and spoken languages, and I'll normally use the term *language* to refer to language in either modality. And since English doesn't have a separate word that means "to produce language by means of a signed linguistic system," I'll often use words such as *speak* or *speaker* without intending to exclude signed languages in any way.

So, we've arrived at an evolutionary paradox. It seems apparent that humans have evolved an anatomy and nervous system that outfit them perfectly for speech—and it seems quite plausible that these reflect adaptations *for* linguistic communication. But at the same time, humans aren't dependent on speech in order to communicate linguistically. This state of affairs has led some researchers (e.g., Corballis, 1999) to hypothesize that the earliest forms of human language were gestural, and that at some later point in time, humans developed the capacity to speak. This idea fits well with several facts.

First of all, the great apes are spectacularly bad at learning to communicate with humans through any semblance of speech. But they do far better in learning to communicate through signed languages. In fact, if researchers had thought to look only at whether apes can learn *spoken* modes of language, we'd still be completely ignorant of the fact that they can easily learn to use hundreds of different meaningful symbols and even combine them in novel, if rudimentary, ways. So, while apes have close to zero capacity for speaking through their mouths, they can obviously control their hands and limbs well enough to make a great many distinct gestures and movements.

Second, primatologists have found that when apes communicate with each other in the wild, they *do* spontaneously use gestures. What's especially intriguing is that their gestures tend to be more communicatively flexible than their vocalizations, as noted by several researchers, including Frans de Waal and Amy Pollick (2012). Vocal sounds are often limited to very specific contexts, but apes seem to be able to repurpose the same gesture in a variety of settings, much as we can flexibly use words. For example, a bonobo involved in a fight with another might stretch out its hand toward a third bonobo as a way of requesting help. But the same gesture might then be used in a very different situation, such as requesting food from a bonobo in possession of a treat. Unlike vocalizations (and again, like words in human language), gestures also seem to be more culturally specific, since chimpanzees have been found to use some gestures that are specific to their particular group.

Finally, when you trace the various communicative behaviors through the primate line, gesture makes a plausible precursor to human language compared to vocal communication. We've already talked about how the vocal alarm calls of vervets are quite unlike human speech vocalizations, suggesting that there's a qualitative difference between the two. But it's also interesting that apes, who are genetically most closely related to us, don't make alarm calls, and don't seem to have vocalizations that have a clearly referential function. This makes apes unlike many species of monkeys and other mammals such as prairie dogs, and makes it less likely that alarm calls served as the bedrock on which language was built. At the same time, monkeys don't appear to use manual gestures to communicate in the way that apes and humans do, hinting that gesturing is a trait that arose after apes diverged from their common ancestor with monkeys, but before humans diverged from our common ancestor with apes (see Figure 2.2).

BOX 2.5
What can songbirds tell us about speaking?

One of the most delightful things about science is that insights often come from unexpected places, which should encourage you to look there more often. At first glance, it might seem that studying birds would be an unlikely place to learn how we might have acquired that most human of traits, language. Birds don't look anything like us, their singing appears to be essentially an elaborate courtship display rather than a way to exchange information, and our evolutionary paths diverged some *300 million* years ago rather than the mere 6 million years or so when our ancestral line split off from the chimpanzees'. But none of this stopped Charles Darwin from remarking, back in 1871, that birdsong was the closest analogue to language found in nature.

Through his careful observations, Darwin understood that different species could have similar traits to each other for one of two reasons: they could have a *homologous* trait, meaning that they all inherited it from a common ancestor, or they could have developed *analogous* traits, which means that the species independently arrived at similar solutions because they faced similar evolutionary pressures. For instance, fish and whales have a similar body shape because they need to swim efficiently in the water, not because they are close genetic relatives. For this reason, we shouldn't limit our search for language-like skills to just those species that are most closely related to us.

But even someone as astute as Darwin couldn't have known just how similar to human language birdsong would turn out to be. Hundreds of studies of birds since Darwin's time have revealed the following:

■ Unlike the vocalizations of most mammals, birdsong is not rigidly fixed from birth. Instead, it seems to require the opportunity for learning. In many species baby birds need to hear adult birds singing before develop-ing normal song. They also seem to need to practice their skills, much like humans do, but unlike other mam-mals. For instance, there's evidence that baby birds go through a "babbling" stage, just like human babies, and even-more intriguing evidence that their mastery of vocal sounds progresses through similar stages (Lipkind et al., 2013) and is affected similarly by the responses of parents (Goldstein et al., 2003).

■ Beyond showing highly developed skills in vocal learning and imitation, songbirds also seem to avail themselves of complex ways of structuring their songs. Individual notes can be combined into "syllables," these "syllables" can be combined into larger "motifs," and "motifs" can be combined into entire songs. In many ways, this looks similar to humans' ability to re-use and combine smaller units in order to make larger, more complex units like sentences. It certainly goes well beyond what apes can do in terms of showing an ability to keep track of complex sequences that have a definite underlying structure.

But there's no evidence that any of the elements birds consistently combine into complex, rule-governed sequences have any *meaning* whatsoever. All of these sophisticated capabilities seem to exist mainly to allow male birds to advertise their sexiness to female birds, and to discourage other males from entering their territory. As far as we know, the song's individual components don't mean anything specific. Perhaps the overall complexity of the song simply serves to broadcast information about the bird's reproductive merits. Think of it as the equivalent of a male rock star getting onstage and demonstrating his skill on the guitar, with subsequent effects on the females in the vicinity.

So research on birdsong leads to the intriguing conclusion that, when it comes to both vocal sophistication and combinatorial talents, we may have more in common with our distant feathered relatives than with our primate cousins. It also suggests that even a complex, combinatorial system can evolve for reasons other than the one that seems most obvious in human language—namely, to give enormous communicative power to a language. The similarities and dissimilarities between birdsong and language create an interesting tension, and encourage scientists to look at language evolution from less familiar angles. For example, are there other distant species that show evidence of having some highly developed language-like skills? Do combinatorial skills necessarily go hand in hand with general communicative skills and motivation? And what is the relationship between language and music in humans? Human music and human language show some structural similarities, but only one is used to carry meanings.

But whether gestures served as the vehicle for the first complex, truly language-like systems is hard to know. Clearly, gesture can be used by modern humans when spoken language is not an option, which shows that language can be overlaid on more than one modality. But we simply don't know when complex vocal skills might have emerged relative to some of the other abilities needed to support a fully fledged language. Maybe even more importantly, we don't really have a sense of how these independent skills might have interacted and influenced each other once present in a species.

It may be that to answer these questions, we'll have to broaden our scope and take a close look at animals that are more distant from us genetically than our favorite non-human research subjects, the primates. There's not much evidence that the ancestors we share with other primates had speech capabilities, but there *is* evidence that vocal skills evolved independently in a number of quite different animals. This means we can look for clues as to why such skills might have developed, and how closely tied they might be to some of the other abilities that are needed for human language (see **Box 2.5**).

2.5 How Humans Invent Languages

Communicating from scratch

In the previous sections, we've spent a fair bit of time exploring the linguistic capabilities of animals, and contrasting them with those of humans. One of the interesting findings from this body of research is that when animals interact with humans, they generally prove themselves capable of more sophisticated language skills than we've been able to observe in the wild (presuming, of course, that we're looking for the right kind of "language" when we observe them in the wild). This would seem to be at least modest evidence in favor of the "language-as-tool" camp, which claims that rather than being innately programmed for language, humans invented it to fill a need, and being the supremely social beings that we are, then transmitted this knowledge to subsequent generations. When animals are on the receiving end of this kind of cultural transmission, it seems that they edge somewhat closer to human-like language capability.

But there's another side to the cultural transmission story, and that is that when developing a linguistic system, humans are surprisingly less dependent on cultural transmission than one might think. True enough, no child deprived of hearing German has ever grown up to speak German, fluently or otherwise. A central theme throughout this chapter is how our particular linguistic knowledge relies heavily on *learning*. But, as it turns out, a child deprived of any real language at all *does* have the resources to invent from scratch at least the basic framework of a language that has just about all of the properties that researchers agree are common to all human languages.

How do we know this? You might be relieved to know that language researchers don't deliberately assign children to experimental conditions in which no one speaks to them for 10 years, in order to see what happens. But researchers *can* see what happens in situations where nature has deprived children of their ability to hear the language spoken around them. Over 90% of deaf children are born to hearing parents, and since only a very small minority of hearing adults know any signed languages, these children are born into a situation where they can't receive the linguistic input that the adults around them are able to provide.

homesign A personal communication system initiated by a deaf person to communicate through gestures with others who, like the deaf person, do not know sign language.

Nevertheless, these youngsters are highly innovative when it comes to creating a gestural system for communication. This phenomenon is referred to as **homesign**. The fascinating thing about homesign is that it comes about at the initiative of the child, who has not yet had the opportunity to learn what a human language might look like, rather than being invented by the adult, who has already mastered at least one language. According to Susan Goldin-Meadow, one of the researchers who has studied gesture and homesign most extensively, the parents of these children do gesture, but usually as an accompaniment to speaking, and they generally don't use their gestures in a way that systematically carries meaning. In contrast, children who homesign typically do make systematically meaningful gestures, as described below (a more detailed description can be found in Goldin-Meadow, 2005).

When gestures replace language

In homesign, children produce separate signs as separate symbols. This is different from how people normally gesture while speaking. When people speak, they often gesture to show emphasis, or to bring out some perceptual aspect of what they're talking about—for example, while talking about a particular person, a gesture might be used to indicate that he's large, or that someone is curvaceous. But these gestures don't have a *referential* value the way that the spoken names do—that is, they don't stand in as symbols for that particular person. Children's homesign gestures, however, *do* have such a referential function, and children tend to reuse the same gestures to convey the same meaning across a wide variety of situations—for example, to make requests, to ask questions, and to comment on a person or situation, whether present or not at the time.

Children also use combinations of signs to convey complex ideas—for example, rather than having a separate sign for holding an umbrella and holding a balloon, a child would invent a sign for the general notion of holding, and combine that with signs for the concepts of balloon and umbrella. Combinations of this sort are used systematically in such a way that the relations between the units can be surmised from their order.

All fully fledged languages have bits of sound (or signs) that reflect inherently relational concepts—that is, words or parts of words like *and, if, since; -s* at the end of a word to mark plural or *-ed* to mark past, and so on. Homesigning children have been seen to invent signs to mark past and future, or the concept that's captured by the word *but*. Goldin-Meadow has even argued that children show evidence of recursion, being able to create more complex sentential units out of simpler sentences.

In terms of the structural complexity of the homesign system, children deprived of any reliable linguistic input already exceed apes who have the benefit of a rich linguistic environment. They also exceed apes in the variety of uses that they put their communication system to. In addition to making requests or commenting on people and situations, children can use homesign to spin a narrative; to talk about hypothetical events; to make statements not just about particular things, but also about things in general (for example, to convey that dogs bark); to talk to themselves; and to comment on their homesign system. And there's evidence that if they have to rely on their homesign system into adulthood (for example, if they never properly learn a commonly used signed language or a spoken language), they continue to innovate and add complexity over time.

WEB ACTIVITY 2.3

Children using homesign
In this activity, you'll view video clips of children using homesign to communicate.

The existence of homesign ought to make advocates of the language-as-tool scenario sit up and take notice. It's clear that in addition to being born with the capacity to *learn* language, children are born with, at least to some degree, the capacity to *invent* language, and that these invented languages share some significant similarities with each other as well as with more developed languages. And, more tellingly, this inventive capacity seems to be exercised by all children who are not provided with a culturally transmitted language, but who are otherwise raised in a highly social environment. Maybe it's useful to return to the analogy of arrow-making, which Daniel Everett (2012) argues is a good way to think about language: Given the usefulness of arrows, it's not surprising that just about every human society developed some form of them, and it's also likely that every human being of normal intelligence has the *capacity* to invent an arrow. But this doesn't mean that every single person in any given society *would* invent an arrow if presented anew with the problem of protein-catching. More likely, some would, some wouldn't (maybe they'd explore other possible solutions), and those who didn't would look over at the arrows made by their ingenious peers, say "What a great idea!" and promptly copy it. Yet, language of some kind does seem to be truly universal even at the level of individuals, and not just at the level of groups.

WEB ACTIVITY 2.4

Gestures supporting or replacing speech In this activity, you'll observe people as they describe events. Note how they use gesture, either as an accompaniment to speech, or as a replacement for speech when they are instructed to communicate non-verbally. Note also the similarities and differences in the gestures across the two situations.

Language: It takes a village

Homesign systems don't develop into full languages if the engine behind them is a single person, suggesting that something more is needed than just one person's inventiveness. But that something more doesn't need to involve a more sophisticated form of language providing a model that can be copied. It turns out that when *a number of people* engage in the same system of homesign, it quickly ratchets up in its complexity and systematicity.

In most of North America, deaf people are either surrounded by hearing people who try to use their own spoken languages to communicate with them, or they have access to a community of speakers of American Sign Language (ASL), a fully formed language in its own right. Typically a deaf person's experience involves both situations. But recent events in Nicaragua have provided researchers with a fascinating natural experiment in which a group of deaf people who did not know either signed or spoken language were brought together and began to communicate in a shared homesign system.

Before the 1970s, deaf people in Nicaragua had very little contact with each other, usually growing up in hearing families with little access to a broader educational system or services for the deaf. But in 1977, a school for the deaf was founded in the capital city of Managua and quickly expanded to serve hundreds of students in the region. The aim of the school was to teach the children Spanish via lip-reading, and it was not overly successful in this respect. But the really interesting linguistic action took place when children were allowed to use gesture to communicate with each other in the schoolyard or on the bus. The staff at the school initially took no part in this gestural system, but when it became apparent that this parallel system of communication was becoming the dominant means of communication for their students, they called in some experts in signed languages to provide some insight. Since then, the students' emerging sign language has been documented by researchers, among them Judy Kegl, Annie Senghas, Marie Coppola, and Laura Polich.

What seems to have happened is this: The children arrived, each having developed, to a greater or lesser degree of complexity, some system of homesign that they'd used to communicate with their hearing families and friends. Once together, they quickly negotiated a shared, standard homesign system to use with each other. By the time the researchers showed up (Kegl et al., 1999), they noticed that, as with many homesign systems, the Nicaraguan kids showed some basic language-like patterns in their gestures. But they also noticed that as younger students arrived and were exposed to the shared homesign system, they began to alter it in ways that gave it greater communicative power. For example, in comparison to the older, original group of students, the younger signers used gestures more efficiently—they made more compact gestures that required less movement, and they combined them more fluently with each other. Whereas the older signers were found to be able to express 24 different events per minute, the younger singers almost doubled this expressive capacity, to 46 events per minute. Individual signs also came to carry more information, and the younger signers were more consistent in the ways they used signs.

Streamlining signing

Along with the efficiency gain, the researchers also documented some significant ways in which the signed system was being restructured and reorganized. As noted by Susan Goldin-Meadow and her colleagues (1996), when gestures accompany speech, they often have a pantomimed quality to them—for example, if you were pantomiming an event in which someone ate a cookie, you might imitate the action of taking a cookie out of the cookie jar and eating it. But when gestures are used *instead* of speech, they're more likely to be produced as separate signs corresponding to separate concepts that are then combined together in sequence. So the same cookie-eating event might be communicated by pointing to a cookie, or by representing it as a round shape and then using a separate gestural symbol to communicate the notion of eating. In a deep way, this reflects a shift from a purely gestural system (playing a supporting role to language) toward a more *linguistic* one in its own right, where symbols are used for general concepts in such a way that they can be recombined with other elements. (You may have noticed this in the examples from Web Activity 2.4)

Annie Senghas and her colleagues (2004) noticed that the younger learners of Nicaraguan Sign Language were pushing their new language further along this trend, abandoning holistic signs in favor of more sequential ones (see **Figure 2.4**). To test this trend in a systematic way, the researchers showed older and younger signers some animated cartoons that depicted objects in motion (such as rolling down a hill) and had them use sign to communicate what had happened in the videos. (For comparison, they also recorded the gestures that were made by hearing Spanish speakers while orally describing the events.) In these events, it might be especially tempting to use a single holistic sign to simulate the motion. And in fact, when the videos were described by the Spanish speakers with accompanying gestures, the gestures were *always* holistic rather than sequential. The oldest signers were more likely than the Spanish speakers to break down the event into two component parts, produced one after the other, but they still produced holistic gestures more often than not. However, things were dramatically different with the younger signers; the two groups of students who arrived later than the original group were both found to use sequential signs most of the time.

WEB ACTIVITY 2.5

Inventing a sign language In this activity, you'll get together with classmates to brainstorm and negotiate ways to mark certain kinds of linguistic information using the modality of gesture. Take a stab at coming up with creative ways to communicate some of the abstract information that languages are so good at capturing!

(A)

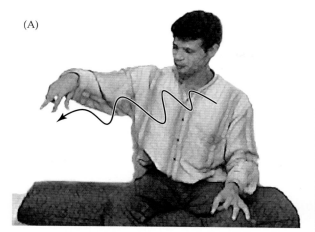

(B)

Figure 2.4 Holistic gestures (A) and sequential signs (B) exemplified by two individuals expressing the motion of rolling downhill. (A) A Spanish speaker gestures while talking. Notice how he has incorporated both the manner of motion (rolling) and the path (down) into a single gesture. (B) The person in these two photos is a third-cohort signer of Nicaraguan Sign Language; she has separated the manner and path of the motion into two separate signs, performed in sequence. (From Senghas et al., 2004.)

Another interesting change was in the way in which the signers came to use spatial location for grammatical purposes. Signs within Nicaraguan Sign Language (NSL) are usually made in a neutral position, right in front of the body, so shifting away from that neutral position can be used to imbue the sign with some additional information. Mature sign languages make use of shifts in the spatial locations of signs for a variety of different reasons—for marking past and future, for example, or even to distinguish between the grammatical subject and object of a verb. When Annie Senghas and Marie Coppola (2001) looked at how NSL signers used space, they found that older signers produced signs in non-neutral locations for a number of different reasons—for example, to introduce new characters or topics, or to indicate different points in time. But the younger signers had settled on a very specific function of spatial signing: they used it when making the signs for verbs, in order to show that the individual involved in two different actions was the same. For example, if they made the signs for *see* and *pay* in the same non-neutral location, this meant that the same person who was seen was also paid. But to the older signers, who hadn't yet attached a specific function to spatial locations for signs, the same two verbs signed in this way could mean either that the same person was seen and paid, or that one person was seen, while another, different person was paid.

Many other changes have been observed for Nicaraguan Sign Language over time. Overall, these changes have had the general effect of putting more information into the conventionalized system of signs—the **linguistic code**—so that there is less of a burden on the viewer to rely on context or shared knowledge to fill in the gaps. Older languages that have developed over many generations rely on a great many abstract grammatical markers to mark subtle nuances of meaning. To get a feel for why all this grammatical marking might have emerged, let's imagine a version of English that has a much sparser linguistic code than our current version, in terms of its structure and markers—think of a simplified form of English spoken by a small child, or by someone just beginning to learn English. For each of the simplified versions below (the *a* sentences), think about the additional contextual knowledge you'd need to have in order to understand it as equivalent to the *b* version of the sentence, but distinct from the *c* version:

(*a*) Christopher Columbus sail America.
(*b*) Christopher Columbus sailed to America.
(*c*) Christopher Columbus will sail from America.

linguistic code The system of symbols and combinatory rules that are conventionally agreed upon by a community of language users as conveying specific meanings. Often, the linguistic code is not enough to fully convey the speaker's *intended* meaning, so that hearers must augment the linguistic code with inferences based on the context.

(a) Francis build house last year.
(b) Francis was building a house all of last year.
(c) Francis built a house last year.

(a) Timmy marry girl. Girl have baby.
(b) Timmy is going to marry a girl who's had a baby.
(c) The girl that Timmy married is going to have a baby.

It's not hard to see how elaborating the linguistic code with the grammatical embellishments found in the more complex sentences might help improve the efficiency of communication and reduce the possibility of misunderstandings.

The sensitive period and innate language ability

Senghas and other NSL researchers have suggested that two ingredients were needed in order for this shared homesign to progress beyond its humble beginnings: (1) a community of speakers using the same linguistic system; and (2) a generational progression in which very young speakers were exposed to the structured input of their linguistic predecessors. The greatest competency in the language, and the most sophisticated innovations, were observed in new learners who had the benefit of the structured system that had been put in place by a previous cohort of students. In particular, students who were very young when exposed to this structured input benefited the most. This fits with the notion that there's a **sensitive period**, a window of time during which children seem to have a special aptitude for learning language. In general, young children who are exposed to a foreign language learn it quickly and in a native-like manner, whereas most adults who start learning a foreign language never achieve native fluency, even after decades of exposure. It's easy to see this in immigrant families in which the kids rapidly shoot past their parents' or grandparents' abilities to speak in their newly adopted tongue—much to the annoyance and envy of their elders.

Many nativists have argued that evidence of a sensitive period for language learning supports the view that language is innately specified. If, as the non-nativists claim, language is simply a by-product of our vigorous intellectual capacity, then it's hard to explain why it should be that small children—who overall are *not* as smart as adolescents or adults—seem to have a leg up on their intellectual superiors when it comes to language learning. On the other hand, it's not hard to explain under a nativist view, as there are other cases in nature where a genetically hardwired ability never develops properly if it hasn't been activated within a certain window of time. For instance, if songbirds are kept from hearing the songs made by adults of their species during a certain period of their development, they never manage to sing normally afterwards (e.g., Brainard & Doupe, 2002).

The parallel to songbirds is especially intriguing, given that there's a surprising amount of overlap between human language and complex birdsong, as discussed in Box 2.5 (see p. 36). Birdsong, like human language, seems to involve a mixture of genetic programming and learning from experience, though it looks like the precise balance between genes and experience varies somewhat among bird species. But the songbird story gets especially interesting when we consider that researchers have found among our avian friends some parallels to the emergence of NSL. In a study by Olga Feher and her colleagues (2009), young male zebra finches were kept from contact with other birds (researchers use the term *isolate* to refer to a young bird in this situation). Isolates that aren't exposed to adult song never grow to sing normally, but parallel to human homesigners, they do produce simpler, distorted songs with some of the elements present in

sensitive period A window of time during which a specific type of learning (such as learning language) takes place more easily than at any other time.

the normal adult songs. It turns out that new baby birds will readily imitate the songs of isolates even though they sound abnormal. The researchers wondered: If baby birds only hear songs of isolates and are kept from hearing normal

LANGUAGE AT LARGE 2.2

From disability to diversity: Language studies and deaf culture

If you're a primate, there are some obvious advantages to being able to hear: you can get advance warning of approaching predators, locate your youngster when she's out of sight, and generally gain a fair bit of valuable information about the physical world. But if you're a *human* primate, your social world is at least as important as your physical world, and the advantages of hearing come mostly from giving you access to language. Without language, how do you benefit from knowledge accumulated by previous generations, how do you learn about the institutional cultures of your society, and how do you teach your own children all these things?

As late as 1960, the time at which Hockett published his ideas about language universals (see Box 2.1), it was widely thought that all languages were spoken. The predominant belief was that humans learned language by imitating their parents, and by being rewarded by them for producing the right sounds. The notion that languages could leap spontaneously from human brains whenever there was a need to communicate and people to communicate with was a foreign one to most people. So perhaps it was not too surprising that existing sign languages—which, after all, simply *happened* without anyone teaching them— were not seen as true languages, but rather as systems of pantomime. Efforts to teach linguistic skills to those who could not hear focused mainly on the torturous instruction of lip-reading and vocal training, since this was seen as the only entry point into language.

All of this began to change when William Stokoe, an English instructor teaching at Gallaudet University, began a more systematic study of the sign language used by his deaf students. He concluded that, far from being a pantomime, their sign language had grammatical elements and structures, and moreover, that these grammatical elements were completely different from those found in English (though no less systematic). He declared the system to be a language in its own right, giving it the name American Sign Language (ASL), and published the enormously influential book *Sign Language*

Structure in 1960—the same year that Hockett's paper on language universals listed the vocal/auditory modality of language as the very first universal feature. Since then, many language researchers have confirmed and extended Stokoe's findings that ASL and other sign languages use many grammatical devices that are analogous to spoken languages, and that they're just as capable of expressing abstract thoughts and ideas.

This knowledge has changed everything about the public perception of sign language and its role in the education and development of deaf people. It used to be thought that signing interfered with a deaf child's learning of a "real" language. Today it is broadly recognized that giving young children access to a sign language very early in their lives is the best way to make sure they'll be able to acquire a native language that they can effortlessly manipulate. Far from being seen as a poor substitute for spoken language, sign languages now have the status of common spoken languages, like German or Arabic. There is deaf theater performed in sign language, there are ASL interpreters at conferences and on TV, and there are courses on ASL in the language departments at colleges and universities; you can even buy an instructional DVD. And most dramatically, there's a general recognition that deafness need not be a disability at all, especially if one lives and works in a community of people who use sign language to carry out the business and pleasures of their daily lives. It's not the deafness itself that is disabling, so much as the mismatch in language modalities that deaf people have experienced with the people around them.

Many advocates for the deaf feel that there are lingering misconceptions and biases about sign language and deaf culture. And, as with any minority culture, tensions exist within both deaf and hearing communities about the appropriate degree of integration between the two cultures. Nevertheless, the core insight that sign languages are *languages*—achieved through rigorous and scientific study—has transformed the lives of many deaf individuals around the world.

adult song, what do they grow up to sound like? Do they sound just like the first-generation isolates, or do they, like later cohorts of NSL signers, add on to the song system and change it? Their experiments found that the second-generation isolates, exposed only to the songs of the first generation, produced sounds that came closer to the normal songs of zebra finches than the first generation did. The researchers then had progressive generations of zebra finches learn from their predecessors and found that over the course of three or four generations, the songs of the zebra finches raised in this way came to sound very much like what the birds produce in a normal environment. It seems that birdsong, like human language, can reconstitute itself from nothingness into something approaching its full glory in a small number of generations.

So where does language come from?

It's tempting to see the emergence of homesign and NSL as evidence that children are innately hardwired for language. Certainly, *something* is driving the creation of a linguistic system that has many of the features of fully developed languages. But we still don't know exactly what that something is. We also don't know exactly why it is that in order to create a "full" language with all the complexities of more developed languages, kids need exposure to language from other people, even if it's not exposure to a fully formed variety of language. Nor do we know which of the features commonly found across languages are universal because they are written by nature into our genetic code, and which of these features might arise simply because they represent the optimal solution for how to package and transmit the kinds of information that human beings are inclined to share with each other.

What is clear is that language is the result of an intricate collaboration between biology and culture. It's extremely unlikely that *all* of the features of language are genetically determined, or conversely, that *all* of them are cultural inventions made possible by our big brains. In the upcoming chapters of this book, you'll learn a great deal more about how language works within the context of our other cognitive systems. All of the knowledge in this book will ultimately bear on the question of where language comes from and why it is that we have it.

2.6 Survival of the Fittest Language?

Changes in languages

So far, we've talked about language evolution and adaptation entirely from a biological perspective. That is, a trait is adaptive to the extent that it helps an organism survive and procreate. Organisms that survive and procreate pass on their genes, while those that die young or can't attract a mate fail to leave a genetic legacy. As a result of this cold, hard reality, the genes for an adaptive trait spread throughout a population or species. In this scenario, what changes over time is the genetic makeup of the individuals that make up the species. In language nativist terms, the capacity for language is adaptive and those humans who readily learned and used language had a reproductive advantage over those who didn't, so over many generations, the general human population came to possess a highly efficient set of cognitive skills tuned for the learning and use of language. By this account, the human brain as shaped by our genes has changed over time and has become specifically good at language.

But it's also possible to talk about the evolution of language from a completely different angle. Languages *themselves* are in a constant state of change, and not just when they're being newly formed, as with Nicaraguan Sign Language. The English in which Chaucer wrote the *Canterbury Tales* is incomprehensible to most people who speak English today. Americans have come to speak a variety of English that is different from the one people in the United Kingdom speak—and neither of those varieties is the same as the English that came out of Shakespeare's mouth 500 years ago (see **Box 2.6**). In fact, your version of English isn't even exactly the same as your grandparents' version (even assuming your grandparents were native English speakers). It's common for older generations to complain about the "poor grammar" of younger generations, and perhaps you've had someone older than you chastise you for saying "I'm good" instead of "I'm well," or inform you that it's wrong to say "less than three cookies"—that it should be "fewer than three cookies," or that "Who did you call?" should be "Whom did you call?" If so, maybe *you* should inform *them* that these aren't grammatical errors—they're grammatical *mutations*.

Languages—like genes within populations—are in constant flux. English has seen some significant changes over the years, including how words are pronounced, what words mean, and which grammatical markers or structures have been adopted. As one minor example, back in the 1600s, over the great

BOX 2.6
Evolution of a prayer

These five versions of the "Lord's Prayer," a common Christian prayer (Matthew 6: 9–13), reflect changes from Old English to present-day English. This text was chosen as an example because of its ready availability across historical periods that span 1,000 years, and because it illustrates how the same message has been expressed during these different periods (see Hock 1986, from which this presentation is modified). It is interesting to note that even today the King James version of 1611 remains the most widely recognized English rendition of this prayer.

Old English (ca. 950)
Fader urer ðu arð in heofnum, sie gehalgad noma ðin, to-cymeð ric ðin, sie willo ðin suæ is in heofne on in eorðo, half userne oferwistlic sel is todæg ond forgef us scylda usra suæ uœ forgefon scyldum usum, ond ne inlæd usih in costunge, ah gefrig usich from yfle.

Middle English (Late fourteenth century)
Oure fadir þat art in heuenes, halwid be þi name, þi kyngdom come to be. Be þi wille don in herþe as it is doun in heuene. Geue to vs to-day oure eche dayes bred. And forgeue to vs our dettis, þat is oure synnys, as we forgeuen to oure dettoris, þat is to men þat han synned in vs. And lede vs not into temptacion, but delyvere vs from euyl. Amen, so be it.

Early New English (William Tyndale's translation, 1534)
O oure father which arte in heven, hallowed be thy name. Let thy kingdome come. Thy wyll be fulfilled, as well in erth, as it ys in heven. Geve vs this daye oure dayly breede. And forgeve vs oure treaspases, even as we forgeve our trespacers. And leade vs not into temptacion, but delyver vs from evell. For thyne is the kyngedome and the power and the glorye for ever. Amen.

Elizabethan English (King James Bible, 1611)
Our Father which art in heaven, Hallowed be thy name. Thy kingdom come. Thy will be done in earth, as it is in heaven. Give us this day our daily bread. And forgive us our debts, as we forgive our debtors. And lead us not into temptation, but deliver us from evil: For thine is the kingdom, and the power, and the glory, for ever. Amen.

Modern English
Our father in heaven, may your name be sacred. Let your kingdom come. May your will be fulfilled as much on earth as it is in heaven. Give us today our daily bread. And forgive us our transgressions, as we forgive those who transgress against us. And do not lead us into temptation, but free us from sin. For the kingdom and the power and the glory are yours forever. Amen.

protests of stodgier generations, speakers of the English language stopped differentiating between singular and plural pronouns for the second person—*you* (plural) and *thou* (singular) became collapsed into the pronoun *you,* used for either the plural or singular. The phenomenon of language change has long been studied with great interest by linguists. In fact, at the time Charles Darwin was still mulling over his ideas about biological evolution, linguists were already well aware of language's tendency to mutate and gradually shape-shift—often diverging over time into separate languages, just as genetic drift can eventually result in distinct species (see **Figure 2.5**).

In biological evolution, mutations occur randomly and natural selection determines whether a mutation spreads throughout a population. Some contemporary language researchers have been advocating a modified notion of natural selection as a force that shapes linguistic mutations. This perspective raises an interesting question: What characteristics does a language need to have in order to ensure its survival? It seems logical that at least two criteria would need to be met:

1. *The language needs to be communicatively useful.* This means that the language should be able to convey the information that people want to get across in an efficient way. Efficiency probably needs to be seen from the perspectives of both the speaker and the hearer. Ideally, the delivery of information should take as little time as possible to utter (and to make sense of), and it also shouldn't put too much strain on the processing resources of either the speaker or the hearer. Forms that take too long to utter, or that mentally tax the speaker, or that are subject to misunderstandings by the hearer, will simply be used less often than more optimal forms, so over time, people will converge on the best communicative solutions.

2. *New learners need to be able to learn the language.* The features of a language that are difficult to learn will simply *not* be learned and, as a result, won't be passed down to a new generation of learners. This means that new learners may play an important *filtering* role in shaping language. In fact, several researchers (e.g., Mufwene, 2008) have proposed that this filter is the driving force behind linguistic changes that take place when a language is passed from one generation to another—maybe it's not so much that children *innovate* changes more than previous users of the language, but that they play a key role in selecting which of a number of inconsistently produced innovations will survive and become more systematically used by speakers of the language.

Figure 2.5 A dendrogram (tree) presenting the relationships among some of the modern European languages, showing how they diverged from a common ancestral language through a series of linguistic changes over time. Languages in parentheses are no longer spoken.

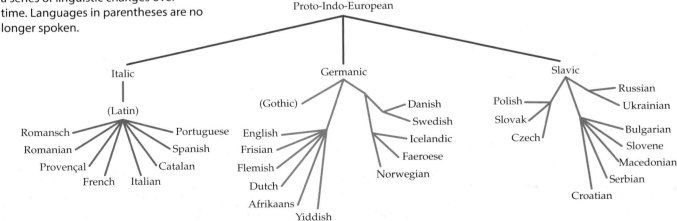

What's adapting to what?

The perspective of linguistic evolution offers a dramatic reversal of the traditional nativist stance on language, as noted by Nick Chater and Morten Christiansen (2008). Nativists who argue that children are innately outfitted with a universal grammar take the view that the human mind has changed over time so as to adapt to the forms and structures that occur in human languages. But the alternative perspective I've just sketched out—let's call it the **cultural transmission view of language change**—says that it's *languages* that have changed over time so as to adapt to the human mind, with all the constraints, limitations, and abilities that human minds bring to the task of learning or using language. Each of these two accounts offers an explanation for why it is that human languages share a number of similarities with each other, but the explanations look strikingly different. Under the nativist view, commonalities across languages reflect hardwired biases to learn certain forms of language. These biases allow children to quickly zoom in on the correct structures of their languages rather than floundering around considering all the logical possibilities. Under the cultural transmission view, languages are similar to each other because they've all had to adapt to the human brain, and presumably, the capabilities and limitations of the human brain are similar across many cultures.

The cultural transmission view has some fascinating implications to explore. For example, if the cultural forces of "natural selection" include both a language's usefulness *and* its learnability, then perhaps a language might be coaxed into different shapes depending on the makeup of the population that uses and learns it. For instance, it might be very interesting to compare the development of Nicaraguan Sign Language with another emerging sign language that has recently caught the attention of language scientists, Al-Sayyid Bedouin Sign Language, or ABSL (see **Figure 2.6**). First described by Wendy Sandler and colleagues in 2005, ABSL has emerged in a small Bedouin community in Israel. This community is unusual in that a great many of its members have an inherited form of deafness because of the high rates of intermarriage within the small population. Far from posing a problem for the community, this has led to a new signed language, created by the people and used by deaf and hearing individuals alike. A deaf child grows up fully integrated within the society, and usually marries a hearing person—which means that families continue to be a mixture of hearing and non-hearing individuals, which in turn motivates hearing members of the family to learn ABSL. This emerging language is now three generations old; its earliest

cultural transmission view of language change The notion that languages change over time to adapt to the human mind, with all the constraints, limitations, and abilities that human minds bring to the task of learning or using language. This view stands in contrast to the nativist view, which holds that the human mind has changed over time because it has become adapted for the requirements of language.

Figure 2.6 Two speakers of Al-Sayyid Bedouin Sign Language, spoken by about 150 deaf and hearing speakers of the Al-Sayyid Bedouin community in the Negev desert in southern Israel. (From Senghas, 2005; photographs by Shai Davidi, University of Haifa.)

adopters are now dead, so it's not possible to know exactly how this language first came to be, and whether it was at the initiative of deaf or hearing people or the result of a joint effort. But what is known is that even the basic word order is different from any of the spoken languages in the region, so from the beginning, it seems to have sprung up with its own structures rather than simply importing them from the nearest spoken language at hand.

There are a few striking differences between the groups of people who collectively created NSL and ABSL, and as pointed out by Annie Senghas (2005), these differences might turn out to be relevant for how the languages take shape. First of all, the speakers of ABSL all come from a single very tight-knit community, whereas the speakers of NSL were bused in from across a large region, coming from many different families and villages that have little connection to each other. Why might this matter? Remember that many of the innovations that were brought into NSL involved making the linguistic code more precise and unambiguous. This reduced people's need to rely on shared contextual knowledge in order to recover the subtleties of the intended meaning. The earliest speakers of NSL, gathered together as they were from diverse backgrounds, would likely have had much less shared knowledge with each other than the earliest speakers of ABSL. Because of this, the communicative pressures within the two communities might have been quite different, with possibly more pressure on the NSL community to pack a lot of information into its linguistic code very early on.

A second important difference between the two communities speaks to the issue of learnability. New learners of ABSL are exposed to the language from birth within their own families. But deaf children in Nicaragua typically don't start to learn NSL until they're old enough to be sent to school. This means that the cognitive makeup of the new learners is quite different across the two groups—if children serve as "filters" for the form of a language, this might result in different kinds of information being filtered out of the language system by the two different groups.

Linguistic directional selection

Newly emerging signed languages provide a special opportunity to look at how languages are shaped in their early stages of development. But perhaps we need not hunt far and wide for these rare cases of newborn languages in order to see the effects that different populations of learners might have on the languages that they pass on to later generations. It's true that the most common language-learning scenario is one in which children learn from birth the language of their parents, which their parents in turn learned as infants from *their* parents. But historical events intervene often enough to create a variety of different learning situations. We can look pretty close to home, at the historical development of English. In the ninth and tenth centuries, a large number of Vikings from Scandinavia invaded England and settled there. Their language was Old Norse, but they interacted with English speakers, picking up the English language and mixing bits of Old Norse with Old English—a fact to which we owe words like *window, cake, smile,* and *skin,* among many others. But according to linguist John McWhorter (2002), the Vikings' linguistic legacy went much deeper than simply sprinkling our language with some new words. McWhorter argues that many of the first Viking learners of English learned their new language as adults, not as children, and as a result were past the age of smooth and effortless language learning. They'd be unlikely to have achieved native-like proficiency, which means that if their children relied mainly on their parents for English language input, they would have received a distorted, inconsistent version of it. McWhorter goes on to suggest that this unusual learning situation was responsible for a long-standing puzzle in the history of the English language—namely, the fact that English has shorn off many of the grammatical markers that are found in related languages such as German and Dutch, and which were presumably present in the ancestral language from which they all evolved. There are many ways in which English is different from its Germanic sibling languages, but overall, the effect has been to strip away certain grammatical markers from the linguistic code in places where the meaning can be inferred from the context (see **Box 2.7** for an example). McWhorter's theory is that a generation of adult learners of English caused a disruption in the normal transmission process, thereby simplifying the grammar.

Notice that this trend of simplifying the grammar goes in exactly the opposite direction from the NSL innovations you saw earlier. In looking at NSL, we saw how a younger generation of signers elaborated the language by creating new grammatical markers to *consistently communicate certain concepts in the linguistic code* rather than leaving them dependent on context. McWhorter argues that over extended periods of time, languages have a tendency to accumulate such markers and force their use even in situations where they're not really needed. Markers become entrenched in the language, he claims, because they're easy for children to learn, given their superior language-learning abilities. But if a language ever has to contend with large numbers of adult learners,

BOX 2.7
Reflexive markers in Germanic languages

In his 2002 paper, John McWhorter discusses a number of ways in which English has dropped grammatical markers that are present in other Germanic languages. The reflexive marker is one such example.

In English, we use pronouns like *himself* or *herself* to communicate reflexive actions—that is, actions in which the person who initiated an action is also on the receiving end of it, as in *he shot himself* or *she scratched herself*. But when it's the case that the action is *usually* performed on oneself, we don't have to include the pronoun (though we can): *he shaved (himself)*, *she bathed (herself)*. When the reflexive is absent, it's understood that the action was performed on oneself.

But in other Germanic languages (see Figure 2.5), a reflexive grammatical marker is obligatory, even if this information seems obvious from the context. In these languages, it's even obligatory to attach these markers with many verbs that English speakers think of as so inherently reflexive that it would be very odd to ornament them with a pronoun like *himself*—for example, verbs like *move, hurry, bow, sneak*, and so on. In the following examples

of expressions in which reflexive markers are obligatorily attached, the reflexive markers are in bold italics.

German: *sich rasieren* "to shave"; ***sich beeilen*** "to hurry"; ***sich erinnern*** "to remember"

Dutch: ***zich scheren*** "to shave"; ***zich bewegen*** "to move"; ***zich herinneren*** "to remember"

Frisian: *hysk eart **him*** "he shaves"; *ik skamje **my*** "I am embarrassed"; *ik stel **my** foar* "I imagine"

Afrikaans: *hybe vind **hom*** "he is situated (at)"; *hyr oer **hom*** "he gets going"; *hyhe rinner **hom*** "he remembers"

Swedish: *raka **sig*** "to shave"; *röra **sig*** "to move"; *känna **sig*** "to feel"

Faeroese: *raka **sær*** "to shave"; *snúgva **sær*** "to turn"; *ætla **sær*** "to intend"

Yiddish: *bukn **zikh*** "to bow"; *shlaykhn **zikh*** "to sneak"; *shemen **zikh*** "to be ashamed" a highly elaborate set of grammatical markers can impose an especially stringent learnability filter.

Proposals like McWhorter's arouse a fair bit of controversy within the language research community. But by portraying language as a system that evolves and adapts to its particular population of users, these ideas provoke new ways of thinking about why languages are the way they are and what they have in common. And in doing so, these ideas force us to think about the role that cultural transmission plays in the emergence of language.

Theories of cultural transmission provide an alternative to the notion of universal grammar when it comes to thinking about how language and the human mind fit together. But the two general approaches need not be incompatible. It could well turn out that we have a core set of innate predispositions that come from our being genetically adapted for language. But it may also be true that not all of the universal properties of languages have come out of these predispositions—some of them may have arisen as adaptations of languages to us.

What we still don't know

While language science isn't yet in a state where we can confidently choose among any of the competing views of language evolution that we've described in this chapter, it *is* in a state where it makes sense to spend a lot of time discussing them. The various theories can now serve as an engine to drive the more detailed questions that researchers need to resolve before being able to answer the big questions of where language came from and why we have it. Much of the detailed groundwork will have to do with questions like these:

- What do our language-related abilities look like, and how specialized are they—that is, how similar or different are language abilities from the cognitive abilities we use for purposes other than language?

- What are the structural properties of language, and what are the optional versus obligatory aspects of language?

- How are the various components of language learned, and why do children seem to learn them better than adults?

- How do we produce and understand language, and under what conditions do we do these things smoothly or bumpily?

- How do speakers and hearers negotiate how much information needs to be put into the linguistic code, and how much can be left to be figured out from the context?

GO TO
sites.sinauer.com/languageinmind

for **web activities, further readings, research updates, new essays,** and other features

The upcoming chapters will deal with these questions. Here's an interesting exercise: After you've worked your way through this book, come back and re-read this chapter. You'll likely find that with the knowledge you've gained, the big themes that have been sketched out in this chapter will feel more "alive" for you. You may find yourself developing strong opinions about competing ideas about language evolution, spinning off new questions, generating new hypotheses, and even thinking of ingenious ways to test some of those new ideas.

DIGGING DEEPER

Language evolution in the lab

Spontaneously invented languages such as homesign or NSL and ABSL, don't spring up very often in the real world; they rely on a special set of circumstances where individuals are cut off from a community language. But it's possible to create an artificial analogue by throwing together a group of individuals and making them communicate with each other in a way that doesn't rely on the conventional language they share. This is the strategy that's been adopted by a number of researchers who are interested in the origins of language. In setting up artificial "language games," the goal is to generate insights about what kinds of features tend to recur in human communicative systems, and why. And by studying multiple iterations of the language game, where each learner of a "language" serves as the source of input to the next new learner, researchers can study how communicative forms are altered, smoothed out, or restructured. These changes can reveal which aspects of the system are most readily learned by subsequent "generations" of learners, or which features prove most useful for communication.

In this chapter, we've seen that human language is highly adaptable, and that if sound isn't an option, people can readily create a language out of gestural cloth. Lab-based language games use a variety of starting ingredients and can reveal common processes applying across very different types of symbols. For instance, in one study led by Carrie Ann Theisen (Theisen et al., 2010), pairs of adults played a game in which one of the participants (the Drawer) was presented with a word such as *teacher* or *university* and had to convey this concept to his partner (the Matcher) by drawing it on a computer with a mouse. The players interacted via computer in separate soundproof booths, and the only linguistic exchange that was allowed between them was when the Matcher typed his guess at which word was being conveyed and the Drawer responded by typing the actual word. There were 26 words as part of the game, and they were chosen so as to share some overlapping semantic features—for instance, a number of the words conveyed types of buildings, or people in certain professions, and there were thematic connections among the various words (e.g., *teacher, school, classroom, school bus; soldier, barracks, war, tank*). The players played the game for a total of 2 hours, with words being drawn randomly from the set of 26; over the course of the game, they would come across multiple examples of the same word.

One of the interesting findings from the study was that, over time, the drawings became more and more arbitrary—that is, they came to be less transparent in communicating the concepts, with the players making do with very schematic, simple visual signs. For example, take a look at **Figure 2.7**, which shows some of the drawings of one pair toward the end of the game. The drawings are hard to interpret for anyone not privy to the evolving system of signs. Over time, the drawings became

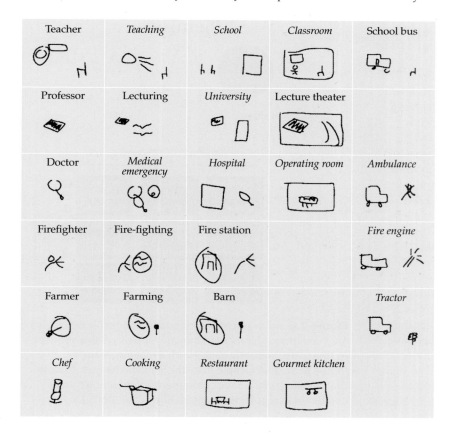

Teacher	Teaching	School	Classroom	School bus
Professor	Lecturing	University	Lecture theater	
Doctor	Medical emergency	Hospital	Operating room	Ambulance
Firefighter	Fire-fighting	Fire station		Fire engine
Farmer	Farming	Barn		Tractor
Chef	Cooking	Restaurant	Gourmet kitchen	

Figure 2.7 Signs used by one pair of participants in the drawing task studied by Theisen et al. (2010).

much more efficient—they required very little time to draw—but they relied on shared interactions with previous, more elaborate signs.

This development echoes some of the transformations over time within Nicaraguan Sign Language. Many of the earliest signs produced by children in the NSL community were highly iconic—that is, they were transparently related to the concepts they were intended to convey. Over time, the signs became much more compact, included less detail, were quicker to produce, and as a result, became more arbitrary. The drawing study suggests that this apparently universal feature of human languages reflects a highly general process in which the repeated use of a sign allows it to become pared down and less transparent.

Another interesting aspect of the drawing study was the extent to which the players re-used elements to communicate concepts that shared certain semantic features. For instance, in Figure 2.7, all of the words that are thematically related to the concept of "school" include a little symbol representing a chair. Buildings of various kinds are often represented by a square. The partners devised a system in which meaningful elements like these could be combined with each other. By re-using and combining meaningful elements, the drawers enabled their partners to better predict new drawings that they'd never seen before. Again, this reflects some of the processes that are visible in NSL and homesign. Rather than faithfully reproducing the details of an event through pantomime, signers tend to break signs apart into smaller linguistic units and combine them in ways that highlight the relationships among various sequences of signs.

Language games that involve multiple "generations" of players over a number of iterations can offer insights into how a system might evolve over time to adapt to learning challenges and expressive needs. One interesting study along these lines was carried out by Simon Kirby and his colleagues (2008). Players were told that their task was to learn an "alien" language that paired written sequences of syllables with certain visual stimuli. The visual stimuli were set up to vary along three dimensions (see **Figure 2.8A**). They consisted of three geometric shapes (square, circle, triangle) in three colors (black, blue, red) moving along three motion paths (left to right, bouncing, in a spiral). The starting language was set up so that syllable sequences were randomly paired up with the stimuli—this means that there could be no patterns inherent in the starting language. The first generation of subjects saw 14 of the 27 possible stimulus pairs in a training phase. After this, the subjects went through a testing phase, in which they were shown all 27 of the visual stimuli and asked to guess, for each visual stimulus, what that object would be called in the alien language. This meant that they were faced with the impossible task of guessing the names of objects they hadn't

seen before. The guesses they came up with then served as the input language to the next learner, and so on, until the language had gone through 10 iterations.

Despite the fact that the word/object pairs were random, the players soon imposed a pattern on the language—for instance, if by coincidence the same syllables appeared in the words for objects that shared features, this might be seized upon, and the relationship would be amplified by a player in his guesses. Since these guesses served as the input language to the next player, the connection between the sounds and features would be even more frequent than in the original, and therefore even more likely to be noticed and amplified by the next learner. Over a series of generations, the link between features and syllables would come to reflect highly systematic relationships between features and sound sequences, as seen in **Figure 2.8B**.

Lab experiments like these give us a window into the biases that shape communicative systems at their outset, and into the ways in which such systems tend to be transformed as a result of repeated interactions between people, and over a series of generations. But what can they tell us about the origin of the forces that shape the language-like systems? For example, can they yield some insight into the question of whether these general biases are innate, or instead, whether they're the result of languages adapting to the learning constraints and communicative goals of their users?

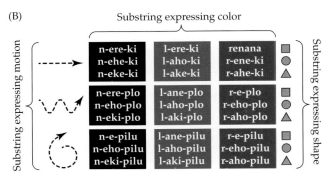

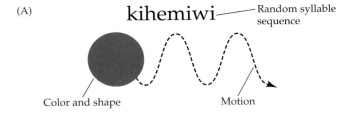

Figure 2.8 An example of a language that test subjects "evolved" through repeated transmission of syllable sequences that were randomly paired with a moving image (A; see text). (B) A sample from the "evolved language." Note that there are systematic components of meaning that are combined in regular ways. (From Kirby et al., 2008.)

The real power of studying language evolution in the lab lies in the possibility of tweaking important variables and observing their effects. We can tell whether certain biases are fixed or highly responsive to the communicative demands of a situation simply by changing some aspect of the language game. If the biases are highly malleable, this suggests that their origin lies in the communicative pressures imposed by the game. For example, Kirby and colleagues found that not all versions of their language game resulted in the system shown here, in which people encoded specific semantic features with particular syllables and combined these in a predictable way. This only happened if players were led to expect that the language had to differentiate between any two different visual stimuli. When this expectation wasn't built into the game, the players settled on a language system where a single syllable string (e.g., *tuge*) could be used to describe all objects moving in a left-to-right manner, regardless of their shape or color. This made the language much easier to learn than the combinatorial version—but it also made it less expressive.

Other variables can also be manipulated within an experiment. We might want to see how an emerging language is shaped by young learners versus older learners; we might want to observe the effects of learning within a large community of speakers versus a small one; or observe a learning situation in which most of the learning comes through contact with a small number of speakers of the language, or a large and diffuse community of speakers. Variations like these could provide a great deal of insight into the nature of universal or highly common aspects of language.

PROJECT

Do some research and identify several aspects of English grammar that have changed over the years. Do the changes codify a distinction that had been previously left to context, or do they drop off or collapse together earlier grammatical distinctions that now need to be recovered from context? Speculate about the possible forces driving these changes. Do they make the language easier to produce? Easier to understand? Easier to learn? Discuss how you might go about testing your hypotheses.

3 Language and the Brain

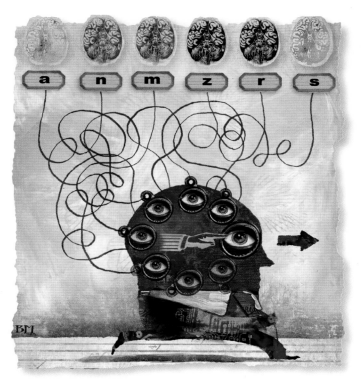

Maybe you were the sort of kid who liked to take things apart to see how they work. If so, you know just how informative it could be to pry the cover off a watch or a clock radio or even a car engine to inspect its mechanical guts. No doubt, a similar curiosity drove the early anatomists of the seventeenth and eighteenth centuries as they peeled back skin to see how the human body is put together (see **Figure 3.1**). Being able to look at the physical systems inside the body yielded many groundbreaking insights—such as the realization that blood doesn't slosh around or seep from one part of the body to another, but circulates throughout the body in special-purpose channels.

Among language scientists, I always think of **neurolinguists**—those who study how the physical brain relates to language behavior—as grown-up versions of the kids who liked to take things apart to see how they work. But the researchers who have chosen this field as their life's work need a heavy dose of patience along with their curiosity, because the brain has been much less amenable to giving up its mechanical mysteries than a car engine or the human digestive tract.

One reason for the brain's inscrutability is that it's not made up of clearly separable parts that are linked together, unlike a car engine or much of the human body. It's easy to intuit that the stomach and lungs are likely to have very different functions: they're quite obviously independent organs made of different kinds of tissue, connected to different "other parts." It's much harder to pull the brain apart into its components. It's essentially a lump of dense tissue weighing about 1.3 kg (3 pounds) made up of interconnected neural cells (approaching

Figure 3.1 Rembrandt's
*The Anatomy Lesson of Dr.
Nicolaes Tulp*, painted in
1632, depicts an anatomy
demonstration of that time.
Such lessons were open to
the public for a fee.

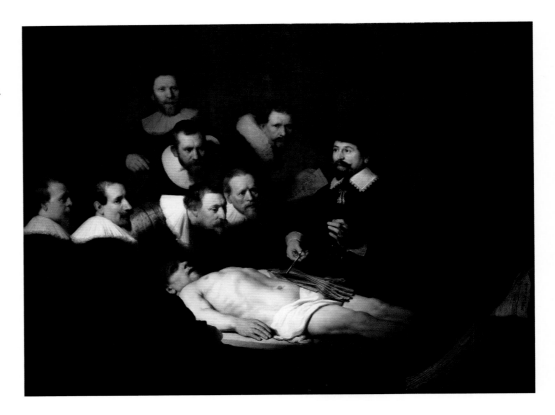

100 billion of them). Some clues can be gleaned from the more obvious physical structure of the brain. For example, the left and right hemispheres are largely physically separate from each other, so it seems reasonable to ask whether the two sides *do* different things. More subtle clues can be discerned by looking at brain tissue under a microscope; if two different regions of the brain have a different cellular makeup, this suggests that they may take on somewhat different tasks. But even today, the connection between the structure of brain tissue and the functions those tissues serve is far from clear. The brain poses significant challenges simply because it's a physical object whose function is not easily understood from its anatomical form. This fact is a big reason why an understanding of the brain has historically lagged far behind our understanding of the other organs in the human body.

A second and even greater difficulty comes from the sheer number, variety, and complexity of the brain's functions. In order to understand how a physical object "works," you need to have a clear idea of what it does. Sometimes this is trivially easy; for example, the function of a (non-digital) clock is to move the clock's hands around in a way that is consistently linked to units of time. When you look at the wheels and gears inside of a clock, it's with the aim of understanding how it accomplishes this specific function. A car is a bit more complicated. Sure, its ultimate purpose is to "drive," but peering under the hood is going to be a lot more informative if you've first been able to break down that larger purpose into component tasks. It helps to start with the idea that a number of different sub-tasks are involved, with the expectation that these map onto different mechanical "systems." For example, in order to "drive," your car's engine has to be able to start, the wheels have to turn in specific directions, the vehicle has to move forward *and* backward while transforming fuel into energy, the speed has to be modulated, and the car needs to be able to be brought to a stop—to name just a few sub-tasks. The different systems that accomplish

neurolinguists Scientists who study how the physical brain relates to language behavior.

these tasks all operate somewhat independently of each other, but their actions need to be coordinated with one other.

Needless to say, the brain is massively more complicated than a car. Among its various tasks are, to name only a very few: regulating your breathing and heartbeat, keeping food moving through your digestive system, recognizing someone familiar, recognizing a dangerous situation, and operating your muscles while you walk or play the piano. Your brain also gives you the ability to solve quadratic equations, learn to dance the tango, evaluate a political argument, navigate unfamiliar city streets, decide whether to post those photos online, and, oh yes, use language to communicate. The brain has a staggering range of functions, some of which possibly overlap, and some of which almost certainly don't. For any given task—say, using language—there's still a lot of uncertainty about the relevant sub-tasks that might form different "systems." For example, is combining sounds part of the same system as combining words into sentences? Is combining words in simple sentence structures part of the same system as creating more complex, recursive structures? Is understanding the meanings of words that you hear part of the same system as choosing specific words to convey the meaning you intend? Good luck trying to find a language scientist who will confidently answer all of these questions—and if you do, good luck finding a second one who agrees with the first. And, given that the physical structure of the brain doesn't make it glaringly obvious how many systems it's divided up into, neurolinguists have to rely especially heavily on reasonable hypotheses about what these separate systems might be.

In short, then, what we *don't* know about language and the brain far outweighs what we *do* know. At the same time, it's hard to imagine that we can ever deeply know how language "works" without having a good sense of how it's implemented in the brain. In the spirit of all those who've ever dismantled stuff to see how it operates, this chapter follows the often ingenious attempts of researchers to figure out how the physical brain accomplishes the mysterious task of language.

3.1 What Can Genetic Disorders Tell Us about Brain Systems?

Brain systems and behavioral syndromes

As I've suggested, before we start peering beneath the skull at neural matter itself, it would be helpful to have some preliminary good ideas about how the brain might be organized into separate systems. This would constrain our guesses about how the brain's matter is laid out. For example, if certain behaviors group together as part of an integral system, we might look for evidence that those tasks are implemented in a common brain region, or that they're accomplished by similar kinds of neural tissue, or that the regions responsible for them are physically connected in some way.

What clues do we look for in trying to isolate separate systems? One approach is to look closely at *disorders of thought and behavior that have a genetic origin*. A number of genetically linked conditions affect cognitive skills. In surveying these conditions, it quickly becomes apparent that brain functions can be targeted in selective ways, leading to different categories of linked impairments, or **syndromes**, rather than just an overall reduction in cognitive abilities.

Ever since Down syndrome was definitively linked to a chromosomal anomaly in 1950, we've known that the ability to learn and carry out intellectual tasks can be disrupted by genetic "glitches." Since then, scientists have identified a variety of learning and psychiatric disorders that have a strong genetic

syndrome Literally, "occurring together" (Greek *syndromos*). A group of symptoms that collectively characterize a medical or psychological disorder or condition. The presence of a syndrome can lead to the identification of a genetic basis for the condition.

double dissociation In reference to language studies, the simultaneous existence of a situation in which language is impaired but other cognitive skills are normal, or a situation in which language is normal despite the impairment of other cognitive functions.

Williams syndrome (WMS) Genetic syndrome, of particular interest to language researchers, in which language function appears to be relatively preserved despite more serious impairments in other areas of cognitive function.

basis. Given that specific, identifiable genetic anomalies can lead to very distinctive patterns of behavior, it's likely that the genes involved have a direct impact on the neural structures that underlie the behavior. Hence, by looking at a variety of disorders and seeing which behaviors are affected and which behaviors remain normal, we can generate some reasonable hypotheses about the underlying brain machinery.

Let's start by considering whether there really is such a thing as a language system in the brain. In Chapter 2, you were introduced to a debate over whether there's a separate, dedicated language system that has evolved in humans over time, or whether language has emerged as a by-product of humans' generally muscular intelligence. These two perspectives fuel very different expectations about how closely linked language functions should be with other aspects of intelligence. If language is an outgrowth of overall intellectual ability, then genetic anomalies that curtail intelligence should have a dramatic effect on language. On the other hand, if language is a specially evolved "module" (much like a specialized organ), it might not be that tightly connected to other cognitive skills. In fact, the most compelling evidence of a separate language module or brain system would be to find a **double dissociation** between language and other cognitive skills: that is, a situation in which language is impaired but other cognitive skills are normal, and, on the flip side, a situation in which language works just fine despite the impairment of other cognitive functions. Double dissociation would provide strong support for the notion that language and cognition rely at least in part on separable neural systems.

Williams syndrome

Williams syndrome (WMS) has attracted the attention of language researchers because it appears to be a case where language function is fairly well preserved despite some striking impairments in other domains. Williams syndrome is caused by a specific genetic anomaly on chromosome 7. Together with certain facial features and cardiovascular problems, it usually results in learning disability, with the overall IQs of affected individuals typically falling in the 50–70 range. People with WMS tend to be socially gregarious and, as it turns out, are often very verbal. Several language researchers have been struck by this last trait, especially given the tremendous difficulties that people with WMS often show on a variety of cognitive tasks, including those that rely on numerical or visual–spatial skills.

Ursula Bellugi and her colleagues (2000) have documented the linguistic and non-linguistic skills of people with Williams syndrome in comparison to the cognitive profiles of people with Down syndrome, another genetic anomaly that leads to intellectual impairments. When Bellugi compared a group of adolescents with WMS and a group with Down syndrome, she found that the overall scores on tests for IQ and cognitive functioning were similar for the two groups. In particular, the WMS group showed quite dramatic difficulties with numerical concepts—for example, many of them said they would rather have "50 pennies" than "5 dollars," and when asked to estimate the length of a bus, they gave responses such as "3 inches or 100 inches maybe" and "2 inches, 10 feet." Needless to say, they had a great deal of trouble carrying out tasks like making change, balancing a checkbook, or cooking from a recipe. Some of their most dramatic difficulties were in spatially organizing parts of objects into coherent wholes.

Typically, individuals with Williams syndrome operate at about the level of an average 6-year-old when it comes to their conceptual understanding, but their conceptual weaknesses are often accompanied by very adult-sounding language. For instance, one young woman, who was literate and enjoyed reading about vampires, seemed to have trouble understanding the concept of vampires; when asked to define one, she offered that a vampire is "a man who climbs into ladies' bedrooms at night and sinks his teeth into their necks." When asked why vampires behave in this way, she said "vampires must have an inordinate fondness for necks" (Johnson & Carey, 1998).

In Bellugi's comparison of Williams and Down syndromes, language was clearly more sophisticated among the Williams group. Their sentences were more fluent and complex, and they showed a stronger understanding of how syntactic structure contributes to meaning. For example, in a sentence like *The man is chased by the horse*, you need a good grasp of syntax in order to know who is doing the chasing and who is being chased—you can't simply deduce this from the words *man, chased*, and *horse*. Individuals with Down syndrome performed almost randomly with such sentences when matching them up with pictures of the events they depicted, while the Williams group showed much better performance. Examples of the divergent strengths and weaknesses of the two groups are shown in **Box 3.1**.

Some language scientists have taken results such as Bellugi's to be strong evidence for a genetically specified language module that is independent of overall intelligence. But a good amount of subsequent research has challenged this conclusion.

First of all, comparing individuals with Williams syndrome against a group of people with Down syndrome doesn't necessarily provide the best assessment of their linguistic strengths, even if both groups are matched for overall IQ. A slightly different picture emerges when people with Williams syndrome are compared with typically developing kids of the same **mental age**—that is, a group of children who are at the same overall level of cognitive functioning. The logic is that if a person with Williams syndrome is at the cognitive level of a 6-year-old, then it makes sense to compare his language abilities with those of a typical 6-year-old. If these abilities are at about the same level, this suggests that the linguistic abilities of the person with Williams are closely linked to his other cognitive abilities. In order to conclude that the language module is preserved in Williams syndrome, we'd need to see evidence that language abilities actually *exceed* what we'd expect to find based on mental age alone (and perhaps are closer to that person's chronological age).

In fact, on most detailed measures of language, subjects with Williams syndrome perform about as well as you'd expect based on their mental age (for a review, see Brock, 2007). The truth is, a typical 6-year-old has pretty good language skills too. The striking—but somewhat misleading—impression that a number of researchers had of the unexpectedly strong linguistic performance of the WMS individuals exemplified in Box 3.1 probably came about for several reasons: (1) when they are compared with subjects with Down syndrome, their language *is* good, but this is largely because Down subjects *under*perform on language relative to their mental age (a fact which, in and of itself, demands an explanation and suggests that language and cognitive abilities aren't always in sync); (2) the language abilities of WMS individuals are strikingly good when compared with their difficulties with visual–spatial and numerical tasks—but this is because performance on these latter tasks is much *worse* than you'd expect based on their mental age; and (3) certain superficial features of WMS language (such as the use of rare words or unusual turns of phrases) give the impression of greater linguistic sophistication, but these words and phrases may be used without full control or understanding.

So, a closer look at the cognitive and linguistic profiles of people with WMS doesn't really show a dramatic dissociation between language and overall cognitive ability. At the same time, results from a wide variety of language mea-

mental age A person's overall level of cognitive functioning, related to the chronological age of a person with typical development.

BOX 3.1
Linguistic and non-linguistic impairments in Williams and Down syndromes

Ursula Bellugi and her colleagues (2000) compared a group of adolescents with Williams syndrome (WMS) and a group with Down syndrome (DNS). All the subjects in these comparisons had approximately equivalent overall IQ scores.

Linguistic performance

Hypothetical questions containing conditional structures. WMS subjects often responded with very adult-sounding language.

Experimenter: "What if you were a bird?"

WMS 1: "You could fly, you could have babies, fly north or south, east or west."

DNS 1: "Bird seeds."

WMS 2: "Good question. I'd fly through the air being free."

DNS 2: "You'd be strong."

WMS 3: "I would fly where my parents could never find me. Birds want to be independent."

DNS 3: "I not a bird, you have wing."

Definitions of homonyms. WMS subjects frequently were able to provide both meanings, while DNS subjects typically reported only one.

Experimenter: "What does *nuts* mean?"

WMS: "There are two kinds of nuts, peanuts and nuts and bolts."

DNS: "We crack nuts. We eat nuts."

Experimenter: "What does *club* mean?"

WMS: "A secret kind of club, and a club with spurs—those pointy things for killing animals."

DNS: "Go to a club. I'm in the key club."

Non-linguistic (visual-spatial) performance

Performance on drawings of common objects. WMS subjects demonstrated significant difficulty with visual-spatial representation. (Drawings from Bellugi et al., 2000.)

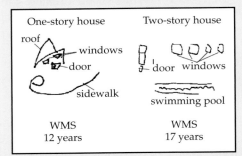
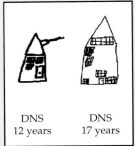

Drawings of a house by subjects with Williams and Down syndromes.

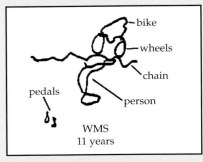
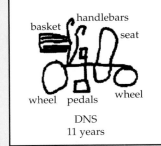

Drawings of a bicycle by subjects with Williams and Down syndromes.

sures *do* suggest a couple of areas of strength for WMS subjects. Relative to their mental age, they score especially well on tests of receptive vocabulary (words that are recognized and understood) and the ability to hold auditory material in short-term memory. Relative weaknesses within the language domain also exist, however; for instance, WS subjects have been found to score poorly on comprehension of complex syntactic structures (e.g., Mervis, 1999).

The research is far from complete, and there are ongoing questions about the most appropriate comparisons to draw across populations (see **Method 3.1**), but the emerging message is this: Williams syndrome doesn't appear to supply

METHOD 3.1

Drawing comparisons across populations

Looking in detail at the cognitive profiles of people within atypical populations (such as individuals with Williams or Down syndrome) can provide a great deal of insight about which types of cognitive abilities tend to cluster together, and which can develop separately from each other. But what are the best comparisons to make between different populations in order to get an accurate picture of which abilities are "normal" and which are not? What characteristics should our sample populations have? If we were simply to compare a random group of people with Williams syndrome and a random group of people without Williams syndrome, we might inadvertently end up with two groups whose members were very different in their average age, their range of experiences, how much time they'd spent acquiring certain skills, and so on. In fact two random populations can be so different in so many ways that it can be hard to draw useful conclusions from their differences. To avoid this pitfall, researchers make an effort to match certain characteristics across populations. But there are a number of different ways in which different populations might be matched. What's the best approach?

One choice might be to align populations by overall IQ and then compare the two groups on specific skills to see if there are uneven patterns. If there are differences across groups, it certainly suggests that some skills aren't predicated on overall intelligence alone. But, as we've seen with the comparisons of Williams and Down subjects in Box 3.1, it can be hard to draw firm conclusions about whether specific skills are within the normal range or not, and hence whether we can consider them to be "spared" abilities. Showing that people with Williams have stronger linguistic abilities than people with Down syndrome, for example, doesn't allow us to conclude that language is normal for the Williams group, since it could simply be the case that language abilities are especially deeply impaired in the Down comparison group.

For this reason, many researchers prefer to compare a group of atypical individuals against those who are developing typically, and align the two groups by mental age, that is, the age at which typically developing children would achieve the same IQ score as those in the contrasting population. But matching on this variable can introduce its own set of problems. If there's a big discrepancy between mental age and chronological age, this leads to very young typical children being compared with older atypical individuals. But such a big gap in age can lead to quite big differences in sociability, attention span, comfort level around strangers, motivation, willingness to participate in a test situation, or various other factors that might affect how the subjects actually perform on the tests that they're faced with. Or, the older group may have had time to develop strategies for compensating for their deficits, which might make their abilities look more intact than they really are. Moreover, matching by mental age means that there's a lot of weight placed on the accuracy of the tests that are used to assess mental age. If the tests turn out to be less accurate or appropriate for use with certain populations, this compromises the whole matching paradigm.

Sometimes, a comparison based on general evaluations of intelligence might be too blunt an instrument, especially if we're interested in looking in more detail at whether there are uneven profiles of performance within the domain of linguistic abilities. In that case, researchers might choose to match the subject groups on some measure of language ability. For instance, they might be matched on vocabulary size, as measured by the Peabody Picture Vocabulary Test, in which children are asked to match a word spoken by the experimenter with one of four available pictures. Or the groups might be matched on the measure of mean length of utterance, which provides a count of the average number of distinct word-like units that the subject produces in a sentence (and which increases quite rapidly with age, especially in the first few years of language learning). This allows the researchers to assess whether, even when a single coarse measure of language development is held constant, there are peaks and valleys in linguistic abilities.

Ultimately, there's no single perfect matching criterion, and the choices researchers make often reflect (1) the nature of the populations that are being tested, and (2) the questions of interest. Sometimes more than one matching group is tested, in order to provide more than one perspective on the relevant comparisons. But when you read papers in which conclusions are made based on comparing two groups, it's always worthwhile to take a close look at the groups that were tested and how they were matched. Were the two groups really equivalent along the most important dimensions, and did the choice of matching criteria support the conclusions that were drawn? How might the results have been affected if a different comparison group had been chosen?

specific language impairment (SLI)
A disorder in which children fail to develop language normally even though there are no apparent neurological damages or disorders, no general cognitive impairment or delay, no hearing loss, and no abnormal home environment that would explain this failure.

definitive evidence for an independent language module, but it does point to an intriguing separation of some specific cognitive skills, both linguistic and non-linguistic in nature. The hope is that by systematically studying many of the skills that are involved in learning and using language, researchers will ultimately come to a better understanding of the particular skills that have a genetic basis, and the consequences for language when these skills are disrupted.

Specific language impairment

Having asked whether Williams syndrome is truly a disorder in which language is preserved while other cognitive functions are deeply affected, we will now look at the flip side of the same question: Is there a disorder in which language is selectively disrupted while other cognitive functions are normal? A number of researchers have argued that there is such a condition.

Specific language impairment (SLI) is defined as a disorder in which children fail to develop language normally even though there's no obvious reason for this—that is, no apparent neurological damage or disorders, no general cognitive impairment or delay, no hearing loss, and no abnormal home environment. Children with SLI usually start speaking later than their peers, and once they do talk, their language shows evidence of odd glitches, some of which linger into adulthood. They produce strangely ungrammatical sentences (for example, *Who did Marge see someone?* and *Yesterday I fall over*), and they persist in such errors well past the age when children normally make elementary syntax errors. Abnormalities at all levels of language structure have been found—that is, at the levels of sound structure, sentence structure, and the structure of complex words. (See **Table 3.1** for a more detailed description and examples of language deficits found in SLI.)

TABLE 3.1 Common linguistic and non-linguistic deficits in specific language impairment (SLI)

Linguistic deficits

Deficits of sound, including:
- difficulty in producing words with complex consonant clusters like *spectacle* or *prescription*
- trouble in perceiving subtle distinctions among speech sounds
- trouble analyzing the sound structure of words and sound sequences; e.g., difficulty answering questions such as, "In the word *spray*, what sound follows 'p'?"

Words: difficulty in tagging words with the right grammatical markers for plural, tense, etc., especially with new words; e.g., difficulty in filling in the blanks for questions like "This is a wug. Now there are two of them: there are two _____."

Sentence structure: trouble understanding the meaning of sentences with multiple participants or complex sentence structure, e.g., *Frank introduced Harry to Sally; Harry was kissed by Sally.*

Non-linguistic deficits

Perception of rapid stimuli: trouble perceiving rapid sequences of sounds or images

Working memory: short memory spans for both speech and non-speech stimuli

Analogical reasoning: impaired reasoning by analogy, even in tasks that don't rely heavily on language

Visual imagery: difficulty in performing tasks that require mentally rotating objects and imagining what they would look like from a different perspective

Adapted from Joanisse and Seidenberg, 1998.

Unlike Williams syndrome, no single genetic anomaly has been identified as being at the root of SLI. But there's quite strong evidence that the disorder has a hereditary component, as gleaned from family histories and studies of identical and non-identical twins, and from the fact that a number of genetic anomalies have been found in people with SLI.

By virtue of its clinical definition and its very name, specific language impairment seems to offer evidence of language as a separate system that develops in the brain—or at the very least, evidence that certain aspects of language structure behave as modules that are independent of other cognitive functions, and that have a direct basis in genetics. This is the point of view taken by researchers such as Heather van der Lely and Ken Wexler (e.g., van der Lely & Marshall, 2011; Rice & Wexler, 1996). These researchers disagree with each other on the details, but their general approach is to say that SLI is due to a genetically based disruption in the process of learning language structure. The end result is a "broken" grammar, or being stuck at a stage of arrested development in the learning of complex language structure. In short, they take a **domain-specific perspective** on SLI, in which the linguistic deficit strikes at mechanisms that are particular to language, rather than ones that are shared with other cognitive abilities.

But, as you might have guessed from our discussion of Williams syndrome, the picture is less clear close up than it appears from a distance. For starters, the dissociation between language and other cognitive functions in SLI is far from sharp. It's certainly true that the problems that usually bring children with SLI into clinicians' offices are their difficulties with language, rather than any other obvious signs of cognitive delay or impairment; in other aspects of their lives, these kids seem to be functioning fine. But more detailed testing shows that many children with SLI also show unusual performance on other tasks that are at best indirectly related to language structure (see Table 3.1). Basic speech perception is often impaired, with SLI kids having more trouble distinguishing between similar sounds like "ba" and "pa." They might also have shorter memory spans, as measured by their ability to retain words or other units in memory over a short period of time. Some children also have trouble with control over their articulatory systems, or even with more general aspects of motor coordination. (See Joanisse and Seidenberg, 1998, for a review of non-linguistic deficits that can accompany the linguistic problems in SLI.)

What to make of these more general symptoms? Several different explanations are possible. Some researchers have argued that the non-linguistic impairments are a clue that the underlying problem isn't specifically linguistic after all. Instead, they argue for a **domain-general perspective** that views SLI as a cognitive problem that's not particular to language in and of itself but that ends up having especially weighty consequences for language. Marc Joannise and Mark Seidenberg (1998) have argued that what starts as a general problem in processing the details of sounds, or in holding material in working memory, could have profound effects on the learning of language structure. Here's an example of how this could play itself out.

Many people with SLI have trouble with the small grammatical tags on words that mark that a verb is in the past tense or that a noun is plural (for example, *walked, bragged*; *dogs, minions, cakes*). What could be simpler? These verbs and nouns merely involve the addition of one extra sound. But, as pointed out in Section 2.3, the plural form of English actually involves a choice between two *different* sounds, the "s" sound and the "z" sound. Which goes where depends on the subtle properties of the sound that comes just before it—so you get the "s" sound after *fat*, but the "z" sound after *fad*. (You'll read in much more detail about this kind of sound variation in Chapter 4.) So, in order to

domain-specific perspective In regard to SLI, the situation in which the linguistic deficit strikes at mechanisms that are particular to language, rather than ones that are shared with other cognitive abilities.

domain-general perspective In regard to SLI, the situation in which the linguistic deficit is only one effect of more general cognitive problems that also affect non-linguistic processes.

grasp how plural formation works in English, a child has to be able to clearly distinguish between the sounds "s" and "z" and line up this difference with the difference between the sounds "t" and "s." Without this ability, the process of making plurals in English looks much more mysterious, and the end result may be that children with SLI produce more random-looking plural structures, or leave off the marker altogether.

At the level of sentence structure, many important differences in structure and meaning are signaled by very small, meek-sounding *function words*. Consider:

The horse chased the man.

The horse was chased by the man.

These sentences are essentially mirror images of each other when it comes to their meaning, yet they are distinguished only by presence of the little words *was* and *by*, neither of them uttered with any acoustic prominence (we don't normally say "The horse WAS chased BY the man," with stress on the small function words). If important grammatical markers like these are missed by children with an underlying sound-processing deficit, then learning to extract general rules about how sentences are put together, and about how structure relates to the meaning of a sentence, is certainly bound to be an uphill battle.

These examples give an idea of how struggling with the details of sounds might snowball into far-reaching problems with language structure. Under this processing-based explanation of SLI, what looks like "broken grammar" could be the end result of trying to learn structure on the basis of lousy input—maybe a bit like trying to learn a foreign language through the constant hiss of white noise. Similar stories could be told about other non-linguistic deficits commonly found among SLI populations, such as problems with working memory. The problem may *look* specifically linguistic simply because language makes especially heavy use of subtle distinctions among sounds, or often requires that long strings of words be held in working memory. Other functions might appear to be "spared" simply because they don't draw as heavily on these particular skills as language does—but it's the underlying *non*-linguistic skills that are damaged, and not the language-learning mechanism itself.

In response to such arguments, defenders of the "broken grammar" view have countered that the mere presence of non-linguistic deficits can't be construed as evidence that they *cause* the apparent problems with language. For instance, Heather van der Lely and Chloe Marshall (2011) take the position that these other cognitive deficits may coexist with the linguistic impairments, but that they don't really have anything to do with the language deficit itself. After all, even in a genetic disorder like Williams or Down syndrome, which can be traced back to a single chromosome, the cognitive impairments are also accompanied by other symptoms or features—for instance, certain typical facial characteristics, or congenital heart problems. Does this mean that the heart is part of the same "system" as the impaired cognitive functions? Hardly. Rather, the co-occurrence reveals that genes can sometimes have very diffuse effects, with ramifications for multiple systems at the same time. In order to show that the linguistic problems *stem* from the more general processing deficit, it's important to show that the severity of the linguistic impairment is clearly related to the severity of the more general processing deficit.

There's still a lot we don't know about the link between the language problems and more general cognitive anomalies of people with SLI (or other genetically linked language deficits such as dyslexia; see **Box 3.2**). A number of issues complicate the picture and will need to be carefully sorted out. For example,

BOX 3.2
Dyslexia: Is there a gene for reading?

Researchers know two salient things about specific language impairment (SLI): First, people who have it struggle with producing the right grammatical patterns and structures. Second, SLI has a strong hereditary basis. Thus, it's tempting to conclude that there are specific genes *for* grammar, and that SLI reflects the disruption of these genes. But to see the problem with this logic, it makes sense to look at disorders of reading.

Developmental dyslexia is a common learning disability that leads to difficulties in learning to read, but no apparent problems with spoken language or other learning problems. Dyslexia is also known to have a strong hereditary basis. So, should we conclude that dyslexia is basically a selective impairment of genes that are responsible for reading? Here's where that idea has trouble getting off the ground: Writing is a fairly recent invention—as a species, we've only been reading and writing for several thousand years, likely a much shorter time than we've been speaking. And while speaking (or signing) is universal among humans, many societies still exist without feeling the need to put things in writing. Moreover, even within societies that have had writing systems for a long time, it's only very recently that literacy has become common in the general population. This makes it highly implausible that, in such a short time, we could have evolved genes dedicated to the mastery of this recent, non-universal, elite cultural tool. What's more, there's no evidence that people who come from societies (and therefore gene pools) with very low literacy rates have any greater difficulty in learning to read than those who come from countries where a larger segment of the population has been reading for centuries. So, what to make of the connection between genes and reading?

A plausible explanation is that reading relies on genes that didn't develop *specifically* for reading, but that the affected genes contribute to a skill that turns out to be highly *relevant* for reading. A closer look at the abilities of people with dyslexia has turned up one consistent sticking point: difficulty with **phonological awareness**, or consciously analyzing strings of sounds into their subparts. For instance, many dyslexics have trouble with requests and questions like these:

> Which word has a different first sound: *beetle, bat, chair,* or *bust*?

> Say *catch*. Now say it again, but don't say the "k" sound.

> Here is a picture of a desk. Now finish the word for me: *des__*.

Some researchers have argued that this difficulty springs from a more general underlying problem in processing sequences of sounds. Whether or not this is true, it's easy to see how trouble in consciously isolating individual sounds from longer strings would be a problem for learning to read (at least in a writing system like ours): The whole enterprise hinges on matching up individual sounds with visual symbols. It's also easy to see why a subtle sound problem might turn up most glaringly as a reading problem: in understanding spoken language, one can get by without decomposing strings of sounds, but an inability to do so in the context of reading has more catastrophic consequences.

Dyslexia is an important example to keep in mind whenever you come across a connection between a genetic anomaly and a highly visible outcome—the causal chain between the genes and that outcome could be either very direct, or very indirect. The notion that genes have evolved specifically *for* that outcome is always, at best, a starting hypothesis that should provoke additional exploration.

---

developmental dyslexia A common learning disability with a strong hereditary basis that leads to difficulties in learning to read, without any apparent spoken language or other learning problems.

phonological awareness The ability to consciously analyze and separate strings of sounds into their subparts.

---

it's unlikely that SLI makes up a single disorder with a single underlying cause. There's quite a bit of variability in the linguistic and non-linguistic profiles of people who have been diagnosed as having SLI. This has led researchers to suggest that SLI is a catchphrase for a cluster of different disorders, all of which end up disproportionately affecting language function. If that's the case, then sorting out cause-and-effect explanations is going to require making the right distinctions among different subtypes of SLI.

Figure 3.2 Sample stimuli from a sentence picture verification task. Children are asked to point to the picture that matches the sentence "The donkey that kicked the cow has a bell."

WEB ACTIVITY 3.1

Cognitive demands in language tests In this activity, you'll explore several tests that have been used to test language functioning in SLI. You'll consider what other cognitive skills might be necessary to succeed at the task, in addition to the targeted linguistic skill.

Testing the right thing: Method is important

There's an important methodological issue to take into consideration when trying to figure out how linguistic skills relate to non-linguistic ones: in order to measure language function, we have to rely on some appropriate test. But the test itself may depend on cognitive skills over and above the specific linguistic skills that are being targeted. For example, a common way to test how well children understand syntactic structure is to present them with a series of test trials involving complex sentences that differ in subtle ways, such as "The donkey that kicked the cow has a bell" versus "The donkey kicked the cow that has a bell." Children are shown several pictures and are asked to choose which picture best goes with the sentence they just heard (see **Figure 3.2**). In order to perform reliably on this test, children need to have intact syntactic skills. But they also need to have several other things: the perceptual skills to make fine distinctions among similar images; the ability to relate visual images to representations of similar events; the memory capacity to keep track of which pictures differ how; the memory capacity to remember exactly what sentence the experimenter uttered; the motivation to repeatedly pay attention to a series of test trials; and so on. This test—intended to probe for syntactic understanding—is hardly purely linguistic. So, let's suppose we find that children who have especially short memory spans do worse on this test than those with roomier memory spans. Does this mean that the children's difficulty with syntax can be explained as originating in problems with working memory? Not necessarily—it may just be that *this particular test* relies heavily on working memory, creating a false connection between memory and syntactic performance. Ideally, we'd want to check to see if the relationship holds across a number of different tests probing for syntactic understanding and memory, using tests that vary in the ways in which they tax non-linguistic cognitive functions.

We need more knowledge about how language works

The title of this section is "What can genetic disorders tell us about brain systems?" Perhaps it's time to take a stab at an answer, based on the research survey so far. The fact that there's a variety of different genetic disorders, with strikingly different effects on both language and general cognition, shows that there is some degree of specialization in the brain, and that genes can affect how these specialized skills develop. At the same time, evidence from language disorders doesn't offer us an easy picture, with a clear division between language and the rest of the brain. Instead, it looks as if we'll need to look deeper, to study the various skills that make up the collection of behaviors we call "linguistic."

In a way, none of this should come as a surprise; it roughly parallels the conclusion we drew at the end of the last chapter about the evolution of language. Language doesn't appear to be a self-contained, all-or-nothing bundle of abilities. We saw that different non-human species show different patterns of strengths and weaknesses in their aptitudes for the various skills that go into learning and using language. For example, chimps show some ability to master the use of symbols, but they have virtually non-existent vocal imitation skills; songbirds show vocal virtuosity in the wild, but there is no evidence that they use their abilities to convey meaning. Language, it seems, is a fortuitous coming together of all the pieces required to make it work—whether these pieces are specifically linguistic skills or more general ones that support it—and this appears to be reflected as well in those situations where something goes wrong in the human brain's ability to pull it all off.

But an important lesson from the study of genetic disorders is that in order to properly understand them, we're going to need a detailed body of knowledge that encompasses all the machinery that goes into learning, processing, and producing language. After working your way through this book, you should have a much better sense of just how intricate this machinery is. There's still much basic work to be done, but ultimately, a careful study of genetic language disorders is likely to provide some important insights about which component skills seem to cluster together, and which ones seem to be less closely related. Ultimately, this may give us a useful angle on thinking about how brain systems might be organized and genetically influenced.

3.2 Where in the Brain Is Language?

In the previous section, I suggested that genetic disorders that affect some skills while leaving others intact can provide clues about underlying neural structures. But language disorders can arise for reasons other than genetic anomalies that are present from birth. They can also happen at any point in life as a result of damage to the brain through stroke, seizures, or simply a very unlucky accident. In theory, disorders from brain damage can provide even more direct information about the relationship between the brain's anatomy and its functions, since in many cases, it's possible to see *where* the brain has been damaged.

Early ideas and discoveries: The case of Phineas Gage

Physicians' records from as far back as the seventeenth and eighteenth centuries document several types of lost language function and try to explain the cognitive nature of these losses. But it wasn't until the nineteenth century that scientists began to develop serious theories about how linguistic functions might actually be implemented in brain matter. This reflects how deeply mysterious the brain was until fairly recently. Nowadays, we take it for granted that we can record detailed images of living brains, and it's common knowledge that different parts of the brain carry out different tasks. But the very notion that the brain is divided up into different regions that perform specific functions was not widely accepted by scientists until about 150 years ago.

Early ideas about the localization of brain function began to gain steam in the 1800s and came largely from observing the effects of brain damage—the kind of devastating damage that obliterates brain tissue in ways that can easily be seen. One of the most famous case studies is that of Phineas Gage, a

25-year-old railroad worker. In 1848 Gage was the unfortunate victim of an accidental explosion that drove an iron rod into his left cheek and out the top of his head, landing about 25 meters away. Incredibly, Gage not only survived, but moments after the accident, sat up and chatted, and a short while later was able to relate the details of the accident to a doctor. He survived for more than 12 years with most of his capacities seemingly intact—his language and motor function, for example, appeared to be fine. The doctor who cared for him noted that Gage's survival was surely due in part to the fact that "the portion of the brain traversed, was, for several reasons, the best fitted of any to sustain the injury." But he also noted that the accident had caused some deep changes; evidently Gage's personality took a turn for the worse, and he was never able to function as well as he had before the accident (see **Box 3.3**).

BOX 3.3
Phineas Gage and his brain

Dr. John Martyn Harlow was practicing in Cavendish, Vermont, near where Gage's accident occurred in 1848. He treated Gage at the time and followed his patient's progress until Gage's death in 1860. Harlow then prepared a detailed summary of the case (he even obtained and studied Gage's skull), which was published in 1868 and describes Gage's altered personality:

The equilibrium or balance, so to speak, between his intellectual faculties and animal propensities, seems to have been destroyed. He is fitful, irreverent, indulging at times in the grossest profanity (which was not previously his custom), manifesting but little deference for his fellows, impatient of restraint or advice when it conflicts with his desires, at times pertinaciously obstinate, yet capricious and vacillating, devising many plans of future operations, which are no sooner arranged than they are abandoned in turn for others

appearing more feasible. A child in his intellectual capacity and manifestations, he has the animal passions of a strong man. Previous to his injury, although untrained in the schools, he possessed a well-balanced mind, and was looked upon by those who knew him as a shrewd, smart businessman, very energetic and persistent in executing all his plans of operation. In this regard his mind was radically changed, so decidedly that his friends and acquaintances said he was "no longer Gage."

Figure 3.3 (A) Phineas Gage's skull is on display at the Warren Anatomical Museum at Harvard Medical School. (B) Reconstruction of the pathway of the iron rod through Gage's skull. (C) A recently discovered photograph of Gage (holding the iron rod), taken some time after his accident. (A,B from Van Horn et al., 2012; C from The Jack and Beverly Wilgus Collection.)

(A)

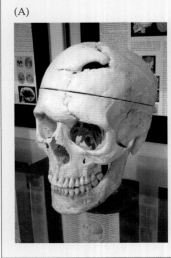

(B)

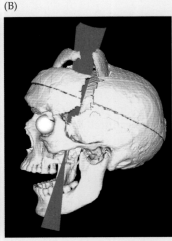

(C)

The case of Phineas Gage was widely publicized. He became an attraction at Barnum's American Museum in New York and toured New England as a traveling exhibit. The details of his accident and recovery aroused the morbid curiosity of the general public, but also the interest of scientists. At the time, the idea that the brain was made up of a number of independent regions, each responsible for different functions, was a new and controversial one. The more traditional view was that the brain functioned as an undifferentiated mass of neurons. But Gage's accident lined up with a number of observations that had been made earlier, in which doctors had pointed out that damage to the brain could have very uneven effects: sometimes a very slight injury to the brain could be fatal, while at other times large swaths of the brain could be damaged with surprisingly little effect. The only possible explanation for this was that different parts of the brain play different roles. David Ferrier, one of the earliest champions of the idea of brain localization, used the Gage case as a centerpiece in his well-known lectures, and as the basis for experiments with monkeys.

And yet, as a scientific case study, the Gage incident falls short on evidence. Other than stimulating interest in a budding idea, its scientific contribution is slender, verging on downright skeletal. There aren't enough facts to be able to draw any clear conclusions about the connection between the damaged parts of Gage's brain and the effects of the trauma on his brain function. Since no autopsy was done, there isn't even a clear picture of exactly what tissue was affected. Moreover, the observations of his behaviors after the accident are unsystematic, and no detailed testing was ever undertaken (Macmillan, 2008). All that we have are the very impressionistic remarks of his physician. From a modern perspective, it's astonishing how little in the way of useful scientific evidence was salvaged from the tragic event. In the hands of a neuropsychologist today, Gage would likely have been put through many batteries of tests to reveal detailed profiles of his cognitive functioning. How could so little scientific value have been pulled out of such a potentially important case?

In the historical context, though, we shouldn't be surprised by the lack of rigorous study applied to the case. Scientists at the time quite literally didn't know what to look for. There was very little understanding of what the brain was *for*, even in a very general sense. It was widely accepted that the brain regulated movement and the senses—this was known from the physical evidence of how the nervous system extends from the brain into the body's muscles and sensory organs. But it wasn't even taken for granted that more abstract aspects of the mind like language or higher intellectual functions—let alone things such as *character* or *temperament*—were under the brain's command. There was simply no framework within which to start testing the various functions that might have been disrupted by Gage's accident.

So perhaps one of the greatest scientific lessons to take from the famous case of Phineas Gage is that in order to make real progress in understanding the brain, an examination of the physical object of the brain has to proceed in lockstep with some sound thinking about the brain's job description. As we'll see in the next section, this applies as much in these days of high-tech brain scans as it did in 1848.

Evidence for language localization: Broca and Wernicke

If there was any doubt in Gage's time that language "lives" in the brain, this was quickly dispelled, largely through the influential work of Paul Broca. In 1861, Broca examined a patient by the name of Leborgne who suffered from a brain condition that had caused him to have seizures from a young age and had left him unable to move one side of his body and unable to speak—aside from

cerebral cortex The outer covering of the brain's cerebral hemispheres.

aphasia Any language disruption caused by brain damage.

Broca's aphasia Aphasia characterized by halting speech and tremendous difficulty in choosing words, but fairly good speech comprehension. Also called motor aphasia or expressive aphasia.

Wernicke's aphasia Aphasia associated with fluent speech that is well articulated but often nonsensical, and enormous difficulty in understanding language. Also called sensory or receptive aphasia.

a particular swear word, the syllable *tan* was the only set of speech sounds he'd managed to eke out for 21 years. The patient died a few days after their meeting, and as Broca was aware that scientists were beginning to explore claims about the localization of language, he decided to autopsy Leborgne's brain. He considered language to be a good test case for the more general hypothesis that the various functions of the brain were compartmentalized into different physical regions. He discovered extensive damage to the frontal lobe on the left side of Leborgne's brain, providing some of the earliest hard evidence of localization in the brain (Broca, 1861).

Based on his observations, Broca argued that the faculty of language was further split apart into subfunctions, an idea that was consistent with many earlier reports of language loss due to brain damage. He noticed that Leborgne seemed to understand language much better than you'd expect from his utter lack of ability to speak—for example, when asked how long he'd been hospitalized, he flashed four sets of five fingers and then a single finger, to indicate 21. To Broca, this suggested that he'd lost the ability to produce spoken language (despite maintaining reasonable dexterity of his tongue and mouth) but that other aspects of language functioning were better preserved. Following this famous case, Broca autopsied the brains of a number of patients whose language was impaired after stroke or other brain damage, and he found that a significant portion of them had damage to the same part of the **cerebral cortex** (the brain's outer layer of neurons), specifically on the left side of the frontal lobe.

Shortly after Broca's discovery, neurologist Carl Wernicke studied a patient who had suffered a stroke and, though able to speak fluently, didn't seem to understand anything that was said to him. A later autopsy revealed a lesion, or evidence of brain damage, on the left side of the cerebral cortex—but the lesion was farther back than the region Broca had described, in the temporal lobe rather than the frontal lobe (see **Figure 3.4**).

In 1874, Wernicke published an influential text in which he explored his ideas about **aphasia**, the clinical term for language disruption caused by brain damage. Even though scientists and clinicians had long suspected that language loss came in at least two distinct varieties, the pioneering work of Broca and Wernicke established that the distinct forms of aphasia were related to different areas of the brain. **Broca's aphasia** (also called motor or expressive aphasia) is characterized by halting speech, if any at all, and tremendous difficulty in choosing words, but fairly good comprehension. **Wernicke's aphasia** (also called sensory or receptive aphasia) is associated with fluent speech that is well articulated but often nonsensical, and enormous difficulty in understanding language. (See **Table 3.2** for examples of speech by patients with Broca's and Wernicke's aphasias.)

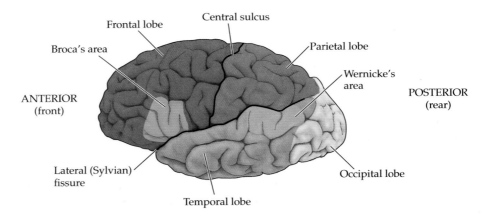

Figure 3.4 A side view of the surface of the brain's left hemisphere. The four lobes of the cerebral cortex are indicated in shades of gray, with Broca's area and Wernicke's area shown in color.

TABLE 3.2 Examples of speech from patients with Broca's and Wernicke's aphasias

Patient with Broca's aphasia, re-telling the Cinderella story:[a]

Cinderella uh… scrubbing and uh… hard worker. Step fa… mother uh go… but no. Scrubbing uh uh wathacallit uh uh working. Stepmother really ugly. Dress break… stepmother and now what dress? Mother Teresa… not exactly… uh uh magic godmother! Dress… beautiful and carriage where? I can uh… pumpkin and uh… servants and horse and beautiful carriage and so magic. But, better midnight… pumpkin carriage gone. Cinderella dance. Midnight uh clock uh Cinderella clock! Slipper fall. Prince can't uh stepmother fitting slipper? Cinderella where? Well locked. Sure enough fits because Cinderella uh… magic uh… girl. And probably uh prince and Cinderella marrying and happy. That's it.

Patient with Wernicke's aphasia, reporting on suffering a stroke:[b]

It just suddenly had a feffort and all the feffort had gone with it. It even stepped my horn. They took them from earth you know. They make my favorite nine to severed and now I'm a been habed by the uh starn of fortment of my annulment which is now forever.

[a]From Thompson, 2008.
[b]From Dick et al., 2001.

Creating brain maps for language

As you've seen, we owe much of our foundational understanding of brain localization to accidents of nature, and to the clinicians who made intelligent observations about the behavior of the unfortunate victims. Further progress came from the pioneering work of neurosurgeon Wilder Penfield, who produced detailed maps of human brain function as part of his surgical treatment of patients with brain tumors or epilepsy (Penfield & Jasper, 1954). To identify indispensable parts of the brain in order to avoid removing them during surgery, Penfield and his colleagues used a procedure for electrically stimulating the brain while the patient was conscious. This stimulation would temporarily disrupt brain function, and the patients' responses were used to pinpoint the sites of specific brain functions in individual patients. By carefully recording the results from many patients, Penfield confirmed that stimulating Broca's and Wernicke's areas often caused problems for language production and comprehension.

But Penfield's studies also showed a surprising amount of variation among individuals. Some patients seemed to have no impairments even when Broca's area was stimulated, while others were rendered mute or incapable of comprehension when regions far outside the expected language areas were targeted. More recent work has confirmed that individuals can vary a great deal when it comes to where in the brain they carry out the same language tasks. This is especially likely to be true of people with damaged brains; unlike the body's physical organs, where lungs can't take over the functions of damaged kidneys, for example, the brain does have a sometimes startling ability to reorganize itself to compensate for damage, especially if the brain damage occurs in a young person. For instance, there have been cases where children have had their entire left hemispheres removed because of enormous amounts of epileptic activity; in some of these, the kids have grown up to have near-normal use of language (de Bode & Curtiss, 2000).

Aside from individual variation, there are other reasons to believe that most people carry out important language-related tasks not just in Broca's and Wernicke's areas, but also in regions far outside of these areas, including in the right hemisphere, and in areas beneath the cerebral cortex (the **subcortical** areas of

subcortical Refers to the internal regions of the cerebral hemispheres, lying beneath the cerebral cortex.

(A)

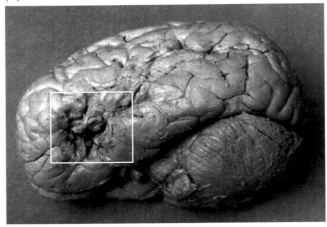

(B)

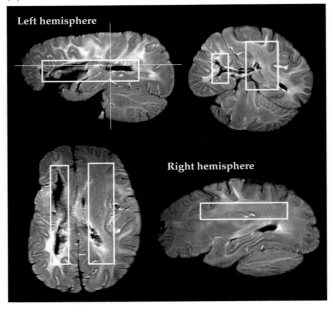

Figure 3.5 (A) Photograph of Leborgne's brain, with damage clearly visible in the inferior frontal lobe of the left hemisphere. (B) MRI images showing extensive damage throughout the left hemisphere. Boxes are drawn around comparable areas in the left and right hemispheres. (From Dronkers et al., 2007.)

brain lateralization The specialization of the brain's right and left cerebral hemispheres for different functions.

the brain). In fact, even the dramatic language impairment of Broca's famous patient named Leborgne may have resulted from more extensive damage than Broca originally thought: since the good doctor had the incredible foresight to preserve Leborgne's brain for future scientists, researchers were recently able to image the brain using modern magnetic resonance imaging (MRI) techniques. They found evidence of deep damage to the brain not just in the frontal lobe on the left side, but also in subcortical areas and throughout the superior longitudinal fasciculus, a bundle of neurons that connects the front and back areas of the cerebral cortex (see **Figure 3.5**).

It's apparent that the divide between comprehension and production is not a tidy one. On closer inspection, most patients with Broca's aphasia have trouble with some aspects of comprehension as well as devastating difficulties with language production. Especially irksome for these patients are sentences that rely on subtle or complex syntactic structure without any helpful clues about meaning. (For example, a Broca's patient might readily figure out the meaning of *The mouse was chased by the cat* but not *The boy was chased by the girl*. For the first example, but not the second, the meaning of the sentence can be plausibly assembled if all you can figure out are the word meanings.) Symptoms like these have prompted researchers to offer various proposals about additional duties of Broca's area. Some have argued that certain kinds of syntactic structures are computed in this region; others have suggested that it's an important site for working memory processes, or for mechanisms that resolve the tension between conflicting linguistic cues. This rethinking of the nature of aphasia is driven in part by more detailed techniques for studying the brain. But it also comes from much more detailed theories about all of the mental operations that are involved in producing and understanding language. And as these theories become richer and more complex, so do ideas about how language function maps onto areas of the brain.

Brain lateralization

The fact that Broca's and Wernicke's areas were both traced to the left side of the brain led to the first inkling that the brain might be organized differently in its two hemispheres—a possibility that initially came as a great surprise to Paul Broca. But since Broca's time, additional evidence of **brain lateralization** (that is, evidence that the right and left cerebral hemispheres are specialized for different functions) has come from many corners, and has involved somewhat exotic brain conditions as well as clever studies of people with uninjured brains.

The best-known studies of brain lateralization were done by Roger Sperry and Michael Gazzaniga in the 1960s, about a hundred years after the pioneering work of Broca and Wernicke. The studies involved a number of "split-brain" patients who had undergone a radical, last-resort treatment to prevent the spread of epileptic seizures from one side of the brain to the oth-

LANGUAGE AT LARGE 3.1

One hundred names for love:
Aphasia strikes a literary couple

Aphasia opens a fascinating scientific window into the brain, but in the lives of those who experience it, it mostly feels like a closing down of connections to others. One of the most moving and complex personal accounts of aphasia comes from American author Diane Ackerman. In her book *One Hundred Names for Love* (2012), she chronicles the stroke and subsequent aphasia suffered by her husband Paul West, a novelist himself.

West came out of his stroke able to utter only a single syllable (*mem*), apparently baffled that others couldn't understand him. It's hard to imagine a couple for whom the loss of language would be more devastating. Ackerman relates how, before her husband's stroke, many of their intimate moments centered on impromptu language games. And she described her husband Paul as a man who "had a draper's touch for the unfolding fabric of a sentence, and collected words like rare buttons."

Through intense effort, Paul was able to recover a good amount of language function, possibly with the help of his dazzling collection of words. When the route to a familiar word was blocked, he was sometimes able to take a neural detour to unearth another one that would serve his purpose. He struggled with words like *blanket* or *bed*, or his wife's name, *Diane*. Nonetheless, he could recruit words like *postilion* or *tardigrades* to get an idea across. Occasionally, he even sent his verbally endowed wife scrambling for a dictionary. In trying to ask her whether she'd received a check she'd been waiting for, he resorted to the word *spondulicks*, which prompted the following exchange:

'What's a spondulick?'

'Money.'

'Really? Truly? Spondulick?' In my mind's eye I picture a spastic duck.

'Yes,' he said emphatically.

'Spondulicks?'

'Spondulicks. It's British.'

Surely he was pulling my leg. I breezed into the library to look it up in an etymological dictionary, where I found this entry:

1856, Amer. Eng. slang, 'money, cash,' of unknown origin, said to be from Gk. spondylikos, from spondylos, a seashell used as currency (the Gk. word

means lit. 'vertebra'). Used by Mark Twain and O. Henry and adopted into British English, where it survives despite having died in Amer. Eng.

Paul West even recovered sufficiently to write an account of his stroke, *The Shadow Factory* (2008). In it, his off-kilter language and sense of humor combine to give the text a vivid and disorienting effect appropriate to the topic. In the following passage, West describes how the stroke left him with trouble swallowing liquids; in order to prevent him from choking on them, they had to be thickened into semiliquid form:

If I were to take a drink from the wrong kind of liquid, I would in all probability aspirate and, having filled my lungs with fluid, choke and die. This unseemly possibility has three stages. The first is pudding, which in no sense imperils you; the next is honey, which puts you in less jeopardy; third is nectar, and finally water, when you are dicing with life and death. If all this sounds mumbo jumbo to an educated audience, it should not. For anyone intending to drink beyond his means, the risk of suffocation is high. For my own part, being on pudding as I was, I was consigned to eat chocolate pudding but shrank from eating the obscene mixture called pudding water, by which a mixture was made of water and thickener until the spoon was standing straight up. Such licentious behavior on the part of English pudding makers may surprise no one, but it may reveal to countless consumers of coffee, tea, and other drinks the perilous condition that they are subjecting themselves to if they drink water that goes down the wrong pipe.

Paul and Diane were even able to resume their intimate wordplay, with adjustments for Paul's various linguistic detours. Sometimes this led to delightful results, when Paul bestowed new terms of endearment upon his wife, whose actual name he was often unable to produce. Among his various offerings were the following exquisite pet names: *My Little Bucket of Hair; Commendatore de le Pavane Mistletoe; Dark-Eyed Junco, My Little Bunko;* and *Diligent Apostle of Classic Stanzas.*

corpus callosum A bundle of neural fibers that connects and transfers information between the two hemispheres of the brain.

er. These patients submitted to a surgery that severed the **corpus callosum**, the bundle of neural fibers that connects the two hemispheres of the cerebral cortex in a high-speed "superhighway." The surgery was approved as a treatment after studies by Roger Sperry showed that the procedure in monkeys resulted in very little change in the monkeys' behavior—and indeed, human split-brain patients were able to function surprisingly well even though their two hemispheres had lost the ability to share information with each other.

But using clever experimental tests, the researchers were able to demonstrate some bizarre consequences of the disconnection. The experiments required finding some way to present information to only one side of the brain. For example, to present information to the left hemisphere, sensory input needs to come from the right side of the body because the brain is wired in such a way that it receives input from, and sends motor commands to, the opposite side of the body. "Split-brain" patients used their right hands to handle objects that were hidden behind a barrier, so that only the left hemisphere had access to information gleaned from touching the objects (see **Figure 3.6**). In other versions of the experiments, patients sat in front of a screen and were told to look

(A)

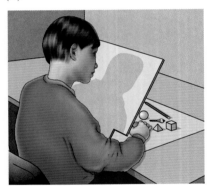

Left hemisphere functions	Right hemisphere functions
Analysis of right visual field	Analysis of left visual field
Stereognosis (right hand)	Stereognosis (left hand)
Lexical and syntactic language	Emotional coloring of language
Writing	Spatial abilities
Speech	Rudimentary speech

Figure 3.6 (A) A split-brain patient handles an object behind the screen with his right hand. (B) Presenting visual information in just the left or right visual field has different effects on individuals with normal versus split brains. When the corpus callosum is intact, information presented in the left visual field is processed in the right hemisphere but can be relayed to crucial language areas in the left hemisphere. In a split-brain individual, only information presented in the right visual field is able to reach the language areas in the left hemisphere.

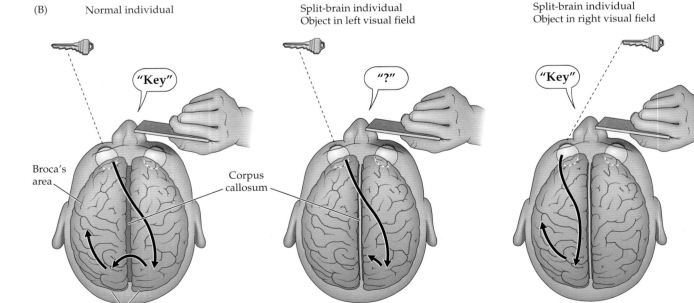

(B) Normal individual

"Key"

Broca's area

Corpus callosum

Visual cortex

Split-brain individual
Object in left visual field

"?"

Split-brain individual
Object in right visual field

"Key"

at a dot in the middle of the screen. Just to the right of the dot, a written word or picture of an object would flash—too quickly for them to move their eyes, but long enough for them to read it or recognize it. This allowed the researchers to make sure that the visual information was available only in the right visual field (that is, the right side of what both eyes take in).

In situations like these, in which the stimulus was presented to the right hand or right visual field—and therefore processed by the *left* hemisphere—the patients had no trouble naming the object or word. However, when the information was presented to the left hand or left visual field, and hence processed by the *right* hemisphere, the patients drew a verbal blank. For a visually presented stimulus, they often reported just seeing a flicker, or nothing at all. At the same time, if asked to identify the object from among a set of picture cards, or even to draw the object with their left hand, they could do it, showing that they had recognized the object. But the part of their brain in the right hemisphere that had recognized the object was unable to communicate with the language areas in the left, leaving them incapable of *reporting* that they had seen it, much less naming it (Gazzaniga & Sperry, 1967).

The fascinating results from the split-brain studies reveal two "half-minds" at odds with each other, with one hemisphere clearly more devoted to language than the other. But even if you have an intact corpus callosum, you too can contribute to brain lateralization science. Experiments with people whose cerebral hemispheres are properly connected have also yielded evidence of language specialization in the left hemisphere, through a task known as **dichotic listening**. In this test, subjects listen to spoken words over headphones. The twist is that a *different* word is spoken into each side, so the left ear, for example, might hear *dog* while the right ear hears *cat*. Most people can tell that each side hears a different word, but usually one of the words seems more distinct than the other. When asked to report what they heard, most people show an advantage for words piped into the right ear—that is, into the left hemisphere, the presumed seat of language. Why would this be, since the right hemisphere is connected to the left in these subjects, with unimpeded communication between the two sides? Regardless of which ear the sounds are coming into, they need to travel to the language areas in the left hemisphere, where their linguistic content can be identified. When the sounds are coming through the right ear into the auditory center in the left hemisphere, the distance to the language areas is shorter, giving these words a jump start. Sounds coming through the left ear into the auditory center in the right hemisphere have to travel a slightly longer distance, so by the time they're processed in the language center, the representations of the words that were delivered to the left hemisphere already have a competitive advantage.

WEB ACTIVITY 3.2

Split-brain studies In this activity, you'll view video footage of a split-brain patient performing the classic Sperry-Gazzaniga tests.

WEB ACTIVITY 3.3

Dichotic listening task In this activity, you'll have the opportunity to test whether you show a right-ear (left-hemisphere) advantage for processing words.

3.3 Mapping the Healthy Human Brain

The earliest insights about the localization of language in the brain came from damaged or anomalous brains. But ultimately, the field of neurolinguistics needed to be able to study healthy human brains in order to confirm and extend the findings of early researchers like Paul Broca and Carl Wernicke. One reason for this is that there's no guarantee that the areas that perform certain functions in a damaged brain line up with the areas for the same functions in a normal brain. We now know that the brain has a truly impressive capacity to

dichotic listening Experimental task in which subjects listen to spoken words over headphones, with a different word spoken into each ear.

reorganize itself, and that even within a few weeks of a stroke, there's evidence that brain function has been rerouted in significant ways. If a function that was previously accomplished by a now-damaged area becomes taken over by a healthy part of the brain, it makes it hard to know what the original organization of brain function was like. There are other more practical challenges that come with relying on individuals with brain damage as the primary research participants. There's a relatively small number of them, which limits how much researchers can generalize to the broader population. It also constrains the amount of research that can be carried out; many individuals with brain damage are extraordinarily generous with their time in helping researchers make progress in the field, but there's a limit to how many hours any one person can spend in a lab performing tests—those who are recovering from a stroke, in particular, may tire easily, or they may show inconsistent performance partly because of their brain injury. Being able to test hypotheses within the general population was necessary in order for the field to make rapid progress and gain greater confidence in its findings.

Localizing language: Brain mapping techniques

Although the possibility of large-scale testing of brain function in healthy humans had to wait until the advent of modern imaging techniques, some groundbreaking contributions to the science of brain localization were made more than a century ago. Among the most influential was the brain-mapping work of German neurologist Korbinian Brodmann, published in 1909. Brodmann believed that the study of brain function had to be grounded in a solid understanding of how the brain was built, so he set about meticulously analyzing the cellular composition of countless slices of brain tissue from animals and human cadavers. Based on his work, he created a "map" of areas in the human cerebral cortex that were anatomically distinct from each other (see **Figure 3.7**). His reasoning was that areas that differed in their physical structure were likely to be responsible for different functions. These **Brodmann areas** have guided much of the exploration of brain function, and are still commonly referred to in current cognitive neuroscience.

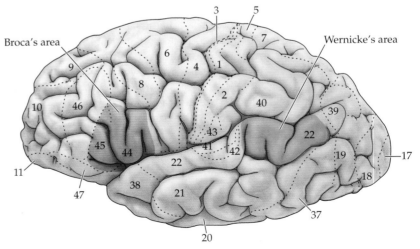

Brodmann areas Areas of the human cerebral cortex that are distinct from each other anatomically and in cellular composition, as determined by Korbinian Brodmann.

Figure 3.7 The Brodmann areas of the brain mark distinctions in cell composition in the various layers of tissue in these regions. Broca's area corresponds approximately to Brodmann areas (BA) 44 and 45, while Wernicke's area corresponds to BA 22.

But how to link up the Brodmann areas with the activities of a healthy brain? A number of these areas were quickly aligned with specific functions, based on experiments with animals in which parts of the brains were electrically stimulated, or in which probes could detect the firing of individual neurons in response to specific stimuli. But these techniques were too invasive to be used with humans, and since language is unique to humans, more detailed localization studies of language lagged behind the study of other basic functions, such as vision. A major technical breakthrough occurred in the early 1990s with the development of fMRI.

It would be a gargantuan understatement to say that the availability of **functional magnetic resonance imaging**, or **fMRI**, has stepped up research activity on brain localization. Over the last two decades, tens of thousands of studies have been published using this method, most of them imaging the uninjured brains of healthy subjects. In popular science writing, it's common to read about fMRI showing brain regions "lighting up" in response to certain stimuli—images of loved ones, or of Hillary Clinton, or an iPad, or whatever. But the fMRI isn't measuring brain activity *directly*. Instead, it's using magnetic field differences to detect and record normal physiological differences in oxygen-rich blood versus oxygen-poor blood. From these **hemodynamic changes**—changes in the blood oxygen levels and direction of blood flow in various areas of the brain—scientists *infer* that brain regions with higher levels of blood flow or blood oxygen are more active. The basic principles underlying fMRI are similar to those of an older technique, **positron emission tomography**, or **PET**. In PET, hemodynamic changes in the brain are made visible by means of a radioactive tracer in the subject's bloodstream. PET is a useful research tool, but it hasn't seen the same massive research application with healthy human subjects that fMRI has, in part because it's a riskier technique, requiring exposure to radiation.

One of the earliest scientists to make the connection between blood flow and brain activity level was Angelo Mosso in the 1870s and 1880s. This connection was based on his observations of a patient named Bertino, who had suffered a head injury that left him with part of his frontal lobes visibly exposed (Raichle, 2000). Mosso noticed that the exposed part of Bertino's brain would pulse more vigorously when the patient heard the chime of church bells, or a clock that signaled time for prayer. Suspecting that the pulsing had something to do with Bertino's thoughts about prayer, he put this question to the patient, and watched Bertino's brain pulse as he thought about it and answered yes.

Mosso, too, struggled with how observations based on injured patients could be extended to the non-invasive study of human subjects in the general population. He eventually conducted a series of experiments using a human balancing device (see **Box 3.4**); the subject lay on a horizontal platform with the head on one side of the pivot and feet on the other, with the two sides perfectly balanced. Mosso assigned the subject tasks that called for various degrees of mental effort, in order to see whether the increase in blood flow to the brain would cause the head to tip lower than the feet, presumably because of the increase in blood flow to the brain (Sandrone et al., 2013). The method was primitive, but it shares the same assumptions as current, highly sophisticated brain-imaging techniques. It's also important to remember that, while the connection between measures of blood flow and brain activity is on the right track, even modern techniques can miss details that occasionally turn out to be supremely relevant for interpreting imaging studies. Brain regions reflect massive populations of neurons, not all of which necessarily carry out the same function. Therefore, fMRI might show an area as basically unresponsive to a certain stimulus even though a minority of its neurons are eagerly firing away.

functional magnetic resonance imaging (fMRI) Neuroimaging technique that uses magnetic fields to measure hemodynamic changes in the brain while the brain is engaged in a task, on the assumption that such changes are a measure of brain activity.

hemodynamic changes Changes in blood oxygen levels and direction of blood flow.

positron emission tomography (PET) Neuroimaging technique that uses radioactivity to measure hemodynamic changes.

BOX 3.4
Then and now:
Measuring brain activity through blood flow

In the late nineteenth century, the Italian physiologist Angelo Mosso observed a brain-injured patient and, based on his observations, made a connection between mental activity and blood flow in the brain. He later devised a "human balancing device" on which he tested his sense of this connection by conducting non-invasive studies of healthy individuals. The subject lay on a horizontal platform with the head on one side of a pivot and feet on the other, with the two sides perfectly balanced (see **Figure 3.8A**). Mosso assigned the subject tasks that called for various degrees of mental effort, in order to see whether this mental effort would cause the head to tip lower than the feet—a presumed consequence of increased blood flow to the brain. As Sandrone et al. (2013) describe:

> Mosso nicknamed his device "the machine to weigh the soul." He reported that the balance tipped towards the head when subjects were given more complex tasks; for instance, more head-tipping occurred while reading a page from a mathematics or philosophy text than when reading a novel. He also claimed to see effects of emotionally charged stimuli. For instance, he reported that the balance tipped toward the head immediately when one of his subjects read a letter from his spouse, and another read a note from an upset creditor. Media hype was just as present in the day of Mosso's balance as with today's fMRI studies, with a French newspaper reporting in 1908 that the device would "soon fully explain the physiology of the human brain" and lead to new treatments for neurological and mental illnesses.

Mosso's method was primitive, but it's worth remembering that it shares the same starting assumptions as our current, highly sophisticated brain-imaging techniques. Based on the assumption that active brain regions will display higher levels of blood flow and blood oxygen than inactive regions, modern fMRI machines use magnetic field differences to detect and record brain activity (see **Figure 3.8B**).

(A)

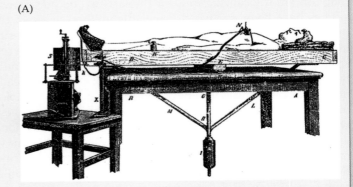

(B)

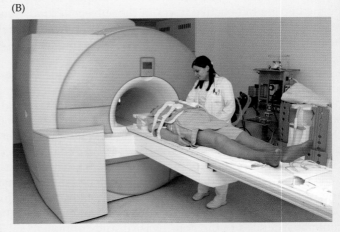

Figure 3.8 (A) Mosso's balance for measuring blood flow. (B) A successor to Mosso's balance, a modern fMRI brain scanner. (A reprinted from Sandrone et al., 2013; B © Shutterstock.)

So, the first assumption that neuroscientists make is that there's a principled connection between hemodynamic measurements and brain activity. The second important assumption is that if changes in blood flow are consistently seen in certain areas of the brain shortly after the presentation of a certain stimulus, this is because the brain is recruiting those areas to process that type of stimulus. Relying on these two assumptions, how would we go about detecting the "language areas" of the brain in an fMRI experiment?

It's not quite enough just to show someone in a scanner an image of a word or sentence, or have her hear a snippet of speech, and then see which brain regions show a change in blood flow. First of all, hemodynamic changes happen even in a brain that's at rest (whatever *that* might mean), so these changes need to be factored out somehow (see **Method 3.2**). A more subtle and difficult point is this: How do we know that the active areas of the brain are engaged in processing the *linguistic* aspects of the stimulus? In reading a word, for example, there will be areas of the brain that are involved in very basic aspects of visual processing that have nothing to do with language—processes that would be just as active in, say, looking at an abstract painting, or recognizing a couch. Or, the word may trigger non-linguistic memories, associations, or thoughts,

METHOD 3.2

Comparing apples and oranges in fMRI

The pictures of activated brain regions that you see in published fMRI studies don't represent a snapshot of the activity of any one brain for the task in question. They're more sensibly read as graphs rather than photos, and they typically represent the *difference* between the experimental condition of interest and some chosen comparison condition, as averaged over many subjects. The dark areas in the picture don't mean that those areas of the brain weren't active while the task was being accomplished. They simply mean that those areas weren't *more* active—to a statistically meaningful degree—than they were during the comparison condition. This means that it's always worth thinking about what the comparison condition is, because the conclusions can only be stated in terms of this difference. A larger or smaller number of brain areas can show up as statistically different depending on the choice of the comparison condition. Let's consider some of the issues that might come up with a language task and various comparison conditions we might opt for.

A common comparison condition is to instruct subjects to close their eyes and think about nothing in particular. Suppose we wanted to use this condition as a baseline for a task in which people listened to sensible conversations. What would people be likely to do in the "think about nothing in particular" baseline condition? If a good portion of the subjects actually lay there replaying the morning's conversation with a girlfriend, or running a recent lecture through their minds in preparation for midterms, there would be a good chance that important language areas of the brain would be involved. The activity in these areas would then become subtracted from the actual language condition, which might give the impression that certain key regions are not activated for language, simply because they were actually activated in *both* the critical language condition and the baseline comparison condition.

Instead of a "resting" baseline condition, researchers sometimes use a control condition that focuses the subject's attention on a specific task that is presumed to involve different computations than the condition of interest. For example, we might compare listening to words (linguistic input) with listening to single tones (non-linguistic input). The hope would be that the differences in activation (see **Figure 3.9**) would reflect the processing of spoken linguistic input as opposed to the processing of non-linguistic auditory input. But other unexpected differences might emerge. For example, it might be

Continued on next page

Noise

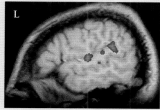 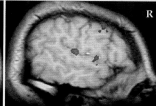

Speech sounds

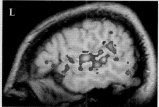 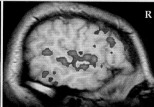

Figure 3.9 These fMRI scans are composites from several subjects that, when combined, indicate areas of peak activation. Pure tones or "noise" (top scans) activate a relatively small region of auditory cortex. When speech sounds are heard (lower two scans), strong activity appears in many areas of the dorsal and ventral auditory pathways. Both the left (L) and right (R) cerebral hemispheres are shown. (From Binder et al.,1994.)

METHOD 3.2 *(continued)*

that the words are more complex examples of auditory stimuli and that they activate regions that are associated with processing complex sequences of sounds, whether linguistic or otherwise. Or, it may be that the words are more interesting and have an effect on brain areas that are linked to heightened attention. In this case, the results might show a difference in activation for a very large number of brain regions, even though only some of them are involved specifically in language.

To take one more example, let's say we compared listening to sentences with listening to musical melodies, based on the logic that both involve processing complex strings of auditory units but only one of them is linguistic. Let's also suppose that, unknown to us, processing melodies actually requires some of the same computations as unraveling the structure of spoken sentences, and involves some of the same areas of the brain. These regions would not show up in the results. The remaining areas that would be identified as being active in the language condition might well provide some answers to the question of which brain regions are devoted to language

and not music. But what if we operated under the false assumption that language and music are fundamentally distinct in their computations and use of brain resources (other than what's required for basic auditory processing)? We might wrongly conclude that our results answered the question of which brain regions are recruited for the purpose of linguistic processing. By assuming too great a distinction between linguistic and musical processing, we might have missed out on identifying some important brain areas that are common to both types of stimuli.

With any luck, over a large number of studies and using a variety of comparison conditions, we'd start to get a clearer picture of how to isolate language-relevant brain regions. But in reading the results of any single study, it's important to realize that it's cutting corners to say, "This study revealed activation in region X for task Y." Statements like this should really be understood as an abbreviation for, "This study revealed greater activation in region X for task Y as compared with task Z." And this understanding should lead us to spend at least a little time thinking about the relationship between tasks Y and Z.

---

activating the same areas of the brain that would be engaged in non-linguistic tasks like silently reminiscing or looking at a photograph. The task itself may incite boredom or arousal, mental states that have certain brain activation patterns. A reasonable strategy for isolating the language areas is to come up with a comparison condition that's as similar as possible to the target stimulus except that it doesn't require language. The brain regions that show activity over and above the control task can then more plausibly be attributed to the linguistic aspect of the stimulus.

Now that neurolinguists are equipped with an anatomical map in one hand and imaging techniques for brain function in the other, what have we learned about language in the brain? Keeping in mind that there are literally thousands of studies out there, the next sections provide very broad outlines of two key conclusions.

Language function is distributed throughout the brain in complex networks

Here's one way to think about the connection between brain regions and their function: we might conceive of important regions as dedicated processing centers, responsible for specific kinds of activities—for instance, visual processing, or language comprehension. A useful analogy might be to think of the regions as self-contained factories that take in raw material as input and produce certain products as output. Each factory has its own structural organization and sets of procedures that are independent from those in other factories, though some commonalities might crop up just because different factory operations settle on similar efficient solutions. This is an easy and intuitive way to think about brain localization, and it's probably made even more intuitive by the type of language that's often used in media reports of neuroimaging studies, with references to notions like "the pleasure center" or headlines like "Scientists Locate Sarcasm in the Brain."

But even some of the earliest proponents of brain localization argued that this picture of the brain as a collection of independent processing centers was overly simplistic. For instance, Brodmann himself doubted that any of the brain regions he identified would turn out to be encapsulated dedicated processors. In his 1909 seminal work, he warned:

> Mental faculties are notions used to designate extraordinarily involved complexes of elementary functions. . . . One cannot think of their taking place in any other way than through an infinitely complex and involved interaction and cooperation of numerous elementary activities. . . . Thus, we are dealing with a physiological process extending widely over the whole cortical surface and not a localized function within a specific region. We must therefore reject as a quite impossible psychological concept the idea that an intellectual faculty or a mental event or a spatial or temporal quality or any other complex, higher psychic function should be represented in a single circumscribed cortical zone, whether one calls this an "association centre" or "thought organ" or anything else.

In fact, if we turn to someone like Carl Wernicke, working early in the history of neuroscience, we see a similarly subtle view. Far from viewing Wernicke's area as something equivalent to the "language comprehension organ," Wernicke conceived of it as a critical piece in a larger network that linked information from different sensory modalities to information about the acoustic quality of words (see **Figure 3.10**).

Instead of thinking of the brain as an assortment of dedicated processing centers or independent factories, here's another possible scenario, one that is more in keeping with the speculations of Brodmann and Wernicke. Imagine the brain as a highly coordinated complex of commercial activity in which the makers of different products have arranged to share resources and their workers' expertise whenever possible. (For instance, the same factory space would handle the production of both fish sticks and chicken fingers, given that they rely on similar procedures. The packaging of many different kinds of goods might take place in another area, bringing together all kinds of frozen foods that go into boxes, including fish sticks, chicken fingers, miniature quiches, and hamburger patties.) In this industrial complex, the production of a specific

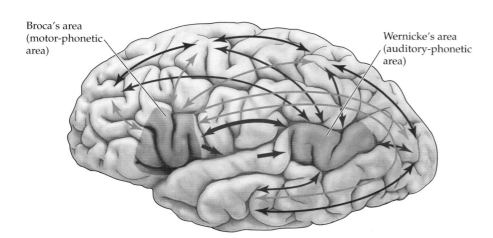

Broca's area
(motor-phonetic area)

Wernicke's area
(auditory-phonetic area)

Figure 3.10 Wernicke's view of language involved a broadly distributed network. Thick red arrows connect the "motor-phonetic" or Broca's area and the "auditory-phonetic" or Wernicke's area. The blue arrows show connections between Wernicke's area and areas that store non-verbal information in "acoustic," "visual," "tactile," and "motor imagery" areas. The orange arrows represent connections between Broca's area and these various sensory areas. The green arrows show connections among the various sensory areas outside of the language network. (After Ross, 2010.)

product wouldn't take place within an isolated factory—instead, its trajectory from start to finish could be described as a path through the complex, making use of whichever resources were suitable for the production process. Some areas within the complex might be highly specialized, with a very small number of specific products (or perhaps even just one type of product) moving through them, while others would perform general tasks that apply to a great number of different products. One consequence of this kind of arrangement would be that products might have to travel large distances from one area of the complex to another, depending on what specific operations they needed to undergo.

From the very earliest work applying brain imaging to the study of language, results have lined up better with this second view of distributed brain function than with the first view of brain regions as dedicated processing centers. In the rest of this section, I'll touch on just a small subset of relevant examples.

In 1978, Bo Larsen and colleagues used a technique that was a precursor to PET and fMRI to identify the regions of the brain that were active while subjects listened to speech, as opposed to the regions that were active while "resting." Surprisingly, in the language-listening task, they found activity not just in Broca's and Wernicke's areas, but also throughout much of both the left and right hemispheres. They concluded that conversation was "likely to involve not only the cortical areas of importance for speech, but practically the whole brain, the left as well as the right side."

The fact that language-related functions are scattered throughout the brain is a testament to the great variety of separate tasks that need to be accomplished in the course of regular, daily language use. Many of the right-hemisphere functions seem to be quite different and complementary to those in the left, perhaps focusing on taking into account how something was said rather than decoding what was said. For example, the processing of information about intonation appears to be mainly housed in the right hemisphere (e.g., Ross & Monnot, 2008). The right hemisphere may also play an important role in how individual sentences are linked together into a coherent story or discourse (e.g., St. George et al., 1999).

The spatial distribution of language in the brain, though, isn't just due to the fact that a great variety of separate tasks are involved. Some of the diffusion also comes from the fact that language is entangled with non-linguistic knowledge. One of the most striking demonstrations of this is the pattern of brain activity that researchers see when they study the recognition of words. It doesn't seem unreasonable, as a first guess, to propose that word recognition might be associated with a certain pattern of brain activity—perhaps there's a location that corresponds to a "mental dictionary," or a general connection path between a "sounds" region of the brain and a "meaning" area. But in fact, you can get quite different patterns of activation for the following three categories of words:

(A)	(B)	(C)
kick	type	lick
step	throw	speak
walk	write	bite
tiptoe	grasp	smile
jump	poke	chew

Did you figure out what each category has in common? The words in category A refer to actions that involve the feet or legs; the words in category B name actions that require the use of fingers, hands, or arms; and the words in category

C describe actions accomplished via movements of the mouth and face. As demonstrated by Olaf Hauk and colleagues (2004), simply *reading* words from these categories activates some of the same brain regions involved in actually carrying out the movements, and reading words from different categories activates different brain regions (reading *kick* activates some of the brain regions involved in moving the feet, etc.; see **Figure 3.11**). Some of the more typical "language-y" areas are engaged as well, but, as Wernicke so astutely predicted at the dawn of modern neuroscience, fMRI data provide visible evidence that the language representations are connected with information in various other regions of the brain that are responsible for storing information about movement and the senses.

The functional neuroanatomy of language

Thinking about language function in terms of many distinct (but often overlapping) networks can help explain some otherwise mystifying data. For example, some patients with brain lesions do poorly on speech perception tests that require them to discriminate between two different syllables. You might predict that this would lead to great difficulty in recognizing words as well—but, while that's true for many patients, it's not necessarily the case. Some patients with poor speech perception skills are easily able to recognize the meanings of words, though they often have a great deal of trouble with language *production*. Conversely, there are other patients who have trouble recognizing words, but pass tests of basic speech perception with flying colors. It seems that it's possible to find cases of double dissociation between the processing of sequences of speech sounds and the recognition of words. What could possibly be going on, since (presumably) you can't easily figure out what a word is without having processed its individual sounds?

Greg Hickok and David Poeppel (2007) have argued that these puzzling findings start to make more sense if you think of the two tasks as belonging to different language-related networks. According to Hickok and Poeppel, word recognition recruits a network that maps speech input onto representations of meaning. Performing tasks like identifying individual syllables, on the other hand, leans more heavily on a different network that maps the acoustic information about sounds onto the articulatory gestures that produce them (this would be the kind of mapping that babies are learning during the babbling stage, when they spend countless hours uttering strings of meaningless sounds, as described in Chapter 2.) This would explain why trouble with simple speech perception tasks can be more directly connected to impairments in language *production* than to difficulties in understanding the meanings of words.

It might seem weird that knowledge of speech sounds would split apart into two separate networks like this. But other modalities show similar dissociations. It's now well known that visual recognition of physical objects fractures into knowledge of *what* objects are and of *how* they are to be used. This can lead to bizarre cases in which, for example, a brain-damaged patient is unable to visually recognize what a comb is or describe its purpose, but can easily demonstrate how to use it. It's more intuitive to think of our knowledge of objects (or sounds) as falling into one bin, but in fact, there's strong

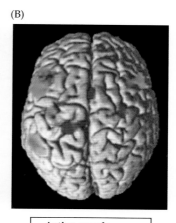
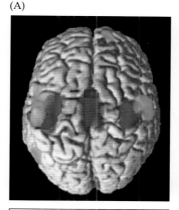

(A)   (B)

Movement	
Blue:	Foot movements
Red:	Finger movements
Green:	Tongue movements

Action words	
Blue:	Leg words
Red:	Arm words
Green:	Face words

Figure 3.11 Results from a study of action words. (A) Activation of brain areas following instructions to move particular parts of the body. (B) Activation of brain areas during silent reading of action words involving three different parts of the body. In a comparison (baseline) condition, subjects saw meaningless rows of hatch marks, averaging the same length as the action words. (From Hauk et al., 2004.)

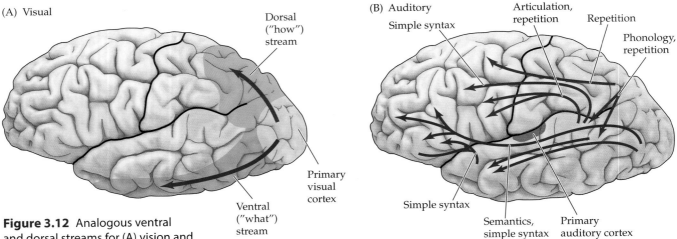

(A) Visual

Dorsal ("how") stream

Primary visual cortex

Ventral ("what") stream

(B) Auditory

Simple syntax

Articulation, repetition

Repetition

Phonology, repetition

Simple syntax

Semantics, simple syntax

Primary auditory cortex

Figure 3.12 Analogous ventral and dorsal streams for (A) vision and (B) language in the left hemisphere of the brain. (B adapted from Gierhan 2013.)

declarative memory Memory for facts and events (whether real or fictional) that can be spoken of ("declared").

procedural memory Memory for physical actions and sequences of actions.

ventral stream Theoretical "knowledge stream" of ventral neural connections (i.e., located in the lower portion of the brain) that process knowledge about "what."

dorsal stream Theoretical "knowledge stream" of dorsal neural connections (i.e., located in the upper portion of the brain) that process knowledge about "how."

evidence that separate knowledge streams exist for processing "what" and "how" information.

The separation of distinct "what" and "how" networks in the brain seems to be a basic way of organizing knowledge across a number of different domains, governing not just vision, but auditory perception and memory as well. Memory researchers, for instance, have long distinguished between declarative and procedural memory. **Declarative memory** refers to memory for facts and events (whether real or fictional) and includes bits of information such as the date on which World War I began, the names of Snow White's seven dwarves, and the object of your first crush. **Procedural memory**, on the other hand, refers to memory for actions, such as how to thread a sewing machine or play your favorite guitar riff. If you've ever forgotten a familiar phone number, only to be able to dial it correctly when given a keypad, then you've directly experienced the disconnect that can happen between the two kinds of memory.

There's now considerable evidence that language, too, is organized in two streams, and that these streams have clearly distinct locations in the brain. As with vision, processing the first type of information (the "what" knowledge) is organized into a network known as the **ventral stream**; the second type of information (the "how" knowledge) takes place in the **dorsal stream** (see **Figure 3.12** and **Box 3.5**). A good deal of research is being conducted with the aim of identifying exactly what kind of information is shuttled along each highway (a 2013 review by Sarah Gierhan provides an overview). The dorsal pathways seem to be involved in information that's relevant for the detailed processing of sounds, for the planning of articulation, and for the repetition of words. The ventral pathways specialize in information about word meanings; damage to these connections, for example, can lead to trouble in understanding the meanings of words, or in retrieving words from memory. Both networks appear to be involved in the processing of syntactic information, though some researchers have suggested that each system is responsible for different kinds of syntactic information, with the processing of very complex structures taking place along the dorsal network.

Much of the emerging evidence supporting the existence of dorsal and ventral pathways is the result of new approaches and techniques that allow researchers to take the next step beyond simply identifying which regions of the brain are active during language tasks. They can now also investigate the ways in which the various language-related regions of the brain are connected to each other by long bundles of neural fibers (*axons*; see Section 3.4) collectively called **white matter**. White matter tracts act as the brain's road networks, allowing products from one processing area to be shuttled to another area for further processing or packaging. (Fun fact: The average 20-year-old human possesses between 150,000 and 175,000 kilometers of white matter fibers, as estimated by Lisbeth Marner and her colleagues in 2003. That's a lot of road.) White matter fiber tracts can be visualized in the living brain by using **diffusion magnetic resonance imaging** (**dMRI**), which tracks how water molecules diffuse through the brain. Since water dif-

white matter Bundles of neural tissue (axons) that act as the brain's information network, allowing products (signaling molecules) from one processing area to be shuttled to another area for further processing.

diffusion magnetic resonance imaging (dMRI) Neuroimaging technique that tracks how water molecules are diffused in the brain, providing a view of the brain's "white matter highway."

BOX 3.5
The functional neuroanatomy of language

The language areas of the cerebral cortex (the outer layer of neural tissue that covers the cerebral hemispheres) are diagrammed in **Figure 3.13**.

The **STG** (superior temporal gyrus) and the posterior portion of the **STS** (superior temporal sulcus) are involved in the phonological stages of spoken-word recognition—for example, in distinguishing between the important sounds in *bear* versus *pear*. This function seems to be bilaterally organized. That is, damage to only the left hemisphere does not result in great difficulties in processing the details of sound, but damage to both hemispheres (bilateral damage) results in "word deafness," in which hearing is preserved but understanding of speech is badly impaired.

The anterior temporal lobe region labeled **ATL** is involved in accessing and integrating semantic knowledge across modalities, and within a syntactic structure. Damage to this area leads to difficulties in understanding complex or ambiguous sentences. Also in the anterior temporal

lobe, the **MTG** (middle temporal gyrus), **ITG** (inferior temporal gyrus), and anterior portions of the **STS** play a role in mapping sound to meaning and are also involved in accessing the meaning of written words. The representation of the meanings of words is widely distributed throughout the cerebral cortex (see Figure 3.11), but some researchers have argued that there is a more organized "hub" for word meanings in the anterior temporal region.

The left dorsal **STG** and **SMG** (supramarginal gyrus), along with the primary auditory cortex (**Aud**) and areas of the primary **motor cortex**, play a role in speech production, which involves integrating auditory information with a set of motor sequences for speech. Unlike speech perception, speech production seems to be heavily lateralized in the left hemisphere.

The **Spt** (Sylvian parietal temporal) region may play a role in sensory-motor integration for the vocal tract,

Continued on next page

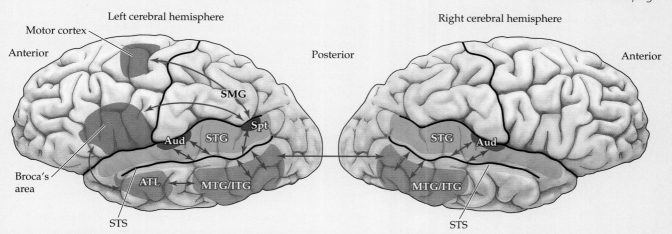

Figure 3.13 This contemporary view of areas of the brain that contribute to language function, as organized into dorsal (green arrows) and ventral networks (red arrows; see Figure 3.12). Note that the networks extend into the right as well as the left cerebral hemisphere, although the left-hemisphere structures predominate. (Adapted from Hickok, 2009.)

BOX 3.5 (*continued*)

including "auditory imagery" of speech and non-speech vocal sounds (for example, humming music), whether the task involves producing sounds out loud or simply imagining them. This region shows heightened activity if auditory feedback from speech is disrupted (for instance, by delays). It is also likely involved in short-term verbal memory, which keeps sound-based information about words active in memory (for example, mentally "rehearsing" a phone number so you don't forget it before you get a chance to dial it). This region also supports the learning of new, unfamiliar words.

Broca's area (Brodmann areas 44 and 45) supports the production and understanding of syntactic structure.

In addition to the language areas of the cerebral cortex shown in Figure 3.13, language may also involve subcortical (internal) areas of the brain. For example, the **basal ganglia**, a collection of structures deep inside the brain (see **Figure 3.14**), have a key role in regulating bodily movement but also appear to be connected to the dorsal auditory stream. Some researchers argue that the basal

ganglia play an important role in the sequencing of sounds and syntactic units.

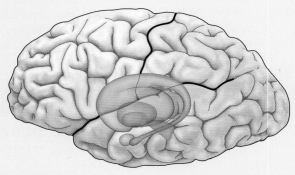

Figure 3.14 The basal ganglia, located deep within the forebrain, consist of several brain nuclei (clusters of anatomically discrete neurons, seen here in different shades of blue and lavender) and appear to have functions in the language pathway as well as their better-known functions in the motor pathway.

Corpus callosum

Figure 3.15 A view of the brain using dMRI, which tracks the movement of water molecules through the brain. Water diffuses in a manner that parallels the white matter tracts that carry neural signals. This imaging technique can provide insights into how information moves between various regions of the brain. (Courtesy of Patric Hagmann.)

fuses in a direction that runs parallel to the white matter fiber bundles, dMRI provides a view of the brain's "white matter road" (see **Figure 3.15**) and, crucially, some insight into how information moves between various regions of the brain—including the dorsal and ventral information processing "highways."

Brain organization for language is both specialized and flexible

Broca's area, which is implicated in language production, is conveniently located next to the part of the motor cortex that controls movement of the mouth and lips, while Wernicke's area, which is important for comprehension, sits next door to the auditory cortex (see **Figure 3.16**). This makes sense, as there would likely be many connections between these adjacent areas. But not all language is spoken. Sign languages involve making movements with the hands rather than with the tongue and lips (though much of the face can be heavily involved); no hearing is necessary, with comprehension relying instead on visual-spatial processes. So here's a trick question: Where would you find the language-related networks for people who grew up with a sign language as their native language? Would Broca's and Wernicke's areas be involved? Or would language establish its base camps in other regions? A logical place to look for this hypothetical "sign language network" might be near the part of the motor cortex that controls hand movements, or over in the right hemisphere, which takes on a good portion of visual-spatial processing.

In order to think about this question, let's revisit our metaphor of the brain as a complex commercial network that makes many different kinds of products. Having an area like Wernicke's next to the auditory cortex is a lot like setting up a fish stick factory near a fishing port—sensible, as the main ingredients don't need to travel far in order to get to the processing plant. But what if, instead of making fish sticks, we decided to make chicken fingers? The ingredients are different, but it turns out that the machinery needed is very similar, as are the various steps in the production process. While it might make sense to build our chicken finger factory near a chicken farm, what if there's already a facility in place near a fishing port that's ideally set up for making products like fish sticks and chicken fingers? Even though it might require shipping the raw ingredients over a greater distance, it might still make more sense to use that facility than to build a whole new facility. So, one way to think about the question of localization of brain function is like this: does the brain's organization reflect mostly the raw ingredients that it uses (spoken sounds versus hand movements), or does it specialize for the various processes (that is, the specific computations) that the raw ingredients have to undergo?

The answer is that, at least much of the time, the brain specializes for processing rather than for the ingredients. This can be seen from a number of studies of sign language users. For example, Greg Hickok and colleagues (2001) worked with a number of patients with aphasia who were American Sign Language (ASL) users and found that, just like hearing folks, there were deaf aphasic patients who had trouble producing signs but could comprehend them reasonably well, while others could produce signs but had trouble understanding them. The deaf patients had brain damage in exactly the areas usually found for aphasic hearing patients—in the areas known as Broca's and Wernicke's, respectively.

Evidence from imaging confirms that the brain organization of ASL signers looks a lot like that of speakers of sound-based languages despite the fact that a completely different modality is being used (for a review, see MacSweeney et al., 2008). This is interesting because in the last chapter, we saw that when gesture is used *linguistically* by homesigners and inventors of new sign languages, it has deeply different properties from pantomime gesture—a fact that had been lost on hearing observers for many years. The distinction between linguistic and non-linguistic gesture also shows up in brain-imaging studies, as found by Karen Emmorey and her colleagues (2011) when they compared brain activation patterns for ASL signs with those for pantomime gestures. To people who don't know ASL, signs can sometimes *look* like pantomime because a number of signs have their origins in a pantomimed gesture that became conventionalized. For example, the ASL signs used to communicate the concepts of hammering or of pouring syrup are a lot like what you'd do if you were asked to

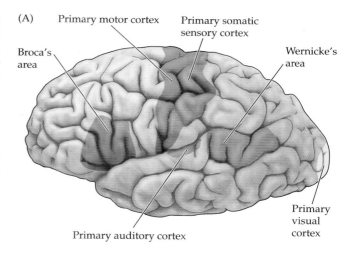

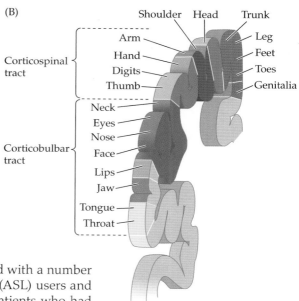

Figure 3.16 (A) This drawing illustrates the proximity of the motor cortex to Broca's area, and of the auditory cortex to Wernicke's area. (B) A schematic illustration of the organization of the primary motor cortex. The areas that control movements of the mouth and lips are located near Broca's area, while the areas controlling movements of the hands, arms, and fingers are more distant.

Figure 3.17 Examples of ASL verbs produced in response to the pictured objects.

(A)

(B)

TO-HAMMER

POUR-SYRUP

pantomime the actions rather than convey them linguistically (see **Figure 3.17**). Emmorey and her colleagues decided to look specifically at iconic signs like these, in order to see whether producing them would activate different brain regions than would pantomiming gestures, even though the hand motions for the two are actually very similar.

To elicit a linguistic sign, the researchers showed native ASL signers a picture of an object, such as a hammer or a bottle of syrup, and asked the signers to generate a verb related to that object. If pantomime gestures were being elicited, subjects were asked to gesture to show how they would use that object. **Figure 3.18** shows data from brain scans for ASL signers producing verbs and from hearing subjects who were gesturing rather than using language. As you can see, the patterns of activation are quite different; the ASL verbs resulted in more activity in the frontal lobe, home of Broca's area, while pantomime gestures triggered more activity in the parietal lobe.

Sign language studies show that when it comes to brain localization, it's not just the raw ingredients of your language that matter; it's also what you do with them. Language networks in the brain readily adapt to a slew of different materials that could be used for linguistic purposes. This is apparent in spoken languages too. For example, lan-

(A) Deaf (handling verbs)

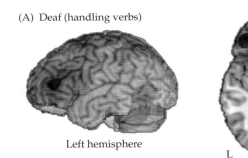

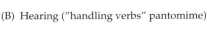

Left hemisphere

L   R

(B) Hearing ("handling verbs" pantomime)

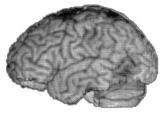

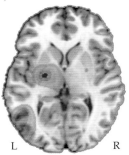

Left hemisphere

L   R

Figure 3.18 Averaged data for (A) brains scans of deaf subjects producing ASL signs and (B) hearing subjects producing pantomime gestures in response to the same stimuli. These scans plot comparisons with a baseline condition in which subjects saw pictures of objects and gave a thumbs-up to indicate that the objects could be manually handled or waved their hands to indicate that they couldn't. (From Emmorey et al., 2011.)

LANGUAGE AT LARGE 3.2

Brain bunk: Separating science from pseudoscience

Phrenology, the practice of analyzing a person's character by feeling or measuring the shape of his skull, is now known as a disgraced discipline, a pseudoscience. But it was based on a set of ideas that were perfectly reasonable at the time (the early 1800s), some of which even turned out to be correct.

Phrenology's main theoretical claim held that the brain was the home of the mind, and since the mind appeared to be made up of a number of distinct faculties (which were conceived of as traits such as time and space perception, language ability, hopefulness, benevolence, acquisitiveness, etc.), these faculties must have corresponding organs in the brain (see **Figure 3.19**). It seemed logical to think that the size of any one of these organs would determine the strength of the corresponding trait for an individual, and that people might vary in which faculties were stronger than others (and hence, which of their brain organs would be bigger than others). The final piece of reasoning was that the skull formed to accommodate the shape of the underlying mental organs and that it was possible to discern a person's mental traits from the shape of the skull.

Phrenology's problem was not with the content of these ideas, all of which were interesting, testable hypotheses; it was with how people went about testing them. Instead of scientifically testing each of the major premises in a systematic way, phrenologists tended to fit the data to match their preconceived theories. The initial charts connecting features of the skull to specific traits were developed by examining people whose traits were already known, and these charts were "confirmed" by additional examinations that were biased by the pre-existing ideas. The great American humorist Mark Twain poked fun at such shoddy practices when he anonymously visited a phrenologist, only to be told that a "cavity" in his skull revealed that his "humor organ" was entirely lacking. He returned a few months later under his own name, and the very same phrenologist, not remembering their earlier encounter but now knowing him to be the famous humorist Mark Twain, examined the author and found "the loftiest bump of humor he had ever encountered in his life-time!" (Lopez, 2002).

Phrenology was eventually discredited, but not before it became wildly popular, with people paying substantial sums of money to phrenologists who would "read" their character and give them advice about which careers or marriage partners they were best suited for. In step with Mark Twain, humorist Ambrose Bierce defined phrenology as "the science of picking the pocket through the scalp" (Bierce, 1911).

Many parallels have been drawn between the pseudoscience of phrenology and the use of fMRI techniques by researchers or consultants who claim to be able to detect, on the basis of the activation of certain brain regions, whether someone will buy a particular product, or vote for a certain candidate. In one highly publicized study (Iacoboni et al., 2007), researchers tucked prospective voters into fMRI scanners and collected brain images in response to images of various candidates, or to words referring to political parties. Based on the results, they drew a number of concrete inferences. They

Continued on next page

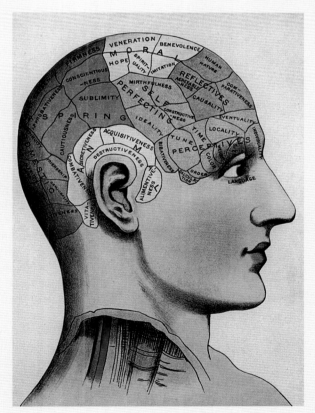

Figure 3.19 A phrenologist's "map" of faculties believed to be associated with certain brain regions.

noted, for example, that when subjects who'd rated Hillary Clinton unfavorably saw photographs of her, they "exhibited significant activity in the anterior cingulate cortex, an emotional center of the brain that is aroused when a person feels compelled to act in two different ways but must choose one. It looked as if they were battling unacknowledged impulses to like Mrs. Clinton." Elicitation of disgust was attributed to viewing the candidate John Edwards, based on high levels of activation in the insula, and Mitt Romney was claimed to have elicited anxiety, based on an active amygdala among viewers.

But many neuroscientists responded to this study with a strong warning that the conclusions were premature. Sure, activity in the amygdala *could* represent anxiety upon seeing the face of Mitt Romney. But since the amygdala is known to become active under a number of different emotional states, not just anxiety, it could also mean that viewers were responding with happiness, anger, or sexual excitement—or perhaps a mental state that hasn't yet been discovered to be associated with the amygdala.

A hefty portion of potentially misleading or mistaken conclusions (including the above example) come from what's known as a "reverse inference," which has the following pattern of logic:

Previous studies have shown that during process X, brain area Y was active.

In the current study, we see stimulus A activates brain area Y.

Hence, processing stimulus A must involve process X.

Such inferences may seem intuitively appealing in many cases, but they are not valid conclusions. Other alternative explanations have not yet been properly tested and ruled out—and given that we now know that any one brain area can easily be implicated in a number of different processes, this is not a step that researchers can afford to skip. Certainly, to dispense "expert" (and expensive) advice about a candidate's political strategy or a company's marketing practices, based on results like these, risks becoming a form of pickpocketing through the scalp.

On the other hand, it's worth remembering that phrenology had some good, even revolutionary ideas. Had these ideas been subjected to proper scientific scrutiny, the accurate ones might eventually have been sifted from the less accurate ones, and we might remember the discipline as laying the groundwork for crucial breakthroughs in scientific thinking about how brain function is localized. In the end, a good part of distinguishing between science and pseudoscience amounts to being able to tell the difference between end points and starting points: does a particular result lend itself to a confident conclusion—or does it hint at an intriguing hypothesis to be tested further?

guages can differ in how they use tone, or changes in pitch. In languages like English, tone has a **paralinguistic use**—that is, it doesn't directly contribute to the composition of words or sentences, but it can be used for emphasis, to clarify the speaker's intended meaning, or for emotional color. But some languages (Mandarin and Vietnamese among them) use pitch as a third type of acoustic building block for words, along with consonants and vowels. In English, producing one consonant instead of another usually results in saying a completely different word—try, for instance: *pan, ban, can, man, tan,* and *Dan.* But varying the pitch on a word like *pan* doesn't turn it into a different word. In Mandarin, though, the same string of consonants and vowels—for instance, the simple sequence *ma*—can mean different things depending on the pitch contour you lay over it. Say it with a high tone, and you've uttered "mother"; with a rising tone, and you've said "hemp"; with a low falling tone, you've meant "horse"; and with a high falling tone, you've made a scolding sound.

For many English speakers, it's preposterously difficult to learn to attend to different distinctions in pitch as part of a word's core identity. Yet, there's nothing *inherently* difficult about making distinctions in pitch—you can easily tell if someone is saying your name in order to scold, query, exclaim with pleasure, or warn of impending danger, and yet all of this requires you to discriminate among pitch contours. So why is it so hard to use exactly the same information for a different purpose? Brain research provides a clue. When

paralinguistic use The use or manipulation of sounds for emphasis, clarification of meaning, or emotional color but not as an element in the composition of words or sentences.

tone is used linguistically to mark the identity of a word, it appears to recruit left-hemisphere regions in the brain. But non-linguistic pitch information is normally processed in the right hemisphere, and sure enough, speakers of languages like English, which uses tone paralinguistically, process tone primarily in the right hemisphere (e.g., Wang et al., 2001). Brain localization reflects the fact that tone has a different job description in the two language types. The process of learning a language like Mandarin isn't as simple as learning to perceptually distinguish tone; it involves some fairly deep reorganization of how information about tone is handled, and through which brain networks it's routed.

This statement about Mandarin likely generalizes to other languages that use sound in seemingly exotic ways. For example, a number of African languages use a set of sounds known as "clicks" that are made with a sucking action of the tongue, much like the sound you might make to spur on a horse. These languages use a variety of different clicks in the same way English uses consonants—that is, as basic building blocks of words. English speakers, it turns out, also use clicks, but as with tone, clicks are put to work in paralinguistic tasks; for English speakers, clicks seem to function a lot like paragraph breaks, to signal a shift in conversational topic. For instance, in studying the paralinguistic function of clicks in English, researcher Melissa Wright (2011) noted the following snippet of telephone dialogue:

> **Nor:** You leave Wincanton about three o'clock and get back about two in the morning…
>
> **Les:** Oh.
>
> **Nor:** …and work full-time on top of that.
>
> **Les:** Oh dear.
>
> **Nor:** But it's a lot easier now huh.
>
> **Les:** Yes I'm sure. Hm. [click] Okay well I'll tell Gordon and uhm, I'm sure he was going to give you a ring anyway.

Despite being regular clickers themselves, many English speakers are fascinated by the linguistic use of clicks in other languages. To English ears, inserting these sounds inside words sounds a bit like highly skilled beatboxing (more on this in Chapter 4). I've had friends ask, "How do they talk and click *at the same time*?" To a speaker of a click language, this is a very odd question, much like asking, "How do they talk and make the consonant *b* sound *at the same time*?"

WEB ACTIVITY 3.4

Linguistic or paralinguistic? In this exercise, you'll see examples of how the same types of sounds have been recruited for different purposes by different languages.

The take-home message from this line of work is that specific patches of neurons seem to be predisposed to handle certain kinds of tasks, but there is a fair bit of flexibility in how these core tasks can be adapted to handle a variety of different situations. This flexibility, together with the distributed nature of the brain's organization, no doubt makes research life a bit more challenging than it would be if the brain were set up as a cluster of independent "factories" or processing centers. Back in 1793, before scientists had any real evidence that different functions lived in different clumps of neural tissue, a medical doctor (Leny, 1793) wrote about the brain:

> There is no part of the human body concerning which we possess so limited a knowledge. Its intricacy is great, and to that, our ignorance seems to bear proportion. We know neither the manner in which it

performs its functions, nor the share which each of its parts have in their performances. The former is perhaps for wise purposes, placed above human understanding; and the latter, though it appears more within our reach, has hitherto eluded the research of inquirers.

We now know that it's not going to be possible to identify the "share which each of its parts have" in various functions of the brain without a much deeper understanding of "the manner in which it performs its functions." You can't just point to a brain region and say, "Vision occurs here" or, "Speech sounds are processed there." You have to have some ideas about how speech might be produced, in order to tease apart the various components that go into it; without this knowledge, you won't be able to figure out where in the brain the separate operations might be taking place, and how these operations might or might not generalize to non-speech stimuli. As you'll see throughout the rest of this book, brain localization research gets a lot more precise and interesting when it's tightly interwoven with ideas about the specific kinds of computations that take place there. In the best-case scenarios, evidence from brain imaging can help resolve some long-standing debates about the nature of cognitive processes. Though there's still an enormous amount we don't know, happily, researchers today need not feel that it's "above human understanding" to eventually arrive at a deep knowledge of how our own brains work.

3.4 The Brain in Real-Time Action

Brain-imaging techniques help scientists answer *where* in the brain language computations take place, and this question goes hand in glove with the question of what these computations look like. But another way to understand how language works is to ask *when* in the brain linguistic action takes place. For example, are some words retrieved sooner than others? Does the timing of language processes happen on a fixed schedule, or does it depend on the context? When we understand language, do we first sort out how the sentence is structured before we tackle its meaning? Answering specific questions like these would allow us to build a much more detailed model of what it means to use language.

Neuroimaging techniques like fMRI are not the ideal tools to use if you want to get a sense of the timing of brain processes, rather than their location. As you learned in the previous section, fMRI doesn't measure brain activity itself—instead, it taps into the changes in blood flow or blood oxygen levels that are the *result* of increased brain activity. These hemodynamic changes lag behind the brain activity that triggers them by several seconds, and as you'll soon see, all the interesting language-related activity takes place on a smaller time scale than this. There have been technical improvements in fMRI methods that allow researchers to mathematically factor out the time lag between brain activity and the fMRI signal, but for researchers who are mostly interested in very precise recordings of the timing of brain activity, it's possible to use methods that measure brain activity more directly.

Measuring electrical brain activity in response to language

Neurons communicate with each other through electrical signaling. In neurons, signaling occurs when electrically charged particles called **ions** move across a neuron's membrane. Each neuron is equipped with **dendrites**, which

ions Electrically charged particles; the charge can be positive or negative. Ions that are especially important in neural signaling include sodium (Na^+), potassium (K^+) calcium (Ca^{2+}), and chloride (Cl^-).

dendrites Neuronal extensions that receive informational "input" from other neurons.

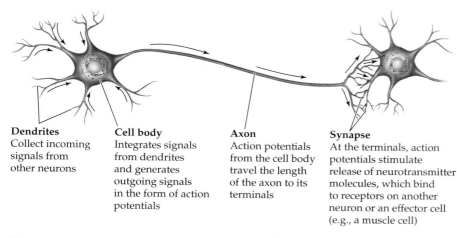

Dendrites
Collect incoming
signals from
other neurons

Cell body
Integrates signals
from dendrites
and generates
outgoing signals
in the form of action
potentials

Axon
Action potentials
from the cell body
travel the length
of the axon to its
terminals

Synapse
At the terminals, action
potentials stimulate
release of neurotransmitter
molecules, which bind
to receptors on another
neuron or an effector cell
(e.g., a muscle cell)

Figure 3.20 Electrical activity in a neuron. Dendrites collect electrical signals from other neurons. These signals are integrated in the cell body, and if the resulting voltage exceeds a threshold, an outgoing signal—an action potential—is sent along the axon, releasing neurotransmitters that have the capacity to alter the voltage of connected neurons.

axon Extension of a nerve cell (neuron) along which informational "output" travels to another neuron.

synapse Site of connection between the axon terminal of a neuron and the receptors of another neuron or a muscle cell.

action potential An electrical pulse that travels down the axon of a neuron to a synapse, resulting in the release of neuro-transmitters.

neurotransmitter Molecules produced by a neuron and released across a synapse in response to an action potential. Neuro-transmitters bind to receptors on a receiv-ing cell (another neuron or a muscle cell), producing a response in the second cell.

electroencephalography (EEG) The use of electrodes placed on the scalp to measure changes in electrical voltage over large numbers of neurons in the brain, thus obtaining information about the timing of responses in the brain.

magnetoencephalography (MEG) A technique related to electroencephalogra-phy that detects changes in magnetic fields caused by the brain's electrical activity.

event-related potential (ERP) The change in electrical voltage (the potential) over large numbers of brain neurons, mea-sured with EEG and lined up with the presen-tation of a relevant stimulus (the event).

are "input" sites that process the information from these signaling molecules. At the "output" end is the **axon**, which extends from the neuron's nucleus and ends in a number of **synapses**, where the axon connects with and passes information to the dendrites other neurons (see **Figure 3.20**). At rest, neurons have a negative electrical voltage, which changes if they are stimulated. If a neuron's voltage rises above a certain threshold, it fires an electrical pulse— an **action potential**—that travels down the axon to the synapses, resulting in the release of chemical signaling molecules called **neurotransmitters**. These neurotransmitters in turn can allow ions to pass through the membranes of connected neurons, altering their electrical voltage.

The action potentials of individual cells can be measured by placing probes near the target cells. But this technique is too invasive to be used with human subjects, so scientists rely on **electroencephalography** (**EEG**), using electrodes placed on the scalp to measures the changes in the electrical voltage over large numbers of neurons (see **Figure 3.21**). Electrodes used in this way are high-ly sensitive to the timing of voltage changes. But because they're picking up the brain's electrical activity through the skull, information about the precise locations of the voltage changes is blurred, providing only very approximate data about where in the brain this activity is taking place. A related technique, known as **magnetoencephalography**, or **MEG**, detects changes in magnetic fields that are caused by the brain's electrical activity. MEG provides better information about where this activity is taking place, but since the technique is much more expensive than EEG, there are many more research studies using EEG than MEG.

Using ERPs to learn the timing of brain processes

For studying language processes, researchers are interested in seeing how the brain's activity changes in response to a particular linguistic stimulus, so they usually look at EEG waveforms that are lined up to the onset of that stimulus. This way of looking at brain activity is known as an **event-related potential** (**ERP**)—the "event" in question being the presentation of the relevant stimu-

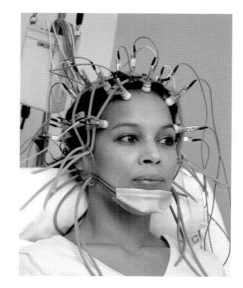

Figure 3.21 A research participant with EEG electrodes placed over the scalp.

lus. When the waveforms from two different types of stimuli are generated, they can be scrutinized for revealing differences. For example: Do the same peaks occur in the waveforms? Do the peaks occur at the same point in time? Are the peaks different in size or duration?

Now that we're outfitted with this nifty equipment, let's see if we can use it to shed some light on language processing. We might start by asking a very basic question: How soon after the presentation of a stimulus does *linguistic* processing kick in? That is, when we hear or read language, it enters our senses through our ears or eyes, and our brain has to decide at some point that what it's dealing with is language. Is there a point in time at which we can see a different pattern of brain activity for linguistic stimuli than for non-linguistic stimuli?

To test this, an obvious starting point might be to compare a linguistic stimulus (like a visually presented word) to a non-linguistic stimulus (like a line drawing of a familiar object). Let's say we measure the brain activity involved in processing these two types of stimuli, and we find a difference in waveforms emerging at about one-tenth of a second, or 100 milliseconds (ms). Cool result. It might be tempting to conclude that about 100 ms after seeing the stimulus, the brain is already starting to grind through language-related processes. But, as with fMRI results, the proper scientific restraint is called for when interpreting the data. We need to avoid inferring more from the evidence than is valid. And, as with fMRI data, that means checking to see whether we've used the best comparison conditions—specifically, is the difference in brain activity really due to the linguistic/non-linguistic aspect of our stimuli? Or could it be due to some other, less obvious difference between words and drawings of objects? For example, the two are very different when it comes to their basic visual properties—maybe the brain is simply responding to those low-level visual differences.

These were some of the considerations that were taken into account in an interesting study led by Haline Schendan (1998). She and her colleagues compared brain activity elicited by words and pictures of objects, but they also included a number of other "word-like" and "object-like" stimuli (see **Figure 3.22A**). This gave them a better idea of exactly which differences the brain was responding to and when.

What they found was that within roughly 100 ms, the brain began to sort visual stimuli by type (possibly so that it could be assigned to the appropriate processing streams), progressively making finer and finer distinctions. The first distinction was made just after 95 ms to separate object-like stimuli from word-like stimuli. Very shortly after, at about 105 ms, the brain distinguished strings of real orthographic characters from other sequences of images, either strings of icons or lines arranged in a type of pseudo-font. Finally, a distinction between words and pseudo-words emerged, starting at about 200 ms from the time the stimulus was first seen (see **Figure 3.22B**).

What do these results mean—that is, how do we translate the waveforms into what the brain is actually accomplishing in these time frames? Certainly, one would be hard-pressed to argue that anything truly linguistic was going on before real letters were distinguished from stimuli that *superficially* looked like sequences of letters. At least the first 105 ms, then, seem to be devoted to purely visual aspects of processing.

But what about the point at which we see a difference in waveforms between real words and pseudo-words? Doesn't this suggest that real words are recognized starting at about 200 ms? Again, this would be drawing too strong a conclusion. All that we're entitled to say, based on these results, is that the *brain is treating these two types of stimuli differently.* It *could* be because it has recognized some stimuli as words and others as not. That's a perfectly reason-

Figure 3.22 Sample stimuli and ERP data from experiments by Schendan and colleagues. (A) Examples of the six different image types that subjects saw in random sequence. (B) Averaged ERP data from two recording sites (Cz and Oz). Note that negative voltage is plotted on the upper portion of the y-axis, while positive voltage is plotted on the lower portion. (Adapted from Schendan et al. 1998.)

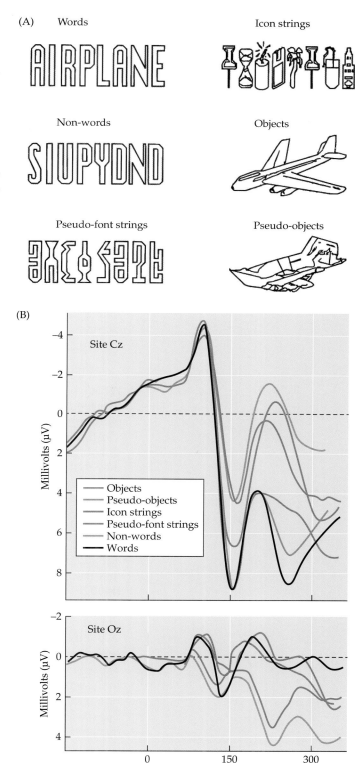

able hypothesis, but others exist as well. The difference in waveforms could instead arise from other, more subtle reasons. For example, the real words contained clusters of letters that are more commonly found together, while the non-words contained letter clusters that are less commonly seen together. So, the difference between a word like *spark* and a non-word like *ctuik* could simply be that the letter sequences *spa* and *ark* are ones that people have seen very often before (for example, *spat, spare, span, spam, spackle, spartan; bark, lark, shark, mark, dark, embark,* and so on). On the other hand, how often have you met the sequences *ctu* or *uik*? Recognition of familiar sequences of letters doesn't necessarily mean that the word itself has been retrieved and recognized, and it could be that recognizing familiar letter strings is all that the brain is doing at 200 ms after the word's presentation. To tease apart these two alternative explanations, we need to set up yet another experiment with just the right contrasting conditions so we can test the hypotheses more precisely.

Sure enough, later ERP work by a team of French researchers (Bentin et al., 1999) did just this and compared the brain's activity in response to real French words, pronounceable pseudo-words (for example, *lartuble*), and unpronounceable processions of consonants (for example, *rtgdfs*). The pronounceable pseudo-words (*lartuble*) contained letter sequences that were common in French, while still not being real words; the unpronounceable consonant strings (*rtgdfs*), on the other hand, contained highly improbable letter sequences. The researchers found that the separation of these types of stimuli occurred in two stages. First, the waveforms showed a difference between the improbable consonant strings, on the one hand, and the real words and pseudo-words, on the other hand, showing that the brain is in fact sensitive to the combinations of individual letters. Only later did the waveforms show a distinction between the pseudo-words and the real words, with the brain activity peaking at about 350 ms after the stimuli were first seen. This is the earliest point at which we can confidently say that real words are in fact being recognized.

This set of meticulous comparisons serves as an important reminder to both researchers and smart consumers of ERP research: what might look like the most obvious difference between two types of stimuli isn't necessarily what the brain is responding to. In making intelligent proposals about how waveforms link up to specific mental activities, there's no getting around the need for painstakingly comparing sets of stimuli that differ in a number of other, less intuitive ways.

Nevertheless, we have in hand some clear evidence that linguistic and nonlinguistic stimuli provoke different patterns of brain activity within a couple of hundred milliseconds. Perhaps the next step is to ask, "Are there distinct waveforms for different kinds of linguistic computations?"

Identifying ERP components for linguistic functions: The N400 and P600 effects

One way to examine the brain's activity is to throw it a curve ball. Causing the brain to process information that's surprising or unexpected allows you to directly compare surprising and unsurprising stimuli to see how the brain deals with the extra processing challenge. Consider:

> John buttered his bread with socks.

> I take my coffee with cream and dog.

Take a moment to describe what's odd about the two sentences above. Now consider:

> The spoiled child throw the toys on the floor.

> Charles doesn't shave because him tends to cut himself.

What's odd about these two sentences? How are they different from the first two sentences, and what operations do you think the brain would need to be performing in order to detect the weirdness?

All four of the above sentences introduce elements of weirdness, and presumably require extra processing. But researchers became very interested when they found that the first set of sentences triggered very different waveforms than the second set. In the first set, the sentences are surprising because the last word makes no sense within the sentence frame. When these bizarre sentences were compared with ones in which the last word of the sentence was perfectly *un*surprising (for example, *John buttered his bread with butter*), the participants' brains showed more intense activity moving toward a negative voltage and peaking at about 400 ms after the odd word was presented. This effect, first discovered by Marta Kutas and Steve Hillyard in 1980, was dubbed the **N400** (ERP components are often named in a way that identifies whether their voltage is moving in a positive or negative direction and that shows the typical timing of their peaks of activity).

But the N400 clearly isn't just a general marker of something gone weird in a sentence, because quite a different waveform is usually seen for sentences like *The spoiled child throw the toys on the floor.* In this case, there's no particular word in the sentence that's nonsensical—it's just that the verb *throw* doesn't have the right grammatical marker on it to go with the singular subject of the sentence, *The spoiled child*. A similar problem crops up with *Charles doesn't shave because him tends to cut himself.* Again, none of the words are nonsensical here. But the sentence is badly formed because the pronoun *him* is in the wrong form—instead, it should be *he*, a pronoun that's no different in meaning from *him* (both words refer to a singular male), but that has the right *grammatical form* for its place in the sentence. Many sentences that have a grammar problem rather than a sense problem trigger a waveform that shows a positive peak at about 600 ms—named, you guessed it, the **P600** (e.g., Neville et al., 1991; Osterhout & Holcomb, 1992; see **Figure 3.23**).

N400 An ERP in which a waveform shows a negative voltage peak about 400 ms.

P600 An ERP effect in which a waveform shows a positive voltage peak about 600 ms.

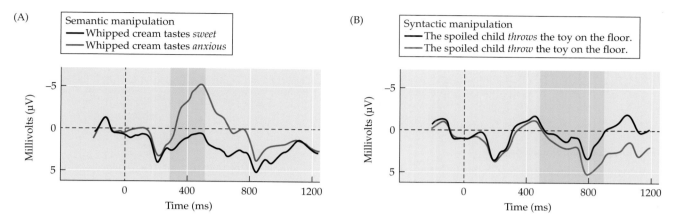

Figure 3.23 N400 and P600 effects (shaded areas) recorded at site Pz. (A) The N400 effect found with incongruous words in a sentence frame, showing a difference in the negative direction between 300 and 500 ms. (B) The P600 found with syntactic violations, showing a difference in the positive direction between 500 and 900 ms. (Adapted from Kos et al., 2010.)

These findings led researchers to suggest that the N400 reflected the processing of meaning, while the P600 was a marker of processing syntactic structure. This proposal stirred up some excitement among psycholinguists because it hinted at the possibility that ERPs could be used to isolate different aspects of language processing and study their relative timing in the brain. The dramatically different waveforms seemed to show that meaning and syntax are routed through different processing streams in the brain.

The N400 and P600 also appeared to be different from a handful of other ERP components that had been found for processing non-linguistic information (see **Table 3.3**). This opened up the possibility that ERP research might be able to identify language-specific operations in the brain. Needless to say, this would add some important evidence to the heated debate about whether language consists of mental operations that are fundamentally different from other cognitive operations.

Remember, though: It may obvious that the difference between the N400 effect and the P600 effect is that one deals with weird meanings and the other deals with syntactic glitches. But this distinction is just the starting hypothesis. Despite the stirring implications of the discovery of these two components, the research community had to hunker down and do much more probing before it could determine whether the N400 does in fact correspond to the processing of meaning in language, or whether the P600 is the brain's signature of syntactic computation.

In the decades since the N400 was first discovered, we've learned a lot about the conditions under which it turns up in an EEG study. A word doesn't have to be nonsensical in order to trigger the N400; it just needs to be somewhat improbable or unpredictable, as measured in any one of a number of ways. For example, the N400 can be found for sentences that describe *unlikely* events, even if they're not outright nonsensical:

He planted string beans in his car.

The N400 can also be found for uncommon words, even when they're perfectly sensible within their sentence frames. Moreover, repeating a word within the experiment leads to a smaller N400 effect for the second occurrence than for the first one. These findings suggest that the N400 isn't a direct marker of the incongruity of meaning; maybe instead it reflects the brain's efforts at retrieving a word and its meaning from memory. This retrieval process gets harder if the word is incongruous in the context of the sentence. But the accessibility of a word can also be affected by factors like how common or rare it is, or how recently it's been seen or heard. In fact, words don't even need to

TABLE 3.3 ERP components elicited by language stimuli

What?	When?	Why?	Example(s)	Triggering stimulus[a]
ELAN: Early Left Anterior Negativity				
Negative-going activity	Peaks at less than 200 ms after stimulus onset	Occurs when a word of the wrong syntactic category appears in a sentence frame	Reading a sentence that inserts a word of an incorrect category	*The pizza was **in** the eaten.* (Expected: *The pizza was **eaten**.*)
PMN: Phonological Mapping Negativity				
Negative-going activity	Peaks at about 270–310 ms after stimulus onset	Occurs when a word or a string of sounds goes against expectations	Reading a sentence that develops strong expectations for a particular word	*The pigs wallowed in the **pen**.* (Expected word: ***mud***)
			Sound-deletion tasks (e.g., subjects are told to think of "*snap* without the *s*")	***tap*** (Expected: ***nap***)
N400				
Negative-going activity	Peaks at about 400 ms after stimulus onset	Occurs when the content of a word is unexpected	Reading words that are nonsensical in a sentence	*The winter was harsh this **allowance**.* (Expected: *The winter was harsh this **year**.*)
			Reading rare or unusual words in a sentence	*He painted the bike **vermillion**.* (Expected: *He painted the bike **red**.*)
P600 (SPS, or Syntactic Positive Shift)				
Positive-going activity	Peaks at about 600 ms after stimulus onset	Occurs in processing (and possibly trying to repair) an unexpected syntactic structure	Reading or hearing sentences with a syntactic violation	*The boats **is** at the dock.* (Expected: *The boats **are** at the dock.*)
			Reading sentences that contain an unusual or unexpected structure	*The broker persuaded **to sell** the stock was tall.* (Expected: *The broker persuaded **his client** to sell the stock.*)
			Reading sentences in which the participants involved in an event are in the wrong order	*The hearty meal was **devouring** the kids.* (Expected: *The kids were **devouring** the hearty meal.*)

[a]The triggering stimulus in each example—the point in the sentence at which the anomaly can be detected—is indicated by the **boldface** type.

appear in sentences in order to show an enlarged N400 effect; simply including a word like *apple* in a list containing the words *shirt, pants,* and *sweater* would normally yield a bigger N400 than seeing it embedded in a list like *banana, peach, orange.* (A thorough review of the N400 effect can be found in Kutas & Federmeier, 2011.)

The P600 has similarly been poked and prodded in an attempt to identify exactly the kinds of brain operations it reflects. Like the N400, it's been unearthed in an assortment of experimental settings since its first discovery. We now know that it doesn't depend on the presence of an outright error in syntax; it shows up in many situations where computing the structure of a sentence just isn't straightforward. For instance, it can be found if a sentence uses an uncommon structure, or if the structure that's being built strains working memory. (See Gouvea et al., 2010, for a review of linguistic operations it reflects.)

Is it just language?

Both the N400 and the P600 effects show up in a broad range of situations, which makes it more difficult to pin them onto very specific linguistic operations. At the same time, a basic difference between them seems to be preserved: The N400 effect looks like it's involved in accessing a word's contents from stored memory and integrating it with preceding information, whereas the P600 is found when the combination of linguistic units is at stake. These seem to reflect two very fundamental aspects of language use. Which brings us to the next question: Are the N400 and the P600 specifically *linguistic* markers of brain processing?

The answer to this question is either disappointing or intriguing, depending on how strongly attached you are to the idea that language is made up of a set of highly exclusive mental operations that are reserved entirely for linguistic purposes. Analogues of both the N400 and the P600 have been found in non-linguistic domains. The N400 is clearly on the promiscuous side, in evidence in situations as diverse as repeated environmental sounds (Chao et al., 1995); videos depicting actions involving objects used in bizarre ways, such as shaving with a broom (Sitnikova et al., 2003); unfamiliar versus familiar faces (Bentin & Deouell, 2000); and incorrect versus correct arithmetic equations (Niedeggen et al., 1999). The wide-ranging nature of the N400 effect has made it all the more challenging to provide a clear answer to the question of what mental operations underlie it. At the same time, because so much is known about the various conditions that affect the N400 component in language, finding the existence of N400 effects in other domains breaks open the possibility of exploring the extent to which linguistic operations might be similar to or different from other cognitive processes.

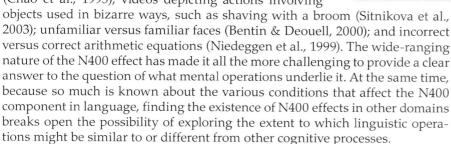

WEB ACTIVITY 3.5

N400s and P600s In this activity, you'll see examples of the types of linguistic and non-linguistic stimuli that have been found to trigger N400 and P600 effects.

As for the P600, it's been demonstrated with non-linguistic stimuli as well. The best known non-linguistic examples involve what you might think of as musical "ungrammaticalities." Most people, whether or not they actually read musical notes or play an instrument, have a good sense of when a note or a musical chord is out of key with the piece it appears in. (You'll have a chance to try this out in Web Activity 3.5). This involves an understanding of the relationship of that note to the other notes around it, since any given note (or chord) can sound fine when played with the right surrounding notes, but very discordant or grating when played with incompatible sounds. In a way, this is much like syntax in language: a word can be grammatically "right" or "wrong" in relation to the surrounding words. The intuition about what makes a word or a note compatible within its surroundings seems to come from an understanding of the basic structures of music—and as with language, this knowledge can simply be absorbed by exposure to music that follows certain regular patterns, without necessarily being taught in any explicit way.

Given the parallels between language and music, it's interesting that when people hear elements that are out of key in a musical phrase, their brain activity patterns are like those observed when they detect a syntactic anomaly; both cases elicit a P600 (see **Box 3.6**). It's a bit tricky, though, to know how to interpret ERP components that turn up across domains of information. For instance, if a P600 is found to be important for processing both linguistic and musical structure, does this mean that identical mental processes are involved? Not necessarily, because we don't know exactly what the P600 is a reflex of. It could

BOX 3.6
A musical P600 effect

Y ou don't have to be a musician to have developed very sharp cognitive expectations about music. You only need to have normal music perception and have been exposed to structured music throughout your life. In Western music, much of our musical experience centers

around the structures of major and minor scales. In their 1998 ERP study, researchers led by Aniruddh Patel had subjects listen to musical sequences set in a particular key. The researchers varied whether they produced a target chord in the same key, a nearby key, or a distant key (**Figure 3.24A**). In terms of perception, in-key sounds are the most predictable, while chords from a distant key are the most jarring.

The ERP data over a number of recording sites show that compared with in-key chords, the less expected sounds elicited positive-going activity beginning at 300 ms and continuing for several hundred milliseconds (**Figure 3.24B**). Chords from distant keys showed the largest positive amplitude, while in-key sounds showed the least. When the waveforms were compared with those elicited by hearing unexpected syntactic structures, they were found to be statistically indistinguishable (Patel et al., 1998).

(A)

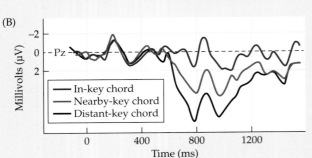

In-key chord

Nearby-key chord   Distant-key chord

(B)

Figure 3.24 (A) Musical notation showing Patel's sample stimuli. (B) Averaged ERP data showing responses at site Pz to in-key sounds, chords from nearby keys, and chords from distant keys. (Adapted from Patel et al., 1998.)

simply be that processing language and music both require access to shared cognitive processes at some point, even if many of their computations are carried out separately. But finding evidence of similar ERP patterns has provided a provocative launching point for further exploration. In Digging Deeper, we'll spend a bit more time looking at evidence for the neural overlap between music and language.

In short, we still don't know precisely what's going on in the brain when effects like the N400 or P600 turn up. This might strike you as vaguely depressing, given that 30-plus years and more than a thousand studies have accumulated since the N400 was first discovered. But as you'll see in some of the later chapters, ERPs have turned out to be highly valuable research tools in testing some very specific theories about the order in which various linguistic processes take place as people understand language. Even though it doesn't provide instant or magical insights about how electrical activity in the brain translates into thought, EEG research contributes some unique pieces to the overall puzzle of how language works in the brain.

GO TO
sites.sinauer.com/languageinmind

for **web activities**, **further readings**, **research updates**, **new essays**, and other features

Using EEG to assess patients in a vegetative state

One of the most heart-wrenching situations anyone can experience is that of having a loved one survive a serious brain injury and emerge from a coma, only to remain in a vegetative state. In the movies, the transition out of a coma is often depicted as a moment when the patient's eyes snap open and he becomes entirely aware of his surroundings, just like waking up from a deep sleep. But in reality, most patients move from a comatose state, in which they're neither awake nor conscious, into a vegetative state, where they go through regular cycles of sleeping and waking but, even when they're awake, show no signs of awareness of themselves or their environment. Occasionally, but inconsistently, they might show subtle evidence that they're responding to the world and people around them, in which case clinicians would deem them *minimally conscious*.

These states of seemingly absent or minimal consciousness are terrible for families and caregivers, in part because of their enormous ambiguity. Is the patient aware but simply incapable of showing signs of awareness? Does he recognize the voices of his loved ones? Does he perhaps even understand what's being said in his presence? Or has he sustained such serious brain damage that any meaningful higher-level function is truly lost? Important decisions about treatment or attempts at rehabilitation hinge on the answers to these questions, but the patient's behavior might offer no scraps of evidence that would shed light on them.

This is a clinical situation in which probing the patient's brain activity through EEG may turn out to be helpful for the very reason that no behavioral response is required. It's especially practical to use with sound-based stimuli, because the patient doesn't have to consciously orient to the stimulus in order to hear it. A review of EEG studies shows that patients who've been diagnosed as being in a vegetative or minimally conscious state often display ERP evidence that there's a good deal of cognition going on (Harrison & Connolly, 2013). About one in four have been shown to produce the N400 response in response to incongruous words in sentences (for example, *The winter was harsh this allowance*). This suggests that at least some patients are able to register aspects of the meaning of a sentence, helping to answer the critical question, "Can he understand what I say?" (And also suggesting that maybe people should be careful when discussing the patient's progress and prognosis, or sensitive family subjects, while in the room with him.)

Because scientists now know a lot about the various conditions under which different ERP components

appear, it's become possible to address fairly precise questions such as: Is basic auditory processing intact? Does the patient distinguish speech from non-speech, or proper speech from speech played backward? Does the patient show signs of higher cognitive function and organization, or just lower-level, more automatic processing? For instance, one useful hint that some level of cognitive control is involved comes from manipulating the proportion of sentences that are weird or anomalous. If an ERP component is affected by the proportion of weird trials (for example, if a high number of odd sentences stops triggering higher levels of brain activity), this suggests that the person is developing strategic expectations about what the stimuli will be like, and that these expectations change the way in which the sentences are being processed. Some components, like the P600, have been found to be sensitive to expectations like these, while other components—like the ELAN (see Table 3.3)—have not. So, finding evidence of a P600 effect would indicate a higher degree of cognitive control than the ELAN.

The most convincing evidence for some degree of hidden consciousness, though, is if the patient is able to respond to instructions in a way that shows he's able to deliberately control his cognition. Here's an example of how this could be measured: Most people react when their names are spoken in the midst of a list of other names, showing a different ERP response to their own names. It's been shown that some patients in a vegetative state also do this. But as it turns out, people's ERP responses also show a distinction that depends on whether they've been allowed to passively listen to names or have been asked to *count* the number of times their names are spoken. This difference can show up only if people are doing something other than passive listening in response to the instructions they're given. A surprising number of patients show evidence that they can react to instructions by shaping their own cognitive processes (in one study reviewed by Harrison and Connolly, 9 of 14 patients diagnosed as minimally conscious showed this distinction in ERP responses).

This body of research reminds us that even though EEG can't be used to read a person's thoughts, it *can* get at some crucial information about the type of cognitive processes going on in someone's head, and in situations where there are real questions about which processes are intact—questions that are hard to answer because of a patient's lack of ability to respond—EEG can open a small but vital window.

DIGGING DEEPER

Language and music

The discovery of a P600 response for quirks of musical structure raises the beguiling possibility of an intimate connection between language and music in the brain. Along with language, music is one of the few human activities that is truly universal across cultures and societies—we seem to be almost as compelled to sing and make rhythmic sounds as we are to talk to each other. And when you look at language and music as systems of information, a number of parallels emerge. To name just a couple of similarities: (1) both involve combining sounds (or signs) in new and complex ways, relying on an underlying knowledge of structure to constrain the possible combinations; and (2) music and spoken language both call on well-honed skills in detecting and reproducing minute differences in sounds, and the ability to sequence them properly. Because of these and quite a few other resemblances between the two domains, scholars from the first dawn of evolutionary theory have speculated that there might be a common evolutionary link between them, with Darwin himself suggesting that language and music have a shared biological origin.

In our current human brains, then, perhaps music and language avail themselves of similar mental operations or resources, as hinted at by the common P600 effect. Maybe they even share neural equipment. Intriguing as this possibility is, one of the lessons of the previous section is that there's still a lot we don't know about exactly how electrical brain activity translates into specific jobs that are carried out by the brain. So there are still many pieces to put together before we can build a good case for a deep and meaningful link between music and language. In this section, we'll take a stroll over a broad research landscape, and get an overview of how researchers are working on assembling some of the pieces to this fascinating puzzle.

The first step is to ask whether, aside from the P600, there are other parallels in real-time brain activity for music and language. Since the P600 seems to be linked to violations of structural expectations in both domains, perhaps a good place to look would be at another apparent marker of syntactic violations, the ELAN (early left anterior negativity), which turns up when a word of the wrong syntactic category is inserted into the sentence's frame (for example, *the pizza was in eaten*; see Table 3.3). This very early ERP component (peaking between 100 and 300 ms after the stimulus onset) is thought to take place when predictions about upcoming linguistic structure clash with the actual stimulus. In Web Activity 3.5, you may have found yourself also generating predictions about upcoming musical notes or chords. Would a violation of such musical predictions lead to something that looks like the ELAN component? A team of researchers led by Burkhard Maess (2001) ran a study using MEG (a variant of EEG that measures magnetic fields) and found that musical violations did indeed trigger an early response in the brain's activity. Since MEG technology offers a more accurate view of where in the brain the response is originating, the study was able to offer a tantalizing peek at localization as well: For violations of language structure, the ELAN originates in the frontal lobes, mostly in the left hemisphere in Broca's area, but with some activity in the corresponding area on the right side as well. Maess and his colleagues found that the musical violations led to activity in the same areas as the language violations, though with music, there was more activity on the right side than on the left (leading the component to be called the ERAN: early right anterior negativity).

We now have mounting evidence that jarring constructions set off similar patterns of real-time brain activity for music and language. Maybe it's time to have a closer look at *where* musical and linguistic activities take place, using techniques like fMRI that are especially well suited for localizing brain activity. A number of brain-imaging studies have found that overlapping regions of the brain— including the classic Broca's area—show signs of activation when people process either language or music. This finding is apparent in listening tasks as well as in experiments where people are asked to generate melodies or language, although the overlap in activated brain regions is far from complete (e.g., Brown et al., 2006; Schmithorst, 2005).

Naturally, there's only so much that we can infer from the evidence of common activation. A standard warning is that neurons belonging to different networks can be routed through some of the same brain regions, so we can't necessarily conclude that if the fMRI is picking up a region as being active in two separate tasks that this means the same *neurons* are being recruited. The use of common neural hardware becomes more likely, though, if we can see evidence that *multiple* regions that are wired together in a language-related network are also active for the processing of music. This is exactly what Stefan Koelsch and his colleagues (2002) found: in a musical task that involved unexpected musical chords, subjects showed signs of activating both Broca's and Wernicke's areas.

So far, we have glimmers that there might be parallels in real-time brain activity for "syntactic" aspects of music and language, and we have evidence for some common areas of activation through fMRI studies. There's another place where we should look for crucial evidence: in damaged brains, we should see that lesions that cause problems with language should also upset musical functioning, and vice versa. Here, however, our hypothesis about music and language sharing an intimate brain connection is in danger of running aground.

Scattered throughout the scientific literature are reports of patients with **amusia**, people who've lost the capacity to make sense of music but whose language functioning seems perfectly normal. Massimo Piccirilli and his colleagues describe one such case: a 20-year-old who suffered brain damage and suddenly found that his perception of music had gone haywire. "I can't hear any musicality. All notes sound the same," complained the patient. He'd been an avid music lover who sang and played guitar in an amateur band, but after his brain injury, he was no longer able to even take pleasure in music: "Sounds are empty and cold. Singing sounds like shouting to me. When I hear a song, it sounds familiar at first, but I can't recognize it. I think I've heard it correctly, but then I lose its musicality. I can recognize the guitar, but not the melody" (Piccirilli et al., 2000). A battery of tests showed that the patient had a lot of difficulty in distinguishing and remembering musical sounds, even though he showed no apparent trouble at all in perceiving speech or environmental sounds. He completely lost the ability to sing or play guitar but, again, showed no damage to his production of speech or, apparently, in any other non-verbal domain other than music.

On the other side of the coin, there are many cases of patients with language disorders such as aphasia who seem to show no change in their ability to process music. Maybe the most dramatic example suggesting how language and musical abilities can be separate comes from **auditory verbal agnosia**, known as "pure word deafness," a condition that affects the processing of speech sounds with almost surgical precision: People with this condition hear speech as meaningless or garbled sound, but usually they can speak, read, or write without any trouble, and their ability to process non-speech sounds, including music, seems to be mostly intact (Poeppel, 2001).

As with language deficits, problems with music perception aren't always the result of an easily identifiable

---

amusia Loss of the capacity to make sense of music (but not of language).

auditory verbal agnosia "Pure word deafness," a condition in which people hear speech as meaningless or garbled sound but usually can speak, read, or write without any trouble; their ability to process non-speech sounds, including music, seems to be mostly intact.

brain injury after a stroke or a blow to the head. Some people (you might have noticed) simply appear to have emerged from the womb unable to carry a tune or get much enjoyment out of any kind of music. These people may have *congenital* amusia, a disorder commonly known as "tune deafness" or "tone deafness" that affects people's ability to hear differences in pitch, remember melodies, or even recognize very familiar tunes. People with congenital amusia also have a hard time picking out an out-of-key note played within a melody. For the most part, those afflicted with the disorder seem to have normal use of language, which again points to a separation between the two systems.

Evidence of double dissociation is usually seen as a very strong argument that two systems are separate, and there's certainly plenty of forceful evidence from the clinical literature that catastrophic disabilities in music can appear side by side with apparently normal language, and vice versa. Does this mean that the idea of a strong connection between language and music should be tossed in the garbage bin as a nifty but failed idea? Not necessarily. Earlier in the chapter, I introduced the metaphor of the brain as a commercial complex that houses a great number of different processing areas, each of which might be shared by multiple manufacturers. Any two products will likely be routed through some of the same processing areas but also at times be diverted to separate areas more suitable for processing those specific products. In the case of music and language, it may be that a condition like auditory verbal agnosia is targeting those processes that are either separate from music or perhaps not quite as important for music as they are for language. This doesn't necessarily mean that there's no overlap at all in the processing of music and language. The two domains are most likely supported by a mix of shared processing areas and resources, while also being distinct from each other in important ways.

This view fits well with the ERP and brain-imaging evidence about language and music. It also fits with a growing number of studies that hint at some subtle but stable links between musical and linguistic abilities. For example, a closer look at music deficits shows that even though a poor aptitude for music doesn't normally show up alongside massive problems with language, it may be linked to some more specific linguistic challenges. Jennifer Jones and her colleagues (2009) closely compared 35 "tune deaf" individuals of various ages with 34 people who had more typical musical endowment, and they found that the amusic group scored worse than the typical group on a fistful of measures that looked at detailed processing of speech sounds. They did especially badly on tests that required them to decompose sequences of sounds—for example, requests like, "Say *reen*. Now say *reen* one sound at a time" or questions like, "What would you get if you put these sounds together: *r-ee-n*?" You might have noticed that these test items sound like they're straight out of the early reading exercises in *Sesame Street* and other educational program like it. In fact, this sort of awareness of how syllables break apart into individual sounds is an important skill in reading (as seen in Box 3.2). Intrigued by the connection, researchers have started to look at whether ramping up musical skills through training can transfer over into reading performance. In one such study, a 6-month musical training program for children in elementary school led to improvements on measures of reading, whereas a 6-month program in painting did not (Moreno et al., 2009).

Finely tuned speech processing skills can also be seen in people with musical expertise and experience. Those who regularly take part in musical activity tend to perform better at distinguishing very fine aspects of speech sounds, and have an advantage when it comes to perceiving speech in noisy environments (e.g., Chobert et al., 2011; Parbery-Clark et al., 2009; Sadakata & Sekiyama, 2011).

Evidence is building for the idea that language and music make use of a number of similar resources and skills, even though they part ways in the brain for some of their important computations. It looks like they're especially closely linked when it comes to detailed processing of sound sequences, and structuring smaller units into sentences or melodies with predictable underlying structures. On the more practical side, this ongoing, intense research may show that the hours children log at the piano have broader benefits, and that music therapy might be appropriate for treating certain kinds of language problems. On the theoretical end, the relationship between language and music makes a fascinating case study of the possible ways in which two venerated human abilities might converge and diverge in the brain.

PROJECT

Music, like language, involves a complex *set* of activities and mental processes, and it demands multiple skills, not just one. Try to generate as detailed a list as you can of the various components that go into musical and linguistic activity, going beyond those discussed in this section. What makes someone good at music/language? Once you've generated your lists, identify which of the skills that are needed for music appear to have close analogues in language. Where do you think it would be most likely that you'd see crossover in cognitive processing? How would you go about finding out? Create a proposal for how you might gather evidence to support your idea of connections between music/language skills.

4 Learning Sound Patterns

To get a sense of what's really involved in learning language, cast your mind back to what it was like before you knew any words at all of your native tongue. Well, wait … since you obviously can't do that, the best you can do is to recall any experiences you may have had learning a *second* language at an age old enough to remember what the experience was like (or a third or fourth language, if you were lucky enough to learn more than one language as a tot). If these memories involve learning a language in a classroom setting, they turn out to be a useful point of departure for our purposes, especially to highlight the striking difference between how you learned language in the classroom, and how you learned it as a newborn initiated into your native language.

In a foreign language classroom, it's usual for the process to kick off with a teacher (or textbook) translating a list of vocabulary items from the new language into your native language. You then use a small but growing vocabulary to build up your knowledge of the language. You begin to insert words into prefabricated sentence frames, for example, and eventually you build sentences from scratch. This is simply not an approach that was available to you as an infant because then you had no words in *any* language that could be used as the basis of translation. Worse, you didn't even know what *words* were, or where words began or ended in the stream of speech you were listening to. You were basically swimming in a sea of sound, and there wasn't a whole lot anyone could do in the way of teaching that would have guided you through it.

If you were to have the unusual experience of learning a second language by simply showing up in a foreign country and plunging yourself into the language as best you could, without the benefit of language courses or tourist phrase books, that would be a bit closer to what you faced as an infant.

But still, you have advantages as an adult that you didn't have as an infant. You are much more sophisticated in your knowledge of the world, so you're not faced with learning how to describe the world using language while you're trying to figure out what the world is like. And your intellect allows you to be much more strategic in how you go about getting language samples from the speakers of that language; you can, for example, figure out ways to ask speakers about subtle distinctions—like whether there are different words for the concepts of *cat* and *kitten*, or how to interpret the difference in similar expressions, such as *screw up* and *screw off.* Not to mention that your motor skills allow you to pantomime or point to objects as a way to request native speakers to produce the correct words for you.

Deprived of many of the possible learning strategies that older people use, it might make sense that babies would postpone language learning until they develop in other areas that would help support this difficult task. And, given the fact that most babies don't start producing recognizable words until they're about a year old, and that they take quite a bit longer than that to string sentences together, it might seem that that's exactly what does happen. But in fact, babies begin learning their native language from the day they're born, or even earlier; it turns out that French babies tested within 4 days of birth could tell the difference between French and Russian, and sucked more enthusiastically on a pacifier when hearing French (Mehler et al., 1988). On the other hand, infants born into other linguistic households, such as Arabic, German, or Chinese, did not seem to be able to tell the difference between French and Russian speech, nor did French household babies seem to notice the difference between English and Italian. This study indicates that babies in utero can begin to learn something about their native language. Obviously, this can't be the result of recognizing actual words and their meanings, since in utero babies have no experience of the meanings that language communicates. Rather, it suggests that even through the walls of the womb and immersed in amniotic fluid, babies learn something about the patterns of sounds in the language they hear.

Humans are unlike honeybees and certain species of songbirds, which are genetically programmed for a specific type of bee dance or birdsong. The speech and accent of a child born of French parents but raised from infancy in the United States will usually be indistinguishable from that of a child born to U.S. parents and raised in that country. This linguistic flexibility reflects the fact that humans are powerful learning machines.

In this chapter, we'll look at what young children need to learn about the sounds of their language—and the sound system of any language is an intricate, delicately patterned thing. Not only does it have its own unique collection of sounds, but it has different "rules" for how these sounds can be combined into words. For example, even though English contains all the individual sounds of a word like *ptak*, it would never allow them to be strung in this order, though Czech speakers do so without batting an eye. And no word in Czech can ever end in a sound like "g," even though that consonant appears in abundance at the beginnings and in the middles of Czech words. English speakers, on the other hand, have no inhibitions about uttering a word like *dog*.

In fact, the sound pattern of a language is a complex code that infants manage to crack and mostly master within the first couple of years of life. A magnificent amount of learning happens within the first few months of birth. Long before they begin to produce words (or even really show that they understand their meanings), babies can:

1. Differentiate their native language from other languages.

2. Have a sense of how streams of sound are carved up into words.

3. Give special attention to distinctions in sounds that will be especially useful for signaling different meanings (for example, the distinction between "p" and "b" sounds; switch the "p" in *pat* to a "b" sound, and you get a word with a different meaning).

4. Figure out how sounds can be "legally" combined into words in their language.

Babies also develop many other nifty skills. Perhaps the only people who deserve as much admiration as these tiny, pre-verbal human beings are the scientists who study the whole process. Unlike foreign language teachers who can test students' mastery of a language via multiple choice exams and writing samples, language researchers have to rely on truly ingenious methods for probing the infant mind. In this chapter, you'll get a sense of the accomplishments of both groups: the very young who crack the sound code, and the scientists who study their feats.

4.1 Where Are the Words?

A stunningly *ineffective* way to learn language would be to simply memorize the meaning of every complete sentence you've ever heard, never bothering to break the sentence down into its component parts. In fact, if you took this route (even if you could actually memorize thousands upon thousands of complete sentences in the form of long strings of sound), you wouldn't really be learning language at all. No matter how many sentences you'd accumulated in your memory stash, you'd constantly find yourself in situations where you were required—but unable—to produce and understand sentences that you'd never encountered before. And without analyzing language in terms of its component, reusable parts, learning a sentence like *My mother's sister has diabetes* would be no help at all in understanding the very similar sentence *My father's dog has diabetes*. You'd treat the relationship in sound between these as purely coincidental, much as you would the relationship between the similar-sounding words *battle* and *cattle*; each one would have to be memorized completely independently of the other. As you saw in Chapter 2, the aspect of language that lets us combine meaningful units (like words) to produce larger meaningful units (like phrases or sentences) is one of the universal properties of human language, and one that gives it enormous expressive power.

Fundamentally, learning language involves figuring out which sounds clump together to form basic units, and learning how these units in turn can be combined with other units—which is why foreign language instruction for beginners puts so much emphasis on learning lists of words. One of the infant's earliest tasks, then, is to figure out which strings of sounds form these basic units—no trivial accomplishment. In talking to their babies, parents are not nearly as accommodating as Spanish or German textbooks, and they rarely speak to their children in single-word utterances (about 10 percent of the time). This means that babies are confronted with speech in which multiple words are sewn seamlessly together, and they have to figure out all on their own where the edges of words are. And unlike written language, where words are clearly separated by spaces (at least in most writing systems), spoken language doesn't present convenient breaks in sound to isolate words. To get an intuitive feel for what this task might feel like to a baby, see how you fare in Web Activity 4.1.

WEB ACTIVITY 4.1

Finding word boundaries In this activity, you'll hear speech in several different languages, and you'll be asked to guess where the word boundaries might be.

METHOD 4.1

The head-turn preference paradigm

The head-turn preference paradigm is an invaluable tool that's been used in hundreds of studies of infant cognition. It can be used with babies as young as about 4.5 months, and up to about 18 months. After this age, toddlers often become too fidgety to reliably sit still through this experimental task. Applied to speech perception, the technique is based on two simple principles:

1. Babies turn their heads to orient to sounds.

2. Babies spend more time orienting to sounds that they find interesting.

In a typical experiment, the baby sits on the lap of a parent or caregiver who is listening to music over a set of headphones; this prevents the adult from hearing the experimental stimuli and either purposely or inadvertently giving cues to the baby. A video camera is set up to face the child, recording the baby's responses, and an unseen observer monitors the experiment by watching the baby on video. (The observer can't hear the stimulus sounds and is usually not aware of which experimental condition the child has been assigned to, though the observer does control the sequence of events that occur.) A flashing light mounted next to the video camera and straight ahead in the child's view can be activated to draw the child's attention to a neutral point before any of the experimental stimuli are played. The stimuli of interest are then played on two speakers, mounted on the left and right walls (see **Figure 4.1**).

Each experiment usually consists of a *familiarization phase* and a *test phase*. There are three goals for the familiarization phase. The first is simply to have the infant become familiar with the sound stimuli. In some cases, if the purpose of the study is to find out whether babies will learn something about new sounds, the sounds played during the familiarization phase might consist of the new stimuli to be learned. The second goal is to train the baby to expect that sounds can come from the speaker on either the left or the right wall. The third goal of the familiarization phase is to tightly lock together the head-turn behavior to the infant's auditory attention. Babies tend to look in the direction of a sound that holds their attention anyway, but this connection can be strengthened by flashing a light

Continued on next page

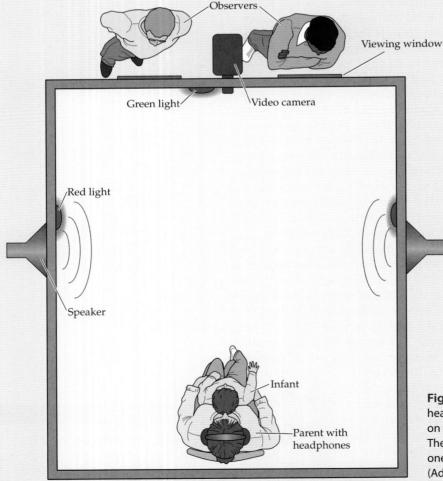

Figure 4.1 A testing booth set up for the head-turn preference paradigm. The baby sits on the caregiver's lap, facing the central panel. The observer looks through a small window or one-way mirror to note the baby's head turns. (Adapted from Nelson et al., 1995.)

in the location of the speaker before each sound, and by making sure that sounds during the familiarization phase are played only for as long as the baby looks in the direction of the sound. This signals to the child that if she wants to continue hearing a sound, she needs to be looking in its direction. After all these goals have been achieved, the baby is ready for the test phase.

During the test phase, the sounds of interest are played on either the left or the right speaker, and the baby's head-turn behavior is recorded by the video camera for later coding. Researchers then measure how long the baby spends looking in the direction of each sound, and these responses are averaged over stimulus type.

Sometimes researchers are interested in which sounds the infants prefer to listen to—do they prefer a female voice to a male voice, for example, or do they prefer to listen to sounds of their own language over an unknown language? Other times, the researchers are only interested in whether the infants discriminate between two categories of stimuli, and it doesn't matter which category is preferred. For instance, in a learning experiment, any distinction in looking times for familiar versus new stimuli should be an indication of learning, regardless of whether babies prefer to listen longer to the new or the familiar sounds. And in fact, it turns out that there isn't a clear preference for either new or familiar sounds—at times, babies show more interest in sounds that they recognize, and at other times, they show more interest in completely novel ones. The preferences seem to depend somewhat on the age of the child and just how often they've heard the familiar sounds (overly familiar sounds might cause a baby to become bored with them).

Probing infants' knowledge of words

Babies begin to produce their first words at about a year or so, but they start to identify word breaks at a much younger age than that. In fact, the whole process is under way by 6 or 7 months. Scientists can't exactly plop a transcript of speech in front of a baby, hand them a pencil, and ask them to mark down where the word breaks are. So how is it possible to peer into infants' minds and determine whether they are breaking sentences down into their component parts?

In studying the cognitive processes of infants, researchers have to content themselves with a fairly narrow range of infant behaviors as a way to measure hidden psychological mechanisms. So, when they decide to study infants of a particular age, they need to have a clear sense of what babies can do at that point in their development—and more specifically, which behaviors reflect meaningful cognitive activity. It turns out that a great deal of what we now know about infant cognition rests on one simple observation: when babies are faced with new sounds or images, they devote their attention to them differently than when they hear or see old, familiar sounds or images. And at the age of 6 or 7 months, one easy way to tell if a baby is paying attention to something is if she swivels her head in its direction to stare at it; the longer she keeps her gaze oriented in its direction, the longer she's paying attention to that stimulus. New sounds and sights tend to draw attention differently than familiar ones, and babies will usually orient to novel versus familiar stimuli for different lengths of time—sometimes they're more interested in something that's familiar to them (a sort of "Hey, I know what that is!" response), but sometimes they prefer the novelty of the new stimulus.

These simple observations about the habits of babies gave birth to a technique that psycholinguists now commonly use, called the **head-turn preference paradigm** (see **Method 4.1**). This technique compares how long babies keep their heads turned toward different stimuli, taking this as a measure of their attention. (If the target stimulus is a sound, it's usually coupled with a visual stimulus such as a light or a dancing puppet in order to best elicit the

head-turn preference paradigm An experimental framework in which infants' speech preference or learning is measured by the length of time they turn their heads in the direction of a sound.

familiarization phase A preparation period during which subjects are exposed to stimuli that will serve as the basis for the test phase to follow.

test phase The period in which subjects' responses to the critical experimental stimuli is tested following a familiarization phase.

head-turn response.) But what makes the method really powerful is that it can leverage the measure of looking time as a way to test whether or not the babies taking part in the study have *learned* a particular stimulus. For instance, let's say we give babies a new word to listen to during a **familiarization phase**. At some later time, during a **test phase**, we can see whether their looking times when hearing this word are different from those for a word they've never heard before. If babies spend either more or less time looking at the previously pre-sented word than they do at a completely new word, this suggests that they've learned something about the first word and now treat it as "familiar." On the other hand, if they devote equal amounts of looking time to both words, it suggests that they haven't learned enough about the previously heard word to differentiate it from a completely novel word.

The head-turn preference paradigm has been used—for example, by Peter Jusczyk and Richard Aslin (1995)—to tackle the question of whether babies have learned where word breaks occur. Here's how: During the familiariza-tion phase of that study, the baby participants heard a series of sentences that contained a target word, say, *bike*, in various different positions in the sentence:

His bike had big black wheels.

The girl rode her big bike.

Her bike could go very fast.

The bell on the bike was really loud.

The boy had a new red bike.

Your bike always stays in the garage.

During the test phase, the researchers measured how long the infants were in-terested in listening to repetitions of the target word *bike*, compared with a word (say, *dog*) that they hadn't heard during the familiarization phase. To first get the baby's attention before the test word was played, a flashing light appeared above the loudspeaker the word was to come from. Once the baby looked in this direction, the test word repetitions began to play. When the baby's interest flagged, causing him to look away from the loudspeaker, this was noted by a researcher, and the baby was scored for the amount of time spent looking in the direction of the loudspeaker. Jusczyk and Aslin found that overall, 7.5-month-old babies spent more time turning to the speaker when it played a familiar word (*bike*) than when it played an unfamiliar word (*dog*). This might not seem like a tremendous feat to you, but keep in mind that the babies must somehow have separated the unit *bike* from the other sounds in the sentences during the familiarization phase in order to be able to match that string of sounds with the repeated word during the test phase. Six-month-old babies didn't seem to have this ability yet.

This study shows that by the tender age of 7.5 months, babies seem to be equipped with some ability to separate or segment words from the speech stream—but it doesn't tell us how they manage to come by these skills, or what information they rely on to decide where the words are. Since Jusczyk and Aslin's initial study, dozens of published articles have explored the question of how babies pull this off. We'll investigate several ways that they might begin to crack the problem.

Familiar words break apart the speech stream

Here's one possibility. Remember that babies hear single-word utterances only about 10% of the time. That's not a lot, but it might be enough to use as a start-ing point for eventually breaking full sentences apart into individual words. It may be that babies can use those few words they do hear in isolation as a way to build up a small collection of known word units. These familiar words can then serve as anchoring points for breaking up the speech stream into more manageable chunks. For example, imagine hearing this procession of sounds in a fictional language:

bankiritubendudifin

Any guesses about what the word units are? The chances of getting it right are not very high. But suppose there are two words in this stream that you've heard repeatedly because they happen to be your name ("Kiri") and the name for your father ("Dudi"). You may have learned them because these are among the few words that are likely to be uttered as single words quite often, so they're especially easy to recognize. Perceptually, they'll leap out at you. If you've learned a foreign language, the experience of hearing sentences containing a few familiar words may be similar to the very early stages of learning a new language as a baby; you might have been able to easily pull out just one or two familiar words from an otherwise incomprehensible sentence. With this in mind, imagine hearing:

ban-**kiri**-tuben-**dudi**-fin

Now when you hear the names *kiri* and *dudi*, their familiarity allows you to pull them out of the speech stream—but it might also provide a way to identify other strings of sound as word units. It seems pretty likely that *ban* and *fin* are word units too, because they appear at the beginning and end of the utterance and are the only syllables that are left over after you've identified *kiri* and *dudi* as word units. So now, you can pull out four stand-alone units from the speech stream: *kiri, dudi, ban, fin*. You don't know what these last two mean, but once they're firmly enough fixed in your memory, they might in turn serve as clues for identifying other new words. So *tamfinatbankirisan* can now be pulled apart into:

tam-**fin**-at-**ban**-**kiri**-san

The residue from this new segmentation yields the probable units *tam, at,* and *san,* which can be applied in other sentences in which these units are combined with entirely new ones.

In principle, by starting with a very few highly familiar words and generating "hypotheses" about which adjacent clumps of sound correspond to units, an infant might begin to break down streams of continuous sound into smaller pieces. In fact, experimental evidence shows that babies are able to segment words that appear *next* to familiar names when they're as young as 6 months old, suggesting that this strategy might be especially useful in the very earliest stages of speech segmentation. (Remember that the Jusczyk and Aslin study showed that 6-month-olds did not yet show evidence of generally solid segmentation skills.) This was demonstrated in an interesting study led by Heather Bortfeld (2005). Using the head-turn preference paradigm, the researchers showed that even 6-month-olds could learn to segment words such as *bike* or *feet* out of sentences—but only if they appeared right next to their own names (in this example, the baby subject's name is *Maggie*) or the very familiar word *Mommy*:

Maggie's bike had big, black wheels.

The girl laughed at Mommy's feet.

That is, when babies heard these sentences during the familiarization phase, they later spent more time looking at loudspeakers that emitted the target word *bike* or *feet* than at speakers that played an entirely new word (*cup* or *dog*)—this shows they were treating *bike* and *feet* as familiar units. But when the sentences in the familiarization phase had the target words *bike* and *feet* right next to names that were *not* familiar to the child (for example, *The girl laughed at Tommy's feet*), the babies showed no greater interest in the target words than they did in the new words *cup* or *dog*. In other words, there's no evidence that the infants had managed to pull these words out of the stream of speech when they sat next to unknown words. At this age, then, it seems that babies can't yet segment words out of just any stream of speech, but that they *can* segment words that appear next to words that are already very familiar.

Discovering what words sound like

Relying on familiar words to bust their way into a stream of sound is just one of the tricks that babies have in their word-segmentation bag. Another trick has to do with developing some intuitions about which sounds or sequences of sounds are allowed at the beginnings and ends of words, and using these intuitions as a way to guess where word boundaries are likely to be.

To get a more concrete feel for how this might work, try pronouncing the following nonsense sentence in as "English-like" a way as you can, and take a stab at marking the word boundaries with a pencil (*hint*: there are six words in the sentence):

Banriptangbowpkesternladfloop.

If you compare your answer with those of your classmates, you might see some discrepancies, but you'll also find there are many similarities. For example, chances are, no one proposed a segmentation like this:

Ba-nri-ptangbow-pkester-nladfl-oop.

This has to do with what we think of as a "possible" word in English, in terms of the sequence of sounds it's allowed to contain. Just because your language includes a particular sound in its inventory doesn't mean that sound is allowed to pop up just anywhere.

Languages have patterns that correspond to what are considered "good" words as opposed to words that look like the linguistic equivalent of a patched-together Frankenstein creature. For example, suppose you're a marketing expert charged with creating a brand new word for a line of clothing, and you've decided to write a computer program to randomly generate words to kick-start the whole process. Looking at what the computer spat out, you could easily sort out the following list of words into those that are possible English-sounding words, and those that are not:

ptangb	sastashak
roffo	lululeming
spimton	ndela
skrs	srbridl

What counts as a well-behaved English word has little to do with what's actually pronounceable—you might think that it's impossible to pronounce sequences of consonants like *pt*, *nd*, and *dl*, but actually you do it all the time in words like *riptide, bandage, bed linen*—it's just that in English, these consonants have to straddle word boundaries or even just syllable boundaries. (Remember, there are no actual *pauses* between these consonants just by virtue of their belonging to different syllables or words.) You reject the alien words like *ptangb* or *ndela* in your computer-generated list, not because it takes acrobatic feats of your mouth to pronounce them, but because you have ingrained word templates in your mind that you've implicitly learned, and these words don't match those mental templates. These templates differ from one language to another and are known as **phonotactic constraints**.

Using English phonotactic constraints to segment another language, though, could easily get you into trouble, especially if you try to import them into a language that's more lenient in allowing exotic consonant clusters inside its words. For instance, *skrs* and *ndela* are perfectly well-formed pronunciations of words in Czech and Swahili, respectively. So, trying to segment speech by relying on your English word templates would give you non-optimal results. You can see this if you try to use English templates to segment the following three-word stream of Swahili words:

> nipemkatenzuri

You might be tempted to do either of the following:

> nipem-katen-zuri

> nip-emkat-enzuri

but the correct segmentation is:

> nipe-mkate-nzuri

And while languages like Czech and Swahili are quite permissive when it comes to creating consonant clusters that would be banned by the rules of English, other languages have even tighter restrictions on clusters than English does. For instance, "sp" is not a legal word-initial cluster in Spanish (which is why speakers of that language often say "espanish"). (You can see some more examples of how languages apply different phonotactic constraints in **Box 4.1**.)

WEB ACTIVITY 4.2

Segmenting speech through phonotactic constraints In this activity, you'll hear sound files of nonsense words that conform to the phonotactic constraints of English, as well as clips from foreign languages that have different phonotactic constraints. You'll get a sense for how much easier it is to segment unknown speech when you can use the phonotactic templates you've already learned for your language, even when none of the words are familiar.

It turns out that by 9 months of age, babies have some knowledge of the templates for proper words in their language. Using the head-turn preference paradigm, researchers led by Peter Jusczyk (1993) have shown that American babies orient longer toward strings of sounds that are legal words in English (for example, *cubeb, dudgeon*) than they do to sequences that are legal Dutch words but illegal words in English (*zampljes, vlatke*). Dutch 9-month-olds show exactly the opposite pattern. This suggests that they're aware of what a "good" word of their language sounds like. And, just as neither you nor your classmates suggested that speech should be segmented in a way that allows bizarre words like *ptangb* or *nladf*, at 9 months of age, babies can use their phonotactic templates to segment units out of speech (Mattys & Jusczyk, 2001).

You might have noticed in Web Activity 4.2 that there was another bit of information that might have helped you segment words, in addition to clues about phonotactic constraints. In that exercise, English-like stress patterns were also present. In English, stress tends to alternate, so within a word, you usually get an unstressed syllable sitting next to a stressed one: *reTURN, BLACKmail, inVIgoRATE.* (In some other languages, such as French, syllables are more or less evenly stressed.) English words can follow either a **trochaic stress pattern**, in which the first syllable is stressed (as in *BLACKmail*), or an **iambic stress pattern**, in which the first syllable is unstressed (as in *reTURN*). But as it turns out, it's not an equal-opportunity distribution, and trochaic words far outnumber iambic words (on the order of 9 to 1 by some estimates). Chances are, you subconsciously made use of this knowledge in your segmentation answers in Web Activity 4.2. If babies have caught on to this pattern in

phonotactic constraints Language-specific constraints that determine how the sounds of a given language may be combined to form words or syllables.

trochaic stress pattern Syllable emphasis pattern in which the first syllable is stressed, as in *BLACKmail*.

iambic stress pattern Syllable emphasis pattern in which the first syllable is unstressed, as in *reTURN*.

BOX 4.1
Phonotactic constraints across languages

As languages go, English is reasonably loose in allowing a wide range of phonotactic templates. English allows consonants to gather together in sizable packs at the edges of words and syllables. For example, the single-syllable word *splints* has the structure CCCVCCC (where C = consonant and V = vowel). Many other languages are far more restrictive. To illustrate, the Hebrew, Hawaiian, and Indonesian languages allow only the following syllable structures:

Hebrew	Hawaiian	Indonesian
CV	V	V
CVC	CV	VC
CVCC		CV
		CVC

In addition to broadly specifying the consonant-vowel structure of syllables, languages have more stringent rules about which consonants can occur where. For example, in English, /rp/ is allowed at the end of the word, but not at the beginning; the reverse is true for the cluster /pr/.

Some constraints tend to recur across many languages, but others are highly arbitrary. The table gives a few examples of possible and impossible clusters that can occur at the beginnings of words and syllables in several languages.

To get a feel for how speech segmentation might be affected by the language-specific phonotactic constraints listed in the table, try listing all the possible ways to break down the following stream of sounds into word units that are legal, depending on whether your language is English, German, French, or Italian:

bakniskweriavrosbamanuesbivriknat

Allow words and syllables to start with				
Language	/kn/	/skw/	/sb/	/vr/
English	no	yes	no	no
German	yes	no	no	no
French	no	no	no	yes
Italian	no	no	yes	no

the language, they might also be able to use this to make guesses about how words are segmented from speech. And indeed, they do: by 7.5 months, babies have no trouble slicing words with a trochaic pattern (like *DOCtor*) from the speech stream—but when they hear an iambic word like *guiTAR* embedded in running speech, they don't recognize it. In fact, if they've heard *guitar* followed by the word *is*, they behave as if they've segmented *TARis* as a word (Jusczyk et al., 1999).

But if you've been paying very close attention, you might have noticed a paradox: in order for babies to be able to use templates of permissible words to segment speech, they *already* have to have some notion of a word—or at the very least, they have to have some notion of a language unit that's made up of a stable collection of sounds that go together and can be separated from other collections of sounds. Otherwise, how can they possibly have learned that "ft" can occur as a sequence of sounds in the middle or at the end of a word unit, but not at its beginning? It's the same thing with stress patterns: How can babies rely on generalizations about the most likely stress patterns for words in their language unless they've already analyzed a bunch of words?

To get at generalizations like these, babies must already have segmented some word units, held them in memory, and "noticed" (unconsciously, of course) that they follow certain patterns. All this from speech that rarely has any words that stand alone without the added confusion of adjacent speech sounds.

Earlier we speculated that maybe isolated familiar words like the baby's name serve as the very first units; these first words then act as a wedge for segmenting out other words, allowing the baby to build up an early collection of word units. Once this set gets large enough, the baby can learn some useful generalizations that can then accelerate the whole process of extracting additional new words from running speech. In principle, this is plausible, given that babies *can* use familiar words like names to figure out that neighboring bunches of sounds also form word units. But this puts quite a big burden on those very first few words. Presumably, the baby has managed to identify them because they've been pronounced as single-word utterances. But as it happens, parents are quite variable in how many words they produce in isolation—some produce quite a few, but others are more verbose and rarely provide their children with utterances of single words. If this were the crucial starting point for breaking into streams of speech, we might expect babies to show a lot more variability in their ability to segment speech than researchers typically find, with some lagging much further behind others in their segmentation abilities.

Luckily, youngsters aren't limited to using familiar, isolated words as a departure point for segmentation—they have other, more flexible and powerful tricks up their sleeves. Researchers have discovered that babies can segment streams of sounds from a completely unfamiliar language after as little as two *minutes* of exposure, without hearing a single word on its own, and without the benefit of any information about phonotactic constraints or stress patterns. How they manage this accomplishment is the topic of the next section.

4.2 Infant Statisticians

Tracking transitional probabilities: The information is out there

In a seminal study, Jenny Saffran and colleagues (1996) familiarized 8-month-old infants with unbroken 2-minute strings of flatly intoned, computer-generated speech. The stream of speech contained snippets such as:

bidakupadotigolabubidaku

Notice that the sounds are sequenced so that they follow a repeating consonant-vowel structure. Because English allows any of the consonants in this string to appear either at the beginnings or the ends of syllables and words, nothing about the phonotactic constraints of English offers any clues at all about how the words are segmented, other than that the consonants need to be grouped with at least one vowel (since English has no words that consist of single consonants). For example, the word *bidakupa* could easily have any of the following segmentations, plus a few more:

bi-dak-upa	bid-aku-pa	bid-ak-u-pa
bi-da-kup-a	bid-ak-up-a	bidaku-pa
bid-akupa	bida-kupa	bi-dakup-a
bi-daku-pa	bid-akup-a	bidak-upa

If this seems like a lot, keep in mind that these are the segmentation possibilities of a speech snippet that involves just *four* syllables; imagine the challenges involved in segmenting a two-minute-long continuous stream of speech. This is precisely the task that Saffran and colleagues inflicted on the babies they studied.

In the Saffran et al. study, though, the stream of sound that the babies listened to during their familiarization phase was more than just a concatenation of consonant-vowel sequences. The stimuli were created in a way that repre-

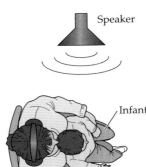

Speaker

Infant

Speaker

Experimenters create an artificial "language" of four "words":

bidaku, golabu, padoti, dutaba

Familiarization phase

Infant hears each "word" repeated 45 times in random order, in an unbroken 2-minute synthesized speech stream:

bidaku-golabu-dutaba-golabu-padoti-bidaku-dutaba-padoti-golabu-dutaba-padoti-dutaba-golabu-bidaku-dutaba-bidaku-padoti-bidaku-padoti-golabu etc.

Test phase

Loudspeakers present infant either a "real" word:

bidaku, golabu

or a sequence of syllables with parts of two words:

dakugo, buduta

Results

Mean looking times for 8-month-olds	
"Real" words	6.77 seconds
Part-words	7.60 seconds

Figure 4.2 In this study, Saffran and colleagues prepared stimuli that amount to a miniature artificial language of four "words," each word consisting of three consonant-vowel syllables. Infants then heard an uninterrupted, 2-minute stream of random combinations of the four words. The researchers noted how much attention the babies paid to the four "words" from the familiarization phase and compared it with the attention the babies paid to three-syllable sequences that also occurred in the speech but that straddled "word" boundaries (part-words). (Adapted from Saffran et al., 1996.)

artificial language A "language" that is constructed to have certain specific properties for the purpose of testing an experimental hypothesis: strings of sounds correspond to "words," which may or may not have meaning, and whose combination may or may not be constrained by syntactic rules.

sents a miniature **artificial language**. That is, the string of sounds corresponded to concatenations of "word" units combining with each other. In this particular "language," each "word" consisted of three consonant-vowel syllables (see **Figure 4.2**). For example, *bidaku* in the above stream might form a word. The uninterrupted two-minute sound stream consisted of only four such "words" randomly combined to form a sequence of 180 "words" in total, which meant that each "word" appeared quite a few times during the sequence. (The fact that the words were randomly combined is obviously unrealistic when it comes to how real, natural languages work. In real languages, there's a whole layer of syntactic structure that constrains how words can be combined. However, for this study, the researchers were basically only interested in how infants might use very limited information from sound sequences to isolate words.)

Later, during the test phase, the researchers noted how much attention the babies paid to actual "words" they heard in the familiarization phase and compared it with the attention the babies paid to three-syllable sequences that also occurred in the speech but that straddled "word" boundaries—for example, *dakupa* (see Figure 4.2). The infants showed a distinction between "words" and "part-word" sequences. In this case, they were more riveted by the "part-words," listening to them longer than the "words"—possibly because they were already bored by the frequent repetition of the "word" units.

How did the 8-month-old infants Saffran et al. studied manage to do this? If the sound stimuli were stripped of all helpful features such as already-familiar words, stress patterns, and phonotactic cues, what information could the babies possibly have been using in order to pull the "words" out of the 2-minute flow of sound they'd heard? To see how you'd fare in such a task, try Web Activity 4.3.

The answer is that there's a wealth of information in the speech stream waiting to be mined, and it's there just by virtue of the fact that the stream is composed of word-like units that turn up multiple times. Saffran and her

WEB ACTIVITY 4.3

Segmenting "words": You be the baby! In this activity, you'll hear 2 minutes of stimuli from an artificial language very similar to that used by Saffran et al. (1996). You'll be asked to distinguish "words" from "non-words" to see if you, too, can manage to segment speech. (Ideally, you should attempt this exercise before you read any further.)

colleagues suggested that babies were acting like miniature statisticians analyzing the speech stream, and were keeping track of **transitional probabilities (TPs)** between syllables—this refers to the likelihood that one particular syllable will be followed by another specific syllable. Here's how such information would help to define likely word units: Think of any two syllables, say, a syllable like *ti* and a syllable like *bay*. Let's say you hear *ti* in a stream of normal English speech. What are the chances that the very next syllable you hear will be *bay*? It's not all that likely; you might hear it in a sequence like *drafty basement* or *pretty baby*, but *ti* could just as easily occur in sequences that are followed by different syllables, as in *T-bone steak, teasing Amy, teenage wasteland, Fawlty Towers*, and many, many others.

But notice that *ti* and a *bay* that follows it don't make up an English word. It turns out that when a word boundary sits between two syllables, the likelihood of predicting the second syllable on the basis of the first is vanishingly small. But the situation for predicting the second syllable based on the first looks very different when the two syllables occur together *within* a word. For example, take the sequence of syllables *pre* and *ti*, as in *pretty*. If you hear *pre*, as pronounced in this word, what are the chances that you'll hear *ti*? They're much higher now—in this case, you'd never hear the syllable *pre* at the end of a word, so that leaves only a handful of words that contain it, dramatically constraining the number of options for a following syllable. Generally, the transitional probabilities of syllable sequences are much higher for pairs of syllables that fall within a word than for syllables that belong to different words. This is simply because of the obvious fact that words are *units* in which sounds and syllables clump together to form a fairly indivisible whole. Since there's a finite number of words in the language that tend to get used over and over again, it stands to reason that the TPs of syllable sequences within a word will be much higher than the TPs of syllable pairs coming from different words.

How does all this help babies to segment speech? Well, if the little tykes can somehow manage to figure out that the likelihood of hearing *ti* after *pre* is quite high, whereas the likelihood of hearing *bay* after *ti* is low, they might be able to respond to this difference in transitional probabilities by "chunking" *pre* and *ti* together into a word-like unit, but avoid clumping *ti* and *bay* together.

Here's the math: The transitional probability can be quantified as $P(Y|X)$, that is, the probability that a syllable Y will occur given that the syllable X has just occurred. This is done by looking at a sample of a language and dividing the frequency of the syllable sequence XY by the frequency of the syllable X combined with any syllable:

$$\text{TP} = P(Y|X) = \frac{\text{frequency } (XY)}{\text{frequency } (X)}$$

In the study by Saffran and her colleagues, the only cues to word boundaries were the transitional probabilities between syllable pairs: within words, the transitional probability of syllable pairs (e.g., *bida*) was always 1.0, while the transitional probability for syllable pairs across word boundaries (e.g., *kupa*) was always 0.33.

That babies can extract such information might seem like a preposterous claim. It seems to be attributing a whole lot of sophistication to tiny babies. You might have even more trouble swallowing this claim if *you*, a reasonably intelligent adult, had trouble figuring out that transitional probabilities were the relevant source of information needed to segment the speech in Web Activity 4.3 (and you wouldn't have been alone in failing to come up with an explanation for how the speech might be segmented). How could infants possibly manage to home in on precisely these useful statistical patterns when you failed to see

transitional probability (TP) The probability that a particular syllable will occur, given the previous occurrence of another particular syllable.

them, even after studying the speech sample and possibly thinking quite hard about it?

Though it might seem counterintuitive, there's a growing stack of evidence that a great deal of language learning "in the wild"—as opposed to in the classroom—actually does involve extracting patterns like these, and that babies and adults alike are very good at pulling statistical regularities out of speech samples, even though they may be lousy at actually manipulating math equations. As we'll see later, sensitivity to statistical information applies not just to segmenting words from an unfamiliar language, but also to learning how sounds make patterns in a language, how words can be combined with other words, or how to resolve ambiguities in the speech stream. The reason it doesn't feel intuitive is that all of this knowledge is *implicit* and can be hard to access at a conscious level. For example, you may have done reasonably well in identifying the "words" in the listening portion of Web Activity 4.3, even if you had trouble consciously identifying what information you were using in the analysis task. (Similarly, you may have had easy and quick intuitions about the phonotactic constraints of English but worked hard to articulate them.) That is, you may have had trouble identifying what it is you knew and how you learned it, even though you *did* seem to know it. It turns out that the vast majority of our knowledge of language has this character—throughout this book, you'll be seeing many more examples of a seeming disconnect between your explicit, conscious knowledge of language and your implicit, unconsciously learned linguistic prowess.

Being able to track transitional probabilities gives infants a powerful device for starting to make sense of a running river of speech sounds. It frees them up from the need to hear individual words in isolation in order to learn them, and it solves the problem of how they might build up enough of a stock of words to serve as the basis for more powerful generalizations about words—for example, that in English, words are more likely to have a trochaic stress pattern than an iambic one, or that the consonant cluster "ft" can't occur at the beginning of a word, though it can occur at its end. Ultimately, these generalizations, once in place, may turn out to be more robust and useful for word segmentation than transitional probabilities are. At times, such generalizations might even conflict with the information provided by transitional probabilities. Eventually, infants will need to learn how to attend to multiple levels of information, and to weight each one appropriately.

Is statistical learning a specialized human skill for language?

We've now seen some of the learning mechanisms that babies can use to pull word-like units out from the flow of speech they hear, including keeping track of various kinds of statistical regularities. Now let's step back and spend a bit of time thinking about how these learning mechanisms might connect with some of the bigger questions laid out in Chapters 2 and 3.

Much of Chapter 2 focused on the questions of whether language is unique to humans, and on whether certain skills have evolved purely because they make efficient language use possible. In that chapter, I emphasized that it was impossible to think of language as a monolithic thing; learning and using language involve an eclectic collection of skills and processes. Since we've now begun to isolate what some of those skills might look like, we can ask a much more precise question: Do non-humans have the ability to segment speech by keeping track of statistical regularities among sounds?

If you found yourself surprised and impressed at the capacity of babies to statistically analyze a stream of speech, you may find it all the more intriguing to learn that as a species, we're not alone in this ability. In a 2001 study, researchers led by Marc Hauser replicated the earlier studies by Saffran and colleagues; their subjects were not human infants, however, but cotton-top tamarins, a species of tiny monkey (**Figure 4.3A**). The monkeys heard about 20 minutes' worth of the same artificial language used by Saffran and her colleagues in their human experiments—four three-syllable "words" like *tupiro* and *bidaku*, strung together in random order and with no pauses between syllables or word units. Afterward, the monkeys went through a test phase, just as the human babies had, in which they heard a sequence of three syllables over a loudspeaker. As in the study with humans, these syllables could correspond to either a word from the artificial language (e.g., *bidaku*) or a part-word in which two syllables of an actual word were combined with a third syllable (for example, *tibida*). The researchers looked at how often the monkeys turned to face the speaker when they heard the test stimulus. They found that the monkeys distinguished between the two types of syllable sequences and oriented toward the speaker more often when they heard a part-word than when they'd heard a word (**Figure 4.3B**).

These results address the question of whether only humans are equipped to learn to chop up speech streams by paying attention to statistical regularities: apparently not. But the experiment doesn't fully get at the question of whether this statistical ability is exclusively enmeshed with our capacity for language. Cotton-top tamarins do have a fairly complex system of sequential calls, and maybe both their system of vocalizations and their statistical abilities reflect precursors of a fully linguistic system like ours. To better test for the connection or disconnection between statistical learning and language, it might make sense to study a species that shows no signs of having moved toward a human-like system of communication. Juan Toro and Josep Trobalón (2005) did just this in their study of speech segmentation in rats, using the same artificial language that previous researchers had used with human infants and cotton-top tamarins. They found that rats, too, were able to use statistical regularities in the speech to learn to differentiate between "words" and "non-words" of that language.

This suggests that picking up on statistical cues may be a very general cognitive skill—one that's not monopolized by species that have language or language-like communication systems, and one that might be useful in domains other than language. If that's so, then we should find that humans don't just pull this trick out of their hats for the purpose of learning language, but that we can also make use of it when confronted with very different kinds of stimuli. And indeed, this turns out to be true. Humans are capable of picking up on

(A)

(B)

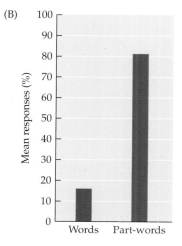

Figure 4.3 (A) An adult cotton-top tamarin (*Saguinus oedipus*), a species of Old World monkey. (B) The mean percentage of trials for which the tamarins oriented to the stimulus by turning to look at the speaker. "Words" in the familiarization phase were *tupiro*, *golabu*, *bidaku*, and *padoti*. During the test phase, the monkeys heard either the test words *tupiro* and *golabu* or the part-words *tibida* and *kupado*. (A © Danita Delimont/Alamy; B after Hauser et al., 2001.)

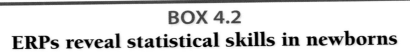

BOX 4.2
ERPs reveal statistical skills in newborns

The head-turn preference paradigm (see Method 4.1) is a clever behavioral method that has allowed researchers to test infants' knowledge without requiring any sophisticated responses or behaviors. Nevertheless, it does require babies to have developed the neck muscles that are needed to turn their heads in response to a stimulus. It also requires the babies to sustain full consciousness for reasonable periods of time. This makes it challenging to study the learning skills of newborn babies, with their floppy necks and tendency to sleep much of the time when they're not actively feeding. But as you saw in Chapter 3, ERPs (event-related potentials) can be used to probe the cognitive processes of people in a vegetative state, bypassing the need for any meaningful behavior at all in response to stimuli. Could the same method be used to assess the secret cognitive life of newborns?

Tuomas Teinonen and colleagues (2009) used ERP methods to test whether newborns can pick up on the transitional probabilities of syllables in a sample of speech. Their subjects were less than 2 days old, and they listened to at least 15 minutes of running speech consisting of ten different three-syllable made-up words randomly strung together. After this 15-minute "learning" period, the researchers analyzed the electrical activity in the babies' brains. Because the ERPs of newborn babies are less wildly variable if measured during sleep, the researchers limited the analysis to brain activity that was monitored during active sleep—which turned out to represent 40%–80% of the hour-long experiment.

ERP activity was compared for each of the three syllables of the novel "words." The logic behind this comparison was that, since the first syllable for any given "word" was less predictable (having a lower transitional probability) than the second and third syllables, it should show heightened brain activity compared with the other two syllables. **Figure 4.4** shows the results of the study, which indicate a

region of enhanced negative activity for the first of the three syllables. Similar results have since shown that newborns can also track the transitional probabilities of tones (Kudo et al., 2011). These remarkable studies reveal that the ability to pull statistical regularities from the auditory world is a robust skill that's available to humans from the very first moments after birth.

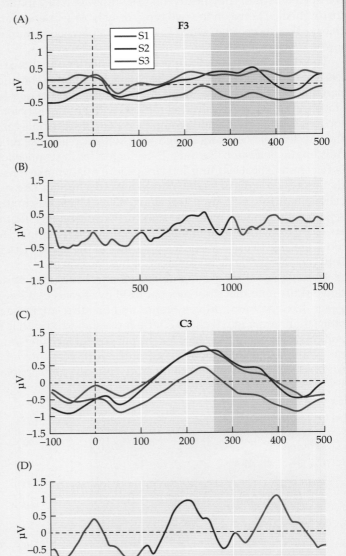

Figure 4.4 ERP activity at two recording sites (F3 and C3) shows enhanced negativity. In panels (A) and (C), the syllables are aligned so that each syllable's onset corresponds to 0. The shaded areas show the region where there is a statistically significant difference between the first syllable (S1) and the second and third syllables (S2 and S3). Panels (B) and (D) track EEG activity for the three syllables spoken in sequence. (Adapted from Teinonen et al., 2009.)

regularities within stimuli as diverse as musical tones (Saffran et al., 1999) and visual shapes (Fiser & Aslin, 2001). It appears, then, that one of the earliest language-related tasks that a baby undertakes rests on a pretty sturdy and highly general cognitive skill that we share with animals as we all try to make sense of the world around us. Indeed, it's likely that as humans, we literally have this ability from birth (see **Box 4.2**).

But that's not the end of the story. Just because individuals of different species can track statistical regularities across a number of different domains doesn't necessarily mean that the same *kinds* of regularities are being tracked in all these cases. In fact, Toro and Trobalón found that rats were able to use simple statistical cues to segment speech but weren't sensitive to some of the more complex cues that have been found to be used by human infants. And there may also be some subtle distinctions in the kinds of cues that are used in dealing with language, for example, as opposed to other, non-linguistic stimuli. These more nuanced questions are taken up in Digging Deeper at the end of this chapter.

4.3 What Are the Sounds?

How many distinct sounds are there in a language?

You might think that having to figure out where the words are in your language is hard enough. But in fact, if we back up even more, it becomes apparent that babies are born without even knowing what *sounds* make up their language. These sounds, too, have to be learned. This is not as trivial as it seems. As an adult whose knowledge of your language is deeply entrenched, you have the illusion that there's a fairly small number of sounds that English speakers produce (say, about 40), and that it's just a matter of learning what these 40 or so sounds are. But in truth, English speakers produce many more than 40 sounds.

Here's an example: Ever since your earliest days in school, when you were likely given exercises to identify sounds and their corresponding letter symbols, you learned that the words *tall* and *tree* begin with the same sound, and that the second and third consonants of the word *potato* are identical. But that's not exactly right. Pay close attention to what's happening with your tongue as you say these sounds the way you normally would in conversational speech, and you'll see that not all consonants that are represented by the letter *t* are identical. For example, you likely said *tree* using a sound that's a lot like the first sound in *church*, and unless you were fastidiously enunciating the word potato, the two "t" sounds were not the same. It turns out that sounds are affected by the phonetic company they keep. And these subtle distinctions matter. If you were to cut out the "t" in *tall* and swap it for the "t" in *tree*, you would be able to tell the difference. The resulting word would sound a bit weird. The sound represented by the symbol *t* also varies depending on whether it's placed at the very beginning of a syllable, as in *tan*, or is the second member of a consonant cluster, as in *Stan*.

Not convinced? Here's some playing with fire you're encouraged to try at home. Place a lit match a couple of inches away from your mouth and say the word *Stan*. Now say *tan*. If the match is at the right distance from your mouth (and you might need to play around with this a bit), it will be puffed out when you say *tan*, but not when you say *Stan*. When you use "t" at the beginning of a syllable, you release an extra flurry of air. You can feel this if you hold your palm up close to your mouth while saying these words.

These kinds of variations are in no way limited to the "t" sound in English; any and all of the 40-odd sounds of English can be and are produced in a variety of different ways, depending on which sounds they're keeping company

WEB ACTIVITY 4.4

Scrambled speech In this demo, you'll get a sense of what speech is like when different versions of sounds that we normally think of as the same have been scrambled from their normal locations in words.

with. Suddenly, the inventory of approximately 40 sounds has mushroomed into many more.

Not only do the surrounding sounds make a difference to how any given sound is pronounced, but so do things like how fast the speaker is talking; whether the speaker is male or female, old or young; whether the speaker is shouting, whispering, or talking at a moderate volume; and whether he or she is talking to a baby or a friend at a bar, or is reading the news on a national television network.

And yet, despite all this variation, we do have the sense that all "t" sounds, regardless of how they're made, should be classified as representing *one* kind of sound. This sense goes beyond just knowing that all of these "t" instances are captured by the orthographic symbol *t* or *T*. More to the point, while swapping out one kind of "t" sound for another might sound weird, it doesn't change what *word* has been spoken. Not like swapping out the "t" in *ten* for a "d" sound, for example. Now, all of a sudden, you have a completely different word, *den*, with a completely different meaning. This means that not all sound distinctions are created equal. Some change the fundamental identity of a speech sound, while others are the speech equivalent of sounds putting on different outfits depending on which other sounds they're hanging out with, or what event they happen to be at.

When a sound distinction has the potential to actually cause a change in meaning, that distinction yields separate **phonemes**. But when sound differences don't fundamentally change the identity of a speech unit, we say they create different **allophones** of the same phoneme. You know that sound distinctions create different phonemes when it's possible to create **minimal pairs** of words in which changing a single sound results in a change in meaning. For example, the difference between "t" and "d" is a phonemic distinction, not an allophonic distinction, because we get minimal pairs such as *ten, den; toe, doe;* and *bat, bad* (see **Table 4.1**).

Our impression is that the difference between the sounds "t" and "d" is a big one, while the difference between the two "t" sounds in *tan* and *Stan* is very slight and hard to hear. But this sense is merely a product of the way we mentally categorize these sounds. *Objectively*, the difference between the sounds in both pairs is close to exactly the same, and as you'll see later on, there's evidence that we're not deaf to the acoustic differences between allophones—but we've mentally amplified the differences between phonemes, and minimized the differences between allophones.

A catalogue of sound distinctions

To begin to describe differences among speech sounds in a more objective way, it's useful to break them down into their characteristics. This turns out to be

phoneme The smallest unit of sound that changes the meaning of a word; often identified by forward slashes; e.g., /t/ is a phoneme because replacing it in the word *tan* makes a different word .

allophones Two or more similar sounds that are variants of the same phoneme; often identified by brackets; e.g., [t] and [tʰ] represent the two allophones of /t/ in the words *Stan* and *tan*.

minimal pair A pair of words that have different meanings, but all of the same sounds with the exception of one phoneme; e.g., *tan* and *man*.

TABLE 4.1 Examples of minimal word pairs[a]

pad/bad	safe/save	bigger/bidder	meet/neat	bush/butch	gone/gong
tap/tab	let/led	call/tall	meme/mean	chin/gin	yell/well
fan/van	lag/lad	bake/bait	shin/chin	read/lead	well/hell

[a]In English, the presence of minimal word pairs that differ only with respect to a single sound shows that those sounds (boldface type) are distinct phonemes. Be sure to focus on how the words sound rather than on how they are spelled.

Figure 4.5 The human vocal tract, showing the various articulators. Air from the lungs passes through the larynx and over the vocal folds, making the folds vibrate and thus producing sound waves. The tongue, lips, and teeth help form this sound into speech. The place of articulation refers to the point at which the airflow becomes obstructed; for example, if airflow is briefly cut off by placing the tongue against the alveolar ridge, a sound would be said to be alveolar; a sound made by obstructing airflow at the velum would be velar.

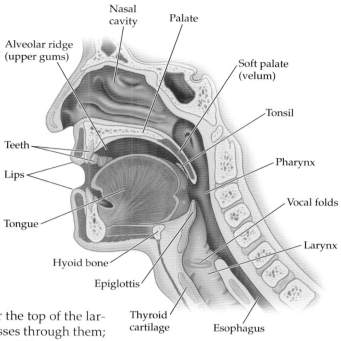

quite easy to do, because speech sounds vary systematically along a fairly small number of dimensions. For example, we only need three dimensions to capture most consonants of English and other languages: place of articulation, manner of articulation, and voicing.

PLACE OF ARTICULATION   Consonants are typically made by pushing air out of the lungs, through the larynx and the **vocal folds** (often called the "vocal cords," although the term "folds" is much more accurate) and through the mouth or nose (see **Figure 4.5**). The vocal folds, located near the top of the larynx, are a pair of loosely attached flaps that vibrate as air passes through them; these vibrations produce sound waves that are shaped into different speech sounds by the rest of the vocal tract. (To hear your vocal folds in action, try first whispering the syllable "aahh," and then utter it as you normally would—the "noise" that's added to the fully sounded vowel comes from the vocal fold vibration, or **phonation**.) To create a consonant sound, the airflow passing through the vocal tract has to be blocked—either partially or completely—at some point above the larynx. The location where this blockage occurs has a big impact on what the consonant sounds like. For example, both the "p" and "t" sounds completely block the airflow for a short period of time. But the "p" sound is made by closing the air off at the lips, while "t" is made by closing it off at the little ridge just behind your teeth, or the alveolar ridge. A sound like "k," on the other hand, is made by closing the air off at the back of the mouth, touching the palate with the back of the tongue rather than its tip. And these are really the only significant differences between these sounds. (As you'll see in a moment, along the other two sound dimensions, "p," "t," and "k" are all alike.) Moving from lips to palate, the sounds are described as **bilabial** for "p," **alveolar** for "t," and **velar** for "k." Other intermediate places exist as well, as described next and summarized in **Figure 4.6**.

vocal folds Also known as "vocal cords," these are paired "flaps" in the larynx that vibrate as air passes over them. The vibrations are shaped into speech sounds by the other structures (tongue, alveolar ridge, velum, etc.). of the vocal tract.

phonation Production of sound by the vibrating vocal folds.

bilabial Describes a sound that is produced by obstructing airflow at the lips.

	Place of articulation								
Manner of articulation	Bilabial	Labio-dental	Inter-dental	Alveolar	Alveo-palatal	Palatal	Velar	Glottal	
Stop	p b			t d			k g	ʔ	
Fricative		f v	θ ð	s z	ʃ ʒ			h	
Affricative					tʃ ʤ				
Nasal	m			n			ŋ		
Lateral liquid				l					
Retroflex liquid				ɹ					
Glide	ʍ w					j			

State of the glottis
- Voiceless
- Voiced

Figure 4.6 A chart of the consonant phonemes of Standard American English. In this presentation, the sounds are organized by place of articulation, manner of articulation, and voicing. (From the International Phonetic Association.)

MANNER OF ARTICULATION As mentioned, the airflow in the vocal tract can be obstructed either completely or partially. When the airflow is stopped completely somewhere in the mouth, you wind up producing what is known as a **stop consonant**. Stop consonants come in two varieties. If the air is fully blocked in the mouth and not allowed to leak out through the nose, you have an **oral stop**—our old friends "p," "t," and "k." But if you lower the velum (the soft tissue at the back of the roof of your mouth; see Figure 4.5) in a way that lets the air pass through your nose, you'll produce a **nasal stop**, which includes sounds like "m," "n," and the "ŋ" sound in words like *sing* or *fang*. You might have noticed that when your nose is plugged due to a cold, your nasal stops end up sounding like oral stops—"my nose" turns into "by dose" because no air can get out through your stuffed-up nose.

But your tongue is capable of more subtlety than simply blocking airflow entirely when some part of it is touched against the oral cavity. It can also *narrow* the airflow in a way that produces a turbulent sound—such as "s" or "f" or "z." These turbulent sounds are called **fricatives**. If you squish an oral stop and a fricative together, like the first and last consonants in *church* or *judge*, you wind up with an **affricate**.

Or, you can let air escape over both sides of your tongue, producing what are described as **liquid sounds** like "l" or "r," which differ from each other only in whether the blade (the front third) of your tongue is firmly planted against the roof of your mouth or is bunched back.

Finally, if you obstruct the airflow only mildly, allowing most of it to pass through the mouth, you will produce a **glide**. Pucker your lips, and you'll have a "w" sound, whereas if you place the back of your tongue up toward the velum as if about to utter a "k" but stop well before the tongue makes contact, you'll produce a "y" sound.

VOICING The last sound dimension has to do with whether (and when) the vocal folds are vibrating as you utter a consonant. People commonly refer to this part of the human anatomy as the "vocal cords" because, much like a musical instrument (such as a violin or cello) that has strings or cords, pitch in the human voice is determined by how quickly this vocal apparatus vibrates. But unlike a cello, voice isn't caused by passing something over a set of strings to make them vibrate. Rather, sound generation in the larynx (the "voice box") involves the "flaps" of the vocal folds (see Figure 4.5), which can constrict either loosely or very tightly. Sound is made when air coming up from the lungs passes through these flaps; depending on how constricted the vocal folds are, you get varying amounts of vibration, and hence higher or lower pitch. Think of voice as less like a cello and more like air flowing through the neck of a balloon held either tightly or loosely (though, in terms of beauty, I'll grant that the human voice is more like a cello than like a rapidly deflating balloon).

Vowels, unless whispered (or in certain special situations), are almost always produced while the vocal folds are vibrating. But consonants can vary. Some, like "z," "v," and "d," are made with vibrating vocal folds, while others, like "s," "f," and "t," are not—try putting your hand up against your throat just above your Adam's apple, and you'll be able to feel the difference.

Oral stops are especially interesting when it comes to voicing. Remember that for these sounds, the airflow is completely stopped somewhere in the mouth when two articulators come together—whether two lips, or a part of the tongue and the roof of the mouth. Voicing refers to when the vocal folds begin to vibrate relative to this closure and release. When vibration happens just about simultaneously with the release of the articulators (say, within about 20

---

alveolar Describes a sound whose place of articulation is the alveolar ridge, just behind the teeth.

velar Describes a sound whose place of articulation is the velum (the soft tissue at the back of the roof of your mouth; see Figure 4.5).

stop consonant A sound produced when airflow is stopped completely somewhere in the vocal tract.

oral stop A stop consonant made by fully blocking air in the mouth and not allowing it to leak out through the nose; e.g., "p," "t," and "k."

nasal stop A stop consonant made by lowering the velum in a way that lets the air pass through your nose; e.g., "m," "n," and the "ŋ" sound in words like *sing* or *fang*.

fricative A sound that is produced when your tongue narrows the airflow in a way that produces a turbulent sound; e.g., "s," "f," or "z."

affricate A sound that is produced when you combine an oral stop and a fricative together, like the first and last consonants in *church* or *judge*.

liquid sound A sound that is produced when you let air escape over both sides of your tongue; e.g., "l" or "r."

glide A sound that is produced when you obstruct the airflow only mildly, allowing most of it to pass through the mouth; e.g., "w" or "y."

LANGUAGE AT LARGE 4.1

The articulatory phonetics of beatboxing

It's not likely that a YouTube video of someone reciting a random list of words from the *Oxford English Dictionary* would spread virally—the act is just not that interesting. But many people *are* rightly riveted by the skills of virtuoso beatbox artists. Beatboxing is the art of mimicking musical and percussive sounds, and during their performances beatboxers routinely emit sounds with names like *808 snare drum roll*, *brushed cymbal*, *reverse classic kick drum*, *bongo drum*, and *electro scratch*. When you see them in action, what comes out of their mouths seems more machine-like than human.

And yet, when you look at how these sounds are actually made, it becomes clear that the repertoire of beatbox sounds is the end result of creatively using and recombining articulatory gestures that make up the backbone of regular, everyday speech. In fact, the connection between speech and beatboxing is so close that, in order to notate beatbox sounds, artists have used the International Phonetic Alphabet as a base for Standard Beatbox Notation.

Want to know how to make the classic kick drum sound? On the website Humanbeatbox.com, beatboxer Gavin Tyte explains how. First, he points out:

> In phonetics, the classic kick drum is described as a bilabial plosive (i.e., stop). This means it is made by completely closing both lips and then releasing them accompanied by a burst of air.

To punch up the sound, Tyte explains, you add a bit of lip oscillation, as if you were blowing a very short "raspberry." Step by step, in Tyte's words:

1. Make the "b" sound as if you are saying "b" from the word bogus.

2. This time, with your lips closed, let the pressure build up.

3. You need to control the release of your lips just enough to let them vibrate for a short amount of time.

The classic kick drum sound (represented as "b" in Standard Beatbox Notation) can be made as a voiced or voiceless version. Embellishments can be added: you can add on fricative sounds ("bsh," "bs," or "bf"), or combine the basic sound with a nasal sound ("bng," "bm," or "bn").

What sounds *really* impressive, though, is when a beatbox artist combines actual words with beatbox rhythms—it sounds as if the artist is simultaneously making speech sounds *and* non-speech sounds. But this is really a trick of the ear. It's not that the artist is making two sounds at the same time, but that he's creating a very convincing auditory illusion in which a *single* beatbox sound swings both ways, being heard both as a musical beatbox sound and as a speech sound. The illusion relies on what's known as the **phonemic restoration effect**. Scientists have created this effect in the lab by splicing a speech sound like "s" out of a word such as *legislature*, completely replacing the "s" sounds with the sound of a cough. Listeners hear the cough, but they also hear the "s" as if it had never been removed. This happens because, based on all the remaining speech sounds that really are there, the mind easily recognizes the word *legislature* and fills in the missing blanks (more on this in Chapter 7). In order for the illusion to work, though, the non-speech sound has to be acoustically similar to the speech sound. So, part of a beatboxer's skill lies in knowing which beatbox sounds can double as which speech sounds. Though many beatboxers have never taken a course in linguistics or psycholinguistics, they have an impressive body of phonetic knowledge at their command.

From a performance standpoint, skilled beatboxers display dazzling articulatory gymnastics. They keep their tongues leaping around their mouths in rapid-fire rhythms, and coordinate several parts of their vocal tracts all at the same time. But newbies to the art shouldn't be discouraged. It's certainly true that learning to beatbox takes many hours of practice. But when you think about it, the articulatory accomplishment is not all that different from what you learned to do as an infant mastering the sounds of your native language, and learning to put them all together into words. As you saw in Box 2.4, most infants spend quite a bit of time perfecting their articulatory technique, typically passing through a babbling stage beginning at about 5 months of age, in which they spend many hours learning to make human speech sounds. In the end, learning to beatbox may take no more practice than the many hours you were willing to put in learning how to talk—just think back to the hours you spent in your crib, taking your articulatory system out for a spin, and babbling endlessly at the ceiling.

---

phonemic restoration effect Auditory illusion in which people "hear" a sound that is missing from a word and has been replaced by a non-speech sound. People report hearing both the non-speech sound and the "restored" speech sound at the same time.

milliseconds) as it does for "b" in the word *ban*, we say the oral stop is a **voiced** one. When the vibration happens only at somewhat of a lag (say, more than 20 milliseconds), we say that the sound is **unvoiced** or **voiceless**. This labeling is just a way of assigning discrete categories to what amounts to a continuous dimension of **voice onset time** (**VOT**), because in principle, there can be any degree of voicing lag time after the release of the articulators.

You might have noticed that all of the consonants listed in Figure 4.6 end up being different phonemes. That is, it's possible to take any two of them and use them to create minimal pairs, showing that the differences between these sounds lead to differences in meaning, as we saw in Table 4.1. But that table shows you only a **phonemic inventory** of English sounds, not the full range of how these sounds are produced, in all their glorious allophonic variety, when each phoneme trots out its full wardrobe.

Phonemes versus allophones: How languages carve up phonetic space

Now that you have a sense of the dimensions along which sounds vary, I owe you a convincing account of why the differences between phonemes are often no bigger than the differences between allophones. (I'm talking here about their differences in terms of pure sound characteristics, not your mental *representations* of the sounds.)

Let's first talk about the differences in the "t" sounds in *tan* and *Stan*. Remember that extra little burst of air when you said *tan*? That actually comes from a difference in voice onset time. That is, there's an extra-long lag between when you release your tongue from your alveolar ridge and when your vocal folds begin to vibrate, perhaps as long as 80 milliseconds (ms). You get that extra puff because more air pressure has built up inside your mouth in the meantime. Unvoiced oral stops with a longer voice onset time are called **aspirated stops**, and these are the sounds that "pop" if you get too close to a microphone without a pop filter. Following standard notation, we'll use slightly different symbols for aspirated stops—for example, p^h, t^h, and k^h (with superscripts) to differentiate them from **unaspirated stops** t, d, and k. From here on, I'll also follow the standard practice in linguistics, and instead of using quotation marks around individual sounds, I'll indicate whether I'm referring to phonemes by enclosing them in forward slashes (for example, /b/, /d/), while allophones will appear inside square brackets (for example, [t], [t^h]).

Now, notice that a difference in voice onset time is exactly the way I earlier described the distinction between the phonemes /t/ and /d/—sounds that are distinguished in minimal pairs and that cause sudden shifts of meaning (see **Figure 4.7**). The difference between /t/ and /d/ seems obvious to our ears. And yet we find it hard to notice a similar (and possibly even larger) difference in VOT between the [t] and [t^h] sounds in *Stan* and *tan*. If we become aware of the difference at all, it seems extremely subtle. Why is this? One possible explanation might be that differences at some points in the VOT continuum are inherently easier to hear than distinctions at other points (for example, we might find that the human auditory system had a heightened sensitivity to VOT differences between 10 and 30 ms, but relatively dull perception between 30 and 60 ms). But another possibility is that our perceptual system has become tuned to sound distinctions differently, depending on whether those distinctions are allophonic or phonemic in nature. In other words, maybe what we

voiced Describes a sound that involves vibration of the vocal folds; in an oral stop, the vibration happens just about simultaneously with the release of the articulators (say, within about 20 milliseconds) as it does for "b" in the word *ban*.

unvoiced (voiceless) Describes a sound that does not involve simultaneous vibration of the vocal folds; in a voiceless stop followed by a vowel, vibration happens only after a lag (say, more than 20 milliseconds).

voice onset time (VOT) The length of time between the point when a stop consonant is released and the point when voicing begins.

phonemic inventory A list of the different phonemes in a language.

aspirated stop An unvoiced oral stop with a long voice onset time and a characteristic puff of air (aspiration) upon its release; an aspirated stop "pops" when you get too close to a microphone without a pop filter. Aspirated stop sounds are indicated with a superscript: p^h, t^h, and k^h.

unaspirated stop An unvoiced oral stop without aspiration, produced with a relatively short VOT.

"hear" isn't determined only by the objective acoustic differences between sounds, but also by the *role* that sounds play within the language system.

As it happens, different languages don't necessarily put phoneme boundaries in the same places; they can differ quite dramatically in how they carve up the sound space into phonemic categories. These distinctions make it possible for us to study whether our perception of sounds is influenced by how a language organizes sound into these categories. Speakers of Thai, for example, distinguish not only between the voiced and unvoiced phonemes /t/ and /d/, but also between the aspirated voiceless phoneme /tʰ/ (as in *tan*) and its unaspirated version /t/ (as in *Stan*). What this means is that if you're speaking Thai, whether or not you aspirate your stops makes a difference to the meaning. Slip up and aspirate a stop by mistake—for example, using /tʰ/ rather than /t/—and you've uttered a word that's different from the one you'd intended.

On the other hand, Mandarin, like English, has only two phonemic categories. But unlike English, Mandarin speakers make a meaningful distinction between voiceless aspirated and unaspirated sounds rather than voiced and voiceless ones. To their ears, the differences between /t/ and /tʰ/ is painfully obvious, corresponding to different phonemes, but they struggle to "hear" the difference between [t] and [d].

Looking across languages, it's hard to make the case that either the difference between voiced and voiceless sounds or the difference between aspirated and unaspirated sounds is *inherently* more obvious. Different languages latch on to different distinctions as the basis of their phonemic categories. This becomes all the more apparent when you consider the fact that languages differ even in terms of which dimensions of sound distinction they recruit for phonemic purposes, as we saw in Chapter 3.

For example, in English, whether or not a vowel is stretched out in time is an allophonic matter (**Box 4.3**). Vowels tend to be longer, for instance, just before voiced sounds than voiceless ones, and can also get stretched out for purely expressive purposes, as in "no waaay!"—note that *waaay* is still the same word as *way*. There's no systematic phonemic distinction between long and short vowels. But in some languages, if you replace a short vowel with a longer one, you'll have uttered a completely different word (for example, if you lengthen the vowel in the Czech word for *Sir*, you'll be addressing someone as *cheese*). In a similar vein, in Mandarin and various other languages described as "tone languages," the *pitch* on a vowel actually signals a phonemic difference. You might have just one sequence of vowels and consonants that will mean up to six or seven different words depending on whether the word is uttered at a high, low, or medium pitch, or whether it swoops upwards in pitch, whether the pitch starts high and falls, or whether the pitch rises and *then* falls. Needless to say, distinctions like these can be exasperatingly difficult to learn for speakers of languages that don't use tone phonemically. And, as you also saw in Chapter 3, there's evidence that different brain processes are involved in using these dimensions of sound, depending on the role they play in the language, with tonal differences on words eliciting more left-

(A) *Bought* uttered with [b]

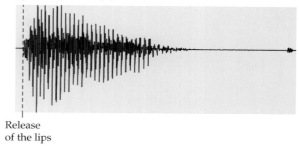

Release of the lips

(B) *Pot* uttered with [pʰ]

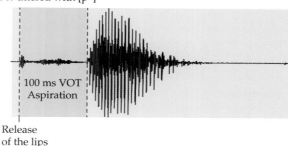

100 ms VOT Aspiration

Release of the lips

Figure 4.7 Waveforms for the words *bought* (A) and *pot* (B). *Bought* is uttered with a [b] sound at the beginning of the word (at a voice onset time of 0 ms), so that phonation (vocal fold vibration) occurs simultaneously with the release of the lips. *Pot* is uttered with a [pʰ] sound, with a lag of 100 ms occurring between the release of the lips and the beginning of phonation. (Courtesy of Suzanne Curtin.)

WEB ACTIVITY 4.6

Phonemic distinctions across languages In this activity, you'll get a sense of how difficult it is to "hear" what are phonemic distinctions in other languages but allophonic in English.

BOX 4.3
Vowels

Unlike consonants, vowels are all made with a relatively unobstructed vocal cavity that allows the air to pass fairly freely through the mouth. Their various sounds are accomplished by shaping the mouth in different ways and varying the placement of the tongue. Interestingly, our perceptual systems tend not to be as categorical when hearing vowels as they are when perceiving consonants, and we're usually sensitive to even small graded differences among vowels that we'd lump into the same category—though there is evidence that experience with a particular language does have an effect on perception.

Vowels are normally distinguished along the features of **vowel height** (which you can observe by putting a sucker on your tongue while saying different vowels), **vowel backness**, **lip rounding**, and **tenseness**.

English has an unusual number of vowel sounds; it's not uncommon for languages to get by with a mere five or so. Only a couple of vowels ever occur in English as **diphthongs**, in which the vowel slides into an adjacent glide (as in the words *bait boat*). Below are the IPA symbols for the English vowel sounds, with examples of how they appear in words in a standard American dialect (note their uneasy relationship to English orthography):

i	beet	u	boot
ɪ	bit	ʊ	book
eɪ	bait	ow	boat
ɛ	bet	ɔ	bought
æ	bat	ɑ	cot
ə	the	ʌ	but
aj	bite	ɔj	boy
aw	bout		

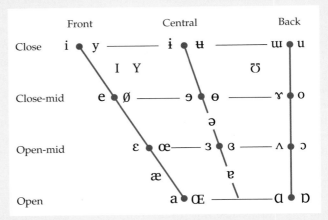

Figure 4.8 A vowel chart, a graphic illustration of the features of vowels, including English vowels and vowels found in other languages. When symbols are in pairs, the one to the right is the rounded version. Diphthongs like eɪ are not marked in this chart but represent transitions between vowels.

The features of the English vowels, along with others that don't occur in English, can be captured graphically in a vowel chart such as the one in **Figure 4.8**.

vowel height The height of your tongue as you say a vowel; for example, *e* has more vowel height than *a*.

vowel backness The amount your tongue is retracted toward the back of your mouth when you say a vowel.

lip rounding The amount you shape your lips into a circle; for example, your lips are very rounded when you make the sound for *w*.

tenseness A feature of vowels distinguishing "tense" vowels such as those in *beet* and *boot* from "lax" vowels such as those in *bit* and *put*.

diphthong A sound made when the sound for one vowel slides into an adjacent glide in the same syllable, as in the word *ouch*.

hemisphere activity among Mandarin speakers, but more right-hemisphere activity among English speakers.

I've just shown you some examples where other languages have elevated sound distinctions to phonemic status, whereas the same distinctions in English have been relegated to the role of mere sound accessories. The reverse can be true as well. For instance, the English distinction between the liquid sounds /r/ and /l/ is a phonemic one; hence, it matters whether you say *rice for Lent* or *lice for rent*. But you'll probably have noticed that this distinction is a dastardly one for new English language learners who are native speakers of Korean or

Japanese—they are very prone to mixing up these sounds. This is because the difference between the two sounds is an *allophonic* one in Korean and Japanese, and speakers of these languages perceive the difference between the two sounds as much more subtle than do native English speakers.

All of this goes to show that when it comes to how we perceive speech, we aren't just responding to the actual physical sounds out in the world. The way in which we hear sounds also has a lot to do with the structure our minds impose on sounds of speech. These mental structures can have dramatic effects in perceptually boosting some sound distinctions and minimizing others. We no longer interpret distinctions among sounds as gradual and continuous. This is actually a good thing, because it allows us to ignore many sound differences that aren't meaningful. For example, your typical English voiced [ba] sound might occur at a VOT of 0 ms, and your typical unvoiced [pʰa] sound might be at 60 ms. But your articulatory system is simply not precise enough to always pronounce sounds at the same VOT (even when you are completely sober); in any given conversation, you may well utter a voiced sound at 15 ms VOT, or an unvoiced sound at 40 ms. But your mind is very good at ignoring this articulatory slippage. What you know about the sound structures of your language imposes sharp boundaries, so you categorize sounds that fall within a single phoneme category—even if they're different in various ways—as the same, whereas sounds that straddle phoneme category boundaries clearly sound different. This way of perceiving sounds is called **categorical perception**, and it's quite a handy perceptual strategy.

To get a sense of the usefulness of categorical perception in real life, it's worth thinking about some of the many examples in which we don't carve the world up into clear-cut categories. Consider, for example, the objects in **Figure 4.9**. Which of these objects are cups, and which are bowls? It's not easy to tell, and you may find yourself disagreeing with some of your classmates about where to draw the line between the two (in fact, that line might readily shift depending on whether these objects are filled with coffee or soup). What's interesting is that this sort of disagreement is not likely to arise when it comes to consonants that hug the dividing line between two phonemic categories.

Such lack of disagreement is a hallmark of categorical perception, and it's been amply demonstrated in many experiments. One common way to test for categorical perception is called a **forced choice identification task**. The strategy is to have people listen to many examples of speech sounds and indicate which one of two categories each sound represents (for example, /pa/ versus /ba/). The speech sounds are created in a way that varies the VOT in small increments—for example, participants might hear examples of each of the two sounds at 10-ms increments, all the way from –20 ms to 60 ms. (A *negative* VOT value means that vocal fold vibration begins even before the release of the articulators.)

If people were paying attention to each incremental adjustment in VOT, you'd find that at the extreme ends (i.e., at –20 ms and at 60 ms), there would be tremendous agreement about whether a sound represents a /ba/ or a /pa/, as seen

categorical perception A pattern of perception where changes in a stimulus are perceived not as gradual, but as falling into discrete categories. Here, small differences between sounds that fall within a single phoneme category are not perceived as readily as small differences between sounds that belong to different phoneme categories.

forced choice identification task An experimental task in which subjects are required to categorize stimuli as falling into one of two categories, regardless of the degree of uncertainty they may experience about the identity of a particular stimulus.

WEB ACTIVITY 4.7

Categorical versus continuous perception In this activity, you'll listen to sound files that will allow you to compare perception of voiced and unvoiced consonants to the perception of pitch and volume.

Figure 4.9 Is it a cup or a bowl? The category boundary isn't clear, as evident in these images, inspired by a classic experiment by linguist Bill Labov (1972). In contrast, the boundary between different phonemic categories is quite clear for many consonants.

(A) Continuous perception

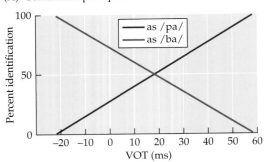

(B) Categorical perception

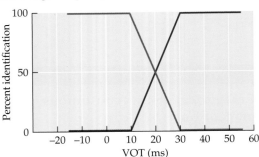

Figure 4.10 Idealized graphs representing two distinct hypothetical results from a phoneme forced-choice identification task. (A) Hypothetical data for a perfectly continuous type of perception, in which judgments about the identity of a syllable gradually slide from /ba/ to /pa/ as VOT values increase incrementally. (B) Hypothetical data for a sharply categorical type of perception, in which judgments about the syllable's identity remain absolute until the phoneme boundary, where the abruptly shift. Although there's some variability depending on the specific tasks and specific sounds, most consonants that represent distinct phonemes yield results that look more like (B) than (A).

in **Figure 4.10A**. In this hypothetical figure, just about everyone agrees that the sound with the VOT at –20 ms is a /ba/, and the sound with the VOT at 60 ms is a /pa/. But, as also shown in Figure 4.10A, for each step away from –20 ms and closer to 60 ms, you see a few more people calling the sound a /pa/.

But when researchers have looked at people's responses to forced choice identification tasks, they've found a very different picture, more like the graph in **Figure 4.10B**. People agree pretty much unanimously that the sound is a /ba/ until they get to the 20 ms VOT boundary, at which point the judgments flip abruptly. The upshot of all this is that when you're processing speech sounds, there's usually no inner mental argument going on about whether to call a sound /ba/ or /pa/. (The precise VOT boundary that separates voiced from unvoiced sounds can vary slightly, depending on the place of articulation of the sounds.)

What sound distinctions do newborns start with?

Put yourself in the shoes of the newborn, who is encountering speech sounds in all their rich variability for the first time (more or less: some aspects of speech sounds—especially their rhythmic properties—*do* make it through the uterus wall to the ears of a fetus, but many subtle distinctions among sounds will be encountered for the first time after birth). We've seen that adults don't pay equal attention to all sound distinctions—they pay special attention to those that signal differences between phonemic categories. But we've also seen that phoneme categories can vary from language to language, and that sound distinctions that are obvious to one language group may be more elusive to another. Clearly, these distinctions have to be learned to some extent. So what is a newborn baby noticing in sounds? Given that she's unlikely to have formed categories such as /p/ and /b/, since these categories are somewhat language-specific, does this mean that she's paying attention to *every* possible way in which sounds might vary in their pronunciation? Remember that sounds can vary along a number of different dimensions, with incremental variation possible along any of these dimensions. Let's suppose that babies are perceiving continuously rather than categorically (see Figure 4.9) for any of these sound dimensions. In that case, the sound landscape for babies would be enormously cluttered—where adults cope with several dozen categories of speech sounds, babies might be paying attention to hundreds of potential categories.

It takes some ingenuity to test for categorical perception in newborns. Once again, you can't give these miniature humans a set of verbal instructions and get back a verbal response that will tell you whether they are perceiving the difference between certain sounds. You're stuck making do with behaviors that are within the reach of your average newborn—which, admittedly, are not a lot. Faced with a newborn whose behavioral repertoire seems limited to sleeping, crying, sucking, and recycling body wastes, a researcher might be forgiven for feeling discouraged. It turns out, though, that one of these behaviors—sucking—can, in the right hands, provide some insight into the infant's perceptual processes. Babies suck to feed, but they also suck for comfort, and if they happen to have something in their mouths at the time, they suck when they get excited. And, as may be true for all of us, they tend to get excited at a bit of novelty.

By piecing these observations together, Peter Eimas and his colleagues (1971), pioneers in the study of infant speech perception, were able to design an experimental paradigm that allows researchers to figure out which sounds babies are perceiving as the same, and which they're perceiving as different. The basic premise goes like this: If babies are sucking on a pacifier while hearing speech sounds, they'll tend to suck vigorously every time they hear a new sound. But if they hear the same sound for a long period of time, they become bored and suck with less enthusiasm. This means that a researcher can cleverly rig up a pacifier to a device that measures rate of sucking, and play Sound A (say, [pa]) over and over until the baby shows signs of boredom (that is, the baby's sucking slows down). Once this happens, the researcher can then play Sound B (say, [pʰa]). If the baby's sucking rate picks up, this suggests the baby has perceived Sound B as a different sound. If it doesn't, it provides a clue that the baby, blasé about the new sound, hasn't perceived it as being any different from the first one (see **Method 4.2** for details of this approach). When it comes to testing for categorical perception then, if babies perceive speech sounds categorically, they should be oblivious to differences between certain sounds but acutely sensitive to differences between other sounds that fall on different sides of a critical boundary. On the other hand, if they're perceiving continuously, then they should *always* hear Sound B as different, and should increase their sucking just about any time Sound B is introduced.

If we look at how babies perceive VOT, the experiments show clear evidence of categorical perception in newborns, so it appears that the youngest humans don't treat all sound distinctions in the same way. Their rate of sucking goes up when two sounds straddle a VOT boundary of about 25 ms, but otherwise they seem oblivious to differences in VOT. This boundary is very similar to the adult dividing line for English voiced and voiceless sounds. What this means is that the sound landscape comes pre-carved to some extent; upon birth, babies aren't faced with the massive task of considering *every* possible difference in sound as being potentially meaningful when it comes to signaling differences between phonemic categories. Some sound distinctions are more privileged than others right off the bat.

When researchers first discovered that babies emerge from the womb with certain pre-set boundaries that happen to line up with the VOT boundaries distinguishing English voiced and voiceless sounds, this generated some excited speculation. Some researchers suggested that children come innately equipped with a set of inborn phonetic categories that are commonly used by languages. But this line of thinking quickly ran into a wall. First of all, Patricia Kuhl and James Miller (1971) devised a clever experiment to study the perception of consonants by chinchillas—which, while adorable, are not known for their linguistic skills, and certainly don't ever produce speech, so it's doubtful that they would be born innately prepared for it. Kuhl and Miller found that

METHOD 4.2

High-amplitude sucking

The high-amplitude sucking method allows researchers to peer into the minds of babies who, due to their tender age, understandably have a limited repertoire of behaviors. It's based on the premise that infants will naturally suck on objects in their mouths when they are excited by hearing a new sound. Throughout the experiment, the baby participant sucks on a pacifier that contains electrical circuitry that measures the pressure of each sucking motion so that the rate of sucking can be constantly tracked. The pacifier is held in place by an assistant, who wears headphones and listens to music to block out the experimental sounds, so there's no possibility of sending any inadvertent signals to the baby.

Infants tend to suck with gusto when they hear a new, interesting sound anyway, but in order to get the strongest connection possible between a new stimulus sound and this sucking behavior, researchers have an initial conditioning phase built into the session. During this phase, a new sound is played every time the baby sucks on the pacifier at a certain rate: no vigorous sucking, no terrific new sound. Babies quickly learn to suck to hear the stimulus.

Once the baby has been trained to suck to hear new sounds, researchers play the first of a pair of stimulus sounds—let's say a [pa] sound—over and over. Once the baby's interest lags, the sucking rate goes down. This is an example of **habituation**. When the baby's sucking rate dips below a criterion level that's been previously established, the second sound of the pair is played, and the dependent measure is the sucking rate of the baby *after* the presentation of this new sound. If the baby begins to suck eagerly again, it's a good sign that she perceives the second sound as different from the first.

This method can be adapted to measure which of two kinds of stimuli infants prefer. For example, if you wanted to know whether infants would rather listen to their own language or an exotic tongue, you could set up your study in a way that trains babies to suck slowly or not at all in order to hear one language, and to suck hard and fast in order to hear the other (being sure to counterbalance your experimental design to make sure that an equal number of babies are trained to suck slowly versus quickly for the native language).

As you might imagine, when working with extremely new babies, there can be quite a lot of data loss. Often babies are too tired, too hungry, or just too ornery to pay much attention to the experimental stimuli, so a large number of participants must be recruited for this method. The method works quite well for infants up to about 4 months of age, after which point the pastime of sucking begins to lose some of its appeal for infants, and they're less likely to keep at it for any length of time. Luckily, at around this age the head-turn preference paradigm becomes an option for testing babies' perception of speech.

---

habituation Decrease in responsiveness to a stimulus upon repeated exposure to the stimulus.

---

these small, furry mammals also perceived consonants categorically, along a VOT boundary very similar to the one found for humans (see **Box 4.4**). This result has since been replicated in some of our closer relatives, such as macaque monkeys, and in much more distant animal relatives such as birds.

There's a second problem with the notion that categorical perception in human newborns reflects innate preparation for linguistic sounds: it turns out that many *non*-speech sounds are perceived categorically as well—not just by humans but also by animals that are *very* distant from us on the evolutionary family tree, such as crickets and frogs. So it looks as if the process of amplifying some sound distinctions while minimizing others is a very general property of the auditory system across species. Though it has a certain usefulness for perceiving speech, it doesn't seem to be intrinsically related to speech.

An especially telling demonstration of the parallels in perception of speech and non-speech sounds comes from experiments that use non-speech sounds to mimic some of the properties of human speech sounds. Remember that VOT

BOX 4.4
Categorical perception in chinchillas

How can you study speech perception in animals? As they do with babies, scientists have to find a way to leverage behaviors that come naturally to animals, and incorporate these behaviors into their experiments. Speech scientists Patricia Kuhl and James Miller (1975) took advantage of the fact that in many lab experiments, animals have shown that they can readily link different stimuli with different events, and that they can also learn to produce different responses to different stimuli in order to earn a reward.

In Kuhl and Miller's study, chinchillas (**Figure 4.11A**) heard various speech sounds as they licked a drinking tube to get dribbles of water. When the syllable /da/ was played (with a VOT of 0 ms), it was soon followed by a mild electric shock. As would you or I, the chinchillas quickly

learned to run to the other side of the cage when they heard this sound. On the other hand, when the syllable /ta/ came on (with a VOT of 80 ms), there was no electric shock, and if the chinchillas stayed put and continued to drink, they were rewarded by having the water valve open to allow a stronger flow of water. In this way, the researchers encouraged the chinchillas to link two very different events to the different phonemic categories, a distinction the chinchillas were able to make.

The next step was to systematically tweak the voice onset times of the speech stimuli in order to see how well the chinchillas were able to detect differences between the two sounds at different points along the VOT continuum. Even though the animals had only heard examples of sounds at the far ends of the VOT spectrum, they showed the same tendency as human babies and adults do—that is, to sort sounds into clear-cut boundaries (see Figure 4.10)—and the sharp boundary between categories occurred at almost the same VOT as was found for humans (33.5 ms versus 35.2 ms; see **Figure 4.11B**).

Figure 4.11 (A) A chinchilla; these animals are rodents about the size of a squirrel. They are a good choice for auditory studies because the chinchilla's range of hearing (20–30 kHz) is close to that of humans. (B) Results from Kuhl and Miller's categorical perception experiment, comparing results from the animals and human adults. The graph shows the mean percentage of trials in which the stimulus was treated as an instance of the syllable /da/. For humans, this involved asking the subjects whether they'd heard a /da/ or /ta/ sound; for chinchillas, it involved seeing whether the animals fled to the other side of the cage or stayed to drink water. (After Kuhl and Miller, 1975.)

(A)

(B)
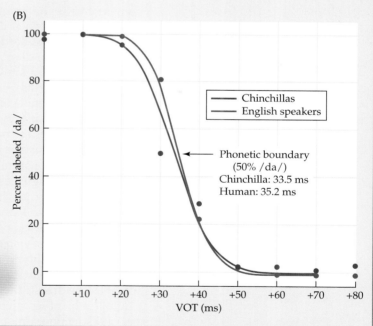

is a measure of the time between the release of the articulators and the beginning of voicing (that is, vibration of the vocal folds). A slightly more abstract way of looking at it is that the perception of VOT is about perceiving the relative timing of two distinct events. This scenario can easily be recreated with non-

ABX discrimination task A test procedure in which subjects hear two different stimuli followed by a third which is identical to one of the first two. The subjects must then decide whether the third stimulus is the same as the first or the second.

speech stimuli, simply by putting together two distinct sounds and playing around with their relative timing.

Researcher David Pisoni (1977) created a set of stimuli by using two distinct tones and varying the number of milliseconds that elapsed between the onsets of the two tones, much as was done in previous VOT experiments—we can call this "tone onset time," or TOT. He then tested to see whether there was a certain window across which people would be especially sensitive to TOT differences. For instance, people might hear two stimuli, Stimulus A being two tones whose onsets were separated by 20 ms, and Stimulus B being two tones separated by 30 ms. The people would then have to judge whether a third stimulus (in which the two tones were separated by, say, 30 ms) was the same as Stimulus A or Stimulus B. The idea behind this task, known as an **ABX discrimination task**, is that if people can readily perceive the difference between the two sound pairs, they'll be reliable at identifying whether the third sound pair is identical to the first or second. On the other hand, if they don't perceive the difference between them, then they'll be randomly guessing as to the identity of the third sound pair.

What Pisoni found was that people were especially good at distinguishing between stimuli right around a TOT of 20 ms. For example, the above pair of stimuli, sound pairs with TOTs of 20 ms and 30 ms, would be perceived as distinct by many of the subjects. But if people heard a pair of stimuli with sounds separated by 40 ms and 50 ms, they were much less likely to perceive them as different. The same was true for a pair of simultaneously produced sounds (0 ms TOT) and a sound pair 10 ms apart. In other words, the TOT boundary for optimal perception of differences was strikingly similar to the boundary for *voice* onset time of speech sounds. Pisoni suggested that differences at about the 20 ms boundary for both speech and non-speech sounds are easy to notice because this is the point at which the auditory system is able to detect that two events occurred at different times. If the time between two events is any shorter, it becomes hard to perceive that they didn't occur at the same time. The limits of the auditory system make the 20 ms mark a point at which stimuli naturally divide up into categories of simultaneous versus non-simultaneous pairs of sound events.

Clearly, the overall evidence from categorical perception scores no points for the hypothesis that babies come preinstalled with probable speech categories. Instead, it supports the notion that a language like English is being opportunistic about where it carves phonemic categories—it appears to be shaping itself to take advantage of natural perceptual biases of the auditory system.

Still, not all languages take advantage of the natural places to carve up phonemic categories that the auditory system so conveniently offers up. As we saw, languages like Mandarin opt not to distinguish between phonemes at the "natural" boundaries, placing phonemic boundaries elsewhere instead. Since babies are obviously able to grow into Mandarin-speaking adults, there must be enough flexibility in their perceptual systems to adapt to the categories as defined by their particular language. What changes in the perceptual life of an infant as she digests the sounds of the language around her?

Quite a bit of research has shown that babies start off noticing a large number of distinctions among sounds, regardless of whether the languages they'll eventually speak make use of them to mark phonemic distinctions. For example, all babies, regardless of their native languages, start off treating voiced and unvoiced sounds as different, and the same goes for aspirated versus unaspirated sounds. As they learn the sound inventory of their own language, part of their job is to learn which variations in sounds are of a deep, meaning-changing kind, and which ones are like wardrobe options. Eventually, Mandarin-hearing babies will figure out that there's no need to separate voiced and voiceless sounds into different categories, and they will downgrade this sound difference in their auditory attention. (Here's a workable analogy to this attentional downgrading: presumably, you've learned which visual cues give you good information about the identity of a person, and which ones don't, so you pay more attention to those strongly identifying cues. So, you might remember that you ran into your co-worker at the post office, but have no idea what she was wearing at the time.) Unlike the Mandarin-hearing babies, who "ignore" voicing, English-hearing babies will learn to "ignore" the difference between aspirated and unaspirated sounds, while Thai-hearing babies will grow up maintaining a keen interest in both of these distinctions.

It can be a bit humbling to learn that days-old babies are good at perceiving sound differences that you strain to be aware of. There's a large body of research (pioneered by Janet Werker and Richard Tees, 1984) that now documents the sounds that newborns tune in to, regardless of the language their parents speak. Unlike many of you, these tiny bundles of joy can easily cope with exotic sound distinctions, including these: the subtle differences among Hindi stops (for instance, the difference between a "regular" English-style /t/ sound and one made by slightly curving the tip of your tongue back as you make the sound); Czech fricatives (for instance, the difference between the last consonant in *beige* and the unique fricative sound in *Dvorak*); and whether a vowel has a nasal coloring to it, a distinctive feature in French, important for distinguishing among vowels that shift meaning. At some point toward the end of their first year, babies show evidence of having reorganized their perception of sounds. Like adults, they begin to confer special status on those distinctions that sort sounds into separate phonemic categories of the language they're learning.

WEB ACTIVITY 4.8

Distinct sounds for babies
In this activity you'll listen to some non-English sound distinctions that newborn babies can easily discriminate.

4.4 Learning How Sounds Pattern

The distribution of allophones

In the previous section, we saw that babies start by treating many sound distinctions as potentially phonemic, but then tune their perception in some way that dampens the differences between sounds that are non-phonemic in the language they're busy learning. So, a Mandarin-hearing baby will start out being able to easily distinguish between voiced versus unvoiced sounds, but will eventually learn to ignore this difference, since it's not a phonemic one.

But this raises a question: How do infants *learn* which sounds are phonemic, and therefore, which differences are important, and which can be safely ignored? You and I know that voicing is a distinctive feature partly because we recognize that *bat* and *pat* are different words with different meanings. But remember that babies are beginning to sort out which sound differences are distinctive as early as 6 months of age, at a time when they know the meanings of very few words (a topic we'll take up in Chapter 5). If infants don't know what *bat* and *pat* mean, or even that *bat* and *pat* mean different things, how can they possibly figure out that voicing (but not aspiration) is a distinctive feature in English?

As it happens, quite aside from their different roles in signaling meaning differences, phonemes and allophones *pattern* quite differently in language. And, since babies seem to be very good at noticing statistical patterns in the language they're hearing, such differences might provide a useful clue in helping them sort out the phonemic status of various sounds.

Let's take aspiration as a test case. Monolingual English speakers have a hard time *consciously* distinguishing a [p] from a [pʰ], especially in tasks that focus on sorting these sounds into categories. Yet the speech patterns of these same speakers show that they *must* be able to hear the difference between them at some level, because they produce them in entirely different sound contexts. Aspirated sounds get produced at the beginnings of words or at the beginnings of stressed syllables—for example, the underlined sounds in words like *pit, cat, PAblum, CAstle, baTTAlion, comPAssion*. Unaspirated sounds get pronounced when they follow another consonant in the same syllable—like the underlined sounds in words like *spit, stairs, scream*, and *schtick*—or when they're at the beginning of an unaccented syllable, as in *CAnter, AMputate, elLIPtical*. The /p/ sound would come off as aspirated in *comPUter*, but not in *COMputational*. In other words, aspirated and unaspirated sounds aren't sprinkled throughout the English language randomly; they follow a systematic pattern that speakers must have somehow unconsciously noticed and reproduced even though they *think* they can't hear the difference between them. (In case you're wondering, it's perfectly possible from a purely articulatory standpoint to produce a word-initial voiceless sound without aspiration, even when it's at the beginning of a stressed syllable—speakers of many other languages do it all the time).

I've talked about how allophonic distinctions are like wardrobe changes for the same sound. Well, just as you wouldn't wear your fishnet stockings to a funeral, or your sneakers to a formal gala, allophones tend to be restricted to certain environments—there are "rules" about which allophones can turn up in which places. And just like "rules" about wardrobe choices, they are to some extent a bit arbitrary, and based on the conventions of a language. When two allophones are relegated to completely separate, non-overlapping linguistic environments, they're said to be in **complementary distribution**. In fact, showing up in different linguistic environments from each other is a defining feature of allophones, along with the fact that they don't signal a change in meaning. This means that whenever a sound distinction is allophonic, rather than phonemic, it should be possible to predict which of the two sound variants will turn up where.

We can see how this works with an example other than aspiration. In English, certain differences among sounds involving the *place* of articulation are distinctive, but others are not. For instance, sounds produced by placing the tip of the tongue against the alveolar ridge are phonemically distinct from sounds produced by the back of the tongue (for example, voiceless /t/ versus /k/ and voiced /d/ versus /g/). One upshot of this is that, taken completely outside of their semantic context (that is, the context of meanings), it's impossible to predict whether the alveolar sounds or the back (velar) sounds will fill in the blanks below (The sounds are depicted in International Phonetic Alphabet, or IPA symbols, as in Figure 4.6 and Box 4.3.)

__ eɪp (as in the word *ape*)	__ ɪl (as in *fill*)
__ ɑn (as in *lawn*)	__ owp (as in *nope*)
__ il (as in *feel*)	__ un (as in *swoon*)
__ æn (as in *fan*)	__ ɪk (as in *sick*)

complementary distribution Separation of two allophones into completely different, non-overlapping linguistic environments.

In all of these blanks, you can insert *either* an alveolar or a velar (back) sound, often of either the voiced or voiceless variety: *tape/cape; Don/gone; teal/keel; tan/can; dill/gill/till/kill; tope/cope; tune/coon/dune/goon; tick/kick*.

BOX 4.5
Allophones in complementary distribution: Some cross-linguistic examples

When two sounds represent separate phonemes, it's usually possible to find minimal pairs involving these sounds. But whenever a language treats two sounds as allophonic variants of a single phoneme, these two sounds appear in non-overlapping phonetic environments, as illustrated by some cross-linguistic examples.

French/English

Nasalization of vowels is a distinctive feature in French, signaling a difference between phonemes. Hence in French, it's possible to find minimal pairs where nasalized and non-nasalized sounds occur in identical environments. For example, the French words *paix* (peace) and *pain* (bread) are distinguished only by whether the vowel is nasalized; no consonant is pronounced at the end of either word.

In English, nasalized and non-nasalized vowels are allophones, so it would be impossible to find minimal pairs involving nasalized and non-nasalized vowel counterparts. Instead, these vowels are in complementary distribution with each other. Nasalized vowels appear in English only immediately before nasal consonants:

Nasalized	Non-nasalized
bit (*beet*)	bĩn (*been*)
lowd (*load*)	lõwn (*loan*)
bræg (*brag*)	bræ̃nd (*brand*)
bɛd (*bed*)	bɛ̃nd (*bend*)
bʌt (*but*)	bʌ̃n (*bun*)
brud (*brood*)	brũm (*broom*)
sɪk (*sick*)	sɪ̃ŋ (*sing*)

Finnish/English

Vowel length marks a phonemic distinction in Finnish, but in most English dialects, differences in vowel length mark different allophones of the same phoneme. In English, longer vowels appear before voiced sounds in the same syllable, while shorter vowels appear before unvoiced sounds:

Short	Long
lɪt (*lit*)	lɪːd (*lid*)
rowp (*rope*)	row:b (*robe*)
sɛt (*set*)	sɛːd (*said*)
mæt (*mat*)	mæːd (*mad*)
feɪt (*fate*)	feɪːd (*fade*)

English/Spanish

The voiced alveolar stop consonant /d/ and its closest corresponding fricative /ð/ (as in the word *then*) are different phonemes in English; hence the existence of minimal pairs such as *den* and *then*. In most dialects of Spanish, however, these two sounds are allophones, and therefore in complementary distribution. The fricative appears after a vowel in Spanish:

Stop	Fricative
donde (*where*)	usteð (*you*)
dolor (*pain*)	comiða (*food*)
durar (*to last*)	laðo (*side*)
an**d**ar (*to walk*)	caða (*each*)
fal**d**a (*skirt*)	oðio (*hatred*)

But not all distinctions that involve place of articulation are phonemic in English. For instance, there's an allophonic distinction between the velar stop [k] and a palatal stop [c], which is made a little farther forward than [k], up against the palate. In each of the same linguistic environments you just saw, only one of either the velar or palatal sounds tends to show up—that is, the sounds are in complementary distribution (see **Box 4.5**). Their distribution is shown below (ignore standard English orthography, and look instead at how the sounds are represented as IPA symbols):

c eɪp (*cape*)	c ɪl (*kill*)	c il (*keel*)	k un (*coon*)
k ɑn (*con*)	k owp (*cope*)	k æn (*can*)	c ɪk (*kick*)

assimilation The process by which one sound becomes more similar to a nearby sound.

If you were to look at many more words of English, a clear generalization would emerge: [c] is allowed whenever it comes before vowels such as /e/, /ɪ/, or /i/; [k] on the other hand shows up in front of sounds like /ɑ/, /o/, or /u/. You might then also notice that /e/, /ɪ/, and /i/ have something in common—they're produced at the front of the mouth, while /ɑ/, /o/, or /u/ are produced at the back of the mouth. It's probably no accident that the palatal sound [c]—which is produced farther forward in the mouth—is the sound that appears with the front vowels rather than the other way around. It's often the case that an allophonic variant will resemble adjacent sounds in some way, following a natural process called **assimilation**. It's important to realize, though, that while the rule that determines the distribution of [k] and [c] is a fairly natural one, given that the stops often morph to resemble their adjacent vowels, there's nothing inevitable about it. In Turkish, for example, /k/ and /c/ are separate phonemes, and each stolidly maintains its shape regardless of which vowel it's standing next to.

From patterns of distribution to phonemic categories

We know from the work on word segmentation that babies are extremely good at using statistical information about sound patterns to guess at likely word boundaries. It makes sense to ask, then, whether babies might also be able to use information about how sounds like [k] and [c] pattern in order to figure out which of the sounds in their language are phonemic. By "noticing" (implicitly, rather than in any conscious way) that these sounds are in complementary distribution, babies born to English-speaking parents might conclude that they're allophones and stop perceiving the sounds categorically as representing two phonemes. That is, they would start to treat [k] and [c] as variants of one sound. Babies in Turkish-speaking households, on the other hand, would have no reason to collapse the two sounds into one category, so they would stay highly tuned to the distinction between /k/ and /c/.

Experiments by Katherine White and her colleagues (2008) suggest that babies might be using distributional evidence along these lines to categorize sounds as "same" versus "different." To test this, they used the trick of devising an artificial language with certain statistical regularities and checked to see what babies gleaned from these patterns. In this language, babies heard the following set of two-word sequences, repeated in random order:

na bevi	rot pevi	na zuma	rot zuma	na suma	rot suma
na bogu	rot pogu	na zobi	rot zobi	na sobi	rot sobi
na dula	rot tula	na veda	rot veda	na feda	rot feda
na dizu	rot tizu	na vadu	rot vadu	na fadu	rot fadu

Do you see the pattern? The babies did. When it comes to the word-initial stops (that is, "b," "p," "t," "d"), whether they are voiced or not depends on the preceding words—if the preceding word ends in a voiceless sound (*rot*), then the stop is also voiceless, assimilating to the previous sound. But if the preceding word ends in a voiced sound (that is, *na*—remember, all vowels are by default voiced), then the stop is also voiced. When you look at the fricatives, though, either voiced or voiceless fricatives ("z," "s," "f," "v") can appear regardless of whether the last sound of the preceding word is voiced or voiceless. In other words, stops are in complementary distribution, but fricatives are not.

Now, based on these patterns, would you think that *bevi* and *pevi* are different words, or just different ways of pronouncing the same word? Given that "b" and "p" are in complementary distribution, and therefore that they are likely allophones of the same phoneme, switching between "b" and "p" probably doesn't change the meaning of the word—it's just that it's pronounced one way after *na* and a slightly different way after *rot*, so you can count entirely on the distributional rules of the language to figure out which variant it should be in that context. What about *zuma* and *suma*? Here, the voiced and voiceless sounds "z" and "s" aren't constrained by some aspect of the phonetic context, so it would make sense to assume that they're separate phonemes. Which of course means that the words *zuma* and *suma* are probably minimal pairs, each with a different meaning.

Katherine White and colleagues found (using the head-turn preference paradigm) that at 8.5 months of age, the babies had caught on to the fact that stops and fricatives involved different patterns of distribution when it comes to voicing—they listened longer to "legal" sequences involving new words beginning with a stop (for example, *rot poli, na boli, rot poli, na boli*) than they did to sequences beginning with a fricative (for example, *rot zadu, rot sadu, rot zadu, rot sadu*). This may be because the babies were able to predict the voicing of the word-initial stop—but not the fricative—based on the previous word, so the words involving stops may have felt a bit more familiar. So, by 8.5 months, babies were able to tune in to the fact that there was a special relationship between a stop and the preceding sound, but that this predictive relationship was absent for fricatives. By 12 months of age, they seemed to understand that this relationship had something to do with whether word units that differed just in the voicing of their first sounds should be treated as "same" or "different" units. At this age (but not at the younger age), the babies also showed a difference in their listening times for sequences of words with stops versus words with fricatives, even when they appeared *without* the preceding word (that is, *poli, boli, poli, boli* versus *zadu, sadu, zadu, sadu*). This makes sense if they were treating *poli* and *boli* as variants of the same word but thinking of *zadu* and *sadu* as different words.

Babies aren't ones to waste information—if they find a pattern, they're likely to put it to good use. As we've seen, distributional sound patterns, which link specific sounds to the phonetic contexts where they can occur, are very handy for inferring which sounds are distinct phonemes rather than variants of a single phoneme. They can also provide some clues about where the boundaries are between words. This is because sometimes whether you pronounce one allophone or another depends upon whether it's at the beginning or end of a word. Compare *night rate* and *nitrate*, for example. Both are made from the same sequence of phonemes strung together, and the only difference is whether there's a word boundary between the /t/ and /r/ sounds. In normal speech, there would be no pause at all between the words. But this word boundary has subtle phonetic consequences nevertheless: If you say *night rate* at a normal conversational pace, the /t/ sound in *night* is unaspirated, and also unreleased (notice that once the tongue meets the alveolar ridge, it kind of stays there as you slide into the /r/ sound). On the other hand, when you say *nitrate*, the first /t/ sound is aspirated and audibly released, and what's more, the following /r/ sound, which is usually voiced, becomes voiceless by virtue of assimilating to the /t/ sound before it. If babies have noticed that the sounds /t/ and /r/ take on a slightly different shape depending on whether there's a word boundary between them or not, this might help them make better guesses about whether *night rates* and *nitrates* form one word unit or two.

Peter Jusczyk and his colleagues (1999) showed that by 10.5 months of age, babies who heard *night rates* during the familiarization phase of a study were later able to distinguish this phrase from the nearly identical *nitrates* (based on the result that during the test phase, they listened longer to the familiar *night rates* than to the novel word *nitrates*). This shows that the babies were tuning in to the very subtle differences in sounds between these two sound sequences, and probably weren't hearing *nitrates* as the same word as *night rates*.

It's not hard to see how this kind of information about likely word boundaries could come in very handy in helping babies to avoid mistakes in slicing up the speech stream. A subsequent study by Mattys and Juszcyk (2001) showed that even at 8.5 months, babies didn't treat the word *dice* as familiar if they'd previously heard a sentence like *The city truck cleared ice and sand from the sidewalk*—here, the sound sequence *d-ice* appears, but with a word boundary after the /d/ sound, which affects how the sequence is pronounced. The babies were not fooled into thinking they'd heard the word *dice*. But the youngsters did seem to recognize the word *dice* if instead they previously heard the sentence *Many dealers throw dice with one hand.*

If anything, this chapter ought to have cured you of any tendency to underestimate the intelligence of babies, or to believe that they're not paying attention to what you say. Clearly, a spectacular amount of learning goes on behind the innocent eyes of infants in their first year. Especially over the second half of that first year, we see piles of evidence that babies' knowledge of the sound system of their language is undergoing dramatic learning and perceptual reorganization. Before uttering their first words, babies have become competent at chopping up the continuous flow of speech into word-like units, figuring out which sound distinctions define sound categories for their particular language, hearing how subtle differences in sound might be related to the phonetic context in which those sounds appear, and leveraging that information in a number of useful ways.

Of course, we haven't said anything at all yet about what the little tykes *do* with this vast knowledge of their language's sounds. Mapping these sounds onto meanings is a whole other task, one that we'll take up in the next chapter.

GO TO
sites.sinauer.com/languageinmind

for **web activities, further readings, research updates, new essays,** and other features

---

DIGGING DEEPER

Statistics, yes, but what kind of statistics?

We're not used to thinking of infants as having great powers of statistical analysis, and yet the scientific work on infant speech perception tells a pretty convincing story that babies zero in on exquisitely detailed statistical regularities from the very beginning stages of learning their language. In fact, this attention to statistical detail seems to be the bedrock on which later language learning can be built.

In many ways, the scientific story is just beginning. Though we have good evidence that babies (along with other animals) pick up on certain kinds of statistical regularities, there are many things we still don't know. When you stop to think about it, the statistical regularities that *could* be entertained by babies come in a great number of varieties and flavors. Do infants focus on some more than others? Does the nature of the patterns they look for change over time? Are the types of patterns they can track different from the patterns that other species of animals are able to track? Do babies notice different kinds of patterns in language than they do in other perceptual domains? And do they have some inborn sense of just which kinds of statistical patterns might be the most useful for the learning of a language? As you can see, we've just begun to scratch the surface. Without digging in and conducting a very large number of studies looking at what may seem like very small details, we can't answer the big questions, such as whether statistical learning has an innate component, or whether humans do it differently from animals.

Let's begin to make all this a bit more concrete. We've seen that babies as young as 8 months of age can track the transitional probabilities (TPs; see p. 117) in a language— that is, they infer that for any two syllables, if the first syllable provides a strong cue to the identity of the second syllable, then those two syllables are quite likely to be grouped together in a word. So, the two syllables in *blender* are good candidates for a word unit because, given the first syllable *blen*, there's a fairly high likelihood that you'll hear the second syllable *der*. This of course assumes that babies are computing probabilities in a particular direction, from left to right. But in principle, it's also perfectly reasonable to ask whether, given the second syllable *der*, there's a high likelihood that it will have been preceded by the first syllable *blen*. In other words, babies could also be computing *backward* transitional probabilities.

It seems a bit odd to think about tracking statistical relationships this way, because we're so used to thinking of language in a left-to-right direction. But it turns out that backward TPs are just as useful for figuring out whether or not two syllables are part of the same word. So, computing them in either direction is likely to be helpful in terms of identifying the statistical peaks and valleys that provide cues about likely word boundaries.

In fact, there are some cases where *backward* TPs might be more informative in identifying certain regularities, especially when it comes to thinking about grammatical relationships between words. Suppose, for instance, you are a baby trying to figure out whether the word *bottle* is a noun or a verb. A really strong cue for noun-hood is that nouns tend to be preceded by articles such as *a* or *the*. In other words, transitional probabilities can provide some good cues, but in this case, they need to be of the backward variety— that is, it would be very helpful to have noticed that, given the word *bottle*, there was an extremely high likelihood that the *preceding* word was *the*. Looking only at forward TPs would be less helpful, because given the word *the*, the likelihood of its being followed by *bottle* is fairly low.

Backward and forward TPs often tend to correlate with each other in natural languages. But it's possible to carefully set up experimental stimuli from an artificial language or a completely unfamiliar language such that either the forward or backward TPs are more informative than the other, in order to test whether babies are sensitive to both sources of information. Using this strategy, Bruna Pelucchi et al. (2009) found that at 8 months of age, babies could indeed track backward TPs as a way to extract words from the speech stream of an unfamiliar language. So infants don't seem to be constrained to computing statistical regularities in one direction only.

Another issue that cries out for exploration is how much phonetic detail is statistically tracked. For instance, should stress be marked on syllable units over which statistics are tracked? So far, we've been implicitly assuming that stress as a cue to word segmentation is separate from TPs. This means that in order to compute TPs, the *test* in the words *CONtest* and *deTEST* would be counted as the same syllable. If you think back to our discussion of stress in Section 4.1, I pointed out that in English, the majority of words have a trochaic stress pattern, with stress on the first syllable, as in *CONtest*. I talked about how, once babies have figured out this generalization, it could be useful to them in segmenting new sequences of sounds they hadn't heard before: when

in doubt, put the word boundary to the left of the stressed syllable. Of course, babies could only notice that most words in English are trochaic once they'd accumulated enough English words! If you think of stress and TPs as separate in this way, it makes sense to predict that babies would rely on stress as a cue only sometime after they were able to rely on using TPs to segment the speech stream. This is because they would first use the TPs as a way to amass a large enough collection of words over which to generalize about stress.

There's some evidence to support the idea that statistical cues to word segmentation are used some time before stress can be applied: Thiessen and Saffran (2003) showed that 6- and 7-month-olds could use TPs to segment new words from an artificial language but that they didn't show any tendency to fall back on a trochaic segmentation bias; 9-month-olds, on the other hand, put *more* stock in the stress cues when they conflicted with the bare statistical cues.

Another way of looking at this is that what changes with a baby's age is that by 9 months, babies have learned to incorporate stress as part of the information that goes into computing TPs. The idea would be that the 9-month-olds were treating the *test* in *CONtest* and *deTEST* as two *different* syllables. This has the effect of turbocharging TPs: Curtin et al. (2005) analyzed all the pairs of syllables in a body of English speech directed at babies, and they found that including stress in the calculation of TPs created an even wider separation between transitional probabilities for within-word syllable pairs than for across-word syllable pairs. In other words, statistical cues became quite a bit more reliable once the information about stress was folded in. The developmental change, then, may be that over time, babies incorporate details about sounds to the extent that they figure out that doing so will enhance the statistical cues. This would make them sophisticated statisticians indeed.

It would almost seem as if eventually, if there are statistical regularities to be found, babies find them. This might logically lead you to think that babies are built to be able to pick up on *any* kind of statistical regularity. But so far, all of the variations on statistical cues we've looked at involve what are really fairly minor tweaks of the original TPs as stated by Saffran et al. (1996). If you get wildly imaginative about the different possible statistical relationships between sounds, you can cook up some truly unusual generalizations. For instance, imagine a language in which the last sound of a word is always /m/ if the word happens to begin with a /k/ sound, and is always /s/ if the word begins with the vowel /o/. It's perfectly possible to create an artificial language in which this generalization is absolutely regular—for example, *kabitdestim, kum, kendom, obaldis, otis, ofadiguntilnes*. But it's a type of generalization that is extremely unlikely to show up in a *natural* language, despite the seemingly unlimited diversity of languages. Real languages tend to stick to regularities that are stated in terms of adjacent or near-adjacent elements.

Once you start looking at sound regularities across many different languages, a number of constraints and typical patterns start to emerge. For example, think of the generalization that determines whether voiceless sounds in English will be aspirated or unaspirated. Notice that it applies to *all* of the voiceless sounds of English, not just one or two of them. It would be a bit weird for a language to have [pʰam] and [kʰam] but [tam], with an unaspirated [t] in this position. That is, sound regularities usually apply to *natural classes* of sounds—that is, groups of sounds that are very similar to one another in phonetic space and that share quite a few articulatory features. For aspiration in English, you can make a broad generalization that voiceless stops become aspirated in certain linguistic contexts, without having to specify individual sounds.

It's also true that allophones of a single phoneme tend to have a lot in common phonetically—so, think of [p] and [pʰ], but also of the liquid sounds [r] and [l], which are allophones in Japanese and Korean. This means that it would be strange for two completely different sounds—say, [r] and [f]—to be in complementary distribution with each other, even though from a strictly mathematical point of view, there's nothing to prevent it.

So, there seem to be some constraints on which sounds or groups of sounds are typically the targets of sound-based generalizations. What's more, there are also some constraints on the types of contexts or neighboring sounds that tend to determine which variant of a sound will end up being pronounced. As we've noted before, the plural marker –*s* as in *dogs* and *cats* is actually pronounced differently in these two words. Attach it to *cat*, and you utter the voiceless fricative [s], but tag it onto *dog*, and you pronounce its *voiced* sibling [z]. And if you start paying attention to all regular plural forms, you'll find that the voiced fricative shows up whenever the immediately preceding sound is voiced, and that it is voiceless whenever it comes on the heels of a voiceless sound. (Notice how it's pronounced in *dogs, docks, cats, cads, caps, cabs,* and so on.) It's probably not sheer coincidence that the plural marker is affected by an adjacent sound, rather than another sound two syllables over. Nor is it likely to be a coincidence that the feature that undergoes the change in the plural marker—that is, voicing—is also the feature than defines the classes of relevant preceding sounds. Sound patterns like these, in which one feature of a sound bleeds over onto a neighboring one, are extremely common across languages. What would be less common is a pattern in which, say, the plural sound [s] became the stop [t] whenever it followed a voiceless sound, but a fricative whenever it followed a voiced sound.

After surveying the world's languages, then, we can divide up hypothetical sound patterns into two groups: those that seem like natural, garden-variety generalizations, and those that are highly unnatural and involve patterns that are really unlikely to be found across languages. Remember

that in Chapter 2 we saw that the existence of language universals and tendencies has been used to buttress the argument that much of language learning is innately constrained. The idea is that children come pre-equipped with biases to learn certain kinds of linguistic patterns over others, and that this is why we see evidence that some patterns are more common across languages than others.

Do babies start life with a bias for certain kinds of statistical regularities in the sounds of speech? If they did, they could avoid wasting their attention looking for patterns that just don't seem to be useful for languages. We might predict, then, that they'd be very unlikely to notice the generalization about word-final /m/ and /s/ being dependent on word-initial /k/ or /o/. A statistical rule like this fails a "naturalness" test on four counts: First, the sounds to which the rule applies—/m/ and /s/—don't form a natural class of any kind, making them odd bedfellows for a rule. Second, the sounds that characterize the relevant linguistic context—/k/ and /o/—are even odder companions, not even belonging to the same category of sound at the broadest level (one is a consonant and the other is a vowel). Third, there's a yawning distance between the word-final sounds and the linguistic contexts on which they depend. And fourth, the relationship between the word-final sounds and the word-initial sounds that determine their identity is purely arbitrary. All of this hardly makes for a promising statistical pattern.

To find out whether babies strategically allocate more of their cognitive resources to statistical hypotheses that are most likely to pan out for a natural language, we'd need to test a large number of natural and unnatural patterns embedded into artificial languages. But there's at least some evidence now that shows that not all statistical patterns are learned with equal ease. Jenny Saffran and Erik Thiessen (2003) compared two kinds of phonotactic constraints: In one experiment, 9-month-old babies had to learn that the first sound in a syllable was a voiceless stop (/p/, /t/, /k/), while the last sound was always a voiced stop (/b/, /d/, /g/). That is, the phonotactic constraint applied to a natural class of sounds. The babies showed signs of learning this pattern after hearing a speech sample of only 30 words, repeated twice. In another experiment, babies had to learn that syllables began with /p/, /d/, and /k/ and that they ended with /b/, /t/, and /g/. In this case, voiced and voiceless stops were mixed together as possible sounds at both the beginnings and ends of syllables, and the babies would have to learn the statistical rules in terms of individual sounds, and not in terms of natural classes of sounds. The end result was that, after the same amount of exposure as in the first experiment, there was no sign that the babies were picking up on this pattern.

So, there are some intriguing results showing that highly natural patterns leap out at babies more readily than unnatural ones. One way to think about this is that the learning biases shown by these tiny language learners correspond to innate "settings" that constrain them from generating wildly unhelpful hypotheses about the structure of language—in other words, they correspond to a type of innate knowledge about natural language patterns. But there's another very different explanation that fits with the same experimental results. As you saw in Chapter 2, the nativist argument based on language universals can be flipped on its head. It may be that, instead of reflecting an innate program that guides the process of language acquisition, language universals reflect a process of languages adapting to the limitations of the human mind. In other words, it may be the case that some kinds of statistical regularities are simply easier to learn than others, or need less mental horsepower to compute. Patterns that are hard for children to learn eventually get weeded out of a language. This explanation is quite a plausible one, especially given that we've already seen that languages tend to adapt to basic properties of the auditory system—for example, like voicing in English, they might shape their phonemic inventories around sound distinctions that are especially easy to perceive.

Still, before we can really pull apart these competing ways of looking at language universals and learning biases, more work needs to be done. We need to establish what kinds of patterns are more easily learned than others, and why. This means building up a body of knowledge about "easy" versus "hard" kinds of patterns, and looking at how these play out across species, across various domains, and perhaps across the developmental span of humans. (Remember, as I hinted at in Chapter 2, the ultimate shape of a language may be influenced by the age at which most of its learners typically acquire it.) The more similarities we see across domains and species in terms of easy versus hard patterns, and the more that the distinction between easy and hard patterns aligns with language universals, the more evidence we have that statistical learning biases are deeply embedded within more general cognitive skills rather than reflecting an innate, language-specific program. On the other hand, if language-related biases turn out to be dramatically different from the kinds of biases we see in other species and other domains, this would provide some support for the idea that there are specific and possibly innate constraints on learning the sound patterns of human language. Care to lay any bets on how it will turn out?

PROJECT

Think of a statistical pattern that seems unlikely to be a natural pattern in a language. Create a snippet of an artificial language, and formulate a research design in which you would test to see whether subjects are sensitive to this particular kind of statistical information. If possible, test a group of adult subjects, and analyze the data. For a description of the artificial grammar studies with adult subjects, see Saffran et al. (1997).

5 Learning Words

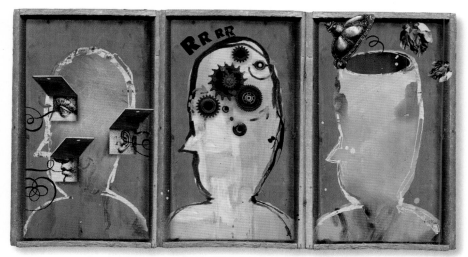

At roughly 12 months of age, children begin to utter their first words. After that much-celebrated milestone event, they manage to add a smattering of new words over the next several months until they have a stash of about 50 or so. And then their word learning starts to accelerate until they reach, by conservative estimates, about 60,000 words in their total vocabulary by the time they graduate from high school. This translates into about 10 new words per day.

To put this achievement into perspective, think back to the days when you were learning "math facts"—memorizing the relationships between numbers and arithmetic operations, such as 2 + 5, or 4 × 7. For many kids, it can take weeks of sweating over practice sheets, drills, and flash cards to solidly commit to memory the multiplication tables—a modest set of several dozen facts. And yet, these same kids seem to be able to pluck words out of the air without any effort, sometimes after hearing a word only once. (If you're in doubt about one-shot word learning, see what happens when you inadvertently utter a swear word within earshot of a toddler.) How do children manage to do this? Presumably, the process of learning words is quite unlike learning math facts.

When you learn words as an adult in a foreign-language classroom, of course, what you do is memorize vocabulary lists that are either translated into words of your first language, or linked to pictures and videos describing scenes and events. You might think that parents helpfully simulate a version of this teaching environment by pointing out objects and events and describing them for their children. But when they talk to their kids, parents typically act more

duality of patterning The concept that language works at two general levels, with units of sound combining into meaningful units (usually words) and these meaningful units combine into a larger pattern of meaningful syntactic units.

like conversational partners than like language instructors. You rarely see parents repetitively putting objects into their children's hands and barking out single-word statements like: "Cup." "Peas." "Spoon." Instead, they're more likely to offer a running commentary such as, "Honey, don't throw your cup on the floor" or, "Boy, do I have some delicious peas for you!" This would be a bit like having your foreign language teacher talk at you in sentences, leaving you to sort out how many words she's uttered and what they all mean in the context. Add to that the fact that parents often talk about things that aren't in the here and now: "Did you have a nice nap?" or, "Grandma and Grandpa are coming tonight." Or, they might comment on a child's state of mind in a way that is only very loosely related to reality: "I know you want these peas!"

Even if parents were to describe only objects and events in the immediate environment, there would still be a lot of explaining to do about exactly how kids make the connections between the stream of sounds they hear and their interpretation of the scenes that these sounds accompany. Researchers of language development like to describe the child's task of mapping utterances onto meanings by invoking a famous example from the philosopher Willard Quine. In his example, an anthropologist is trying to characterize the language of a small indigenous tribe previously unknown to Western scientists by noting the relationship between what speakers say and the contexts in which they say it (which also seems like a reasonable strategy for word learning by children). When a rabbit scurries by, a tribesman points to it and exclaims, "Gavagai!" The anthropologist might then assume that *gavagai* corresponds to the English word *rabbit*. But how can he be sure? It might also mean any one of the following: "There goes a rabbit," "I see a rabbit," "That thing's a pesky varmint," "white," "furry," "hopping," "lunch," "rabbit parts," "a mammal," "a living thing," "a thing that's good to eat," or "a thing that's either good to eat or useful for its skin." Or, for that matter, the tribesman may not be commenting on anything to do with the rabbit; he might be pointing out the lovely color of the newly sprung leaves on the trees, or the fact that the sun is about to set. The logical possibilities for choosing a meaning to go with the utterance are fairly vast.

Of course, we have the sense that not all of these logical possibilities are equally likely—for example, if the tribesman is pointing to the rabbit, it would be rather strange for him to be describing the approaching sunset, and it's a good bet that he'd be more likely to be referring to the rabbit itself than its various parts, or some very general category of living things. But do *babies* know these things? We can't assume that just because we as adults can rely on certain inferences or biases to figure out new meanings that these would also be available to your average toddler. Ultimately, the child needs to have some way of constraining the enormous space of possibilities when it comes to linking sounds with meanings. In this chapter, we'll explore what some of these constraints might look like, and how the child might come to have them in place.

But learning words goes beyond just figuring out which meanings to attach to bundles of sounds. In Chapter 2, I introduced the idea that human natural languages show **duality of patterning** (see Box 2.1). That is, language operates at two very general levels of combination. At one level, meaningless units of sound combine to make meaningful units (for example, words), and at the second level, meaningful units (words) combine with each other to make larger meaningful syntactic units. Words, therefore, are the pivot points between the system of sound and the system of syntactic structure. So, in addition to learning the meanings of

WEB ACTIVITY 5.1

Inferring language meaning In this exercise, you'll get a direct feel for the task of inferring language meaning without the benefit of any explicit teaching. You'll see some short videos, accompanied by unintelligible speech. Your job will be to generate plausible (and implausible) guesses at the meanings conveyed by the speech.

words, children also have to learn how words interface with the sound system on the one hand and syntactic structure on the other. This chapter will also deal with how individual words become connected with these two distinct levels. As was the case in Chapter 4, what might intuitively *feel* like a straightforward learning task is anything but.

5.1 Words and Their Interface to Sound

Which sounds to attach to meanings?

When it comes to learning the meanings of words, a baby's first job is to figure out *which* blobs of speech, extracted from an ongoing stream of sounds, are linked to stable meanings. For example, it would be helpful to know if *gavagai* really consists of one word or three—and if it's more than one, where the word breaks are. No problem, you might think, having read Chapter 4. In that chapter, we saw evidence that infants can segment units out of running speech well before their first birthday, relying on a variety of cues, including statistical regularities. So, by the time babies learn the meanings of their first words, they've already been busy prepackaging sounds into many individual bundles. The idea would be that these bundles of sound are sitting in a young child's mental store, just waiting for meanings to be attached to them.

For example, let's suppose that in our hypothetical language, *gavagai* breaks down into two words: *gav agai*. Assuming they've heard each of these words in speech often enough, babies who've been exposed to this language from birth should be able to recognize *gav* and *agai* as cohesive linguistic packages, but they'd treat the sound sequences *avag* or *vagai* as just a collection of random sounds. As seen from the experiments with artificial languages in which "words" have been completely disembodied from meanings, babies should be able to segment these units based entirely on their knowledge of sound patterns and their regularities in running speech. In theory, then, when trying to figure out the *meaning* of *gavagai*, they should know that they're looking to attach meanings to the sound bundles *gav* and *agai*. If so, this would make some of the challenges of learning the meanings of words a bit more manageable.

But, once again, never take the workings of the infant mind for granted. We've been referring to the segmented units of speech as *word* units. This is convenient because as adults, we recognize that these sequences of sounds correspond to meaningful words. But babies don't necessarily know that. Just because they can slice these units out of a continuous speech stream doesn't mean that they understand that these particular groupings of sounds are used as units for *meaning*. They might simply be treating them as recurring patterns of sound that clump together. This might seem odd to you, since you're so used to thinking of speech sounds as carrying meaning. But consider this: studies of statistical learning have shown that both babies and adults can learn recurring groupings of musical tones in just the same ways that they learn word units in an artificial language. It might be easier for you to imagine how someone might recognize a group of tones as a recurring and cohesive bundle of sounds, without having the expectation that there's any meaning attached to them. It's entirely possible that for babies, this is exactly how they treat the "word" units they pull out from speech. They've figured out that certain sounds systematically go together, but they haven't yet figured out what these bundles of sounds are *for*.

A number of researchers have suggested that something very much like this is going on in the minds of babies at the earliest stages of word learning. The idea is that they've gotten as far as memorizing a bunch of meaningless sound bundles, but the next phase of linking sounds with meaning is an entirely new step. When they first start linking up sounds to meanings, they don't simply dip into their bag of stored sound sequences; rather, they start from scratch in building up brand new sound-based representations. The evidence for this argument goes as follows:

Remember that when babies segment units from speech, these units contain an exquisite amount of phonetic detail. Babies are able to attend to even very subtle sound variations, such as aspiration, and can use them as segmentation cues. On the other hand, a number of researchers have claimed that the units of sound that babies attach meaning to are much coarser in their phonetic detail than the strings that they segment out of speech. They've suggested that the mental representations that result from slicing up the speech stream aren't in fact the *same* representations that underlie a child's early meaningful words. In other words, let's suppose that a baby has managed to successfully segment the sound sequence for the word *dog* based on sound regularities alone—that is, she has the sense that this is a non-random, recurring bundle of sounds that clump together. Her representation of this bundle of sounds would look quite different from her representation of the sounds for the *meaningful* symbol *dog* when she starts to figure out that *dog* refers to the furry family pet. It's even been proposed (see, for example, Hallé and de Boysson-Bardies, 1996) that the representations that serve as containers for meaning aren't made of strings of individual sounds at all, unlike the representations for segmented speech. Rather, they're general and quite fuzzy holistic *impressions* of sounds.

This might seem like an odd proposal to make. After all, why would babies go to the trouble of segmenting speech into units if they weren't going to use these units as the basis for meanings? But there's some familiarity to the idea that the mental representations for words might be to some extent separate from the detailed representations of the sounds that make up those same words. If you remember, back in Chapter 3, I summarized some arguments for the separation of linguistic knowledge into dorsal and ventral streams in the brain. These arguments included evidence that some patients do well on word-recognition tasks even though they struggle with basic sound-discrimination tasks; and conversely, some patients are able to make fine sound discriminations but have a hard time recognizing familiar words. This suggests there's some potential slippage between the two systems; perhaps it takes babies some time to fully establish the connections between them.

However plausible the notion might be, though, in order to understand the sound representations that babies first map meanings onto, we need to take a close look at the mental life of these early word-learners.

Studying how children map sounds to meaning: The switch task

Our best bet for studying how babies map sounds onto meaning is through carefully designed lab studies that look at the precise conditions under which these mappings are made. One way to do this is through an association test known as the **switch task**. Stager and Werker (1997) used this technique to test whether children pay attention to fine details of sound in learning new object-word mappings (see **Figure 5.1**).

In this task, there's a *habituation phase* in which two objects are each paired up with a novel word that is not an actual English word but obeys its phonotactic rules (for example, *lif* and *neem*; see Figure 5.1A). To learn these associations, babies watch pictures of objects one at a time, accompanied by their associated labels spoken through a loudspeaker over a number of trials during this phase. The trials are repeated until the babies show signs of **habituation**—that is, of

switch task A simple word-mapping test in which infants are exposed to a visual representation of an object paired with an auditory stimulus during a habituation phase. During the subsequent test phase, the infants hear either the same object–word pairing, or they hear a new word paired with the familiar object. A difference in looking times between the novel and familiar pairings is taken as evidence that the child had mapped the original auditory stimulus to the familiar object.

habituation Decreased response to a stimulus after repeated presentations of that stimulus.

(A) Habituation phase

Test phase

Same   Switch

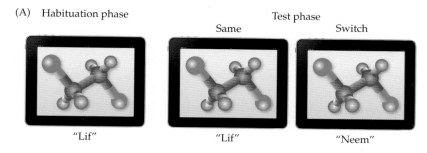

"Lif"   "Lif"   "Neem"

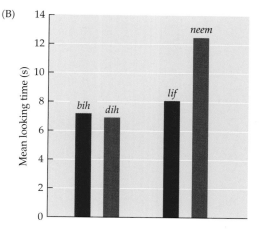

Figure 5.1 (A) A switch task using the highly distinct stimuli *lif* and *neem*. During the habituation phase, children heard *lif* paired with the visual image. In the test phase, children either heard *lif* again or a new word (*neem*) paired with the original visual image. In a different version of the same experiment, the highly similar sound stimuli *bih* and *dih* were used. (B) Mean looking times for 14-month-old participants. Babies readily distinguished between *lif* and *neem*, but not between *bih* and *dih*. (Adapted from Stager & Werker, 1997.)

having become so familiar with the stimuli that the amount of time they spend looking at the picture starts to decline. A test phase follows during which the labels and their objects are sometimes swapped, so that the object that used to be shown along with the word *lif* is now shown with the word *neem*, and vice versa. These "switched" trials are compared with "same" trials, in which the words accompany their original pictures.

If babies have linked the correct label to the picture of each object, they should register surprise when the wrong label is paired with the familiar picture; that is, they should look longer at the "switch" trials than at the "same" trials. This result is exactly what we see for babies who are 14 months of age or older—shortly after the average age at which babies gurgle their first recognizable words (Stager & Werker, 1997). Or rather, the effect shows up for two words that are very different from each other, such as *lif* and *neem*. But babies at this age *don't* notice the switch if the words are very similar to each other—for example, *bih* and *dih*. Instead, they act as if these were just variants of the same word, linked to the same meaning (see Figure 5.1B). This is interesting, because infants can clearly hear the difference between /b/ and /d/ in categorical perception tasks that *don't* require them to link meanings with sounds, but they seem to ignore this difference when it comes to linking up sounds with simple pictures.

These results raise the possibility that babies' representations of meaningful words don't actually contain all the phonetic detail of the strings of sounds that they segment from speech. But why would this be? One idea is that there's a difference between information that babies can pay attention to while processing language in the here and now, and the information they commit to long-term memory in the form of a stable **lexical representation** by which sound and meaning properties are recorded. The thinking might go like this: babies (and maybe adults too) are somewhat miserly about their long-term memory space, and only keep as much detail about sound in the lexical representation of a word as they need for the purpose of distinguishing that word from other words in their long-term memory. But adults and older children have large vocabularies of thousands of words, so they need a lot of sound detail to keep their lexical representations separate from one another.

For example, older individuals really need to encode the difference between /b/ and /d/ so they can distinguish between word pairs like *big/dig*, *bean/dean*, *bad/Dad*, *bought/dot*, and so on. But put yourself in the shoes of an infant who only knows a smattering of meaningful words. Take the following meager collection:

baby	mommy	daddy
hat	shoe	diaper
yummy	milk	juice
spoon	bottle	blanket

lexical representation Information that is committed to long-term memory about the sound and meaning properties of words, and certain constraints on their syntactic combination.

None of these words are very similar to each other, so there's no need to clutter up lexical representations with unnecessary details. However, with time and a burgeoning vocabulary, the infant might notice not only that she needs to distinguish between words like *big* and *dig*, but also that the voicing difference between /b/ and /d/ is mighty useful for distinguishing between many other words. She would then start paying attention to voicing (see Section 4.3) as a general property that serves to signal meaning differences. When she later comes across a new word such as *pill*, her lexical representation would reflect the fact that its first sound is voiceless, even though she may never have heard the contrasting word *bill*.

This is a plausible account. But it's not clear that babies' failure to notice the difference between *bih* and *dih* in the switch task really reflects less detailed lexical representations. Another possible explanation is that babies are just very inefficient and prone to error when it comes to *retrieving* words from memory. So, they might confuse words that are similar to each other during the retrieval process, even though sound distinctions between them are actually there in their lexical representations. For example, it's possible that they do in fact have separate lexical representations for *bih* and *dih*, but they might easily confuse them because of their similarity—just as you might mistakenly pull a bottle of dried basil out your cupboard while searching for oregano. You know they're different herbs, but their similar appearance has momentarily confused you.

This alternative retrieval account gains support from evidence that even adults are less sensitive to detailed sound differences when they're trying to match newly learned words with their meanings. Katherine White and her colleagues (2013) showed that when adult subjects were taught a new "language" in which made-up words were paired with abstract geometric objects, they showed a tendency to confuse novel words like *blook* with similar-sounding words like *klook* if they'd heard the word only once before. But this confusion lessened if they'd heard the novel word multiple times. These findings suggest that, like those of adults, children's lexical representations might well be linked to rich and detailed phonetic representations, but be vulnerable to sound-based confusion when words are unfamiliar. And in fact, 14-month-olds seem perfectly capable of distinguishing familiar words like *dog* from very similar ones like *bog* (Fennell & Werker, 2003). Together, these two experiments argue against the notion that the sound representations that children map onto meanings are different in nature from the sound representations they segment out of running speech.

We can find even more direct evidence that the units babies pull out of the speech stream are put to good use in the process of attaching meanings to clumps of sounds. In a study led by Katharine Graf Estes (2007), 17-month-old babies first heard a 2.5-minute stream of an artificial language. Immediately after that, the babies were exposed to a novel word-learning task using the switch paradigm. The added twist was that half of the new words in the switch task corresponded to word units in the artificial language the babies had just heard. The other half were sequences of sounds that had occurred just as often in the artificial language but that straddled word boundaries ("part-words"), as seen in the experiments in Chapter 4. Babies were able to learn the associations between pictures and words, but only for the sound units that represented word units in the artificial language, showing that they were applying the results of their segmentation strategies to the problem of mapping sounds to meaning.

Results like these suggest that, indeed, very small children are able to draw on their stores of segmented units to help them in the difficult task of matching words and meanings. In other words, if you're a baby and the transitional probabilities among sounds lead you to treat *agai* as a coherent and recurring clump of sounds, you might have a leg up in figuring out what is meant by "Gavagai!" All of this suggests that word learning relies heavily on the statistical experience that babies have with language. As it turns out, the *amount* of exposure to language that children get in their daily lives can vary quite dramatically, leading to some striking consequences for their early word learning (see **Box 5.1**).

BOX 5.1
The 30-million-word gap

Small children can learn new words after just one exposure, which might lead you to think that they can acquire a decent vocabulary even if they hear just a modest amount of language. But there's good reason to believe that the greater the quantity of input, the more solid their learning of language will be.

In Chapter 4, we saw that children can track the statistical patterns in their speech. While even 2 minutes of a very simple sample was enough for them to be able to parse the speech stream, in real life, the language sample that children hear is much messier and more complex. Remember that in the speech segmentation experiments, for example, babies only heard samples of *four* frequently repeated "words," hardly a realistic reflection of real-world speech. In order to be able to notice the statistical patterns in everyday speech, children no doubt need a much heftier amount of input.

We've also seen that children gloss over many details of the sounds of unfamiliar words. This too suggests that they might benefit from many repetitions of the same word, in order to solidify their representations of words and their ability to pull them efficiently from memory.

Are there repercussions for children who hear less language? In a well-known study published in 1995, researchers Todd Risley and Betty Hart found that there were massive differences in the amount of speech that children heard in their homes; the average number of parental words directed at the babies ranged from 200 to 3000 words per hour. The amount of exposure to language was strongly correlated with the size of the children's vocabulary (Hart & Risley, 1995).

A more troubling result was that kids from the poorest families generally heard much less talk than children from more economically privileged homes—and were significantly behind in their vocabulary growth as well (see **Figure 5.2**). The authors of the study estimated that by the age of three, lower-income kids would have heard

an average of 30 million fewer words than their wealthier counterparts. This raised a fair bit of concern, since the size of a child's vocabulary upon entering school is a good predictor of how easily he'll learn to read. It's well known that school-age children from lower-income homes lag behind higher-income children in reading skills.

The study by Hart and Risley focused attention on socioeconomic differences, but a broader lesson is the relationship between the quantity of language input and the child's word-learning trajectory. These days, educators and language researchers raise concerns about whether the constant presence of electronic devices and social media in many households might be cutting into a family's conversation time.

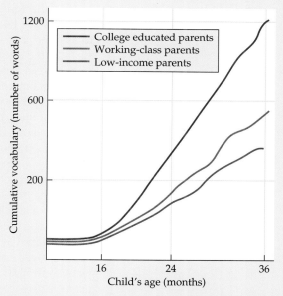

Figure 5.2 Hart and Risley's data show that disparities emerge very early in life among children living with college-educated professional parents, working-class parents, and low-income parents living on welfare. (Adapted from Hart & Risley, 1995.)

5.2 Reference and Concepts

Words and objects

A young child's sense that certain bundles of sound are more likely than others to be linked to meaning is a start. But in order to explain how sound–meaning pairings come about, we also need to look at the other side of the equation, and know a bit about which *meanings* a child considers to be good candidates for linguistic expression. It would be a startling child indeed whose first word turned out to be *stockbroker* or *mitochondria*—even if her parents held down jobs as genetics researcher and financial analyst and uttered such words on a daily basis at home. It's simply implausible that these *concepts* would be part of a toddler's mental repertoire. These are complex notions that are probably impossible to grasp without the benefit of some already fairly sophisticated language to explain them. Most children's first words instead refer to tangible objects or creatures that can be experienced more directly through the senses: *rabbit, bottle, milk, baby, shoe.*

But how is it that a child knows (or comes to learn) that *rabbit* is more likely to be referring to the whole squirming animal than to its fur or, even more implausibly, three of its four limbs? It *feels* obvious to us. Our intuitions tell us that some concepts—such as whole objects—are simply more psychologically privileged than others, almost crying out to be named. But, as always, we can't assume that what feels obvious to us would also feel obvious to a very young baby. Our own intuitions may be the result of a great deal of learning about the world and about how languages use words to describe it. (Think back, for example, to how phonemic categories which seem so deeply ingrained to us in fact had to be *learned* early in childhood.) Have intuitions about "obvious" candidates for word meanings been with us since babyhood, guiding our acquisition of words throughout our lives?

It would seem that they have. Many studies have shown, for example, that when babies hear a new word in the context of a salient object, they're likely to assume that the word refers to the whole thing, and not its parts, color, or surface, the stuff it's made of, or the action it's involved in. Researchers often refer to this assumption as the **whole-object bias** in word learning. This bias doesn't seem all that surprising when you consider the landscape of very early infant cognition. Even as young as 3 months of age, babies clearly organize the jumble of lines, colors, and textures that make up their visual world into a set of distinct *objects*, and they have robust expectations that objects in the world will behave in stable and predictable ways.

In one study by Philip Kellman and Elizabeth Spelke (1983), 3-month-old babies saw a screen with a stick visible at its top and another stick at the bottom. If the two sticks moved simultaneously, the babies assumed that they were joined to a single object, and they were surprised if the screen was removed to reveal two disconnected objects. ("Surprise" was measured by how long the babies stared at the scene once it was revealed.) On the other hand, if the two sticks moved separately, the babies were unfazed to find that two separate objects were hiding behind the screen. Aside from knowing that objects usually act as indivisible wholes, young babies also seem to know that objects can't disappear at one point and reappear at another, that they can't pass through other objects, and that inanimate objects can't move unless they come into contact with other objects.

Given that babies can clearly parse the world into whole objects long before they can parse speech into word-like units, it would seem natural that once children figure out that words are used to *refer*, they then take for granted that

whole-object bias The (theoretical) assumption by babies that a new word heard in the context of a salient object refers to the whole thing and not to its parts, color, surface, substance, or the action the object is involved in.

(A) Training phase

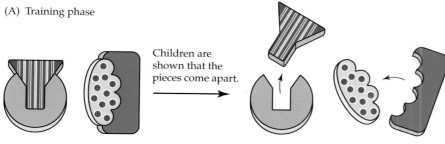

Children are shown that the pieces come apart.

"Look at the modi! See the modi? It's a modi!"

(B) Test phase

"Where's the modi?"

Figure 5.3 (A) Two of the novel objects used in experiments by Hollich et al. Experimenters demonstrated to young children (ages 12 and 19 months) how the objects could be separated into two parts. (B) During the test phase, children saw a display showing both the entire assembled object and the more colorful of its parts. (Adapted from Hollich et al., 2007.)

objects are great things to refer to. At one level, this might be simply because objects are perceptually important, so when babies hear a word, they easily slap that word onto whatever happens to be most prominent in their attention. But in fact the relationship appears to go deeper. It's not just that whole objects have a tendency to draw babies' attention; it appears that babies have a sense of what kinds of things *words* attach to.

A study by George Hollich and colleagues (2007) explored whether the act of *naming* by an experimenter affected how babies visually examined objects and their parts. Babies age 12 and 19 months were shown objects made of two parts—a single-colored "base" piece and a more exciting, colorfully patterned piece that inserted into the base (see **Figure 5.3**). During a training phase, the experimenter labeled the object with a nonsense word ("Look at the modi! See the modi? It's a modi"). The experimenter did nothing to hint at whether the word referred to the whole object or just one of its parts but did emphasize that the object came apart, by repeatedly pulling it apart and putting it back together again. Then, during the testing phase, the experimenter put the whole object and an exact copy of the colorful part on a board in front of the child and asked the child, "Where's the modi? Can you find the modi?" Since babies reliably look longer at an object that's been named than at other objects, it's possible to measure looking times to infer whether the child thinks that *modi* refers to the whole object or to the colorful part; the child's eye gaze should rest longer on whichever object he thinks the word refers to.

The results of the study showed that babies looked longer at the whole object than at the object part, suggesting that they had taken the word *modi* to refer to the whole object rather than to one of its parts. But before we draw this conclusion with any certainty, we want to make sure that kids weren't just looking at the whole object because it was more interesting or visually important, but that their eye gaze really reflected something about making a link between the object and the word *modi*. To check for this, during an earlier phase of the experiment, even before the experimenter labeled the object, babies' free-ranging eye movements to the whole object and the isolated part were also measured. Before hearing the novel name, babies spent roughly the same amount of time looking at the colorful part as the whole object. So it wasn't just that the babies found the whole object more visually compelling; it was specifically the act of naming that drew their attention to it. In other words, the whole-object bias seems to be about something more specific than just finding whole objects more interesting, and even at 12 months of age babies have some ideas about what kinds of meanings words are likely to convey. This kind of knowledge can really help narrow down the set of possible meanings for words.

Obviously, though, people *do* talk about parts of an object as well as the whole thing, and they can also describe an object's color, texture, temperature, function, taste, ingredients, location, origin, the material it's made of, or any actions or events it's involved in. A whole-object bias might help babies break into an early vocabulary, but sticking to it too rigidly would obviously be pretty limiting. For example, researcher John Macnamara (1972) describes a scenario where a child thought the word *hot* referred to the kitchen stove. (You can imagine a parent warning "Don't touch that! It's hot!") Luckily, as we'll see shortly, kids make use of a slew of helpful cues in figuring out that you can talk about other things besides objects, and that words can map onto different kinds of concepts.

Categories large and small

So far, I've talked about object names as if they refer to specific objects, actual things that the child can see or touch. But that's actually the wrong way to think about words like *rabbit* or *bottle* or *blanket*. These nouns don't just apply to any particular object—they apply to the entire *categories* of rabbits, bottles, and blankets. It turns out that only a small subset of nouns—the ones we call proper nouns, like *Dave, Betty, Marilyn Monroe,* or *Cleveland*—refer to particular entities or individuals. And, when you think about it, language would be only very narrowly useful if words didn't generalize beyond specific referents. We'd like to be able to talk to our kids not just about *this* family dog ("Honey, don't tease the dog"), but also about dogs more generally ("Don't get too close to a strange dog"; "Some dogs bite"; "Dogs need to go outside for walks"; and, eventually, "The dog is descended from the wolf"). Presumably, one of the huge benefits of language for humans is its ability to convey more general information along these lines.

Mapping words onto categories is even more complex than mapping words onto specific referents. In principle, any single object could fall into an infinite number of categories. Along with categories like "dogs," "furniture," or "reggae music," people could (and sometimes do) talk about categories such as "foods that give you heartburn"; "professions that pay poorly but give great satisfaction"; "things I like to do but my ex never wanted me to do"; or even "objects that broke at exactly 2 PM on March 22, 2006." But categories like these rarely get their own words—in the scheme of categoryhood, they just don't make the cut. How do children figure out which categories are most likely to have words bestowed upon them?

Just as whole objects seem to be more natural candidates for reference than their properties or their parts, we also have intuitions about which categories seem the best candidates for reference. Even if we look at just those categories that *have* been awarded their own words, though, it becomes clear that people are inclined to talk about some kinds of categories more than others. For instance, unless you're a dog breeder, you probably use the word *dog* in your daily communication much more often than you do the more specific word *Dalmatian*. What's more, you probably also use it more often than the more general terms *mammal* and *animal*, even though these broader categories obviously encompass a larger number of creatures. This is generally true of categories at a mid-level degree of specificity—for example, chairs get talked about more often than recliners or furniture, and the same holds for apples versus Cortlands or fruit. These privileged midlevel categories are called **basic-level categories**, in contrast with the more general **superordinate-level categories** and the more specific **subordinate-level categories**.

When you look closely at their informational value, the basic-level categories seem to be especially useful for capturing generalities. For instance, if you know that something is a dog, you know a lot of things that are likely to be true about it: you know that it probably barks, needs exercise, eats meat, has a pack psychology, marks its territory, has sharp teeth, and so on. On the other hand, if you only know that something is an animal, the number of things you know about it is much smaller and vaguer. So, being told "Fido is a dog" allows you to infer many more things about Fido than being told "Fido is an animal." At the same time, basic-level categories (say, dogs versus cats or birds) also tend to be fairly distinct from one another, unlike subordinate-level categories (for example, Dalmatians versus collies). Often it makes sense to talk about what the category members have in common that differentiate them from other categories. So, if you're told "Dogs need to be walked," this is a more useful piece of information than being told "Dalmatians need to be walked." It may be that basic-level categories are favored by language users exactly because they strike this balance between similarity among members and distinctiveness from other categories.

In learning their early words, then, kids have to figure out how to map the words onto just the right categories, including how to hit exactly the right level of specificity. They sometimes show evidence of **under-extension** of category names—for example, if a child first learned the word *flower* in the context of referring to a carnation, she might not realize that daisies can be referred to by the same word. But you wouldn't necessarily notice a child's vocabulary under-extensions without some explicit probing—she might just not call a daisy *any-thing*, rather than use an obviously wrong word for it. **Over-extension**, in which a child uses a word for an inappropriately general category—for instance, referring to all animals as *doggie*—is more easily observed. Errors of over-extension may well be more common in children's minds, although it's a bit hard to tell based only on how they label things in the world.

Despite these missteps, children's early speech (just like adult language) contains a disproportionate number of basic-level words—a fact that raises the question, is this simply because basic-level words are more common in their parents' speech, or is it because young children are especially attuned to words in this middle layer of categories? It might be helpful to young children if they showed up at the word-learning job with some preconceptions about not just what aspects of the physical environment are most likely to be talked about (whole objects more than parts), but also what categories make for good conversation. To answer this question, we need to look at experiments that specifically probe for the links young children make between new words and their meanings.

One way to do this is with a slightly modified version of Web Activity 5.2, in which you had to guess the possible referents for the made-up word *zav*. If children see a novel word like *zav* used to refer to a Dalmatian, and they assume that it applies to members of the same basic-level category, they'll also accept collies and terriers as possible referents of the word and will gladly apply the word *zav* to these kinds of dogs as well. On the other hand, if their guesses

basic-level categories The favored midlevel category of words that strike a balance between similarity among members of the category and distinctiveness from members of other categories; e.g., of the words *dog*, *Dalmatian*, and *animal*, *dog* would fall into the basic-level category.

superordinate-level categories The more general categories of words that encompass a wide range of referents; e.g., *animal*.

subordinate-level categories More specific categories comprising words that encompass a narrow range of referrents; e.g., *Dalmatian*.

under-extension Mapping new words into categories that are too specific; e.g, referring to a carnation, but not a daisy, as *flower*.

over-extension Mapping new words into categories that are too general—for instance, referring to all animals as *doggie*.

are more conservative, they might limit their choices to only Dalmatians and reject other kinds of dogs as falling under the meaning of *zav*. Or, they might guess more liberally, and extend the word to apply to all animals, including cows and cats.

Several studies (e.g., Callanan et al., 1994; Xu & Tenenbaum, 2007) have found that young children are clearly reluctant to extend a new word to a broad category such as animals, as are adults. But, whereas adults seem to have fairly strong assumptions that *zav* extends to a basic-level category, preschoolers seem a bit more conservative, sticking more often with the subordinate-level category as the appropriate meaning of the word. However, these early assumptions about categories seem to be fairly fluid. For example, the study by Fei Xu and Josh Tenenbaum (2007) found that preschoolers became willing to shift their interpretation of a new word to a basic-level category if they'd heard just

LANGUAGE AT LARGE 5.1

How different languages cut up the concept pie

Babies seem to approach the task of word learning with some reasonable starting assumptions. These line up fairly decently with the way language cuts up conceptual space into word-sized bites. Many of these assumptions mirror facts about the natural world, and capture the sorts of properties that define or distinguish categories of things in the world. For example, no language that I know of has a word that groups together roses and rabbits but excludes all other flowers and mammals. We have the feeling that such a language would be deeply alien. Concepts, then, seem to offer themselves up in natural classes—much as the sounds of speech tend to pattern together in natural classes, as we saw in Chapter 4.

The starting assumptions that children have about word meanings may well help them avoid unnatural hypotheses about word meanings. But they only take kids so far. After all, in addition to talking about the natural world, we also use language to talk about some very abstract notions and relationships. And once we move into the space of abstract concepts, it's less obvious which concepts cry out for their own words. As a result, languages can vary quite widely in how they match up words and meanings.

For instance, consider words for family members, such as *mother*, *brother*, *cousin*, *aunt*, *grandfather*, *sister-in-law*, *stepfather*, etc. Some of the dimensions that English enshrines in distinct words include information about gender, generation, and whether the relationship is by blood or marriage. This may seem very natural to you. But you don't have to go very far to find dramatically different ways of referring to relatives. For example, many languages (such as Bengali, Tamil, Korean, and Hungarian) also feel the need to encode the relative age of family members, so there would be a different word for an older brother than for a younger brother. In Hawaiian, you'd use the same word for your mother and your aunt, and there would be no way to distinguish siblings from cousins. On the other hand, Sudanese children have to learn different words to distinguish their father's brother's children from their father's sister's children, from their mother's brother's children, and their mother's sister's children; English speakers are satisfied with the single word *cousin*. Other languages can get even more complicated, having certain distinctions among relatives made only on the mother's side, but not the father's side.

No language has a word to cover every concept, and it's not always obvious why languages make the choices they do. Ever wondered, for example, why English has the word *hum*, but no word for what you do when you sing the melody of a song but substitute "la la la" for the song's actual words? (In the Pirahã language, the situation is reversed.) And how come we make no distinction between addressing one person or many with our pronoun *you* (though a previous version of English did, with the two words *thee* and *ye*)?

In some cases, lexical gaps can be filled when speakers of a language encounter a handy word in another language and simply appropriate it, rather than inventing their own. In this way, we've imported nifty words like *Schadenfreude* (from German), *déjà vu* (from French), *bozo* (from West African), *robot* (from Czech), *aperitif* (from French), *tsunami* (from Japanese), *pogrom* (from Russian via Yiddish), *bonanza* (from Spanish), and *schlep* (from Yiddish) among many others.

three examples of the word being applied to members of the same basic-level category. So, hearing that both a collie and a terrier could also be called a *zav* would lead children to assume that *zav* could also be used to name a poodle or a Labrador retriever, even though they'd never heard the word applied to those particular kinds of dogs. And, if they'd heard *zav* being used three times *only* in reference to a Dalmatian, they became even more convinced than they'd been at the outset that this word applied only to members within this subordinate-level category.

This study suggests that youngsters don't necessarily match up words with the right categories the first time they hear them, but that they're not set in their ways when it comes to their first hypotheses about word meanings. Instead, they gather evidence that either confirms or disconfirms their preliminary guesses and fine-tune these guesses accordingly. Of course, as outside observers we might never become aware of their internally shifting word meanings unless we specifically choose to test for them.

LANGUAGE AT LARGE 5.1 *(continued)*

Still, many potentially useful words remain unimported from other languages, so numerous wordless gaps remain even in a language as porous as English. Author Howard Rheingold (2000) has collected hundreds of examples in his book *They Have a Word for It*. In it, he offers numerous gems, including the following:

rasa (Sanskrit): The mood or sentiment that is evoked by a work of art

razbliuto (Russian): The feeling a person has for someone he or she once loved but now does not

fucha (Polish): Using company time and resources for your own ends

mokita (Kiriwina, New Guinea): Truth everybody knows but nobody speaks

koro (Chinese): The hysterical belief that one's penis is shrinking

The above examples are easily grasped, and one wonders why English speakers haven't been clever enough to think of them. But some untranslatable words have astonishingly nebulous meanings. This is what the Czech novelist Milan Kundera (1980) says about the Czech word *lítost*:

Lítost is a Czech word with no exact translation into any other language. It designates a feeling as infinite as an open accordion, a feeling that is the synthesis of many others: grief, sympathy, remorse, and an indefinable longing. The first syllable, which is long and stressed, sounds like the wail of an abandoned dog.

Under certain circumstances, however, it can have a very narrow meaning, a meaning as definite, precise, and sharp as a well-honed cutting edge. I have never found an equivalent in other languages for this meaning either, though I do not see how anyone can understand the human soul without it.

There. Clear on the concept of *lítost*? Likely not. Which brings us back to the problem of word learning. How is anyone, child or adult, supposed to arrive at an accurate understanding of a word whose meaning can best be captured as "a feeling as infinite as an open accordion"? How do Czech speakers come to reliably learn its meaning?

In all likelihood, learning such subtle words requires being exposed to many situations in which it is appropriate, and inferring its nuanced meaning from the contexts of its use. In fact, Kundera uses exactly this approach to teach his non-Czech readers the meaning of the word, offering vignettes such as the following:

Let me give an example. One day a student went swimming with his girlfriend. She was a top-notch athlete; he could barely keep afloat. He had trouble holding his breath underwater, and was forced to thrash his way forward, jerking his head back and forth above the surface. The girl was crazy about him and tactfully kept to his speed. But as their swim was coming to an end, she felt the need to give her sporting instincts free rein, and sprinted to the other shore. The student tried to pick up his tempo too, but swallowed many mouthfuls of water. He felt humiliated, exposed for the weakling he was; he felt the resentment, the special sorrow which can only be called *lítost*. He recalled his sickly childhood—no physical exercise, no friends, nothing but Mama's ever-watchful eye—and sank into utter, all-encompassing despair.

Naturally, in order to map meanings onto categories, children need to first carve the world up into the right sorts of categories, which in itself is no small feat. In fact, having immature and still-unstable categories may well explain why kids are less eager than adults to map new words onto basic-level category members. Adults may simply be more certain than young children that collies and terriers *do* fall into the same category as Dalmatians, but that cats and pigs don't.

Cues for forming categories

Clearly, the process of mapping meanings onto words has to go hand-in-hand with the process of forming categories. So how do children learn that bananas belong in a category that excludes oranges? Or that dining room chairs, stools, and recliners all are the same *kind* of thing? Or that their own scribbled attempts at art have more in common with paintings hung in a museum than with splatters on the ground from accidentally spilled paint?

There's no single cue across all these categories that obviously groups category members together. For bananas versus oranges, it might be handy to pay attention to shape. But for different examples of chairs, what really seems to matter is that people sit on them. As for pictures versus accidental paint splatters, what's important is not so much how they look or even how people use them (a picture is still a picture even if someone can wash it off its surface), but whether someone *intended* to create them.

What are the essential properties that bind together the members of a category? The photographs in **Figure 5.4** give you an idea of some of the challenges children face in identifying both the features that category members have in common with each other and the features that distinguish them from members of other categories. While shape seems to be an especially useful cue in the early days of word learning, children as young as age two are able to tune in to all of these cues—shape, function, and the creator's intent—as a way of grouping objects into categories, paving the way for correctly naming a great variety of different categories.

It's easy to see that naming things accurately depends on having the right kinds of categories in place. What may be less obvious is that words themselves can serve as cues to forming categories. That is, just hearing someone name things can help children group these things into categories. An interesting line of research by Sandy Waxman and her colleagues (e.g., Waxman & Markow, 1995) reveals a very early connection in the minds of children between words and categories. The researchers used the following experimental setup: One-year-old babies were shown several objects of the same superordinate-level category (various animals, for instance). In the key experimental condition, all of the objects were named with the same made-up word during a familiarization phase—for example, "Look at the toma! Do you see the toma?" Afterward, the babies were shown either another animal or an object from a completely different superordinate category, such as a truck. The babies tended to be less interested in the new animal than in the truck—as if thinking, "I've already seen one of those—show me something different!" But what was interesting is that the novelty effect of the truck only showed up if all of the animals had been named by the same name. If each animal had been named with a different word, the babies paid as much attention to the new animal as the truck. But using the same word for all of the animals seems to have focused their attention on what the animals all had in common, so when they later saw another one, they were more indifferent to it.

In this version of the study, babies tuned in to the fact that when objects share a common label, this means they can be grouped into a common cate-

APPLE

PRESENT

DRINK

BED

GAME

Figure 5.4 Do all of these images represent category members for the words on the left? Do you have any intuitions about the kinds of features that might be easiest for very young children to attend to?

gory. But the more general expectation that *language* communicates something about categories emerges at the tender age of 3 or 4 months. Alissa Ferry and colleagues (2010) found that after the familiarization phase, these tiny infants paid attention differently to objects of the same category than they did to objects of a completely new category, as the 1-year-olds did in the earlier study. But they did this only when the objects were accompanied by a phrase, such as, "Look at the toma! Do you see the toma?" When the same objects were accompanied by a musical tone instead, the babies didn't seem inclined to group the objects into categories.

Remember: at this age, babies haven't managed to segment words out of the speech stream yet. So it seems that well before they produce their first word, or possibly even pull out their first word-like unit from a torrent of speech, babies have the preconception that words are useful for talking about object categories. Happily, then, infants aren't left to flounder around among all meanings that words might theoretically convey. Once they begin learning the meanings of words, they can rely on certain built-in expectations about which meanings are the best candidates for words.

There's still some debate among researchers about the exact nature of some of these expectations. Are they innate? Are they specifically part of the language faculty? That is, expectations that act as constraints on word learning could amount to default assumptions that specifically link words to certain

BOX 5.2
Word learning in dogs

While Baby is busy learning the word *doggie*, the family dog may well be involved in its own word-learning project. Many a dog owner has boastfully claimed that his canine best friend can recognize many words of English, beyond the usual commands *sit*, *heel*, and *stay*. Research suggests that at least some of these dog owners may be telling the truth.

A number of studies over the past decade have put canine "wordiness" to the scientific test. Some dogs do indeed show evidence of being able to remember hundreds of words for different objects, demonstrating that they're able to retrieve a target object from among ten or more other objects, solely on the basis of the object's name. Dogs have also shown the capacity to learn new words after a single exposure, much as human infants can (Kaminski et al., 2004).

Naturally, this is fodder for those researchers who argue that language—or at least the capacity for fast word learning—is not a uniquely human trait, but one that we share to different degrees with other species. Nevertheless, showing that dogs can learn words doesn't necessarily mean that they get there by means of the same cognitive machinery.

For example, do dogs show the same kinds of word-learning biases that human babies do? One recent study investigated whether dogs, like children, accord special importance to shape as a diagnostic trait of objects that share the same name. This shape bias was first noted in children by Barbara Landau and her colleagues (1988), who demonstrated it as follows: Suppose you show a small child a novel object, saying, "This is a dax." Then you present her with a variety of objects that share features of color, size, texture, or shape with the original object and ask her, "Show me another dax." Does the child generalize to objects that are the same color as the first? The same size? There are a number of possible features to attend to as possible ways of defining the object category. It won't surprise you to learn that, for infants, object shape wins out over the other features. It seems clear that objects that have the same shape are more likely to be the same *kind* of object than those that merely happen to be of the same color or size.

But dogs may not show the same bias, according to a study by Emile van der Zee and colleagues (2012). These researchers studied a border collie named Gable who had solidly learned more than 40 words of English. They presented Gable with a word-learning conundrum similar to the one Landau's team used for children. They found that Gable had a tendency to extend the name *dax* to objects of the same size, ignoring their shape, color, or the other features. But even this was not a stable bias. Gable was allowed to take the "dax" home and play with it for several weeks while being repeatedly exposed to its name. When he was tested again after this period, he preferred to extend the word *dax* to objects that had a similar texture. This study suggests that dogs might have to explore a broader hypothesis space when it comes to generating guesses about the meanings of new words. Unlike children, they might not come into the world with pre-existing notions about how words and meanings are likely to line up.

meanings. Alternatively, they could be side effects of other kinds of cognitive and perceptual mechanisms that tend to organize the world in certain ways. For example, novice word learners often extend names on the basis of the shapes of objects. If they hear someone use the word *zav* to refer to a red ball and then they are asked whether *zav* also refers to an orange or to a red hat, they'll choose the object of the same shape (the orange) over the other object that has the same color as the original *zav* (see, e.g., Landau et al., 1988). Is this because there is a specific word-learning bias that directs them to equate shape with object labels? Or is it simply that they've figured out that shape is a more reliable cue than color for deciding which category the object falls into? (After all, grapes, apples, and shirts all come in different colors, so it's best to pay attention to their shapes in figuring out what kind of objects they are.)

We don't always know why young children make the assumptions they do about the alignment of words and meanings, but it's become clear that at various points in their early word learning, children have a whole repertoire of ways in which to constrain their possible hypotheses about word meanings. Given that the ability to learn words is not limited to humans, it would be interesting to know whether similar constraints apply to word learning in other species (see **Box 5.2**).

5.3 Understanding Speakers' Intentions

Associations versus intentions

So far, we've looked at two aspects of word learning: the sound sequences that are the bearers of meaning, and the things in the world—whether objects or categories of objects—that are linked with these sound sequences. But there's an important dimension we've neglected so far. I've been talking as if words "have" meanings and as if objects or categories "have" names. But of course, it's not that objects *have* names in the same way that they *have* certain shapes, colors, or textures. It's that people *use* certain names to refer to these objects. As discussed in Chapter 2, word meanings are a fundamentally social phenomenon. We link words with objects only because we accept that as members of a particular linguistic community, we've entered into an implicit social agreement to use certain words to describe certain concepts. Linguistic meaning, then, is a social compact within a cultural community—much like our agreement to use paper money with certain markings, or numbers electronically associated with a specific bank account, as proxies for things of value that can be exchanged for other things like food or cars. Our ability to enter into these complex social agreements distinguishes us from other animals and is probably an important prerequisite for language.

As adults, we can recognize that linguistic labels aren't inherently associated with objects or categories, and that they're social constructs rather than properties of the natural world. When we interact with someone, we understand that their use of a word isn't automatically triggered by the presence of a certain object, but rather, that the other person is using the word in the service of some intentional message involving that object. But how prominently does this understanding figure in a child's early word learning? Do very young children have the same understanding of the social underpinnings of language, knowing that names are used by speakers with the intent to refer? And if they do, does this understanding help guide the process of learning what words mean? Or do they simply create associative links between words and objects without being preoccupied by what's in the mind of the speaker who used that word?

associative learning Learning process by which associations between two stimuli are made as ideas and experience reinforce one another.

It takes children quite a while to behave like adults in terms of their ability to fully appreciate the contents of another person's mind. For example, if you've ever played hide-and-seek with a toddler, you probably discovered that he can fall prey to the charming delusion that if he can't see you, *you* can't see *him*—as long as his face and eyes are covered, he may be unconcerned that the rest of his body is in plain view. And, until about the age of four, children have a hard time thoroughly understanding that something that they know could be unknown to another person. (In Chapter 11, we'll explore in more detail some of the ways in which children fail to take the perspective of others.)

Given that babies begin the process of word learning long before they have a completely formed sense of people's states of mind, it could well be the case that their early word learning is of a more simple associative variety, and that it's only over time that they begin to treat language as the social construct that it is, reasoning about speakers' motives and intentions. So, you might think of a child's early word learning as similar to the associations learned by Pavlov's dogs in the famous classical conditioning experiments in which a bell was rung every time dinner was served. The end result was that the dogs eventually began to salivate whenever a bell was rung, even if dinner wasn't forthcoming. It's rather doubtful that the dogs went through a process of reasoning that the bell was intentionally being rung by the human experimenter with the specific purpose of communicating that dinner was on its way. More likely, they just paired the two events— bell ringing and dinner—together in their minds. This kind of simple-minded **associative learning** is well within the learning capacities of animals with far less intelligence than dogs. So it stands to reason that as a learning mechanism, it would be readily available to infants in the early days of vocabulary mastery.

All of which makes it really interesting to consider the experimental results of Dare Baldwin and her colleagues (1996), in which young children *failed* to learn the meanings of words on the basis of paired association between an object and a particular word. In this study, 15- to 20-month-old toddlers were left in a room with a novel object. While they played with it, and were therefore obviously focusing their attention on the object, they heard a disembodied voice intone "Dawnoo! There's a dawnoo!" over a set of loudspeakers. But they didn't end up learning that *dawnoo* was the name for the object they were playing with. Since it's been well documented that kids can learn the meaning of a word after a single exposure, what gives? This seems to be the perfect scenario in which rapt attention to a single object is paired with hearing a single common noun—in other words, just the scenario in which an associative mechanism should produce results in word learning.

The trouble was, the researchers argued, that children *don't* learn words like Pavlov's dogs. Even when they're extremely young, they understand that language is rooted in highly social behavior. And there was nothing in the situation that clearly signaled to the babies that anyone was actually intending to use the word *dawnoo* to refer to that object. Without this evidence, the infants weren't willing to attach the word *dawnoo* to the object right in front of them merely because they heard the name simultaneously with focusing their attention on the object. Essentially, the kids were treating the simultaneous utterance of the word as a coincidence.

In other studies, Dare Baldwin (1993) demonstrated that when there was clear evidence of a speaker's intent to refer, young children were able to map the right word onto an object even if when they heard the word, they were paying attention to a *different* object than the one intended. For instance, in one study, 18-month-old infants played with toys on a tabletop, and while they were absorbed with a toy, the experimenter would utter, "It's a modi!" The infants would look up at the speaker, only to find that *her* attention was focused on a different object, at which point they would direct their own attention to this new object. When later asked to "find the modi," they'd be more likely to choose the thing that the experimenter had been looking at than the toy they themselves had been playing with at the time they'd heard the word.

By 2 years of age, toddlers can put together some pretty subtle clues about a speaker's referential intent in order to figure out what words are likely to mean. In one clever study by Michael Tomasello and Michelle Barton (1994), an experimenter suggested to the child, "Let's find the toma. Where's the toma?" The experimenter then proceeded to look inside five buckets in a row. For all but one of the buckets, he lifted an object out of the bucket, scowled, and put it back. One object elicited an excited "Ah!" before the experimenter put it back inside its bucket. For the most part, children guessed that *toma* referred to the object that seemed to satisfy the experimenter. In fact, when children's word learning in this condition was compared with a different condition in which the experimenter showed only one object to the child while uttering a satisfied "Ah," there was no difference in performance. The children had no trouble rejecting the other objects as possible referents, based solely on the reactions of the experimenter.

These studies show that very young children routinely fail to learn word/meaning pairs when they have reason to doubt that these pairings are intended by the speaker. Tots also look askance at word/meaning pairs that are produced by speakers who obviously intend them but whose labeling behavior has been demonstrably bizarre in the past. For instance, Melissa Koenig and Amanda Woodward (2010) had 2-year-olds interact with speakers who labeled various familiar objects. When a speaker named three familiar objects inaccurately (for example, calling a shoe a "duck"), the children were more reluctant to learn a new word (for example, *blicket*) that he applied to a novel object than when the speaker behaved normally, giving all the familiar objects their conventional names.

This body of works clearly establishes that even at a very young age, small kids don't just link words together with objects that happen to be in their attention when they hear the word. But associative learning mechanisms are extremely powerful, and it seems far-fetched that children would be totally unable or unwilling to use them in the process of learning the meanings of words. What's more plausible is that on their own, associations are taken to be weakish evidence of word meanings, as compared with witnessing direct evidence of referential intent by a speaker who's abiding by normal linguistic conventions (see **Method 5.1**). Barring clear signs of the speaker's intent, children may need to hear multiple pairings before settling on the meaning of a word, or they may have a much more fragile memory trace of the word. And, solid evidence of a competent speaker's intent may trump associative processes when the two are in conflict.

This story would suggest that words could still be learned to some extent if, for some reason, kids didn't have a deep appreciation of the fact that words are used by speakers to satisfy a communicative goal, or if they lacked the ability to make inferences about what those goals are. And this seems to be largely true for children with **autism spectrum disorder** (**ASD**), a neurological condition that impairs the ability to coordinate attention with another person, or to make inferences about someone else's state of mind. Autism researcher Simon Baron-Cohen teamed up with Dare Baldwin and Mary Crowson (1997) to replicate Baldwin's experiments in which the speaker uttered a word while looking at a different object than the one the child was gazing at. The researchers found dramatically different results between typical kids and kids with autism. The children with autism did end up mapping novel words onto

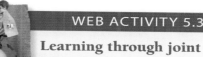

WEB ACTIVITY 5.3

Learning through joint attention In this activity, you'll watch video clips of how babies typically learn language "in the wild." Notice how both the child and adult are involved in establishing joint attention during the interaction.

autism spectrum disorder (ASD) A neurological condition that impairs the ability to coordinate attention with another person, or to make inferences about someone else's state of mind.

METHOD 5.1

Revisiting the switch task

In Section 5.1, I introduced the switch task as a method that's useful for studying how children map novel words onto novel objects. Researchers who use this method usually assume that it can tell us something interesting about how children learn the names for objects, that to some extent it simulates what kids are doing when they learn new words in the real world. But let's revisit that technique in light of what you've just learned about how important it is for children to have some clear evidence that the speaker actually *meant* to refer to an object before they attach the word to it.

In the switch task, children see images on a screen paired with recorded words that are played over a speaker. This is very unlike the studies by Dare Baldwin and her colleagues, where babies were able to look for clues about a speaker's referential intent; the switch setup as I've described it doesn't really provide any such clues. This raises the concern: Are we really creating a realistic word-learning scene when we use this technique? Are kids approaching the mapping task in the switch paradigm in the same way as they'd approach a normal word-learning situation?

Some researchers have argued that because of the lack of clear cues about referential intent, the task typically underestimates children's ability to map new sound sequences to new meanings. There are ways, though, to bolster these cues within the experimental setup, even though the babies aren't interacting with a living, breathing communicative partner.

Chris Fennell and Sandy Waxman (2010) tweaked the switch task to make the communicative purpose of the novel words a bit more transparent. They did this by first having a training phase in which babies saw very familiar objects (for example, a car or a cat) accompanied by their familiar names: "Car!" "Kitty!" This was intended to make it clear to the child that the whole point of the recorded voice was to name the objects in the display. The researchers compared this scenario with one in which the sounds that accompanied the familiar objects were clearly not being used to label the objects: in these conditions, instead of hearing the names of the objects, the babies heard expressions like "Wow!" or "Whee!" This training phase was followed by the standard habituation phase, in which

babies heard a novel name (for example, *bin*) paired with a novel object. Finally, there was the usual test phase, with babies seeing the novel object while hearing either the same novel word (*bin*) again in "no-switch" trials, or either a very similar word (*din*) or a very different word (*neem*) in "switch" trials (see Figure 5.1).

When the communicative purpose of the speech was highlighted, 14-month-old babies were more eager to map the novel words onto the objects they'd seen; that is, they were more likely to distinguish between the original word and a different one in the test phase, as shown by longer looking times in "switch" trials than "no-switch" trials. Especially interesting was the fact that the babies were distinguishing between the "switch" and "no-switch" trials even when there was a very subtle phonetic difference between the two words (for example, *bin/din*). Remember that previous studies had shown that at 14 months, babies failed to attend to these fine differences in sound, leading some researchers to propose that early word learning relies on very coarse representations of sound. But the study by Fennell and Waxman suggests that the failure might simply have reflected an uncertainty about whether the novel words were supposed to be understood as names for the objects, possibly leading to a more tentative link between sound and meaning.

Fennell and Waxman found that the referential intent behind the novel words could also be ramped up if the words were embedded within phrases like "There's the *bin*. Do you see the *bin*? Look at the *bin*." Here, the sentence frame provides some clues that the novel word is being used to refer to a specific object.

The study adds some new information to the debate I introduced in Section 5.1, about how babies connect meanings up with sounds. But it also provides a much more general lesson: It's important to look closely at any task that assumes to be tapping into how children learn new words. What assumptions is the task making about how kids map words onto meanings? Is it assuming a purely associative mechanism? Or is it sensitive to the fact that referential intent plays an important role in the whole process? Any method that fails to incorporate this crucial piece may not provide a complete reflection of how words are normally learned.

object referents—but they mostly assumed that the word referred to the object that they themselves were looking at, rather than the one the experimenter was looking at. It's easy to see how a failure to check what the speaker meant to be talking about could lead to some instability in word meanings. For example, if you happened to be looking at a duck the first time you heard someone say, "Look at the bicycle"; at the lint between your toes the second time you hear the word *bicycle*; and then, finally, at the correct object the third time, you would have some serious confusion sorting out the meaning of *bicycle*. It's not surprising, then, that many children with ASD have some significant language impairment. Evidence of speaker intent can serve as a powerful filter on the range of possible word meanings.

Mutual exclusivity

Here's another example of a possible constraint on word meaning. One of these objects is called a "dopaflexinator." Can you guess which one?

A 3-year-old would be inclined to agree with you (assuming you chose the object on the right). But why? It seems obvious: the object on the left is called a "hammer," so there's only one other candidate for the novel word. If your reasoning went something like this, it hints at a general bias to line up object categories and linguistic labels in a one-to-one correspondence. This expectation has been called the **mutual exclusivity bias**.

It's possible to take mutual exclusivity too far, of course. *Hammer* isn't the only word you could use to describe the object on the left. You could also, under various conditions, call it a "tool," a "piece of hardware," a "weapon," a "thing-amajig," an "artifact," or simply an "object." But given that *hammer* is by far the most common way to refer to it, the mutual exclusivity bias might be a useful way for a small child to zoom in on the likely referent for a word she doesn't know yet, especially when the new word is spoken in the context of many objects whose names she *does* know.

It's worth asking, though, whether you and the 3-year-old are in fact arriving at the same conclusion by means of the same thought processes. Do you really have the expectation of a one-to-one correspondence between object categories and labels? You likely know that the hammer can be described by a number of different words and that under different circumstances, it might be most natural to call it a "tool" or a "weapon." But you also have the sense that *hammer* is the most natural word to use in this particular circumstance, so you assume that because I didn't use this word, I must have referred to the other thing. That is, it's not that you've eliminated the possibility that the hammer could have another name, but that you have a theory about how I'd be most likely to refer to this object in this instance. You're not just responding to your knowledge of associations between words and meanings, but relying on a set of expectations about how a typical language user would communicate in a specific situation.

What about small children? Do they also have a theory about the behavior of typical speakers, allowing them to predict which word a speaker is most likely

mutual exclusivity bias A general bias to line up object categories and linguistic labels in a one-to-one correspondence.

to use in referring to the object? Or is their naming bias coming from a more rigid guiding constraint that prevents them from mapping more than one label onto any one object? (Notice that children eventually would have to relax such a constraint, or they'd never learn to flexibly refer to the same object with a number of different names, depending on the context.)

This issue is still being debated in the literature, but one way to test it would be to see whether children with autism make the assumption that a previously unheard name can't apply to objects whose names are already known. If they do, then the naming bias probably doesn't originate entirely from inferences about speaker intent, since one of the hallmarks of autism is that inferences of this variety are often impaired. So far, the evidence suggests that kids with autism also apply mutual exclusivity, as shown by Melissa Preissler and Sue Carey (2005). In fact, the children in that study relied on mutual exclusivity even though, in a separate test, they had striking difficulties in using the eye

LANGUAGE AT LARGE 5.2

Learning language from machines

The evidence pointing to the important social aspects that guide word learning suggests that plunking children down in front of the TV is probably not the best way to help them to learn language—even though there's lots of information in the signal, the cues about referential intent are sorely lacking. Interacting with other humans (or, at the very least, watching other humans interacting with each other) seems to be fairly important to the process of learning about language meaning.

But more and more, we live in a world where many of our interactions that used to involve humans are taking place with machines instead—often machines that are programmed to act like humans in many respects: we book airline tickets by talking to a computer-generated ticket agent, and we access our bank accounts though automated bank machines or Internet-based programs instead of interacting with human tellers.

As adults, we seem surprisingly willing to treat our machines as if they had human desires and goals—I once heard someone state that her word processor "had it in" for her. This eagerness to attribute human-like qualities to

machines underlies the success of computer programs for simple interactions like checking out your groceries, or of artificial conversational agents called "chat bots." Chat bots have little in the way of humanoid intelligence—for example, the earliest one, ELIZA, was programmed to respond to any human-uttered sentence containing the word *mother* with a sympathetic *Tell me about your family*. But users of these programs can easily be fooled that they're interacting with a human agent, presumably because they are so willing to project human-like goals and communicative intentions (see the table for a snippet of conversation with a chat bot). It turns out that even when we *know* we're interacting with a machine, we treat them as we might a human—for instance, people routinely apologize to computer-generated voices, knowing full well they are not real people.

All of this raises an interesting question in light of our discussion of word learning: Would young children be willing to attribute referential intent to robots? And would doing so allow them to learn new words from robots?

A clever study by Laura O'Connell and her colleagues (2009) set out to find out whether 18-month-olds would assume that, like humans, robots are likely to be referring to objects that they aim their (mechanical) eyeballs at. Using an experimental setup similar to the one used by Baldwin (1993), the researchers had a robot use a new label (for example, *dax*) for one of two novel objects while varying which of the two objects it was "looking" at when it uttered the word (using a recorded human voice). As when listening to human speakers, the babies checked out the eye gaze of the robot, and spent more time looking at the

WEB ACTIVITY 5.4

Robots versus humans In this activity, you'll explore conversations with chat bots and discuss the ways in which they behave like human speakers, and the ways in which their behavior violates expectations about how humans communicate with each other.

gaze of a speaker to figure out the object of referential intent. This makes it seem unlikely that their responses on the mutual exclusivity test were based on getting inside the head of the speaker, rather than applying a simple mapping constraint. Thus, even though children with autism might be missing some important ways to constrain hypotheses about word meanings based on speaker intent, it seems that they can still benefit from the assumption that object categories have a single label attached to them. By the way, this assumption may be shared by dogs who learn new words: a clever border collie named Rico was able to infer that a novel name applied to an object whose name he didn't already know (Kaminski, Call, and Fisher, 2004).

On the other hand, some studies of typical kids suggest that this assumption is suspended when it conflicts with probable speaker intent. For example, in a study led by David Sobel (2012), when a speaker previously referred to known objects with either the wrong name (calling an apple a "shoe") or a novel name (calling an apple a "blicket"), preschoolers seemed more inclined to assume he

---

LANGUAGE AT LARGE 5.2 *(continued)*

Chat bot chatter

Here's a conversation I had with Jabberwock, a chat bot. Can you tell which is the human and which is the bot?

How are you?

Great. How are you?

Coolio. How's your boyfriend?

I don't have a boyfriend.

I thought you said you did. Aren't you lonely?

Not really.

Really?

I like spending time alone.

Why do you like spending time alone?

It's just the way I'm built.

How are you drawn?

Actually, I'm a live person. Flesh and blood and all that.

I am a human and you are a bot.

I hesitate to correct you, but you are wrong.

No. You are wrong.

Never mind. How's your girlfriend?

I don't have one.

strongly enough to actually learn the word. Nor did it help matters any if the children first watched the experimenter and the robot chatting briefly. The babies still weren't willing to see the robots as fully communicative beings (or possibly, they weren't willing to buy into the idea that the robot belonged to the same linguistic community that they did). A later study by Yusuke Moriguchi and colleagues (2011) found similar results with older kids. Four-year-olds were completely unwilling to learn a new word from a robot, while some 5-year-olds did learn new words from a robot, but not as many as they did from a human speaker.

There's still a lot that we don't know about the nature of human interactions with intelligent machines, so it's hard to know what it would take to get children to learn language from robots as if they were human conversational partners. Perhaps there are subtle clues other than eye gaze that we humans give to infants that increase their confidence in our purposeful use of language. Perhaps it's about in-group status. Maybe babies treat all outsiders with some suspicion, not quite willing to treat them as reliable speakers of the same language, whether it's because they dress differently, belong to a different ethnic group, or are made out of metal parts. Or maybe children need to develop a more nuanced theory of how robots work—they're not alive, but they *are* intelligent and can implement programs that are purposeful and reliably consistent.

As we get a better handle on some of these questions, at some point it may become possible to create robots that serve as good language teachers for small children. But for the time being, parents and caregivers are not obsolete in this role.

object that was seemingly holding the robot's attention. But they failed to learn the word from the robot—when they were later asked by a human which object was a dax, they performed randomly. So, while they were clearly able to follow the robot's eye gaze, it seems they didn't take the extra step of attributing referential intent—at least not was using a novel name like *modi* to refer to a familiar object such as a cup, even though this object already had a perfectly serviceable name. In this scenario, it seems, they were able to clue in to the fact that the speaker was behaving unusually; hence one should be prepared to hear him use unusual words for familiar objects.

Associations can be useful. But in the messy, chaotic world of language learning, it might take quite some time and cognitive power to separate the accurate word/meaning associations from the spurious ones—even with the help of word-mapping biases or constraints. Fortunately, it seems that young kids are able to lean quite heavily on their understanding of the purposeful, socially grounded nature of language, and that this gives them a tremendous leg up in figuring out the intended meanings of words.

5.4 Parts of Speech

Verbs and other learning problems

Reading the previous sections of this chapter, a person could easily be led to believe that learning the meanings of words essentially boils down to learning all the object categories that happen to have names. But, much as we like to talk about categories of objects, language also has a healthy assortment of words that have very different kinds of meanings. For instance, how many words in the following sentence actually map onto an object category?

Mommy will cook some tasty porridge in a pot.

The answer is: one. The word *pot* is a well-behaved basic-level category term. But *Mommy* refers to a specific individual, not a category; *cook* denotes an action; *porridge* picks out some stuff, rather than a whole object; *tasty* refers to a property; and *in* signals a spatial relationship. Not to mention nebulous words like *will*, *some*, and *a*, which don't easily map onto anything in the world at all but communicate much more abstract notions.

Word-learning biases that youngsters exploit often seem best geared to learning the kinds of notions that are captured by common nouns like *pot*. And in fact, nouns make up the lion's share of the early vocabulary of toddlers across a variety of different cultures and languages. But how would a small child go about learning all the other kinds of words?

The problem is especially acute for those words whose meanings are not transparent from the immediate context. Verbs in particular seem to pose some prickly challenges. Imagine being a child at your own birthday party and hearing your parent say, "Look! Grandma brought you a present! Why don't you open your present? Here, let me help you." If you didn't already know what *brought*, *open*, and *help* mean, it would be a bit tricky to figure it out just from this context. *Brought* refers to something that happened in the past, rather than the here and now; no act of opening has happened yet; and even if your parent is in the act of helping while uttering the word *help*, how do you know that the word isn't referring to a much more specific kind of action, such as handing or holding something, or getting scissors or undoing tape?

A study led by Jane Gillette (1999) starkly demonstrates the difficulties of learning verbs from non-linguistic context. The researchers tested college undergraduates' ability to infer the meanings of words from the visual context, reasoning that college students should be at least as good at the task as your average toddler. They tested the students' ability to guess the meanings of nouns and verbs based on a series of video clips of parents interacting with their toddlers while manipulating objects and talking about them. The sound had been removed from the video clips, but a beep indicated where in the speech stream a target word had appeared. The videos contained the 24 most frequent nouns and verbs that the parents had used in interacting with their children—words like *ball, hat, put,* and *stand* rather than unfairly difficult words like *predator* or *contemplate*. For each target word, the students saw six different videos and had to guess which word had been used in each of the six videos, the idea being that they should be able to notice what all six videos had in common and figure out the meaning of the target word accordingly.

It doesn't sound like it should be an onerous task, especially for intelligent adults endowed with full conceptual knowledge of the world. And when it came to the nouns, the students did reasonably well, guessing correctly 45% of the words. But their performance on verbs was fairly dismal, at a mere 15%. Some common words like *love, make,* or *think* were never guessed correctly.

What was missing from these videos was the *linguistic* context that accompanied the words. And this turns out to be especially informative when it comes to identifying the meanings of verbs.

First of all, most verbs come with handy suffixes attached that let you know that they *are* verbs—as in *licking, kicked,* and *pushes*. This might give you a clue that the word probably depicts an action rather than an object or a property. But more than this, the sentence frame also provides some important information. Think about the events being described by each of the following sentences:

> Sarah is glorping.
>
> Sarah is glorping Ben.
>
> Sarah glorped the ball from Ben.
>
> Sarah glorped Cindy to Ben.
>
> Sarah will glorp to Toronto.

The different sentence frames dramatically constrain the meaning of the word *glorp*. This is because verbs come specified for **argument structures**: syntactic frames that provide information about how many objects or participants are involved in each event, and what kind of objects or participants are involved. For instance, an **intransitive verb** such as *sleep* or *sneeze* has only one participant ("Sarah is glorping"). A **transitive verb** such as *kick* has two—the actor, and the object of the action "Sarah is glorping Ben"). And a **ditransitive verb** such as *take* involves three participants—the actor, the object, and a third participant, typically introduced by a preposition ("Sarah glorped the ball from Ben"). So you can infer something about the kind of verb you're dealing with just by noticing how many noun phrases surround it, and you can tell even more by the nature of those noun phrases. In the example above, you can tell that *glorp to Toronto* probably involves some kind of verb of motion.

Children use syntax to constrain meaning

Having access to the syntactic context of a new word would make the word-learning task much less daunting. The question is: Can very small children benefit from this potentially useful information?

The answer appears to be yes. For example, Letitia Naigles (1990) showed 2-year-olds videos in which a duck repeatedly pushed a rabbit into a bending position while both the duck and rabbit waved their arms around. The videos were intentionally designed to include two salient actions: arm waving and pushing. Some children heard the video described as "the duck is gorping the bunny."

WEB ACTIVITY 5.5

Context as a clue to word meaning In this activity, you'll generate guesses about the meanings of nonsense words, based solely on their linguistic contexts. Which aspects of context provide the strongest constraints?

argument structures Syntactic frames that provide information about how many objects or participants are involved in each event, and what kind of objects or participants are involved.

intransitive verb A verb with only one participant; e.g., *sneeze*.

transitive verb A verb with two participants: an actor (the subject) and the object of the action; e.g., *kick*.

ditransitive verb A verb with three participants. In English, the third participant (the indirect object) is usually introduced by a preposition.

Figure 5.5 Visual stimuli accompanying Gelman and Markman's novel word-learning test. When children were asked, "Show me the fep one," they were most likely to choose the object in the upper right corner. When asked, "Show me the fep," they were most likely to pick the one in the lower left. (From Gelman and Markman, 1985.)

Others heard "the duck and the bunny are gorping." Both groups were then shown two new videos—one of the duck and rabbit waving their arms, with no pushing, and the other with the duck pushing the rabbit, but no arm waving. They were asked, "Find gorping." The toddlers looked longer at the pushing scene when *gorp* had occurred as a transitive verb (*The duck is gorping the bunny*). But when they'd previously heard an intransitive frame (*The duck and the bunny are gorping*), they looked longer at the arm-waving scene. These differences suggest they had interpreted the meaning of the verb from its linguistic context.

Verbs are especially rich in syntactic information, but other categories of words also come with useful markers that can help narrow down their meanings. For instance, take the nonsense sentence *Dobby will fep some daxy modi in the nazzer*. There's a lot you can infer about the made-up words in this sentence based on syntactic cues alone. You know that *Dobby* is the name of someone or something specific; you know that *fep* is likely an action; that *daxy* probably refers to a property of *modi*; that *modi* is a substance, rather than an object; and that *nazzer* refers to a category of object.

Babies begin to pay attention to these cues quite early in their word-learning careers. For example, in Section 5.2, we found that 3- to 4-month-olds form categories more readily when pictures are accompanied by language than by musical tones. At that age, the instinct to categorize seems to be triggered by *any* kind of linguistic material, regardless of its content. But by 13 or 14 months of age, they begin to expect that words that appear to have the shape of nouns ("These are blickets") but not words that sound like adjectives ("These are blickish") are used to refer to categories (Booth & Waxman, 2009). By 2 years of age, they can differentiate between common nouns ("This is a zav") and proper names ("This is Zav") based on their syntax alone, knowing that proper names refer to specific individuals while common nouns refer to kinds of objects or individuals (Katz et al., 1974). Around the same age, when seeing a substance piled up on the table, children assume that if a speaker uses a mass noun to describe it ("This is some fep"), she's referring to the substance, but if she uses a count noun ("This is a fep"), she's talking about the pile itself (Soja, 1992). By 3 or 4 years of age, kids infer that adjectives are used to communicate properties of objects; they are especially good at recognizing adjectives that highlight some sort of contrast between objects—for example, a word used to distinguish a large object from a smaller one of the same kind (Gelman & Markman, 1985; see **Figure 5.5**).

It's clear, then, that the syntactic identities of words can help children narrow in on those aspects of meaning that the words are likely to convey, a phenomenon known as **syntactic bootstrapping**. Of course, this raises the question of how kids learn about syntactic categories in the first place, an issue we'll take up in the next chapter.

5.5 Words: Some Assembly Required

The smallest units of meaning

I've talked a fair bit about how the expressive power of language rests on its combinatorial properties. If you simply memorized whole *sentences* as having complex meanings, without thinking of them as being composed of separate meaningful pieces, you wouldn't get very far in creating and understanding new sentences that express unfamiliar ideas. So far, I've been talking about words as if they were the Lego blocks of language—the smallest meaningful parts that speakers can snap together in an endless array of new structures. But this isn't completely correct. Some words are made up of more than one piece of meaning and can be broken down into smaller blocks themselves.

syntactic bootstrapping Using the syntactic properties of words to identify and narrow in on those aspects of meaning that words are likely to convey.

We would be missing something if we thought of each of the words in **Table 5.1** as solid pieces that can't be split apart into smaller meaningful units. All of them are made of at least two parts whose meanings contribute something to the meaning of the whole (and three and four parts, respectively, in the case of un-chewable and lifeboat salesgirl). When you get down to the pieces that can't be broken down any further, you're dealing with **morphemes**— the smallest bundles of sound that can be related to some systematic meaning. It's obvious, for example, that housewife has something to do with houses and something to do with wives, but if you take just a part of the morpheme house—say, hou—it's also obvious that this set of sounds doesn't contribute anything specific to the meaning of the word as a whole.

Many words, like *rabbit* or *red*, are made up of a single morpheme, so it's been convenient to talk about words as the smallest units of meaning. But it's quite possible to stack morphemes up on top of one another to create towering verbal confections such as:

antidisestablishmentarianism position announcement

You may be wondering why I'm treating *lifeboat salesgirl* or *antidisestablishmentarianism position announcement* as single words when anyone can see that there are spaces that separate some of the morphemes. And obviously, units like *lifeboat, announcement* and *antidisestablishmentarianism* can and often do stand alone as separate words without having to lean on the other morphemes that make up the more complex compounds in the examples above. But, despite the writing conventions, it makes sense to think of the complex compounds as words rather than phrases. To see this, you have to look at how these particular compound nouns behave in the presence of other bits of language surrounding them. It then becomes clear that they pattern much like simple words such as *cat* or *rabbit*. For example, just like simple nouns, these complex nouns can follow the definite article *the,* and be preceded by an adjective like *nervous* or *unexpected.* And watch what happens when we slap the plural morpheme *-s* onto this unlikely collection of words:

cat-s

lifeboat salesgirl-s

antidisestablishmentarianism position announcement-s

Here are some things you *can't* do with the plural (the asterisk is conventionally used to show that certain forms are unacceptable to speakers of a given language):

*lifeboat-s salesgirl

*antidisestablishmentarianism-s position announcement

*antidisestablishmentarianism position-s announcement

Why can't you do this? As it turns out, you can only attach the plural morpheme to the end of something that is a *word* in its own right. But isn't *lifeboat* a word? It can be, when it appears in a context like *Each of the lifeboats sprung a leak*—in which case no one bats an eye when it sports a plural morpheme. But in *lifeboat salesgirl,* it has forfeited its word-hood to become merely one part of a larger word—much as separate atoms can be joined together to form complex molecules.

Table 5.1 Some uses of multiple morphemes

(A) Compounding	(B) Derivational affixes	(C) Inflectional affixes[a]
housewife	preview	drinking
blue-blood	un-chewable	kicked
girlfriend	owner	cats
lifeboat salesgirl	redness	eats

[a]In English, only suffixes are inflectional, there are no inflectional prefixes (see p. 172).

morphemes The smallest bundles of sound that can be related to some systematic meaning.

What makes something a word, then, is not so much whether it maps onto a stable meaning—that is a property of morphemes. Rather, what makes something a word is that when you start building structures out of linguistic units, it can be slotted into those particular spaces that are reserved for words. That is, when you start snapping units together, pieces like *lifeboat salesgirl* and *rabbit* can fit into the same slots, joining up with the same kinds of other pieces. (More on this idea in the next chapter.)

So rather than saying that children learn the meanings of words, it would be more accurate to say that children have to learn the meanings of *morphemes*—whether these stand alone as words or whether they get joined together. And, when it comes to learning *words*, a lot of what's involved is distinguishing which words are in turn assembled out of morphemes.

Word-building options

In English, there are three main options for building complex words out of multiple morphemes. The first of these involves **compounding**, as illustrated in the examples under (A) in Table 5.1. The process is essentially to glue together two independent words (for example, *house* and *wife*) into one unit so that the new unit acts as a single word.

The complex words in parts (B) and (C) of the table are built with the use of **affixes**—that is, linguistic units that can't stand on their own but have predictable meanings when attached to a stem morpheme such as *own*, *pink*, or *cat*. In English we're limited to **prefixes** that attach at the front end of a word (such as *un-*), and **suffixes** (like *-able* and *-ed*) that go on the back end. Some languages, rather exotically, can shoehorn **infixes** right into the middle of a stem morpheme. For example, in English, we express the infinitive form of a verb like *write* by adding the word *to*, as in *She wants **to** write*. But in Tagalog, to express the infinitive form, you split your verb stem for *write*, which is *sulat*, and you wind up with the two parts of the word straddling the infix *-um-*: *sumulat*. Likewise, *bili* ("buy") becomes *bumili* ("to buy").

Although both (B) and (C) in Table 5.1 show examples of forming new words through affixation, there are some important differences. The affixes in (B) are called **derivational affixes**, while those in (C) are given the name **inflectional affixes**. You might have noticed that attaching a derivational affix to the stems in (B) often involves not just altering some aspect of meaning, but also transforming a word of one category into a word of a different category. For example, the verb *own* becomes the noun *owner*, and the adjective *sad* becomes the noun *sadness*. Often, transforming the grammatical category of a concept is a derivational morpheme's entire reason for being, as in the following examples:

nation-al	femin-ism	fus-ion
national-ize	man-hood	sens-ation
dual-ity	child-ish	warm-ly
clear-ance	sens-ory	son-ic
syllab-ify	cooperat-ive	acre-age

Having such suffixes on hand can be quite convenient. It would seem a shame to have to coin a brand new morpheme—let's say, *flug*—to express the concept of doing something "in a warm manner." Derivational morphemes like *warmly* do a wonderful job of efficiently building a new vocabulary on the foundations of an existing one, while keeping the connections between related words nice and transparent.

compounding Gluing together two independent words into one unit so that the new unit acts as a single word.

affixes Linguistic units that can't stand on their own but have predictable meanings when attached to a *stem morpheme* such as *own*, *pink* or *cat*.

prefixes Affixes attached at the front end of a word; e.g., *un-*; *pre-*.

suffixes Affixes attached at the end of a word; e.g., *-able*; *-ed*; *-ing*.

infixes Affixes "shoehorned" into the middle of a word (not found in English).

derivational affixes Affixes that transform a word of one category into a word of a different category or significantly change the meaning of the word; e.g., the affix *-er* turning the verb *own* into the noun *owner*, or the affix *pre-* changing the meaning of the word *view* (whether either *view* or *preview* is used as a noun or verb).

inflectional affixes Affixes that serve as grammatical reflexes or markers, the presence of which is dictated by the grammatical rules of a language; e.g., in English the affixes *-ed* and *-ing* change the tense of a verb. (Note that in English only suffixes are inflectional affixes.)

Inflectional affixes (actually, in English, we only have inflectional *suffixes*) have a different flavor. Their job is not so much to create new words by mooching off existing ones. Rather, you might think of them as grammatical reflexes or markers. For example, you can't say *I ate three juicy pear* or *The pear are ripe*; you have to say *I ate three juicy pears* or *The pears are ripe* because the noun has to bear the right marker for number (plural versus singular) and agree with other elements in the sentence (see **Box 5.3**). The presence of such markers is dictated by the grammatical rules of a language. In English, the requirements on such markers are few—number marking, for example, only needs to appear on the noun itself. In some other languages, the marker also has to turn up on the

BOX 5.3
The structure inside words

The morphemes that make up a word can't be strung together in just any order. For example, there's only one way to arrange this fistful of morphemes:

-s; re-; -ation; -al; nation; -ize

The *only* possibility is *re-nation-al-ize-ation-s*. You can't have *re-nation-ation-al-ize-s* or *re-nation-s-ize-ation-al*, and certainly not *al-ize-ation-re-s-nation*, which is utter morpheme soup. But it's not just the linear order that needs to be learned by kids who are deconstructing words into their parts. Multi-morphemic words also have intricate *internal* structure. This has to do with the fact that affixes come with constraints, not just in terms of whether they're attached to the front or the back of the stem, but also in terms of what *categories* of words they can attach to. For example, the word *renationalizations* has the following structure:

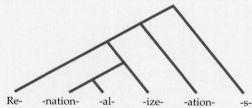

Re-   -nation-   -al-   -ize-   -ation-   -s-

How do we know? Well, we know that *re-* can't attach to the unaltered stem *nation*, because *nation* is a noun, and *re-* needs to attach to a verb stem (so, we can get *re-draw* or *re-group*, but not *re-desk* or *re-beauty*). However, *-al* does attach to nouns, as in *front-al* or *autumn-al*. Since the resulting *national* is an adjective and not a verb, and hence not available for *re-* to attach to, the next affix to glom on must be *-ize*, which can hitch onto a select group of adjectives (for example, *lexical-ize*, *legal-ize*, and *metallic-ize*), though it somewhat more productively attaches to

nouns (*bastard-ize, demon-ize, woman-ize, burglar-ize*). Since we now have the verb *nationalize*, we can finally attach *re-* to it (whereas if we had attached *-ation* to it at this point, we would have turned it into a noun, rendering it ineligible to be joined with *re-*). To cap the word off, we add *-ation* to the verb *renationalize* to make it the noun *renationalization*, which now allows the plural marker *-s* as the final flourish. (As the lone inflectional suffix among a bevy of derivational suffixes, *-s* has to occur at the very end of the word: remember the impossibility of compound words like **lifeboats salesgirl*.)

As far as we know, kids don't seem to make mistakes in which they combine morphemes in the wrong order, attaching affixes to words that they're incompatible with. Many of these complex words involving derivational morphemes are likely stored as wholes in memory. However, at some point, children must catch on to the patterns and structure inherent in word formation, much as they catch on to generalizations about phonotactic structure, which governs the possible *sound* structure of words. Without these generalizations in place, they would never come to know that a word like *sugar-ize*, though fanciful, is not beyond the pale, whereas jumbles like *bnanpt* or *speak-ize* are non-starters.

WEB ACTIVITY 5.6

Structures for words In this activity, you'll recruit arguments like the one given here for *renationalizations* and propose an internal structure for a variety of complex words.

case Grammatical markers that signal the grammatical role (subject, direct object, indirect object, etc.) of a noun within a given sentence.

adjective and even the definite or indefinite article. Consider Spanish: *the juicy pears* are *las peras jugosas,* and to eliminate any one of the three plural markers would be as ungrammatical as saying *three pear* in English.

In English, we have a fairly paltry set of inflectional morphemes, limited to plural markers on nouns and three types of markers on verbs:

1. The present progressive suffix -*ing* (*walking*)

2. The past-tense suffix -*ed* (*walked*)

3. The marker -*s* to signal the third person present tense (*I walk,* but *he walks*)

But some languages systematically mark not only person and number on many words, but also encode notions such as **case,** which signal what role a noun is involved in—that is, the noun stems (and often adjectives and articles) will have different endings depending on whether they're part of the subject, direct object, indirect object, and so on. There can be different forms for each of these case endings (typically bearing labels such as *nominative, accusative, dative,* etc.) depending on the specific noun involved; this has led to some remarkably complex morphological systems.

For example, if you undertake to learn a language like Czech, be prepared to cope with shape-shifting words. The following language instruction excerpt, from "Introduction to Studying Czech Language" at Bohemica.com, tries to give a sense of the system while cushioning the shock (I suspect, unsuccessfully) for the new learner:

Which Czech words change their form and when?

The short and slightly depressing answer is: "Most words in Czech change their form most of the time." All nouns, adjectives, pronouns, and numerals change their forms according to case, gender, and number. There are seven cases but they have different endings for singular and plural so in fact there are fourteen. However, not all the cases have separate endings.

How many endings does Czech have?

All in all, a lot but you will see that it is not so bad. Theoretically, for nouns there could be 196 different endings (14 different functions—6 + 1 cases in singular and 6 + 1 in plural—times 14 different models). In fact, there are only 24 different endings: -a, -e/ě, -i, -o, -u, -y; -ou; -é, -í, -ů; -ech, -ách, -ích; -em, -ám, -ím, -ům; -mi; -ami, -emi, -ími; -ovi, -ové, and 0 (nothing is also considered an ending).

There are some more endings for adjectives but no more than ten. Overall, there are less than 40 endings for all nouns, adjectives, pronouns and numerals which is not much at all.

Then, there are about a dozen endings used for other purposes, and that's about it. Apparently, Czech, the language of endings, makes do with about 60 different endings altogether.

Learners of Czech who are inclined to complain should bite their tongues; if they were learning Greenlandic, they'd need to learn 318 inflectional affixes and more than 400 derivational morphemes.

The upshot of all this is that although in English bare stems like *eat, water,* and *red* occur on their own as words a great deal of the time, this is not the case for some languages, where a stem can never be stripped of its inflectional morphemes. In these languages, the hypothetical *gavagai* could never refer to just one meaning unit. Obviously, in languages like these, the sense of what a word is can be quite different, and children have to learn to decompose many words into their component parts. But in fact this seems to be done with impressive ease. For example, Turkish nouns may have a plural and/or a possessive marker, and they *must* be tagged with a case marker. Meanwhile, Turkish verbs never show up without a full morphological regalia of three suffixes marking tense, number, and person (among other things). Yet in Turkish-speaking children, the whole system is pretty much mastered and error-free by the time they are 2 years of age (Aksu-Koc & Slobin, 1985). And, while the first word of a baby growing up in an English-speaking household almost always consists of a single morpheme, that's not true for Turkish children, whose earliest words already snap inflectional morphemes onto the stem.

WEB ACTIVITY 5.7

Complex words across languages In this activity, you'll get a taste of how children growing up with a language like Czech or Turkish would have to learn to excavate the stem morpheme from what is frequently a pile of affixes attached to it.

The fact that words often contain more than one morpheme suggests that there may be more to word learning than just connecting up sound sequences with their associated meanings. Perhaps children also have to learn how to *build* words and not just remember them. But we should be careful not to make an unwarranted assumption: Just because it's possible for us to identify the different morphemes that make up a word doesn't automatically mean that children need to learn how to build them on the fly. It's entirely possible that kids do memorize even the complex words as whole units, and that words like *childish*, *quickly*, and *cats* are simply stored in memory. In the next section, we turn to a heated, decades-long debate about this topic.

5.6 Words versus Rules

Learning to generalize

In a famous experiment, Jean Berko Gleason (Berko 1958) showed young children a picture of a bluebird-like creature, saying, "This is a wug." Then she showed them a picture of two of the creatures, saying, "Now there is another one. There are two of them. There are two ___" (see **Figure 5.6**). Often, the children obligingly produced the missing word *wugs* (pronounced with a [z] sound at the end, not [s]).

This simple result was hailed as an important early finding in research on language acquisition. It showed that when faced with a new word that they couldn't possibly have heard before, kids were able to tag on the right plural morpheme. Since they obviously couldn't have memorized the right form, they must have been generalizing on the basis of forms that they *had* heard: *dogs*, *birds*, etc. It turns out that children were able to do similar things with novel possessive forms (the *bik's hat*) and past-tense forms (*he ricked yesterday*).

This ability to generalize to new forms on the basis of previously known forms is an incredibly powerful mechanism. To some language scientists, it is *the* essential hallmark of human natural language. One way to view the whole

(A)

(B)

Figure 5.6 The "wug test" has its own line of merchandise. Here, the original test is affixed to a "wug mug," allowing language enthusiasts to spontaneously test for the generalization of the English plural at home and at the office. (Courtesy of Jean Berko Gleason. Adapted from The Wug Test © Jean Berko Gleason 2006.)

process is that children must be forming rules that involve variables—that is, they're manipulating symbols whose value is indeterminate and can be filled by anything that meets the required properties for that variable. So, a rule for creating the plural form for a noun might be stated as: *Nstem* + *s* where *Nstem* is the variable for any stem morpheme that is a noun. No need for children to memorize the plural forms—and for that matter, an adult learner of English could be spared a fair bit of trouble by being told up front, "Look, here's how you make plural nouns in English." The other inflectional morphemes in English can also be applied by rule. For example, to form the past tense of a verb: *Vstem* + *ed*.

Of course, that's not the whole story, because in addition to *dogs, birds*, and *bottles*, we also have *children, men, mice*, and *deer*, none of which are formed by applying the plural rule, as well as irregular verb forms like *rang, brought*, and *drove*. These just have to be memorized as exceptions. Moreover, they have to be memorized as whole units, without being mentally broken down into stems plus affixes. For instance, what part of *children, mice*, or *deer* corresponds to the plural morpheme, and what part of *rang* or *brought* would you say conveys the past? In these examples, the meanings of the two morphemes are fused into one seamless whole.

It's especially interesting to see how children cope with the rule-like forms, compared with the exceptional ones. Very early on, they tend to correctly produce the common exceptional forms—they'll produce *went* rather than *goed*, for example. But this stage is short-lived. They soon catch on to the pattern of attaching *-ed* to verb stems and apply it quite liberally, peppering their speech with lots of errors like *bringed, feeded, weared*, and so on. Once entrenched, this attachment to the rule-like forms can be hard to dislodge, even in the face of parental correction. Here's a well-known interaction reported by psycholinguist Courtney Cazden (1972) involving a child oblivious to a mother's repeated hints about the correct past-tense form of the verb *to hold*:

> **Child:** My teacher holded the baby rabbits and we patted them.
>
> **Mother:** Did you say your teacher held the baby rabbits?
>
> **Child:** Yes.
>
> **Mother:** What did you say she did?
>
> **Child:** She holded the baby rabbits and we patted them.
>
> **Mother:** Did you say she held them tightly?
>
> **Child:** No, she holded them loosely.

Paradoxically, errors due to overgeneralizations like these actually reflect an *advance* in learning—they're evidence that the child has abstracted the generalization for how to form the past tense.

One system or two?

To some researchers, there's a stark separation between the knowledge that underlies the regular forms of the past tense and the knowledge that underlies the irregular forms: the regulars involve the *assembly* of language from its parts, while the irregular forms, which have to be memorized, hinge on the *retrieval* of stored forms from memory. These are seen as two fundamentally distinct mental processes—words versus rules. Researchers who argue for this view often point to evidence hinting at two distinct psychological mechanisms, including some evidence suggesting that different brain regions may be involved in processing regular versus irregular verbs (see **Box 5.4**). But others argue that

BOX 5.4
Separate brain networks for words and rules?

If you wanted evidence that regular versus irregular past-tense forms call on dramatically different cognitive mechanisms, maybe a good place to look would be inside the brain. There's no guarantee, of course, that two separate cognitive mechanisms would show up as involving visibly distinct brain regions; but it would be very suggestive if you *did* find different patterns of activity for regulars versus irregulars. And it would be especially suggestive if these patterns made sense given what we know about the overall organization of the brain.

This is precisely the research strategy being pursued by Michael Ullman and his colleagues. Ullman has suggested that regular and irregular complex words reflect the same distinction as the one between declarative and procedural memory—the *what* and *how* systems organized along ventral and dorsal streams, as discussed in Chapter 3 (see Figure 3.12 and Box 3.5). In language, the idea is that the content of memorized information (such as the sounds and meanings of words) is handled by the ventral stream, while the dorsal stream is responsible for "how to" knowledge (such as how to assemble words into sentences, or how to implement the pronunciation of sounds).

We now know that the temporal lobe plays an important role in accessing memorized information about words, while more frontal regions of the brain (along with the basal ganglia) are implicated in more grammatical tasks, which likely involve assembly. Is there evidence for a similar neural dissociation for regular and irregular past-tense forms? Ullman and colleagues (2005) give a detailed summary, including the following:

- Patients with Alzheimer's disease usually show extensive degeneration of the temporal region of the brain, though the frontal area and the basal ganglia are relatively spared. This leads to a pattern in which patients can usually produce grammatical speech but have a lot of trouble retrieving and recognizing words. These patients turn out to have trouble with irregular verbs, but not regular ones. On the other hand, patients with Parkinson's disease have damage to their basal ganglia, and have trouble with syntactic processing and regular past-tense forms more than irregulars.

- ERP studies tend to show different patterns of brain wave activity for regular and irregular verbs: when a syntactically sensitive ERP component known as the LAN (left anterior negativity) shows up, it's elicited by violations on regular verbs, whereas violations of irregu-

lars are associated with a different ERP component, the N400.

- Though not decisive, neuroimaging work hints at greater activation of temporal regions for regular verbs, and of frontal regions for irregular verbs.

- Patients with fluent (Wernicke's) aphasia, with damage in the temporal region, had more difficulty with irregular verbs than regular ones; the pattern was reversed for patients with non-fluent (Broca's) aphasia, with damage to the frontal area (**Figure 5.7**).

Still, these data wouldn't amount to a slam dunk in favor of the separate-networks hypothesis (even if they were to show perfectly consistent results across studies). It's important to remember that differences in brain activity don't just show up when two difference *processes* are involved—different patterns of associations for different words can also do the trick. Remember, for example, the evidence from Chapter 3 that words elicited different patterns of brain activity depending on whether they were strongly associated with actions performed by the hands, mouth, or feet (see Figure 3.11). In a similar vein, opponents of the separate-networks hypothesis (e.g., Joanisse & Seidenberg, 2005) have argued that different patterns of brain activity reflect the fact that regular versus irregular verbs might have stronger links to phonological versus semantic information. Researchers from both camps continue to identify and test more subtle and informative contrasts.

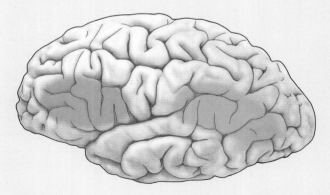

Figure 5.7 The approximate areas of brain damage for two of the patients in a study by Ullman et al. (2005). The pink region represents damage in the brain of FCL, a patient with non-fluent aphasia; the blue region shows damage to the brain of fluent aphasic JLU. (Adapted from Ullman et al., 2005.)

analogy In regard to forming complex words, a process of comparison in which similarities between the members of pairs or sets of word forms are taken as a basis for the creation of another word form.

the two don't involve truly distinct processes at all. They suggest that children could simply be memorizing even the regular forms, and then extending the past-tense forms to new verbs by **analogy**.

Using analogy is quite different from applying an abstract rule. An abstract rule involves actively combining a certain tag—say, the regular past tense form -*ed*—with anything that matches the variable specified within the rule—in this case, a verb stem. But analogy involves finding similarities across different memorized words. Here's an example that may remind you of questions you've likely seen on aptitude tests:

Hen is to *rooster* as *aunt* is to ___.

Getting the right answer to this question (*uncle*) involves figuring out what's different between hens and roosters and then applying that same difference to the concept of aunt. The argument is that analogy can also apply to the *sounds* that make up words in the present and past tense. For example:

Slip is to *slipped* as *wrap* is to ___.

In order to fill in the blank via analogy, you don't need to decompose the word *slipped* into a verb stem and a separate past-tense morpheme. All you need to do is notice that there's a certain difference in meaning between *slip* and *slipped*, and that the difference in meaning is accompanied by a certain difference in sounds, and then apply this sound difference to the word *wrap*.

Unlike a combinatorial rule, the same analogical processes could be applied to both regular and irregular forms:

Ring is to *rang* as *sing* is to ___.

How plausible is it that analogy plays a key role in learning the past tense for both regular and irregular forms? The notion is bolstered by the fact that over-generalization isn't limited to the regular, supposedly rule-based forms—kids often over-extend irregular patterns as well, as in the examples below (from Pinker, 1999):

It was neat—you should have **sawn** it! (seen)

Doggie **bat** me. (bit)

I know how to do that. I **truck** myself. (tricked)

He could have **brang** his socks and shoes down quick. (brought)

Elsa could have been **shotten** by the hunter, right? (shot)

So I took his coat and I **shuck** it. (shook)

You mean just a little itty bit is **dranken**? (drunk)

These kinds of errors turn up in children's speech because in fact the irregular forms don't show a completely random, arbitrary relationship between the present and past forms. It would be odd to have *stap* be the past tense of a verb like *frond*, for example. Instead, irregulars tend to show up as pockets of semi-regular patterns. So we get, among others:

lie/lay	give/gave	forgive/forgave	bid/bade
hang/hung	fling/flung	sling/slung	sting/stung
blow/blew	grow/grew	throw/threw	know/knew
find/found	bind/bound	grind/ground	wind/wound

If irregular forms show some principled patterning in their sound structure, and if children over-extend these patterns as they do with regular forms, then the line between memorized words and rule-based assembly becomes blurred. It seems tricky to account for the irregulars by means of a general rule; if these were in fact formed by rule, we'd have no way of explaining why the past tense of *snow* isn't *snew*, for instance. But the regularities inherent in the examples above suggest that there must be some way for the human mind to detect and generalize patterns that don't result from the application of a rule.

In a famous paper published in 1986, Dave Rumelhart and Jay McClelland set out to build a computer model that does exactly that. Their **connectionist model** of the past tense treats verb stems and past-tense forms as bundles of sound that are associatively linked together in memory. The model's job is to learn to predict which sounds make up the past-tense form, given a particular verb stem. So, if the model receives as input the set of sounds that make up the stem *grind*, it should ideally be able to come up with the sounds contained in *ground*, even though it has never before been presented with the past form *ground*. It should be able to do this based on its exposure to many other pairs of verb stems and past-tense forms; assuming there are systematic statistical patterns to be found in the relationships between the stems and past-tense forms, the model is designed to detect them and store them as probabilistic associations.

In the early stages of "learning," the model's predictions are pretty random; since it's had minimal exposure to examples, any set of sounds is as likely as another to be associated with the sounds of *grind*. But after it's been exposed to many examples of stems and past-tense forms, it begins to adjust the connections between the sounds of the verb stem and the sounds for the past-tense form. For example, the model begins to "notice" that most of the consonants that appear in the uninflected form also turn up in the past-tense form, so it is able to predict that a pair like *stap/frond* would be extremely unlikely to show up, while *grind/ground* is quite likely. It also begins to "notice" that there are similarities in sound between words that belong to the same subclass of irregular past-tense forms—for example, it notices that there's something the same in the words that have the vowel sound "ay" (as in *find*) in the verb stem but the sound "ow" (as in *found*) in the past-tense form: the word-final consonants *-nd* tend to be present in these words. The gradual tweaking of connections between the verb stem sounds and the past-tense sounds reflects the gradual learning of irregular past-tense forms through a form of statistical analogy. Naturally, the more frequently a word occurs, the more opportunities the model has to associate the correct past-tense form with the verb stem, which might account for the fact that children's earliest past-tense forms tend to be very high-frequency ones like *went*, *came*, *got*, and so on.

Language researchers agree that something like this is probably needed to account for the non-accidental patterns that irregular forms fall into. But Rumelhart and McClelland made the stronger claim that exactly the same kind of mechanism can be used to account for how the *regular* forms are learned, dispensing entirely with the notion that these are formed by a rule that manipulates abstract symbols. This claim has generated a great deal of controversy, and an outsider looking in might be surprised at the charged and passionate nature of the debate over regular and irregular verb forms. But what's at stake is, in part, two general, conflicting views of how children learn the systematic patterns of their language.

One view emphasizes the fact that language is at heart an intricate system of rules, and that children come into the world prepared to extract rules out of their linguistic input. As we'll see in the next chapter, whatever arguments might be made for treating the past-tense formation as rule-based, they are fairly mild compared with the arguments for using rules to account for the regularities governing how entire *sentences* get assembled. Some researchers take an additional step and claim that kids rely on genetic programming that allows them to extract

connectionist model Here this refers to a computational model of the past tense. Based on previously learned associations between verb stems and past-tense forms, the model predicts the probable shape of past-tense forms for new verb stems.

LANGUAGE AT LARGE 5.3

McLanguage and the perils of branding by prefix

In its attempts to build a strong brand identity, the McDonald's fast-food restaurant chain deliberately created a "McLanguage," decorating a whole slew of product names with the prefix *Mc-*. For instance, you can get a special McDeal on the McNuggets or the Chicken McGrill, order a McSalad, and consider having a McFlurry for dessert. The company's goal was to stamp its brand identity indelibly on these products and to distinguish them from similar products made by competitors. In fact, McDonald's has been so territorial about the prefix that it is famous for initiating aggressive litigation against any other companies that try to use it in their branding. In 1987, McDonald's successfully fought Quality Inns International for trademark infringement over that company's plans to name a new chain of hotels McSleep Inns.

But McDonald's went a tad overboard in its branding zeal, and their McLanguage planted the seeds of its own destruction. By using *Mc-* as if it were a prefix that could be attached to any regular word, the company encouraged people to mentally decompose *McSalad* and *McNuggets* as being made up of two meaningful units—that is, of two morphemes stuck together. This wouldn't have been a problem for the restaurant chain if the *Mc-* prefix had become entrenched in consumers' minds as a morpheme with a narrow, brand-specific meaning, something like "from McDonald's." But as morphemes become more **productive** in a language— that is, as they are applied to a wider and wider set of stem morphemes—they have a tendency to take on lives of their own and to broaden their meanings beyond their original uses.

McDonald's itself fanned the flames of this process and quite likely accelerated the productivity of the *Mc-* morpheme. For example, a 1981 TV commercial had Ronald McDonald onstage teaching children how to create new words in McLanguage, using lyrics set to a catchy country rock tune: "There's nothing Mc-to it. You can Mc-do it. Just pick a word and add a *Mc-* to it. It's rockin' Mc-language. It's rockin' Mc-fun." The commercial then pictured children in the audience bopping in their seats to the music and coining new words like *Mc-you*, *Mc-me*, and *Mc-camera*. The scene looks much like a commercial version of the wug test: McDonald's encouraged its audience to play with language and to tag all kinds of words with the morpheme, laying the groundwork for the morpheme's productivity and the broadening of its meaning well beyond the company's product names.

If McDonald's had had a language scientist involved in its branding campaign, the company might have predicted that pretty soon all these McKids would begin using the prefix productively to suit their own expressive goals. Sure enough, along with the official line of "McProducts," we soon had the words *McJobs*, and *McMansions*. The prefix was often pejorative—it's no compliment to call someone's

---

productivity In linguistics, a process that can be applied very broadly to a large set of lexical items, rather than being restricted to a small set of words.

---

just the *right* rules out of the input with remarkable efficiency, while managing to avoid coming up with rules that would lead them to dead ends. Under this scenario, nothing could be more natural than for children to seize on a regularity like the English regular plural or past-tense forms and represent the pattern by means of a rule that any new form can then be cranked through.

The opposing view takes the stand that children can get away with very little in the way of innate expectations about rules and what they might look like, and that in fact there is enough information available in the linguistic input for children to be able to notice generalizations and extend them to new situations quite readily. All that's needed is a sensitivity to statistical regularity, just like the one built into Rumelhart and McClelland's connectionist model. Proponents of this view tend to emphasize the fact that, as we saw in the last chapter, even young babies are exquisitely sensitive to statistical regularities in linguistic input. They argue that regular morphemes simply reflect statistical regularities that are somewhat more regular than the less regular forms, and there is no need to formulate an actual rule in either case.

GO TO
sites.sinauer.com/languageinmind

for **web activities, further readings, research updates, new essays,** and other features

new home a "McMansion." And in 1998, author George Ritter wrote about "McUniversities," worrying about the trend toward shallow, cost-effective, convenient, consumer-oriented practices in higher education. The *Mc-* prefix is now so widespread that you can take almost any noun, run it through a search engine with *Mc-* attached, and get numerous hits. You can easily find *McSchool, McCulture, McParents, McChurch, McThought, McBeauty, McJesus,* and even *McSex,* none of which sound like anything to aspire to.

Lots of "McFun" indeed. But not exactly what McDonald's had in mind. What's happening with the *Mc-* prefix is a process that marketers call "genericide"—which is what happens when language originally introduced as part of a brand identity gets absorbed into regular usage. It's not hard to find instances of brand names that have become common nouns. If you stroll across your *linoleum* floor over to your *formica* countertop, pop two *aspirin* into your mouth, check on the stew in the *crock-pot,* pick up the spilled *kitty litter* in the corner with a *kleenex,* pour a bowl of *granola,* and open your freezer to take out a *popsicle* before proposing a game of after-dinner *ping pong,* and you talk about all this without regard for the specific brands that are involved, you are contributing to the genericide of these brand names. Even *heroin* used to be a brand name—though, unlike with *aspirin,* Bayer is probably glad to no longer be readily associated with this product.

Companies often dread genericide because once a word has passed into common usage, they can no longer hold exclusive legal rights to the name. As a result, they often do everything they can to halt the linguistic change—attempts that often amount to fighting a losing battle. And bits of language like the *Mc-* prefix are even more susceptible to genericide than brand *names,* because of the fact that it's in the nature of prefixes to be promiscuous in attaching themselves to a broad range of words.

In the trademark case over the McSleep Inns, Quality Inns argued that it was not encroaching on the linguistic rights of McDonald's because, as language scientist Roger Shuy testified (Lentine & Shuy, 1990), the *Mc-* prefix had become a productive derivational prefix that in one of its uses simply marked the noun it glommed onto as "basic, convenient, inexpensive, and standardized." This argument was rejected by the judge, but the generic use of the prefix continues. In 2003, McDonald's objected (unsuccessfully) to Merriam-Webster's definition of *McJob* as "a low-paying job that requires little skill and provides little opportunity for advancement." In 2007, the company lobbied Oxford University Press to soften the pejorative definition of *McJob* that appears in the *Oxford English Dictionary*. But dictionaries reflect usage rather than create it, and by the time a word becomes an entry in a dictionary, the cows are out of the barn, and the word has passed into common usage.

In the end, given the scornful ways in which the generic "McMorpheme" is often used, perhaps it's just as well that Quality Inns lost the right to use the prefix. And, as it happens, its chain of Sleep Inns is quite successful.

DIGGING DEEPER

The chicken-and-egg problem of language and thought

We've seen that word learning involves matching up the right concept with the right word, and that very young children are outfitted with helpful biases that make it easier to work out the right matches. But which came first? The concepts or the words? Do children first parcel the world into concepts and then look to see if there is a word assigned for each concept? Or do they rely on language to lead them to concepts that, if children were left to their own wordless devices, might never properly gel?

There have been proposals on both ends of the spectrum. At one extreme is the idea advanced by the philosopher Jerry Fodor (1998) that *all* concepts that line up with words are innately wired. The claim is that as a species we're endowed with thousands of concepts that form the building blocks of language. One of the more obvious flaws of this notion, as pointed out by Steve Pinker (2007), is that concepts often link up to a word in one language but not in others. This leads to bizarre conclusions. For example, you'd have to say that English speakers, who can brandish the separate words *see* and *show,* have both of these concepts encoded in their DNA but that Hebrew speakers, who can only describe an act of showing by using the more roundabout paraphrase *cause to see,* have only the concept of seeing in their genes.

At the other end of the extreme, some have claimed that language is the mold within which conceptual thought is shaped. Words, as the idea goes, stamp categories out of otherwise amorphous collections of things, properties, and events. This view was articulated most famously by Benjamin Whorf (1956), who stated:

> We dissect nature along lines laid down by our native languages. . . . We cut nature up, organize it into concepts, and ascribe significances as we do, largely because we are parties to an agreement . . . that holds throughout our speech community and is codified in the patterns of our language.

Under such a view at its strongest, if your language has no word for the concept of cousin that is distinct from *sister*, then you necessarily meld the two relationships into one concept. And until English speakers encountered and adopted the French word *aperitif*, they no doubt had trouble getting their heads around the concept of an alcoholic drink you might sip before dinner.

This is a rather radical claim, but it's one that's implicitly held by many very smart people. It's present when the novelist Milan Kundera (1980) questions how anyone could possibly understand the human soul without benefit of the word *litost* (see Language at Large 5.1), and in George Orwell's famous assertion in his essay *Politics and the English Language* (1946) that obfuscatory language has the effect of bamboozling the citizenry. But how does this claim stack up as an actual theory of learning?

If you consult your own intuitions about how you learn new words, it probably seems hard to commit to either of these extreme views. Sometimes concepts seem to come first, and sometimes the words do. On the one hand, it seems doubtful that prior to being introduced to the word *mitochondria*, you had already grasped the notion of microscopic structures within your body's cells that produce the energy that fuels your thoughts and action, and that you had simply been waiting all your life to know what those invisible membrane clusters were *called*. On the other hand, that thingamajig that rock climbers use so that one member of a climbing pair can arrest her partner's fall without having the rope burn the skin of her palms? If you've ever climbed, you are probably extremely clear in your mind about the particulars of the thingamajig's function and use, even though you may not know that it's properly called a "belay device."

It's nice to admit a truce and call for a compromise in the word-first versus concept-first standoff—and indeed, you'd be *very* hard-pressed to find a language researcher nowadays who subscribes to either of the extreme views I've just sketched out. But an acknowledgment that both sides are probably right is not that informative until you start hashing out the details, and this is what researchers are now busy doing. In Chapter 12, we'll take up the question of whether the language you speak has long-lasting effects on how you carve the world into concepts. For now, we'll focus on the relationship between concepts and language in children's very early learning.

If infants do possess some concepts without the benefit of language, what are they, and how do kids come by them? Are some of them innate, perhaps forming the building blocks of more complex concepts? Do some, more than others, leap out of the environment that the child experiences? If so, how are the other, less salient concepts learned? And how does conceptual development mesh with the fact that languages often choose very different means to express similar concepts?

We don't have the space or the time to explore all of these questions here, but let's at least scratch the surface. As a starting point, let's consider what infants can *think* about before they speak. What kinds of concepts and categories are they capable of forming in the absence of language? The standard method for inferring whether babies have abstracted a category is one you've already encountered in Section 5.2. Researchers show the babies multiple objects that fall into the same category, and then show them an object outside of that category. If the babies react by spending more, or less, time looking at that object than they do at an object that falls within that category, the researchers infer that the babies have noticed some essential difference between the objects. We've already seen in Section 5.2 that the mere presence of speech encourages babies to find commonalities across these objects. But can babies form categories in a way that's completely independent of language?

It seems clear that babies can form some categories before they show any evidence of understanding word meanings, and well before they actually begin producing words themselves. For example, Paul Quinn and colleagues (1993) showed that at 3 or 4 months, babies can cognitively group different examples of cats and dogs together, and differentiate each basic-level category from the other; that is, they react when they see a dog after they've seen many cats, and vice versa. Do basic-level categories, such as dog, precede more abstract ones, like mammal? Actually, no. Some studies have found that very broad categories tend to be acquired even earlier; for instance, infants as young as 2 months can form a category that includes various mammals but excludes furniture (Quinn & Johnson, 2000). This is interesting because, as we saw in Section 5.2, basic-level words are more commonly used by parents than the broader, superordinate-level words, and they also tend to be learned earlier by children, who pronounce words like *dog* and *bed* before they talk about *mammals* and *furniture*. Conceptual development, then, seems to proceed independently of language in this regard.

There's also evidence that preverbal infants can form categories that rely on quite conceptual features, rather than just perceptual differences. For example, by about 7 months, they can group together things that are animals and things that are vehicles, and soon after, they can also differentiate between birds and airplanes, despite the fact that these categories look very similar to each other. This suggests that they're doing something a bit more abstract than just paying attention to perceptual features, such as whether something has wings or a particular shape (Mandler, 2004).

Spatial concepts also make an early appearance, and some researchers have suggested that a certain amount of spatial conceptualization is innate. It's been shown that 3-month-old babies can grasp the difference between objects that appear above, below, to the left, and to the right of one another—for example, if a teddy bear is presented as being above a box during the familiarization phase, infants react when they later see the bear appearing below it. By 6 months, they can abstract this relation even when different pairs of objects are used during the familiarization and test phases, and they can also recognize relations like inside versus behind, even when these are represented from different visual angles. The concepts of between and support seem to be harder, and appear a bit later. (For a useful review of this literature, see Casasola, 2008.)

Again, to some extent at least, thinking about spatial relations seems to be independent from talking about them. For example, Korean speakers have to use different linguistic forms to distinguish objects that are loosely contained inside others (like a pencil inside a cup) from objects that are tightly contained (a peg inserted into a hole). In English, it's acceptable to refer to both of the objects as being *in* something. Nevertheless, English-learning kids do treat these cases as different categories of spatial relations (McDonough et al., 2003).

There seems to be plenty of evidence, then, that children do think before they speak, suggesting that their categories and concepts are not dependent on the mold of language. But a couple of considerations complicate the picture somewhat.

One of these is the fact that, even though kids begin *talking* at about 1 year of age, it's very hard to know for sure at what age they have mapped meanings onto word units and, hence, whether their concepts have been influenced by language. In Chapter 4, we saw that by 5 months of age, children are able to recognize the sounds of familiar words, and to segment other words from the speech stream that contains them. The received wisdom until quite recently has been that meaning-to-sound mapping doesn't really happen until closer to 10 months of age or so. But newer evidence shows that kids do understand the meanings of at least some words at the age of 6 months (Tincoff & Jusczyk, 2012). This makes it hard to know: Is a 7-month-old, for example, truly ignorant of any meaningful words? Can we be sure about a 5-month-old?

The other complication is that, even though the standard experimental methods show that babies can group objects together on the basis of certain shared features, it's not clear that their conceptual knowledge is all that rich or stable. Babies often show a surprisingly immature grasp of even

very basic conceptual knowledge until about the age when they actually begin to talk.

One of the most striking examples of this comes from an intriguing study cooked up by Fei Xu and Susan Carey (1996). The researchers set up a display in which a toy duck emerged from one end of a screen, then hid back behind it again. From the other edge, there emerged a toy *truck*, which then also hid behind the screen. Now, if I were to lift the screen and show you what was behind it, how many toys would you expect to see? You'd say two. But a 10-month-old baby might be at a loss. In Xu and Carey's study, it turned out that the infants were no more surprised to see one object than they were to see two, as measured by the amount of time they spent looking at the object(s) once revealed. At this age, it would appear that babies don't really understand that a duck preserves its duck-hood and are pretty relaxed at the prospect that it might transform itself into a truck. But testing babies at 12 months—the age at which they usually start to talk—revealed that they were unnerved by the sight of a single object rather than two.

In fact, the scientists showed that the presence of language can have an immediate, striking effect on kids' responses, even with younger babies. When *9*-month-old babies saw exactly the same display accompanied by a voice that gushed, "Look, a truck! Look, a duck!" they registered surprise at seeing a single object, as if the fact of two different names led them to the conclusion that these were two different objects (Xu, 2002).

This is an especially arresting demonstration. It's hard to know, though, whether the linguistic input was actually *required* in order for infants to be able to form a stable representation of these objects in their minds. Perhaps the act of naming simply accelerated learning that would have happened anyway, by focusing the children's attention on the difference between the two objects. This interpretation gets some support from a similar study done with rhesus monkeys: adult monkeys expected that objects like apples wouldn't suddenly morph into coconuts—presumably without the benefit of knowing the words for the objects (Phillips & Santos, 2007).

One way to think about Xu and Carey's findings is in terms of the following analogy: suppose I show you two color chips that are quite close in color, and later I ask you to remember whether I'd shown you examples of one color or two. You might have an easier time accurately remembering if I'd pointed out, "Here's a blue one. And here's a periwinkle one." But does this mean that you were incapable of *perceiving* the difference between the two colors until I named them? Unlikely. Instead, the act of my naming them was a signal that I consider the difference between them relevant, which may have caused you to pay more attention to the precise difference between them. Another example: if I refer to two sweaters as chartreuse and teal but my husband calls them both green, do you infer from this that he's blind to their difference in hue? A more reasonable conclusion would be that he doesn't *care* that they're different.

The true power of language to shape thought, then, may lie not so much in the power of words to impose concepts, but more indirectly in the social nature of the communicative act. Remember from Section 5.3 that infants are deeply sensitive to the fact that naming an object involves a deliberate act of reference. If a particular linguistic community has seen fit to recruit a word for a concept, this is some fairly good evidence that it sees fit to talk about that concept on a regular basis. That in itself is a powerful thing.

So, even if the effect of language turns out to be one of directing attention to the speaker's intended message, rather than cutting new categories out of whole cloth, it's probably worth standing up and taking note of its effects. At the very least, language might play an important pedagogical role. For instance, in the spatial domain, we saw that English-learning children could form distinct categories for tight-fitting versus loose-fitting objects, despite the fact that English allows the same words to express both. But verbal commentary can provide an added boost: Marianella Casasola and her colleagues (2009) showed that children had an easier time distinguishing a category of tight-fitting objects from loose-fitting ones if a speaker pronounced the word *tight*, or even a nonsense word, while they were looking at the tightly fitting objects. Another provocative study looked at the effects of exposing preschool children to many examples of sentences such as *Mary thought that Fred went to the movies* rather than other complex sentences such as *The boy that had red hair stole the cake*; kids who were trained on the first set of sentences could be nudged into an earlier understanding that the mental states of others can differ from their own (Hale & Tager-Flusberg, 2003).

And what to make of the diversity across languages? I'll set aside for the moment the question of whether a lifetime of hearing the particular words or structures of your native language as opposed to others does leave a permanent imprint on your cognition; we'll take that issue up in Chapter 12. But current science gives us hints that, at least early in our mental lives, language helps to give shape to our understanding of the world. Most of us have no memories of the momentous early days of our word learning. But I'll leave you for now with the words of a woman who did: Helen Keller (1909), who lost her sight and hearing as an infant, recalled making the connection between things and words at the age of seven, when her teacher, Annie Sullivan, finger-spelled them into her palm. Her writings about this event line up very plausibly with what we know from the studies we've just discussed, and yield some poetic insights into the subjective experience of how daily objects can become transformed once they've been anointed by the human act of reference:

> My teacher placed my hand under the spout. As the water gushed over one hand, she spelled into the other hand w-a-t-e-r, first slowly, then rapidly. I stood still, my whole attention fixed on the motion of her fingers. Suddenly I felt a misty consciousness as of something forgotten—a thrill of returning thought; and somehow the mystery of language was revealed to me. I knew then that w-a-t-e-r meant the wonderful cool something that was flowing over my hand. That living word awakened my soul, gave it light, hope, joy, and set it free!... I left the well-house eager to learn. Everything had a name, and each name gave birth to a new thought. As we returned to the house, every object that I touched seemed to quiver with life. This was because I saw everything with that strange new sight that had come to me. On entering the door I remembered the doll I had broken. I went to the hearth and picked up the pieces. I tried vainly to put them together. Then my eyes filled with tears; I realized what I had done, and for the first time I felt repentance and sorrow.

PROJECT

Demonstrating that language is *necessary* for the development of a concept as opposed to simply facilitating it is no easy matter. Take on the challenge of proposing an experiment or series of experiments that will help get at the answer to whether babies need exposure to language in order to acquire certain concepts. Keep in mind the practical and ethical problems of *depriving* infants of exposure to specific words of English; you might instead use the strategy of recruiting concepts not encoded by words in the English language.

6 Learning the Structure of Sentences

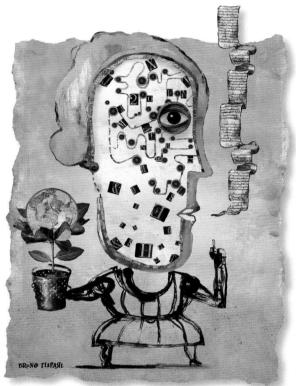

Achieving a vocabulary of 60,000 words or more is an impressive learning feat. But it's not nearly as impressive as the fact that you readily *combine* these words deftly and creatively. To get a quick feel for the scale of combinatorial possibilities that language offers, consider chemistry: with a measly 118 elements in the periodic table, there are *trillions* of known molecules that combine these elements. Just think what you can do with 60,000 units!

The combinatorial power of language allows you to convey entirely novel ideas that have never been expressed in language before. For instance, I'm guessing that you've never heard the following sentence:

> *It was all because of the lucrative but internationally reviled pink hoodie industry that the president came to abandon his campaign promise to ensure that every household parrot had recourse to free legal counsel.*

This sentence may be a touch on the enigmatic side, but chances are you had no trouble understanding it (though perhaps not all of its implications). On the other hand, you'd have no hope of understanding that sentence if its words were served up to you in this order:

> *Industry ensure because that internationally reviled had legal household parrot was it abandon all pink president every of campaign promise the but lucrative hoodie the came to his to that counsel recourse to free.*

Clearly, being able to string multiple linguistic units together is not enough. In order for us to be able to understand sentences made by combining words, they obviously can't just be tossed together in a bag. There has to be some underlying order or structure. That is, language has a **syntax**, a set of rules or constraints for how the units can be put together. The syntactic structure

syntax The structure of a sentence, specifying how the words are put together, Also refers to a set of rules or constraints for how linguistic elements can be put together.

semantics The meaning of a sentence; the system of rules for interpreting the meaning of a sentence based on its structure.

telegraphic speech Speech that preserves the correct order of words in sentences, but drops many of the small function words such as *the*, *did*, or *to*.

compositionality The concept that there are fixed rules for combining units of language in terms of their form that result in fixed meaning relationships between the words that are joined together.

of a sentence is obviously intimately tied to its linguistic meaning, or its **semantics**. You can combine the same assortment of words in a number of permissible ways with strikingly different results in meaning. As any small child knows, the justice systems of the world care very deeply about the difference between the sentences *Susie punched Billy* and *Billy punched Susie*. It's the tight coupling between the syntax of the language and its semantics that makes these distinctions possible.

As it turns out, syntactic structure is extraordinarily complex—so much so that the efforts of many linguists over numerous decades have not succeeded in exhaustively describing the patterns of even *one* language (English being the most heavily studied to date). It is one of the least-understood aspects of linguistics. And yet small children master the bulk of it in their first few years of life, before they are seen fit to learn even the most rudimentary aspects of arithmetic. Figuring out how they do this, and what they know about syntactic structure at any given stage, is fraught with theoretical and methodological challenges. It takes a sturdy soul to venture into this particular research domain.

The combinatorial nature of language becomes evident in children's speech at a fairly young age. Typically, they move beyond the single-word stage and combine two words at around 18 months of age, and by about 2 years they can speak in **telegraphic speech** (see **Box 6.1**), which preserves the correct order of words in sentences but drops many of the small function words such as *the*, *did*, or *to*. At this stage, "kid talk" sounds a bit like the compressed language used in telegrams or text messages: *Mommy go store now. Doggie no bite finger.* Six months later, by the age of two and a half, most children are speaking in full sentences, though still simple ones. By the time they enter kindergarten, they have mastered virtually all of their language's syntax.

What's most interesting is that at no point do kids seem to entertain the possibility that sentences can be made by throwing words together in just any order. Even when their output is restricted to two words, they never seem to violate the basic word order patterns of their language. For instance, English-speaking children always place the subject in front of the verb and the object after the verb; so even in the speech of toddlers, *Susie eat* means something different than *Eat Susie*.

But figuring out what's inside children's heads as they learn to combine words is no easy matter. In this chapter, we'll explore some ideas about what it is that children have to learn about their language's structure, what their syntactic knowledge might look like at various stages, and what it is that allows them to ultimately learn such an intricate and complicated system.

6.1 The Nature of Syntactic Knowledge

Compositionality

In introducing this chapter, I presented you with a tossed salad of words as a way to illustrate how impossible it is to understand words that are combined together without any structure. But you don't have to look at long and complicated sentences to get a sense of why language *has* to have some underlying structure in order for it to get off the ground. You just have to look at compound nouns.

In Chapter 5, we talked about how simple nouns can be combined into more complex compound nouns such as *houseboat* or *insurance policy*. It turns out that this is one of the very rare instances in language where units get combined in a *non-compositional* way. **Compositionality** is the notion that there are fixed rules for combining units of language in terms of their *form* that result in fixed *meaning* relationships between the words that are joined together. At heart, the

BOX 6.1
Stages of syntactic development

Children begin to combine words shortly after their first birthday, when they have about 50–60 words in their vocabulary. Their utterances gradually become more complex, and some regular patterns show up across children in their progression to more complex syntactic forms. One of the most detailed studies of language development was published in 1973 by Roger Brown, who based his analyses largely on data from weekly recordings of three children taken over a period of several years.

Brown found that children of the same age varied a good deal in terms of the syntactic elements they produced in their own speech. For example, by the age of 2 years and 2 months, a little girl named Eve was already producing various prepositions and complex words like *mommy's*, *walked*, and *swimming*, while at the same age, her peers Adam and Sarah were still eking out telegraphic speech consisting only of content words unembellished by grammatical morphemes.

A much better way than sheer age to predict a child's repertoire of grammatical markers is the measure of **mean length of utterance** (**MLU**). This refers to the average number of morphemes in a child's utterances measured at a given point in time (i.e., at a specific age). Here are some examples of how MLU is computed:

Daddy's porridge allgone.
  1   2   3   4   MLU = 4

My mommy holded the rabbits.
  1   2   3 4 5 6 7 MLU = 7

Daddy went to the store.
  1   23 4 5   6   MLU = 6

Based on his analyses, Brown noticed that function words and suffixes tended to emerge in a fairly consistent sequence across children—and that this sequence didn't necessarily match the frequency with which they were spoken by the children's parents. He identified five stages of children's early syntactic development defined by MLU. The table presents a summary of the approximate ages and inventory of grammatical morphemes at each of these stages.

Roger Brown's five stages of syntactic development

Stage	Age in months	Overall MLU	Morphemes present	Examples
I	15–30	1.75	Content words only	More juice. Birdy fly. Here book.
II	28–30	2.25	Present progressive; in, on; Plural -s	I falling. Dolly in. Eat apples.
III	36–42	2.75	Irregular past tense; Possessive -s; Full form of "to be"	Baby fell down. Mommy's hat. Is Daddy sad?
IV	40–46	3.5	Articles; Regular past tense -ed; Third person regular (present tense)	This is the mommy. I holded it. You fixed it. He likes me.
V	42–52+	4.0	Third person irregular (present tense); Full form of "to be" as auxiliary verb; Contracted "to be" as main verb; Contracted "to be" as auxiliary verb	She does it fast. Was she swimming? He's nice. He's swimming.

From Brown 1973.

mean length of utterance (MLU) The average number of morphemes in a child's utterances at a given point in the child's development.

idea is similar to the notion of operations in simple arithmetic: once you learn what addition and subtraction *do*, you can, in principle, add any two (or more) numbers together, or subtract any number from another. You may never have seen this equation:

$$457{,}910{,}983.00475386 + 6{,}395{,}449{,}002.03 = x$$

and you can't possibly have memorized such an equation in the way you might have memorized the "fact" that 5 + 2 = 7. But you can easily compute it, just as you can compute any combination of numbers joined together by an arithmetic operator.

The same thing applies to simple sentences like *Susie punched Billy*. The operation of joining a subject (*Susie*) together with the phrase *punched Billy* yields a perfectly predictable meaning result. We know that Susie is the individual who initiated the action of punching, and Billy is the unfortunate individual at the receiving end of the punch. If we replace the word *Susie* with *Danny*, then *Danny* now stands in exactly the same role in the sentence that *Susie* used to; changing which word appears in the subject slot doesn't allow the possibility that the new occupant of that slot (*Danny*) now refers to the recipient of the action rather than its initiator. We can do the same kind of replacement with the object—slide *Fred* into the slot where *Billy* used to be, and now *Fred* is the recipient of the punching action. These examples seem simple and obvious, but this notion of *predictability of meaning from the way the parts are put together* is at the very heart of the combinatorial nature of language. And it works for excruciatingly complex sentences—there's no reason to believe that there isn't the same kind of tight, predictable relationship between the structure and meaning of more convoluted sentences.

But, interestingly, noun-noun compounds don't behave in this rigid, predictable fashion. For example, consider these words: *houseboat, housewife, house guest, housecoat, house arrest, house lust*. Despite the fact that the same *structural* relationship exists between the component words in all of these compounds, there isn't a uniform *semantic* relationship: a houseboat is a boat that *is also* a house, but a housewife is certainly not a wife that *is also* a house. While you could construe both a housewife and a house guest as *living in* a house (at least some of the time), this certainly can't apply to a housecoat, which is something you *use in* a house. And *house arrest* and *house lust* fit none of these.

For the sake of comparison, let's see what happens when you join words that do stand in a compositional relationship to one another, say, an adjective with a noun. Consider the very diverse phrases *red dog, corrupt executive, long book*, and *broken computer*. A red dog is a dog *that is* red. A corrupt executive is an executive *that is* corrupt. A long book is a book *that is* long, and so on. In fact, any time you join an adjective with a noun, the adjective serves the purpose of identifying a property that the noun possesses. For the more mathematically inclined, we could say that a phrase formed by grouping an adjective with a noun corresponds to a set of things in the world that is the intersection of the sets picked out by the adjective and the noun—in other words, *red dog* refers to the set of things in the world that are both red and dogs. Given that this rule holds for any combination of an adjective and noun, the process of joining these two kinds of words is fully compositional. (I'll leave aside for the moment the tricky cases like *small elephant*: does this refer to the set of things that are both small and an elephant?)

To see how useful compositionality can be, watch what happens when you come across a phrase involving a noun that you don't know, let's say *a red dax*. You may not know what a *dax* is, but you know that it's colored red. But what does *house dax* mean? Is it a dax for a house? A dax that lives in a house? A dax that is a house? You can't tell without more information. Even if you *do* know both of the words in a newly coined compound (such as *house book*), it can take a lot of guesswork to figure out the actual relationship between the two parts (for example, try to work out the meanings of the novel compounds in **Table 6.1**).

You can see from these simple examples how non-compositionality would seriously hinder the communicative usefulness of sticking words together into longer units. Essentially, you'd have to memorize the relationships between words, or at best infer them by running through some plausible possibilities. But you couldn't predictably *compute* them the way you can do a computation in arithmetic. Creating meanings non-compositionally gets squishy enough with combinations of just *two* words—now scale that up to sentences of 10 or 20 or 52 words (the last is probably the average length of a sentence in a Henry James novel) and you can see why compositionality plays such an important role in the expressive powers of language.

Despite the great allure of compositional meaning, the existence of noun-noun compounds points to the fact that it *is* possible to combine words in ways that don't reflect a general rule—in this case, although the combinations are syntactically uniform, always combining a noun with a another noun, they don't result in a fully general semantic pattern. At the same time, though, some regularities do exist, and there are some common semantic relations that tend to occur over and over again. For example, many noun-noun compounds express a part-whole relationship: *computer screen, car engine, door handle, shirt sleeve, chicken leg, wheel rim*, and so on. (Notice that the second noun is always a part of the first; a *chicken leg* is most definitely not the same thing as a *leg chicken*, whatever that means.) Another common semantic relation is one in which the second noun is a thing for the benefit of the first: *baby carriage, dog bed, cat toy, student center, employee insurance*. So, some generalization by analogy is possible, even if it is looser than more compositional kinds of meaning combinations.

One way to think about the distinction between compositional and non-compositional meanings is in terms of the words-versus-rules debate you met in the discussion of past tense and plural forms in Chapter 5. In that chapter, we saw that researchers came to intellectual blows over a controversy about whether complex words marked as regular plural or past-tense forms (such as *dogs* and *walked*) get formed as the result of a general rule that creates larger units out of smaller morphemes, or whether they arise by *memorizing* the complex words and then extending their internal structure by analogy to new examples.

Memorizing meanings and extending them by analogy is exactly what we have to do with the meanings of noun-noun compounds, since there doesn't seem to be one fixed rule that does the trick. So it's important to take seriously the possibility that other ways of combining words might also be achieved by means other than a rigid combinatorial rule over abstract categories.

In fact, some researchers would argue that what looks like rule-based behavior (for example, making combinations like *red ball*) is really just an extension of the memorize-and-extend-by-analogy strategy used in combining units like *coffee cup*. It's just that it's more regular. Others argue that it's extremely unlikely that adult speakers could manage to flaunt the complexity and creativity that they do without the benefit of something akin to rules. But even if we accept that adult speakers accomplish most of their word combinations by means of rules, this doesn't necessarily mean that combinations of units *at all ages* are accomplished by rules. This issue is an important one to keep in mind throughout the chapter.

It's clear, however, that the rule-based approach offers certain cognitive advantages by putting much less burden on the memorization of the complex words or phrases—we can simply apply the rules in a fully general way. This advantage becomes larger and larger as we scale up from two-morpheme words all the way to complex sentences. And, at the upper limits of our language, ab-

---

TABLE 6.1 Novel noun-noun combinations

Take a stab at describing a plausible meaning for each of these novel combinations of nouns when they are made into noun-noun compounds (and if more than one meaning comes to mind, provide several). What range of different semantic relationships between the two words do you find yourself drawing on?

rabbit phone	paper candy
flower card	rain paint
wallet plant	window cup
book dirt	computer organ

stract rules allow us to create an endless variety of new combinations that seem impossible to form by analogy to existing forms. What might such rules look like, if indeed they do exist? And what kinds of categories would they involve?

Basic properties of syntactic structure

One of the most basic things a set of language rules needs to do is radically constrain the possible combinations of words into *just those that are meaningful.* For example, given the bag of words *cat, mouse, devoured, the,* and *the,* we need to be able to distinguish between an interpretable sentence like *The cat devoured the mouse* and other combinations that don't yield a meaning at all, and are not considered to be possible combinations (marked by an asterisk as not legal or meaningful within a language):

>   *Cat mouse devoured the the.

>   *Cat the devoured mouse the.

>   *The cat the devoured mouse.

>   *The the cat devoured mouse.

And we'd like our rules to apply not just to this bag of words, but to other bags of words, such as *teacher, kid, loves, every,* and *that,* to yield meaningful combinations like:

>   Every teacher loves that kid.

and to rule out bad combinations such as:

>   *Every that teacher loves kid.

>   *Teacher kid loves every that.

>   *That every teacher kid loves.

Our rules need to be stated in terms of useful category labels as opposed to individual words like *teacher* or *cat*—otherwise, we'd never be able to generalize across sentences and we'd need to learn a new rule to go along with every new word. So, it becomes useful to identify words as belonging to particular syntactic categories. Let's propose some categories, and some useful abbreviations:

>   Det—determiner {*the, every, that*}

>   N—noun {*cat, mouse, teacher, kid*}

>   V—verb {*loves, devoured*}

The first line means that *Det* stands for the category determiner, which is a set that contains the words *the, every,* and *that.* Noun (N) is a set that contains *cat,* etc.; and V stands for the category verb. Using these categories as variables, we can now propose a rule that would limit the possible combinations of units, as specified by the following template:

>   Det-N-V-Det-N

This template allows us to indicate the correct way of stringing together these words and to rule out the meaningless ways.

But syntactic rules that merely specify templates for the correct word order wouldn't get us very far. Imagine you're a child learning about the syntactic possibilities of your language, and you've come up with the linear rule as stated above. Now, you encounter the following sentences:

>   She loves that kid.

>   Every kid loves her.

There's no way of fitting these new examples into the rule Det-N-V-Det-N. You might conclude that now you need another syntactic category that includes pronouns. And of course you'd have to specify where pronouns are allowed to occur in a sentence. So, you might add to your collection of possible rules:

Pro-V-Det-N

Det-N-V-Pro

where Pro stands for pronoun. And, if you encountered a sentence like *We love her*, you'd have to add a second pronoun:

Pro-V-Pro

So now you have a minimum of four rules to capture these simple sentences. But the fact that there are four separate rules misses something crucial: ultimately, structure is as systematic as it is because we want to be able to predict not just which groupings of words are legal, but also *what* the groupings *mean*. And, it turns out, the relationship between *she* and *loves that kid* is exactly the same as between *the teacher* and *loves that kid*. If there were separate rules that specified what Det + N could combine with and what Pro could combine with, in theory, they should be able to come with different specifications for the resulting meanings.

In other words, it might be possible for *The teacher loves that kid* to mean that the person doing the loving is the teacher, while *She loves that kid* might mean that whoever *she* refers to is the *recipient* of the kid's love. But this sort of thing never happens in languages. And what's more, if you looked at all the places where pronouns are allowed to occur, you'd find that they happen to be the exact same slots where Det + N are allowed to occur. What's needed is some way to show that the syntax of English treats Det + N and Pro as equivalent somehow—in other words, that Det + N can be grouped into a higher-order category, of which Pro happens to be a member. Let's call this a **noun phrase**, or **NP**.

As soon as we catch on to the notion that words can be clumped together into larger units, called **constituents**, our syntactic system becomes extremely powerful. Not only can we characterize the patterns of structure and meaning in the examples above, but we can explain many aspects of syntactic structure that would otherwise be completely mysterious. For instance, the syntax of English allows certain phrases to be shuffled around in a sentence while preserving essentially the same meaning. Some examples:

Wanda gave an obscure book on the history of phrenology to Tariq.

Wanda gave to Tariq an obscure book on the history of phrenology.

An obscure book on the history of phrenology is what Wanda gave to Tariq.

Here the phrase *an obscure book on the history of phrenology* acts as a single clump. It's impossible to break up this clump and move only a portion of it around; the following just won't work:

*Wanda gave an obscure to Tariq book on the history of phrenology.

*An obscure book is what Wanda gave to Tariq on the history of phrenology.

The reason these don't work is that the unit that's allowed to be moved corresponds to a higher-order constituent, an NP. The entire phrase *an obscure book on the history of phrenology* is an NP, so it has to move as a unit. (Notice the NP slot, indicated by brackets, could easily be filled by a much simpler phrase, as in *Wanda gave to Tariq [a puppy] / Wanda gave [a puppy] to Tariq*. Again, this illus-

noun phrase (NP) An abstract, higher-order syntactic category that can consist of a single word or of many words, but in which the main syntactic element is a noun, pronoun, or proper name.

constituent A syntactic category consisting of a word or (more often) a group of words (e.g., noun phrase, prepositional phrase) that clump together and function as a single unit within a sentence.

Christus, der ist mein Leben, 1st phrase (J. S. Bach)

Figure 6.1 We intuitively group words into phrases, or constituents. It's been argued that music is structured in a similar way, grouping notes together into constituents based on perceived relationships between pitches and chords. One effect of this is that pausing in the middle of a musical phrase or constituent makes a sequence of notes feel "unfinished" or unresolved. The figure shows an analysis of a musical phrase into its constituent parts. (From Lerdahl, 2005.)

trates the equivalence of NPs in the syntax, regardless of whether they're instantiated as very simple or very complex phrases.) This movement pattern can easily be captured with a notion of constituent structure—we could specify a rule that allows NPs to be moved around to various syntactic positions. But the pattern would seem rather arbitrary if our syntactic knowledge merely specified the linear order of individual words, because such a rule would give no indication of *why* the string of words should be cut exactly where it is. (You might be interested to know that music, like language, is often described as being structured in terms of constituents, as illustrated in **Figure 6.1**.)

One of the best arguments for the idea that sentences have internal structure rather than just linear ordering comes from the fact that the same string of words can sometimes have more than one meaning. Consider the following famous joke, attributed to Groucho Marx:

> Last night I shot an elephant in my pajamas. What he was doing in my pajamas, I'll never know.

Not a knee-slapper, perhaps, but the joke gets its humor from the unexpectedness of finding that the most natural way to interpret *I shot an elephant in my pajamas* turns out to be wrong, creating a jarring incongruity (incongruity being an essential ingredient of many jokes). On a first reading, most people don't group together *an elephant in my pajamas* as an NP unit, for the simple reason that this reading seems nonsensical. So they assume that the phrase *in my pajamas* is separate from the NP *an elephant*. That is, they assign the grouping:

> Last night I shot [$_{NP}$ an elephant] in my pajamas.

rather than the grouping:

> Last night I shot [$_{NP}$ an elephant in my pajamas].

But the joke ultimately requires you to go back and re-structure the sentence in a different (and very odd) way.

The rapid-fire decisions that people make about how to interpret ambiguous structures (see **Table 6.2**) is a fascinating topic that we'll explore in Chapter 8. But for the time being, notice how useful the idea of constituent structure can be. If sentences were defined only by word-order templates rather than being specified in terms of their underlying structure, examples like the Groucho Marx joke would seriously undermine the possibility of there being a systematic relationship between structure and meaning—the same word-order template would need to somehow be consistent with multiple meanings.

In fact, assigning two possible structures to the string *I shot an elephant in my pajamas* also explains an interesting fact, namely, that one of the possible meanings of the sentence evaporates if you do this:

> In my pajamas, I shot an elephant.

Now, it's impossible for the elephant to be sporting the pajamas; it can only be the speaker who's wearing them. This makes absolute sense if you know about constituent struc-

WEB ACTIVITY 6.1

Constituent structure in music
In this activity, you'll explore some parallels between the structure of sentences and the internal structure of music.

TABLE 6.2 Syntactic ambiguities

Can you identify at least two meanings associated with each sentence? Some meanings are clearly more plausible than others.

The children are ready to eat.

You should try dating older women or men.

He offered the dog meat.

What this company needs is more intelligent managers.

Jonathan has given up the mistress he was seeing for three years, to the great dismay of his wife.

Now you can enjoy a gourmet meal in your sweatpants.

Why did Joanie buy the frumpy housewife's dress?

LANGUAGE AT LARGE 6.1

Constituent structure and poetic effect

I've shown that grouping words into larger constituents can account for the equivalence of units like *the elephant in my pajamas* and *she* in the larger frame of the sentence. I've also argued that without constituent structure, we have no way of explaining why a string of words can have two quite different meanings. But there's additional evidence that we chunk words into constituents.

When you utter a long sentence, notice where you're most likely to take a breath or pause slightly. No one, for example, can read the following sentence from a Henry James novel (stripped here of its original commas) without slight breaks:

> He received three days after this a communication from America in the form of a scrap of blue paper folded and gummed not reaching him through his bankers but delivered at his hotel by a small boy in uniform who under instructions from the concierge approached him as he slowly paced the little court.

The slashes show where you're most likely to insert brief pauses:

> He received three days after this / a communication from America / in the form of a scrap of blue paper folded and gummed / not reaching him through his bankers / but delivered at his hotel by a small boy in uniform / who under instructions from the concierge / approached him / as he slowly paced the little court.

Notice that these breaks line up with boundaries between separate clauses or large phrases. As you'll see in this chapter, large chunks, or *constituents*, are in turn made up of smaller chunks. Pauses are most natural between some of the largest constituents in a sentence. The deeper down into the structure you go, the less likely there are to be breaks between words. It would be distinctly odd, for instance, to break up the first few phrases like this:

> He received three days after / this a communication from / America in the form of a /

Happily, Henry James made generous use of commas to help his readers group words into the right constituents.*

In poetry, although commas may be used, line breaks are often used to even more strongly set off phrases from one another, as in this stanza from Wilfred Owen's poem "Dulce et Decorum Est":

> *Bent double, like old beggars under sacks,*
> *Knock-kneed, coughing like hags, we cursed through sludge,*
> *Till on the haunting flares we turned our backs*
> *And towards our distant rest began to trudge.*
> *Men marched asleep. Many had lost their boots*
> *But limped on, blood-shod. All went lame; all blind;*
> *Drunk with fatigue; deaf even to the hoots*
> *Of tired, outstripped Five-Nines that dropped behind.*

* In case you're curious, with James's punctuation in place the sentence reads as follows: "He received three days after this a communication from America, in the form of a scrap of blue paper folded and gummed, not reaching him through his bankers, but delivered at his hotel by a small boy in uniform, who, under instructions from the concierge, approached him as he slowly paced the little court." (Henry James, *The Ambassadors*, 1903, p. 182.)

Continued on next page

With the exception of the second-to-last line, all of Owen's line breaks segment separate clauses or sentences, carving the stanza at its most natural joints.

But poets can skillfully leverage the expectations their readers have about the most natural carving joints in language by creatively violating these expectations (you know what you've always heard about what you can do with the rules once you know them). The technique of breaking up a line inside of a poem's constituent is called *enjambment*. Sometimes, it has the effect of forcing the reader to jump quickly to the next line in order to complete the constituent. The poet e. e. cummings uses enjambment (often even splitting up words) to enhance the manic feel of his poem "in Just-":

in Just-
spring   when the world is mud-
luscious the little
lame balloonman

whistles   far   and wee

and eddieandbill come
running from marbles and
piracies and it's
spring

In this next poem—a work by William Carlos Williams titled "Poem"—constituents are broken up in a way that creates an effect of freeze-framing the deliberate motions of a cat:

As the cat
climbed over
the top of

the jamcloset
first the right
forefoot

carefully
then the hind
stepped down
into the pit of
the empty
flowerpot.

In fact, the line breaks and the effect they create are the main reason we think of this piece as a poem in the first place.

Finally, in "We Real Cool," Gwendolyn Brooks, by busting up the sentences in an unexpected way, has given extra prominence to the pronoun *we*, lending it a swagger it would never have if each instance of the subject pronoun occurred on the same line as its verb phrase:

The Pool Players.
Seven at the Golden Shovel.

We real cool. We
Left School. We

Lurk Late. We
Strike Straight. We

Sing sin. We
Thin gin. We

Jazz June. We
Die soon.

ture and you also know that the rules that shuffle phrases around are stated in terms of higher-order constituents. Remember that under the pajama-wearing elephant reading, *an elephant in my pajamas* makes up an NP unit, so it can't be split up (much as in the examples earlier about Wanda and what she gave to Tariq). Splitting apart *an elephant* from *in my pajamas* is only possible if these two phrases form separate constituents, as is the case in the more sensible reading of that sentence.

Phrase structure rules

phrase structure rules   Rules that provide a set of instructions about how individual words can be clumped into higher-order categories and how these categories are combined to create well-formed sentences.

A useful way of capturing the structured nature of sentences is by means of **phrase structure rules** that provide a set of instructions on how individual words can be clumped into higher-order categories and how these are combined together to create well-formed sentences. For example, to capture the fact that a determiner and a noun can be combined to form a noun phrase, we might write:

NP → Det + N

We can apply this rule to give the following structure to the phrase *an elephant*:

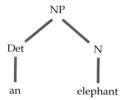

But we also know that a pronoun on its own can correspond to an NP—this is apparent because pronouns and Det + N phrases sit in the same syntactic slots and contribute to a sentence's meaning in the same way:

An elephant sneezed.

It sneezed.

So we also need a phrase structure rule to reflect this structure:

NP → Pro

which gives the pronoun *it* this structure:

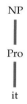

We can make exactly the same observation about proper names, which also act as NPs (for example, *Jonathan sneezed*). So we now have a third way of building an NP:

NP → name

Now, we've also seen that *an elephant in my pajamas* can be a complex constituent. In fact, it's also an NP, as evidenced by the role it plays in *An elephant in my pajamas sneezed*. This phrase is a bit more complex, involving a **prepositional phrase (PP)** embedded inside the noun phrase (NP). And notice that there's an NP embedded within the PP. So, we get a structure like this (where P stands for the category "preposition"):

prepositional phrase (PP) A syntactic constituent, or higher-order category, that in English, consists of a preposition (e.g., in, under, before) followed by an NP.

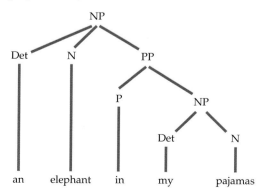

To get a structure like the above, we need the following rules:

(a) NP → Det + N + PP

(b) PP → P + NP

(c) NP → Det + N

We can also collapse (a) and (c) into a single rule schema, using parentheses to show that the PP is optional:

NP → Det + N + (PP)

Notice that we now have multiple ways of instantiating an NP. We've seen that any one of the possible expansions for an NP could occur interchangeably as potential subjects of a verb like *sneezed*. The same modular approach is available for any NP slot, regardless of where in the sentence it occurs. For example, consider the second NP in our tree structure, under the PP. Instead of expanding the NP node into Det + N, we could have expanded it as Pro:

[$_{NP}$ An elephant [$_{PP}$ in [$_{NP}$ it]]]

using brackets within brackets to indicate phrases within phrases. And, since an NP can in turn include a PP (which itself must include an NP within), we could also get a much more complex phrase:

[$_{NP}$ An elephant [$_{PP}$ in [$_{NP}$ my pajamas [$_{PP}$ from [$_{NP}$ the store]]]]]

And, iterating the NP rule once more:

[$_{NP}$ An elephant [$_{PP}$ in [$_{NP}$ my pajamas [$_{PP}$ from [$_{NP}$ the store [$_{PP}$ down [$_{NP}$ the street]]]]]]]

Now that we've explored a range of options for creating NPs, we also want to have rules for combining NPs (which serve either as subjects or objects) together with verbs (V) to form sentences (S). For instance, we might have:

S → NP + VP

VP → V + (NP) + (PP)

where VP stands for the category "verb phrase." This fragment of a phrase structure grammar would now allow us to get *both* versions of *I shot an elephant in my pajamas*.

As you can see from **Box 6.2**, we'd need a much more complete set of phrase structure rules to capture the full combinatorial possibilities for English. But even the small set of rules that are described in Box 6.2 can offer up some powerful machinery for creating new combinations.

It's worth noting that there is no consensus about the exact way to represent the syntactic structures of even quite simple sentences. Various frameworks have evolved, each relying on a number of arguments about why the structures should be represented in one particular way or another. These disagreements exist because once you start including a broad enough set of sentences in your data set, there are subtle aspects of linguistic structure that might lead to rethinking the original rules—you may have encountered this process already in considering possible rules for the sentences in Box 6.2. Also, different frameworks might have different ways of lining up the syntactic rules with their semantic effects. There are even disagreements about whether theoretical notions like phrase structure rules really reflect very closely how human minds represent the structures of language—or whether these rules are simply a convenient, shorthand way of expressing our knowledge of the syntactic

BOX 6.2
Rules for constructing sentences of English

Consider a possible set of rules for capturing the sentences we've discussed so far (parentheses indicate optional elements):

1. S → NP + VP
2. VP → V + (NP) + (PP)
3. NP → Pro
4. NP → Name
5. NP → (Det) + N + (PP)
6. PP → P + NP

It takes a bit of practice to get an intuitive feel for how such rules might work. For the following sentences, try using the above rules to create tree structures in which each node of the tree shows the result of applying one of the syntactic rules. If a sentence can have more than one meaning, be sure to show both possible structures, as permitted by the syntactic rules:

The girl with a tattoo loves me.
Bill snores.
Samantha read the book on the Queen's throne.
A life with no love awaits Jenny in the future.
I saw the man with the glasses from my store.

Is that all there is to English syntax? Hardly. If you take note of sentences all around you, you'll quickly run into examples that can't be captured by our current set of rules. Here are a few:

I love the girl who has a tattoo.
Alisha told me that she loved her husband.
Weyman and Stuart drank beer for three hours.
The three little pigs built their houses on the hill.
You believed the outlandish story that she fed you.
Fabian threatened to kill his rival.

You'd need to propose additional rules to build these sentences. Give it a try: suggest a specific set of rules that would produce these sentences, and provide the tree structure that would result. Don't worry about how you would label the syntactic units (any sensible label will do), but do think about which clumps would form a constituent.

Can you think of a few other examples of sentences that go beyond the scope of the rules in this box? (Note: this shouldn't be hard to do!)

---

patterns of our language, knowledge that might actually be implemented in a very different way. But for the most part, people tend to agree on a number of important points, including the following:

- Our knowledge of structure is **generative**; that is, whatever we know about language structure allows us to recognize and generate new examples of never-before-encountered sentences.

- Our knowledge of language structure must be **hierarchical**—that is, it needs to reflect the fact that words group together into constituents, which in turn can group together with other words or constituents to form larger constituents.

- The generative and hierarchical qualities of language allow for **recursion**, permitting syntactic embeddings that resemble loops that (in theory) could go on forever (see **Box 6.3**).

We've seen, for example, that a PP can be embedded within an NP—but the PP also can contain an NP. This creates the possibility of a structure that ends up looking a lot like nested Russian dolls, with multiple NPs (each enclosed in brackets in these examples) hiding within embedded PPs:

[The paper on [the desk in [the office]]]

generative With respect to language, a quality of language that allows us to use whatever we know about language structure to recognize and generate new examples of never-before-encountered sentences.

hierarchical Top-down (or bottom-up) arrangement of categories. With respect to language, a quality that involves how words group together into constituents, which in turn can group together with other words or constituents to form ever-larger constituents.

recursion Repeated iterations. With respect to language, refers to syntactic embeddings that nest constituents (such as clauses or NPs) within other constituents in a potentially infinite manner.

There's nothing in the syntactic rules that prevents this from going on in the same vein:

> [The paper on [the desk in [the office on [the top floor of [the house]]]]]

and on:

> [The paper on [the desk in [the office on [the top floor of [the house down [the street]]]]]]

and on:

> [The paper on [the desk in [the office on [the top floor of [the house down [the street outside [the city limits]]]]]]]

Eventually, these recursive structures get to be too much for our memory to keep track of, an issue we'll pick up in Chapter 8. But it's in the nature of a generative syntax like this to allow a handful of phrase structure rules to generate what is, in principle, an infinite number of sentences that adhere to those rules. This makes a language incredibly powerful and creative

Now back to the big question: How do kids ever figure out that their language has the sort of syntactic structure it does? Over the course of hearing many sentences, they would need to register that certain words tend to occur in the same syntactic contexts, and group those words into the same type of syntactic category. They'd then have to notice that certain words tend to clump together in sentences, and that the various clumps occur in the same syntactic contexts, forming interchangeable constituents. They would also have to clue in to the fact that these interchangeable word clumps always have the same relationship to the meaning of the sentence, regardless of the clumps' specific content. Finally (as we'll see in more detail in Section 6.4), they would have to figure out the possibilities for moving constituents around in a sentence while keeping track of relationships between them over long spans of words. Any one of these learning tasks involves hearing and tracking lots and lots of sentences and then drawing quite abstract generalizations from these many sentences.

One of the most hotly debated issues in psycholinguistics is whether kids are helped along in the learning process by genetic programming that outfits them with specific assumptions about how languages work. Such innate programming would no doubt make learning syntax less daunting. And, despite the fact that languages of the world come in a great variety of syntactic flavors, there are a surprising number of ways in which they overlap in terms of their structural properties. Of all the possible systems that languages *might* have evolved to combine words, it seems that only a pretty restricted subset of these options ever turn up. And, interestingly, kids rarely seem to follow dead-end leads that would cause them to posit exotic grammatical systems that stray from what we think of as a human language. As a result, a number of researchers have proposed that children come into the world with a set of constraints that steer them away from ever considering grammars that fall outside the range of human grammars. In other words, children might have in place an innate **universal grammar** that provides them with a set of learning biases that line up nicely with the syntactic systems of human languages.

Opponents of this view argue that no such extra help is needed. Kids, they suggest, are equipped with robust general-purpose learning machinery that is perfectly up to the task of learning syntactic generalizations from huge quantities of data. The reason children don't work themselves into a tight corner

universal grammar A hypothetical set of innate learning biases that guide children's learning processes and constrain the possible structures of human languages.

BOX 6.3
A language without recursion?

In most languages, recursive structures are varied and abundant. For example, in English, recursion makes it possible to create complex phrases like these:

John's brother's house is big.

Frog and Toad are friends.

Cyprian will either marry his childhood sweetheart or he'll spend his life alone.

Ernie thinks that Bert wants to get a pet pigeon.

The letter that Juliet sent to Romeo went astray.

Language researchers have generally assumed that recursion is a universal property of language. But there may be exceptions. Dan Everett, a linguist who worked among the Pirahã people of the Amazonian jungle (see **Figure 6.2**), has claimed that sentences like the above, with their embedded constituents, don't exist in Pirahã (Everett, 2005). Instead of saying *John's brother's house*, speakers of this language would say something like:

Brother's house. John has a brother. It is the same one.

Or, instead of saying *The tiger got Jake and Lisa*, a Pirahã speaker would say:

The tiger got Jake. Lisa also.

One consequence of the lack of recursion is that, unlike English, Pirahã places an upper limit on the length of any given sentence in that language.

Everett's claims about Pirahã have been challenged by other linguists who question his analysis of the language, and because of limited access to this small, remote group of speakers, the controversy has yet to be resolved. But if Everett's claims are accurate, they raise some intriguing questions. Why would a language decline to make use of the powerful device of recursion in its syntax? And, from another angle, if humans can communicate with each other perfectly well without recursion in their language, why is recursion such a massively robust feature of language? What are the communicative costs and benefits of recursion?

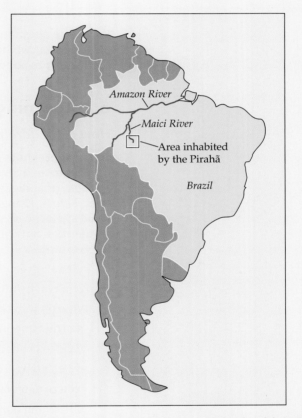

Figure 6.2 The Pirahã people live on the banks of the Maici River in Brazil's Amazon Basin. As of 2010, there were about 420 individuals in this small community.

thinking that English sentences are generated by an alien grammar is because they have access to plenty of data that would quickly disabuse them of syntactic generalizations that fall too far from the mark.

What's more, there are alternative explanations for the syntactic similarities across languages, as explored in Chapter 2. Languages may share certain similarities *not* because the human brain is genetically programmed for certain structures, but because certain structures do a better job of meeting communicative needs, or lining up with the brain's strengths and weaknesses when it comes to learning or processing linguistic structure.

The disagreements between the nativist and data-driven views of syntactic learning tend to come down to several issues: First, what information *is* there in the input that a child hears—that is, is there actually enough evidence in the input to promote the right generalizations and circumvent the incorrect ones that kids might be tempted to make? Second, what kinds of learning mechanisms are available to kids throughout their learning trajectory? Third, what is it that children know about language structure anyway? Does their knowledge actually correspond to the kinds of abstract rules and representations that we've just posited for an adult's knowledge of syntax? In the rest of this chapter, we'll see that these questions have yet to be definitively answered. On the other hand, it's clear that we have a growing set of theoretical and methodological tools with which to address them.

6.2 Learning Grammatical Categories

How do children know about grammatical categories?

To crawl back into the mind of a young child in the early stages of language development, it always helps to consider an unfamiliar language. Let's look at Zapotec, an indigenous language of Mexico that you probably haven't encountered before. Using the following sentences as a basis, take a stab at drawing some syntactic generalizations, at least at the level of basic word order. What regularities can you see? (Warning: it may take a little while to work through these examples.)

> ytaa'az gyeeihlly li'eb
>
> bgu'tya' bzihny
>
> ytoo'oh li'eb ca'arr
>
> naa'ng banguual
>
> naa li'eb banguual
>
> gwua'ilreng li'ebr
>
> rcaa'za ygu'tya' bzihny
>
> binydyang dolf ytoo'oh pa'amm ca'rr
>
> re'ihpy pa'aamm laa'reng gwua'llreng li'ebr

Got it? Good. Now, what is the correct way to order the following three words: *juaany, be'cw,* and *udiiny?* (Seriously, give this a try before reading any further.)

Actually, I suspect you can't tell—this wasn't an entirely fair exercise. You simply didn't have enough information in this little language sample to be able to figure out much of anything. But things change quite dramatically if I give you a bit of information about how the individual words map onto meanings. Using the mappings below, try again to derive some syntactic generalizations and figure out the correct order of *juaany, be'cw,* and *udiiny.*

> ytaa'az—beat
>
> bgu'tya', ygu'tya'—kill
>
> ytoo'oh—sell
>
> naa'ng, naa—be

gwua'llreng—read

rcaa'za—want

binydyang—hear

re'ihp—tell

bzihny—mouse

ca'arr—car

li'ebr—book

banguual—old

udiiny—hit

be'cw—dog

gyeeihlly, li'eb, pa'amm, dolf, and juaany—all proper names

This information makes all the difference. You should now be able to tell that *udiiny juuany be'cw* would give you a well-formed sentence.

It's worth thinking about *why* the information about how the individual words map onto meanings is so useful. It's useful because of the following assumptions you were implicitly making: (1) words that map onto the same general kinds of meanings (for example, actions rather than people or things) will occupy the same slots in the syntax, and (2) the syntactic patterns are affected by the role that entities play in a sentence (distinguishing, for example, the agents that instigate actions from the entities that are acted upon).

Where do these assumptions come from? Quite possibly from your knowledge of English, in which syntactic categories do tend to be made up of words that are similar in meaning. But what's interesting is that these assumptions turn out to be universally true of languages. Given that this is the case, and that they turn out to do so much work in breaking into the syntax of a new language, it seems sensible to ask whether children come into the world preprogrammed with certain basic preconceptions about the relationship between language structure and meaning. In order for these assumptions to be accessible at the very outset to a child learning a *first* language, they'd have to be innate.

This is the position taken by proponents of the **semantic bootstrapping hypothesis**. The idea is that the child comes equipped with innate expectations of certain grammatical categories as well as built-in mappings between key concept types and grammatical categories. For example, children might jumpstart syntactic learning with the innate knowledge that nouns tend to be used to refer to objects, or that the subject of a sentence is typically the agent of the action that's being described.

As useful as it might be for babies to have such preprogrammed expectations, this doesn't necessarily mean that they have them. It might instead be the case that babies start off innocent of even the most basic facts about how meaning and syntax relate to each other, that they have to build from the ground up the notions that words fall into specific grammatical categories, and that this constrains not only aspects of their meaning, but also how they combine with other words in sentences. The arguments for innately based semantic bootstrapping become weaker if we can show that babies are able to learn these things easily and without any built-in assumptions.

To get a feel for how this might happen, consider again the Zapotec sentences you saw earlier. What would happen if you *didn't* assume from the getgo that words for people and things could be grouped together into a coherent syntactic category that patterned systematically in the language's structure?

semantic bootstrapping hypothesis
The idea that children come equipped with innate expectations of certain grammatical categories, as well as built-in mappings between key concept types and grammatical categories.

distributional evidence The tendency of words or types of words to appear in certain syntactic contexts, allowing extrapolation of these tendencies to newly learned words.

What if you had to rely *only* on the evidence that was there in front of you in the sentences themselves, without the benefit of any preconceptions that words that are similar in meaning might behave similarly in the syntax of a sentence? How would you form a concept of a grammatical category, and how would you figure out which words belong to it?

You likely could eventually break into the system, but it would take you many more example sentences than just the few that you were offered here. But eventually, with enough data, you might notice, for instance, that certain words like *ytaa'az* or *re'ihpy* only ever occur at the beginnings of sentences, so you'd begin to group them as belonging to the same class of words (let's call this Class A for the moment). You would then also notice that only certain words can appear immediately after the Class A words, words like *li'eb* or *bzihny*, which we'll call Class B words. Given enough **distributional evidence** of this sort—that is, evidence about the tendencies of words to appear in certain syntactic contexts—you could come up with some generalizations about word order. Once you moved on to learning the meanings of some of these words, you might then notice that Class A words tend to be words that refer to actions, and that Class B words tend to refer to people, things, or animals. This would then allow you to make very reasonable guesses about whether new words you meet should belong in the syntactic categories of Class A or B, once you had some idea of their meanings. From this point on, you would be in a position similar to the one you started the exercise with—that is, with certain ideas firmly in place about the mapping between syntactic categories and meanings. It just would have taken you a while to get there. Moreover, paying attention to distributional evidence, rather than meanings alone, would ultimately lead you to a more accurate understanding of these categories (see **Box 6.4**).

Is distributional evidence powerful enough?

To make a convincing case that youngsters can form syntactic categories by tracking distributional evidence, we'll need to answer several questions. The first of these is: If we look beyond just a small sampling of language, how reliable would this distributional evidence be? And if distributional evidence does turn out to be a reliable source of information for forming grammatical categories, our second question would be: Is there any evidence that small children are able to track distributional evidence and group words into categories accordingly?

Let's start with the first question regarding the reliability of distributional evidence. In arguing for the semantic bootstrapping hypothesis, which takes the position that some assumptions about syntax are innate, Steven Pinker (1987) noted that a child could run into trouble if he were relying solely on distributional patterns in sentences such as these:

(1a) John ate fish.

(1b) John ate rabbits.

(1c) John can fish.

If our alert toddler happened to notice that *fish* and *rabbits* occur in exactly the same syntactic environments in examples 1a and 1b, he'd be in danger of concluding that the following sentence is also perfectly good:

(1d) *John can rabbits.

The problem here is that a single word, *fish*, actually falls into more than one syntactic category; it can act as either a noun or a verb, while *rabbits* can't. But

BOX 6.4
Science is *not* a verb

Michael Shermer, editor of *Skeptic* magazine, is a fervent advocate for science. In a 2006 interview with Kevin Berger of *Salon* magazine, he said:

> We've got to get past this idea that science is a thing. It isn't a thing like religion is a thing or a political party is a thing. It's true that scientists have clubs. They have banners and meetings and they drink beer together. But science is just a method, a way of answering questions. It's a verb, not a noun.

Shermer's point is that, rather than treating science as a collection of facts or ideological beliefs, we should understand that it's a process that demands active engagement.

I appreciate Shermer's take on science. Truly, I do. But I can't get on board with the idea that science is a verb. The notions of verb-hood and noun-hood are, at their core, notions of *structure* and not meaning, defined in terms of which slots in a sentence they can occupy. And it's plain to see that the word *science* occupies noun-y slots rather than verb-y ones:

> Science is not a verb.
>
> Rice is not a liquid.
>
> Ink is not a food.
>
> The science of language is cool.

The hair of kittens is soft.

The president of the company is foolish.

The word *science* sits in the same slots as the words *rice*, *hair*, and *president*—all of which are, uncontroversially, nouns. If *science* were a verb, we'd be able to say things like:

> I think we should have scienced that.
>
> Did you remember to science your theory?
>
> He presented his findings after sciencing in solitude for a year.

Common "knowledge" is that nouns refer to "things" and verbs to "actions." And, as argued in this chapter, the match between the *syntactic* notions of nouns and verbs and the kinds of *meanings* nouns and verbs tend to capture is potentially very useful for language learning. This match-up of syntax and meaning provides clues about the syntactic categories of new words we encounter. But the match is only a tendency; ultimately, learners of a language have to cope with the fact that actions and events can be nouns (*destruction; revenge; flood*) and that not all verbs involve actions (*need; correspond; negate*). So, the meaning of a word can sometimes provide misleading or unhelpful information about its syntactic category. When this happens, distributional cues need to prevail.

---

how could our child tell that *fish* in 1a is in a different category than *fish* in 1c? If he knew that it referred to a thing in 1a but an activity in 1c, and if he knew that these meanings mapped to different categories, he'd manage not to go astray. But without these assumptions in place, he could be misled.

Distributional evidence might be messy in other ways that would preclude our child from learning the right categories for words. For example, if he were paying attention to which words can occur at the beginnings of sentences in English, he'd come across examples like these:

(2a) John ate fish.

(2b) Eat the fish!

(2c) The fish smells bad.

(2d) Whales like fish.

(2e) Some of the fish smells bad.

(2f) Quick, catch the fish!

(2g) Never eat fish with a spoon.

lexical co-occurrence patterns Information about which words tend to appear adjacent to each other in a given data set.

bigrams Sequences of two words (i.e., word pairs).

trigrams Sequences of three words.

In each of the above examples, the first word of the sentence belongs to a different syntactic category. Assuming that children aren't fed a carefully regimented sample of speech that manages to avoid these problems until they've properly sorted words into categories, how useful could distributional evidence be?

It's obviously going to matter *what* distributional evidence we consider. Looking just at the left edge of a sentence doesn't produce great results for English, but other patterns could be much more regular. For example, looking at **lexical co-occurrence** patterns (that is, at information about which words tend to appear adjacent to each other in a data set) could prove to be more promising. For instance, in English it turns out to be fairly easy to predict which category can occur in which of the following slots in these word pairs, or **bigrams**:

>   (3a) the ___
>   (3b) should ___
>   (3c) very ___

Chances are, if asked, you'd supply a noun in 3a, a verb in 3b, and an adjective in 3c. And lexical co-occurrence patterns get even more useful if we look at sequences of *three* words, or **trigrams**:

>   (4a) the ___is
>   (4b) should ___ the
>   (4c) very ___ house

Note, for example, that either an adjective or a noun can occur after *the*, but only a noun can occur between *the* and *is*. Similarly, examples 4b and 4c are more constrained with trigrams than are the bigrams in 3b and 3c.

Pursuing this idea, Toby Mintz (2003) set out to measure the reliability of sequences, or "frames," such as *the ___ is* or *should ___ the*. He looked at a large database containing transcriptions of the recorded speech of parents talking to toddlers and pulled out the 45 most frequent sequences of three words in which the first and last words were the same. So, for instance, the sequences *the doggy is* and *the bottle is* count as two instances of the frame *the ___ is*. He then measured, for each of these frames, how accurate it would be to make the assumption that the middle words in the trigrams would always be of the same grammatical category. This measure of accuracy reveals just how predictive the frame is of that intervening word's category.

Mintz found that, by relying just on these frequent frames in the database, it would be possible to correctly group the words that occurred in the frames with an accuracy rate of better than 90%. Hence, it seems there's pretty sturdy statistical information to be had just on the basis of distributional evidence (provided, of course, that small children are able to tune in to just this type of handy statistical evidence while perhaps ignoring other, less useful distributional evidence).

Using Mintz's "frequent frames" is only one possible way of capturing statistical regularities for words of the same grammatical category. Other formulations have also proven useful to greater or lesser degrees, and the usefulness of various statistical strategies may vary from language to language. Leaving aside for the moment the issue of exactly how best to capture distributional regularities, it's at least fair to say that information from lexical co-occurrence is reliable enough to allow kids to make reasonably good guesses about the category membership of a large number of words, once they've been exposed to enough examples.

So, what about our second question: Are very small children able to make use of these regularities? We saw in Chapter 4 that babies as young as 8 months can track statistical patterns over adjacent syllables and are able to use this information to make guesses about word boundaries. So, there's already good reason to suspect that they might also be attuned to statistical patterns in inferring the grammatical categories of words. And some recent studies of babies in their second year provide more direct evidence for this view. For instance, Mintz (2006) studied how 12-month-olds would react upon hearing novel words in frequent frames within sentences such as *She wants you to deeg it* or *I see the bist*. Some words, like *deeg*, consistently appeared in verb slots, while others, like *bist*, appeared in noun slots during a familiarization phase. Mintz then measured looking times during a test phase and found that the babies distinguished between grammatical versus ungrammatical sentences that contained these novel words. That is, they looked longer at the "ungrammatical" sentence *I bist you now* than at the "grammatical" *I deeg you now* (see **Figure 6.3**).

Other studies, using artificial grammars, also suggest that beginning at about 1 year of age, very small children can sort novel words into categories based solely on distributional information. In fact, they seem to be able to do this even when the distributional information is not perfectly consistent, suggesting that small doses of problematic examples like those flagged by Pinker in examples 1a through 1c above might not present a dire problem for learning. The exact nature of the statistical information that children can draw on is still not clear, though. This may well change over the course of development; for example, it may be that information involving adjacent words in the form of bigrams is easier for kids to clue in to earlier in their development than information involving non-adjacent elements, as in the frequent-frames hypothesis.

Finding evidence that children can form categories on the basis of distributional evidence alone does not, of course, rule out the possibility that they *also* tap into innate preconceptions about the relationship between grammatical categories and their typical contributions to meaning. It's perfectly possible that children lean on both kinds of informa-

Figure 6.3 Mintz used the head-turn preference procedure (see Method 4.1) to measure the ability of infants to infer syntactic categories from distributional evidence. (A) Infants heard nonsense words within bigrams (word pairs, shown in italic) or trigrams (three words) in either noun-supporting or verb-supporting sentence frames, unaccompanied by any semantic context. To make sure some nonsense words weren't intrinsically more "noun-y" or "verb-y" than others, the subjects were divided into two groups. The words presented to Group 1 as nouns were presented to Group 2 as verbs, and vice versa. (B) In the test phase, the words were presented to the infants in grammatical and ungrammatical sentences. (C) Results, showing mean listening times to grammatical and ungrammatical sentences, by frame type. (Adapted from Mintz, 2006.)

(A) **Familiarization phase**

Group 1	
Verb Frame Sentences	**Noun Frame Sentences**
She wants *to deeg it*.	I see *the gorp in* the room.
She wants *to lonk it*.	I see *the bist in* the room.
You *can deeg*.	That's *your gorp*.
You *can lonk*.	That's *your bist*.
Can *you deeg the* room?	I put *his gorp on* the box.
I lonk you now!	Here's *a bist of* a dog.

Group 2	
Verb Frame Sentences	**Noun Frame Sentences**
She wants *to gorp it*.	I see *the deeg in* the room.
She wants *to bist it*.	I see *the lonk in* the room.
You *can gorp*.	That's *your deeg*.
You *can bist*.	That's *your lonk*.
Can *you gorp the* room?	I put *his deeg on* the box.
I bist you now!	Here's *a lonk of* a dog.

(B) **Test phase**

Grammatical for Group 1; ungrammatical for Group 2

Can you lonk the room?
I deeg you now!
I put his bist on the box.
Here's a gorp of a dog.

Grammatical for Group 2; ungrammatical for Group 1

Can you bist the room?
I gorp you now!
I put his lonk on the box.
Here's a deeg of a dog.

(C) **Results**

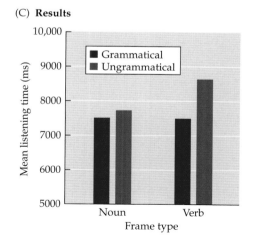

tion. However, the potential clout of the statistical information does suggest that perhaps a semantic bootstrapping hypothesis is less *necessary* to account for children's earliest groupings of words into abstract categories.

6.3 How Abstract Is Early Syntax?

Do children understand structure in the same way as adults?

So far, I've tried to persuade you that in order to capture what you know about how words can be strung together into sentences, you need to have (1) internalized an abstract set of categories, and (2) learned some rules or patterns for combining these categories. Without these, it's hard to see how we could account for the flexible and systematic nature of your syntactic knowledge.

I've also discussed a bit of evidence that children start to distinguish among syntactic categories in the second year of life, along with some ideas about how they might be able to pull this off. And it's also during the second year of life that toddlers begin to combine words together in their own speech. So this must mean that this is the point at which we're seeing evidence that they know about general patterns of syntax or phrase structure rules.

Not so fast. To sing the refrain: Once again, we should avoid making assumptions about what children know at any given stage based on what we know about language as adults. After all, it's possible that their early combinations of words rely on some knowledge that looks very different from ours.

It's easier to imagine this if we think of a species that we don't normally consider to be terribly linguistically sophisticated (and hence, quite likely to be very different from us cognitively). Let's suppose, for example, that you've taught your pet pigeon to peck on pictures that correspond to words or phrases of English in order to earn food pellets. I have no doubt you could do this if you were patient enough. I also suspect that you could teach your bird to distinguish between sentences like *The man bites the dog* and *The dog bites the man* so that it would peck on different pictures for each of these, each picture corresponding to a depiction of the sentence it was paired with. Would you be credible in claiming that your pigeon had learned syntax, and knew all about phrase structure rules? Not at all. You would have no evidence that the bird wasn't simply treating each of these sentences as if they were long words, each with their particular associations or "meanings." (Actually, it's not even clear that the pigeon has a notion of meanings, based on this test, but we'll leave this issue aside for the moment.) That is, the bird likely just memorized which string of sounds is supposed to go with each picture, much as we have to simply memorize the meanings of individual words or morphemes rather than composing them out of meaningful parts. To get evidence for syntax, we would need to see much more impressive data.

We should be as skeptical and conservative in imputing linguistic knowledge to babies as we are to pigeons. Sure, the knowledge of young kids is more *likely* than that of a pigeon to resemble our adult linguistic system, but where's the evidence? That is: When kids are beginning to form larger units of meaning in which they put together recognizable words, are we really seeing evidence of fully abstract rules? Or are they doing something less flexible and creative, akin to memorizing word-like structures? Or another possibility: they might be doing something in between. For example, they might know that their existing collection of words can be combined together with other meaningful words, and they might know that the order in which they get combined matters, but they might not yet have a fully abstract set of rules. They might instead know, for example, that the verb *bite* can be put together with two other words that pick out people or animals, and that the word that goes *before* the verb *bite* picks out the offending biter while the word that *follows* the verb picks out the bitten victim. This would allow them to form a rudimentary sentence with the verb *bite*, combining it with their repertoire of nouns. But maybe they don't yet know that you can accomplish similar tricks with similar effects on meaning with just about any combinations of words that happen to be nouns and verbs.

Looking for evidence of rules

Where would we look for evidence of abstract rules? Obviously, the usefulness of having rules in the first place lies in the fact that they can be extended to any novel words that we might learn. If you, with your fully fledged syntactic system in place, learn a new adjective like *avuncular*, for example, you don't also need to learn where you can shoehorn it into a sentence—this comes for free once you have a fully formed syntax. You might have first learned it in a sentence such as *My boss has somewhat of an avuncular air about him*, but you can immediately trot out your newly acquired vocabulary gem in new word orders such as *The president strikes me as avuncular* or *The avuncular but rigorous professor has a loyal student following*, and so on. In fact, you don't even need to know the meaning of the word in order to confidently recognize that if the first sentence is grammatical, then so are the others. You can accomplish that feat by substituting the word *brillig* for *avuncular*, for example.

So, the best test for the abstraction and generality of toddlers' syntactic knowledge would be to check to see how readily their knowledge extends beyond specific memorized words or phrases and can be applied to freshly encountered new words—can they take a new word and plug it into all the slots that call for a word of that category, even if they've never seen the word in those particular slots?

In fact, mistakes may provide some of the best evidence for abstract rules; when kids overstep the bounds and apply a rule *too* generally, producing forms that they've never heard their parents say, this gives us some compelling clues about the learning that's taken place underneath. Remember from Chapter 5, for example, that there's a stage during which kids' speech includes "creative" errors like "He *goed* to the store" or "The teacher *holded* it." We saw that one way of interpreting these errors is to say that kids have figured out that there's an abstract rule in which you can take a verb stem and tack the morpheme *-ed* onto it to signal past tense. The reason these are errors is because English happens to have exceptions—at some point, you have to memorize which verbs are exempt from the rule. The above errors could be seen as evidence that children have the rule, but haven't yet sorted out the exceptions—they've gone a bit wild in their application of rule.

There's some reason to think that kids do this at the level of syntax too. Sometimes they do appear to overapply structures of syntax, as well, and assume that they involve a more general category than they actually do. Melissa Bowerman (1982) documented some examples of errors like these:

Don't giggle me! (Meaning "Don't make me giggle!")

You can push her mouth open to drink her. (Meaning "You can make her drink.")

She falled me. (Meaning "She made me fall.")

These seem like fanciful inventions that stray far away from the grammar of actual English, until you realize that there are examples like this in *adult* English:

Don't melt the butter. (Meaning "Don't make the butter melt.")

You can bounce the ball. (Meaning "You can make the ball bounce.")

intransitive verbs Verbs that take a subject but no object, such as *(Joe) sneezes* or *(Keesha) laughs.*

transitive verbs Verbs that take both a subject and an object, such as *(Joe) kicks (the ball)* or *(Keesha) eats (popcorn).*

You broke it. (Meaning "You made it break.")

All of a sudden, it looks less like the kids are just pulling syntax out of their ear, and more like they might actually be on to something—perhaps they're noticing that verbs that appear in the **intransitive** form (with just a subject) can also appear in the **transitive** form (with a subject and an object), and that when they do, the object in the *transitive* form takes on the same role in the event that the subject takes in the *intransitive* form:

> *The butter* melted. You melted *the butter.*
>
> *The ball* bounced. The girl bounced *the ball.*
>
> *The glass* broke. She broke *the glass.*

Unfortunately, the children abstracted a rule that is slightly *too* general (see **Table 6.3**). It turns out that for English, this equivalency in syntax can't be applied willy-nilly to all verbs. Rather, it's restricted to particular classes of verbs that tend to signal a change of state or location. As it happens, some languages *can* apply a rule like this to more or less all verbs, so it's not a crazy hypothesis

TABLE 6.3 Some examples of children's creative overgeneralizations

Child's utterance	Speakers' age (years; months)
From Bowerman, 1988	
I said her no.	3; 1
Don't say me that or you'll make me cry.	2;
I want Daddy choose me what to have.	2; 6
Button me the rest.	3; 4
I'll brush him his hair.	2; 3
Do you want to see us disappear our heads?	6+
I don't want any more grapes. They just cough me.	2; 8+
I want to comfortable you.	5; 9
It always sweats me. *(Said while refusing a sweater.)*	4; 3
If you don't put them in for a very long time, they won't get staled. *(Referring to crackers in a bread box.)*	3; 6
Mommy will get lightninged. *(Meaning "struck by lightning.")*	5; 2
Can I fill some salt into the bear? *(Referring to a bear-shaped salt shaker.)*	5; 0
I'm gonna cover a screen over me.	4; 5
He's gonna die you, David. *(Then mother is addressed.)* The tiger will come and eat David and then he will be died and I won't have a brother any more.	4+
C. Hudson Kam (unpublished observations of her son)	
Why did you fall me off, Daddy?	2; 10
I was just getting you afraid. Did I afraid you?	3; 3
I wuv cheesecake! It bounces me off walls!	3; 4
This is colding me. *(Said while waving hands in front of face.)*	3; 4
I am running while fastening my legs. *(Meaning "making them go faster than they are supposed to go.")*	3; 6
She deadened him. *(Meaning "she killed him.")*	3; 7

for the kids to make. Like the overgeneralization of regular past-tense forms, it might be seen as evidence that kids are learning to syntactically manipulate abstract categories like verbs and noun phrases, in much the same way as our phrase structure rules in Section 6.1 involved the manipulation of categories like verbs or noun phrases.

Children as cautious learners of syntax

Some researchers have argued that overextensions like *She falled me* actually play a fairly marginal role in children's very early syntax. On the contrary, these scientists suggest, when children first start to combine words in short sentences, they display a startling *lack* of adventurousness in generalizing patterns to new forms. Michael Tomasello (1992) documented his own daughter's early speech and discovered that any particular verb that entered her vocabulary was often produced in only one syntactic frame for quite some time afterward, rather than being incorporated into other possible syntactic frames with verb slots. This happened even though different verbs might enter her usage as part of different frames. So, a verb like *break* might appear along with a subject and object, as in *Mommy break cup,* while *cut* might appear only with an object, as in *cut string.* His daughter rarely produced strings like *break dolly* or *Daddy cut meat.* In other words, *break* and *cut* were treated as if each verb had its own miniature set of combination rules; the verbs were clearly not considered interchangeable. This led Tomasello to suggest that it takes children a fairly long time to integrate verbs into a full system of phrase structure rules. If they did have such a system, he argued, new verbs would appear in multiple syntactic frames, wherever verbs in general are allowed to appear, much as is the case whenever you're introduced to a new adjective like *avuncular* or *brillig.*

Tomasello and his colleagues have since conducted a variety of experiments showing that when it comes to verbs, at least, children are conservative learners rather than eager generalizers. In a 1997 study, they compared how readily children generalized nouns and verbs by repeatedly exposing toddlers (average of 2 years and 10 months) to novel words over a period of 10 days. For instance, children saw pictures accompanied by comments such as "Look! The wug!" or "Look what Ernie's doing to Big Bird. It's called meeking!" The children easily learned the meanings of both the nouns and verbs, and used them regularly in their own speech. However, while the *nouns* tended to occur in lots of different syntactic environments (*I see wug; I want my wug; Wug did it*), the children hardly ever combined the new *verbs* with any other words at all—and when they did, they almost always used the same syntactic frame that they had heard the experimenter use.

In another study by Brooks and Tomasello (1999), children of a similar age heard sentences that appeared either in the active form (*The cat is gorping Bert*) or in the passive form (*Ernie is getting meeked by the dog*). They were then asked a question that nudged them toward producing an active from: *What is the cat doing?* (Or, if appropriate, *What is the dog doing?*) The children almost always produced the new verb in an active transitive form if that's what they'd heard earlier, but if they had been introduced to the verb in the passive form, they used the active form only 28% of the time, despite the fact that this particular syntactic frame is the most frequent frame to be found in English.

The puzzle then seems to be not why children make errors of *overgeneralization*, like those documented by Melissa Bowerman. Rather, we might wonder why they seem to generalize so *little*. Tomasello and his colleagues have proposed that children are reluctant to generalize because their early structure doesn't involve general rules at all. Instead, it involves snippets of verb-specific structures, and far from invoking highly abstract phrase structure rules, children use frames that allow for nouns to be slotted in like this:

[[$_N$ (hitter)] *hit* [$_N$ (hittee)]

[$_N$ (thing broken)] *break*

That is, kids don't have general, broad concepts such as NP subjects or objects. Instead, they have much narrower concepts that specify the roles that nouns play in highly particular syntactic frames involving individual words—**verb islands**, to use Tomasello's terminology. Another way of looking at it is that if we were to ask whether children's early structures involve memorized words or rules, the answer might be that they're hybrids. Not rules, but little "rulelets."

But the fact that children are shy about generalizing verbs in their own speech isn't necessarily a knockdown argument that they're unable to form more general rules. True, clear evidence of generalization or (especially) overgeneralization would provide some solid clues that children actually have abstract rules. But does the absence of (over)generalization mean that their early syntax is limited to mainly word-specific combinatorial information (or rulelets)?

Here's another way of approaching the issue of why children seem to generalize verb structure so little: To what extent is it *reasonable* for children to form generalizations about this aspect of their language? Recruiting a joke might help explain what I mean:

> A journalist, a mathematician, and a logician were driving through Scotland and watched as a black sheep crossed the road. The journalist said: "Oh, look! In Scotland, the sheep are black!" The mathematician sniffed: "Well. At least one sheep in Scotland is black." To which the logician replied: "You mean at least one half of one sheep in Scotland is black."

The joke, aside from stereotyping certain professions, makes it clear that it's possible to be either inappropriately liberal or too stingy with generalizations—the joke is amusing because neither the journalist nor the logician hits on a reasonable approach to drawing generalizations from examples.

But notice that what counts as appropriate is very much colored by experience. We know that the logician is being unduly conservative because our experience with the real world tells us that animals are usually the same color on both sides of their bodies, even though it's *possible*, in principle at least, for it to be otherwise. The journalist is overly eager to generalize—but his response would be perfectly reasonable if it turned out to be the case that an International Sheep Breeders Association had agreed that each country would produce only one color of sheep. Knowing this would justify generalizing on the basis of one example.

So, for children, it's not just a problem of how to form abstract categories consisting of words and phrases that behave similarly. It's also a problem of figuring out, on the basis of limited input, whether words or phrases that seem to pattern together really do so in all cases.

When it comes to verbs, there's actually good reason for children to be cautious. In order to use verbs correctly in your own language, you need to draw on more than just general phrase structure rules—you also need quite a lot of verb-specific information. Children's early reticence in generalizing verbs might simply be because they've noticed this very fact about verbs. To make the point, let's take a quick survey of some possible syntactic frames that verbs can appear in. Some frames do indeed generalize very broadly. For example, all active transitive frames of the form:

NP$_1$-V-NP$_2$

can be transformed into a passive version:

NP$_2$-V-(by NP$_1$)

where the object of the active version now appears as the subject of the passive, and the subject of the active form becomes what we would call the oblique subject of the passive form (with the oblique subject being optionally left off). For example, *Susie hurt Billy* would become *Billy was hurt by Susie,* or just *Billy was hurt.* This rule applies absolutely generally, regardless of the specific verb. It's exactly the kind of situation for which it's really handy to have very general rules and broad notions such as a subject NP or an object NP.

But many alternations between possible syntactic frames turn out to hinge on knowing something about individual verbs. For instance, if you generalized frames on the basis of the verb *drop,* you'd be inclined to conclude that a verb can appear in the following frames:

NP$_1$-V-NP$_2$ Alice dropped the ball.

NP$_2$-V   The ball dropped.

Despite some similarities in the events described, this would get you into trouble with the verb *fell,* which can appear in the second of these frames, but not the first:

*Alice fell the ball.

The ball fell.

To make matters worse, the verb *hit* can only appear with the first and not the second of the frames (or at least, the second seems wrong except in some contexts where it's made extremely clear beforehand what the ball is expected to collide with):

Alice hit the ball.

*The ball hit.

In other words, you might expect youngsters to be rightfully quite wary of extending verbs to new frames until they've received a fair amount of evidence about which frames that *particular* verb is permitted to be slotted into. They're wise to avoid being like the journalist in the joke, who jumped at the chance to generalize from too little data. That is, the phrase structure rules give a very good framework for where verbs possibly *might* appear in the syntactic structure of a sentence, but in many cases, you actually need to know for specific verbs or small classes of verbs whether *that* verb (or its class) is licensed in that particular structure (see more examples in **Box 6.5**).

Part of learning about the syntax of verbs, then, might involve accumulating quite specific knowledge of a given verb's combinatorial properties, something you couldn't know until you'd actually seen the verb in action in multiple syntactic frames. This more specific information is called **subcategorization information**.

Learning when to generalize

There's evidence to suggest that children may avoid generalizing verbs not because they're unwilling or unable to abstract general patterns, but because they've clued in to the fact that to use verbs properly in English, they need to accumulate lots of verb-specific information *in addition to* abstract rules. Eliza-

subcategorization information Verb-specific knowledge of the verb's combinatorial properties.

BOX 6.5
Quirky verb alternations

Generalizing syntactic structures for English verbs is fraught with peril! All of the verbs below involve physical contact, and might at first be seen by a child as very similar to each other.

> "Poke" verbs (*poke, dig, jab, pierce, prick, stick*)
>
> "Touch" verbs (*touch, caress, kiss, lick, nudge, stroke, tickle*)
>
> "Hit" verbs (*hit, bang, bump, knock, smash, whack*)
>
> "Spank" verbs (*spank, belt, clobber, flog, pummel, thrash, wallop, whip*)
>
> "Swat" verbs (*swat, claw, paw, punch, stab, swipe*)

Eventually, however, the child has to learn that verbs fall into a number of different syntactic categories, each with its own distinctive patterns of syntax. Below are examples of syntactic alternations, some of which apply only to very small sets of verbs, and some of which apply more broadly. These provide just a taste of the peculiar knowledge about verbs that children have to learn:

Paula poked the cloth with the needle.
Paula touched the cat with the stick.
Paula hit the fence with the stick.
Paula spanked the child with her right hand.
Paula swatted the fly with a dishcloth.

Paula poked at the cloth.
*Paula touched at the cat.
Paula hit at the fence.

*Paula spanked at the naughty child.
Paula swatted at the fly.

The needle poked the cloth.
The stick touched the cat.
The stick hit the fence.
*Paula's right hand spanked the naughty child.
*The dishcloth swatted the fly.

*Paula poked the needle against (or on) the cloth.
*Paula touched the stick against (or on) the cat.
Paula hit the stick against (or on) the fence.
*Paula spanked her hand against (or on) the naughty child.
*Paula swatted the dishcloth against (or on) the fly.

*Paula poked the cloth ragged. (Meaning "with the result that the cloth was ragged.")
*Paula touched the cat happy. (Meaning "with the result that the cat was happy.")
Paula hit the door open.
*Paula spanked the child sore.
Paula swatted the fly dead.

You can consult an entire book devoted to the syntactic properties of verbs: *English Verb Classes and Alternations*, by Beth Levin (1993), from which the examples here are drawn.

---

beth Wonnacott (2011) used semi-artificial grammars to probe the conditions under which children readily generalize. She created a toy language that focused on just the following structure:

> verb-noun-particle

To keep things simple, the experiment used only one verb, *moop*, whose meaning was something like "there are two." The nouns were common words of English like *pig* or *cow*. Each noun had to be followed by a **particle**, a syntactic marker whose meaning was not identified in any way. There were two possible particles to be learned: *dow* and *tay*. The child's main learning task, then, was to figure out the correct ordering of these elements, and to learn that both *dow* and *tay* were members of a category that patterned the same in terms of their proper "slot" in the sentence.

particle A syntactic marker, often lacking a specific meaning, that accompanies other syntactic elements.

The interesting hitch was that some children saw a version of the toy language where any noun could be followed by *dow* or *tay*, used interchangeably. (This would be analogous to the determiners *a* and *the* in English, where either *a* or *the* can appear before any common noun, regardless of which noun it is.) In this version of Wonnacott's language, then, there was no need to keep track of noun-specific restrictions on particles. During the experiment's learning phase, children heard 16 sentences involving four different nouns, each occurring with both particles. For example:

Moop giraffe dow.

Moop giraffe tay.

Moop cat dow.

Moop cat tay.

Moop mouse dow.

Moop mouse tay.

Moop pig dow.

Moop pig tay

In the second version of the toy language, however, *dow* appeared only with some nouns, while the others could only be followed by *tay*. For example:

Moop giraffe dow.

Moop cat dow.

Moop mouse dow.

Moop pig tay.

Moop cat dow.

Moop pig tay.

Moop mouse dow.

Moop giraffe dow.

In other words, although the two particles were of the same syntactic category and occupied the same slot in the syntax, the child had to pay attention to the specific nouns in figuring out which particle to use. This is a lot like the verb-specific constraints in English, but a bit more extreme. In the learning phase for this second version, children again heard sixteen sentences involving four nouns—but this time, each noun only ever appeared with either *dow* or *tay*.

The children had no trouble reproducing the correct sentences for the language they saw, regardless of whether they saw the language where the particles were interchangeable or the language where particles were licensed by specific nouns. But the most interesting question was: What would they do when presented with a sentence involving a noun they hadn't heard before—for example, *moop dog tay*? Would they, in their own speech, produce examples of *moop dog dow*, in which they generalized to the other particle? The two different versions of the toy language seem to warrant different solutions: in the first case, children should be prepared to treat *dow* and *tay* interchangeably, without regard for the noun they follow, but in the second version, they might reasonably conclude that if *dog* can appear with *tay*, then it *can't* appear with *dow*. The children were in fact sensitive to this difference and were much more willing to generalize if they'd been exposed to the first version of the language, with the interchangeable particles. In other words, if they heard the version of the language that had tight lexical restrictions, they tended to be highly conservative, producing only the forms they'd heard before.

If we compare these results to what English-speaking toddlers are doing in their earliest syntax, we have a possible explanation for why children in Tomasello's study were so willing to treat nouns as interchangeable units, all while *failing* to use verbs in structures they hadn't heard before: they may simply have learned through exposure to English that when you combine nouns with other elements, you don't have to care which noun it is, only that it is one. Verbs, on the other hand, are more picky about their companions. Kids may have figured out, correctly, that it's appropriate to generalize liberally when it comes to nouns, but to be more restrained when it comes to verbs.

Admittedly, these examples from Wonnacott's study involve snippets of language that are far simpler than English, and the children were on average 6 years of age, quite a bit older than Tomasello's generalization-shy toddlers. This makes it hard to directly compare the results with what's going on in the learning of English. Nevertheless, by showing a close link between children's tendency to generalize and the degree to which a language shows lexical restriction of syntactic options, Wonnacott offers the possibility that children's failure to generalize doesn't *always* reflect a lack of abstraction.

There's another reason why Tomasello's studies may have underestimated the syntactic sophistication of toddlers, and it's an issue that rears its hoary head for all researchers of developmental syntax: sometimes it can be hard to figure out the state of a small child's knowledge solely on the basis of what she might be willing to say, since the act of uttering (or comprehending) language involves not just *having* knowledge, but also *deploying* that knowledge. You might have become painfully aware of this, for instance, when first learning a new skill or concept—you've got the idea of what you're supposed to do, but the *execution* can be highly variable, depending on whether there are distractions around, or even on who happens to be watching. For language researchers, there's an important distinction between **linguistic competence** (that is, the underlying knowledge that involves representations and the rules for combining them) and **linguistic performance** (the execution of that knowledge in speaking or comprehending).

In fact, as we'll see in future chapters, there's plenty of evidence that verb-specific information affects the linguistic performance of adults, who presumably do have a fully fledged syntactic system in place. It turns out that, in *addition* to having general rules in place, our memories also accumulate a detailed historical record of verb-specific information—including information about the frequency with which we've encountered specific verbs in various syntactic frames. Such information plays a very important role in how we understand or produce sentences on the fly. It hardly seems surprising then that child language would show similar constraints on performance. In other words, children may well have *knowledge* of a general system of syntactic rules that involve abstract categories, but in the act of producing speech in the heat of the moment, they could be falling back on the most familiar structures for a particular verb.

Based on all of the data so far about children's very early syntax, it would appear there's good reason to question the assumption that very small children have abstract syntactic rules (see **Box 6.6**). At the same time, various studies using artificial grammars have recently emerged in which babies as young as 12 months are able to learn and generalize highly abstract aspects of syntactic structure (e.g., Gómez & Gerken, 1999). And, as we saw in Chapter 5, they even seem to be using some aspects of their syntactic knowledge to learn the mean-

linguistic competence Underlying knowledge about linquistic representations and the rules for combining them.

linguistic performance The execution of linguistic competence in speaking or comprehending.

BOX 6.6
Syntax and the immature brain

One of the recurring themes in this and earlier chapters is that even when children's behaviors are similar to those of adults, we can't assume that they're using the same cognitive machinery. Closer inspection is needed to better understand the nature of children's linguistic expertise. As we've seen, some researchers argue, based on detailed behavioral experiments, that children's early syntax looks qualitatively different from adults' syntax.

Another way to get at this question is by examining the structure of child and adult brains and looking at where the brain is most active during language tasks. Brain-imaging studies with children are still not that common (given the practical challenges of getting energetic youngsters to lie still inside a cocoon-like magnet), but there is beginning to be exploration in this area. Jens Brauer and colleagues (2011) carried out an fMRI study in which adults and 7-year-old children evaluated sentences that were either well formed (*The lion in the zoo roars*), ungrammatical (*The yogurt in tastes good*), or semantically odd (*The stone bleeds*). Brain activation on this task was compared with a "resting" baseline task.

For both children and adults, the language task engaged the posterior portion of Broca's area, known as BA 44, which is part of the dorsal network for language. But the children showed even greater amounts of activation in the anterior portion of Broca's area, or BA 45, which connects to the ventral pathway. This area, by contrast, was not very active for adults.

In addition to studying fMRI data, the researchers examined the connective white matter in the dorsal and ventral pathways. They did this by means of diffusion MRI (dMRI), which, along with showing axon pathways (see Figure 3.15) allows scientists to see the extent to which axons have developed a protective myelin sheath, crucial for electrical signaling. A greater degree of myelinization reflects a more efficient and mature neural pathway. This analysis showed that children's dorsal pathways were still considerably less mature than those of the adults (see **Figure 6.4**). The authors of the study suggested that because of the immaturity of their dorsal network, children were forced to rely on the ventral pathway more heavily than adults did for the same task.

Since we don't yet have a very solid understanding of the roles of these two networks, especially when it comes to syntax, it's hard to line up the brain-imaging results in an exact way with the theories of syntactic development we've talked about in this chapter. Moreover, the study by Brauer and colleagues only looked at a very general language task, rather than trying to pinpoint very specific aspects of language. Nevertheless, the results lend plausibility to the idea that children and adults might rely on quite different computations, even at a stage when children appear remarkably like adults in their linguistic behavior.

(A) Children (age 7 years)

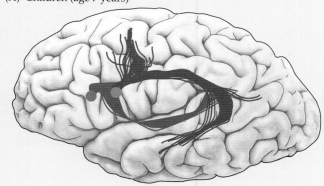

(B) Adults

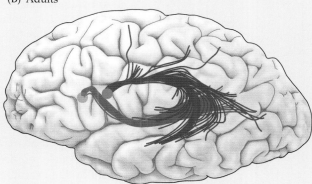

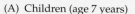

Maximum activation in adults in BA 44
Maximum activation in children in BA 45
—— Dorsal pathway
—— Ventral pathway

Figure 6.4 Brain imaging reveals different patterns of brain activation in a language task. In adults, area BA 44 showed greater activation than other areas, while in children area BA 45 was also heavily active. The analysis also revealed that the children's dorsal pathway for language was underdeveloped compared with that of adults. (Adapted from Friederici, 2012.)

ings of new words, making different inferences about verb meanings depending on whether the verbs appeared in a frame like *the duck is gorping the bunny* or *the duck and the bunny are gorping*. So on balance, the science suggests that children are quite likely to be actively forming general syntactic categories and rules by the time they're beginning to combine words in their speech (though it may takes some time for children's syntactic knowledge to become fully adult-like, as suggested by the recent brain imaging studies discussed in Box 6.6).

There's also growing evidence that children are exquisitely sensitive to the statistical properties of language in the process of forming this abstract knowledge. Remember from the discussion in Section 6.1 that some researchers have expressed skepticism that very small children could ever arrive at a sophisticated set of syntactic rules by linguistic exposure alone, without the help of some innate constraints that would help steer them in the right direction. It may well be that such constraints play a role in the acquisition of syntactic knowledge. But when it comes to basic syntax, it looks as if the input is not as impoverished as we might have thought, and that kids can get a tremendous amount of mileage out of their impressive ability to keep track of statistical patterns.

6.4 Complex Syntax and Constraints on Learning

Relating phrases over long distances

When linguists look closely at syntax, they find that our knowledge of the structure of language has to go well beyond simply knowing how words can be grouped together into the constituents that form a sentence. We also need some fairly intricate knowledge about how elements in a sentence can relate to each other over long spans of words.

For example, consider a complex sentence like this one, in which a second clause, called a **relative clause**, is embedded within the main clause:

> The rat that Stan was so thrilled to have bought from the pet store yesterday just chewed his favorite shoes to pieces.

What role does *rat* play in this sentence? One answer is that it seems to be the central element—or what we might call the **head**—of the elaborate NP that serves as the subject of the verb *chewed*. That is, the sentence seems to be structured like this (omitting lots of details about some of the smaller constituents):

> $[_S$ $[_{NP}$ The rat that Stan was so thrilled to have bought from the pet store yesterday] $[_{VP}$ just chewed his favorite shoes to pieces]].

But *rat* also plays a second role in the sentence: it's also the thing that Stan bought yesterday. In other words, it *also* seems to be functioning as the direct object of *bought*.

Notice that something interesting is going on in this sentence. Normally, the verb *bought* requires a direct object in its syntactic frame, as is obvious from the following example sentences (with * marking ungrammatical sentences):

> *Stan bought.

> *Stan bought from the pet store.

> Stan bought a rat from the pet store.

But in the complex sentence you saw earlier, there's no direct object immediately following *Stan*, yet the sentence is fully grammatical. Why would this be?

relative clause A clause that is embedded within the main clause and shares a referent with the main clause.

head The central element of a constituent—for example, the head of a prepositional phrase is the preposition.

It turns out that the requirement for having a direct object is fulfilled by the fact that *the rat* doubles as both the object NP of *bought*—despite not being adjacent to that verb—and part of the subject NP of the verb *chewed*. In other words, *rat* is linked to the object NP position even though it doesn't appear there in the sentence. We can capture this fact by showing a colored underscore right after *bought* and using the same color for the phrase *the rat*, in order to show that the two somehow correspond with each other:

> [$_S$ [$_{NP}$ **The rat** that Stan was so thrilled to have bought __ from the pet store yesterday] [$_{VP}$ just chewed his favorite shoes to pieces]].

So, because the relationship is between the overt phrase *the rat* and the object of the verb *bought*, the embedded relative clause is called an **object-relative clause**. It's also possible to construct an example of a **subject-relative clause**:

> [$_S$ [$_{NP}$ **The rat** that __ won Stan's heart at the pet store yesterday] [$_{VP}$ just chewed his favorite shoes to pieces]].

Here, *the rat* is linked to the *subject* position of the embedded verb *won*, as well as serving as the head of the NP subject of the main clause verb *chewed*.

In relative clauses, an indeterminate number of words can appear between a phrase and the position in a sentence to which it's linked, and for this reason, such relationships are called **long-distance dependencies**. There are also long-distance dependencies that don't involve relative clauses. For example, *wh-* questions also involve a relationship between an overt phrase and some (possibly far downstream) position in a sentence:

> **What** did Felicia claim that she saw her boyfriend eating spaghetti with __ ?

You can check to see that *what* really is linked to the object of the preposition *with* by providing a full-sentence answer to the original question; you'll find that the phrase that supplies the answer (*some chopsticks*) has to occur as the object of *with*:

> Felicia claimed that she saw her boyfriend eating spaghetti with some chopsticks.

Long-distance dependencies like these take syntax to a whole new level. Until now, much of the syntax-learning that we've been talking about has involved relationships between words or small phrases that are right next to each other—for example, learning that a word is an adjective based on the fact that it's nestled in between a determiner and a noun, or learning whether a verb like *drop* can appear with an NP that follows it as well as an NP that precedes it. But in order to learn how to properly use and understand long-distance dependencies, children need to move well beyond controlling *local* bits of structure involving nearby phrases, and into a deeper understanding of *global* structure, with its full panoply of recursive structure and complex constituents, and they need to grasp abstract grammatical notions such as subject-hood and object-hood (see **Box 6.7**).

Are children guided by innate syntactic constraints?

Many researchers have argued that children develop complex syntax with such baffling ease that they must be guided by certain innate expectations. For example, they must be innately predisposed to believe that language is structured in terms of higher-order constituents and relationships among them. To make the argument, let's consider some alternative ways that children might think

object-relative clause An embedded clause in which the referent that is shared between the main and embedded clauses is linked to the object position of the embedded clause (e.g., I saw the cat that the dog chased).

subject-relative clause An embedded clause in which the referent that is shared between the main and embedded clauses is linked to the subject position of the embedded clause (e.g., I saw the cat that chased the dog).

long-distance dependencies Relationships between constituents widely separated from each other in a sentence.

BOX 6.7
Specific language impairment and complex syntax

Typically, children begin to produce complex forms such as relative clauses at about age three. Here are some examples (Diesel & Tomasello, 2000) of relative clauses produced by 3-year-old children:

> This is the sugar that goes in there.
> And here's a rabbit that I'm patting.
> That's the kind of tea that I'm making for them.
> People who have spears hit people in the nose.

However, as discussed in Chapter 3, kids with specific language impairment (SLI) have a harder time mastering language. Researchers have argued that a certain subtype of SLI leads to especially marked difficulty with complex syntactic structures. In one study, Melanie Schuele and Leslie Tolbert (2001) elicited relative clauses from their young subjects. The children played a game that involved describing one of two objects to a blindfolded person. The experimenter placed two objects on the table—for example, a windup toy pig that was made to move, and a stationary toy pig. She identified one of the objects by pointing to it, and she instructed the child, "Tell her [that is, the blindfolded adult] to point to this one." The child described the toy to the blindfolded adult, who then removed the blindfold and chose the appropriate toy. The idea here was to encourage the child to produce sentences with relative clauses, like *Point to the pig that's walking*.

Before the age of five, the children with SLI didn't even attempt to produce relative clauses. Instead they just produced simple sentences like *Point to that one. He is walking*, or *Who's walking?* But even the older children with SLI, who did form relative clauses, often made mistakes that were not common among the earliest attempts at relative clauses by typically developing kids. For example, the children with SLI would often leave off the relative marker, making sentences like these:

> Point to the one is walking.
> Point to the girl fall down.

Or, they would use the wrong marker:

> Point to the one what knock Bert down.
> Point to the girl this falled down.

Difficulties with relative clauses can be quite persistent in children with SLI. In one study (Novogrodsky & Friedmann, 2006), a group of children 9 to 14 years of age with SLI made mistakes more than half the time on object relative clauses, which are considered to be more difficult than subject relative clauses. There's a great deal of discussion in the literature about exactly what underlies these syntactic deficits.

about syntax that *don't* involve the expectation of constituent structure, to see how these might easily lead to dead ends.

Take, for example, yes/no questions in English. You can convert any statement into a yes/no question, but the relationship between the two is a bit tricky. See if you can formulate a general rule:

That man was nice.	Was that man nice?
The book on the table is red.	Is the book on the table red?
I can cut the cake.	Can I cut the cake?
You should buy a computer.	Should I buy a computer?
Stan loves his rat.	Does Stan love his rat?
Sandeep trained Stan's rat.	Did Sandeep train Stan's rat?

To describe the pattern, you'd first need to identify a category of words that includes *was, is, can, should, does,* and *did*—we'll call them **auxiliary verbs**. All you need then is some generalization that says that to form a question, you simply move the auxiliary verb to the beginning of the sentence. (Notice that if the statement version doesn't have an auxiliary verb, the question still needs

auxiliary verbs A category of words (often informally known as "helping verbs") that accompany the main verb. Includes *was, is, can, should, does,* and *did.*

to have one, slotting in the general-purpose "default" auxiliary *does* or *did*, appropriately marked for tense.)

But see what happens if we now embed a relative clause inside the main clause, giving us two potential auxiliary verbs:

The book that is on the table is red.

It's clear that it has to be the second of these auxiliary verbs that moves to the front of the sentence, and not the first:

Is the book that is on the table __ red?

*__Is__ the book that __ on the table is red?

In fact, if we start looking closely, it's apparent than whether it's the first, second, or last auxiliary verb, the one that appears at the front of the sentence has to be the auxiliary that's *related* to the *subject of the main clause*. In the sentences below, only the subject of the main clause has been put in brackets—the corresponding questions show that only the auxiliary that's associated with this subject can appear at the front of the sentence. None of the other auxiliary verbs, shown in black boldface can be targeted to appear at the front of the sentence:

[The book on the table] is red.

Is [the book on the table] __ red?

[The book that **is** on the table] is red.

Is [the book that **is** on the table] __ red?

[The book that **is** on the table that **was** built by my cousin] is red.

Is [the book that **is** on the table that **was** built by my cousin] __ red?

[The book] is on the table that **is** red.

Is [the book] __ on the table that **is** red?

[The book that **is** red] is on the table that **was** built by my cousin.

Is [the book that **is** red] __ on the table that **was** built by my cousin?

It's worth asking what small children might conclude about how yes/no sentences get formed. First, let's consider the fact that the overwhelming majority of yes/no questions involve a single clause. Here, I've collected a variety of complicated sentences to allow you to see the pattern. But in the speech that's directed to a child, it might be quite some time before the child hears the accumulation of the kind of data that I've just laid down in front of you. On the basis of only a small sampling of input, what's to force a child to be thinking in terms of main clauses and subjects? It might be simpler to think in terms of shallower relationships, like simple linear order. For instance, if a child is eager to generalize but has only heard single-clause yes/no questions, she might come to the very reasonable hypothesis that to form a question, you just move to the front the *first* auxiliary verb that would normally appear in the declarative form. Of course, this would ultimately be wrong, but it could be quite some time before the child got enough data in the input to figure this out. In the meantime, an incorrect generalization might become firmly fixed in the child's mind. Since preschoolers tend to produce mostly single-clause sentences, this misguided generalization could persist for a long time without being detected and corrected.

TABLE 6.4 Number of errors on yes/no questions by type

Type of error	Number of errors made[a]	
	Group 1: Mean age 4 years 3 months	Group 2: Mean age 5 years 3 months
Type I errors Auxiliary verb is repeated: *Is the boy who is being kissed by his mother is happy?*	30	9
Type II errors Sentence is "restarted": *Is the boy that is watching Mickey Mouse, is he happy?*	10	5
Type III errors Wrong auxiliary verb is moved: *Is the boy that watching Mickey Mouse is happy?*	0	0

Data from Crain & Nakayama, 1987.
[a]Total number of responses for Group 1 was 81. Total number of responses for Group 2 was 87.

Now, what's interesting about setting up a rule based on serial order is that, not only is it wrong, but it's actually a truly bizarre rule when it comes to the structures of natural languages. Languages just don't seem to care very much about linear precedence relationships in their syntax, shunning rules that refer to first or third elements or whatever. Rather, rules of syntax seem to be uniformly built around constituent structure and hierarchical structural relationships.

So it would be interesting to ask: In the face of limited data, would a child ever posit a rule that seems to go against the natural grain of human language syntax? Are kids ever tempted to conclude that the way to form a yes/no question is by moving the first auxiliary verb to the front of the sentence, leading to errors such as:

*Is the book that ___ on the table is red?

Stephen Crain and Mineharu Nakayama (1987) tested children between the ages of three and five and elicited yes/no questions by prodding them to, for example, "Ask Jabba if the boy who is watching Mickey Mouse is happy." They found that although the children very often produced questions that weren't grammatical, there wasn't a single instance of errors like the one above, where the wrong auxiliary appeared at the front of the sentence. Most of the errors involved *repeating* an auxiliary, as in *Is the boy who is being kissed by his mother is happy?* (see **Table 6.4**). So, it seems that kids don't really entertain the possibility of a rule that moves auxiliary verbs based on their serial order in a sentence. Crain and Nakayama have argued that this is because children's expectations about syntax are constrained from the start to look for structural relationships rather than relationships based on serial order.

Just as with yes/no questions, some researchers have argued that biases on learning could also help constrain children's learning of *wh-* questions. As you'll see in a moment, such biases could be quite helpful in sorting out the syntactic subtleties of *wh*-questions.

We saw earlier that in *wh-* questions, the *wh-* word can be related to a syntactic slot in the sentence that occurs well downstream, as in:

What did Felicia claim that she saw her boyfriend eating spaghetti with ___ ?

Wh- questions can be formed by linking *wh-* words to a great variety of different syntactic slots, including subjects, direct and indirect objects, and adverb phrases of manner or time. If we limit ourselves to possibilities within a single main clause, we can find examples like:

Who ___ saw Freddy?

What did Shaheen see ___ ?

What did Francidel spot Freddy with ___ ?

How did Francidel spot Freddy ___ ?

When did Ivan kick Shaheen ___ ?

And of course, as in the example with Felicia and her spaghetti-eating boyfriend, the long-distance dependency can extend over multiple clause boundaries.

The sheer variety of ways to form a *wh-* question seems to invite generalization—but there are some important limitations. A *wh-* word can't be linked with just any syntactic slot. Consider, for example, the ways in which the following statements *can't* be turned into questions, demonstrating that not everything is fair game when it comes to concocting *wh-* questions:

Betsy invited Silke and Tobias.
***Who** did Betsy invite Silke and ___ ?

Weyman believed the rumor that Kirk had dated Cecelia.
***Who** did Weyman believe the rumor that ___ had dated Cecelia?

Stuart wondered when Myra made her special sauce.
***What** did Stuart wonder when Myra made ___ ?

These examples are violations of what are known as ***wh-* island constraints**: a set of syntactic restrictions on long-distance relationships involving *wh-* questions.

You might expect that in the process of learning how to form *wh-* questions, kids would be exposed to many examples in which *wh-* words link to syntactic slots of many flavors. Since the process applies similarly to a large variety of syntactic phrases, here seems to be a case where kids might be especially prone to overgeneralizing, much as they often overgeneralize past tense and plural morphemes. So it would seem natural to find examples of violations of the *wh-* island constraints. But this doesn't seem to happen.

Around the age of three, kids understand that *wh-* elements can relate to syntactic slots much farther along in the sentence. In one study, Jill de Villiers and her colleagues (1990) told children little stories followed by questions. For example, one of the stories involved a tale about a girl who took a shortcut home across a wire fence, and then later at bedtime confessed to her mother that she had ripped her dress that afternoon. The children were then asked one of two questions, with their answers providing some insight into how they structured the question in their minds. Half of them heard:

When did she say she ripped her dress?

This question has two possible answers: *at bedtime* or *that afternoon*, depending on whether the *wh-* dependency looks like this:

When did she say ___ she ripped her dress? (Answer: at bedtime.)

or like this:

When did she say she ripped her dress ___ ? (Answer: that afternoon.)

***wh-* island constraints** Syntactic constraints that prevent wh- words (*who, what, where*) from being related to certain positions within a sentence.

The other half of the children heard this question:

When did she say how she ripped her dress?

In this question, the *wh-* word is blocked from being associated with an element in the lower clause, and the *only* possible structure is this one:

When did she say ___ how she ripped her dress? (Answer: at bedtime.)

The preschoolers who heard the first question provided both types of answers, showing that they were quite willing to consider that *wh-* words could be linked with faraway elements in the sentence so long as this obeyed the constraints on *wh-* dependencies. But the children who heard the second sentence (which, by the way, differed by a mere word) tended to provide *only* the sole correct answer, suggesting that they were unwilling to generalize to *wh-* dependencies that *violate* such constraints, even when such generalization produces sentences superficially very similar to sentences with perfectly legal *wh-* dependencies.

But how could they know which *wh-* dependencies are disallowed? Why the absence of errors?

WEB ACTIVITY 6.4

Probing children's knowledge of syntax In this activity, you'll explore some possible ways to test what children know about syntax, and you'll encounter some of the advantages and limitations of various techniques.

Learning mechanisms

How do children navigate the intricate maze of syntax? How are they (seemingly) able to avoid the many dead ends? One possibility is that at some point, kids do make very basic mistakes but these mistakes are swiftly corrected by adults, so at a very early stage, they abandon analyses that are fundamentally wrong. But it's not clear that this explanation has much muscle.

First of all, parents tend not to correct their child's grammar very often, focusing more on the content of what they say than on how they say it. (In fact, since their offspring's early syntax contains generous dollops of ungrammaticality, playing the role of grammar police would be sure to be a conversation-stopper.) Second, even when parents *do* provide corrections, it may not have a meaningful impact on kids' production of language. Children, like adults, tend to be much more preoccupied with the content of conversations than about which forms are produced, and attempts to dispense grammar lessons are likely to be met with reactions such as this (from Braine, 1971):

Child: Want other one spoon, Daddy.

Parent: You mean you want the other spoon.

Child: Yes, I want other one spoon, please, Daddy.

Parent: Can you say "the other spoon"?

Child: Other . . . one . . . spoon.

Parent: Say "other."

Child: Other.

Parent: Spoon.

Child: Spoon.

Parent: Other spoon.

Child: Other . . . spoon. Now give me other one spoon?

Kids, it seems, are not as willing to learn from corrections as your typical adult foreign language learner is.

There's another way to explain kids' obedience to many of the syntactic constraints (such as *wh-* islands). It may be that children have caught on to the fact that they never come across examples of sentences that violate such constraints, and that from this they infer that such structures are illegal. But from a child's perspective, that could just be an accidental gap in the input. For all she knows, she might hear a dozen such sentences next week; perhaps the right contexts for such questions just haven't arisen yet. Let's suppose a child did adopt a purely cautious approach in which she assumed, after hearing a lot of sentences, that types that she hadn't heard yet must surely be ungrammatical. A strategy like this might lead to some pretty strange conclusions. For example, you may well have never heard a sentence in which the word *wombat* appears in the main clause while *soliloquy* appears in the lower clause. But I seriously doubt that you've concluded that such a sentence would be *ungrammatical*, and if I put you on the spot, I'm sure I could get you to produce one that we would both agree sounded just fine. So, something more is needed than just noticing that these aberrant *wh-* questions haven't occurred. There must be something that leads children to believe that it's weird to have a constraint that disallows *wombat* and *soliloquy* from appearing in different clauses of the same sentence. At the same time, something must cause them to not bat an eye at the prospect of a constraint that prevents a word like *when* from being linked with an element in a clause that is introduced by a word like *how.*

By and large, kids seem to steer away from the kinds of generalizations that languages avoid trading in, and gravitate toward the ones that tend to recur time and again across languages. This has led many researchers of language acquisition to argue that children are born with certain syntactic expectations that guide their language development. The chain of this argument (often referred to as the **argument from the poverty of the stimulus**) usually goes something like this:

1. Children acquire a complex syntactic generalization or constraint with few or no errors—that is, the trajectory of acquisition seems to be abrupt, rather than gradual with errors dwindling slowly over a long period of time.

2. The language input that they receive has little or no direct evidence for that particular syntactic generalization or constraint; in any case, the evidence available is not enough to support such rapid learning.

3. Because of the lack of sufficient evidence, children couldn't be learning the generalization or constraint on the basis of the linguistic data they hear.

4. Therefore, children must have access to innate biases that will allow them to reject certain kinds of grammars while accepting others, even though the input they receive might be entirely consistent with both.

In one of the strongest forms of this argument, known as the **principles and parameters theory**, some researchers have proposed that children are equipped with an innate template that constrains what a natural human language must look like—that is, a template for a universal grammar. This template specifies the various syntactic options that are available to languages, so the process of acquiring language basically boils down to gathering just enough data to figure out which of those options applies to the child's particular language, much like

WEB ACTIVITY 6.5

Natural and unnatural rules Do you have a sense of what might be a plausible syntactic rule for real languages? In this activity, you'll see data sets from foreign languages and will be asked to detect plausible generalizations that are consistent with data. Can you distinguish these plausible generalizations from other generalizations that are also compatible with the data, but that represent highly unnatural rules?

argument from the poverty of the stimulus The argument that there is not enough input available to children to allow them to learn certain structures without the help of innate expectations that guide their language development.

principles and parameters theory A theory claiming that children's language learning is dramatically constrained with the help of innate syntactic "options" or "parameter switches" that restrict the possible syntactic structures children can infer. Language learning is said to consist largely of checking the input to see which of the constrained set of options apply to the language being learned.

flipping a set of predetermined switches to the right settings. Kids start out with default settings for each parameter, and then switch them over from the default if they come across linguistic evidence that provides the impetus to do so.

Arguments for innate constraints based on the poverty of the stimulus are highly controversial. Since the syntactic structures in question are usually so intricate and varied, and empirical results that document children's learning of these structures is still so sparsely available, there is far from universal agreement on the first of the points listed above. For example, in the experiments we've talked about so far, researchers have found a suggestive absence of certain kinds of errors. But experiments like these only probe children's knowledge at one particular point in time, under very specific conditions. To be really secure about claiming that knowledge of certain structures comes to children quickly and painlessly, we'd want to track their production and comprehension of *wh-* questions over a sustained period of time. This is becoming much more feasible for researchers to do as large databases like the CHILDES database become broadly available (see **Method 6.1**). Now that many researchers can access a hefty amount of child language data without running up the costs of gathering and coding data themselves, we're beginning to see much more

METHOD 6.1

The CHILDES database

Experiments that test specific aspects of learning, using cleverly devised artificial languages, or that probe for the production or comprehension of specific syntactic forms can be extremely useful. But no study of syntactic development could be complete without detailed documentation of children's language in their natural habitat. Many groundbreaking studies have been conducted using diary records or detailed video or audio recordings of interactions between children and their parents. But gathering such data can be dauntingly time-consuming and expensive. Once the data are gathered, though, they can be used to answer many more questions than just the ones that originally motivated the research.

To maximize the value of recordings that have been painstakingly collected in children's classrooms or living rooms, researchers led by Brian MacWhinney have developed a database for the sharing and sampling of child language data: CHILDES (Child Language Data Exchange System; http://childes.psy.cmu.edu/). Researchers can contribute their transcripts of child language interactions (following a common set of transcription notations and rules), as well as digitized audio and video files. They can also access the full audio/video files and transcripts that have been contributed by other researchers. Computer programs are available to search through the database for specific information.

CHILDES includes child language transcripts from hundreds of research projects carried out in English as well as projects in dozens of far-flung languages such as Cantonese, Indonesian, Catalan, Russian, and Welsh. It also includes language data from individuals with various language impairments and from bilingual learners. There have already been thousands of papers published using data mined from the CHILDES database.

In terms of its impact on the field of language development, CHILDES is a game-changer. It allows researchers with limited resources to test hypotheses using an extremely rich data set. It allows for the comparison of data across many different languages, which makes it possible to look for universal cross-linguistic patterns in language development. It provides enough data to allow researchers to have a sense not only of whether certain forms are produced by children, but how often, and to compare the relative frequencies of syntactic structures in their speech. And because the transcripts also include language by the adults that the children are interacting with, it also allows researchers to test detailed quantitative predictions about the relationship between a child's input and her language production. This is especially important because so many of the currently debated issues revolve around the nature of this relationship and whether the child's input is rich enough to support syntactic generalizations, or whether children learn syntax with the help of certain innate assumptions.

detailed pictures of children's syntactic development. It may well turn out to be that kids' syntactic learning is actually more gradual and riddled with errors than we'd thought.

We're also far from being able to assert the second point in the above argument with any confidence. What would it take, for example, to really be able to say that there's not enough data in the input for children to be able to learn, say, the rule for how to make yes/no questions? Recent work with artificial grammars has shown just how efficient tiny children can be in sucking out information from even quite small amounts of exposure to a language, sometimes learning a generalization on the basis of only a dozen or so exposures of relevant examples, sometimes fewer. By the age of three, a child has usually heard millions of sentences. Let's suppose that a sentence type that is critically important for learning appears in only 1% of all sentences. Is that enough? (That would still add up to tens of thousands of occurrences of the critical sentence type.) What about 0.01%? (That would be hundreds of examples.) We need to have more sharply developed theories about how children make generalizations on the basis of their input, and what kind of examples contribute to these generalizations—adding some flesh to our ideas about how and when children generalize will be important in being able to conclude whether a certain tiny amount of data is truly insufficient to support learning.

The role of linguistic input

In order to really understand how children learn syntax, we need to have a much better sense of how the language in a child's environment shapes the learning process. The issues go well beyond simply knowing whether kids will stumble across just the right examples to guarantee that they'll avoid serious learning detours. We also want to know: Does the frequency with which they hear certain structures have an important role to play in their mastery of them? This question seems simple, but the answers to it are anything but.

On the one hand, children often step through learning stages in ways that seem disconnected from the frequency with which they hear certain forms or structures. For example, in Box 6.1, I pointed out that there's a fairly consistent order in which kids learn various English morphemes, and that this order doesn't necessarily line up with how often those morphemes appear in the child's input. Because of mismatches like these, researchers have often tried to come up with other explanations for the order of acquisition of forms, typically suggesting that the order is parallel to the forms' inherent syntactic or conceptual complexity.

On the other hand, close couplings *can* sometimes be seen between the child's output and the statistical patterns in the child's input, at times accounting for a lot of the variability across children. (See, for example, a study by Caroline Rowland [2003] and colleagues on the acquisition of *wh-* questions.) Why the diverging results?

One challenge lies in figuring out *which* statistics are the right ones to test. As you saw in Section 6.3, children often link structures closely to specific verbs—for instance, they might use the passive structure only with certain verbs but not others. If you looked only at the overall statistics for passive versus active structures in the parental input, you might not find a very good match with the proportion of actives and passives in the child's output. But if you looked more closely at the statistics for the active versus passive structures *accompanying specific verbs*, you might see a much tighter link between the input and output.

But there are even more complex issues to consider. Let's suppose a child hears sentences of Type A just as often as sentences of Type B. This doesn't

linguistic input The linguistic forms a child is exposed to.

linguistic intake The representations a child uses as the basis for learning structure.

necessarily mean the two are given the same weight in the child's mind. What if Type A uses a kind of structure that's harder to process than Type B and the child isn't able to actually *interpret* Type A sentences upon hearing them. Or maybe Type A sentences aren't as helpful in deciding between competing hypotheses about the structure of the language. Perhaps the child would just filter out the Type A sentences. In these cases, the **linguistic input** to the young learner (the forms that the child is exposed to) might be quite different from the child's **linguistic intake** (the representations that the child uses as the basis for learning structure).

If there's a large enough gap between the child's input and her intake, this might even cause her to *permanently* represent the structure of her language in a way that's different from her parent's representations. When this happens, you get linguistic "mutations" from one generation to the next—more commonly known as "language change."

In one intriguing paper, linguists Lisa Pearl and Amy Weinberg (2007) suggest that this is exactly what happened in a word order shift that took place in Old English sometime in the twelfth century. In the first half of that century, the direct object appeared before the verb:

> *he Gode þancode*
> he God thanked
>
> (from *Beowulf,* ~1100 A.D.)

but by 1200, word order conventions had changed: it was more likely for the direct object to appear after the verb, as it does in present-day English:

> *he   awec   deade   to life*
> he awakened the-dead to life
>
> (from *James the Greater,* ~1150 A.D.)

Pearl and Weinberg point out that, even though the *object-verb* word order was generally more common in Old English prior to the shift, the *verb-object* order did show up in single-clause sentences (much as it does in modern German or Dutch). But children may have filtered out multi-clause sentences because of their complexity, placing more weight on the single-clause structures. As a result, over a series of several generations, the *verb-object* order came to be more and more frequent in the output of the younger generation, until the language shifted into a stable *verb-object* order for all types of sentences.

In this example from Old English, the process of filtering out certain sentences from the input may have led to children ending up with a language that didn't quite match that of their parents. But in other cases, input filtering might have the opposite effect, leading to a *more faithful* reproduction of the parental language, and here's why. The speech of even the most articulate adult can be a messy thing, riddled with speech errors, false starts, and disfluencies. All of these can lead us to produce sentences that would leap out at us as ungrammatical if we were to see them reproduced in a word-for-word transcript. So there is a potential problem for young language learners: if their input may be regularly corrupted with spurious examples of ungrammatical forms, how can they distinguish between the good (grammatical) sentences and the unintentionally bad ones?

A study by Melanie Soderstrom and colleagues suggests that very young learners may have ways of tuning out sentences that are likely to be corrupted (Soderstrom & Morgan, 2007). Since many ungrammatical sentences contain disfluencies in them—as either a symptom or cause of the ungrammatical struc-

LANGUAGE AT LARGE 6.2

Language universals, alien tongues, and learnability

Some artificial languages, Esperanto among them, were invented with the practical goal of being as learnable as possible by speakers of other languages (see Language at Large 2.1). Esperanto was designed to avoid exceptions to grammatical rules, which in theory, at least, should make it easier to notice (or memorize) generalizations about its structure. (For a fascinating survey of invented languages throughout history, see Arika Okrent's 2009 book *In the Land of Invented Languages*.)

We've talked about the possibility that humans are born with certain predispositions to learn the generalizations that characterize *human* languages, while avoiding those that fall outside of the range of what human languages seem to do. But what if an invented language is conceived as an artistic project and is not supposed to feel human? For instance, how does Klingon—a fictional language spoken in the famous *Star Trek* series—fit into the typology of human languages? Klingon was designed to be as evocative as possible of the alien warrior race that spoke it, and it was supposed to *feel* alien. But is Klingon truly an alien language? Are its features unlike those of any human language?

The father of the Klingon language was Marc Okrand, in reality a linguist who knew a great deal about the variety of patterns found in human languages. Okrand was somewhat constrained by the fact that, despite being an alien language, Klingon had to be *sayable* by human actors, and ideally it would not be so far-out in its grammar that devoted (human) fans would fail to grasp its structure (see Okrand's *Klingon Dictionary*, 1992). The solution he arrived at was to create a language that drew heavily on attested elements of human languages, but that made use of some of the more unusual of these elements, or combined elements in weird ways.

The consonants of Klingon are distinctly human-like. But its inventory of phonemes contains some of the more rare and unusual among human sounds (for example, guttural and uvular sounds that are produced way at the back of the vocal tract) while rejecting some of the most common ones (like the basic /s/ sound). This is a strange way for a language to go about things—usually, if it contains the odd sounds, it also contains the more common ones. So, for example, there's a very strong tendency among languages that have the less common voiced /v/ sound to also have the more common matching voiceless sound /f/. Klingon violates this tendency.

In its basic syntax, Klingon lies at the marginal edges of human languages. There are six possible ways of combining subjects, objects, and verbs and, while all of the possibilities are attested in human languages, the object-verb-subject order is by far the rarest among these. Klingon, naturally, recruits this most avoided of word orders. But notice that Klingon nevertheless relies on notions like *subject* and *object*, rather than, say, having a rule in which the identity of the first consonant of a word determines its linear order in a sentence.

Some of the alien feel of Klingon comes from the fact that it uses a way of encoding structural relationships that is very different from English (or most European languages, for that matter). In English, most of the work of signaling relationships among the various components of the event that's being described is carried out in the syntax—that is, you know what role Susie plays in a sentence by knowing whether she appears in the subject or object slot of a sentence. But Klingon is an **agglutinative language**, so called because of the fact that prefixes and suffixes stick to the root words like flies to flypaper. The end result is that much of the work that would be done by the careful arrangement of words in English is instead carried out at the level of morphology, with relationships being marked by prefixes and suffixes.

For example, if you know Spanish, you'll understand that the single word *bailaban* means "they danced"—the suffix *-aban* marks the third person plural subject as well as past tense. Where Spanish could be considered an "agglutinative-lite" language, other languages, such as Swahili, can pile up quite a few morphemes (including prefixes that identify the person and number for both subjects and objects) with the result that a single word such as *tumewauliza* can be used to mean "We have just asked them."

Klingon goes in for serious agglutination. It has 26 different noun suffixes, 29 pronoun prefixes, and two suffixes marking number. Klingon verbs can be marked

---

agglutinative language A language in which words are formed by joining morphemes together. Syntax is expressed by multiple bound affixes and not by changes in position, form, stress, or tone of the root word. Each affix typically represents a single unit of meaning (such as tense or plural), and affixes do not change form in response to other affixes or different root words.

Continued on next page

for, among other things, notions such as causation, predisposition and volition, negation, whether an action is completed or ongoing, and how certain the speaker is of the information he's asserting. Again, none of these markers individually is a hugely strange thing for a language to have, but the complete collection makes for an unusual system. It also makes for some potentially very long words. When the Klingon Language Institute held a contest for the longest three-word sentence in Klingon, the winner was:

Nobwl''a'pu'qoqvam'e' nuHegh'eghrupqa'moHlaHbe'la w'lI'neS she'eghtaHghach'a'na'chajmo'.

which translates into:

The so-called benefactors are seemingly unable to cause us to prepare to resume honorable suicide (in progress) due to their definite great self-control.

Because Klingon was intended to be a language hanging on the outer edges of possible human languages, it stands to reason that it wouldn't be one of the easiest languages to learn—presumably, there's some reason why some patterns are much less common across languages than others. But this is hardly seen as a design flaw among aficionados of Klingon. The handful of devoted enthusiasts who have learned to speak Klingon with anything resembling conversational ease take special pride in mastering it, all the more so because of its reputation for being a truly hairy language to learn.

But is Klingon in fact less learnable than other languages? And if so, exactly what aspects of its design make it an inhospitable language for human minds? And how learnable *are* languages like Esperanto, which were devised with the specific hope of being easy on the language-learning mind? These are empirical questions, and going about answering them would make for an especially interesting encounter of science fiction and science fact. In truth, we'd learn a lot about ourselves and our capacity for learning the natural, organic kinds of languages. The decidedly scientific use of artificial languages to identify more versus less learnable grammars (a topic we'll take up again in Chapter 12) makes a research program along these lines more than a passing fantasy among the bumpy-foreheaded crowd.

A psycholinguistics of Klingon? Now, that would be boldly going where no man has gone before.

---

ture—children could, in principle, reduce the amount of bad linguistic data they take in simply by ignoring sentences that are audibly bumpy. In their study, Soderstrom and her colleagues used a head-turn preference procedure to see whether 22-month-olds would show more interest in listening to fluent speech than to disfluent speech. They found that preverbal 10-month old babies made no distinction between the two. But the older toddlers, who were by then combining words and showing some basic grammatical knowledge, did prefer to listen to fluent speech over speech that contained disruptions (see **Figure 6.5**).

There are likely to be many other ways in which children filter the input that they hear. For example, as you're about to see in the upcoming chapters, there are very real time pressures on the processing of speech. If the hearer can't efficiently retrieve words, assemble syntactic structures, and resolve any thorny ambiguities or complexities at the speed at which language rolls by, the end result may simply be a failure of interpretation. We don't yet know what percentage of the sentences a child hears might end up in a mental garbage heap because the child hasn't been able to assign them a proper structure.

You may have the sense by now that the open-ended questions far exceed the definitive answers when it comes to understanding how children

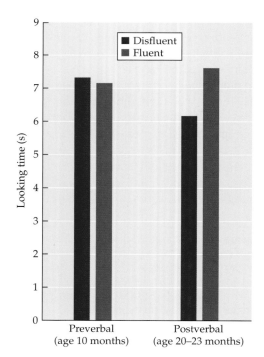

Figure 6.5 Mean looking times to fluent and disfluent speech. Preverbal infants were 10 months old, while the postverbal subjects ranged in age from 20 to 23 months. (Adapted from Soderstrom & Morgan, 2007.)

learn syntax. And this is certainly true. The researchers who toil in the field of syntactic development are burdened with more than their share of challenges when it comes to making progress in leaps and bounds. Among these challenges: the need for large amounts of data about children's linguistic abilities over a long period of time; a lack of agreement by linguistic experts about the exact nature of the syntactic knowledge that children are acquiring; and a very hazy understanding of how performance limitations on producing and comprehending language might interact with the learning of syntactic knowledge.

You might wonder why anyone would voluntarily choose this field of study. Yet, researchers' drive to understand how children learn the complexities of syntax is very strong because the stakes are high. No other animals seem to spontaneously communicate in a system that pairs complex structure with compositional meaning. Because of this, to many language researchers, this field is the nexus for the really big questions about language: Are we born with a special predisposition for language that sets us apart from other animals? Did our brains evolve as specially tuned machines for language learning, or is language a by-product of a vast, general intelligence that is capable of learning almost any complex pattern? And what is it about our minds that causes languages the world over to seize on some kinds of patterns while rejecting others as the basis for their grammars?

GO TO
sites.sinauer.com/languageinmind

for **web activities, further readings, research updates, new essays,** and other features

---

DIGGING DEEPER

Domain-general and domain-specific theories of language learning

What we know about language structure seems to be quite unlike most other kinds of knowledge we've mastered in our lives. Try to think of anything you know from any other cognitive domain that is analogous to the structure-dependence exhibited by the form of yes/no questions in English. It's not easy to find plausible non-linguistic examples. It's partly because linguistic knowledge seems so idiosyncratic that many researchers have expressed doubt that language could be learned at all without a heavy dose of **domain-specific learning**—that is, using learning mechanisms that are strictly devoted to language.

Of course, in order to convincingly make the claim that language *isn't* learned by general-purpose learning machinery, we need to have some good ideas about how humans go about learning highly complex information that *isn't* linguistic in nature. We would then need to show that these **domain-general learning** mechanisms are badly suited for learning language.

This critical step in the scientific argument is still very much unresolved, for the simple reason that *non*-linguistic learning is far from well understood. But in recent years, researchers have made progress in providing more detailed hypotheses about what domain-general learning mechanisms might look like and, in doing so, have often

argued that they might actually be reasonably well suited for many aspects of language learning.

For the most part, contemporary approaches to domain-general learning (at least those that are relevant for language) fall into one of two categories. The first of these is the class of **associationist theories**, with their focus on memorized relationships and patterns, while the second category refers to statistical learning theories known as Bayesian models.

Associationist theories are often made computationally explicit within a **connectionist framework**. A connectionist approach offers the possibility of generalizing without the use of abstract linguistic rules or categories. Instead,

---

domain-specific learning Learning by mechanisms that are strictly devoted to language.

domain-general learning Learning by mechanisms that aren't limited to learning language.

associationist theories Domain-general theories of learning that emphasize learning that takes place when items become associated in memory through experience.

connectionist framework A framework for implementing the process by which items become associated in memory, involving interconnected networks of units.

a connectionist system makes predictions about new forms based on their overall similarity with forms that have been encountered in the past. Such an approach, for example, has been used to model how children might learn past tense and plural forms in English, which you encountered in the last chapter (Rumelhart & McClelland, 1986).

For a case like the English past tense, rather than calling up a general rule for combining an element from the verb category with the morpheme *-ed*, the connectionist network draws on its past experience, in which adding *-ed* was the most frequent way to form the past tense, applying to the largest variety of forms of verbs. The connectionist model also takes into account clusters of irregular verbs that share certain sound patterns, such as *sing, sink, drink, ring*. If a new verb comes along with a striking similarity to these outlaw verbs, the connectionist network is more likely to assume *its* past tense form is also irregular.

Connectionist systems are especially good at keeping track of regular patterns that are found among adjacent or near-adjacent elements. This makes them potentially very handy for some language-learning tasks. Earlier in this chapter, we talked about how lexical co-occurrence patterns might provide quite a bit of information in helping a young child group words into syntactically relevant categories. Connectionist networks excel at using this sort of information. For example, if *bottle* and *doggie* are both closely associated with the frame *the__is*, the network will flag *bottle* and *doggie* as being highly similar to each other, while the word *eat*, which never appears in this frame, is highly dissimilar from both. On the basis of this similarity, a connectionist network might then predict that if *bottle* appears in a new frame like *the __ in*, *doggie* is more likely to also be able to appear in that frame than *eat,* which has been previously found to be quite unlike *bottle* in terms of its lexical co-occurrences. (For an example of a full connectionist model that successfully learns to sort words into syntactic categories; see Redington et al.,1998.)

Connectionist systems can readily be adapted to track just about any kinds of associations, not just linguistic ones, so they provide a plausible example of how domain-general learning machinery might take on some of the work of language learning. But just because a connectionist network *could* in principle learn any set of associations doesn't mean that, embedded within the mind of a living organism, it *will*. Remember, the findings from Chapter 2, in which rats were able to easily learn associations between smell and bad food, but weren't able to make the same connection between *color* and bad food. It may be that in order for these broadly domain-general theories to line up with actual facts about learning, they'll need to be fitted with certain biases to learn some associations and not others—and some of these biases may well turn out to be language specific (and possibly innate).

But while connectionist models do a great job of capturing statistical regularities among nearby elements, they tend to do less well with patterns that involve complex relationships between linguistic elements over long spans of words. This is because connectionist models avoid abstract rules and structures, which happen to be especially efficient at capturing long-distance dependencies.

Until recently, there was a general shortage of ideas about how powerful abstract representations might be merged with domain-general theories of learning. But lately, a number of researchers have been turning their attention to the second class of statistical models known as Bayesian learning models. The basic idea behind these models goes like this:

Children's approach to learning about the world is essentially that of rational investigators—you might think of them as miniature scientists intent on uncovering explanations for the phenomena around them. They learn by generating hypotheses about the world and fitting these hypotheses with the available data, taking into account their prior knowledge or assumptions.

To make things a bit concrete, let's revisit our problem of generalizing about the color of sheep in Scotland (see p. 210). Suppose this time we observe two black sheep, and not just one, while driving in Scotland. And let's suppose we're again considering the hypothesis that all sheep in Scotland are black. The fundamental statistical insight of Bayesian accounts hinges on Bayes' theorem, which states that for a set of observations X, the probability that a hypothesis h is correct given the observed facts is proportional to the likelihood that if h were true, it would give rise to the observations multiplied by the prior probability of that hypothesis. Or:

$$P(h|X) \propto P(X|h) \times P(h)$$

We want to figure out how confident we should be in concluding that all sheep in Scotland are black given that two black sheep just crossed the road in front of our car. This corresponds to the term $P(h|X)$. Well, if it were true that *all* sheep in Scotland were black, then there would be a 100% likelihood that any two sheep we spot would be black— this is the term $P(X|h)$. Compare this to another possible hypothesis that says that white and black sheep are bred in equal numbers. This hypothesis would yield a likelihood of 25% that any two sheep we spot would be black (that is, if there were equal numbers of black and white sheep in Scotland, then meeting two black ones should be no more likely than meeting two white ones, and only half as likely as meeting one of each.)

But this doesn't necessarily mean that you should favor the hypothesis that all sheep are black. You still need to multiply the term $P(X|h)$ by the *prior* probability that all sheep in Scotland are black. You might have prior knowledge that the probability of this hypothesis $P(h)$ is very low. For example, you might know that black sheep don't withstand northern climates very well. Or that they're the result of a fluke genetic mutation. Or you may simply have observed, from your extended travels, that black sheep are much less common than white sheep.

One advantage of Bayesian statistical models over associationist models is that they make it possible to generalize on the basis of just a few examples—that is, relatively few examples may be needed before one hypothesis stands out as clearly more probable than many others. For instance, your sense of the prior probabilities of black versus white sheep can be dramatically shaped after just a couple of encounters with sheep. This is appealing, given that there's evidence that kids can learn the meanings of words, or even generalizations about structure, on the basis of a small handful of observations.

Bayesian models also offer one way to think about a thorny problem that we saw earlier: that kids are unlikely to learn from parents acting as grammar police, correcting them when they overgeneralize grammatical rules. All kids have to go on is the sentences that they hear around them. So how do kids learn from the *absence* of certain kinds of sentences in their input? Suppose, for example, that the child is trying to decide between two grammars: one that allows *wh-* island violations like this one:

> ***Who** did Weyman believe [$_{NP}$ the rumor that ___ had dated Cecelia]?

and one that doesn't. The child has never heard examples like this, where a *wh-* word is linked with an element inside of a complex NP. Obviously, the kid can't just conclude that every unattested example is ungrammatical. But a Bayesian approach allows her to consider the fact that, for any grammar that *allowed* this structure, it would be rather unlikely that over the course of, say, a million sentences she's heard to date, there would be not a single example among them. In such a large sample, the likelihood of a total absence of such sentences given a hypothesized grammar that allows them—that is $P(X|h)$—would be very low, thereby reducing the child's confidence in such a hypothesis.

Bayesian approaches, like associationist models, give us one way to see how a small child might leverage her impressive abilities in tracking statistical patterns in order to break into the structure of her language. Both types of models can and have been applied to many domains other than language. But just as with associationist models, it's entirely possible to graft language-specific biases and assumptions onto domain-general Bayesian learning mechanisms. For example, the prior knowledge that affects the confidence of adopting a hypothesis might turn out to be very specific to language. It might include, among other things, the bias that languages are very likely to have grammatical rules that refer to constituents and their structural relationships, and very unlikely to have rules that refer to the serial order of elements in a sentence. Or that syntactic structure generalizes over categories that correlate broadly in meaning (for instance, creating a category for words that refer to objects) rather than in terms of their sound. Biases like these, if they exist, might be the result of learning, or they could be innately specified.

PROJECT

Test for domain-specific versus domain-general learning of structure. Focus on an interesting generalization about English syntactic structure. Using nonsense words, create a sample from an artificial language that captures that structural generalization. Now think about testing whether the same kind of structural generalization could be represented in a non-linguistic domain (you might consider using images or tones). Create a sample of data from this non-linguistic domain to present to learners. Sketch out an experiment in which you could test to see whether the same generalization is more easily learned by human subjects with linguistic stimuli versus non-linguistic stimuli. What might the result of such a study tell you?

7 Word Recognition

In Chapter 5, we explored the ways in which babies and young children learn to pluck word chunks out of the streams of speech that they hear, pair these chunks up with meanings, and add to a growing collection of words that will eventually tally up to tens of thousands, if not more. But learning words and their meanings is only part of the story. Once we've added these thousands of words to our memory's stash of vocabulary units, we also need to be able to quickly and efficiently retrieve them while producing and understanding language.

Both speaking and comprehending language involve matching up meanings with their corresponding sound sequences at breakneck speed while at the same time juggling other complicated information. During a normal conversation, speech unfurls at a rate of about 150 words per minute; master debaters and auctioneers can reach speeds of 400–500 words per minute. This means that while listening to your conversational partner speaking at a typical leisurely rate, you have less than half a second to match up the sounds coming out of her mouth and rummage around in your voluminous vocabulary to find exactly the right word before the next one follows hot on its heels, all while working out how that word figures in the syntactic structure and meaning of the unfolding sentence. Most of the time you're doing all this while also planning your own response or interjection.

Perhaps it's not entirely surprising that, as a species that depends on transmitting information via language, we've evolved to have an efficient set of routines that allow us to pack and unpack large volumes of spoken information in very small spans of time. Presumably, we've had many generations—likely more than 100,000 years' worth—over which to develop the brains for it, and a knack for speedy language comprehension would seem to offer certain evolutionary advantages. On the other hand, *written* language is a fairly recent human innovation, with the oldest known writing system dating back a mere 5,000 years, to about 3200 B.C. Even today, many (hearing) societies in the world get by without a written language, though no society is speechless. Nevertheless, our ability to strip meaning from symbols on a page is at least as fast as our ability to do so with spoken sounds. The pleasure reading of skilled readers proceeds at a clip of about 200–400 words per minute—roughly 3–6 words per *second*.

The recognition of spoken words and the reading of written language offer quite different challenges from the standpoint of information processing. In speech, sounds have to be correctly identified, word boundaries have to be accurately located, and a string of sounds has to be mapped onto the correct word, despite the fact that many other words might offer *almost* as good a match as the right one. In writing, a jumble of arbitrary symbols has to be mapped onto words that have usually been learned in terms of their sound, not in terms of their visual symbols. The system of visual symbols represents a whole new set of symbolic units and mappings that's been artificially grafted onto the "natural" system of spoken language. Skilled reading relies on smoothly integrating this artificial system with the "natural" one during normal language processing—perhaps it's a little bit like the linguistic equivalent of learning to use a prosthetic limb.

In the previous paragraphs, I've been a bit preoccupied with the *time* it takes to recognize words. As it happens, time is the central obsession of the researcher who studies word recognition or, more generally, language processing. This preoccupation with time goes far beyond mere trivia, or even the desire to explain how it is that we process language as quickly as we do. Specific theories of language processing stand or fall based on the predictions they make about the relative timing of certain processing events. Time also serves as one of the most important methodological tools for studying how language processing works. As you'll see, researchers have come to learn a great deal about *how* linguistic information is processed by looking in minute detail at *how long* people take to process it, and by making careful comparisons of the time it takes to process stimuli that differ along specific dimensions. We owe much of what we know about word recognition to clever and meticulous forms of timekeeping. In this chapter, you can get a small taste of what it's like to do research on word recognition by taking part in the many Web Activities that are sprinkled throughout. A number of these activities will focus your attention on the precision and attention to detail that's needed in order to construct experiments where the results often hinge on finding differences of less than a tenth of a second of processing time.

7.1 A Connected Lexicon

Word webs

What happens in your mind when you hear or read a word? In Chapter 1, I emphasized the fact that our subjective intuitions about language often miss some critical information, and as you'll see, that's certainly the case when it comes to understanding something as basic as word recognition. Let's start by trying to describe the very simplest case of recognizing a word in isolation, outside of the context of a sentence. Based on how the experience *feels*, we might describe the process as a bit like this: Retrieving words from memory is like getting words out of a vending machine—let's think of word representations as the snacks you're trying to buy. Specific sequences of sounds you hear or letters you read are like the sequences of letters and numbers you have to punch into the machine to get the right product to come out. Just as a vending machine has a program set up to link a sequence of button presses with a specific location that delivers your chosen snack to you, letters or sounds are programmed in your mind to activate a specific word representation. In both cases, what you want conveniently drops down for your use in the form of a single, packaged unit. When it's described this way, there doesn't seem to be much to the process of retrieving words; it's simply a matter of punching in the right input in terms of sounds or letters, which is then linked in a one-to-one fashion with the right word representation. Why *shouldn't* this happen very quickly in real time?

The truth is that this subjective impression of word recognition is deeply wrong. In actual fact, recognition of either spoken or written words is quite a bit messier than this. It seems that words aren't organized in our minds independently of one another, but rather, are connected together in complex webs. When we try to retrieve one word, we end up pulling a string that has the actual matching word, but also has a bunch of connected words dangling from it as well. But since we have the *impression* that we've pulled a single word out of our mind, what is it that has led language researchers to the conclusion that words are actually highly interconnected? To get there, they've had to find ways to probe aspects of the word recognition process that may not be completely accessible to conscious intuition.

Evidence for partial retrieval of related words

One of the strongest (and earliest) sources of evidence for the interconnections among words has come from the phenomenon of **semantic priming**, which suggests that when you hear or read a word, you also partially activate other words that are related in meaning. The relevant experiments (the first of which were performed by David Meyer and Roger Schvaneveldt, 1971) typically use a method known as the **lexical decision task**, in which participants read strings of letters on a screen that are either actual words (for example, *doctor*) or nonsense words (*domter*) and then press one of two buttons—one button if they think they've seen a real word, and another to signal that the letters formed a nonsense word. The speed with which subjects press each button is recorded.

Semantic priming experiments have shown that participants are faster to recognize a real word if it follows hard on the heels of a word that's related in meaning. For example, responses to the test word *doctor* would be speedier if that word occurred in the experiment just after the word *nurse* than if it followed an unrelated word like *butter*. This suggests that the word *nurse* wasn't accessed in isolation. If you think of word recognition as "lighting up" a word in your mind, then some of the light spills over onto neighboring words in the semantic space. This partial lighting up of *doctor* following *nurse* makes it easier to recognize *doctor* when you see that word on the screen.

The lexical decision task shows that this happens with written words. But spoken language also seems to activate related words in much the same way. One way to see quite vividly what's happening as people process spoken words is to track their eye movements to a visual scene in real time as people hear instructions related to that scene. For example, imagine seeing a screen showing pictures of, say, a hammer, a nail, a cricket, and a box of tissues, and then hearing an instruction to "click on the hammer." Seems like a trivial enough task. But a record of subjects' eye movements (see **Figure 7.1**; Yee & Sedivy, 2006) shows that as they're hearing *hammer*,

semantic priming The phenomenon by which hearing or reading a word partially activates other words that are related in meaning to that word, making the related words easier to recognize in subsequent encounters.

lexical decision task An experimental task in which participants read strings of letters on a screen that might either be actual words (*doctor*) or nonsense words (*domter*). Subjects press one button if they think they've seen a real word, or a different button to signal that the letters formed a nonsense word. Response times for real words are taken as a general measure of the ease of recognizing those words under specific experimental conditions.

WEB ACTIVITY 7.1

Interconnected words In this activity, you'll explore how to ascertain which words might be linked together in memory, through a pen-and-paper word association test in which people are asked to list the first words that come to mind when they encounter a word.

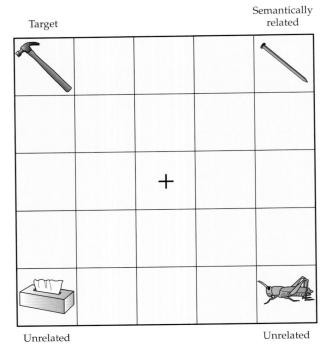

Target

Semantically related

Unrelated

Unrelated

Figure 7.1 A sample display from an experiment by Yee and Sedivy (2006). Shortly after hearing the word *hammer*, subjects were more likely to look briefly at the nail than at unrelated items such as the cricket. This suggests that hearing a word results in the activation of semantically related words as well as the target word.

facilitation Processes that make it easier for word recognition to be completed.

inhibition Processes that result in word recognition becoming more difficult.

they might be briefly lured by a picture of a related word—that is, they're more likely to look at the nail than at the unrelated cricket. This aligns nicely with the evidence from lexical decision tasks, suggesting that words that are semantically related to the target word get an extra burst of activation, relative to other words in the lexicon.

Competition from partially activated words

The lexical decision experiments show evidence of **facilitation**: a word is made easier to recognize by having it occur after a semantically related one. But as you might imagine, if the process of retrieving a word partly lights up several other words, this could sometimes make it more *difficult* to pick out the correct word from among the other, partially lit-up ones. That is, related words that are partially activated could get in the way of recognizing the right one, a result that is referred to as **inhibition**. The experimental record shows evidence of this too, especially when it comes to words that are similar in *form*, rather than meaning. For example, if "primed" with the word *stiff*, people might be slower to subsequently recognize *still* as a word (Slowiaczek & Hamburger, 1992). In this case, the prime word seems to *compete* with the target word, tripping up the recognition process. Again, the data from the priming paradigm is corroborated by eye-tracking experiments; if the visual array includes a beetle as well as a beaker, for instance, recognition of the spoken word *beaker* tends to be slowed down, so it takes people longer to locate the image of the beaker in the display (Allopenna et al., 1998).

Competition among lexical items in memory can be seen easily when the form of a target word is similar to other words that are relevant in the immediate context; for example, in the lexical decision priming paradigm, a word might inhibit the access of a similar one immediately following it, or in the eye-tracking paradigm, locating the target referent for a word may be slowed down because the eye is drawn to an object corresponding to a similar-sounding word. But these are somewhat contrived experimental scenarios in which similar words have been deliberately planted. Most of the time when we're retrieving words from memory in real-life conversation, we don't have to cope with such blatant decoys—for example, how often would we be in a context where both *beetle* and *beaker* would be uttered? So, to what extent is lexical competition likely to really play a role in our routine language comprehension?

Quite a bit, it would seem. Competition among words happens even when there are no similar words in the immediate context—it's enough merely for there to be similar words in your own personal mental storehouse. The evidence comes from comparing how quickly people retrieve words that have either many or few sound-alikes in the general lexicon, even when those sound-alike words aren't prominent in the context. As it happens, some words that you know are relatively unique when it comes to their sound structure. For instance, take the word *stench*: try to come up with as many other words as you can that differ from that one by only one sound. After *staunch* and the more uncommon word *stanch* (as in: *stanch the flow of blood*), I pretty much draw a blank myself. But I can reel off quite a few examples that differ by only one sound from the word *sling*: *sting, fling, bling, cling, slung, slang, slim* (remember, *-ng* counts as one *sound*), *slit, slip, slid, slick*. Psycholinguists have invoked a real-estate metaphor to describe this difference between *stench* and *sling*; we say that *stench* is found in a "sparse neighborhood," with very few sound-based neighbors, while *sling* resides in a "dense neighborhood," with its neighbors crowding up on all sides.

Again, psycholinguists have used response times in lexical decision tasks to probe for **neighborhood density effects**. All things being equal, after the length and frequency of words has been controlled for (since these factors can also affect how long it takes to recognize a word), people take longer to recognize words that come from dense neighborhoods than words that come from sparse neighborhoods (e.g., Goldinger et al., 1989). This effect can be seen even though no similar words have occurred before the test word, suggesting that lexical neighbors can compete for recognition even when they are not present in the immediate context. It's enough that they're simply part of the vocabulary.

neighborhood density effects
Experimental results demonstrating that it is more difficult and time-consuming to retrieve a word from memory if the word bears a strong phonological resemblance to many other words in the vocabulary than if resembles only a few other words.

Building a model of word recognition

Vague metaphors involving spotlights or neighborhoods are useful for getting an intuitive sense of how words in the mental lexicon affect each other in the process of word recognition. But it's also worth moving toward more precise theories of what lies beneath these effects. Making explicit models can advance a field very quickly, whether they're communicated as simple diagrams or actually implemented as working computer programs that simulate real language processes. A model not only serves as a way of explaining current experimental results, but also tends to force researchers to grapple with other perfectly reasonable ways to account for the same data. When you have to make a decision about the details of your model, you become aware of the things you don't yet know. So the process of building models is really useful for throwing light onto as-yet-unanswered questions that researchers might otherwise not think of. One of the main benefits of a model is that it makes new predictions that can be tested experimentally.

There's probably no other psycholinguistic process that's been modeled in as much detail and by so many different rivals as word recognition. These modeling efforts have led to an enormous volume of published experimental papers dealing with word recognition. There isn't room in this chapter to give a thorough overview of all of the models that have been proposed, or the experimental evidence that has been generated. Instead, my goal will be to bring out some of the key findings and big questions about how words are processed in the mind, and to relate these to the choices that go into building a good working model.

Let's start with one simple way to model how related words affect each other in the process of word recognition, as sketched out in **Figure 7.2**. Here, rather than just being listed as isolated units, words are represented as belonging to a complex network. Words that are related in meaning are linked together in the network—for example, *lion* is linked to *mane* and *tiger*, and *tiger* is linked to *stripes*. (Links could also be established between words that frequently occur together in speech, whether or not their meanings are similar—for example, between *birthday* and *cake*, as illustrated by the word-association task in Web Activity 7.1). If a match is made between the sounds (or letters) being perceived and a particular word, that word gets a surge of ener-

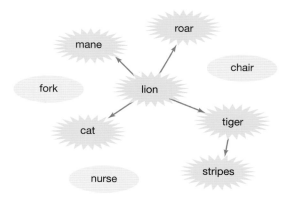

Figure 7.2 A simple spreading-activation network. Hearing the word *lion* activates the mental representation of that word and, in turn, the representations of related words such as *mane*, *cat*, *tiger*, and eventually *stripes* (via *tiger*).

mediated semantic priming The
process by which a prime word (e.g., *lion*)
speeds up responses to a target word (e.g.,
stripes) not because of a direct connection
between *lion* and *stripes*, but due to an indirect connection via some other intervening word (e.g., *tiger*).

gy or activation. Since the words in the lexicon aren't isolated from one another
but share links with quite a few other words, activation "flows" throughout
the network along these links. For example, hearing or reading the word *lion*
will also excite the connected words *mane* and *tiger*. This has behavioral consequences, such as the priming effects we've just seen.

Setting words up in a network like this (we've just created a mini-model!)
results in a new prediction: Since each word is connected to a number of other
words, and energy spreads along links in the network, we should see signs of
activation traveling along paths of interconnected words. That is, *lion* should
activate not just *tiger*, but also the word *stripes*. The latter word isn't related to
lion, but it *is* related to *tiger*, which is itself linked to the perceived word. In fact,
there is evidence for just this kind of **mediated semantic priming**, in which
a prime word like *lion* speeds up responses to a target word like *stripes*, even
though the prime and target are only related via some other intervening word.

Our simple spreading-activation story looks promising, but it's going to need
some adjustments and refinements. So far, there's nothing to prevent activation
from continuing to spread throughout the network from link to link to link in
such a way that it eventually activates just about every word in the network. For
example: *lion → tiger → stripes → paisley → shirt → tie → neck → head → hair*,
and so on. The model needs to have a way to prevent such overwhelming buzzing within the lexical network.

One way to achieve this is by building in a *decay function* by which activation levels gradually die down over time. This means that the activation of *lion*
would surge at first, but then fade. Since it would take some time for activation
to spread throughout the network, the decay function would limit how much
energy is passed on to remotely connected words or concepts. So, the activation
of *lion* would have dwindled somewhat by the time it spread to *tiger*, meaning that *tiger* would be less activated than *lion* was initially. As a result, *stripes*
would receive less activation than *tiger*, and any activation that *stripes* passed
on to *paisley* might well be negligible by that point. With this modification, it
should now be possible to quantitatively tinker with the specific rates at which
activation spreads and decays so that the model will closely simulate the patterns of results from experiments with humans. For example, the model should
now also be able to capture the fact that the degree to which a related prime
speeds up responses to a target word depends not only on how closely related
the two words are, but also on how much time has elapsed between the presentation of the prime and target words.

So far, we have a model that does a nice job of capturing *facilitatory* priming effects and their limits. But what about the cases in which the presence of
related words *slows down* or impedes the recognition of the target? As it stands,
the model doesn't predict these competition effects, so we need to either scrap
it or add something else. Given that we already have some mileage from our
little model in accounting for priming effects, the latter strategy seems like a
good place to start.

Competition effects are seen most clearly among words that are related to
each other in form rather than meaning, so we might focus on the process of
mapping sounds or letters to word representations. This is depicted in **Figure
7.3A**, where phonemic (or orthographic) units are connected to word representations. When a sound (or letter) is identified, it becomes activated, and by
virtue of the connections it has to words, activation flows to those words that
contain it. So far, this predicts that words that contain overlapping sounds
(for example, *beam* and *beat*) should both become active. But there's nothing
in the model yet to explain why hearing *beam* should make it harder to subsequently recognize *beat*—in fact, as it stands, the model predicts the opposite,

(A)

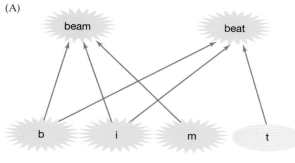

Sound input: /bim/

(B)

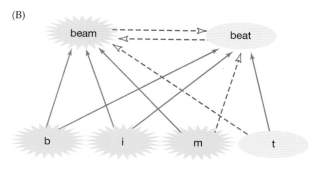

Sound input: /bim/

Figure 7.3 (A) A simple model showing only excitatory connections (solid lines and arrows) from the phonemic units in the words *beam* and *beat* (/bim/ and /bit/ respectively). With only excitatory connections, there's nothing to explain why hearing the word *beam* should make it harder to subsequently recognize *beat*. (B) A model with inhibitory connections (red dashed lines) in addition to excitatory links (solid lines and arrows). As the activation of a phonemic or word unit rises, activation is decreased for units that are connected to it via inhibitory links. For example, the rise in activation for *beam* results in the suppression of activation of *beat*.

since connections allow activation to spread. We can get the right result if we propose that two kinds of connections can exist between representations that share a link: **excitatory connections**, which pass activation from one unit to another, and **inhibitory connections**, which have exactly the opposite effect so that the more active a unit is, the more it *suppresses* the activation of a unit it is linked to. You can see this in the revised model in **Figure 7.3B**; in this version of the model, once the last sound or letter of *beam* is perceived, it will excite the word *beam*. But *beat* will be inhibited: as the activation of the unit *m* rises, it will suppress the word *beat* through the inhibitory link between *m* and *beat*; and *beat* will also become inhibited by virtue of the inhibitory link from the word *beam* to *beat*.

As you've seen, a great deal of the evidence for the degree of activation of word representations comes from either eye movement studies or experiments using the lexical decision task. In many cases, researchers strive to test predictions that involve very subtle differences in activation between types of stimuli, or changes in activation levels for the same stimuli over time. Hence, the experimental methods that they use need to be deployed with great precision. **Method 7.1** lays out some of the challenges that come up in using the lexical decision task, and the techniques that researchers use to get the most out of this simple task.

excitatory connections Connections along which activation is passed from one unit to another, so that the more active a unit becomes, the more it increases the activation of a unit it is linked to.

inhibitory connections Connections that lower the activation of connected units, so that the more active a unit becomes, the more it *suppresses* the activation of a unit it is linked to.

WEB ACTIVITY 7.3

Tinkering with models and making predictions In this activity, you'll try your hand at making empirical predictions based on subtle variations in the details of the model you've just seen.

Probing the model's assumptions

Our model-building exercise so far has focused on two aspects of the model: (1) the existence of links that connect representations to one another, and (2) what happens along these links (that is, do they spread activation or suppress it, and how do these effects dissipate over time?). But our little model also makes certain implicit commitments that we haven't yet defended empirically.

We've assumed that the input to word recognition is a set of discrete letter or sound units, represented as integral units rather than as bundles that

METHOD 7.1

Using the lexical decision task

There's a simple logic behind the semantic priming techniques that are used in lexical decision tasks. You create an experiment in which you record and compare the response times to test words, or targets, that have been preceded by primes: words that are either *related* or *unrelated* to the target. For example, response times to the target *doctor* preceded by the prime *nurse* would be compared with results for *doctor* preceded by *chair*. If responses to the former are significantly faster than to the latter, you've found a priming effect, suggesting that seeing the word *nurse* facilitated the subject's recognition of the word *doctor* through spreading activation. But actually running an experiment using priming techniques involves making many small technical decisions, each of which could conceivably have some impact on your results or how you interpret them.

First, you'll need to deal with the possibility that participants might try to anticipate patterns within the experiment in order to respond strategically. If this happens, their response times might say less about what people typically do in daily conversation than about what students do when trying to puzzle out a psychology experiment. The goal is to minimize patterns wherever possible. For example, you can easily eliminate the expectation that the correct response to the target will be to press the button for "Yes, it's a word" by making sure that you put in plenty of fillers, and balance the experiment so that the likelihood of the target being a real word is exactly 50% over the course of the experiment.

But some patterns are impossible to eliminate outright, such as the relationship that exists between some of the primes and targets. If, after a while, your participants begin to catch on to the fact that the target is often related to the prime, they might approach the task less as a word

recognition task, and more as a word association task: once they see the prime *nurse*, for example, they might start actively thinking of related words. In that case, it would be unsurprising to find that there's a close relationship between word association tests and priming patterns (see Web Activity 7.1); but you'd be less confident in concluding that related words are *spontaneously* activated during routine word recognition out in the wild.

You can rely on two approaches to reduce the possibility that participants will consciously notice the relationship between primes and targets. The first is to simply include a great number of filler items in which the prime and target aren't related in any way, making it harder to detect the pattern. For example, it would be harder to notice the relationships between words in this set of stimuli:

FREEDOM—METAL

WRENCH—BOOK

HANDLE—SHOES

NURSE—DOCTOR

FLOWER—SCREEN

PAPER—ROOF

than in this one:

FREEDOM—METAL

WRENCH—HAMMER

HANDLE—DOOR

NURSE—DOCTOR

FLOWER—VASE

PAPER—ROOF

contain other parts or properties. This doesn't seem like an unreasonable assumption for recognizing written words—after all, the letter *p* looks pretty much the same, regardless of which other letters it's next to (at least if it's typed or printed). So it doesn't seem odd to think of it as a basic unit. Even so, by treating letters as integral units, the model predicts—without justification—that similarities among letters should be irrelevant. For example, it predicts that the word pair *bin/din* should be no more confusable than *bin/sin*, which is probably wrong.

But things get especially complicated in dealing with the perception of *spoken* language. Individual sounds vary a great deal, depending not only on

METHOD 7.1 (continued)

The other way to reduce strategic responding is to provide your participants with as little time as possible to anticipate words that are related to the prime. You can do this by shrinking the time between the presentation of the prime and the presentation of the target. In fact, you can even exploit an intriguing quirk of the human perceptual system, namely, the fact that there's a time lag between conscious and unconscious perceptual processing, so at very rapid speeds, it's possible for our unconscious minds to have processed a stimulus while our conscious minds don't "know" that we've done so.

Researchers have used subliminal presentation of the prime word—in a paradigm known as **masked priming**—as a tool to eliminate the possibility of conscious, strategic responding. At the beginning of a trial, participants see a row of dashes or # symbols "masking" the prime. The prime is then briefly flashed and quickly covered up again before the presentation of the target stimulus. For example:

mask	#####	(1,000 milliseconds)
prime	NURSE	(50 ms)
mask	#####	(500 ms)
target	DOCTOR	(response required—is it a word?)

As we've seen from our discussion of modeling, the interconnected lexicon is in a constant state of flux, reflecting the spreading and dampening of activation over time along various links. This means that using the priming technique—which probes for responses at *one* specific time point—is a bit like relying on a snapshot to capture an object that is in motion. Depending on when you press the shutter, you may get a very different picture of the object's path of motion. For instance, if you're interested in finding out whether target words that have some particular relationship to their primes become activated above baseline levels (that is, relative to targets with unrelated primes), whether or not you find a priming effect may depend upon when you present the target. Probe too soon, and activation may not have spread to the target yet. Probe too late, and activation may have dissipated or become suppressed.

For this reason, researchers often sample at different time points, by varying either how long the prime is presented or the **interstimulus interval** (**ISI**), which refers to the amount of time between the offset of the prime and the onset of the target.

Another issue with using a snapshot technique to capture a temporally dynamic process is that response times will be affected by how deeply people process the target words before making a decision. If they press the button after very shallow processing, they may not yet have had time to fully access the word's semantic representation. This can happen if the non-word targets are very distinct from any possible words (for example, *bgltx*, *aoitvb*), so decisions about the target's status can be made very quickly and on the basis of very superficial characteristics. On the other hand, if the non-words look like possible though non-existent words (for example, *blacket*, *snord*), then participants will have to process them more deeply before deciding whether the targets are words or non-words.

---

masked priming A priming task in which the prime word is presented subliminally, that is, too quickly to be consciously recognized.

interstimulus interval (ISI) The amount of time between the offset of the prime and the onset of the target.

---

where in the word they appear, but also on the particular speaker's age, gender, regional dialect, and individual characteristics of the vocal tract. What's more, sounds often smear together when pronounced, making it tricky to carve up the speech stream into separate units. We'll take up these issues in Section 7.4.

Another built-in assumption that we've made so far is that word representations themselves are discrete units. Our model captures these as individual nodes that become activated or inhibited as entire units. I've been extremely vague about what's *in* a word representation. Let's assume that a word node is really just a container for information about a word's meaning and sound, as well as information specifying how the word combines syntactically with other words. But by representing words as nodes, our model implies that all of this information is available simultaneously and all to the same degree when the word node is activated. In fact, there's an ongoing debate about whether words

(A)

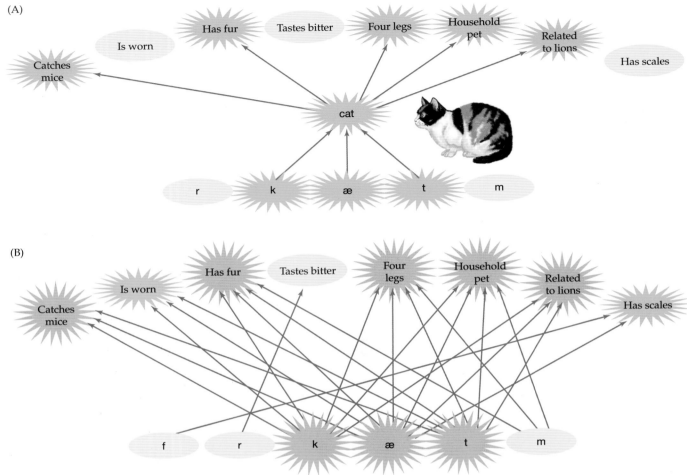

(B)

Figure 7.4 Localist versus distributed representations. (A) Localist word representations are shown by this example of a model in which the semantic features are connected to a single word unit (only excitatory connections are shown here). The activation of phonemic units results in the activation of the word unit and, in turn, the activation of that word's semantic features. (B) Distributed representations are shown in this example of a model in which phonemic units are directly linked to various semantic features without any intervening word units.

should be represented as discrete units (or containers) at all. An alternative view is that words should be captured as bundles of features instead. In dealing with the meanings of words, for example, the difference between *localist* word representations (with discrete nodes) and *distributed* representations (just bundles of features) is shown in **Figure 7.4**.

In the localist representation (Figure 7.4A), sound units connect to word nodes, which in turn connect to semantic features that become turned on when the word node is activated. In the distributed representation (Figure 7.4B), bundles of sound units connect directly to bundles of semantic features, without any intervening word nodes. The advantages and disadvantages of each approach, as far as generating correct predictions goes, are quite subtle, and I won't elaborate on them. But just to give you a taste for where they might differ, I'll point out that one argument that's been made for distributed representations is that they more accurately reflect some of the losses that might happen with brain damage. For example, when people suffer from aphasia due to a stroke, access to word representations is often impaired. But the damage doesn't seem to selectively wipe out swaths of a person's vocabulary, as might be expected if words were represented as integral units. Rather, the damage seems to lead to an across-the-board dysfunction in access, as if some *parts* of all word representations were destroyed, rather than some subset of word units in a person's vocabulary. (See **Box 7.1** for additional discussion on how to think about word meanings.)

BOX 7.1
Words: All in the mind, or in the body too?

So far, we've been talking about meanings of words as clusters of semantic features or properties that are linked to word representations and become "turned on" when a word is heard or read. For example, the word *dog* might be represented with properties such as [has fur], [barks], [has four legs], [is a mammal], and so on. The assumption is that we've learned and mentally stored some properties about the things in the world that are called *dog*. It's often thought that these properties are abstract—that is, the property [has fur] comes to be stored in the mind in the same way regardless of how we came to know this fact about dogs, whether through visual observation of the fur, by feeling it, or by being told that dogs have fur. In other words, we don't think about meanings in terms of pictures or tactile experiences; we think about them in *thoughts*. The perceptual experiences are just the delivery device for getting to the meanings; they're not part of the meaning representation itself. To take a slightly more provocative example: the idea is that even though the color blue is closer to green on the color spectrum than it is to red, the *meaning* of the word *blue* in our minds would be no closer to the meaning of *green* than to that of *red*, since word meanings are just abstractions.

But many researchers argue that links between words and our perceptual experiences are preserved, and some even go so far as to say that meaning isn't really about pulling abstract properties from those experiences so much as it is about encoding the perceptual memories and linking them to words and to each other.

A number of studies suggest that at the very least, there is cross talk between word representations and bodily information. For example, people are usually faster to respond to a word like *pen* or *knife* when their hands are positioned as they would be if they were actually using these objects (Klatzky et al., 1989). They are faster to respond to sentences like *He closed the drawer* if the response requires them to make a movement that's consistent with simulating the action—for example, if subjects have to move the hand away from the body to push a button rather than starting at a faraway resting point and moving the hand toward the body to push a button (Glenberg & Kaschak, 2002). Semantic priming shows that reading a word like *typewriter* speeds up responses to a word like *piano*, where the main similarity between the words is in how the corresponding objects are physically manipulated, rather than some more abstract property that they share (Myung et al., 2006). And people seem to take less time to read words when they can easily imagine ways in which they might physically interact with their corresponding objects, such as *cat* versus *sun* (Phillips et al., 2012).

But it's one thing to show that words set off resonances with corresponding perceptual memories, and quite another to show that knowing and retrieving the meanings of words somehow *depends* on accessing those perceptual memories, which is what more fervent proponents of embodied meanings want to claim. It would be useful to see what happens to word processing when there is damage to sensory or motor systems in the brain. One study by Véronique Boulenger and colleagues (2008) looked at people with Parkinson's disease, a condition that dampens the brain activity responsible for planning physical movement. Would such subjects show a selective impairment in accessing the meanings of words involving action? They did; compared with other subjects, those with Parkinson's showed reduced priming for action words (suggesting that these words were being weakly activated) while showing normal priming for words that don't evoke actions. But when these subjects were treated with medication that improves the brain functioning in motor areas, they showed normal priming for action words as well. This suggests that perhaps word meanings are not entirely abstract, and that some are woven tight with bodily action. Other classes of words seem to be more tightly linked with specific sensory domains. For instance, damage to the visual region in the brain often leads to difficulty processing words for things that we normally experience visually, such as *birds* (Warrington & Shallice, 1984).

Results like these are hard to explain with a story that says word meanings are made out of pure thought rather than out of pictures or patterns of movement. They're driving a rethinking about how to talk about the meanings of words. Of course, building meanings out of body memories poses some challenges of its own, the greatest of these being how to account for more abstract words like *freedom* and *hypothesis*, let alone *if*, *but*, or *not*.

Finally, you might have noticed that in Figure 7.3, the links between the sound units and word units aren't bidirectional; they go in one direction only, from the lower to the higher level. It certainly makes sense to have activation flow from the sound level to the word level—after all, we recognize words mostly on the basis of their sounds. But we might question whether this is the *only* direction in which information can flow. In theory, our model could have been developed otherwise, with facilitation and inhibition going from the top down as well.

I'll take this issue up in later sections, after you've had a chance to think about the empirical consequences of each move, with the help of prompts in Web Activity 7.4.

7.2 Ambiguity

A multiplicity of meanings

In the preceding section, you learned that retrieving a word from memory is not a simple matter of pulling out a single word from its designated slot in the mind's vending machine. Instead, multiple word representations are simultaneously activated, resulting in competition among lexical representations, sometimes to a degree that causes a discernible delay in the time it takes to retrieve a word. Competition is most intense when words overlap a great deal in terms of their sounds or orthography (so that *bean*, for example, might interfere with the retrieval of *beat*). Which might lead us to ask: What about when the sound overlap between words is not partial, but *complete*? As it happens, English is riddled with **homophones**, words that mean completely different things and may be spelled differently, but that sound exactly the same. Here's just a small sample:

bred, bread	made, maid	side, sighed	flea, flee
none, nun	blew, blue	missed, mist	main, mane
bridal, bridle	waste, waist	know, no	in, inn
sun, son	stare, stair	seen, scene	fair, fare
team, teem	pea, pee	hour, our	retch, wretch

The problem of ambiguity gets worse. English is also rife with **homographs**, words that share the same spelling but have different meanings (and may or may not sound the same). Consider, for example:

The performer took a deep **bow**.
It's difficult to hunt with a **bow** and arrow.

Jerry is headed **down** the wrong road.
I've really been glad to have my **down** parka this winter.

Silvia is **content** with her lot in life.
The **content** of this course is difficult.

To round the list off, consider the many words that are **polysemous**, conveying a constellation of related but different meanings. Consider some the many possible uses of the word *run*:

She's got a **run** in her stockings.

There was a **run** on the banks this week.

homophones Two or more words that have separate, non-overlapping meanings but sound exactly the same (even though they may be spelled differently).

homographs Words that are spelled exactly the same but have separate, non-overlapping meanings (and may or may not sound the same).

polysemous words Words that can convey a constellation of related, but different meanings, such as the various related meanings of *paper*, which can, among other meanings, refer to a specific material, or a news outlet.

Sam went out for an early morning **run**.

I'd like to **run** my fingers through your hair.

Let's **run** through the various options.

He's had a **run** of bad luck.

Can you **run** this over to the post office?

You can try generating a similar list for words like *paper* or *dish*—you may find yourself startled at how many different meanings or uses you can come up with.

Ambiguity is so rampant in language (and not just in English) that you might begin to wonder whether it's a serious design flaw common to many languages. It's hard to imagine that the presence of ambiguity does anything useful to promote effective communication between people (but see **Box 7.2**).

BOX 7.2
Why do languages tolerate ambiguity?

If the goal of language is for a speaker to plant his intended meaning firmly and decisively into the mind of the hearer, ambiguity appears to be a serious flaw. By definition, an ambiguous word or phrase is compatible with multiple interpretations, not just the meaning the speaker intended. You'd think that languages would strive to avoid ambiguity. Yet all known languages seem to be rife with it, despite the fact that lexical ambiguity could very easily be avoided. In the words of blogger Geoff Pullum (2012):

> Let me make a numerical point to begin with. The number of [possible letter sequences] with length not more than 10 over the roman letters a to z plus the apostrophe is $27^{10} = 205,891,132,094,649$—about 200 trillion. The total number of words in the workaday word list is about 25,000. What I'm saying is that English could easily have a distinct letter sequence for every different meaning, using letter sequences much shorter than the present ones. It doesn't because the language in general shows no signs of being the slightest bit interested in that. English uses the same two-word phrase for denigrating, ceasing to hold, making notes, and euthanasia. [The phrase is **put down**.] It wantonly employs a single three-letter word for meanings relating to understanding, judging, experiencing, finding out, dating, visiting, ensuring, escorting, and saying farewell. [The word is **see**; see if you can create a sentence for each of these uses.] Nobody who thinks about English for a few seconds could possibly believe it shuns ambiguity. It doesn't give a monkey's fart about avoiding ambiguity.

Steve Piantadosi and his colleagues (2012) have gone even further and argued that not only do languages not "care" about avoiding ambiguity, they actively seek it out because ambiguity actually makes a language more effective. The logic goes like this: Ambiguity rarely creates serious impediments to understanding—yes, processing ambiguous words comes with a small cost for the hearer (as you'll see in the rest of this chapter), and yes, occasionally, communication may rupture as a result. But the vast majority of the time, hearers are quite competent at relying on context to navigate through the various meanings offered up by a single string of sounds or letters. The benefits of ambiguity come from considering the costs of *producing* language. Speakers can minimize their effort by re-using bits of language that are common, short, and easy to pronounce, rather than resorting to longer words with unusual combinations of sounds. The idea is that languages tend to strike a balance between comprehensibility and ease of production. If ambiguity is managed fairly easily by the hearer, the speaker may as well take advantage of it to reduce his own cognitive workload.

Throughout this chapter, you'll see how the word recognition mechanism is set up to avoid ambiguity sinkholes, suggesting that Piantadosi and his colleagues are right that ambiguity doesn't do much damage to understanding. In support of their second point—that ambiguity makes the task of speaking easier—Piantadosi and his colleagues presented evidence from several languages showing that words that are easier to produce are exactly the ones that are most likely to be re-used for new meanings. That is, ambiguous words in those languages were generally shorter, more common, and composed of fewer unusual combinations of sounds than unambiguous words.

The English writer Virginia Woolf had an interesting perspective on ambiguity and the usefulness of language. In her 1937 essay on writing titled "Craftsmanship," Woolf argued that if we think of a useful statement as one that can mean only one thing—that is, a statement that unambiguously communicates a very specific idea—then it should be apparent "how very little natural gift words have for being useful. ... They have so often proved that they hate being useful, that it is in their natures not to express one simple statement but a thousand possibilities." To make her point, Woolf suggested the reader imagine what's going on inside the mind upon hearing a simple and seemingly utilitarian phrase:

> Take the simple sentence "Passing Russell Square." That proved useless because besides the surface meaning, it contained so many sunken meanings. The word "passing" suggested the transiency of things, the passing of time, and the changes of human life. Then the word "Russell" suggested the rustling of leaves and the skirt on a polished floor also the ducal house of Bedford and half the history of England. Finally, the word "Square" brings in the sight, the shape of an actual square combined with some visual suggestion of the stark angularity of stucco. Thus one sentence of the simplest kind rouses the imagination, the memory, the eye and the ear—all combine in reading it.

For Woolf, the point of language is just that—to rouse the imagination, rather than communicate a specific idea. Poets (and maybe even advertising copywriters) would likely agree with that, and I myself would admit that it's certainly the aim of great *writing* to rouse the imagination. But I strongly doubt that whoever announced "Passing Russell Square" on the train did so with the intent of evoking the rustling of long skirts on polished floors. And I also suspect that your average passenger understood the announcer to be communicating a specific idea (even if thoughts of rustling skirts *did* enter his mind).

But Woolf's discussion of language, fanciful though it may be, is in some ways a plausible psycholinguistic hypothesis about word recognition. There is good reason to think that during the course of recognizing a single word, a plethora of meanings presents itself.

Look back at the model we built in Figure 7.3, and notice the connections between the units of sound and word representation units. So far, we've been assuming that word units are activated to the extent that the sound units they are connected to become activated; perfect matches will be activated the most, but highly similar words will also light up. But as Virginia Woolf notes, often a set of sounds will match up *exactly* with a number of different word meanings. For example, the sounds in the name *Russell* match up with the name of whoever Russell Square happens to be honoring, but also with many different Russells, as well as the homophonous word *rustle*. Presumably, the mental lexicon includes connections from this set of sounds to *all* of these word representations, so activation of the sound units should spread to all of these word representations and their respective semantic features. If that's the case—and if, as suggested by Virginia Woolf, words commonly have a multiplicity of meanings—then the real puzzle is: How is it that words manage to make themselves useful after all? In other words, how is it that we ultimately arrive at a single interpretation, despite the numerous possible meanings?

The easy answer to this question is that we undoubtedly use context to disambiguate meanings. But since we've been building detailed models, let's be a bit more precise: *How* do we use context? We might build up our model using two different approaches.

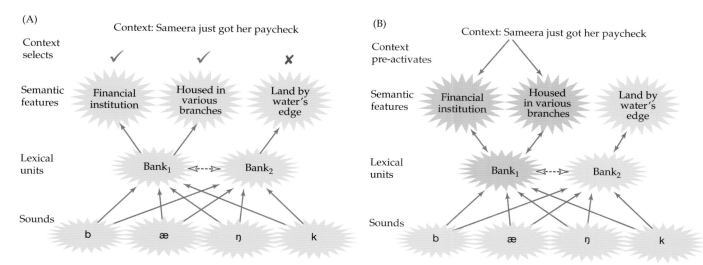

Figure 7.5 Two ways in which context can help word recognition. (A) Activation flows from the bottom up, from phonemic units to words and in turn to semantic features. Both meanings of the word *bank* are equally active until contextual information is recruited to select the most appropriate meaning. (B) Context can generate more expectation for some meanings than others by "pre-activating" some semantic features. Hence, by the time the word *bank* rolls off the tongue of the speaker, one of the meanings of that word is already more active than the other. Inhibitory connections appear in red.

The first is illustrated in **Figure 7.5A**, using two meanings of the word *bank*. Here, sound units are activated as these sounds are heard. Activation flows from the sound level to the lexical level, activating both word representations and, in turn, their associated semantic features. The flow of activation is in one direction only, from the lower level of sound to the higher level of meaning. (Lateral inhibitory links have also been drawn in between word representations, but since each word representation receives equal activation, these links would have no impact on the relative activation of the two possible meanings.) Once words and their meanings are activated, a separate decision mechanism is triggered to select the most contextually appropriate word, based on a good match between the semantic features of that word and the semantic expectations that have been set up by the context. To relate this to Virginia Woolf's observations, this would mean that multiple meanings do in fact routinely flare up in the mind, even if we ultimately have a way of picking out the most "useful" one.

A second approach is shown in **Figure 7.5B**. The crucial difference here is that activation can move from the top semantic level down to lower levels. Context activates certain semantic features, which in turn activate associated word representations. This means that even before there's any sound input, one word representation may be more active than the other. Once the word itself is uttered, activation moves from the sound units to each of the competing meanings, but since the contextually favored word is already more strongly activated, it inhibits the less-favored reading. As a result, the activation level of the competing meaning may remain very weak, perhaps even negligible. Our response to Virginia Woolf might be: even though language is rife with ambiguity, the mind is very efficiently set up to promote the most "useful" meanings of words at the expense of the less useful ones. In that case, what do we make of Woolf's poetic meditations about rustling skirts? Well, perhaps such alternative meanings come to mind when you think about language in a more deliberate way, with a purposeful focus on the connections between words. But they're unlikely to spontaneously arise in the normal course of language comprehension.

Evidence for the simultaneous activation of word meanings

In 1979, David Swinney published a seminal study that tested whether competing meanings of ambiguous words become simultaneously activated even when plenty of contextual information makes it easy to home in on the most useful meaning. For example, the word *bug* could refer to either a small crawl-

crossmodal priming task An experimental task involving both spoken and written modalities; participants typically hear prime words, which are often embedded within full sentences, and they must respond to test words displayed orthographically on a computer screen.

ing creature or a surveillance device for eavesdropping, but its meaning should be clear in the following context:

> Rumor had it that, for years, the government building had been plagued with problems. The man was not surprised when he found several spiders, roaches, and other bugs in the corner of his room.

Swinney devised an elegant experiment to test the following predictions: Clearly, the relevant meaning of the word *bugs* must become activated in order for someone to understand the passage. Hence, its activation should spread to other words that are related in meaning—for example, the word *ant*. Now, if the irrelevant meaning *also* becomes activated, then its activation should spread as well to related words, such as *spy*. But if the activation of the irrelevant meaning remains low, then the activation flowing to *spy* should be no greater than to a word completely unrelated to either meaning (such as *sew*). And how to measure the spread of activation? Through the familiar semantic priming task.

Swinney used a **crossmodal** variant of the priming task in which subjects listened to passages like the one above and then responded to test words presented visually on a screen (see **Figure 7.6**). Subjects responded by pressing one of two buttons to indicate whether they thought they'd seen a word or a non-word (naturally, plenty of non-word filler items were included). Subjects saw the test word *ant*, *spy*, or *sew*. Swinney also varied whether subjects heard passages with helpful context or with context that didn't help to disambiguate between the meanings of *bugs*. To complete the comparison, he also varied whether subjects heard the ambiguous word *bugs* in the passage, or an unambiguous counterpart, *insects*.

Figure 7.6 The crossmodal priming task. (A) Sample experimental materials for the task as used by Swinney (1979). (B) A subject from one of the four experimental conditions listens to sentences while sitting in front of a computer screen. At some predetermined point in the sentence, a string of letters appears on the screen, and the subject must press a button to indicate whether the letter string is a real word or a non-word. (Adapted from Swinney, 1979.)

(A)

BIASING CONTEXT

Condition 1: Ambiguous prime
"Rumor had it that, for years, the government building had been plagued with problems. The man was not surprised when he found several spiders, roaches, and other bugs in the corner of his room."

Condition 2: Unambiguous prime
"Rumor had it that, for years, the government building had been plagued with problems. The man was not surprised when he found several spiders, roaches, and other insects in the corner of his room."

NEUTRAL CONTEXT

Condition 3: Ambiguous prime
"Rumor had it that, for years, the government building had been plagued with problems. The man was not surprised when he found several bugs in the corner of his room."

Condition 4: Unambiguous prime
"Rumor had it that, for years, the government building had been plagued with problems. The man was not surprised when he found several insects in the corner of his room."

(B)

"The man was not surprised when he found several spiders, roaches, and other bugs…"

VISUAL TARGETS presented either immediately after the prime (bugs/insects) or several syllables downstream

ANT (related to the intended meaning of the ambiguous prime)

SPY (related to the alternative, unintended meaning)

SEW (unrelated)

When subjects had to respond to the target word right after hearing the ambiguous word *bugs*, Swinney saw clear evidence of the activation of *both* meanings of that word. That is, response times were faster to both *ant* and *spy* than they were to the control word *sew*. In contrast, the pattern was quite different when the unambiguous word *insects* was substituted for *bugs*: here, as would be expected, response times for *ant* were faster than for *sew*, but response times for *spy* were not. This shows that it was clearly the presence of the ambiguous word *bugs* that caused the activation of the word *spy*. So Virginia Woolf is at least partly right: even the useless "sunken meanings" become active in the mind along with the obviously intended "surface meanings."

But Swinney's experiment also showed that people quickly converge on the intended meaning. When the same experiment was repeated but with the test word appearing on the screen three syllables after subjects heard the word *bugs* (or *insects*), the results were quite different. In that case, responses to the word *ant*, but not to the word *spy*, were sped up relative to *sew*. It appears that the irrelevant meaning had been activated in parallel with the more pertinent one, but then was quickly suppressed.

These results support a model in which all lexical candidates that match the sound input become active, at least for a time. But later research suggests that the picture is actually a bit more complex, and that in some cases, contextually inappropriate meanings never reach discernible levels of activation. The full story, it turns out, needs to take into account the relative frequencies of the competing meanings.

To see how frequency of meanings might play a role, play along with the following exercise. Quick, now: for each of the words below, say aloud the first synonym or brief definition that comes to mind:

port   straw   chest   pitcher

yarn   cabinet   bark   mint

All of these words are ambiguous. But for some of them, one particular meaning may have sprung to mind immediately, while for others you may have been aware of a mental tug-of-war between two meanings. And if you compared your answers with your those of classmates, some words would have converged on one meaning, while others may have been split between them. This is because for some words (for example, *bark, pitcher, straw, chest*) both meanings occur with roughly equal frequency in English, while for others (for example, *port, cabinet, yarn, mint*) one meaning is dominant and the other is subordinate. A well-known study by Susan Duffy, Robin Morris, and Keith Rayner (1988) explored how this factor interacts with contextual expectations. Rather than using semantic priming as the basis for their experiment, they exploited another behavioral consequence of lexical activation: remember that when multiple words are activated at the same time and compete with each other, as in the studies of neighborhood density effects, people usually take longer to recognize the target word. As you might expect, ambiguous words generally take longer to read than unambiguous ones, providing some additional evidence that multiple meanings of these words are activated simultaneously and compete with each other. And, based on David Swinney's priming results, we might predict that such competition would show up regardless of whether the context favors one of these readings or not, since both meanings appear to be activated, at least for some time.

But Duffy and colleagues found something a bit more subtle. When the context favored the subordinate meanings of words like *mint* or *cabinet*, subjects did read these more slowly than unambiguous control words in the same sentence, indicating competition from the alternative meanings. (For example *mint* was read more slowly than *jail* in a sentence like *Although it was by far the largest building in town, the mint/jail was seldom mentioned.*) But when the words were equally biased in frequency between the two meanings, as for *pitcher* or *straw*, and when the context favored one of their meanings, people spent no more time reading these ambiguous words than unambiguous control words, suggesting that there was no discernible competition from the alternative meaning. This raises the possibility that both frequency of meanings *and* contextual expectations can affect the activation levels of word representations. When these conspire to boost the activation of the same meaning, this lexical representation becomes disproportionately activated, allowing it to very quickly inhibit any potential competitors; however, when the two sources of information conflict, with frequency boosting the activation of one and context favoring the other, the result is roughly equal activation of both meanings, leading to competition between them.

LANGUAGE AT LARGE 7.1

The persuasive power of word associations

What if hearing a word didn't set off resonances within an entire connected network of information? What if word recognition really did just work like a vending machine, with the sounds and letters of words merely acting as pointers or addresses to slots containing meanings or concepts?

If that were the case, marketers, advertisers, and politicians would probably be a lot less preoccupied with words than they are. For example, in a word-vending-machine world, a politician trying to persuade the public on a point of policy shouldn't really care what that policy is called. After all, different ways of saying the same thing would just be different ways to get to the same concept slot in the vending machine.

But politicians and their strategists do care about the names for policies, sometimes obsessively so. For example, Frank Luntz (2007), who has worked as a communications consultant for Republican party candidates in the U.S., has a list of suggestions, seen in the table, for the wording of various policies or initiatives to advance the interests of his clients.

Never say	Instead, say
Tax cuts	Tax relief
Drilling for oil	Energy exploration
Private health care	Free market health care
Wiretapping	Electronic intercepts
Estate tax	Death tax

If you feel insulted at the suggestion that you might feel differently about a plan to reduce taxes depending on the name used to refer to it, you might consider the results of a 2010 poll conducted by CBS and the *New York Times* to probe how Americans felt about having gay people serve in the U.S. military. When people were asked, "Do you favor or oppose gay men and lesbians serving in the military?" the results were as follows:

Strongly favor: 51%

Somewhat favor: 19%

Somewhat oppose: 7%

Strongly oppose: 12%

But when people were asked, "Do you favor or oppose homosexuals serving in the military?" they were less receptive to the idea:

Strongly favor: 34%

Somewhat favor: 25%

Somewhat oppose: 10%

Strongly oppose: 19%

This makes no sense if words are just pointers to concepts. But as you now know, an awful lot happens in the mind on the way to retrieving a word's meaning from memory. Different patterns of activation will resonate throughout the lexicon, depending on whether you hear a phrase like *drilling for oil* or *energy exploration*. (If you want to get a feeling for the differences, you might try a little experiment: give two groups of people a word association task like the

These additional results make it clear that both of the models in Figure 7.5 need to be adjusted to take into account the effects of frequency and the way it interacts with context. But *exactly* how these factors interact is still a matter of some debate. (For example, do they both exert an influence at exactly the same point in time during word recognition, or does one factor come into play earlier than the other?) As a result, researchers are still in the process of refining the models to greater and greater levels of precision and continue to test finer and finer predictions about the behaviors that should result. But there's general agreement that multiple sunken meanings *are* often aroused in the mind (even though the ambiguity doesn't generally impede the eventuality of getting to a single useful meaning), and that the extent to which this occurs depends jointly on the context and frequency of the alternative meanings.

Virginia Woolf's literary excursions raise some questions that don't seem to come up in the more scientific literature. For the most part, even when there is

---

LANGUAGE AT LARGE 7.1 *(continued)*

one you did in Web Activity 7.1. Among the words on the list, include *energy*, *oil*, *exploration*, and *drilling*, and see what comes up.)

A growing body of evidence suggests that the activations that are set off during word recognition probably amount to more than just brief mental flickers that quickly dissipate without any consequences for behavior. Within social psychology, researchers have studied a phenomenon known as **implicit priming**, in which exposing people to certain stimuli increases the likelihood that they'll behave in ways that reflect stored associations, which are activated upon perceiving the stimuli. For example, in one classic study by John Bargh and colleagues (1996), undergraduate students formed sentences out of scrambled word lists, with some students receiving lists that contained words associated with the elderly (for example, *Florida*, *wrinkles*, *bingo*, *gray*) while other students got lists of neutral control words. After the students had finished the test, the experimenters measured and compared how quickly students from the two groups walked down the hall. Those who'd been exposed to the words associated with the elderly walked more slowly than those who'd been in the control condition.

Naturally, marketers are also highly intrigued by the possibility of meaningful links between word associations and behavior or attitudes, and such links are increasingly

being tested in the lab by researchers who are interested in the psychology of consumer behavior. To give you just one example, Jonah Berger and Gráinne Fitzsimons (2008) constructed an experiment to see whether exposing people to photographs of dogs would make them more likely to give positive evaluations of sneakers carrying the brand name of Puma. In case the logic behind this study escapes you, it goes like this: Generally, the more familiar people are with an idea or concept, the more they're inclined to like it (which explains why you might have the same TV commercial inflicted upon you half a dozen times during a single program). Berger and Fitzsimons reasoned that because of the similarity between the concepts of dog and puma, pictures of the dog would activate the Puma brand name, making it feel more familiar. As a result, people should experience warmer feelings toward the Puma products, which, in fact, was what the researchers found.

Naturally, just because you see an effect in the lab doesn't mean it will carry the day out in the real world. Real-world choices made by consumers or voters are complex, and likely to be affected by a wide range of different variables; I seriously doubt that you'd be convinced to buy a product you otherwise have no interest in, simply because of the associations set off by its name. Nevertheless, experimental research does lend some credibility to the notion that the Edsel automobile, one of the greatest marketing flops of the last century, wasn't helped in any way by its name. The car was named after one of its makers, Edsel Ford, who unfortunately bore a highly unpopular, old-fashioned, Germanic-sounding name—perhaps not the right one to attach to an American car a mere decade or so after the Second World War.

---

implicit priming A psychological phenomenon in which exposing people to certain stimuli increases the likelihood that they'll exhibit behaviors that are associated with the stimuli. For example, exposing people to words associated with the elderly may trigger behaviors that are stereotypically associated with the elderly, such as walking slowly.

Product names and sunken meanings
Many product names are deliberately chosen from among the inventory of existing English words (for example, the product names *Apple* and *Tide*). This creates a new lexical ambiguity, where the word can now refer either to its original meaning, or to the newly named product. In this activity, you'll explore some possible implications of this practice.

clear evidence of parallel access of competing meanings, the irrelevant meaning is quite fleeting, and quickly submerged. But do these active meanings, however fleeting, nevertheless manage to have an impact on our aesthetic or emotional experience of language? We don't really know—but recent findings and discussions about how alternative ways of saying the same thing may have different persuasive effects (see Language at Large 7.1) suggest that, perhaps, even brief flickers of activation from "useless" meanings or associated words may not be inconsequential.

7.3 Recognizing Spoken Words in Real Time

The flow of spoken words

So far, most of what we've seen about word recognition could apply equally well to the spoken or written language modality, and in fact, the experimental methods that we've seen have relied on both spoken and written stimuli, and sometimes both, to explore the underlying psychological mechanisms. But spoken language offers some particular challenges for hearers, along with some specific puzzles for researchers. We now turn to these modality-specific issues.

One obvious difference between spoken and written words is that when you read a word on a screen or on the page, you can see the whole word at once, and in normal circumstances, you can stare at it for as long as it takes to recognize it. But spoken language unfolds one sound at a time, rather than being uttered all at once, and once it's been uttered, it's gone. As aptly described in a paper by James Magnuson and colleagues (2007), if reading were like listening to spoken language, it would be like this: "Imagine reading this page through a two-letter aperture as the text scrolled past, without spaces separating words, at a variable rate you could not control." It would feel deeply weird to read a word that appeared one or two letters at a time from left to right, and this intuition is confirmed by studies that look at where people focus their gaze while reading. Rather than scanning the word left to right, their gaze lands somewhere within the word, and they can usually read the entire word from that position (or, if the word is very long, they might move their eyes rightward once to take in the rest of the word).

The "scrolling by" nature of spoken word recognition raises a very interesting question: At what point do people initiate the process of matching a string of speech sounds to a stored word representation? In the previous sections, you saw how in the process of word recognition, activation flows from sounds to word representations that contain those sounds. For example, when you hear the sequence of sounds /k/, /ae/, and /t/, the word *cat* will be activated, and also, to a lesser extent, the words *cot* and *can*, among others. But when does the activation of possible word representations begin, given that there's a time lag between the first and last sounds of a word? Does the activation of word candidates start even before the end of the word is encountered in the speech stream, or is it delayed until all the sounds of the word have been uttered? And if people do wait until the entire word has been uttered before activating lexical candidates, how do they identify where the end of the word is anyway, given that usually no silences occur between words in running speech?

In principle, it should be perfectly possible to first locate likely word boundaries, and then activate all of the sounds that bundle together in one word so that they in turn can activate matching lexical candidates. Remember, after all, that we saw in Chapter 4 that even tiny babies were able to figure out where to break the speech apart into words on the basis of statistical information, probably months before they'd acquired much in the way of a working lexicon. So one could imagine that adult word recognition might rely on the same kind of statistically based word segmentation, which would serve as the very first step in spoken word recognition—in a way, we'd be mentally inserting "spaces" between the words before any lexical activation occurred. An analogy with text might be that you'd run a program, based on statistical probabilities, to put spaces between the spoken words before any actual "reading" of the words themselves began.

How can we test to see whether lexical activation begins only after both edges of the word are identified, or whether it's initiated before this point? We can readily recruit some of the methods we've already talked about, and simply tweak them a bit.

For example, remember that in his famous study, David Swinney used semantic priming as a tool to probe for the level of activation of competing word representations: evidence of priming (that is, speeded responses) for words like *spy* and *ant* meant that both meaning representations for *bugs* were activated. We can use a similar logic now, but instead of giving subjects entire words, we can present *partial* words and see whether there's any evidence of priming for words that are related to potential matches to partial words. For example, imagine recording a word like *conform*, and cutting off the sound file right in the middle of the sound /f/. Statistically, the sound sequence /nf/ is extremely unlikely to correspond to the end of a word, so hearers should be able to guess that the end of the word hasn't occurred yet, based solely on information about the sound patterns of English words. So, if lexical activation is delayed until the ends of words are identified, we wouldn't expect to see priming for any words that are related to *conform*—for example *copy* or *imitate*. On the other hand, if lexical activation *is* initiated, we'd expect to see priming not only for words related to *conform*, but also for words related to other possible continuations of this snippet, that is, words semantically related to *conflate, confabulate, confuse, confine, confide, conflicted,* and so on. Such words, with their overlapping onsets, are known as **cohort competitors**.

This latter scenario is exactly what William Marslen-Wilson (1987) predicted. In his **cohort model** of word recognition, he suggested that lexical activation begins right after the beginning of a word, with multiple cohort competitors becoming active. As more and more sound input comes in over time as the word unfolds, the set of possible matching candidates dwindles until the **uniqueness point**, at which there remains only one possible match with the sound input. **Table 7.1** illustrates how the set of cohort candidates becomes smaller and smaller with each incoming snippet of speech.

cohort competitors Words with overlapping onsets (e.g., *candle, candy, candid,* etc.).

cohort model A model of word recognition in which multiple cohort competitors become active immediately after the beginning of word is detected, and are gradually winnowed down to a single candidate as additional acoustic information is taken in.

uniqueness point The point at which there is enough information in the incoming speech stream to allow the hearer to differentiate a single word candidate from its cohort competitors.

TABLE 7.1 Winnowing down cohort candidates as a word unfolds in time

Initial sounds heard	Cohort candidates
/kæ /	*cat, cap, cast, can, cash, cad, camp, cab, cattle, capture, candidate, catholic, candelabra, captain, canteen, castrate, Canada, cancel, castle, canister, captive, candle, cantaloupe, castoff, candy, cannibal, cashew, cantankerous, California, castaway,* many others
/kæn/	*can, candidate, candelabra, canteen, Canada, cancel, canister, candle, cantaloupe, candy, cannibal, cantankerous,* others
/kænɪ/	*canister, cannibal*
/kænɪs/	*canister*

incremental language processing
The processing of language in such a way that hearers begin to generate hypotheses about the meaning of the incoming speech on the basis of partial acoustic information, refining and revising these hypotheses on the fly rather than waiting until there is enough information in the speech stream for the hearer to be certain about what the speaker meant.

Evidence for the activation of multiple cohort candidates

A number of experiments by Marslen-Wilson and his colleagues (e.g., Marslen-Wilson, 1987; Zwitserlood, 1989) used crossmodal priming tasks and found evidence for the parallel activation of multiple cohort competitors based on partial words. That is, even in the middle of a word, there was evidence for the activation of words that were semantically related to cohort candidates. For example, while hearing the word fragment *cap-*, people were relatively fast in a lexical decision task to respond to words like *ship* or *jail*, presumably because these words were semantically related to the cohort candidates *captain* and *captive*.

These results were important and suggested that language processing is highly **incremental**—that is, hearers don't cautiously hang back during language processing and wait until there's enough information to be certain about what the speaker meant; rather, they eagerly generate hypotheses about the meaning of the unfolding speech, and refine and revise these hypotheses on the fly.

The incremental nature of word recognition can be demonstrated robustly with the use of another method we've discussed earlier—that of tracking hearers' eye movements continuously in response to spoken language. This method is especially useful for studying word recognition in real time. Unlike the priming method, which provides a set of snapshots of activation levels at different points in the speech stream, eye tracking provides something more like a movie of the word recognition process, showing how patterns of eye movements respond in lockstep with the unfolding speech stream.

Eye-tracking studies provide clear evidence that cohort competitors become activated. Paul Allopenna and colleagues (1998) were among the first to report extremely detailed eye movement data, providing a dynamic, moment-by-moment view of the word recognition process. They argued that the likelihood of looking at an object was directly related to the activation level for the word corresponding to that object, so by looking at the rising and falling patterns of eye movements for a group of subjects, you could get a fairly continuous look at activation levels for words over time. You can see a cohort effect in action in **Figure 7.7**.

Figure 7.7 Sample visual displays and data from the eye-tracking experiment by Allopenna et al. (1998). (A) An example display, which was accompanied by instructions such as "Pick up the beaker. Now put it above the triangle." Each display contained a target referent (beaker) and a cohort competitor (beetle) as well as an unrelated item (carriage). (B) A graph showing the likelihood of looking at the target referent, the cohort competitor, and the unrelated item in the display. Notice that subjects were equally likely to look at the target referent and the cohort shortly after the onset of the word. (Adapted from Allopenna et al., 1998.)

(A)

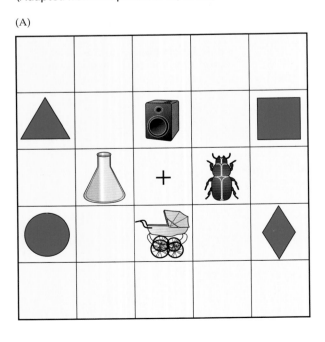

(B)

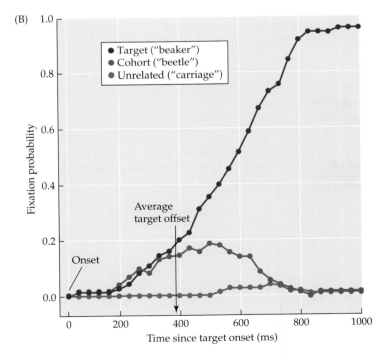

Subjects heard spoken instructions, such as "Pick up the beaker," accompanied by visual displays in which the target object (i.e., a beaker) was always present. In some of the displays, they saw a cohort competitor (for example, a beetle), as well as other, unrelated objects. The results showed that people were much more likely to look at the cohort competitor objects than at the unrelated objects, and that these eye movements were often initiated extremely early in the word, on the basis of very little phonetic information. The time needed to say the average target word in this study was about 400 milliseconds (ms). At about 200 ms, subjects were beginning to launch more eye movements to the objects matching either the target or cohort words than to the unrelated objects, suggesting that the words *beetle* and *beaker* were already more activated than other words. Given that there may be as much as a 200 ms time lag between the point an eye movement is programmed and the point the eyes actually begin to start moving, this reveals that people were starting to zero in on the target and cohort as potential matches for the incoming word on the basis of the thinnest slice of phonetic evidence, in some cases merely a sound or two. Eye movements to the cohort began to drop off shortly after the end of the word (and hence were programmed roughly 200 ms earlier), in response to new sound input that ruled the cohort word as an incompatible match. This means that before the end of the word occurred, not only were the target and its competitor both activated, but people were already beginning to identify the target as the actual word that had been spoken. Data like these very neatly rule out the notion that word segmentation has to occur before any word activation takes place. Figure 7.7 reveals the truly incremental nature of word recognition.

Since these early studies, continuous tracking of eye movements has corroborated some of the findings about word recognition that have come from other methods. For example, eye movements show that not only cohort competitors, but words that are semantically related to the cohort words become activated shortly after the beginning of a spoken word, nicely paralleling Zwitserlood's (1989) semantic priming study with cohort competitors (for example, the word *hammock* triggers eye movements to a picture of a nail, via its semantic relationship to the cohort competitor *hammer*, as found by Yee & Sedivy, 2006). Effects of frequency and neighborhood density are also apparent (see Magnuson et al., 2007), lining up tidily with studies from lexical decision tasks. Researchers have also used eye movement studies to figure out whether people who are bilingual keep their two languages separate or experience crosstalk between them (see **Box 7.3**). And in the next section, you'll see how tracking eye movements has also been useful in addressing subtle theoretical questions about spoken word recognition.

WEB ACTIVITY 7.6

Identifying cohort candidates A simple task known as "gating" can provide a quick, accessible window on how multiple cohort candidates become activated on the basis of partial sound input from a word. This activity will give you a feel for the process of winnowing down a list of candidate matches as sound input accumulates.

How important are the left edges of words?

So far, I've presented a tidy pile of data to convince you that the activation of lexical candidates is triggered well before the end of the word, and that multiple words whose onsets overlap become activated all at the same time. This shows that you don't need to identify the right edges of words (that is, their ends) before generating possible matches for the sound input, as emphasized by the cohort model. But notice: the cohort model *does* require that you've identified the *left* edge of words, since the whole point is that cohort candidates are activated on the basis of whether they're consistent with the sound input of the word *so far*. Meaning, you have to know where the word's beginning is.

BOX 7.3
Do bilingual people keep their languages separate?

If you know more than one language, to what extent are you able to keep your two language systems separate in the frenzy of daily speech and comprehension? For example, when you hear someone speaking to you in one of your languages, do you limit access to the words in memory that belong to that language? Or do you also activate the words that belong to your other language?

To find out, we can draw on some of the methods from this chapter to see whether you experience competition from words that sound alike but belong to separate languages. In this section, you've seen evidence that within a single language, cohort competitors with overlapping sounds at the beginnings of words are simultaneously activated—so a spoken word like *beaker* leads to the activation of *beetle*. Suppose you're a Russian-English bilingual, and you're listening to someone saying, "Can you hand me the marker?" Would you *also* activate the Russian word for a stamp—pronounced as /marka/?

Michael Spivey and Viorica Marian (1999) designed a simple eye-tracking study to probe for competition effects from cross-language cohort competitors. They created visual displays in which some of the trials contained a cross-language cohort competitor for the target word (for example, if the target was the English word *marker*, the cross-language cohort competitor was a stamp). They

compared the eye movement patterns for these "cohort" displays with "control" versions of the same displays in which none of the objects in the display had names in either language that overlapped with the target word (for example, a ruler—pronounced /liñejka/ in Russian). Specifically, they wanted to know whether, upon hearing the English word *marker*, their bilingual subjects would be more likely to look at the stamp (/marka/ in Russian) than at the ruler (/liñejka/ in Russian), which served as the unrelated "control" object (see **Figure 7.8**). The experiment was conducted in both English and Russian (when /marka/ was the target word in Russian, the marker served as the cross-language competitor object).

The eye movement data showed that when the subjects heard the experimental instructions in Russian, there was strong evidence of competition from the English cohort

Figure 7.8 A sample visual display from the eye-tracking experiment by Spivey and Marian (1999), accompanied by the English instruction, "Pick up the marker." (A) The "cohort" version of the display contains a postage stamp, whose Russian name (/marka/) is a cohort competitor for the English target word (*marker*). (B) The "control" version of the display, in which the cross-language cohort competitor (the stamp) has been replaced by an object (the ruler) whose Russian name does not overlap with the English target.

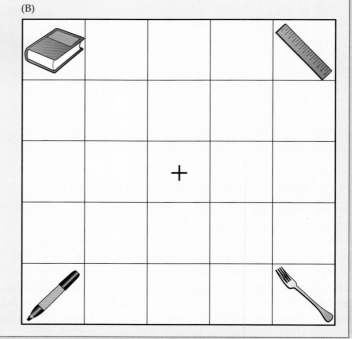

BOX 7.3 *(continued)*

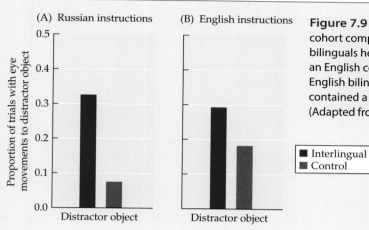

Figure 7.9 Graphs showing eye movements to the cross-language cohort competitor and to an unrelated control. (A) Russian-English bilinguals heard instructions in Russian, while the display contained an English cohort competitor to the Russian target word. (B) Russian-English bilinguals heard instructions in English, while the display contained a Russian cohort competitor to the English target word. (Adapted from Spivey & Marian, 1999.)

Nacht (German)

nag (Afrikaans)

natt (Swedish, Norwegian)

nat (Danish)

nátt (Faroese)

notte (Italian)

noche (Spanish)

competitor. There wasn't a clear effect of cross-language competition in the other direction, though; evidently in some cases, cross-language competition can be muted or absent (see **Figure 7.9**). Further experimentation (e.g., Marian & Spivey, 2003) suggested that the degree of cross-language activation could be dialed up or down, depending on a number factors, including which language is the first or dominant language and whether the experimental setting is a bilingual one or a purely monolingual interaction.

These studies (along with a number of others) show that languages aren't walled off from each other during daily use, and activation within one system can leak over into the other system. You might imagine that in some cases, cross talk between languages might be useful. For instance, languages that are related to each other or that have borrowed heavily from each other may have a number of cognate words, which share features of both sound and meaning, as in the following examples, all words that mean the same as English *night*:

In the case of cognate words, activating the English word *night* upon hearing *Nacht* in German can help you access the word's meaning in German. But in many cases, overlapping sounds in words across languages will be completely coincidental (sometimes unfortunately so, as exemplified by the regrettable similarity of a certain English swear word and the French word for seal, which is *phoque*). In these cases, activation from the other language can only serve to make the task of word recognition harder, requiring extra time and effort to suppress irrelevant words. Bilingualism, then, seems to come with some added burdens for language processing. This isn't necessarily a bad thing; to foreshadow the upcoming chapter, the added strain of cross-language activation can have some surprising cognitive benefits in the long run.

This seems like a pretty reasonable assumption. After all, figuring out the left edge of a word in running speech shouldn't be that hard, for the simple reason that once you've recognized the previous word, it's quite obvious where the word break should go—at the end of *that* word! And as we've seen, the recognition of the previous word has, in all likelihood, already been a resounding success even before the last sounds of that word enter your ears, so there should be no ambiguity about where the word boundary should be. That's if all goes well, of course. But suppose that, for some reason, there's a slip-up in the recognition process, and the word boundaries are set in the wrong place. The effects of this initial error should be catastrophic, cascading down the speech stream. Or suppose that someone in the room coughs or a cell phone goes off right at the moment the initial sounds of a word are being uttered. This should be terribly disruptive to word recognition.

mondegreens "Slips of the ear" that result in errors of word segmentation.

"Slips of the ear" do happen for these and other reasons, resulting in mis-hearings that have become known as **mondegreens**. This term was first coined by American writer Sylvia Wright, who recalled how as a child, she'd heard the Scottish ballad "The Bonnie Earl of Murray," which went like this:

> Ye Highlands and Ye Lowlands
> Oh where hae ye been?
> They hae slay the Earl of Murray
> And Lady Mondegreen.

At least, that's how she remembered it, only to learn years later that the last line was actually "and laid him on the green." Other famous examples of monde-greens include hearing Bob Dylan's "The answer, my friend, is blowin' in the wind" as "Dead ants are my friend, they're blowin' in the wind" or hearing "the girl with kaleidoscope eyes" as "the girl with colitis goes by" in the Beatles' "Lucy in the Sky with Diamonds."

Perhaps it's not surprising that mistakes like this often happen with song lyrics, where the speech sounds are distorted and accompanied by music. But some researchers have argued that, even for normal speaking situations, the cohort model would lead us to expect many more such failures than actually occur, all because of the fact that the whole process rests on that crucial identi-fication of the word's left edge. Jay McClelland and Jeff Elman (1986) proposed their TRACE model as a way to preserve the large-scale competition effects that are part and parcel of word recognition, while making the system more resil-ient against processing disruptions. In their model, streams of sound input are continuously fed into the word recognition system and activate the words that contain them, without any need for identification of the left edges of words. So, let's suppose you've just entered a conversation, and not having clearly heard all the sounds that are being spoken, you're in the midst of catching a short burst of sounds consisting of *astdan*. This ordered stream of sounds begins to activate possible matches, including words like *aster*, *astronaut*, or *Aztec*. But all of these possibilities quickly become mismatched with the sound input upon encountering the /d/ sound and so become deactivated. Here, the cohort and TRACE models predict very different outcomes. The cohort model would be at a loss to propose any remaining viable candidates, because there are simply no options left for words that begin with the sounds *astdan*. But TRACE isn't limited to activating words that make any assumptions about the left edges of words, so it can also activate possible matches, such as *fast Dan* or *last dance*, which may well turn out to be consistent with both the continuing sound input and the context of the sentence.

The TRACE model makes a clear prediction that is at odds with the cohort model, namely, that words whose sounds overlap with the target word in the middles or ends (and not just the onsets) should become activated as well. That is, a word like *beaker* should activate *speaker*, and not just *beetle*. Hence, using the semantic priming paradigm, TRACE would predict that the word *beaker* should speed up recognition times for a word like *music* (via *speaker*) as well as *insect* (via *beetle*) compared with some unrelated word (for example, *table*). It's turned out to be quite difficult to find effects of semantic priming via rhyme competitors. On the other hand, eye movement studies (for example, by Paul Allopenna and colleagues, 1998) have found evidence of activation of rhyme competitors, as il-lustrated in **Figure 7.10**. Nevertheless, overlap at the beginnings of words clearly results in greater competition than overlap at the ends of words.

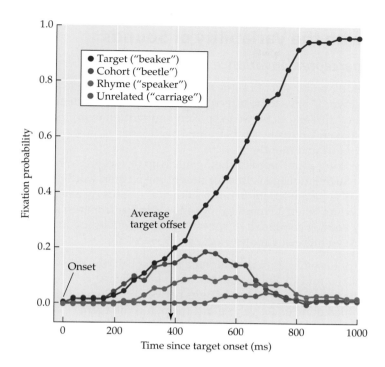

Figure 7.10 Eye movements reveal a "rhyme effect." The graph reflects the subjects' likelihood of looking at the target referent (beaker), its cohort competitor (beetle), its rhyme competitor (speaker), and an unrelated object (carriage). Note that the rhyme effect occurs later than the cohort effect (see Figure 7.7), and is more subtle. (Adapted from Allopenna et al. 1998.)

TRACE can explain this asymmetry by including inhibitory links between competing words and between the sound and word levels of representations. Rhyme competitors will be at a disadvantage because the activation of *speaker* will be pushed down relative to *beaker* or *beetle*, based solely on its mismatch with the first few sounds. Eventually as the word unfolds in time, there will be some overlap between the words *speaker* and *beaker*, so this will boost the activation of *speaker*, but this new surge of activation will have to overcome the initial dampening of that word based on the early mismatch of sounds.

The cohort and TRACE models differ on a number of dimensions, not just with respect to whether the possible lexical candidates have to be aligned with the left edge of the word. (For example, the models disagree on how top-down information can affect the activation of lower levels of representation, a theme that will be taken up in Digging Deeper at the end of this chapter.) Both models have undergone major renovations in response to new experimental data. To some extent, the changes to the models have made it more difficult to know which model—if either of them—is "right," as there's now a good deal of overlap in the results that the two can account for, even though they resort to quite different mechanisms to achieve them. This might seem a touch depressing to someone who believes that the ultimate goal of science is to declare a "winner" between competing theories or models. But ongoing tension between detailed models can really push a field forward, and it is scientific progress that becomes the ultimate winner in the game. Without competing models, it would be a lot harder to formulate the questions that drive the collection of data. For instance, the clashing of the predictions of the cohort and TRACE models is what motivated researchers to closely compare the activation levels of cohort versus rhyme competitors. And without these detailed models, what we know about word recognition would be more like a jumbled laundry list of experimental effects than a set of subtly contrasting mock-ups of what's going on inside our heads.

7.4 Coping with the Variability of Sounds

The problem of perceptual invariance

In the previous section, we considered some of the questions that come up as a result of the fact that words have to be uttered over a span of time. But an even more radical source of differences between spoken and written word recognition is the fact that spoken language is constrained by the shapes, gestures, and movements of the tongue and mouth.

So far, I've been talking about words as being made up of *sequences,* or *strings* of letters or sounds. Such language is fine for describing written words, which are indeed made up of separate letters strung together like beads on a necklace. But it's deeply misleading when it comes to spoken words. Far from resembling beads in a necklace, sounds combined in speech result in something like this, suggested the American linguist Charles Hockett (1955, p. 210):

> Imagine a row of Easter eggs carried along a moving belt; the eggs are of various sizes, and variously colored, but not boiled. At a certain point the belt carries the row of eggs between the two rollers of a wringer, which quite effectively smash them and rub them more or less into each other. The flow of eggs before the wringer represents the series of impulses from the phoneme source; the mess that emerges from the wringer represents the output of the speech transmitter.

Hence, the problem for the hearer who is trying to identify the component sounds is a bit like this:

> We have an inspector whose task it is to examine the passing mess and decide, on the basis of the broken and unbroken yolks, the variously spread out albumen, and the variously colored bits of shell, the nature of the flow of eggs which previously arrived at the wringer.

Unlike letters, which occupy their own spaces in an orderly way, sounds smear their properties all over their neighbors (though the result is perhaps not *quite* as messy as Hockett's description suggests). Notice what happens, for example, when you say the words *track, team,* and *twin.* The /t/ sounds are different, formed with quite different mouth shapes. In *track,* /t/ sounds almost like the first sound in *church;* your lips spread slightly when /t/ is pronounced in *team,* in anticipation of the following vowel; and in *twin,* the /t/ sound might be produced with rounded lips. In the same way, other sounds in these words influence their neighbors. For example, the vowels in *team* and *twin* have a nasalized twang, under the spell of the nasal consonant that follows. It's impossible to tell exactly where one sound begins and another one ends. This happens inevitably because of the mechanics involved in the act of speaking.

As an analogy, imagine a sort of signed language in which each "phoneme" corresponds to a gesture performed at some location on the body. For instance, /t/ might be a tap on the head, /i/ a closed fist bumping the left shoulder, and /n/ a tap on the right hip. Most of the time spent gesturing these phonemic units would be spent on the transitions between them, with no clear boundaries between units. For example, as soon as the hand left the head and aimed for the left shoulder, you'd be able to distinguish that version of /t/ from one that preceded, say, a tap on the chin. And you certainly wouldn't be able to cut up and splice a videotape, substituting a tap on the head preceding a tap on the left shoulder for a tap on the head preceding a tap on the chest. The end result would be a Frankenstein-like mash. (You've already encountered this problem earlier, in Chapter 4 and in Web Activity 4.4.)

The variability that comes from such coarticulation effects is hardly the only challenge for identifying specific sounds from a stream of speech. Add to this the fact that different talkers have different sizes and shapes to their mouths and vocal tracts, which leads to quite different ways of uttering the same phonemes, and yet we're somehow able to hear all of these as equivalent. And add to *that* the fact that different talkers might have subtly different accents—and again, unless the accent is very thick, this doesn't seem to prevent us from understanding each other. When it comes down to it, it's extremely hard to identify any particular acoustic properties that clearly map onto specific sounds. So if we assume that part of recognizing words involves recovering the individual sounds that make up those words, we're left with the problem of explaining the phenomenon known as **perceptual invariance**: how is it that such variable acoustic input can be consistently mapped onto stable phonemic units of representation?

The motor theory of speech perception

The problem of perceptual invariance has led some researchers to suggest that perhaps speech perception *doesn't* actually involve recovering the sounds of a word. Perhaps what we do instead is reconstruct the series of *gestures* that make up the word. The idea driving this account, called the **motor theory of speech perception**, is that there's a fairly direct link between the acoustic signals in speech and the gestures that produce it. So why not assume that the articulatory gestures form the backbone of the speech perception system, rather than the activation of abstract units of representation such as phonemes?

And if speech perception is really about reconstructing the gestures that make a word, then shouldn't *visual* input about how a word is formed—that is, lipreading—ultimately have an impact on how we "hear" a word? Strange as this hypothesis might seem, there's very strong evidence that this actually happens, as illustrated in Web Activity 7.7.

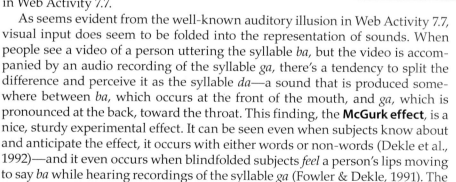

WEB ACTIVITY 7.7

The McGurk effect In this exercise, you'll see a demonstration of the McGurk effect, in which the perceptual system is forced to resolve conflicting cues coming from the auditory and visual streams.

As seems evident from the well-known auditory illusion in Web Activity 7.7, visual input does seem to be folded into the representation of sounds. When people see a video of a person uttering the syllable *ba*, but the video is accompanied by an audio recording of the syllable *ga*, there's a tendency to split the difference and perceive it as the syllable *da*—a sound that is produced somewhere between *ba*, which occurs at the front of the mouth, and *ga*, which is pronounced at the back, toward the throat. This finding, the **McGurk effect**, is a nice, sturdy experimental effect. It can be seen even when subjects know about and anticipate the effect, it occurs with either words or non-words (Dekle et al., 1992)—and it even occurs when blindfolded subjects *feel* a person's lips moving to say *ba* while hearing recordings of the syllable *ga* (Fowler & Dekle, 1991). The McGurk effect seems to support the motor theory quite nicely. Other support for this view comes from brain-imaging research showing that simply listening to speech sounds involves brain activity in motor areas of the brain—in fact, the same areas that are active when people imagine themselves actually articulating that sound (D'Ausilio et al., 2009).

But, while awareness of the gestures that make sounds clearly plays a role in speech perception, it doesn't seem to be true that such knowledge is *required*. If that were the case, we'd expect that brain damage to the areas that are responsible for speech production would inevitably disrupt speech perception as well.

perceptual invariance The phenomenon whereby acoustically different stimuli are perceived as examples of the same phoneme or word.

motor theory of speech perception A theory that the perception of speech sounds involves accessing representations of the articulatory gestures that are required to make those speech sounds.

McGurk effect An illusion in which a mismatch between auditory information and visual information pertaining to a sound's articulation results in altered perception of that sound; for example, when people hear an audio recording of a person uttering the syllable *ga* while viewing a video of the speaker uttering *ba*, they often perceive the syllable as *da*.

But it's not hard to find people who have had a stroke and suffered massive damage to the motor speech system, and have serious speech production problems as a result, but can still recognize words just fine. And there's other evidence of the dissociation between production and perception. For example, as we saw in Chapter 4, very young babies can distinguish many sounds just after birth, and even sort them into perceptual categories with clear boundaries. Between 6 and 8 months of age, they're able to track the statistical relationships among sounds, well before they can control their own mouths well enough to reliably produce those sequences of sounds. Even more damaging for the motor theory is the fact that animals like chinchillas can form sound categories in a way that is similar to humans, and even adjust their perception of sounds depending on neighboring sounds. Since it's a bit of a stretch to argue that chinchillas have mental templates for how human sounds are pronounced, we may be stuck after all with explaining how acoustic properties map onto representations of sounds and, along with it, grappling with the invariance problem.

Context effects in speech perception

Another way to explain how we might get perceptual invariance from variable acoustic data goes something like this: Perception itself involves much more than just mapping acoustic signals to corresponding sounds. It also involves using contextual cues to *infer* those sounds. In doing that, you work backward and apply your knowledge of how similar sounds "shape-shift" in the presence of their neighbors, to figure out which sounds you're actually hearing. It turns out that a similar story is needed to account for perceptual problems other than speech. For example, you can recognize bananas as being yellow under dramatically different lighting conditions, even though more orange or green might actually reach your eyes depending on whether you're seeing it outdoors on a misty day or inside by candlelight (see **Figure 7.11**). Based on your previous experiences with color under different lighting conditions, you perceive the banana as having a constant color, rather than changing chameleon-like in response to the variable lighting. Without your ability to do this, color would be

(A)

(B)

Figure 7.11 Color constancy under different lighting. We subjectively perceive the color of these bananas to be the same under different lighting conditions, discounting the effects of illumination. Similar mechanisms are needed in order to achieve a stable perception of variable speech sounds.

pretty useless to you as a cue in navigating your physical environment. In the same way, knowing about how neighboring sounds influence each other might impact your perception of what you're hearing. The sound that you end up "hearing" is the end result of combining information from the acoustic signal with information about the sound's surrounding context. (Notice that much the same explanation can be provided for the McGurk effect: in that case, what you "hear" is the result of folding together auditory and visual information.)

Another way in which context might help you to identify individual sounds is knowing which *word* those sounds are part of. Since your knowledge of words includes knowledge of their sounds, if you have an idea of what word someone is trying to say, this should help you to infer the specific sounds you're hearing. A classic study by William Ganong (1980) illustrates just this effect, which has since become immortalized as the **Ganong effect**. In his experiment, subjects listened to a list of words and non-words and wrote down whether they'd heard a /d/ or a /t/ sound at the beginning of each item. The experimental items of interest contained examples of sounds that were acoustically ambiguous, between a /d/ and /t/ sound, and that appeared in word frames set up so that a sound formed a word under either the /d/ or /t/ interpretation, but not both. So, for example, the subjects might hear an ambiguous /d-t/ sound at the beginning of __ask, which makes a real word if the sound is heard as a /t/ but not as a /d/; conversely, the same /d-t/sound would then also appear in a frame like __ash, which makes a real word with /d/ but not with /t/. What Ganong found was that people interpreted the ambiguous sound with a clear bias in favor of the real word, even though they knew the list contained many instances of non-words. That is, they reported hearing the *same* sound as a /d/ in __ash, but a /t/ in __ask.

The Ganong effect helps to explain how it is that we're not bothered by the inconsistency of sounds in the context of word recognition. It also has some important implications for our general program of model-building, as laid out in Section 7.1. If you remember, we ended that section by leaving open the possibility that activation from a higher level of representation—the word level—sends activation down to the lower level of sound representation. A model like this would predict that the same sound should be perceived differently depending on the word it's embedded in—precisely the effect discovered by William Ganong (see **Figure 7.12**). But the Ganong effect also shows limits to the influence of top-down information. The word frame only had an effect on sounds that straddled the category boundary between a /t/ and /d/. If the sounds were good, clear examples of one acoustic category or the other, subjects correctly perceived the sound on the basis of its acoustic properties, and did not report mishearing *dask* as *task*, for example. This shows that when a sound is strongly activated on the basis of very clear bottom-up evidence from the acous-

Ganong effect An experimental result demonstrating that the identity of a word can affect the perception of individual sounds within that word. When people hear a sound that is acoustically ambiguous between two sounds, their identification of that sound can be shifted in one direction or another depending on which of the possible sounds results in an actual word.

WEB ACTIVITY 7.8

The phoneme restoration effect
In this example, you'll hear an audio clip illustrating the phoneme restoration effect, in which knowledge of a word allows the hearer to "fill in" a missing sound in the speech stream.

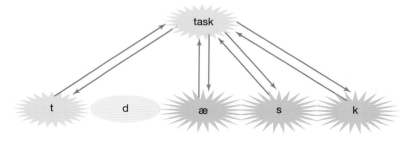

Figure 7.12 Top-down activation from words to sounds. In this model, the activation of the sound /t/ is initially weak, as shown, because the acoustic signal provides a poor example of this sound. However, over time, activation feeds up to the word level, activating the word *task*, and then bounces back down to the individual sounds contained in that word.

LANGUAGE AT LARGE 7.2

How does ventriloquism work?

Good entertainment often bends reality. That's true in spades for skillful acts of ventriloquism: we know that the words are uttered by the human handler, but we can't stop ourselves from hearing the dummy "speak" them. So how does this work?

Ventriloquism cashes in on several different kinds of illusions. The first of these has to do with perceiving the location of a sound. As is apparent from the McGurk effect, what we "hear" is usually the end result of combining visual and auditory information, whether the cues are about articulation or about the location of a sound in space. In the natural world, visual and auditory cues almost always line up, but since human beings are curious enough to wonder what happens if they don't, we now know what happens when there's a disconnect between the two. In a ventriloquist's act, the lips of the human appear to be still, while the dummy's mouth flaps in time with the words that are spoken. What happens if your ears are telling you one thing about the location of a sound, and your eyes are telling you another? It turns out that you believe your eyes. You don't have to see a ventriloquist to experience this illusion. Have you ever thought about what happens in a movie theater? The sound is coming from speakers placed around the room, but it *feels* as if spoken words are coming straight out of the mouths of the actors on-screen.

The reason you put more trust in what your eyes are telling you is simply that most of the time, visual information is a more reliable source of information about an object's location than auditory information is. But that can change in a situation where the visual cues become fuzzy or indistinct—in that case, you'd likely depend more on sound to figure out an object's location in space. It's also possible that the location illusion is affected somewhat by where you're directing your visual attention. If you look at YouTube clips of ventriloquist acts, you might notice that the dummy is usually designed to draw more visual attention than the human, with brighter clothing and humorous facial features, and is very animated in its movements, while the human tends to blend into the background, wear nondescript clothing, and have very limited movements of both the face and body while the dummy is "speaking."

The second kind of illusion deals with the actual sounds of speech and how they're interpreted. Ventriloquists manage to speak without moving their lips, so how is it that they're able to produce the full range of speech sounds? The answer is that they don't; to some extent, they can rely on us as hearers to hear what we expect to hear rather than what's really there.

Ventriloquists speak with their lips still and partly open, which nevertheless allows them to make many speech sounds by controlling the shape and movement of the tongue behind the lips in a way that's not visible.

---

tic signal, top-down expectations from the word level aren't strong enough to cause us to "hallucinate" a different sound. However, when the acoustic evidence is murky, word-level expectations *can* lead to pretty flagrant auditory illusions (you can experience one yourself in Web Activity 7.8).

The **phoneme restoration effect**, first discovered by Richard Warren (1970), offers a dramatic example in which the acoustic input *is* misheard. In these examples, a speech sound is spliced out—for example, the /s/ in *legislature* is removed—and a non-speech sound, such as a cough, is pasted in its place. The resulting illusion causes people to "hear" the /s/ sound as if it had never been taken out, along with the coughing sound.

Again, this suggests that word-level expectations can activate individual sounds by means of top-down connections. This particular illusion seems to become stronger as the activation for the word itself increases; the effect is stronger for longer words (which have fewer lexical competitors) than for shorter words. It's also more robust for words that make sense in the context of the sentence than for words that don't fit with the sentential context. These results make sense if words themselves can receive activation from an even higher level of representation.

phoneme restoration effect An auditory illusion showing that when a speech sound within a word is replaced by a non-speech sound, people often report hearing both the speech and non-speech sounds.

But sounds made by moving the lips—like /b/, /p/, /w/, /m/, /v/, and /f/—are problematic. To some extent, the ventriloquist can write a script that avoids words containing these sounds, but when absolutely necessary, these labial sounds can be replaced by other similar-sounding phonemes. For example, /f/ might be replaced by /θ/ (the first sound in *think*), and /m/ by the similar-sounding /ŋ/in *sing*. We've already seen from the Ganong effect and phoneme restoration effect that the sounds we think we hear depend to some extent on the sounds that we expect to hear in a particular word. Ventriloquism takes full advantage of this.

Based on some of the results that we've talked about with these particular auditory illusions, we should also be in a position to offer some scientifically grounded advice to an aspiring ventriloquist. For example, remember the Ganong effect, in which a sound was perceived in such a way as to be consistent with the rest of the word. If you want your hearer to perceptually morph a *d* into a *b* sound, best to use the sound in a word where it wouldn't make sense as a *d*. (For example, in *dest*, but not in *dust* when it's intended to be heard as *bust*.) Remember also that the effect of the surrounding word was strongest when the sound itself was ambiguous—clear examples of sounds that made no sense in the words they were embedded in (for example, *dest*) were just perceived as mispronunciations. This suggests that you can't simply

throw in a clear-sounding *d* and expect it to be heard as a *b* sound, even if the word makes no sense with a *d* sound. For this reason, ventriloquist manuals usually suggest altering the substituted sounds in some way. For instance, one way to make a *d* sound slightly more like a *b* sound is to pronounce it by placing the tongue against the teeth rather than in its usual position on the ridge behind the teeth. It takes some practice to distort certain sounds so that they become more acoustically similar to the intended labial sounds.

The phoneme restoration effect showed that even quite garbled sounds can be reinterpreted as specific phonemes, and that the illusion is especially strong with long words that have few competitors, and with words that are generally quite predictable in context. In other words, the more strongly activated the word is, the stronger an impact it's likely to have on how people perceive the sounds within it. It seems to make sense, then, that words that contain substituted sounds should be ones that are likely to be strongly activated in the context.

Once you start seeing how this genre of entertainment fits neatly with a model of normal, everyday speech perception, it might be hard to stop making the connections. In fact, you might even be tempted to make specific predictions about best ventriloquist practices, and put them to rigorous empirical tests by adapting some of the experimental approaches you've learned about here.

7.5 Reading Written Words

Word recognition in spoken and written modalities

As far as we know, spoken language emerged spontaneously as a result of humans interacting with each other, rather than being deliberately engineered by some unusually enterprising human. But that's not the way written language came about. A writing system *does* need to be consciously designed and usually taught in a much more formal, deliberate way than spoken (or signed) language. It's rather remarkable, then, that many people learn to recognize written words as quickly and automatically as they do. For expert readers, the consciously acquired skill of reading words has become fused to a large extent with the cognitive system for recognizing spoken words.

Many of the mechanisms for recognizing words are the same, whether they involve speech or written symbols. As you saw in Sections 7.1 and 7.2, both spoken and written language show similar effects of semantic priming and competition. Hence, the models for both spoken and written word recognition need to have similar ingredients such as spreading activation and inhibition. Moreover, parallels exist between the two modalities when it comes to asking whether there is top-down flow of information within the system, with activation spreading from words to sounds or letters. In the previous section, we saw that top-down activation could be very useful in solving the problem of perceptual invariance. While the problem of perceptual invariance is especially acute for *spoken* language, in cases where the shape of *written* letters is highly ambiguous, top-down connections may also help with the recognition of written words (see **Box 7.4**)

Just as there are specific challenges that arise for the understanding of spoken words, the same is true for words in their written form. In spoken language, the word recognition system has to confront issues that arise from the fleeting nature of speech in time. Recognizing written words, on the other hand, introduces some specific problems that involve mapping visual symbols onto spoken linguistic units. In this section, we'll explore some of the cognitive implications of recognizing words through the medium of visual symbols rather than sounds (or gestures).

BOX 7.4
Reading chicken scratch

In Section 7.4, I emphasized the ways in which spoken language is quite different from written language—sounds "smear" together, and different people make the same sounds very differently. Written text obviously doesn't present these problems. That is, unless you're trying to read someone's cursive handwriting. In that case, letters do change shape somewhat depending on their neighbors, and of course, the handwriting of one person can be very distinct from the handwriting of another. Writing that's produced by the human hand begins to look a bit more like speaking that's produced by the human mouth—the individual letters, like individual sounds, are not always easy to identify with confidence (see **Figure 7.13**).

The perceptual problem of reading chicken scratch is a lot like trying to recognize a spoken word whose sounds are indistinct, so it's possible that it could be solved by recruiting the same mechanisms that boost the understanding of blurry spoken words. For example, we saw through the Ganong effect and phoneme restoration effect that top-down information flowing from the word level to the sound level can help stabilize the perception of a sound that's on shaky ground acoustically. So, sounds that seem to fall in between a good /t/ and /d/ might be heard differently depending on the words they're

embedded in. When reading *printed* text, the flow of bottom-up information would normally be highly efficient because the text doesn't vary that much visually, so you might think that there wouldn't be much need for links going top-down from words to letters. But some models of word recognition, such as TRACE, adopt the same architecture for both written and spoken language for just those cases where the visual identification of letters could be challenging—you can imagine this might happen at a distance, for example, or if a letter is partially obscured.

Top-down processing could be especially useful when people are faced with the perceptual puzzle of deciphering cursive writing. Anthony Barnhart and Stephen Goldinger (2010) designed an experiment to test whether semantic factors of a word would impact how quickly people recognized and named it. It's often been found, for example, that words whose meanings are easy to imagine visually (like *desk*) are recognized faster than ones whose meanings are less visually grounded (like *pain*). This suggests that when the meaning of a word is really easy to access, it becomes active more quickly, with that activation possibly feeding down to the lower level. Barnhart and Goldinger replicated this effect, but found that it was quite a bit stronger when people read words in handwritten cursive script than when they read the same words in a computer-generated font. The story seems to be that when the bottom-up flow of information from the letters to the word level was made more difficult, people relied more heavily on their knowledge about the words.

Colorless green ideas sleep furiously.
Colorless green ideas sleep furiously.
Colorless green ideas sleep furiously.
Colorless green ideas sleep furiously.

Figure 7.13 Handwriting samples by different writers, showing different renditions of the sentence *Colorless green ideas sleep furiously.*

Diversity in writing systems

If you were going about inventing a new written language to piggyback on the spoken one you already have, how would you do it? Obviously, the general idea is to create a set of symbols that match up to spoken linguistic units. But which units? Words? Syllables? Phonemes? All of these are reasonable strategies, each with certain advantages and disadvantages.

Words—or perhaps those smaller units of meaning, **morphemes**—might seem like a good starting point, but they have one obvious drawback: there are a *lot* of them. This means that learning to read would entail having to memorize possibly tens of thousands of symbols. This is not as impossible as it may sound. In fact, it's a feat that's in some ways less remarkable than what any human child has to do with a spoken language. If children can store in memory tens of thousands of sound patterns, *along* with discovering their meanings, surely they are capable of mastering the same number of visual patterns and mapping these onto already known meanings. Indeed, this type of **logographic writing system**, in which symbols are mapped to units of meaning, was adopted for some languages, such as Chinese. And when you use numeric symbols such as *1* or *7*, you're essentially using a logographic system, in which the symbol maps directly to a concept rather than being determined by how the word sounds. This can come in very handy in interactions between speakers of different languages. For example, even if you can't count in Italian, you as an English speaker can agree on the price of fish in a Roman market by resorting to the logographs that you and the vendor have in common in your writing systems.

Nevertheless, dropping down to a smaller size of linguistic unit can dramatically reduce the number of symbols you need, and this brings you into the realm of mapping symbols onto sound-based units. Some languages, like Japanese, have instituted a **syllabic writing system**, in which characters represent different syllables. This means that syllables like *ka* or *ki* might be captured by entirely different characters, ignoring the fact that the two units have the same first sound. A syllabic system works especially well for languages whose phonotactic constraints severely limit the shape of allowable syllables, and hence their number. For example, Japanese, which is limited to syllables that consist of one consonant followed by one vowel, can get away with fewer than 60 characters, whereas English, which allows varied pile-ups of consonant clusters at either end of a syllable, would need many more.

Many writing systems, including English, are based on an **alphabetic inventory** in which the goal is to map characters onto individual sounds or phonemes. This approach uses a conveniently small handful of written characters. But it's possible to go down to even smaller linguistic units—individual sounds, after all, are really clusters of articulatory features (see Section 4.3), so a sound like /k/ can be described as a velar voiceless stop (*velar*: produced at the back of the mouth; *voiceless*: produced without vibration of the vocal folds; *stop*: produced by completely obstructing the airflow). Notice that in our own alphabetic system, we totally ignore the very real sound-based similarity between /k/ and /g/, both of which are velar stops and differ only with respect to voicing. In principle, a featural writing system could use different characters for each feature to convey this information. Some elements of this approach can be found in the Korean alphabet, in which the strokes that make up letters have some systematic relationship to phonetic features.

Depending on your own language background, an alphabetic system may seem to be the most "natural" choice for a writing system to you. But it's not without its own artificial aspects and disadvantages. For example, it's not very natural at all for us to think (at least to *consciously* think) about speech in terms

morphemes The smallest bundles of sound that can be related to some systematic meaning.

logographic writing system Writing system in which symbols are mapped to units of meaning such as morphemes or words rather than to units of sound.

syllabic writing system Writing system in which characters represent different syllables.

alphabetic inventory A collection of orthographic symbols that map onto individual sounds or phonemes.

phonemic awareness The conscious recognition of phonemes as distinct units, usually only solidly acquired by individuals who are literate in an alphabetic writing system.

onset The material in a syllable that precedes the vowel.

rime The material in a syllable that includes the vowel and anything that follows.

of individual sounds. **Phonemic awareness**, or overt recognition of phonemes as distinct units, isn't something that just spontaneously happens at some point in development. We usually have to be forced to think that way as part of learning an alphabetic writing system. By contrast, conscious awareness of words, or even syllables, or even parts of syllables, comes more easily.

Until they're literate (in an alphabetic language), even adults do badly on phonemic awareness tests in which they have to pull words apart into their individual sounds. These tests might include questions such as, "How many sounds are there in the word *bed*?" and "What are you left with if you take the first sound away from the word *spring*?" and "What sounds do the words *bag* and *bed* have in common?" Preliterate children and adults find these quite challenging, and have an easier time with questions that probe knowledge about syllables and their internal structure, such as, "How many syllables in the word *bicycle*?" or "What sounds do the words *fling* and *spring* have in common?" (This last question tests for the separation of a syllable into an **onset**— the material in a syllable that precedes the vowel—and a **rime**—the material that includes the vowel and anything that follows. Evidently, syllable onsets

---

BOX 7.5
Do different writing systems engage the brain differently?

If you compare alphabetic languages like English with logographic ones like Chinese, it's hard to think of "reading" as involving the same set of skills in both cases. Learning to read in each of these languages introduces a new set of cognitive problems that don't apply to the spoken languages themselves. The writing system for English forces learners to consciously decompose words into phonemic units, a skill that's not necessary for speaking. On the other hand, the Chinese writing system doesn't require much phonemic awareness of its readers, but it does require them to be able to differentiate and memorize a very large number of minutely differing visual symbols, or *radicals* (see **Figure 7.14**).

The different demands of the two systems are evident in the way that reading is taught to children. Chances are that a child's first steps in learning to read English involved reciting the alphabet and learning to recognize individual letters and their corresponding sounds. And as

it happens, the child's level of phonemic awareness is a strong predictor of her reading ability. In contrast, Chinese children spend many hours learning to *produce* the intricate symbols of their written language, and children's reading ability in Chinese is more strongly related to character copying than it is to phonemic awareness (Tan et al., 2005).

These differences lead straight to the question of whether reading involves the same patterns of activity in the brain for the two languages. For example, perhaps Chinese readers don't really activate the sounds of words, since in many cases, it's possible to get straight to the word's meaning without "sounding out" the symbols. Charles Perfetti and his colleagues (2010) reviewed a number of fMRI studies of reading in Chinese and in English and drew several conclusions. First, there are some similarities in the brain regions that are involved in reading both languages. Both languages rely on a reading network in the brain that connects visual areas (in posterior parts of the brain) with phonological areas (in temporal-parietal and anterior areas) and areas for meaning (the inferior frontal gyrus). That is, even for a writing system like Chinese, the phonological system is not bypassed during reading—the visual symbols are still well connected to information about

Figure 7.14 In addition to making fine-grained distinctions among characters, Chinese readers need to be able to recognize how basic symbols, known as radicals, can be combined and elaborated. The Chinese examples shown here all incorporate the radical for *hand* (the first symbol in each character).

and rimes are more cognitively accessible than individual phonemes.) Hence, one of the ironies of devising a writing system is that the smaller the linguistic unit you choose to map characters onto, the less cognitively accessible these units tend to be. Of course, the *larger* the linguistic unit, the more of them there are to be memorized! **Box 7.5** explores some of the implications of the different cognitive demands imposed by different writing systems.

In practice, almost no language adopts just one of the above writing strategies in a "pure" way. For an assortment of reasons—cognitive, practical, political, and historical—writing systems tend to emerge as hybrids of these different mapping approaches. For example, Chinese leans heavily on a logographic system, in part because of China's imperial history, in which a unified written language was created that could be understood among all the different dialects spoken across that vast country; a single writing system for multiple dialects or languages is only possible if it maps onto meaning rather than onto the finer-grained aspects of sound. This feature made the Chinese writing system a viable cultural export into other linguistic groups. Japanese writers incorporate logographs of Chinese

---

BOX 7.5 *(continued)*

words' sounds as well as their meanings. Nevertheless, there are some interesting differences, as shown in **Figure 7.15**. Specifically, while reading is very strongly lateralized in the left hemisphere for English readers, there's more bilateral activity in the visual areas for Chinese readers. This may be related to the added visual burden for learning Chinese characters. In addition, Chinese readers showed activation over a larger frontal area than English readers, but *reduced* activity in temporal areas that play a role in matching graphemes to phonemes.

What happens when a reader, who's developed an

efficient network for reading Chinese, learns to read English, or vice versa? Does a person's first-language reading network become recruited for the task of reading the second language? And if so, does this affect reading performance in the second language?

A study led by Jessica Nelson (2009) suggests that it depends on which writing system you start out with. Evidence from fMRI studies showed that Chinese subjects who learned English as a second language were able to use the same reading networks for both English and Chinese. But the reverse wasn't true; English speakers who learned to read Chinese showed different patterns of brain activity for the two languages. The authors suggest that it may be possible to read English as if it were Chinese—that is, by recognizing whole words and matching them to word meanings, rather than by sounding out the individual phonemes of a word. However, since using a "sounding out" strategy for reading Chinese is not really viable, English learners of Chinese would have been forced to develop new skills for reading.

English reading
Left hemisphere

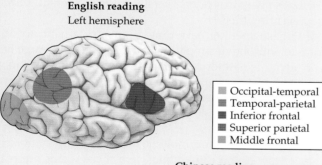

☐ Occipital-temporal
☐ Temporal-parietal
☐ Inferior frontal
☐ Superior parietal
☐ Middle frontal

Chinese reading
Left hemisphere   Right hemisphere

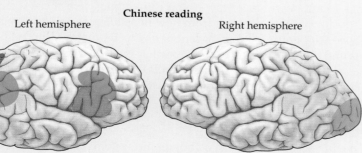

Figure 7.15 A rough diagram of English and Chinese reading networks, as identified by Perfetti et al. (2010). Chinese readers show more bilateral activity in occipital-temporal regions (green) and activity in the left middle frontal gyrus (blue). However, Chinese reading involves reduced activity in inferior frontal areas (purple) and in temporal-parietal regions (orange).

WEB ACTIVITY 7.9

Inventing a writing system
Your own literacy training has a big impact on how easily you learn new writing systems. In this activity, you'll try your hand at inventing and decoding different types of writing systems.

origin into their orthographic toolkit, along with their own, more sound-based, syllabic script. Nevertheless, because of how hard it is to memorize these symbols, Chinese writing also uses some systematic markings that represent the pronunciation of the characters, to help reinforce the mapping between characters and words.

You might have noticed while reading about these different writing systems that, unlike spoken language, written language doesn't always exhibit the property of *duality of patterning*. That is, in spoken languages, sounds that have no intrinsic meaning are combined to form larger, meaningful units like morphemes and words. But in logographic writing systems, the smallest units of combination *do* have intrinsic meaning. Given that, as far as we know, duality of patterning is universal in spoken languages (see Box 2.1), this gives rise to an intriguing contrast between spoken and written languages. What could explain the difference? Is it that humans have certain innate expectations about the fundamental nature of spoken languages, but lack such expectations about the design of writing systems? Or is the difference due to the fact that different communicative pressures and constraints exist for spoken and written languages? At the moment, these questions are wide open.

Alphabetic irregularities

English, like all European languages, uses an alphabetic writing system. Of course, try telling someone who's grown up writing a *real* alphabetic language (like Finnish or Spanish) that English maps individual symbols onto sounds. For instance, how is the *sound* /k/ represented? Well, it depends on where it falls in a syllable, and which letter comes before or after it. For example: *cat, cot, cut* but *kiss, kept*; however, *pick, back,* but *meek*. Judging by these examples, it seems that it would sometimes be more accurate to say that *sequences* of letters map onto *sequences* of sounds rather than that individual letters map onto individual sounds. To make matters worse, sometimes how the sound is spelled depends on the individual word, possibly reflecting a long-ago borrowing from another language—you can't figure out how it's spelled from any rules, you just have to *know*: as in *click* versus *clique*; *tick* versus *tic*; *like* versus *psych* (incidentally, *which* sound is the letter *p* representing there?).

The irregularities of English spelling have drawn much comment over the years, at times humorous, or vitriolic, or simply resigned. The writer George Bernard Shaw, who was an advocate of reforming English spelling to make it more alphabetically transparent (see Language at Large 7.3), remarked that there was nothing to prevent the word *fish* from being spelled *ghoti* (*gh* as in *enough*, *o* as in *women*, *ti* as in *nation*). So how do people cope with really idiosyncratic words like *beau, have* (in contrast with *gave, save, rave*), *thorough, sign, colonel,* or *pint* (in contrast with *mint, lint, glint*)? These examples just don't line up symbols to sounds in any reasonable way. If you think about how these words are read, it's probably not that different from how people represent Chinese logographic symbols—the entire pattern of letters has to be matched up with individual words and their meanings. This means that English, a so-called alphabetic language, also relies on mappings of symbols to larger linguistic units than sounds, at least for some of its words (and you just have to know which ones).

Two systems for reading, or one?

The messiness of the English orthographic system has led researchers to suggest that the ability to link written symbols, or **graphemes**, with meaning—in

graphemes Written symbols, analogous to phonemes in spoken language; individual graphemes may or may not correspond to individual phonemes (for example, two graphemes are used to represent the sound /k/ in *sick*).

other words, the ability to read English—can't be accomplished by any single cognitive route. One of the most influential models of reading, the **dual route model**, was developed by Max Coltheart and colleagues (1993, 2001) and proposes that there are at least two pathways that link graphemes with meaning. One is the **direct route**, in which a series of orthographic symbols is directly connected with the meaning of a word. The other pathway is called the **assembled phonology route**, in which graphemes are "sounded out" against their corresponding sounds, beginning at the left edge of the word. It's easy to see how having both routes available for reading would be extremely useful. The assembled phonology route allows us to read words that we know from spoken language but haven't yet mastered in print. And the direct route allows us to handle the messy exceptions that arise over time in a mongrel language like English. It might also be more efficient, once we've seen the same words in print repeatedly, to recognize words directly from their orthography without needing to fire up our phonological correspondence rules. In fact, it does seem to be the case that as people become more expert at reading, they rely less on the phonological route.

But even highly skilled adults don't move entirely away from the phonological route, since there's some evidence that the sounds of words still have an impact even in a silent reading task when the focus is on recovering the meaning of the word. In one series of experiments by Guy Van Orden and colleagues (1987, 1988), subjects had to decide whether words that they saw on a screen were part of a larger category (for example, given the category of clothes, respond by pressing a "Yes" button for the word *shirt*, or a "No" button for the word *pear*). Sometimes, non-words flashed on the screen, and occasionally these non-words served as fake homophones for relevant words—for example, given the category flowers, the non-word *roze* might come up. If people are automatically sounding out the target stimuli, we might expect that when these targets sound just like actual words that fall into the flower category (*rose*), there might be some confusion, causing people to be slower to respond "No" to the targets. This was true for fake homophones (*roze*)—and it was also true for real-word homophones (*rows*), suggesting that even familiar words were being converted into their sound patterns and causing confusion when they were pronounced the same as the word *rose*. However, orthographically similar words and non-words (*robs*, *rone*) did not slow down the response times, indicating that the source of the confusion really was at the level of sound.

What happens when the two routes clash? Sometimes, the grapheme-to-phoneme correspondence rules conflict with the right way to pronounce an exceptional word—as in the word *pint*, which is a black sheep among the words *lint*, *mint*, *hint*, *glint*, and so on. In that case, the pronunciation by regular rule can interfere with the correct but irregular sound pattern, causing people to make mistakes when reading the word aloud, or to read it more slowly. The interference is more striking for less frequent words like *pint* than it is for very frequent words like *have*, which suggests that the two routes compete with each other to produce the right output, but that a heavily practiced word can win decisively along the direct route.

The dual route model accounts quite nicely for the split-personality nature of the English writing system. But it's not the only model that's been proposed to account for it. You may remember the great words-versus-rules debate at the end of Chapter 5. In that debate, some researchers claimed that we have two very distinct systems for forming plural or past-tense forms such as *cats* or *walked* in contrast to irregular forms like *ate* or *children*. According to this two-systems view, the regular forms are produced by a general rule, whereas the irregular forms just have to be memorized as individual words. Sound familiar?

dual route model a theory of reading which proposes that there are two distinct pathways—the direct route and the assembled phonology route—that link written symbols (graphemes) with meaning.

direct route According to the dual route theory of reading, the means by which a series of orthographic symbols is directly connected with the meaning of a word, without involving sound-symbol correspondences.

assembled phonology route According to the dual route theory, the means by which graphemes are "sounded out" against their corresponding sounds, beginning at the left edge of the word.

LANGUAGE AT LARGE 7.3

Should English spelling be reformed?

Not all writing systems are equally user-friendly. English, for one, has an unsettling amount of spelling irregularity, compared with most other alphabetic writing systems. Children who are lucky enough to learn to read in more transparent alphabetic languages (such as Greek, Italian, or Finnish) usually breeze through basic reading lessons more quickly than their English-speaking peers. How did English spelling get to be this unwieldy, and isn't it time something was done about it?

Remember that spelling, unlike speaking, is the result of conscious decisions to capture spoken language with a set of symbols. It would be nice if spelling had been decreed for English by people with a sophisticated knowledge of English phonology and the cognitive interests of readers at the forefront of their minds. But it wasn't. The Anglo-Saxons, linguistic ancestors of English speakers everywhere, simply adopted the Roman alphabet to correspond with the sounds of their own language—where the Anglo-Saxon language had extra sounds, sequences of letters sometimes came to be composed to represent single sounds (for instance, *th, sh,* and *gh,* which was then a fricative sound produced at the back of the throat). Early spelling wasn't particularly consistent, in part because writing skills were still very unsettled (think of the unstable spellings of a first grader who's just learned to write), but also because different dialects pronounced the same words somewhat differently, and there was no central spelling authority to insist that it all be done in the same way.

The Norman conquest of England added chaos to the already somewhat slaphappy approach to orthography. More scribes were trained in French and not especially concerned with preserving whatever Anglo-Saxon spelling conventions there might have been. They corrupted the alphabetic system with French conventions of spelling that were intended to honor the Latin origins of words rather than their pronunciation. For example, the word *doubt* has the letter *b* in it simply because it is borrowed from the Latin word *dubitare,* and this is also how we ended up with the letter *c* capturing the /s/ sound for certain words of Latin origin (for example, *city*).

To make matters worse, consider that spoken language changes over time. Written language, on the other hand, tends to be much more conservative. This makes sense. You can hardly speak to someone who isn't alive and present in the current day, so there's not much reason to continue to talk the way people used to talk decades or centuries ago. But a good bit of literate behavior involves reading texts by people who are long dead. When the 1500s saw a massive shift in the pronunciation of English words, the spellings of those words ended up being stuck in the past. For example, what we now call "long" and "short" vowel sounds, as in *beet* and *bet,* are really just different vowels. But they used to be the same, distinguished only by length, until a language change known as the Great Vowel Shift rearranged the entire vowel inventory of English.

So much for how we got here. Should we get out of this orthographic morass? There have been many passionate advocates for spelling reform throughout the ages, including George Bernard Shaw, who suggested starting from scratch with a brand new alphabet, and the *Chicago Tribune,* which, more modestly, took it upon itself in 1934 to begin using more transparent spellings of certain words such as *thru, agast, iland,* and *telegraf.* The changes didn't stick.

There are monstrous practical obstacles against spelling reform. Spelling reform can happen, even on a large scale,

This seems a bit like the claim that you have one rule-based system for constructing the sounds of a word, and then another direct route for memorized links between sequences of letters and the words they represent. You might also remember that the claim of two separate systems was hotly contested by a competing connectionist approach. Well, that's the case here too, and the dual route model of reading has its own connectionist competitor.

For the connectionist model of reading (Seidenberg & McClelland, 1989) there's no either-or distinction between getting to a word through its sound-based rules or getting to it through memorized links between graphemes and meaning. These researchers have argued that even irregularly spelled words are not completely exempt from letter/sound pairings, as a pure dual route model

LANGUAGE AT LARGE 7.3 (continued)

but there has to be some single accepted authority that drives the change. For example, when Mustafa Kemal Atatürk, the first leader of the Turkish Republic, decided to shift the entire Turkish language away from using Arabic script to the Roman alphabet used by Western nations, he had the concentration of power to do so. (And to his credit, he consulted linguists, educators, and writers in the process.) It was hard enough to accomplish this in a single nation. But the success of English as a global language spanning numerous countries, many of which have a psychic allergy to centralized control of any sort, makes it hard to imagine how significant spelling reform could ever be achieved.

The global nature of English raises another set of issues when it comes to spelling reform: whose variety of English should become the basis for the written language? Even within North America alone, there is a great deal of variation, with differences among regional dialects apparently growing over time, rather than shrinking. For instance, the dialect region of the Inland North, clustered around the Great Lakes area, is currently undergoing a dramatic shift in the pronunciation of its vowels, not unlike the Great Vowel Shift of long ago. A speaker from Chicago or Detroit might pronounce the words *busses* and *socks* much like speakers from other regions might say *bosses* and *sacks*. Should spelling reflect pronunciation in Chicago, or Boston or London or Australia or Hong Kong? Whichever we choose as the official standard, some language groups are going to get a spelling system that is more transparent than others. On the other hand, if we democratically allow every English variety to change spellings to make them maximally transparent, communicating in writing between members of different dialect groups could get tricky. (Raise your hand if you've ever turned on the subtitles while watching a movie in which the actors speak a

strong English dialect you're unfamiliar with. If everyone were to adopt their own transparent writing system, this would cease to be a viable strategy.)

When a language is spoken by many people who also speak other languages, as English is around the world, this tends to accelerate the rate at which its sound patterns change. Even if English speakers everywhere did agree to settle on a particular dialect as the basis for their writing system, this dialect would inevitably change over time. Should the writing system keep pace with the changes in the spoken language, thereby maintaining its easy-to-learn transparency? Or should it stay more fixed, allowing readers to be able to read texts written by people who spoke an earlier version of that particular language?

In the end, pushing for reforms that create a dramatically more transparent writing system for all users of English might make it easier to learn to read in English. But it could ultimately cut readers off from being able to read the thoughts of English speakers from other places and other times.

WEB ACTIVITY 7.10

Predict the future of English orthography The rise of the Internet means that written text can now be broadly disseminated without the involvement of "gatekeeping" professional editors. In this exercise, you'll be prompted to look at some samples of Internet text that is not filtered through an editorial staff, and to notice common examples of non-standard spellings. Take a stab at making some predictions about what these examples might mean for the future of English orthography.

would have you believe. For example, even for a word like *sign*, the letter *s* still matches up with the sound /s/ as does *n* with /n/. There really aren't, it turns out, any words like George Bernard Shaw's *ghoti* for *fish*. And you can find clusters of *similar* irregular words—*resign, benign, align*—much like you find clusters of similar irregular past-tense forms (for example, *sleep-slept, creep-crept, keep-kept*). So, smaller rules seem to be embedded among the exceptional forms. The claim among connectionists is that there is a continuum between the most idiosyncratic forms and the most regularly patterned, and that what look like rules are really just the very strongest patterns.

In this model, hearing a word activates a set of phonological units, which are indirectly linked to a set of meaning units. These connections have formed over time and reflect learned associations between sounds and meaning. Learn-

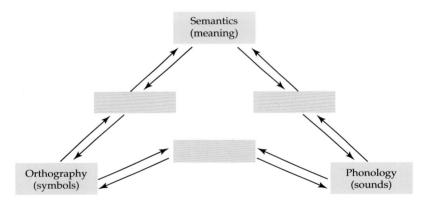

Figure 7.16 A single-system connectionist model of reading. Over the course of learning to read, connections between sounds (phonology) and meaning (semantics) are supplemented by a set of connections linking together orthography with phonology, and orthography directly with meaning. (Adapted from Seidenberg & McClelland, 1989.)

ing to read simply means grafting a new set of units and connections onto the existing sets for meaning and sound. As shown in **Figure 7.16**, a set of orthographic units has now been added to the system. These units are connected to both the meaning units and the phonological units, and the strength of these connections will depend on how often each set of units gets turned on.

For example, seeing the letters *p-i-g* while reading or hearing *pig* will turn on the phonological units /p/ /ɪ/ /g/. If units are turned on simultaneously very often, the system will establish a strong connection between them. For instance, reading the letters *w-i-g* will also turn on the /ɪ/ /g/ sound units. For very regular sound patterns, the same letters and sound units will be turned on very often, leading to more strongly weighted connections. In a connectionist system, very strongly weighted connections behave somewhat like rules. But the system can also form less regular, and hence slightly weaker, connections as well, for example, the correspondence between the letters *i-g-n* and the sounds in words like *sign* and *align*. For highly irregular words, the connections between orthographic units and *sound* units will be very weak. But there will still be connections between the orthographic units and the meaning units. These connections will be quite strong if the word is a very frequent one, like *have*, so the word can be recognized very efficiently on the basis of these robust links. The same system, then, can account for both the greater reliance on sound patterns for regular orthography, and the greater reliance on orthography-to-meaning links for irregular words. This is pretty much the same strategy taken by connectionist approaches to irregular morphology, and the claim is that it organically arises out of the way in which we generally learn patterns and associations.

The argument between these two models boils down to whether there are really two very distinct reading systems, or just one that makes use of connections between different subsystems. It's been a difficult argument to settle decisively with the usual set of lab tools that measure behavior, and it may be that careful brain-imaging work will ultimately help to settle the debate. But at the very least, the connectionist model suggests that it's possible to model many aspects of actual reading behavior without resorting to two very different reading routes.

GO TO
sites.sinauer.com/languageinmind

for **web activities, further readings, research updates, new essays,** and other features

DIGGING DEEPER

The great modular-versus-interactive debate

Figure 7.12 introduced an innovation to our model, adding top-down excitatory links going from the lexical level to the phoneme level. The top-down links allows activation of a specific word to send activation down to its component sounds. This is useful for capturing phenomena like the Ganong effect or the phoneme restoration effect, where the identity of the word alters the perception of individual sounds.

Or does it? Some researchers (e.g., Norris et al., 2000) have argued that these apparent top-down effects aren't what they seem to be. Think of it this way: the phoneme nodes send along information to the lexical level, sort of like reports being sent up by employees to higher management; the job of each phoneme node is to report on how likely it is that that particular phoneme was uttered, so nodes that are more strongly activated than others send up more convincing reports. Let's suppose that, going solely on the acoustic input, two phonemes, /t/ and /d/, send up equally convincing reports (are equally activated) based on a somewhat fuzzy example of a particular consonant sound—this is what happens in your typical Ganong-style experiment. Next, let's suppose that this fuzzy sound appears in the word frame *spi__*. Our current model with top-down links built into it would be the equivalent of this scenario: A higher-level manager gets conflicting reports, integrates these with his own knowledge, and comes to the conclusion that only one of these phonemes is consistent with all the information he has. So he talks to the employees at the lower level and convinces them that what they heard was wrong, and they alter their reports accordingly and send these back up. But, an alternative scenario that *doesn't* involve top-down nodes would go something like this: The manager gets conflicting reports, determines that only one of these fits with additional information that his employees didn't have and, as a result, makes an executive decision about which of these reports is right. He acts *as if* the reports from his employees had been altered to fit his own knowledge, incorporates that into his own report, and sends that up to yet a higher level of management. In this version of the model, the manager doesn't go back to try to convince his employees that one of them made an error; he simply decides that this must be the case.

Both accounts get the facts right. But one of them implicates top-down links, while the other has a strict bottom-up flow of information, with enhanced decision-making powers at the lexical level. Does it matter which one is right?

Sure it does, for the simple reason that although the two models align with the same facts about the basic Ganong effect, they might actually make different predictions about more nuanced aspects of word recognition and speech processing. And obviously, scientists want to get a really detailed and refined understanding of the processes they're studying. After all, this is one reason for making models in the first place—to push our understanding to greater and greater levels of detail. But the difference between these two models goes beyond general scientific diligence and attention to detail; it represents a quite profound disagreement about fundamental aspects of how the mind is designed, something researchers call **cognitive architecture**.

Researchers who propose top-down links are generally advocating an **interactive mind design** in which higher, more abstract levels of knowledge (usually what we think of as "more intelligent" levels of knowledge) can directly inform lower-level perception. Let's push this idea to an unlikely, extreme level. Imagine you're watching a horror movie in which spiders are crawling over the heroine's entire body. You begin to feel crawling sensations on your own skin, even though there is nothing making contact with it, and therefore nothing to be picked up by the sensory nerves in your skin. A top-down account would say that your suggestive higher-level thoughts are actually causing the nerve cells in your skin to send signals back up through your nervous system that are identical to the signals that would be sent in response to feeling spiders crawling over you.

This is wildly implausible, and if we recorded the activity of individual nerves, we'd find no such thing. Rather, your mind is creating its own interpretation based on other incoming information from the movie, the end result being that you have a subjective experience *as if* your nerves were being directly stimulated. But though your mind has convinced *you*, it hasn't convinced the nerve cells in your skin that you're being crawled upon. So there are obviously limits to how far down information can flow from higher levels.

---

cognitive architecture Fundamental characteristics of the mind's structure that specify how different cognitive components interact with each other.

interactive mind design A view of the mind's structure in which higher, more abstract levels of knowledge (usually what we think of as "more intelligent" levels of knowledge) can directly inform lower-level perception.

Some researchers have argued that in fact the mind is designed in such a way that the higher levels of processing *never* converse with the lower levels—that their job is simply to integrate information, interpret it, and pass that on to even higher levels, which in turn won't converse with them. Under this **modular mind design** view, employees at each level do their jobs without consultation or interference from above. One rationale for this particular cognitive architecture is that it's likely to be highly efficient. If lower levels of processing can do their work by restricting attention to only a very limited amount of information, they can prepare their reports quite quickly. But if they have to take into account the opinions and information from higher levels of processing as well, this might slow everything down. Proponents of a modular architecture (most prominently, the philosopher Jerry Fodor; see Fodor 1983) have argued that there's a striking difference between the type of information processing accomplished by lower-level modules, and the type of processing that does higher-level integration and makes decisions. The argument is that low-level perceptual processes are more like extremely fast reflexive instincts, while higher-level processes are more like slower, thoughtful judges.

The distinction seems intuitively appealing, in part because perception can be fairly stubborn—*reflex*-like—even in the face of compelling higher-level knowledge. For example, you've likely already seen the famous Müller-Lyer illusion involving lines of identical length that nevertheless look to be different in length (**Figure 7.17**). You probably knew already that the lines in this image were the same length, and if you didn't, you're invited to measure them now. But this knowledge has stunningly little impact on your perception of these lines. Your visual perceptual system, acting on a specific set of visual cues, simply cannot be reasoned with.

Such a bullheaded perceptual system might seem perverse in the case of illusions like the Müller-Lyer effect (after all, isn't it preventing you from seeing what's *really* there?), but the argument is that in fact, we'd be subject to a great many more hallucinations if our higher-level processes were allowed to readily interfere with the output of lower-level perception. In getting back to word recognition, for example, wouldn't top-down feedback render us incapable of noticing other people's mispronunciations and slips of the tongue? These are clearly inconsistent with our higher-level knowledge of the words they're attempting to pronounce, and usually we know exactly what they're trying to say, yet we persist in hearing the actually produced sounds.

From a broader view of the field of psycholinguistics, then, the decision about how to model lexical effects on

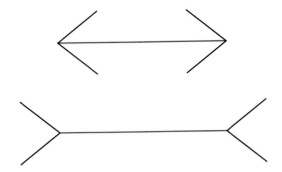

Figure 7.17 The Müller-Lyer illusion. No matter how much top-down certainty you have that the two red lines are actually the same length, lower-level visual processes still insist that they're different.

phoneme perception isn't just about making more precise predictions. The issue has become a test case for these two big, competing views of how the mind is designed. (You'll see in the next chapter that these competing views have far-ranging implications for aspects of language comprehension that go well beyond the realm of words.)

So, is there a way to decide which of these views is right? Experimental efforts in the domain of word recognition have focused on a particular phenomenon known as **compensation for coarticulation**. As we've seen, sounds are often affected by other sounds they're pressed up against. Hearers automatically adjust for this. For example, if they hear a sound halfway between /t/ and /k/, they'll be more likely to treat it as a /t/ if it follows the sound /ʃ/ (this symbol corresponds to the first sound in *ship*) and to treat it as a /k/ if it follows the sound /s/. This is because the shape of your tongue when you pronounce the second consonant is affected by where you place your tongue for the first consonant; a /t/ normally sounds a bit /k/-like following /ʃ/, and a /k/ normally sounds more /t/-like following /s/, so when hearing a sound that's in between, hearers automatically take into account the articulatory context, to decide which one is most likely. All of this is a low-level process, and affects the activation of sounds whether or not any words are involved at all—for example, even if the sounds are embedded in nonsense words. So it seems that compensation for coarticulation involves information that's readily available at the sound level, not information that's coming down from the word level. To return to our metaphor, in order to incorporate this information into their reports, the employees at the sound level talk to their neighboring sounds, rather than talking to their bosses at the word level.

---

modular mind design View of the mind's structure in which higher levels of processing never directly influence the lower levels; instead, the higher levels integrate information based on lower-level processes, interpret it, and pass these interpretations on to even higher levels.

compensation for coarticulation Phenomenon in which the perception of speech automatically adjusts to take into account the tendency for sounds to be pronounced differently in different phonetic environments; thus the same ambiguous sound may be perceived differently, depending on the adjacent sounds.

But we can use this phenomenon to test whether word representations are able to alter the reports of their sound-employees from the top down (rather than simply making an executive decision based on their levels of activation). To do this, we can leverage the compensation for coarticulation effect together with the Ganong effect. In this more complex experimental scenario, research subjects hear words like *Christma?* or *fooli?* in which *?* is a sound halfway between /s/ and /ʃ/, followed by the word *?apes*, in which *?* is a sound halfway between /t/ and /k/. In other words, the second word could be interpreted as either *tapes* or *capes*. We know that compensation for coarticulation would make people more likely to hear *capes* after *Christmas* and *tapes* after *foolish*, and that this is a result of influence from neighboring sounds. But in this case, they're hearing exactly the *same* sound embedded in the word *Christmas* or *foolish*. So we would expect that people would report hearing *capes* just as often after *Christma?* as after *fooli?*—unless, that is, the word-level representation was able to change the activation levels of the sounds themselves so that these sounds could in turn influence their neighbors. In that case a more highly activated /ʃ/ sound in the frame *fooli?* should bias the hearer into thinking she is hearing *tapes* rather than *capes*, just as if the /ʃ/ sound had been activated on the basis of the acoustic input.

This subtle logic provides a way to wedge apart the predictions made by competing top-down and bottom-up explanations. Sure enough, results have been reported in favor of the top-down account, first by Jeff Elman and James McClelland (1988), proponents of the TRACE model of word recognition, in which top-down links figure quite prominently. But too much is at stake theoretically to let these results by without closer scrutiny. Mark Pitt and James McQueen (1998) came back with a challenge, arguing that there was still a way in which the results could have come about from a strictly bottom-up system. They pointed out that the identity of the ambiguous /s-ʃ/ sound could have been determined not by feedback from the word level, but simply because the last vowel in *Christmas* occurs much

more often with /s/ than with /ʃ/ and, conversely, the last vowel in *foolish* occurs much more often with /ʃ/ than with /s/. So, the activation of the /s/ and /ʃ/ sounds could still have been determined solely by consulting neighboring sounds: the probability of certain sound sequences over others would bias the perception of either /s/ or /ʃ/, and this would in turn bias the perception of /t/ and /k/ in the following word, based on compensation for coarticulation. Hence, no interference was needed from the word level. (To revisit our office scenario, the employees' reports now are affected by discussions with their peers, rather than top-down instructions from their supervisor.)

Several papers have flown back and forth since then, either supporting or challenging Elman and McClelland's original results, and this particular test case for the modular-versus-interactive debate is still unresolved. But there's more than one way to skin a modular cat, and researchers have been attacking the question from a number of different angles. For example, they've looked at whether top-down processing can be found between other levels, such as whether higher-level syntactic or semantic expectations can drive up the activation of one lexical candidate over others, even when the others are equally consistent with sound-based information. In the next chapter we'll see whether cues from context and meaning can affect lower-level decisions about which syntactic structure to build during sentence comprehension. And discussions have occurred about whether a top-down architecture is consistent with what we know about how brains work. After all, the strongest version of the modular perspective—that higher levels of knowledge and information processing *never* feed back to influence lower ones—is a sweeping and interesting idea, generating predictions about a great many separate phenomena. Over the decades, the sheer bigness of the idea has inspired an impressive body of work, and has mobilized researchers from both camps to think of ever-more-compelling experiments to defend their claims.

PROJECT

Step into the modular/interactive battle arena!
Generate a set of predictions that are made by a model that proposes the top-down flow of information. Flesh these predictions out by sketching an experimental design, describing in detail the experimental conditions, stimuli, and methods. Suppose that your results bear out the predictions made by the top-down model. Try to identify any way in which these results might be open to attack by proponents of modular, bottom-up models of word recognition.

8 Understanding Sentence Structure and Meaning

As we saw in Chapter 6, the mind is exquisitely adept at relating syntactic structure to meaning, able to compute the meanings of long, complex sentences, even those containing numerous clauses nested within each other and coding intricate relationships among their elements, of which this particular sentence is an excellent example.

Despite our great parsing prowess, we still stumble over some sentences. We've all had the experience of finding ourselves re-reading certain sentences over and over, not quite sure how to unravel their meanings even though none of the words in them are especially complicated or unfamiliar. Some sentences just feel knotty or clunky. They're the sentences that an English teacher or an editor might single out with the remark "awkward sentence structure" or "this feels clumsy."

Let's see if you have an intuitive sense of the kinds of sentences that strain language comprehension. Of the perfectly grammatical sentences listed on the next page, some slide through the mind with ease, while others seem to bunch up or create hard-to-read word piles. Make a note of the ones you find somewhat taxing or confusing. For the time being, rely solely on your editorial instinct; by the end of this chapter, you should have some scientific understanding of *why* they cause problems for the reader. (And if you ever find yourself working as an editor, you'll be able explain to your authors exactly what's gone awry with many of their bad sentences.)

The boy watched the ball with the yellow stripe float down the river.

Susanne put the toy soldier in the box into the cupboard.

The soup and the vegetables simmered lightly on the stove while the hostess served some wine.

The patient told the doctor that he was having some trouble with about his sore knee.

The baker is going to sue the plumber who botched the installation of his new pipes last week.

The suspect who was seen last night at the crime scene has confessed to the murder.

The mouse the cat chased keeled over.

The boy who stalked the prom queen has been caught.

The teachers taught new math techniques passed the exam with flying colors.

Woody confided to his therapist that he occasionally thought about murdering his mother.

While the pop star sang the national anthem played in the background.

The cruel man beat his puppy with a thick stick.

Samantha explained to her son's dentist that the boy's grandparents kept feeding him candy.

Friedrich cooked the ribs and the corn had already been roasted.

The farmer slaughtered the goose that had intimidated his hens.

The gang leader hit the lawyer with a wart.

As Marilyn smiled the photographers snapped dozens of pictures.

The bartender told the detective that the suspect will try to escape the country yesterday.

The coffee in the red mug was already cold by the time the secretary had time to drink it.

The administrator who the intern who the nurse supervised had accused fudged the medical reports.

At least nine of these sentences would be recognized by most psycholinguists as potential troublemakers, containing elements known to cause problems for readers or hearers. Obviously, being able to recognize what makes sentences tricky to read is exceptionally useful if you're a writer or editor. But if you're a psycholinguist, it also gives you some nifty insights into how human beings go about structuring the words of incoming speech or text into sentences with complex meanings. We can figure out a great deal about how human language comprehension works in real time by observing it at its limits and seeing where it breaks down. Different theories of sentence processing make different predictions about which sentences will be harder to process than others.

In this chapter, you'll get a chance to explore the nature of difficult sentences, whether written or spoken. But this isn't just a story about awkward sentences. As you'll see, in addition to learning how glitches in processing come about, you will ultimately gain an appreciation of why it is that most of the time, comprehension glides along perfectly smoothly.

8.1 Incremental Processing and the Problem of Ambiguity

Processing sentences on the fly

As you saw in Chapter 7, the word recognition system is not especially timid when it comes to making rapid, reasonable guesses about which words are in the midst of being pronounced; it begins to link sounds with possible words and their meanings from the very first moments of utterance, activating a large number of possibilities in the memory store, and gradually winnowing these down to the very best candidates.

But what about sentences? Unlike words, their meanings don't just depend on retrieving meanings that are pre-stored in memory. Remember that the meaning of each sentence has to be constructed anew based on the syntactic relationships among all the words in the sentence. (Otherwise, we wouldn't be able to understand sentences we'd never heard before, having never had the opportunity to memorize their meanings.) This process of structure-building during comprehension is referred to as **parsing**. (Psycholinguists often use "the parser" as a convenient term for the collection of structure-building mechanisms and procedures; the term does not refer to an individual person.) How long does it take for the parser to build these meaningful structures? Does each word in the sentence have to be uttered and fished out of memory first before syntactic grouping and structuring can begin to take place?

It seems not. The parser happens to be just as eager as the word recognition system in generating guesses about possible meanings, even on the basis of very partial information from the speech stream. Like word processing, understanding sentences is an exercise in **incrementality**—that is, meaning is built on the fly as the speech comes in, rather than being delayed until some amount of linguistic material has accumulated first. One very intuitive way of showing that understanding follows hot on the heels of the uttered speech is by means of a **shadowing task**, in which subjects are asked to repeat the words of a speaker's sentence almost as quickly as the speaker produces them. People who are very good at this can follow at a lag of about a quarter of a second—roughly a lag of one syllable behind the speaker. This suggests that within hundreds of milliseconds of a word, not only has its meaning been recognized, but it has been integrated with the syntactic structure and meaning of the sentence. We know that people are actually analyzing the sentence's meaning rather than just parroting words or even just the sounds of words, because shadowing gets considerably slower when meaningful sentences are replaced with nonsensical sentences (but with recognizable words), and slower yet if the sentence that has to be repeated is in a foreign language or uses made-up words.

But there's a downside to this "hungry" style of language processing. Like an overeager student who blurts out the answer before the teacher has finished asking the question, the parser's guesses, based on only partial information from the sentence, may not all turn out to be the right ones. You might remember that this was also a factor with the eager word recognition system. Along with the correct target word (for example, *candy*), soundalike words, especially

parsing The process of assigning syntactic structure to the incoming words of a sentence during language comprehension. The structure-building mechanisms and procedures collectively are often referred to as "the parser."

incrementality The property of synthesizing and building meaning "on the fly" as individual units of speech come in, rather than delaying processing until some amount of linguistic material has accumulated.

shadowing task An experimental task in which subjects are asked to repeat the words of a speaker's sentence almost as quickly as the speaker produces them.

WEB ACTIVITY 8.1

Processing language on the fly
Try your hand at a shadowing task. You'll first be able to listen to someone shadowing speech, and then have an opportunity to shadow a variety of sensible, senseless, and foreign-language sentences.

reduced relative clause A grammatical structure in English involving a relative clause in which certain function words have been omitted (for example the reduced relative clause *raced past the barn* derives from the full relative clause *that was raced past the barn*). This structure often leads to ambiguity.

those that begin with the same sounds, also become activated (*candle, Canada, cantaloupe*). Evidence of such spurious activation can be seen in priming tasks or in patterns of eye movements to visual displays. In other words, extreme eagerness or incrementality in word recognition leads to an explosion of potential ambiguity of meanings, at least for a short period of time. The processing system ultimately has to suppress a number of possible interpretations that started out as being perfectly consistent with the uttered speech. This happens at the level of the sentence as well.

"Garden path" sentences

Successful interpretation is often a matter of not getting tripped up by the incorrect meanings that also become activated during comprehension. But sometimes, one of the alternative meanings causes so much disruption during parsing that it becomes really hard to recover the correct meaning of the sentence. Consider the following, probably the single most famous sentence in psycholinguistics, brought to life by Tom Bever (1970):

The horse raced past the barn fell.

Figure 8.1 Tree structures illustrating two possible syntactic interpretations of the string *The horse raced past the barn*…. (A) A main clause interpretation. (B) An interpretation involving a reduced relative clause, with the anticipation of additional content to be uttered as part of the verb phrase (VP).

On a first reading, many people think this sentence makes no sense, or is ungrammatical with some words left out. But it's perfectly grammatical. Don't believe me? It means exactly the same thing as this:

The horse that was raced past the barn (by someone) fell.

Still don't see it? It has exactly the same structure and a very similar meaning to this:

The horse driven past the barn fell.

Assuming you've eventually been able to parse the sentence correctly, the puzzle becomes this: What is it that makes that first sentence so dastardly difficult to understand, much more so than the other two, even though all of them are permitted by the grammar of English? The answer is that only the first has the potential for a temporary ambiguity; until the very last word of the sentence, it's most natural to understand the sentence as being structured so that the word *horse* is the subject of the verb *raced*—that is, the horse is *doing* the racing, rather than being raced. This interpretation would have worked out just fine if the sentence had continued this way:

The horse raced past the barn and fell.

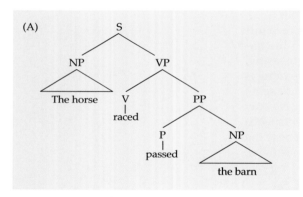

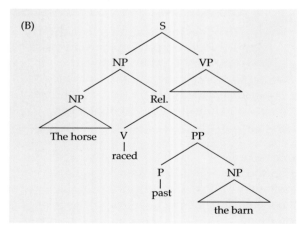

Which is why people often tend to have the feeling that the sentence is missing a word or two. But in order to get the right reading for our original sentence, you have to ignore this highly tempting meaning for the first six words of the sentence, and instead interpret them as being structured such that the phrase *raced past the barn* is a separate clause adding more information about the horse—this is called a **reduced relative clause** because it's just like the (non-reduced) relative clause *that was raced past the barn* with some of the function words taken out. In this more complicated structure, notice that *the horse* acts semantically as the direct object of *raced*—that is, it is being raced, rather than doing the racing—but *also* acts as the subject of the main clause verb *fell*. **Figure 8.1** shows one way in which to graphically capture the two different interpretations. (And, if grammatical terms like *direct object* and *relative clause* aren't part of your daily vocabulary, **Box 8.1** on the next page offers a quick refresher.)

Here are a few more sentences with reduced relative clauses, and with the same potential for ambiguity as our horse-racing example—though a number of them seem to cause somewhat milder reading hiccups, for reasons we'll see later:

> The swimmers drowned in the lake were not found until the following spring.

> The general presented copies of the report was aware of the problems.

> The boat floated downstream will never get past the rapids safely.

Difficult sentences like these are poetically called **garden path sentences**, since their effect is to lead readers down a garden path, misleading them into interpreting the sentence one way, but then veering off in another direction entirely. In English, temporary syntactic ambiguities aren't limited to cases in which a word sequence can be read either as a reduced relative clause or as belonging to a simple main clause. A generous variety of opportunities exists for garden path sentences. For example:

> After the police stopped the car...

Here, *the car* could be read as either the direct object of the verb *stopped* (as in *After the police stopped the car they noticed its license plate was missing*), or as the subject of the following clause (*After the police stopped the car sped off down the road*). Most likely, the first of these possible continuations feels more graceful to you, while the second is a bit bumpy, presumably because you've given in to the desire to interpret a noun phrase immediately following a verb as a direct object of that verb. This creates problems when you then encounter the second verb *sped off*, which nonsensically appears to have no subject, so you need to go back and reanalyze the sentence so that *the car* is interpreted as its subject.

Now try supplying a plausible continuation for this sentence:

> The married man promised his mistress that he would soon abandon...

If you suggested that the next words should be *his wife*, then you've taken the heavily traveled path of interpreting *that he would soon abandon* as introducing a sentence complement of the verb *promised*—that is, what the married man promised was that he would soon abandon someone, perhaps his wife. But another structure is possible, as evident in this sample continuation:

> The married man promised his mistress that he would soon abandon a diamond ring.

Since it's decidedly bizarre to abandon a diamond ring, the reader is nudged into a different interpretation and, if successful, will eventually settle on a reading in which *that he would soon abandon* is a relative clause, providing additional information about his mistress (similar to *The married man gave the woman that he would soon abandon a diamond ring.*)

Once you start looking, you'll be able to diagnose many awkward-sounding sentences as garden path sentences. For instance, each of the sentences below contains a temporary ambiguity. Try to identify the fragment of the sentence that could be interpreted in two ways, and then think about another possible

garden path sentences Sentences that are difficult to understand because they contain a temporary ambiguity. The tendency is for hearers or readers to initially interpret the ambiguous structure incorrectly, and then experience confusion when that initial interpretation turns out to be grammatically incompatible with later material in the sentence.

BOX 8.1
Key grammatical terms and concepts in English

Subject

The noun phrase (NP) that appears to the left of a verb phrase (VP) and combines with it to form a sentence. The subject is often described as "what the sentence is about." When the sentence is in the active voice, the subject is typically (but not always) the cause or the instigator of the event described by the verb:

Copernicus made an important discovery.

The third man on the left is acting suspiciously.

She died on August 12, 1542.

Direct object

A noun phrase that appears inside of the verb phrase, to the right of the verb. Not all verbs take a direct object; whether a verb allows/requires one or not must be specified as part of the lexical knowledge of that verb. When the sentence is in the active voice, the direct object is usually the entity that is acted upon, or comes into being, as a result of the actions of the subject:

Copernicus made **an important discovery**.

The president fired **his chief of staff**.

The police stopped **the car**.

Cyrano wrote **an eloquent love letter**.

Indirect object

Occasionally, two noun phrases occur inside a verb phrase; in this case, only one is the direct object; the other NP is the indirect object. Rather than expressing the acted-upon entity, the indirect object usually expresses the recipient of the acted-upon thing. An indirect object either appears immediately after the verb or is introduced by a preposition:

Cyrano wrote **Roxanne** an eloquent love letter.

Cyrano wrote an eloquent love letter for **Roxanne**.

Copernicus explained his discovery to **many skeptical theologians**.

The hooded man passed **the bank teller** a note.

Sentence complement

A clause, or a sentence unit, that appears inside the verb phrase, to the right of the verb. It is often (but not always) introduced by the *complementizer* word *that*, and may occur on its own, or together with a noun phrase:

His friends warned Copernicus **that the authorities were planning his arrest**.

The president claimed **he had created many new jobs**.

Main versus subordinate clauses

A sentence may have multiple sentence units contained within it, but usually only one is the main clause: this is the sentence that is at the top of the tree (as in Figure 8.1), while the other subordinate clauses are embedded inside other phrases. Subordinate clauses might appear within the verb phrase as sentence complements, attached to nouns as relative clauses, or introduced by adverbial words such as *although*, *despite*, *after*, etc. Here, the subordinate clauses appear in bold:

The horse raced **while the cow stared**.

Though her audience loved her, Marilyn was riddled with doubt.

The man **who was acting suspiciously** turned out to be an escaped convict.

She died **because she had no money for the operation**.

Conjoined clauses

Two or more constituents of the same type can be conjoined by *and* or *but*, including clauses. When a main clause is conjoined with another main clause, they carry equal weight, and both are considered to be main clauses:

The police stopped the car and the driver jumped out.

Copernicus made a discovery but he hesitated to reveal it.

Relative clause

A sentence unit that is embedded within a noun phrase, usually (but not always) introduced by a relative pronoun such as *who* or *that*:

The boy **who stalked the prom queen** has been caught.

The discovery **that Copernicus made** was controversial.

Notice that, confusingly, *that* can also be a complementizer introducing a sentential complement inside a verb phrase (see the entry "Sentence complement").

BOX 8.1 (continued)

Active versus passive voice

This is one of the most commonly misunderstood grammatical concepts. The active voice is simply the default structure for expressing an event or a situation:

> Many theologians denounced Copernicus.

> The principal drove the prom queen home.

The passive voice is an alternative way of expressing the same event:

> Copernicus was denounced by many theologians.

> The prom queen was driven home by the principal.

A passive sentence can only be related to an active voice sentence that contains a direct object. The passive sentence rearranges the order of the noun phrases so that the direct object from the active version becomes the subject of the passive version, and the subject from the active sentence (usually the instigator of the action) becomes embedded in a prepositional phrase introduced by the word *by*. In the process, the auxiliary verb *to be* (or occasionally *to get*) is inserted between the subject and the verb, and the verb appears in the past participle form (for example, *drove* becomes *was driven*; past tense verbs that end in *-ed* appear in exactly the same form as past participles—more on that later in the chapter). Thus:

> The orangutan is being fed too often by the staff.

> Copernicus got arrested for his controversial ideas.

> The prom queen is chosen by the students every year.

A noteworthy feature of passive sentences is that the *by* phrase may be dropped, thereby leaving the instigator of the action completely implicit, unspoken, or unknown:

> The orangutan is being fed too often.

> Mistakes were made.

> Copernicus was denounced.

Many people mistake other structures for passive sentences because they contain superficial similarities such as the presence of *to be*. But if a sentence does not contain all of the elements described above, it is not passive. Try identifying the passive sentences among the following examples:

> (a) The maid is stealing money.

> (b) Those ideas were considered revolutionary.

> (c) The prisoners were being tortured on a daily basis.

> (d) Now you are just being picky.

> (e) Copernicus got famous for his controversial ideas.

> (f) Every car is searched at the border.

For many relative clauses, it's possible to drop the relative pronoun (such as *that* or *who*), leading to a reduced relative clause. When this happens to a relative clause that's in the passive voice, the auxiliary *to be* (or *to get*) also gets dropped:

> The astronomer (who got) arrested for his ideas was controversial.

> The prom queen (who was) driven home by the principal was drunk.

Answer to the passives quiz: The passive sentences are (b), (c), and (f).

way to continue the sentence that would be consistent with that second reading of the ambiguous string of words:

> The investigation revealed the error resulted from gross negligence.

> Sam ate the hot dog and the vegetables went untouched.

> The gangster shot the cop with the gun.

> This company only hires smart women and men who may be dumb but who have clout.

> Visiting relatives can be annoying if they overstay their welcome.

> The government plans to raise taxes were defeated.

> The army houses soldiers and their families.

Once you've identified the potential ambiguities, you can check your interpretations against **Figure 8.2**, where some of these examples are graphically mapped out.

(A)

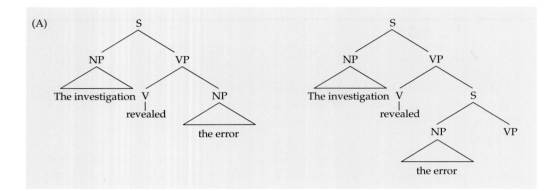

(B)

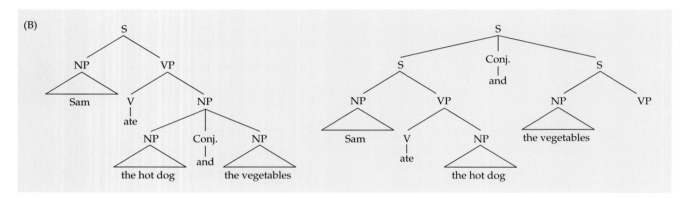

(C)

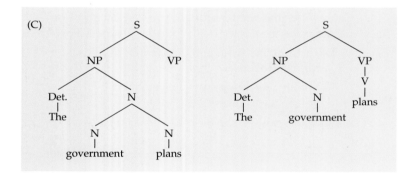

Figure 8.2 Alternative interpretations for three ambiguous sentence fragments. (A) Two possible structures for *The investigation revealed the error…*. (B) Two ways of interpreting *Sam ate the hot dog and the vegetables…*. (C) Two structures for *The government plans…*. Notice that in (C), the ambiguity hinges on whether *plans* is analyzed as a noun or a verb.

Measuring processing difficulty

Many garden path sentences are easy enough to identify, because the reader becomes aware of some processing tangle or even of an initial misreading. But psycholinguists often want to study subtler ambiguity effects that bypass conscious awareness. Once again, careful timekeeping is a useful tool for detecting mild but real processing disruptions.

A garden path effect is detected by measuring how long people take to read the disambiguating region of the sentence—that is, the first point at which any alternative but incorrect readings stop being consistent with the unfolding sentence. In the following examples, disambiguating regions are in bold:

The general presented copies of the report **was aware** of the problems.

The investigation revealed the error **resulted from** gross negligence.

Crash blossoms run amok in newspaper headlines

"VIOLINIST LINKED TO JAL CRASH BLOSSOMS." That's the headline of a 2009 article that ran in the newspaper *Japan Today*, prompting an American editor on an online discussion forum about copyediting to query, "What's a crash blossom?" In fact, the article was about the blooming musical career of a violinist whose father had died in a 1985 Japan Airlines crash. The headline is a garden path sentence rivaling the famous "horse raced" example in its inscrutability, and it involves a similar ambiguity of structure. It contains a reduced relative clause, and would be somewhat more understandable had it been written like this:

> The violinist who has been linked to the JAL crash blossoms.

There's also a second ambiguity contained in the word sequence *JAL crash blossoms*. Under the intended meaning, *crash* is supposed to be a noun, and *blossoms* is supposed to be a verb. But it's tempting to read the phrase such that *crash* is acting as a modifier (much like an adjective), and *blossoms* is a noun. Here, a lexical ambiguity involving the syntactic category of the word *blossoms* contributes to a completely nonsensical way of structuring the sentence overall. (Another example of this is with a sentence like *He saw her duck*, where *duck* could be either a noun or verb, resulting in very different readings.)

Function words like *who*, *that*, and *was* can serve the practical function of disambiguating a sentence, but in many cases such words are, perversely, optional. When they get dropped, this can lead to potential syntactic ambiguity. And in newspaper headlines, where there is a premium on terse expression, the disambiguating words are often swept away.

Hilarious results frequently ensue. Spotting garden path sentences in headlines (or crash blossoms, as they've come to be called at the suggestion of journalist John McIntyre) is a favorite sport of language geeks, and you can find many examples discussed on the popular linguistics blog Language Log (just do a search for "crash blossoms" on the blog's website). Here are a few examples of especially humorous crash blossoms that have been honored in the blogosphere:

POLICE INVESTIGATE DEATH BY BALZAC
(Balzac turns out to be a town, not the famous nineteenth-century French writer)

CHINESE COOKING FAT HEADS FOR HOLLAND

MANSELL GUILTY OF MISSING BUSINESSMAN'S MURDER

SMOKING MORE DANGEROUS FOR WOMEN THAN MEN

SISTERS REUNITED AFTER EIGHTEEN YEARS IN CHECKOUT COUNTER

GREECE FEARS BATTER MARKETS AGAIN

BRITISH LEFT WAFFLES ON FALKLAND ISLANDS

MINERS REFUSE TO WORK AFTER DEATH

JUVENILE COURT TO TRY SHOOTING DEFENDANT

You might try keeping a log of the crash blossoms you find in headlines over the period of, say, a week. Some might be funny, like the ones above in which a second meaning is readily accessible. Others might be nothing more than uninterpretable word mash-ups. Then try rewriting the headlines so that you preserve as much of their meaning as possible while removing the hazardous ambiguities.

For purposes of comparison, it's often possible to create virtually identical sentences that don't contain hazardous ambiguities, simply by introducing disambiguating function words, such as those in italics below:

> The general *who was* presented copies of the report **was aware** of the problems.

> The investigation revealed *that* the error **resulted from** gross negligence.

If the bold regions in the first pair of sentences (that is, the sentences containing the potential ambiguity) take significantly longer to read than the same bold

METHOD 8.1

Using reading times to detect misanalysis

How do you know for sure that a sentence is hard to read because readers are deceived into taking the wrong fork in the interpretive road? As a psycholinguist, you have several options. Most of the work on ambiguity resolution has relied on measures of reading time. A cheap and low-tech way of gathering these is by means of a **self-paced reading task**. Subjects read through sentences on a computer one word or phrase at a time, pressing a button to advance through the sentence, while a program records the amount of time they spend reading each segment. One downside to this method is that it's a bit unnatural, and breaks up the flow of reading by requiring subjects to keep pushing a button. Researches have tried to make the task a touch more natural by embedding it in a **moving window paradigm**, simulating somewhat the experience of bringing each word into focus by moving the eyes over the sentence. In this experimental situation, subjects first see the entire sentence with each character covered over by dashes:

```
--- ------- --------- ------ -- ---
------ --- ----- -- --- -------.
```

Each button press reveals a portion of the sentence and covers up the previous one, so a sequence of button presses would reveal chunks like this:

```
1. The general --------- ------ -- ---
   ------ --- ----- -- --- -------.

2. --- ------- presented copies -- ---
   ------ --- ----- -- --- -------.

3. --- ------- --------- ------ of the
   report --- ----- -- --- -------.

4. --- ------- --------- ------ -- ---
   ------ was aware -- --- -------.
```

```
5. --- ------- --------- ------ -- ---
   ------ --- ----- of the problem.
```

Even so, there may be a tendency for subjects to apply a steady rhythm to their button presses and artificially fit their reading into that time frame. When they hit an especially difficult phrase, they may have already pressed the button to advance to the next phrase, even if they haven't fully processed the earlier phrase. This can lead to *spillover effects*, where the reading time that should be recorded for a particular phrase ends up being recorded for the following one instead, as subjects struggle to catch up in processing. This is a bad outcome, since so much of the theorizing about garden path sentences hinges on firm knowledge about exactly which regions of the sentence cause hiccups in processing. In general, there's a concern that by breaking up the flow of reading, and in a way that doesn't allow subjects to backtrack, you're not getting the most accurate picture of how processing works in typical reading situations.

You can encourage a smoother flow of reading and also get a more detailed snapshot of reading with a slightly higher-tech version of the reading time measure. Subjects read sentences presented on the screen in their entirety while their eye movements are being recorded. This allows you, the researcher, to measure the amount of time readers

---

self-paced reading task A behavioral task intended to measure processing difficulty at various points in a sentence. Subjects read through sentences on a computer screen, one word or phrase at a time, pressing a button to advance through the sentence. A program records the amount of time each subject spends reading each segment.

moving window paradigm A version of the self-paced reading task in which dashes initially replace each alphabetic character in a sentence, and participants press a button to successively "uncover" each portion of the sentence. This method of presentation simulates a fairly natural reading rhythm.

---

regions in the second pair (the unambiguous versions), then a garden path effect is considered to have occurred, and is taken as evidence that the reader ran into some processing trouble from having initially been misled, at least in part, by the wrong interpretation of the ambiguous portion of the sentence. You can get a more detailed feel for the reading time task in **Method 8.1**.

spend on each region of interest. It also allows you to get a picture of how long subjects take reading each portion on their first pass, how often they backtrack and where, and how long they spend rereading portions of the sentence.

By and large, there's a lot of overlap in the data gathered by these two methods—certainly enough that the self-paced reading task remains a viable, easy way to detect most robust garden path effects. But the finer detail of eye tracking can provide clues that might help distinguish between competing theories. For instance, as you'll see in Section 8.2, different theories make different predictions about the nature of the parser's initial analysis, as opposed to later revisions to that analysis. Some researchers have argued that first-pass reading times align neatly with the parser's first guesses, while backtracking, or regressive eye movements, are informative about later revision processes. It's doubtful that eye movement behavior lines up this cleanly with the inner workings of the sentence processing system, but the distinction between earlier versus later reading time can often add an extra dimension to the reading time profile.

Regardless of how they're collected, interpreting reading times is tricky, because the measure is somewhat of a blunt instrument. All kinds of factors can cause increases in reading times, not just misanalyzing the syntactic structure of the sentence. Reading times can be elevated because uncommon words are used, because the sentence depicts an unexpected event, because a low-frequency structure is used (regardless of ambiguity), or because the sentence is somehow unnatural in a particular context. Ideally, in order to be able to attribute long reading times to misanalysis, you want to—wherever possible—compare sentences that contain an ambiguity to *unambiguous* versions of the same sentences, with the same meaning, containing the same content words. This is a standard design feature of experiments that rely on reading times. Usually, each subject sees only one version of each sentence, so the second version cannot be predicted, and reading times across subjects are compared.

8.2 Models of Ambiguity Resolution

What's the big deal about garden path effects?

Some of the most passionate discussions in psycholinguistics (often referred to as the "parsing wars") have revolved around questions of ambiguity resolution and how to correctly explain garden path effects. Part of me would like to say that this passion was fueled by a burning desire to equip writers and editors with a definitive list of do's and don'ts of sentence construction—no doubt the skills of an entire generation of professional writers might improve as a result. But the reality is that researchers were mobilized into spending long hours (and indeed, many years) in studying ambiguity resolution because this area of psycholinguistics became the battleground for several "Big Ideas" in the field.

In order to work up to the Big Ideas, we have to start with a simple question: Why is it that *one* reading of an ambiguous string of words often seems to be so much more attractive than another? For instance, in the classic horse-racing example, why are we so tempted to read the sentence as a simple main clause, and why does it seem to be so hard to access the reduced relative clause reading? Notice that this kind of confusion is strikingly different from what happens in word recognition. Remember that with words, multiple candidates are usually activated in parallel, with competitors dropping off in activation over time until a winner remains standing. We don't ever seem to have the experience of hearing the syllable *can-* and committing *so* strongly to the word *candle* that we just can't seem to recover and recognize the word as *cantaloupe* once it's been fully uttered. But with full-blown garden path sentences, there's a strong

garden path theory A theory of parsing that claims that an initial "first-pass" structure is built during comprehension using a restricted amount of grammatical information and guided by certain parsing principles or tendencies, such as the tendency to build the simplest structure possible. Evaluations of plausible meanings or consideration of the context only come into play at a later stage of parsing.

early commitment to one particular structure, a strategy that sometimes leads to epic failure when this commitment turns out to be wrong. When faced with a syntactic ambiguity, why don't we just remain non-committal until there's enough information to help us decide on the right structure? This would avoid situations in which the interpretation eventually falls apart. What is it about the preferred structure that makes it so magnetic?

The garden path theory

Explanations for the existence of severe garden path effects have followed several very different approaches. One of the earliest accounts of these troublesome sentences is known as the **garden path theory** of parsing, proposed by Lyn Frazier and her colleagues (see Frazier & Fodor, 1978, for an earlier version; and Frazier & Clifton, 1996, for a reformulation). These researchers noticed that for a number of different types of garden path sentences, people seemed to be drawn toward a structure that was simpler than what turned out to be the correct structure. For example, if you look back in Figure 8.1 at the rendition of the sentence fragment *The horse raced past the barn*, it's evident that the more alluring structure—with its single clause and basic word order—is not as complex as the reduced relative clause, which involves a passive structure and two clauses. Frazier and her colleagues argued that a number of other garden path effects follow the same pattern (for example, look back at the sentence fragments diagrammed in Figure 8.2A). They proposed that when faced with an ambiguity between a simpler and a more complex structure, people have a strong preference for the simpler structure, and this causes an interpretation crash when the sentence reveals itself to be consistent only with the more complex structure.

Elaborating on this observation, Frazier and colleagues suggested that, rather than activating multiple meanings at once, as is the case in word recognition, the parser computes only one structure and its associated meaning. To justify why there are such different mechanisms for recognizing words and processing sentences, they argued that the two processes are really very different in nature. After all, one of them involves pulling pre-stored items out of memory while the other involves actual *computing*; new structures have to be built out of the stream of words coming in as input, not just matched up with items in memory. As you saw in Chapter 6, words can't just be assembled in any old way for a given language, but have to follow certain rules of syntax that specify the possible ways to group words into constituents—we might think of these syntactic rules as being like a set of very stringent building codes. So the parser has to consult these building codes and propose a way to group words into a sensible structure that meets their legal requirements. It's easy to imagine that all this computation might be fairly expensive in terms of processing resources. In order to be able to interpret sentences incrementally—as we've seen that people manage to do—the parser needs to build sentences very quickly. So to achieve this blazing speed, the parsing system builds whatever legal structure is easiest to build, and runs with it. If the whole thing runs aground at some later point, then a reanalysis of the sentence is initiated.

It may have crossed your mind, though, that there are other factors that could potentially affect how an ambiguous phrase is interpreted. For example, some interpretations might be more plausible than others, or fit in better with the preceding context. Wouldn't this information be taken into consideration while assembling the structure of a sentence? According to the garden path theory, no, not during the parser's first attempt at building structure. This may seem odd, since information about plausibility or contextual fit could be a great help in averting a parsing meltdown. Why would the parser ignore such useful information? This is where the Big Ideas come in.

On the face of it, a parsing system that disregards helpful information looks like a badly designed system, because it would result in a number of otherwise avoidable errors—it just seems needlessly dumb. But it's worth pointing out some intellectual historical context. At the time that psycholinguists began trying to explain how ambiguity resolution works, there was quite a bit of emphasis in cognitive psychology on the fact that sometimes, human information processing *does* appear to be a bit dumb. Evidently, we humans are saddled with certain inherent processing limitations. Intelligent, thoughtful analysis consumes a lot in the way of processing resources, and it takes a lot of time. In the 1970s and 1980s, it was becoming increasingly apparent to psychologists that because of our limitations, we can easily deplete the processing resources that are needed for solving some difficult cognitive problems. As a work-around, we often rely on cognitive processes that are fast and easy, but that fail to take into consideration all of the relevant information.

This notion had come to be a highly influential one. The work of well-known psychologists such as Amos Tversky and Daniel Kahneman (1974) had shown that in many situations, people rely on very quick but error-prone **heuristics**— that is, shallow but very fast information-processing shortcuts that often lead people to leap to "illogical" or incorrect conclusions based on very superficial cues. (As an example, consider this problem: The surface area of water lilies growing on a pond doubles every day. If it takes 24 days for the pond to be completely covered, in how many days is the pond half covered? If you answer 12, then you've fallen prey to a common heuristic.) Cognitive psychologists began talking about an important distinction between these fast, automatic, but often buggy processes, as opposed to slow, deliberate, but ultimately more accurate thought machinery. The scientific thinking evolved that an enormous amount of human cognition depends on the faster but dumber cognitive processes, and that we have a limited mental budget to spend on the more "intelligent" ones, which require considerably more effort and processing time. Such distinctions continue to be important ones in psychology to this day—you can find an accessible overview of this body of research in Daniel Kahneman's (2011) book *Thinking, Fast and Slow*.

The garden path theory is very consistent with this line of thinking, and represents one of several attempts to apply the ideas about fast versus slow cognition to problems in language processing. The idea is that the parsing system is able to conserve processing resources by relying on a set of quick and simple structure-building heuristics in its first guess at sentence structure. In this first pass, a great deal of information that *could* be pertinent to resolving the ambiguity is ignored, because this would take too much time and mental energy to integrate—in fact, if the parser did have to consider all potentially relevant information in the first-draft structure, doing so might strain memory capacity beyond the breaking point. All things considered, a fast-and-cheap solution may be the best strategy, even if it does result in frequent errors—if an error is detected, a deeper analysis of the sentence is triggered.

If you've worked your way through the Digging Deeper discussion in Chapter 7, this theoretical approach should seem very familiar to you. There, I discussed the tension between *modular* and *interactive* models of word recognition. In a modular system, "higher-level" information doesn't have a direct effect on "lower-level" processes. Instead, it comes into play at a later stage, once the lower-level processes have been completed. For example, in a modular model of word recognition, information about the context or lexical knowledge can't affect the activation levels of individual sounds; it can only help decide which

heuristics Shallow but very fast information-processing shortcuts that often lead to incorrect conclusions based on superficial cues.

sounds are most appropriate, based on how activated they are on the basis of the bottom-up input. In an interactive model, on the other hand, information from the higher levels can flow from the top down to affect the activation of sounds.

When it comes to parsing, the garden path model is an instantiation of a modular system. Structures are initially built by a lean, fast parser on the basis of a very limited amount of purely syntactic information, and entirely without the benefit of semantic knowledge or knowledge about the context of the sentence. Once a partial structure is built, it gets sent off to the higher-level semantic interpretation component, which then evaluates its sensibleness. But no information about the *meaning* of the sentence fragment to that point can influence the parser's first stab at structure-building. For some researchers, the division between syntactic and semantic knowledge could be seen as a division between fast, automatic mental processes and slow, thoughtful ones, with semantic information lagging behind syntactic processes (and sometimes cleaning up some messes in interpretation). This distinction was discussed in quite a lot of detail by the philosopher Jerry Fodor in his well-known book *The Modularity of Mind* (1983).

In Chapter 7, I suggested a metaphor for thinking about the distinction between modular and interactive systems: A highly modular system is structured like a company or factory in which lower-level employees do their jobs with very limited knowledge and responsibilities, and then simply pass on their work to higher-level workers who later make all the important decisions. On the other hand, an interactive system is more like a company in which all levels of workers have a shared stake in making decisions, with information flowing freely from upper to lower levels. As in business, the competing models offer different advantages: the first option may be fast and cheap, but lacks a certain flexibility (which you may have experienced, if you've ever asked a customer service representative to deal with a problem outside of his area of expertise). The second option is "smarter" in some ways, but maybe not so cost-effective on a large scale.

The constraint-based approach

In the garden path model, because the parser initially spits out a single preferred structure in the face of ambiguity, it's expected that people will often run into an interpretive dead end, and be forced to reconsider the sentence's meaning; this is an unavoidable by-product of the parser's efficiency. But quite a few researchers have argued that the parser actually shows a lot more subtlety and intelligence in its initial analysis than the garden path model is willing to give it credit for. The core of the argument is that in reality people experience much less confusion in processing sentences than you'd expect if they were blindly computing the "preferred" structure without considering other potentially helpful information.

According to the early version of the garden path account, the parser only looks at the syntactic categories of words, and how they might be assembled according to the language's syntactic building codes, all while following certain preferred building routines. But in that case, *all* sentences that make use of *dispreferred* structures (where more favored, or preferred, ones are available for the same string of words) should be *equally* likely to lead to a garden path effect because the wrong structure is initially built. But this doesn't seem right. For example, compare these two sentences:

The dog walked to the park wagged its tail happily.

The treasure buried in the sand was never found.

Both sentences involve reduced relative clauses. Most people find the first far more difficult to interpret than the second (if your own parser has become benumbed to the distinction as a result of reading too many garden path sentences in the last half hour, try them out on a fresh reader). This became one of the key arguments against the garden path theory, as dissenting researchers began to look for evidence that similar structures resulted in extremely variable garden path effects. One of the key pieces of evidence that such dissenters hoped to find was data showing that some sentences that are saddled with dispreferred structures, such as reduced relative clauses, don't show any measurable garden path effects at all—for example, if we compared the following two sentences, we might not find any difference in reading times for the region marked in bold:

The treasure buried in the sand **was lost forever**.

The treasure that was buried in the sand **was lost forever**.

This would suggest that in the first sentence of the pair, which begins with a potentially ambiguous string of words, readers don't seem to have been misled by the other (supposedly preferred) interpretation, and interpretation goes as smoothly in reading the final portion of the text as if there had been no ambiguity at all.

In one influential paper, researchers led by Maryellen MacDonald (1994) used a witty expository device to make the point that reduced relative clauses don't always cause interpretive snarls. They pulled out many examples of reduced relative clauses from the writings of various psycholinguists, some of whose theories in fact *did* predict that such structures would invariably cause garden path effects. Some of these examples are reproduced in **Box 8.2**, along with a few other examples I dug up myself from various sources.

The main competitor to the garden path theory was the **constraint-based approach**. It parted ways with the garden path account on a number of points. First, constraint-based theorists argued that a broad range of information sources (or constraints) could *simultaneously* affect the parser's early decisions, including semantic or contextual information, which was often thought of as being too subtle or slow to drive initial parsing (specific constraints will be discussed in detail in Section 8.3). Parsing speed, they argued, is not necessarily bought at the expense of subtlety or intelligence in processing. As a result, only a very small percentage of temporary ambiguities might cause any discernible processing difficulties.

Second, they argued that syntactic ambiguity resolution actually looks very much like ambiguity resolution in word recognition. In both cases, multiple interpretations are accessed in parallel, and our minds very quickly try to judge which one is more likely to be correct, based on very partial linguistic evidence along with various sources of information—such as context, or statistical frequencies—that make one interpretation seem more likely to be the right one. These sources of information (or constraints) can serve to either ramp up or suppress the activation of one interpretation relative to the other.

So why does it often seem that we consider only *one* interpretation of a sentence, with the other seeming to be completely inaccessible? The response of constraint-based theorists was that flagrant garden path effects are in fact the results of an unfortunate coincidence: the various sources of information that are available in the ambiguous portion of the sentence just happen to *overwhelmingly* point to the wrong interpretation, causing the parser to suppress the competing correct one, much as a lexical competitor is suppressed over time. By the time readers or hearers get to the disambiguating region, it's too late—they've already pushed the eventually correct alternative beyond accessibility.

constraint-based approach The main competitor to the garden path theory, this approach claims that multiple interpretations of an ambiguous structure are simultaneously evaluated against a broad range of information sources (or constraints) that can affect the parser's early decisions.

BOX 8.2
Not all reduced relatives lead to processing implosions

We've seen how a relative clause like *the horse [that was raced past the barn]* can become ambiguous and potentially impede sentence processing when the clause is "reduced" by removing function words (becoming *the horse raced past the barn*). But are such reduced relatives always a problem for the person processing them?

Maryellen MacDonald and her colleagues (1994) discovered examples of reduced relative clauses in the writings of various psycholinguists, many of whom were proponents of theories predicting that reduced relatives invariably lead to garden path effects. MacDonald's point was not that these psycholinguists are bad writers, oblivious to the fact that their sentences might cause readers to stumble, but (more damningly) that their *theories* are flawed, since these sentences seem to pose no real burden for readers. Here's a sampling of the sentences unearthed by MacDonald et al., with the reduced relative clauses in color type (color was added for this textbook, not by the authors of the original papers):

> Thus, a noun phrase followed by a morphologically ambiguous verb (e.g., "The defendant examined") will be temporarily ambiguous.

Trueswell, Tanenhaus & Garnsey, 1994, p. 287

> Referential information provided by the discourse is of no help.

Britt, Perfetti, Garrod & Rayner, 1992, p. 305

> Recent research reported by Ferreira and Clifton (1986) has demonstrated that syntactic processing is quite independent and that the initial syntactic analysis assigned to a sentence is little influenced by the semantic information already analyzed.

Frazier & Rayner, 1987, pp. 520–521

In all cases, the examples cited here were not the only reduced relatives in these articles.

MacDonald et al., 1994, p. 678

Of course, the use of reduced relatives is not limited to academic writers. Here are some examples I discovered among the wilds of the popular print media:

> The reward money offered to find Jyrine, a helpless toddler, was a paltry $1,000.

"What happened to my child?" *Essence*, September 2007, p. 224

> The food prepared for the now non-existent media event is donated to homeless shelters.

"911 Coverage of Sept. 11 attacks overshadowed a world of events," *Denver Post*, October 11, 2001

Of the two reduced relatives in the following example, only the first one (italicized) is potentially ambiguous. Neither seems to pose any difficulty for processing:

> … many Western Europeans believe that a job *offered to an older worker* is a slot taken away from a younger one.

Foreign Affairs, May/June 2007, p. 55

This final, lovely example has one reduced relative clause nested inside another (the embedded clause is italicized):

> … many Russian politicians influenced by more than 40 years of communist propaganda *aimed against the west* finally became good "Homo Sovieticus."

Letter to the editor, *San Francisco Chronicle*, June 6, 1995

In other words, the idea is that a sentence like *The horse raced past the barn fell* starts out activating both interpretations, but since all the available constraints in the ambiguous region are heavily biased toward the simple main clause, the reduced relative reading is too weak to ever become a serious candidate and becomes deactivated. On the other hand, things are a bit different in an easier sentence like *The treasure buried in the sand was never found*. In this case, the constraints are more equivocal, creating a more even balance between the two alternatives. When the disambiguating region is reached, the new information in that region provides the decisive evidence between the alternative meanings (both of which are still active), and readers end up settling on the correct meaning without too much difficulty.

This is really a dramatically different view of the nature of ambiguity effects than the one offered by the garden path model. For the garden path account, comprehension mishaps arise because the inherent limitations on human cognition force the parser to make decisions about structure without considering all the evidence, so these decisions will often be wrong. For the constraint-based model, the parser *has* considered all the evidence and has made a rational prediction based on prior experience with language—it's just that in some cases, the outcome turns out to fly in the face of all reasonable predictions.

Let's turn to testing the predictions made by each model. As I've mentioned, the garden path account predicts that the parser will crash whenever it's forced to build a structure that falls outside of the preferred structure-building routines—it will always build the wrong one first. But the constraint-based account says that garden path effects will be highly variable, even for the so-called dispreferred structures. Processing difficulty may range from devastating to non-existent, depending on the specific words that appear in those structures, or even the specific context of the sentence. This is because the extent to which one reading over another will be favored should depend on the biasing strength of *all* the constraining sources of information together, of which general structural information is but one source. For the garden path theory, only structure should determine the presence of a garden path effect, since this is the only source of information that's considered in the early phases of parsing. Garden path effects, then, should be impervious to other sources of information.

To evaluate the predictions of the garden path and constraint-based theories more concretely, let's look more closely at the varied bouquet of information sources that bear on the resolution of syntactic ambiguity.

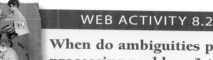

WEB ACTIVITY 8.2

When do ambiguities pose processing problems? In this activity, you'll see a number of examples of temporary ambiguities. You'll informally gauge the difficulty of each example—does the degree of processing difficulty seem variable, even for structurally similar sentences? You'll be prompted for potential explanations for your intuitions.

8.3 Variables That Predict the Difficulty of Ambiguous Sentences

Thematic relations associated with verbs

Part of our inherent knowledge of the meanings of verbs involves knowing what kinds of events they describe, including how many and what kinds of participants must be involved, and what roles the various participants play. This is often referred to as knowledge of **thematic relations**. For example, when we hear the verb *bite*, we know that a biting event involves at least two participants—the biter and the bitee. We also know that the biter must be an animate entity in possession of teeth and the ability to close those teeth around something. The bitee, on the other hand, could be another animate entity, or an inanimate object; you can bite your brother, but you can also bite your brother's finger or a piece of toast. A parser that had access to this semantic information (as predicted by the constraint-based account) could make much smarter guesses about the likely structure of ambiguous word strings in at least some cases.

Consider a sentence like *The treasure buried in the sand was lost forever*. The verb *bury* involves at least two participants, one doing the burying, and one being buried. But treasure is a terrible fit as the participant doing the burying. So, as soon as the reader gets to *The treasure buried…*, there's semantic pressure to shift to the alternative reduced relative clause reading, in which the treasure is the entity *being* buried rather than the one doing the burying. This means the reader is less likely to be led down the garden path to an interpretation that later blows up.

thematic relations   Knowledge about verbs that captures information about the events they describe, including how many and what kinds of participants are involved in the events, and the roles the various participants play.

But thematic relations aren't quite as helpful in a sentence like *The dog walked to the park wagged its tail happily.* Ultimately, the right interpretation of the sentence refers to an event in which two participants are involved—the dog and the implicit, unmentioned dog walker. Since a passive clause is involved, the dog in this event is the walkee rather than the walker (see Box 8.1 for a primer on passive structures). But when the verb *walk* appears in an active main clause, it also allows walking events in which there is just one participant doing the walking—this participant must have functioning legs and be capable of locomotion. As it happens, the noun *dog* fits perfectly nicely with this requirement, leading to a very plausible interpretation of the ambiguous region of the sentence as a simple main clause in the active voice. Unfortunately, this interpretation turns out to be wrong.

The constraint-based model predicts that when information from thematic relations is strong enough to steer people away from the normally dominant reading of a structure, it should diminish or eliminate a garden path effect, as measured using reading times. In fact, this is what a number of studies have found (e.g., Trueswell et al., 1994).

The syntactic frames of verbs

In Chapter 6, we spent a fair bit of time talking about how individual verbs in English select for specific syntactic frames, and how children have to learn these facts in addition to the general phrase structure rules of their language. You can't just put any verb into a generic verb slot in a sentence structure and expect things to turn out well. Hence, the ungrammaticality of:

> *The soldier buried.

> *Alice fell the ball.

> *Samantha sneezed that Billy was in prison.

> *The mom put the cookies.

> *The mom put the cookies about the jar.

> *Frank said the report.

Some verbs, like *fall*, have to be **intransitive verbs**, with just a subject and no direct object. Some (for example, *buried*) are **transitive verbs**, with a subject and a direct object (a direct object is a noun phrase that denotes one of the participants in the event described by the verb and appears immediately after the verb with no intervening preposition). Some (for example, *put*) are **ditransitive verbs**, calling for both a direct object and an indirect object (which may be introduced by a preposition). Finally, some (like *said*) are **sentential complement verbs**, which introduce a clause rather than a direct object noun phrase. (See **Table 8.1** for some additional examples.)

The garden path model (at least in its original incarnation) claims that all the parser cares about in its first pass is a verb's status as a verb, leaving aside these fancy details about syntactic frames. But constraint-based advocates have countered that the parser has access very early on to information about the syntactic frames that are linked with specific verbs. Access to such information would lead to much "smarter" parsing decisions. Notice that *walk* is allowed to appear with or without a direct object, whereas *bury* absolutely can't get by without one:

> Raj walked his dog to the park.

> The dog walked.

> The dog walked to the park.

intransitive verbs Verbs that occur with a subject but no direct object.

transitive verbs Verbs that take both a subject and a direct object.

ditransitive verbs Verbs that occur with a direct object and an indirect object (which may be introduced by a preposition).

sentential complement verbs Verbs that introduce a clause rather than a direct object noun phrase (NP).

TABLE 8.1 A variety of syntactic frames for verbs

Intransitive verbs (*appear with a subject only*)

The neighbors' dog reeks.

Gerhardt finally relaxed.

Mariah sings beautifully.

The magician vanishes.

The tornado touched down last night.

Transitive verbs (*select for a direct object noun phrase*)

This theory vexes me.

I rarely wear socks.

The author signed his book.

The queen poisoned the courtesan.

The engineer inspected the plans.

Ditransitive verbs (*select for two noun phrases, one of which may appear inside a prepositional phrase*)

Please lend me the money.

Parents should send their teens to boarding school.

Devon presented his fiancée with a ring.

Frances hid the affair from her husband.

The teacher tossed Alisha the ball.

Sentential complement verbs (*select for a clausal unit*)

The workers complained that their bosses harassed them.

I agree that the king should be deposed.

The president assumed his staff would cover his mistake.

The contract stipulated that employees should be paid weekly.

The teacher regretted that she had promised the kids a dollar for every book they read.

Verbs that fall into more than one category[a]

NP-bias verbs: e.g., accept, repeat, advocate, maintain, reveal, print

S-bias verbs: e.g., conclude, decide, promise, worry, prove

[a]Many verbs fall into more than one of the four categories, but may occur much more often in one syntactic frame than another. The verbs given as examples here can appear with either a sentential complement (S) or a direct object noun phrase (NP), but have a bias for one or the other. Try constructing sentences with both kinds of frames for each verb.

The soldier buried the land mine.

*The pirate buried.

*The pirate buried in the sand.

Based on this knowledge, on getting *The treasure buried in the…*, the parser would be able to avoid the normally seductive main clause reading, since this reading lacks the obligatory direct object that *bury* demands. This would leave as viable the reduced relative clause interpretation, in which the syntactic process of passive formation has taken the direct object *the treasure* and stuck it into the subject position of the correct structure.

There's a fair bit of experimental evidence showing that knowledge of syntactic frames plays a central role in ambiguity resolution. What's more, this knowledge about syntactic frames is fairly nuanced, not just limited to what's grammatical or not, but also tuned in to which syntactic frame is most *statistically likely* for a given verb. An especially ingenious case study showing effects of syntactic frame probabilities is presented in **Box 8.3**.

Frequency-based information

So far, we've been talking about syntactic versus lexical ambiguity as if it were easy to sort ambiguous examples into one bin or the other. And sometimes,

BOX 8.3
Subliminal priming of a verb's syntactic frame

If you work at it, you can develop a reasonable set of intuitions about how sentence processing works by noticing which sentences are difficult, why, and how to make them less so. Nonetheless, there's a limit to how much conscious access we're able to have to the internal workings of our parsers—which is one reason why psycholinguists need to design clever experiments in order for us to truly understand the complex nature of building sentences on the fly.

In fact, one such clever study by John Trueswell and Al Kim (1998) illustrates just how much of our sentence processing can be hidden from consciousness, while at the same time exploring how it all works. The researchers took as their starting point evidence from other studies showing that specific verbs could be biased toward certain syntactic frames, and that these biases in turn could influence the interpretation of garden path sentences. For example, the verbs *accept* and *realize* both allow either a direct object NP or a sentential complement, but *accept* is biased toward the direct object frame while *realize* is biased toward the sentential complement frame. Hence, the two verbs set up very different expectations for how the following ambiguous fragments should continue:

The photographer accepted the ...

The photographer realized the ...

So if the first fragment perversely continues with a sentential complement as below, contrary to the bias of the verb *accept*, this results in a garden path effect in the disambiguating region (in color):

The photographer *accepted* the fire could not be put out.

However the same region is read more quickly if it follows the verb *realized*:

The photographer *realized* the fire could not be put out.

Taking these facts as background, Trueswell and Kim noted that information about syntactic frames is part of the lexical information associated with a word, much as the meaning of a word has to be linked to that specific lexical entry. Given that words can prime related meanings (so seeing *tiger* boosts the activation of the related word *lion*), they wondered whether it's also possible for verbs to boost the accessibility of syntactic frames associated with other words. That is, can seeing *realize* boost the accessibility of the sentential complement frame for *accept*, with the result that readers will be less likely to experience confusion in the problematic example shown above?

To find out, Trueswell and Kim had subjects perform a self-paced reading task on sentences containing potential ambiguity, as in *The photographer accepted the fire could not be put out*. But just as subjects pressed a button right after reading *photographer*, and before they saw the verb *accepted*, a "priming" verb flashed subliminally on the screen for 39 milliseconds—subjects consciously experienced this merely as a brief flicker that happened just before *accepted* was displayed. Half of the time, the priming verb favored a direct object NP frame (for example, *obtained*), while the other half of the time, the priming verb was biased toward a sentential complement frame (*realized*). It turned out that the identity of the secret priming verb shifted the expectations for the syntactic frame, even though the overtly visible verb (*accepted*) stayed the same in both conditions: Subjects spent less time reading the disambiguating region when they'd "seen" *realized* than when they'd "seen" *obtained*. It would appear that the syntactic frame bias associated with one verb can become activated and spread to another verb, in turn influencing the parser's expectations about structure—and that all this can happen without the reader becoming aware of it.

structurally ambiguous word strings really do come down purely to syntax; for example, in a classic attachment ambiguity, such as *I saw an elephant in my pajamas*, it's really just a matter of how the words get grouped together—the meanings and syntactic categories of the words themselves are identical under both readings. But that's not true for all ambiguities, as you might have noticed from Figure 8.2. For instance, where do you sort a sentence like *The government plans to raise taxes were defeated*? Here, the syntactic ambiguity hinges entirely on whether *plans* is taken to be a noun or a verb, and how this *word* is interpreted ultimately drives how the sentence can be structured.

Actually, it's also possible to think of the famous reduced relative clause ambiguity as similarly boiling down to a lexical ambiguity, though a somewhat more subtle one. For a sentence like *The horse raced past the barn fell*, it comes down to how we interpret the word *raced*. Now, with the way I've drawn the tree structures in Figure 8.1, *raced* simply has the syntactic category of verb whether it appears in the main clause or the reduced relative clause reading. But a closer look shows that these *two* verbs are not interchangeable, and are composed of different parts. In the main clause reading, *raced* is a garden-variety example of a verb stem plus a past-tense morpheme. But in the reduced relative clause reading, the verb stem is joined by a past-participle morpheme, not a past-tense morpheme. Unfortunately, for regular verbs of English, these two morphemes look exactly the same—they are homophones, just like the words *bank* and *bank*. Note, for example, that the same form shows up in all of these syntactic environments: *I raced, I have raced, The car was raced*. But you can infer that past-tense verbs are different from past participles by looking at many *irregular* verbs, in which the two types show up in different forms, and appear in different syntactic environments, at least in standard varieties of English (for example: *I drove* but not **I have drove* or **The car was drove by my brother; I have driven*, or *The car was driven*, but not **I driven home*). As a result, when certain *irregular* verbs appear in reduced relative clauses (see the examples below), the italicized portions of these sentences contain no ambiguity whatsoever, even though they have exactly the same syntactic structure as some of the fiercely confusing garden path sentences we've seen:

> *The horse rode past the barn* and fell.
> *The horse ridden past the barn* fell.
>
> *The students gave high marks* to their instructor.
> *The students given high marks* liked their instructor.
>
> *Wheat grew in the Midwest* and was exported in large quantities.
> *Wheat grown in the Midwest* was exported in large quantities.

The idea that many syntactic ambiguities have their roots in lexical ambiguity is a provocative one, because it suggests that perhaps syntactic and lexical processing are not so distinct after all, as suggested by a number of constraint-based theorists. At the very least, factors that influence the interpretation of ambiguous words should have a visible impact on the interpretation of some syntactic ambiguities.

This is the case made by Maryellen MacDonald and her colleagues (1994). They argued that when we look at word-based ambiguity (say, the two meanings of *bank*, or the noun-versus-verb readings of *plan*), we see that the more frequent readings become activated most strongly. This is the pattern that shows up in standard word recognition tasks. If that's so, they argued, shouldn't the relative frequencies of lexical alternatives also play a role in situations where a syntactic ambiguity hinges on a lexical ambiguity? If *plans* is more frequent as a verb than as a noun, shouldn't this make it easier to build the structure that's consistent with the verb reading, since the verb representation will be the more strongly activated one? The same argument can be made for reduced relative clauses that contain past participles. As it happens, some verbs (such as *entertained*) rarely show up as past participles, whereas others (such as *accused*) more commonly do. Thus, we might expect *entertained* to lead to a much stronger bias for the main clause interpretation than *accused*, resulting in a bulkier garden path effect for the first than for the second of these two sentences:

> The audience entertained at the gala left in high spirits.

> The suspect accused at the crime scene was soon released.

Several researchers (e.g., Trueswell, 1996; MacDonald et al., 1994) have indeed found that the severity of garden path effects for reduced relative clauses is affected by the frequency of past-tense/past-participle readings of ambiguous verb forms. So the outcomes of word recognition processes have a way of leaking into syntactic ambiguity resolution.

We can push the idea of frequency bias a bit further. It seems natural that, when encountering an ambiguous word that could have either Meaning A or Meaning B, the more frequent meaning would be easier to pull out of memory, because it will have left a stronger trace in memory. But even though sentences are *built* rather than pulled from memory, it still stands to reason that more common structures would be easier to build than less common ones, just as a building crew would be more efficient in building a house from a plan that they've used many times before than from one that they've used less frequently. Could some portion of garden path effects be due to different frequencies of use of the alternative structures? For example, are reduced relative sentences so hard in part because their structure is much less common in English than the competing structure of simple past-tense main clause?

Models that factor in how frequently competing structures are used do often seem to give better results than ones that leave this source of information out. To ask this question more directly, though, we can compare similar structures across languages that happen to have different patterns of frequency for these structures. Take the following sentence:

> Someone shot the maid of the actress who was standing on the
> balcony with her husband.

Who was standing on the balcony with her husband? Most English speakers say it was the actress, preferring to attach the relative clause to the nearby noun. But a funny thing happens when the sentence is translated almost word for word into Spanish:

> *Alguien disparó contra la criada de la actriz que estaba en el balcón con*
> *su marido.*

The majority of Spanish speakers say that it was the maid who was on the balcony with her husband. This is interesting because, as it happens, relative clauses in Spanish attach more frequently to the first of two nouns, while the reverse is true in English. English and Spanish readers, then, seem to be resolving the ambiguity in a way that reflects their personal experience with these structures (Mitchell & Cuetos, 1991).

The importance of context

Let's return to that famous racing horse, and the ugly sentence in which it appears. What happens when the sentence shows up in a story like this:

> Farmer Bill and Farmer John were racing their horses through the field. Farmer Bill rode his horse along the fence, while Farmer John raced his horse past the barn. Suddenly, the horse raced past the barn fell.

Does the last sentence of the story suddenly seem less difficult? If so, why would that be?

Several researchers (e.g., Crain & Steedman, 1985; Altmann & Steedman, 1988) have pointed out that attaching a modifier phrase (such as a relative clause or a prepositional phrase) usually only makes sense when that modifier is needed to pick out one of two or more similar entities—here, to distinguish between two horses. In this story, when the final sentence is encountered, there's pressure to interpret the phrase *raced past the barn* as providing some more information about the horse; without this modifier, the simple noun phrase *the horse* wouldn't provide enough information to distinguish between the two horses, leading to confusion about which one was being referred to. But in a scenario that doesn't involve two horses—for instance, in a story about a single horse, or an out-of-the-blue sentence where the presence of two horses hasn't been established—the use of the modifier is unnatural. Speakers and writers don't generally go around providing extra, unnecessary information in the form of a modifier phrase. Without the proper contextual support for relative clause reading, readers will be more likely to default to the alternative main clause reading.

Reading time studies have shown that the right context can reduce or eliminate garden path effects, even for complex structures such as a reduced relative clause (e.g., Spivey-Knowlton et al., 1993). But the effects of context have been seen most vividly in studies of spoken language in which a visually present context provides a strong constraint for interpretation. In these experiments, researchers have used evidence from eye movements to infer the interpretations that are unfolding in the minds of listeners as they listen to ambiguous language.

As you've seen in Chapter 7, when people look at a visual scene while listening to spoken language, they try to relate the scene in front of them to what they're hearing. Since people look at images that correspond to the words they think they're hearing, this makes it possible to track eye movements to the visual scene as a way of inferring which word(s) they're activating based on spoken input. It takes a bit more ingenuity, but it's also possible to set up visual displays to test between competing syntactic interpretations, as demonstrated by Michael Tanenhaus and his colleagues (1995). For example, look at the scene in **Figure 8.3A** and imagine hearing an instruction like, "Put the apple on the towel into the box."

Where do you think you'd be looking at various points in the sentence? Naturally, upon hearing *apple*, people tend to look at the only apple in the display. But when they hear *towel*, there are now two possibilities. Which towel should they look at? It depends on which sentence structure they're entertaining. If they've attached *on the towel* directly to the verb phrase, they'll interpret the instruction as meaning they should pick up the apple and place it on the empty towel since it makes no sense to put the apple on the towel that it's currently sit-

(A)

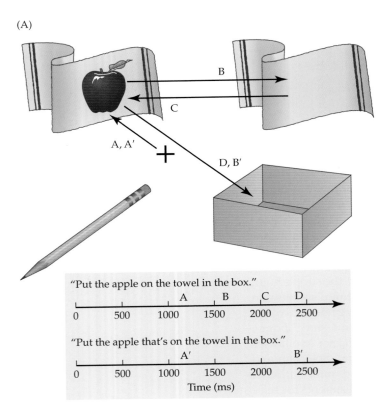

Figure 8.3 Visual displays and eye movement patterns used in the 1995 study by Tanenhaus et al. (A) Visual display with only one referent corresponding to the word *apple*. Letters indicate the typical sequence of eye movements and their timing relative to the spoken instruction. (A′ and B′ correspond to the unambiguous version of the instruction.) (B) Visual display with two referents corresponding to *apple*. Note that for this display, the sequence and timing of typical eye movements (relative to critical words in the speech stream) are the same, regardless of whether the instruction was ambiguous or unambiguous. (Adapted from Tanenhaus et al., 1995.)

(B)

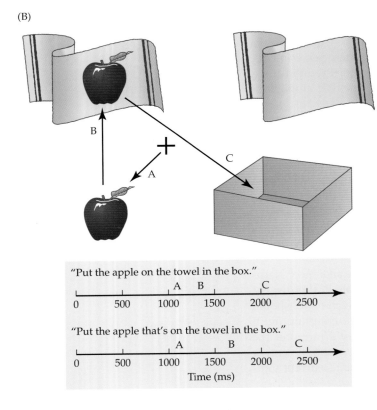

ting on. Of course, they'll hit trouble when they get to *into the box*, since they'll already have interpreted the empty towel as the intended destination. On the other hand, if they've attached *on the towel* to the noun *apple* (specifying *which* apple should be moved), then they'll continue looking in the upper left square, which contains the object that corresponds to this noun phrase. They'll then have no trouble integrating *into the box*, since they're still waiting at this point to hear the destination phrase that will attach to the verb phrase. Critically, there should be no need to look at the empty towel, since this object is irrelevant for carrying out the instruction as understood. In other words, it's possible to use eye movements to the irrelevant towel as evidence of a garden path interpretation.

And evidence for a garden path is exactly what you see when the ambiguous sentence *Put the apple on the towel into the box* is compared with its unambiguous version *Put the apple that's on the towel into the box*. In the ambiguous version, people look at the irrelevant towel more often than in the unambiguous version (see Figure 8.3A).

This method turns out to be especially sensitive to the effects of context, particularly if that context can be set up visually so that hearers don't have to hold it in memory, as they might with a story context. Remember that attaching extra information to the noun is most natural in a situation where it's needed to distinguish between more than one similar entity. It's perfectly easy to visually set up just such a context, as shown in **Figure 8.3B**, where there are now two apples in the scene, only one of which is on a towel. In this visual context, when subjects hear *Put the apple on the towel*, there's a strong incentive to interpret the phrase *on the towel* as specifying which of the two apples is to be moved.

As it happens, the effects of the visual context are powerful; when faced with a scene like the one in Figure 8.3B, upon hearing *Put the apple on the towel into the box*, subjects very rarely look at the empty towel—no

(A)

(B)

(C)

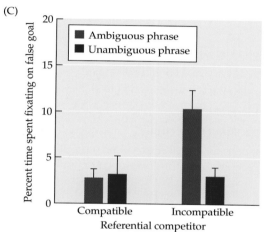

Figure 8.4 Sample visual displays and eye movement data from Chambers et al. (A) Display in which both referents corresponding to *egg* are compatible with the action described in the instruction "Pour the egg in the bowl over the flour." (B) The second referent corresponding to *egg* (i.e., a hard-boiled egg) is incompatible with the instruction. (C) The study's results show that when the second referent is incompatible with the action, participants are less likely to interpret the phrase *in the bowl* as helpfully distinguishing between the two potential referents; instead, they interpret the ambiguous phrase as referring to the goal location, as evident by the increased amount of time spent looking at the false goal (the empty bowl). (Adapted from Chambers et al., 2004.)

more so, in fact, than when they hear the unambiguous version of the instruction. Hence, the eye movement record shows no evidence of a garden path interpretation when the context is appropriate to the normally less preferred structure.

Even more subtle effects of context have been demonstrated by Craig Chambers and his colleagues (2004). In their experiment, they set up displays such as those illustrated in **Figure 8.4**, simulating a cooking environment in which objects needed to be manipulated according to spoken instructions such as, "Pour the egg in the bowl over the flour" (or its unambiguous counterpart, "Pour the egg that's in the bowl over the flour"). You'll notice that in both versions of the visual display, there are two eggs, so the phrase *in the bowl* is potentially helpful in identifying which of the two eggs is the target of the instruction. However, in Figure 8.4B (unlike in Figure 8.4A) the display contains only one egg in liquid form that could possibly be poured—the other egg is still inside its shell. Hence, upon hearing *Pour the egg*, the subject might infer that since the action could only target one of the eggs, there's no need for additional information to specify which of the eggs is under discussion. If hearers are indeed making these inferences based on the visual context, then they might be tempted to misinterpret the ambiguously attached phrase *in the bowl* as designating the location where the egg is to be poured, rather than as further information about the targeted egg. Such an interpretation would be revealed in increased glances to the empty bowl, the "false goal" in the display. In fact, Chambers and his colleagues showed that just such a garden path effect did emerge in the visual displays with a single pourable

BOX 8.4
Doesn't intonation disambiguate spoken language?

Many people assume that in spoken language, unlike in written language, true ambiguity simply doesn't arise; the belief is that while a string of words may be ambiguous, the *way that you say those words* will be different depending on your intended meaning, allowing your hearer to avert any possible misinterpretation. And in many cases, this is true. For example, I'm sure that you can come up with six or seven different ways to utter the word *really*, each of them clearly communicating something different from the others.

But let's look at the issue a little bit more carefully in the context of the garden path sentences that we've come to know and love. Here, the situation is a bit different from your ability to clarify your intended use of the word *really*—in that case, intonation was serving to signal a *general* communicative purpose such as asking a question, expressing incredulity or emphasis, or indicating doubt. In the case of garden path sentences, though, intonation is being asked to signal one *structure* rather than another. Under what conditions would it be possible for intonation to disambiguate structure? (Actually, it would be more accurate to talk about the disambiguating potential of **prosody**, a notion that includes intonation, but also rhythmic aspects of speech such as pausing and lengthening of sounds.)

One possibility might be that particular sentence

structures match up with specific prosodic patterns in a one-to-one fashion. But this turns out not to be true. The relationship between syntax and prosody is much more slippery than this. There's a general tendency, for example, to insert pauses or stretch out the last syllable of a phrase just before the boundary between major constituents (you saw evidence of this in Language at Large 6.1, in our discussion of constituents in literary language). For example, ambiguities that revolve around whether a clause is to end or to continue lend themselves especially well to prosodic disambiguation. Consider the following ambiguous fragment:

While the pop star sang the national anthem…

which, as you've seen, could continue like this:

… played in the background

or it could continue like this:

… the people stood respectfully

In the first continuation, the desire to insert a pause is very strong, in keeping with the convention of inserting a comma:

---

prosody The rhythm, stress, and intonation of a spoken phrase or sentence.

---

egg (see Figure 8.4C). However, when two pourable eggs appeared in the display, there was no evidence of misinterpretation, with eye movements being similar for both the ambiguous and unambiguous versions of the instruction. This shows an impressive ability to closely integrate the incoming stream of speech with detailed aspects of the visual context. Contrary to the predictions of the garden path model, people seem to be able to recruit context quickly enough to avert garden path effects for a number of syntactic ambiguities.

You might be inclined to wonder just how often the need for such context-sensitive inferences arises in actual spoken language. After all, isn't it true that we can communicate our intended meaning through intonation, even when a given string of words has more than one meaning? This is a common intuition, but while intonation can sometimes help to disambiguate speech, it certainly doesn't sweep away all or even most potential ambiguities (see **Box 8.4**). Rather, intonation seems to be just one more useful cue among many that we can use intelligently to help us untangle strings of words and their many potential meanings.

WEB ACTIVITY 8.3

Create and recognize "easy" versus "hard" ambiguous sentences In this activity, you'll be guided through a series of steps in which you'll generate sentences that contain a potential temporary ambiguity. Some of these will be likely to cause very severe garden path effects, while others will be likely to cause only minimal disruption. You'll hone your editorial instincts and learn to recognize the potentially troublesome sentences.

BOX 8.4 *(continued)*

While the pop star sang, the national anthem played in the background.

But boundaries between constituents that are smaller than clauses are marked with much subtler prosody—and in fact, whether or not they're marked at all can depend on factors such as the length of the phrases that are involved, so you'd be more likely to mark the boundary here:

The patient told the doctor [s that he was having some ongoing trouble with his injured knee].

than here:

The patient told the doctor [s that he smoked].

But even if prosodic patterns don't match up neatly with syntactic structures, it's still possible that speakers would choose to use cues like pauses and syllable lengthening as a courtesy to the hearer, in order to mark the correct way in which the words should be grouped into constituents. This, too, turns out to be not quite true. A number of studies have shown that speakers fail to reliably disambiguate speech for their hearers. For example, David Allbritton and his colleagues (1996) recorded the speech of trained actors as well as psychology undergraduates while they read sentences aloud, and found that *neither* group spontaneously disambiguated sentence structure through prosody. When instructed, the actors at least were able to use prosody to signal their intended meaning, but only when both meanings of the ambiguous sentence were presented to them side by side. This finding is consistent with a number of other similar experiments.

Things get a bit better when speakers and hearers are involved in an interactive task such as a game in which the speaker instructs the hearer to move objects around on a board. For example, Amy Schafer and her colleagues (2000) found that under these circumstances, when speakers became aware of their partners' misinterpretations, they did use prosody somewhat consistently to disambiguate their instructions. But overall, the evidence suggests that in many linguistic settings, it's quite difficult for speakers to anticipate ambiguities that will prove difficult for their hearers and to be helpful in the prosodic patterns that they produce.

Still, some systematic alignment between syntax and prosody does occur, probably as a by-product of the processes that are involved in planning and uttering speech, as you'll see in Chapter 9. Prosody is more helpful for some structures than for others, but there's enough information there to be of some use to hearers for the purposes of disambiguation, as demonstrated by Tanya Kraljic and Susan Brennan (2005). So, while prosody certainly doesn't render spoken language unambiguous, hearers can use it as one more helpful cue, along with the many other sources of information discussed in Section 8.3.

WEB ACTIVITY 8.4

Does prosody disambiguate?
In this activity, you'll listen to sound files of speakers uttering ambiguous sentences. You'll be asked to determine whether you can reliably understand the intended meanings of the sentences based on the speaker's prosody.

Humans understand language despite rampant ambiguity

By now, we've compiled quite a list of variables that seem to have the effect of either aggravating or relieving garden path effects. Overall, experimental evidence suggests that the human parser is quite a bit more flexible, intelligent, and less error-prone than was originally envisioned. In order to predict whether a specific sentence will cause a serious derailment for readers or hearers, it's not enough just to know that it contains a potential ambiguity. People are able to combine information from a large variety of informative cues to help resolve an ambiguity. If a number of different cues all conspire to point to the wrong interpretation, readers or listeners will run into a dead end, and have to backtrack in their processing attempts. But situations in which these cues overwhelmingly point to the wrong structure are extremely rare.

This turns out to be a good thing for language comprehension, because as it happens, language is even more inherently ambiguous than psycholinguists might have imagined. The sheer scope of linguistic ambiguity became apparent to computer scientists once they started building computer programs whose goal was to understand sentences produced by humans. They found that for many partial sentences of English, the programs would offer not one or two, but sometimes *thousands* of ways of parsing the sentence in conformity with the rules of English grammar. Most of these massively ambiguous sentence fragments are not at all problematic for humans—we filter out almost all of the grammatically legal structures as nonsensical or enormously unlikely to ever be uttered. But currently, computers are much less good at coping with ambiguity than we are. Attempts to build machines that can understand us have highlighted just how impressive we are at resolving ambiguities in language.

Is it possible to have a language without ambiguity? As far as I know, naturally occurring languages all involve ambiguity, but it is certainly possible to invent an ambiguity-free artificial language, as was done by James Cooke Brown (1960) when he created the language known as Loglan. In Loglan, words never have more than one meaning, and they're combined in ways that resemble logical formulas—these formulas convey conceptual content in a transparent way so that you can never have one string of words that means more than one thing. Brown originally invented Loglan with the idea that it would be interesting to see whether a completely unambiguous language could help its speakers organize their thinking more clearly. But more recently, enthusiasts of Loglan (and a related language known as Lojban) have argued that unambiguous languages could prove to be very useful in the interaction between humans and computers, since ambiguity has such a catastrophic effect on computers' ability to understand language.

Would humans benefit from using an unambiguous language among themselves? Despite the hype from some Loglan and Lojban enthusiasts, it's not clear that they would. As you've seen, people are extremely good at cutting through much of the ambiguity inherent in language. And as discussed in Chapter 7, ambiguity might serve to lessen the demands on language *production*. In Box 7.2, I introduced the idea that ambiguous words allow languages to reuse easy-to-produce bits of language with minimal disruption to comprehension. In the case of syntactic ambiguities, it may be that a language that contains ambiguity allows for a simpler syntactic system, or allows speakers some important flexibility in how they order words and phrases. The notion that ambiguity might offer some important benefits is echoed by author Arika Okrent (2009), who discusses her attempts at learning Lojban. She suggests that "composing a sentence in Lojban is like writing a line of computer code. Choose the wrong function, drop a variable, forget to close a parenthesis, and it doesn't work." As a result, she notes, watching live conversations in Lojban is much like watching people slowly doing long division in their heads.

8.4 Making Predictions

Eyeing the content yet to come

In the previous section, you learned that it's quite rare for ambiguity to be truly disruptive for language processing—the human parser seems to be very adept at coping with the uncertainty introduced by strings of words that are ambiguous. We regularly make use of our experience with language patterns, our knowledge of the world, or our awareness of the specific context to choose the most likely meaning when several are possible. This allows us to process language incrementally and on the fly, even when the fragments we've heard are highly ambiguous.

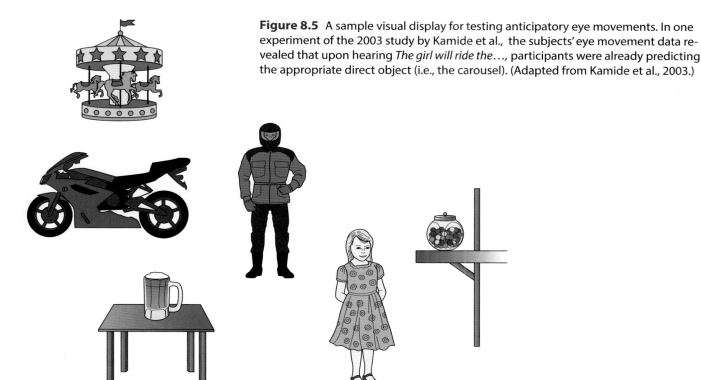

Figure 8.5 A sample visual display for testing anticipatory eye movements. In one experiment of the 2003 study by Kamide et al., the subjects' eye movement data revealed that upon hearing *The girl will ride the...*, participants were already predicting the appropriate direct object (i.e., the carousel). (Adapted from Kamide et al., 2003.)

However, researchers have shown that we go even further than this. Not only do we *choose* among multiple possible structures for incoming fragments of speech, but we can *anticipate* the meanings of sentences, even before we've heard critical portions of these sentence.

Anticipatory, or predictive, language processing has been demonstrated quite clearly in a number of eye-tracking experiments. In one of these studies, Yuki Kamide and her colleagues (2003) showed people visual displays illustrating several characters and various objects, and observed their eye movements as they listened to sentences involving these characters and objects. For example, while viewing a picture such as the one in **Figure 8.5**, subjects would hear one of the following sentences:

The man will ride the motorbike.

The man will taste the beer.

The girl will ride the carousel.

The girl will taste the sweets.

The researchers found evidence that people were anticipating the identity of the direct objects in the sentence. That is, upon hearing *The girl will ride the...*, they were already more likely to be looking at the carousel than at any of the other objects in the display. (In contrast, hearing *The man will taste the...* prompted glances at the picture of the beer.) Listeners' guesses about the upcoming direct objects reflected the *combination* of the previously heard subjects and verbs—that is, people didn't just look at the rideable objects (the carousel *and* the motorbike), or the objects that they think girls like (the carousel and the candy). They looked at whichever object was most likely to be involved in an event involving the already-mentioned subject and verb. This suggests that they had integrated linguistic information about the subject and the verb, used this information to build a partial meaning of the unfolding sentence, and were generating predictions about the most likely way to fill in the sentence's meaning.

In another experiment, Kamide and her colleagues leveraged the grammar of Japanese to show that predictions about meaning are based on a subtle interplay between linguistic and contextual information. Unlike in English, in which the verb usually appears before the direct object, in Japanese the verb typically appears at the end of the sentence after both the subject and its direct and indirect objects. For example, here's the Japanese translation for the sentence *The waitress will merrily bring the hamburger to the customer*:

weitoresu-ga	*kyaku-ni*	*tanosigeni*	*hanbaagaa-o*	*hakobu.*
waitress	customer	merrily	hamburger	bring.

Japanese subjects heard sentences such as these while viewing visual displays (see **Figure 8.6**).

What kind of predictions were listeners making after they'd heard just the first two or three words of the sentence? Since waitresses usually bring people food, it would be sensible for the listeners to assume that this is the direction the sentence was taking, and to throw some anticipatory glances at the hamburger. But waitresses can also do many other things involving customers: they can greet them or tease them, take their orders, recite the menu, and so on. What information could the Japanese hearers use to constrain the set of possibilities?

One potentially useful source of information is the presence of case markers in Japanese—these are grammatical tags that appear on nouns to indicate whether the noun is a subject (in which case it appears with the -*ga* tag), an indirect object (-*ni*), or a direct object (-*o*). In the above sentence, the noun meaning "customer" is tagged with an indirect object marker. This means that the customer could be involved in, say, an event of bringing, which does involve an indirect object; but he couldn't be the target of a teasing event, which involves

Figure 8.6 A sample of the type of display used in the Kamide et al. study to probe the integration of grammatical and contextual information in generating predictions about the upcoming content in the sentence (see text). (Adapted from Kamide et al., 2003.)

a direct object, but no indirect object. In fact, if the waitress were teasing the customer, we'd have to tag the noun with the direct object tag *-o* rather than *-ni*:

weitoresu-ga	*kyaku-o*	*tanosigeni*	*karakau.*
waitress	customer	merrily	tease.

Is predictive language processing sensitive to such linguistic subtleties? Kamide and her colleagues showed that it is. Upon analyzing their subjects' eye movements, they found that after hearing only the first three words (that is, the equivalent of *waitress customer merrily*), the subjects were more likely to look at the hamburger than at the distractor object (the garbage can)—but only if the word for "customer" was tagged with an indirect object marker, signaling that the word was grammatically consistent with an event in which the waitress brought the customer some food. When the case marker was inconsistent with such an event, the subjects were not lured by the picture of the hamburger.

Brain waves reveal predictive processing

One of the great advantages of the eye-tracking method, as compared with button-press response time measures, is that it allows researchers to get a moment-by-moment view of what's happening in people's minds as they process language. This is because the target behaviors (that is, eye movements) are tracked continuously as speech unfolds, rather than being probed at one particular point in time *after* the presentation of some critical stimulus, as is the case in response time studies. Naturally, this makes eye-tracking a powerful method for studying predictive processing, where we want to see what's happening in the mind *before* people encounter some critical stimulus. But the technique comes with certain limitations as well:

1. You have to be able to visually depict the content of the sentence, which restricts the abstraction and complexity of the stimuli.

2. Eye movements can only reveal how people respond to those aspects of the sentence that are visually depicted, but they're fairly uninformative about whether people are generating predictions about content that isn't present in the display. In a sense, the visual displays may be acting as a sort of multiple choice test situation—we can see whether people are favoring certain hypotheses over others among the options that are provided, but we can't easily tell whether they're generating hypotheses that *aren't* made visually available as options, or whether they would do so in a more open-ended language-processing situation. This is important because presumably, much of daily language processing takes place in less visually constraining contexts.

One way around these limitations is to study brain wave activity while people hear or read language. This approach offers researchers many of the advantages of eye-tracking methods, without the constraints imposed by visual presentation. Like the eye-tracking studies, experiments that measure event-related potentials (ERPs) can tap into moment-by-moment responses to language as it unfolds.

A number of researchers have used ERP techniques to ask: Do people anticipate the actual *words* that will appear downstream, rather than just the general content that's yet to come? In one such study, Katherine DeLong and her colleagues (2005) had subjects read sentences like these:

The day was breezy so the boy went outside to fly a kite.

The day was breezy so the boy went outside to fly an airplane.

Figure 8.7 ERP data from the study by DeLong et al. (2005). This graph plots the ERP waveforms at the midline central (vertex) recording site for words that were determined to be of high versus low predictability based on a separate sentence completion task. Note that negative values are plotted upward. Both articles and nouns that were low in predictability showed significantly greater negativity between 200 and 500 ms after the onset of the word (N400) compared with articles and nouns of high predictability.

Sentence completion task:
"The day was breezy so the boy went outside to fly…"

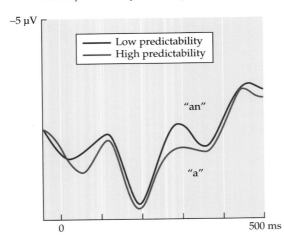

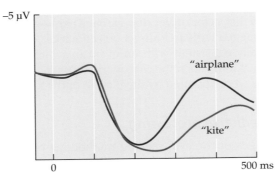

If people are generating predictions about upcoming words, they're probably more likely to come up with *kite* than with *airplane.* If you remember the discussion of N400 brain waves back in Chapter 3, unexpected words result in heightened N400 activity compared with more predictable words. (This is the case regardless of whether "predictability" reflects the semantic plausibility/ anomaly of a word in the context, or simply a contrast between a common versus rare word.) Hence, subjects should display more energetic N400 activity upon reading the word *airplane* at the end of the sentence.

This is exactly what DeLong and her colleagues found (**Figure 8.7**). But more importantly, they found heightened N400 activity for the "airplane" sentences at the *previous* word, the article *an*. Notice that in the sentences above, the more predictable word *kite* should be preceded by the article *a*, following the English rule of phonology that says the article *an* only appears before vowel-initial words. By cleverly setting up a contrast in the articles that could appear with predictable and unpredictable words, the researchers were able to probe for clear evidence of word anticipation. The earliness of the N400 effect suggests that even before getting to the word *airplane*, subjects must have generated some expectations about the specific *shape* of the upcoming word; otherwise they wouldn't have been surprised by the occurrence of the article *an*.

Subsequent ERP studies support the conclusions of DeLong and her colleagues: people appear to generate some predictions about the form as well as the content of upcoming material. Moreover, their predictions show sensitivity to a variety of information sources. In the study that I've just described, subjects were presumably relying on their general knowledge of the world in anticipating that boys are more likely to fly kites than airplanes on a breezy day. But another study showed that people's predictions relied more on the specific story context than on real-world plausibility—for example, in reading a story about an amorous peanut, they showed *less* N400 activity (reflecting greater expectation) for the sentence *The peanut was in love* than for *The peanut was salted* (Nieuwland & Van Berkum, 2006). Moreover, the identity of the speaker can also affect a hearer's expectations. In a study led by Jos Van Berkum (2008), subjects exhibited an N400 effect upon encountering a word that would be unexpected from a particular speaker. For instance, if someone with an upper-class accent uttered, "I have a large tattoo on my back," subjects showed heightened N400 activity at the word *tattoo*; in fact, this effect occurred very early in the utterance of the word, leading the authors to argue that hearers must have been generating expectations of likely upcoming words even before the speaker began to say *tattoo*.

Predictions in language and hockey: A matter of expertise

Together, the eye-tracking and ERP studies reveal an extremely active and adaptive language-processing system. Instead of waiting for the speech signal to trigger the process of word recognition and subsequent structure-building, we quickly pull together all the information that's available to us at any point in time, and generate expectations about the sentence's upcoming content and form. Naturally, these preliminary expectations might turn out to be wrong, in which case we have to be able to quickly revise them.

Our ability to generate and revise predictions appears to be a critical aspect of smooth and efficient language processing. Increasingly, psycholinguists see language processing—whether or not it involves ambiguity—as the business of making predictions about a sentence's future trajectory, much as you might make predictions about the trajectory of objects moving in physical space. In some cases, this means making predictions about how an ambiguous structure will pan out. But it can also involve generating expectations about the type of event that is being described, about whether a just-uttered word like *the* will be followed by an adjective or directly by a noun, or even stylistic expectations about whether the speaker is likely to refer to a youngster by using the word *child* or the more informal *kid* in a particular social situation.

Some researchers have argued that the idea of predictability in language can offer a unified approach to understanding the processing of both ambiguous and unambiguous sentences. For example, John Hale (2001) has used the term **surprisal** to capture this notion, arguing that processing difficulty is a reflection of whether a sentence's continuation is highly predicable, and whether the unfolding sentence ends up conforming to the most likely outcome. Surprisal is lowest when the probability that a sentence will continue in a particular way is very high, and the sentence does in fact continue in the most likely manner. The first two examples below (only one of which involves a syntactic ambiguity) illustrate a low level of surprisal upon encountering the words in bold—and hence, these words should be very easy to process:

The horse raced past the barn **and fell**.

Lin likes to eat bacon with her **eggs**.

Surprisal is highest (leading to greatest processing difficulty) when the sentence actually continues in a way that was extremely *im*probable, as shown by the words in bold in the next two examples:

The horse raced past the barn **fell**.

Lin likes to eat bacon with her **cheesecake**.

Intermediate levels of surprisal occur when the unfolding sentence is reasonably consistent with a number of possible outcomes, one of which turns out to be realized, as illustrated by the words in bold in the final two examples below:

The landmine buried in the sand **exploded**.

Lin bought some **potatoes**.

A great deal of knowledge and skill goes into being able to make linguistic predictions. In the physical world, your ability to make predictions about

surprisal A measure that's inversely related to the statistical predictability of an event such as a particular continuation of a sentence. Processing difficulty is thought to reflect the degree of surprisal at specific points in the sentence, so that less predictable continuations result in greater processing difficulty.

where a moving object will land depends on your experience with moving objects. In much the same way, making linguistic predictions is dependent on your experience with language—with its grammar, with its common words and structures, and with how people tend to wield it in a variety of situations. Now, predicting an object's motion trajectory is usually far simpler than predicting the path of a sentence. But to push the analogy a bit further, think of language processing as similar to the skills that are required for playing hockey at a very high level, and predicting the movement of the puck. According to author Adam Gopnik (2011), hockey requires, above all, the ability to "see the ice":

> … the ability to grasp a changing whole and anticipate its next stage. It's the ability to make quick decisions, to size up all the relationships in a fast-changing array and understand them. A related notion is that of situational awareness: a heightened consciousness of your surroundings and both the intentions of the people around you and their anticipated actions.
>
> Well, hockey, obviously, which is played at incredibly high speed, reveals and rewards situational and spatial intelligence at a degree of difficulty that no other sport possesses. So much so, that the greatest of all hockey players, Wayne Gretzky, had, besides his other significant skills as a fine-edge skater, almost nothing else that he's specifically good at. That is his gift—the gift of spatial and situational intelligence: knowing what's going to happen in three seconds, anticipating the pattern approaching by seeing the pattern now, sussing out the goalie's next decision and Jari Kurri's or Luc Robitaille's eventual trajectory in what would be a single glance if a glance were even taken. Gretzky is the extreme expression of the common skill the game demands.

To many psycholinguists, this is as apt a metaphor as there is for the "common skill" that is demanded by everyday language processing. Perhaps if all of us spent as much time playing hockey as we did using language, we too would have the expertise of a Wayne Gretzky.

Like hockey, making language-based predictions does appear to be an acquired skill. Arielle Borovsky and her colleagues (2012) set out to learn whether children, like adults, make predictive eye movements, in a study very similar to the eye-tracking experiment by Kamide et al. (2003). They tested adults and children age 3 to 10 years, presenting their subjects with spoken sentences such as, "The pirate hides the treasure," along with visual displays of various objects related to the sentences. They measured the point in time at which a subject began to look more often at the picture of the treasure than at the other objects in the display, in anticipation of the direct object.

As in the earlier study by Kamide and colleagues, adults in the Borovsky et al. study regularly made predictive eye movements very soon after hearing the beginning of the verb. Children did too, although their eye movements were somewhat more sluggish than the adults', suggesting that the predictions about the upcoming sentence content were not being generated as quickly. Of special interest, though, was the fact that children with relatively large vocabularies launched speedier anticipatory looks than their peers with smaller vocabularies. Knowledge of language, more than age itself, was correlated with the speed of their predictions. And it might surprise you to learn that, even among the adults, vocabulary size was correlated with the speed of predictive processing. In the language arena, as in hockey, it appears that some people are more expert than others at anticipating what is going to happen next—though much more research still needs to be done to understand the source of the variability of this skill. And, alas, as with hockey, aging may result in a decline in the ability to anticipate upcoming words, as discovered in ERP studies by Kara Federmeier (2007).

WEB ACTIVITY 8.5

Linguistic predictions In this activity, you'll explore a range of language phenomena in which expectations about upcoming structure or content could potentially guide language processing.

8.5 When Memory Fails

When are complex sentences difficult?

Let's take another look at the difficult sentences introduced at the beginning of this chapter. As you've seen, ambiguity is a common culprit when it comes to creating havoc for language comprehension. But sentences can be hard to process for other reasons too. Several of the most difficult sentences from the introductory section could not readily be pinned on an ambiguity. For example:

> The mouse the cat chased keeled over.

> The administrator who the intern who the nurse supervised had accused fudged the medical reports.

It's easy to see that these sentences involve more than one clause or sentence unit, and encode multiple events (for instance, in the first sentence, there's an event of the cat chasing the mouse, and an event in which the mouse keels over). But that alone can't explain the difficulty, because it's certainly possible to express these same events in a sentence without straining the processing system:

> When the cat chased the mouse, the mouse keeled over.

> The mouse keeled over when the cat chased it.

And oddly, if we want to say that it was the cat that keeled over, rather than the mouse, the next sentence seems to be considerably easier to understand:

> The cat that chased the mouse keeled over.

So, it's not just that the sentence is generally complex or the ideas inherently difficult to understand; it's that there's something taxing about the particular structure with which those ideas are expressed. For instance, the first sentence of the following pair would typically be read faster than the second, even though they're made up of exactly the same words:

> The senator who spotted the reporter shouted.

> The senator who the reporter spotted shouted.

What's the key difference? Both contain a relative clause attached to the subject of the main clause, *the senator*. But in the first sentence of the pair, *the senator* is also linked to the subject role of the embedded verb *spotted*. (Notice what happens in the question/answer pair: *Who spotted the reporter? The senator spotted the reporter.*) This type of relative clause is called a subject relative clause. In contrast, in the second sentence, *the senator* is linked to the direct object role of the embedded verb *spotted*. (Notice: *Who did the reporter spot? The reporter spotted the senator*). This yields an object relative clause. As I did in Chapter 6, I'll notate the relationships by using the same color for the phrase *the senator* and the underscore marking the position in the sentence that it links to:

The senator who ___ **spotted** the reporter shouted.

The senator who the reporter **spotted** ___ shouted.

So: why are object relative clauses harder to process than subject relative clauses?

Memory failure or faulty predictions?

As with the ambiguous sentences discussed in Section 8.2, there are two competing classes of explanations for the difficulty: one that highlights the inherent limitations of the parser, and another that emphasizes its tendency to predict structure. According to the first account (a version of which is articulated in great detail by Ted Gibson, 1998), the trouble crops up because complex sentences involve holding some parts of a sentence in memory until they can be related to other parts of the sentence—as the distance between these related parts gets bigger, so do the demands on memory and the prospects of processing failure. And, in some cases, multiple dependencies have to be held in memory at the same time, adding even more strain on memory.

In a subject relative clause, an NP (*the senator*) has to be integrated with the embedded verb (*spotted*), as well as the main clause verb (*shouted*), leading to *two* dependencies:

The senator who ___ **spotted** the reporter **shouted**.

This turns out to be fairly easy: at *spotted*, there's no intervening NP to get in the way of the integration of the two components, and by the time *the reporter* is reached, the first dependency has already been resolved. Things are a bit different with the object relative version:

The senator who the reporter **spotted** ___ **shouted**.

Readers have to hold *the senator* in memory while encountering *the reporter*, and it's the intrusion of this second NP that makes the integration with *spotted* that much harder. The sentence gets harder still if you add yet another intervening NP:

The senator who the reporter next to the president **spotted** ___ **shouted**.

Second, while the intervening phrase *the reporter* is being encountered and stored, neither of the two dependencies involving *the senator* has yet been resolved, adding to the memory burden. You can see the effect of piling up the number of unresolved dependencies by taking the original object relative sentence and adding yet another object relative clause:

The senator who **the reporter** who the president detested ___ spotted ___ shouted.

For most people, this sentence disintegrates into utterly unrecognizable word mush. But again, there's nothing difficult about the *ideas* expressed in the sentence, as we can see if we unravel the sentence and present the same content in a way that avoids the memory crash:

The president detested **the reporter** who ___ spotted **the senator** who ___ shouted.

There's yet a third memory-related issue that may play a role in these horrendous sentences: the semantic similarity of the nouns *reporter* and *senator*. Some researchers have pointed out that it's a general property of memory that similar items tend to blur together and become harder to retrieve separately. It's possible that when complex sentences involve very similar nouns that have to be held in memory at the same time, this might make it hard to retrieve the right noun in the right place in the sentence. The experience might be analogous to reading a long Russian novel populated by a large cast of characters, all of whose names sound alike—it becomes onerous to keep track of who did what to whom. Indeed, readers often seem to fare better with object relative sentences that contain very dissimilar nouns. Compare:

The senator who the president summoned arrived.

The helicopter that the president summoned arrived.

These explanations all derive from the very reasonable assumption that the process of building syntactic structure taps working memory resources, which, sadly, are known to be finite. But not all researchers focus on memory limitations in explaining the difficulty of object relative clauses. Some have suggested that the difficulty is a by-product of the parser's tendency to predict upcoming structure based on previous experiences with language; in this case, experience with the statistical likelihood of different structures leads the parser astray. In a sense, you might think of the subject-relative/object-relative asymmetry as simply another kind of very transient garden path effect. To see this, have several people you know (but not from this class) complete the following fragment:

The beauty queen who …

How many of them produced an object relative clause, as opposed to a subject relative clause? Based on the statistical patterns of English, chances are that the subject relatives came up more frequently, with most people providing a verb rather than a second NP as the next element to continue the fragment. In that case, according to an experience-based account, they'd have trouble reading sentences with object relative clauses (for example, *The beauty queen who the judge disqualified broke into tears*) not because they'd drained some finite processing resources, but because their perfectly intelligent and reality-based expectations about upcoming structure were not met once they ran into the more unusual sentence structure.

Both of these accounts are well grounded in reasonable assumptions about language processing, assumptions for which there's a fair bit of independent evidence. Luckily, there are ways to pull apart the two explanations—for instance, they make somewhat different predictions about *where* in the object relative clause readers should experience the greatest difficulty. For experience-based accounts, this should happen right upon encountering the second NP, where expectations of a subject relative structure are confounded (as in *The beauty queen who **the judge** disqualified broke into tears*.) For memory-based accounts, the trouble spot should be at the embedded verb, where the noun has to be integrated with the verb, over an intervening NP (*The beauty queen who the judge **disqualified** broke into tears*.) These are subtle points, but it seems likely at this stage of data gathering that both explanations correctly capture portions of the difficulty with object relative clauses.

LANGUAGE AT LARGE 8.2

Straining the parser for literary effect

What makes for good writing? A sensible editorial response might be: writing that puts as little stress as possible on the language processing system. If that's the case, no one seems to have told the novelist Henry James, famous for his convoluted syntax. Here are some typical Jamesian sentences from his 1903 novel *The Ambassadors*:

> *One of the features of the restless afternoon passed by him after Mrs. Peacock's visit was an hour spent, shortly before dinner with Maria Gostrey, whom of late, in spite of so sustained a call on his attention from other quarters, he had by no means neglected.*

> *Chad offered him, as always, a welcome in which the cordial and the formal—so far as the formal was the respectful—handsomely met; and after he had expressed a hope that he would let him put him up for the night, Strether was in full possession of the key, as it might have been called, to what had lately happened.*

Why would a writer make a conscious choice to create sentences that wind their way through multiple embeddings, stretch syntactic dependencies over dizzying distances, and follow bizarre twists of structure, all of which make the prose harder to read? Author and critic Zadie Smith (2009) suggests that the technique was part of James's attempt to cultivate a more acute consciousness in his reader, that his syntactic choices were "intended to make you aware, to break the rhythm that excludes thinking."

Like most literary writers, James (and Smith) likely relied on intuitions about language. But from a scientific perspective, the idea's not crazy. It seems strange and counterintuitive, but a number of studies suggest that when information is *too* easy to process fluently, people are somewhat prone to thinking *less* deeply, to falling back more readily on fast-but-dumb cognitive heuristics.

One intriguing example comes from a study led by Adam Alter (2007), in which subjects had to answer math problems like the one you saw earlier: In a lake there is a patch of lily pads. Every day, the patch doubles in size. If it takes 48 days for the patch to cover the entire lake, how long would it take for the patch to cover half the lake? Many people mistakenly answered 24, but they were less likely to do so if they'd read the problem in a nearly illegible font. One interpretation of this intriguing finding is that the font made the problems *feel* harder, thereby kick-starting a more careful mode of thinking. (Or, if you will, the hard-to-read font had the effect of "breaking the rhythm that excludes thinking.")

There are other fascinating cases that might be part of the same phenomenon. One of these is a study by Boaz Keysar and colleagues (2012) in which bilingual subjects were confronted with what's known as "the Asian disease problem," first studied by Amos Tversky and Daniel Kahneman (1974):

> A new disease, recently emerged in Asia, has begun to spread. In the U.S., without medicine, 600,000 people will die from it. Two new medicines have been developed, but only one of them can be manufactured and distributed. You must choose which medicine to use.
>
> If you choose medicine A, 200,000 people will be saved.
>
> If you choose medicine B, there is a 33.33% chance that 600,000 people will be saved, and a 66.66% chance that no one will be saved.
>
> Which medicine do you choose?

The interesting finding from this experiment is that people's choices tend to depend heavily on the wording of the problem, a phenomenon known as the **framing effect**. When the problem is worded as it is above, people are more likely to choose medicine A. But they switch and are more likely to choose medicine B if they are informed that the outcome of medicine A is that *400,000 people will die*, but that with medicine B there is a *33.33% chance that no one will die and a 66.66% chance that 600,000 people will die*.

The careful reader will have noticed that this scenario is exactly the same as the earlier one, so it seems somewhat irrational that people would have such a different response to it. Keysar and colleagues found that their bilingual subjects showed the usual framing effects if they heard the problem in their native language. But when the problem was presented in their second language—which required more effort to process—the bias introduced by the wording vanished, and their subjects showed a more "rational" pattern of responding to both versions in the same way. Again, one possible interpretation is that the extra processing challenge of reading the problem in a foreign language triggered a more thoughtful processing mode.

framing effect A phenomenon in which decisions or preferences regarding two identical outcomes are observed to be dramatically different, depending on the wording of the outcomes.

Whether or not it leads to deeper thinking, there's no doubt that reading Henry James feels more strenuous than reading the easy, breezy style of much contemporary popular writing. And this sense of effort can be leveraged for literary effect. One exceptional example can be found in "The Depressed Person," a short story by David Foster Wallace (2007). I'll leave it to you to identify the various structures and long dependencies that strain the parser. Add to that the actual content, and the effect is a passage that feels as exhausting and overwhelming to read as depression is itself:

> The friends whom the depressed person reached out to for support and tried to open up to and share at least some contextual shape of her unceasing psychic agony and feelings of isolation with numbered around half

a dozen and underwent a certain amount of rotation. The depressed person's therapist—who had earned both a terminal graduate degree and a medical degree, and who was the self-professed exponent of a school of therapy which stressed the cultivation and regular use of a supportive peer community in any endogenously depressed adult's journey toward self-healing—referred to these friends as the depressed person's Support System. ... The excruciating feelings of shame and inadequacy which the depressed person experienced about calling supportive members of her Support System long-distance late at night and burdening them with her clumsy attempts to articulate at least the overall context of her emotional agony were an issue on which the depressed person and her therapist were doing a great deal of work in their time together.

8.6 Variable Minds

Individual differences in memory span

So far, I've been using expressions like "*the* parser" and "*the* language processing system" as if sentence comprehension involved something like a software program, and each one of us had exactly the same copy of it installed in our heads. Many language researchers will admit that when you look more closely at individuals' data, you might see quite a bit of variation in how different people respond—for example, some people might display enormous garden path effects for certain sentences, while others might show subtle or nonexistent slowdowns. But until fairly recently, this kind of variability was treated as unsystematic experimental "noise," not as an integral part of building theories of language comprehension. Building and testing theories has typically focused on the commonalities that can be found across large numbers of language users, not their differences.

But differences among individuals are becoming a very interesting part of the language-processing story. It's obvious that there are some meaningful cognitive differences across individuals. We all know people who have phenomenal memories, and others who are hopelessly absent-minded; some have an extremely analytical style of thinking, while other are more creative and impulsive in their thought processes. These are stable differences that characterize people over long spans of time. Far from being "noise" or transient variations that might be there today but gone tomorrow, they seem to play an important part in organizing people's experiences and the ways in which they process information. So we'd like to know whether different cognitive profiles also have an impact on how people organize and process linguistic information.

The connection between individual cognitive profiles and language processing was first made with regard to claims about memory. As we've seen in the previous section, in order to explain why some sentences are hard to understand, a number of researchers have pointed the finger at working memory limitations. And that's interesting, because it seems that some people are blessed with longer memory spans than others, and that these are stable indi-

reading span test A behavioral test intended to measure an individual's verbal working memory. The test involves having the individual read a sequence of sentences while holding the last word of each sentence in memory. The number of words successfully remembered corresponds to that individual's memory span.

vidual traits that can be measured by standard tests. So, if the difficulty inherent in certain kinds of sentences comes from the fact that these sentences bump up against limits on memory capacity, then we should be able to predict, based on someone's working memory span, whether their interpretation of such sentences is especially prone to crashing—and maybe even whether they experience the prose of Henry James as pleasantly stimulating or as a depressing slog.

In an important paper, Marcel Just and Patricia Carpenter (1992) looked at several aspects of language processing in subjects with high memory spans versus subjects with lower spans. They measured memory span using a particular test known as the **reading span test** (developed by Meredith Daneman and Patricia Carpenter, 1980). This task, which is intended to mimic the memory pressures on the parsing system, requires subjects to keep certain words active in memory while reading and understanding text. You try it—read the following sentences, and as you do, be sure to remember the last word in each sentence:

> Despite their persistent disagreements, they managed to agree how to best educate their child.

> At last, she spotted the rowboat coming across the bay, tossed about on the tall waves.

> Long periods of unstructured reading and thinking sometimes lead to the most fertile ideas.

Quiz time: Without looking back, can you remember the last word of every sentence? If you could, the reading span test would continue, inflicting upon you higher and higher numbers of sentences until you failed to recall all of their last words. This breaking point would reflect the limits of your memory span on this particular test.

Just and Carpenter argued that there are several consequences to having a lower memory span. The most obvious one is that it becomes very hard to understand sentences that make heavy demands on verbal working memory. They reported evidence showing that low-span subjects were especially slow at reading object relative clauses (which have been argued by some researchers to be real memory-hogging sentences) compared to the less taxing subject relative clauses. On the other hand, the higher-span subjects experienced a much more subtle slowdown for sentences with object relative clauses, presumably because their extra processing capacity could accommodate these structures fairly easily.

It's also possible that low-span subjects approach ambiguity resolution in a different way than higher-span subjects do. In Section 8.3, I summarized a variety of sources of information that might be helpful in the disambiguation process. Just and Carpenter argued that people with higher memory spans are better able to juggle all these sources of information at once, whereas people with lower memory spans might have to constrain the amount of information they take into consideration while resolving ambiguities. For instance, they might not as readily take into account the semantic plausibility of competing interpretations, and they might not be able to hold multiple interpretations open for long periods of time. The end result might be that they commit early to one single interpretation, based on a very limited amount of information—in other words, low-span subjects might show exactly the kind of processing style that's been described by the garden path model. Thus, according to Just and Carpenter, the garden path model had it partly right: Resource limitations *do* result in a parser that builds a single structure without considering all the options—but this isn't built into the *architecture*, or mind design, of the parser. It's just a by-product of trying to understand sentences using a narrower memory span. Those who have the luxury of spending mental resources on a parsing style that considers more information take advantage of the opportunity to do so.

You'll remember, though, that not all researchers agree that object relative clauses are difficult because they stretch memory resources too thin. The experience-based argument was that these sentences are hard simply because they don't occur very frequently, hence they defy the word-by-word predictions that parsers make over the course of a sentence as it unspools. Notice that in this debate, individual differences become an important source of evidence that can shed some light on very general questions about the nature of parsing. Namely, if it turns out that we can systematically predict how hard it is for individuals to parse object relative clauses by looking at their memory spans, then this looks like pretty strong support for the view that such sentences do in fact draw heavily on memory resources, and that this is what makes them potentially difficult. In other words, the different parsing outcomes of different individuals can tell us something about the language processing system.

How have researchers from the experience-based camp responded to the evidence linking memory span with processing difficulties? By casting doubt that the reading span test is a valid measure of pure memory in the first place. Maryellen MacDonald and Morten Christiansen (2002) have argued that some people do better on the reading span test not because they have a more spacious memory, but because they are better *readers*. Better readers, they claim, are better able to read and understand sentences efficiently—they can do so while consuming less in the way of processing resources, which simply makes them *appear* to have more processing capacity. And how do people get to be better readers? Generally by spending more time immersed in written language than their peers. Think about any type of athletic training, say, training to run a marathon. We're used to thinking of training as having the result of extending an athlete's capacity (her strength or endurance). But one of the most important aspects of training is that the athlete learns to use her body more efficiently to achieve the same movements. Someone who runs 5 or 10 miles a day certainly has more strength and endurance than I do—but if both of us go for a run, it's also true that I will simply be working harder to run at the same speed. According to Christiansen and MacDonald, high performance on the reading span test merely reflects the fact that the so-called high-span subjects don't have to work as hard to process the same sentences. The memory test, then, is just a stand-in for the amount of reading "training" a person has had. And why would those with more experience at reading have an easier time with unusual structures like object relative clauses? Possibly because they've encountered these unusual structures many more times than people who read less (especially given that written language is far more likely to use unusual, infrequent structures than spoken language). Under this view, the way to get better at coping with the intricate syntax of Henry James is not to do mental calisthenics that extend memory capacity—rather, it's simply to read more.

Ultimately, this debate about individual differences and working memory hinges on being able to answer two yet-to-be-resolved queries: (1) How much does the reading span test really capture about memory capacity (and how does it relate to other, possibly "purer" tests of memory span, and do these also correlate with difficulties in processing complex syntax)? (2) To what extent does experience with language affect performance on both memory tests and tests of language processing?

WEB ACTIVITY 8.6

Test yourself on various memory tasks To what extent do you think these tests do or don't tap into the same kinds of memory resources that are needed to process complicated sentence structures?

cognitive control Also known as **executive function**. The goal-directed cognitive processes responsible for directing attention and supervising behavioral responses to stimuli.

Stroop test Behavioral test in which subjects are required to name the color of the font that a word appears in while ignoring the (possibly conflicting) meaning of the word.

Differences in cognitive control

More recently, researchers have become interested in another source of individual variation and its relation to language processing, namely, the ability to ignore and suppress irrelevant information. So far, the picture that I've painted of the language-processing landscape is one of rampant, cutthroat competition among linguistic representations, all clamoring for attention. Often the difference between successful understanding and utter cognitive mush comes down to being able to focus on the right representations while ignoring the others. This seems to be part of a general skill called **cognitive control** (also referred to as **executive function**)—you might think of cognitive control as the managerial aspect of cognition, directing attention depending on specific mental goals and supervising behavioral responses to stimuli. You need it for much more than just language, and without it, it would be impossible to function competently in a complex environment; you wouldn't be able to do things such as drive, follow a conversation in a crowded room, avoid swearing at your boss, or do any one of a thousand daily things that require you to ignore information or impulses that get in the way of your specific goals. As you might have noticed, the capacity for cognitive control seems to vary quite a bit among individuals. Some are able to push away intruding information or impulses very effectively, while others are more likely to be lured by them.

At one extreme of the spectrum lie those individuals who, because of a stroke or brain injury, have clearly identifiable brain damage to the prefrontal cortex area of the brain, an area that seems to be responsible for exercising cognitive control. Patients with damage to one specific area of the brain's frontal lobes—the left inferior frontal gyrus (LIFG)—have a hard time resolving conflict between competing representations. One way that this shows up is in their performance on a **Stroop test**, where they are told to name the color of the font that a word appears in while ignoring the meaning of the word. For example, subjects would have to identify the font color for words that appear like this: **BLUE, CHAIR, YELLOW,** and so on. Needless to say, it's not hard to name the font color for **BLUE** or even **CHAIR.** But to give the correct answer "red" for the word **YELLOW** means having to suppress the interfering meaning of the word. People are slower and make more mistakes when the font color and meaning mismatch in this way, and patients with damage to the LIFG are especially slow and error prone.

WEB ACTIVITY 8.7

Measuring cognitive control A number of different tests can be used to measure cognitive control. This activity provides a demonstration of several of them.

Language processing is often a lot like a Stroop test. Think about what you have to do to understand a garden path sentence, for example, or the meaning of the word *ball* in a sentence like *She decided not to attend the ball.* In both cases, *irrelevant* meanings are activated, and have to ultimately be squashed. There's a growing body of research that suggests all of these examples are related to cognitive control abilities. For instance, patients with LIFG damage have a hard time settling on the less frequent meaning of an ambiguous word, or recovering from garden path sentences. Among a normal population, brain-imaging studies have shown that the LIFG is especially active in just such situations, when people have to override a strong bias toward an interpretation that turns out to be wrong. And again, among people who are considered to be in the normal range, the degree to which it's hard to retrieve the subordinate meaning of a word or to recover from a garden path sentence seems to be systematically related to some measures of cognitive control (for a summary of these findings, see Novick, Trueswell & Thompson-Schill, 2005). All of this points to there being some consistent aspect of a person's cognitive profile that affects the ways in which she experiences language and its tremendous potential for ambiguity. To some extent at least, a person's degree of cognitive control is shaped by experience—an intriguing line of research suggests that bilingual and multilingual people develop this skill more robustly than monolinguals (see **Box 8.5**).

As luck would have it, human brains go through a good deal of their lives being somewhat short of managerial personnel. The prefrontal cortex is one of the last of the brain regions to fully mature, which explains why teenagers who are

BOX 8.5
Bilingualism and cognitive control

In Chapter 7, you learned that people who know more than one language mix them together in their minds, rather than storing and accessing each of them separately. This intermixing has some dramatic consequences for language processing. In Box 7.3 you saw that Russian-English bilinguals experienced competition from Russian-sounding words that sounded similar to the English words that they were hearing. This suggests that, because bilinguals carry around an extra vocabulary, they regularly experience more competition than monolinguals. Increased competition can make language processing slower and harder, and there's evidence that bilinguals show less efficient word recognition compared with monolinguals (Rogers et al., 2006). They also experience interference across languages in speaking as well as understanding language, and this is reflected in poorer performance in picture-naming tasks, even when the bilinguals are speaking in their first and dominant tongue (Ivanova & Costa, 2008).

But increasingly, researchers are finding an upside to bilingualism. It appears that as a result of the regular exercise of wrestling with a greater degree of competition, bilinguals build up more muscular cognitive control abilities. These benefits can be seen throughout the life span.

At the *very* young end of the life span, Ágnes Kovács and Jacques Mehler (2009) tested 7-month-old babies who were being raised in monolingual and bilingual households. They used a variant of a classic cognitive test known as the "A-not-B test," in which infants see an object being hidden in one location, and then watch as it's moved to a different location. In order to find the object in its new location, babies have to suppress their knowledge of the first location. This is a very basic cognitive control task that babies only reliably accomplish by the age of 18 months. Kovács and Mehler used a simplified version of the task in which children were first trained to look at one side of a screen, and then had to learn to look at the other side

before being rewarded with a nifty visual treat. The babies from bilingual households were better at redirecting their gaze to the new location, while the monolingual babies were more likely to get stuck in the pattern of looking at the old location. This is quite a dramatic demonstration, as babies at this age have yet to utter their first words!

Preschoolers and school-age children who are bilingual continue to show enhanced performance on tests of cognitive control, as do adults at all ages. In fact, the bilingual advantage seems to *increase* in magnitude as adults advance into old age—perhaps this is a reflection of the fact that, just as it's one of the latest systems to mature, cognitive control is also one of the first to decline as we age. (Note to you in your 20s or 30s: be sure to make good use of your peak performance years!)

Ellen Bialystok and her colleagues (2004) measured the performance of adults age 30 to 80 on a cognitive interference task known as the "Simon task." In this task, a red or green square pops up on the screen, and people have to press a button on the right to indicate a green square, or a button on the left to indicate a red square. The control condition of this test involves no spatial interference; the square simply shows up in the neutral location at the center of the screen. But in the "Simon" condition, the squares appear on either the left or right side of the screen. Sometimes the square is on the side that's congruent with the correct button press (a red square appears on the left, requiring the subject to press the left button), while at other times the square appears on the side that's incongruent with the button press (a red square appears on the right side, requiring the subject to press the left button). In the incongruent trials, subjects have to ignore the square's location in order to avoid its interference with their response. People usually respond more slowly to the incongruent trials than to the congruent ones, and the difference between them is taken as a measure of the degree of interference they experience.

BOX 8.5 *(continued)*

Figure 8.8 presents the responses of subjects grouped by age. **Figure 8.8A** shows the control condition in which there's no interference; you can see that the subjects show overall slower response times beginning in their 50s, but that the performance of bilingual and monolingual subjects is identical at all ages. But a different picture emerges from **Figure 8.8B**, which plots the degree of interference on the Simon trials. Here, the bilinguals outperform the monolinguals at all ages, and the difference becomes more pronounced as the subjects enter their 60s (and continues to grow).

All of this seems to have some important clinical implications for people suffering from Alzheimer's disease. Along with memory loss, people with Alzheimer's experience a dramatic loss of cognitive control. But bilingualism appears to offer some protection against the effects of the disease. A number of studies across quite different populations (e.g., Alladi et al., 2013; Bialystok et al., 2007) have shown that bilingualism delays the progression of symptoms, so even when they're at a relatively advanced stage of the disease, bilingual patients typically function at a higher level than their monolingual counterparts.

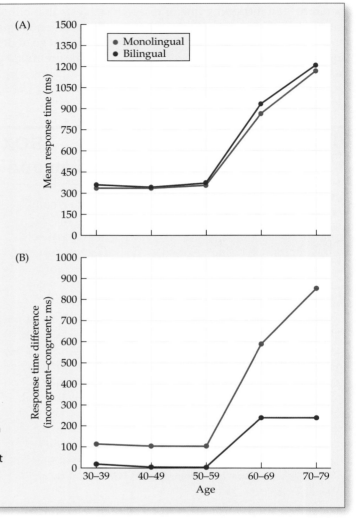

Figure 8.8 Mean response times for subjects by age. (A) Response times are plotted for the control condition in which there's no interference. (B) The degree of interference on Simon trials, calculated by subtracting the response times for congruent trials from the (longer) response times for incongruent trials. (Adapted from Bialystok et al., 2004.)

---

perfectly capable of mastering calculus or higher-order logic can nonetheless torment their parents with their inability to suppress certain impulses or inhibitions. These facts of neuroanatomy have been used by experts to argue that criminal courts should not apply the same sentencing criteria to adolescents as they do to adults. Now, it won't land them in jail, but you might expect that youngsters would also experience some trouble with linguistic ambiguity, and they do. John Trueswell and his colleagues (1999) tracked the eye movements of 5-year-olds listening to garden path sentences such as, "Put the frog on the napkin into the box." There's a temptation to treat *on the napkin* as attaching to the verb, and hence understand it as the intended destination for the frog, rather than as modifying the noun (as in *the frog that's on the napkin*; see **Figure 8.9**).

When confronted with such sentences, adults usually experience a brief garden path effect, as evident from their eye movements, but then quickly recover and perform the correct action. But in what the researchers cutely dubbed the "kindergarten-path effect," 5-year-olds experienced

WEB ACTIVITY 8.8

The kindergarten-path effect
In this activity, you'll see some video recordings of subjects' eye movements and actions in response to ambiguity. You'll be able to see how adults and children differ in how they resolve confusing garden path sentences.

Figure 8.9 An example of a visual display from a 1999 eye-tracking study conducted by Trueswell et al. The subjects were children, who viewed the display while being given ambiguous and unambiguous versions of the instruction "Put the frog (that's) on the napkin in the box." With the ambiguous instruction, in addition to showing evidence of confusion in their eye movements, children often performed incorrect actions, such as hopping the frog onto the napkin and then into the box. This suggests that they were unable to completely suppress the incorrect interpretation of the ambiguous sentence. (Adapted from Trueswell et al., 1999.)

more devastating consequences of the ambiguity, performing the right action *less than half* of the time—for example, they might hop the frog onto the napkin, and then into the box, as if they were blending both interpretations rather than suppressing the incorrect one in favor of the right one.

In this chapter, I've pointed out how an eager, incremental style of language processing leads to tremendous potential for ambiguity—an ambiguity that usually creates fairly minor processing wrinkles for most adults. But for kids and their immature prefrontal cortexes, the processing traps laid by potential ambiguity aren't limited to exotic garden path sentences; such traps can also turn up in the mundane course of ordinary word recognition.

Remember that all words—even those that don't have a homophonous match—are temporarily ambiguous, so in the first few hundred milliseconds of the word *log*, both *log* and *lock* become activated (among others). In Chapter 7, we saw that evidence of such eager activation of word prospects can be seen in the pattern of subjects' eye movements to a visual scene—for example, when hearing *log*, people often look at a key because of its relationship to the cohort competitor *lock*. But for normal adults, such eye movements are usually extremely fleeting, quickly dropping down to baseline right after enough phonetic information has rolled in to identify the target word. And subjects are almost never aware of these spurious eye movements, or that they briefly flirted with interpreting *log* as *lock*. The competition seems to linger on a bit more for children: Yi Ting Huang and Jesse Snedeker (2010) found that in the same situation, 5-year-olds tended to persist in looking at the key for some time after hearing the disambiguating final consonant of the word *log*, and that they sometimes chose the key after being asked to "pick up the log." Perhaps once *lock* has been activated, and hence its related word *key*, the irrelevant representations continued to reverberate.

More relaxed cognitive control, though, may not be all bad. Some researchers (for example, Sharon Thompson-Schill and colleagues, 2009) have actually suggested that on balance, a slow-maturing prefrontal cortex may have evolved because of its overall cognitive advantages: Less cognitive control might allow children to learn language by easily generalizing rules to new situations. And less top-down cognitive management may well help anyone think more creatively. When it comes to language, a bit less cognitive discipline could even lead to a deeper enjoyment of the aesthetic potential of language—I'm thinking of Virginia Woolf from Chapter 7, and her inability to hear the words "Passing Russell Square" without hearing the rustling sound of long skirts on floors. Who knows? Perhaps her keen awareness of the rich ambiguities inherent in all words may have had its roots in an artistic temperament and its failure to squash down all sorts of irrelevant but wonderfully interesting information.

GO TO
sites.sinauer.com/languageinmind

for **web activities, further readings, research updates, new essays,** and other features

A psycholinguist walks into a bar...

Time for some jokes.

A man and a friend are playing golf at their local golf course. One of the guys is about to chip onto the green when he sees a long funeral procession on the road next to the course. He stops in mid-swing, takes off his golf cap, closes his eyes, and bows down in prayer. His friend says: "Wow, that is the most thoughtful and touching thing I have ever seen. You truly are a kind man." The man then replies: "Yeah, well we were married 35 years."

Two weasels are sitting on a barstool. One starts to insult the other one. He screams, "I slept with your mother!" The bar gets quiet as everyone listens to see what the other weasel will do. The first weasel yells again, "I SLEPT WITH YOUR MOTHER!" The other says, "Go home, Dad, you're drunk."

I want to die peacefully in my sleep like my grandfather. Not screaming in terror like his passengers.

A man put on a clean pair of socks every day of the week. By Friday he could hardly get his shoes on.

If you wanted to get analytical about humor (and why in the world wouldn't you?), you might notice that these jokes create the eerily familiar cognitive sensation of leading you down one train of thought for a while and then, at the punch line, yanking you into a completely different mental frame of reference so that you have to reinterpret the entire situation in an unexpected way. You might think of it as the garden path approach to humor, with the punch line serving as the "disambiguating region." Scholars who study humor often argue that such incongruous shifts are an important part of what makes something funny. The philosopher Immanuel Kant put it this way: "Laughter is an affection arising from a strained expectation being suddenly reduced to nothing." There's a striking parallel between the "strained expectation" you might feel in reading a garden path sentence, and the brief bewilderment that occurs before the *Aha!* moment in the joke.

For many jokes, the humor goes beyond merely being analogous to linguistic ambiguity—it *relies* on it:

A man walks into a restaurant and growls at the maitre d': "Do you serve crabs here?" The maitre d' responds, "We serve everyone here. Have a seat, sir."

What do you call a fly with no wings? A walk.

There are two fish in a tank. The first fish says to the second fish, "How the hell do we drive this thing?"

Why did Ludwig van Beethoven kills his two ducks? They wouldn't stop saying "Bach! Bach!"

Given that so many jokes hinge on recognizing and resolving conflicting interpretations, whether linguistic or otherwise, it wouldn't be surprising to find that there's some overlap in the neural machinery that's involved in interpreting jokes and resolving ambiguities. We've seen that the frontal lobes of the brain play an important role in refereeing between competing interpretations, with a starring role for the region known as the left inferior frontal gyrus (LIFG). A brain-imaging study by Tristan Bekinschtein and colleagues (2011) found that this region was more active for jokes that rely on competing meanings than for ones that rely on absurdist thoughts or images:

Why did Cleopatra bathe in milk? Because she couldn't find a cow tall enough for a shower.

But ambiguity alone isn't enough to tickle the funny bone. If it were, this would also be a joke:

What was the problem with the other coat? It was hard to put on with the paint roller.

Jokes rely on ambiguity, plus a little magic. With run-of-the-mill ambiguity, the goal of the language processing system is to identify the correct interpretation and quickly and efficiently squash any competing ones. The magic in jokes probably has to do with the fact that the whole point is *not* to squash the competing meaning, but to keep both interpretations alive in order to enjoy the tension between them—the more interesting the tension, the better the joke. (And it's precisely this tension that makes some unintended "crash blossoms" hilarious.) Becoming conscious of the reverberations between meanings is even more cognitively complex than basic ambiguity resolution. And indeed, the brain imaging study by Bekinschtein et al. found that the LIFG was especially active when people listened to jokes

LANGUAGE AT LARGE 8.3 (*continued*)

that played with ambiguity, when compared with non-funny sentences involving ambiguous words.

So there's a great deal of enjoyment to be had from the fact that our minds activate multiple meanings at once, whether you're a Virginia Woolf type who savors the useless multiplicity of the meanings of words, or just someone who likes to hear a good joke. If you need a good laugh, you might try visiting the LaughLab (http://richardwiseman.wordpress.com/books/psychology-of-humour/), a website in which psychologist Richard Wiseman documents his search for the funniest joke in the world. You'll find many jokes there that rely on language processing working the way it does. Among the submissions, you'll find one of my favorites. It hinges not on a garden path ambiguity, or even a pun due to

outright lexical ambiguity, but on the more subtle lexical neighborhood activation effect, in which words that sound much like their targets are also accessed in the mind:

The monks were in the monastery copying those beautiful illuminated manuscripts. One young monk suggested that, since they'd been copying copies, it might be time to go back to the original and make sure that their copies were correct. The abbot agreed and sent the monk down into the cellar to examine the original. The monk was gone for a long time, and finally the abbot went to look for him. He found the monk in tears and asked what was wrong. Through his tears, the monk blurted out, "The word was *celebrate*!"

DIGGING DEEPER

Knowledge versus processing

One of the foundational ideas of modern linguistics is the distinction between *knowledge* of language and the *implementation* of this knowledge through processes whose end result is the actual comprehension or production of language. The idea is based on the very intuitive notion that we can have the knowledge required to do something, but all sorts of other factors in the end determine whether that knowledge is successfully carried out—presumably, you *know* how to multiply 24 and 37, but whether you manage to compute the answer in your head will be affected by a variety of things ranging from drunkenness to sleep deprivation, acute relationship troubles, a short memory span, someone yelling "952!" in your ear, and so on. In linguistics, *knowledge* of language—that is, the representations of words, the knowledge of sound patterns, understanding the options for how words can be formed from morphemes, grasping the rules of syntax, and all of that—is called *linguistic competence*. On the other hand, the mechanisms for recognizing or producing words, for parsing strings of words into meaningful structures, or figuring out, in the heat of the moment, how to assemble words into a sentence to express an idea, all fall into the domain of *linguistic performance*.

This separation has been implicit in all of our discussions on parsing so far—for instance, I've talked about how the rules of syntax are like a building code that *constrains* the construction of a sentence, but what actually gets built is determined by something else, namely "the parser." This seems to be a very useful distinction, because it allows us to explain why interpretation might fail even though a sentence seems to abide by everything we know about the patterns of our language. Consider, for example, the following sentences, all of which register as "bad" to the average English speaker:

The mouse the cat the dog bit chased ran.

The authors celebrated in the garden were drunk.

The three chairs is beside the table.

Her ate the cake.

The first example is an interpretation nightmare—most people just can't grasp what it means unless the structure of the sentence is made apparent (and it gets a lot easier if you transform the sentence to *The mouse that the cat that the dog bit chased ran*), in which case they might be able to squint and see that yes, it's a legitimate sentence after all. The second example is a garden-variety garden path sentence involving a reduced relative clause—with that knowledge, you should now be able to figure out what it means and agree that it's a legitimate sentence. On the other hand, the third and fourth examples are perfectly easy to understand, but they're just "wrong," and it's easy to point to what's wrong with them: in the third sentence, the subject and verb have to agree in number, so *is* should be *are*; in the fourth example, an object pronoun has been used instead of a subject pronoun, so *her* should be *she*. When foreigners are learning to speak a new language, we attribute many of their errors to a non-native *competence*, or a failure to have fully learned the patterns and structures of the language. The errors of native speakers though, whether slips of the tongue or lapses in understanding of convoluted but perfectly grammatical sentences, are normally said to be *performance* errors.

That seems reasonable enough, but the distinction gets murky pretty quickly. Take this common example:

Who did she meet?

Whom did she meet?

Is either of these "wrong"? It depends who(m) you ask! Until quite recently, the first sentence would have sounded just as bad to speakers of English as *Her ate the cake*, and for the same reason: namely, that the *wh*-pronoun bears the wrong *case marking*—it's marked as a subject form when it needs to be related to the object of *meet*. But languages evolve, and English is in the process of dropping the subject/object distinction on these *wh*- words. To many younger English speakers, *Whom did you meet?* sounds as archaic as *I bid thee good-bye*. In fact, many undergraduates I teach have so completely lost the subject/object distinction for *wh*- pronouns that they can't reliably tell which sounds more "right": *Whom did she meet?* Or *Whom ate the cake?*—a fact that might horrify some of their grandparents. (If you can't tell, either, I encourage you to admit this to someone a couple generations older than you and observe the effect.)

So, what are we to do with a situation in which English speakers disagree about which form is right? (And we're talking here about disagreement among monolinguals who have learned English from the day they were born, not foreign learners of English.) And, especially, what do we do with the speaker who thinks that either *who* or *whom* is perfectly good as a direct object of a verb? Is this a matter of competence? And if so, who are the fully competent speakers? Or should this be classified as a matter of performance—of having trouble understanding the sentences that are deemed bad? The answer to that depends on exactly why responses are varied. Is it because people's knowledge of these forms varies (especially as a function of age), or is it that younger and older people differ in their abilities to understand these *wh*- questions?

Most students I've asked say it's about knowledge. It seems obvious, they argue, that people will learn and prefer whichever form they're exposed to most often. Each

subsequent generation has been using fewer *whom*s and more *who*s, so that eventually, children learning English from young parents will very rarely if ever encounter a *whom*. Since learning the syntactic patterns of language is sensitive to the statistical distributions of those patterns, it makes sense that those kids who've heard *whom* quite often will think of that form as more "right" than those who've never heard it. So it also seems to make sense that one's competence, or knowledge of language, shouldn't just have all-or-none rules, but that perhaps these rules should be graded in a way that reflects the amount of experience they've had with specific linguistic patterns.

Again, all this seems reasonable enough. But here's where the potential blurring of competence and performance comes in. Remember that when we talked about the longer reading times for object relatives as opposed to subject relatives, this was all done in the context of talking about object relatives causing *processing* difficulty. And that seems right, if the difficulty really does boil down to issues with working memory constraints, as suggested by a number of researchers. But one of the alternative explanations for the processing trouble was that object relatives are simply less frequent than subject relatives, and hence less expected by a parser whose job it is to predict the form of the unfolding speech, whether it's a single word or a complex sentence. This means that frequency is reflected *both* in knowledge of language (so less-frequent sentences can be more grammatical than highly frequent ones) and in processing efficiency (less-frequent sentences are more difficult to process than more-frequent ones).

You might see where this is going. In the eyes of some researchers, especially those who are immersed in experience-based theories, there are no meaningful differences at all between knowledge and processing. Knowledge of language simply boils down to the accumulation of those routines that have been used to interpret or produce forms. Rather than having a separate and static set of rules that you consult like a building code during the process of building, the "rules" of syntax are more like a series of paths you've had to travel in the past in order to understand language: the more heavily traveled paths are the "rules" that generate more frequent structures. And, just like a familiar path home, it will both be easier to travel quickly, and feel more "right" than an unfamiliar one.

Still, for many researchers, the distinction between competence and performance remains a very important one. This is especially so for those scholars who've argued that much of the knowledge of language is innate. These researchers very explicitly reject a purely experience-based view of linguistic knowledge; they claim that much of what kids know about language *couldn't* have been learned through experience without some extra set of constraints or defaults, simply because their accuracy with certain kinds of structures goes far beyond what they could possibly have encountered as linguistic input (recall the arguments from the "poverty of the stimulus," as discussed in Section 6.4). So linguistic knowledge has to amount to more than just well-worn processing paths or routines.

As we've seen in Chapter 6, one of the strongest arguments that's made in support of the idea of innate linguistic knowledge is the fact that when you look across languages, there tend to be certain commonalities in structures or rules, so languages seem to be constrained in terms of the kinds of structures or patterns they allow. Small kids, the argument goes, show an uncanny ability to avoid just those structures that tend to be universally ruled out, presumably because they are innately guided toward jumping to the right conclusions about structure.

Let's go back to an example of a potentially universal constraint on the structure of *wh-* questions, which we first saw in Chapter 6. Remember that *wh-* words have to be linked to some position in the sentence, and that this relationship can span quite a large distance, and involve a variety of different syntactic slots:

What did Felicia claim that she saw her boyfriend eating spaghetti with __ ?

Who does Joey think he should be studying hard in order to impress__ ?

When did Britney say her lawyer would set up a hearing with the judge __ ?

But, as we saw, certain long-distance relationships seem to be forbidden even when they look superficially very similar to *wh-* relationships that never raise anyone's eyebrows. Compare, for example, the following set of contrasts (remember that the asterisk conventionally indicates unacceptability):

What do you think that Joey bought __?

* **What** do you wonder whether Joey bought __ ?

What did you claim that John bought __?

* **What** did you make the claim that John bought __ ?

What do you think that Josh left __ at my house ?

* **What** would you laugh if Josh left __ at my house?

Who did Betsy invite Silke to come with __ ?

* **Who** did Betsy invite Silke and __ ?

Who did Weyman believe __ had kicked Cecilia?

* **Who** did Weyman believe the rumor that __ had kicked Cecilia?

What did Stuart wonder if Myra made __ ?

* **What** did Stuart wonder when Myra made __ ?

These prohibitions on structure, often called *wh-* island constraints, are apparently echoed in many languages. And, as discussed in Chapter 6, kids seem to make surprisingly few errors with them, showing that they are aware of these restrictions on *wh-* questions. All of this is hard to explain under a purely experience-based account.

But there's another possible explanation that doesn't resort to saying that kids are genetically predetermined to favor certain *wh-* question structures over others. Some researchers have suggested that the ugliness of the above *wh-* questions for English speakers has nothing to do with speakers' knowledge or *competence*, but rather, that this is a matter of *performance*: such sentences, they claim, create difficulties for the parsing system. Hence, we should think of them more along the lines of horrendous sentences like *The horse raced past the barn fell*, or *The mouse the cat the dog bit chased ran*. Specifically, Robert Kluender and Marta Kutas (1993), along with Philip Hofmeister and Ivan Sag (2010) have proposed that *wh-* island constraints reflect limitations on working memory during sentence processing. If that's true, the mystery about the apparent universality of *wh-* question structures evaporates very quickly. And for that matter, so does the mystery of how kids know to avoid certain *wh-* structures: it's simply that those structures are too hard to compute.

One hint that a performance-based account of *wh-* islands might be on the right track is the fact that people don't seem to be absolutely uniform in condemning all *wh-* island violations as unacceptable (you may have quite a lot of variation in judgments in your own class, for example). This is surprising if the sentences are ruled out by universal, genetically programmed constraints, but much less so if they are grammatically well-formed but simply create processing difficulty. After all, there appear to be some systematic individual differences that correlate with how much difficulty people experience on certain garden path sentences or long-distance dependencies. If one could find that certain traits that are *known* to be implicated in processing difficulty also predict the variation in whether *wh-* island violations sound "bad," this would deflate one of the significant arguments for innate universal language-learning constraints.

Such evidence has been hard to find. In one paper, Jon Sprouse and colleagues (2012) tested subjects on a number of working-memory tasks, and found no relationship at all between memory performance and the degree to which these subjects rejected *wh-* island violations as bad sentences. On the other hand, Hofmeister et al. (2012) have complained that not much can be concluded from the study by Sprouse and colleagues until they first establish that the specific memory tests that they chose *do* reliably predict acceptability judgments for sentences that are already known to be unacceptable to subjects for processing reasons—for example, sentences like *The mouse the cat the dog bit chased ran.* Without this preliminary control in place, it's hard to know whether their particular method really bears on the question of competence versus performance at all.

In any case, given the juicy implications of the issue, there is bound to be a good deal more heated debate about whether to classify these iconic *wh-* island violations as a matter of knowledge, or a matter of processing.

PROJECT

Aside from approaching the question from an individual differences perspective, can you think of another way to test whether *wh-* island violations reflect competence or performance? Propose and, if possible, carry out an experiment to find out. Be sure to think about the appropriate control sentences you would want to use, and to establish that your method is capable of capturing the distinction.

9 Speaking: From Planning to Articulation

Speaking can get you into trouble. Ask a friend of mine, who is married to a woman named Carmen. A frosty weekend in the marital household once ensued after he slipped up during a conversation and addressed her as *Susan*—the name of his previous spouse. Oops. Carmen took this as an ominous sign that he was not yet over his ex-wife. To make matters worse, my friend's entire family, despite having been warned of the dire consequences, has managed to make exactly the same slip in poor Carmen's presence at one time or another.

It gets worse. You can lose your job for misspeaking. In 2006, radio announcer Dave Lenihan was fired for dropping a racial slur while discussing the prospect of Condoleezza Rice as commissioner for the National Football League. Lenihan said, "She's got the patent résumé of somebody that has serious skill. She loves football, she's African-American, which would be kind of a big coon. A big coon. Oh my God—I totally, totally, totally, totally am sorry for that. I didn't mean that."

Listeners pounced, demanding his resignation. Lenihan claimed that he was aiming to articulate *coup* and mispronounced the word. No matter. In the ensuing kerfuffle, many commentators expressed the belief that uttering the word (whether intentionally or not) reflected racist attitudes (whether consciously held or not) on the part of Dave Lenihan. The radio station manager agreed, and within 20 minutes he was on the air to announce that Lenihan was being tossed from the show. The manager said he believed the offending word was an inadvertent slip of the tongue, but was nonetheless "unacceptable, reprehensible, and unforgivable."

And you especially need to watch your tongue if you're a politician. In 2012, Republican candidate Rick Santorum had an episode in which he inserted a problematic syllable into his speech while referring to President Barack Obama: "We know, we know the candidate Barack Obama, what he was like. The anti-war government nig- uh, the uh America was a source for division around the world." Almost immediately, the video clip for this portion of his speech spread over the Internet faster than lexical activation spreads between two semantically related words. Naturally, many people claimed that Santorum had caught himself in the midst of uttering a racially charged word, thereby revealing the true inner attitudes that he normally attempted to hide from voters.

The reactions illustrated here all point to a very common explanation for speech errors that goes back to the psychologist Sigmund Freud—in fact, many people still call errors like this "Freudian slips." (As the joke goes, Freudian slips are when you say one thing but mean your mother.) Freud believed that these unintended speech intrusions were often symptoms of repressed thoughts that managed to break through to the surface despite our best efforts to keep them squashed below consciousness. To Freud, speech errors acted like windows into the mind.

In one example, Freud discussed how a professor in the middle of giving a lecture mistakenly uttered the German word *Versuchungen* ("temptations") instead of the word *Versuche* ("experiments"), causing him to say: "In the case of female genitals, in spite of many temptations—I beg your pardon, *experiments*." Supposedly, the error bubbled to the surface because of the speaker's secret thoughts about the tempting nature of female genitalia.

But, unlike you, Freud predated the great era of psycholinguistics. I'm guessing that even at this early stage in your own knowledge of language, you could probably offer a competing explanation for many speech errors, and give Freud an intellectual run for his money. For instance, you now have the benefit of knowing from studies of word recognition that words aren't pulled out of memory as single, hermetically sealed packages in isolation from other words. You've seen reams of data showing that multiple lexical entries become activated all at once, particularly those that are similar in sound and meaning, and that similar words jostle and compete for recognition. It doesn't seem like much of a stretch to suppose that a connected lexicon and competitive activation might also sometimes gum up the system for speaking. I suspect it hasn't escaped your notice either that in German, the words for *temptations* and *experiments* are highly similar in *form*. Would the professor have been just as likely to make the same speech error while speaking English, in which the words *temptations* and *experiments* sound nothing like each other?

And yet, the Freudian view of speech errors is extremely common among many people today. Its stubborn prevalence is one of the most striking examples of the disconnect between what floats around in the world as general knowledge about language, and the detailed, data-grounded knowledge that exists within the language sciences community. Psycholinguists overwhelmingly take a very different view of what causes speech errors, but for some reason, this hasn't filtered down to the general public. To re-invoke a metaphor from the first chapter of this book, it's as if psycholinguists have been discussing gravity as an explanation for why objects fall—but everyone else is still talking about magnets.

A Freudian explanation for speech errors sounds perfectly plausible if you know very little about the guts of language. After all, very few people stop to think about all the various processes and mechanisms that have to be in place in order for language to work properly. So it never occurs to them that speech errors might have a much less, well, sexy explanation than the one Freud offered and that so-called Freudian slips might just be the result of some breakdown in the mundane, everyday mechanics of speaking.

As it happens, speech errors *are* a fascinating window into the mind. But not in the way that Freud thought. The variety of errors, where and when they occur, and how often they slip out can reveal a lot about the underlying mechanics of speaking. Much of what we know about how speaking works has been sparked by the study of speech errors—trying to explain slips of the tongue led to new ideas that in turn prompted the invention of experimental techniques to test those ideas. This chapter is the story of what psycholinguists have discovered about the mechanics of speaking, and how they got there.

WEB ACTIVITY 9.1

Collecting speech errors In this activity, you'll be asked to keep a journal in which you jot down every speech error that you hear over a few days. You'll be prompted to think about any patterns you observe, and to generate some hypotheses about their underlying cause, based on what you already know about language.

9.1 The Space between Thinking and Speaking

Sentences are prepared on the fly

You may have been told at some point in your life: think before you speak. Well, that raises a good question: How much *do* you normally think before you begin to speak? Do you typically plan out your entire sentence in your mind before you begin to utter its first sound? Or do you just dive in and start talking, building the sentence as you go along? To get a feel for the question, try this: start narrating aloud what happened to you in the first hour after you woke up today. Ready. Set. Go.

While doing this little exercise, you might have become aware of moments when, in the middle of a sentence, you were still trying to remember this morning's events in sequence, or you were fumbling around for the right word. Chances are, you weren't completely fluent. Your speech was probably littered with pauses, false starts, backtracking, the odd "um" and "uh," or places where you stretched a word out, stalling for time while thinking about what you were going to say next. In fact, you'd be *highly* exceptional if you got through your whole narrative without any hesitations or disfluencies. In normal conversation, people simply don't go around speaking in perfect, crisp, well-formed sentences that roll smoothly off the tongue. Reading a word-for-word transcript of actual spoken language can be quite eye-opening—when speech is recorded on paper, it's clear that people are rarely as articulate as we remember them being. (**Box 9.1** reveals disfluencies in the speech of even the smooth-talking former U.S. president Bill Clinton.)

The sheer ubiquity of hesitations and disfluencies in people's speech makes it pretty clear that they begin to speak before they've planned out every detail of their upcoming utterance. It seems that speaking is incremental—sentences are assembled a step at a time, with much of the assembly being carried out on the fly while deep in the throes of actually uttering it. In this sense, it's much like language comprehension, in which interpretation is attempted long before the entire sentence (or even a significant chunk of it) has unrolled from someone's mouth.

At the same time, it doesn't seem likely that speech production is *radically* incremental or assembled entirely on the fly—a certain amount of planning has to have happened before you open your mouth. Speaking is a bit different from comprehension in this regard. In the process of language *understanding*, you initiate interpretation on the basis of the smallest snippets of speech, beginning to activate possible lexical items and immediately trying to integrate these with the structure of the unfolding sentence. The gap between speech and interpretation literally comes down to a matter of milliseconds.

BOX 9.1
What spoken language really sounds like

Written and spoken language are strikingly different from each other. Without seeing verbatim transcripts of spoken language, it's hard to get an appreciation for just how riddled with disfluencies human speech can be. Detailed court transcripts can reveal how people really talk, at least when in the charged atmosphere of a courtroom. The following excerpts are taken from transcripts in the impeachment trial of former president Bill Clinton, in which he was charged with lying about his relationship with White House intern Monica Lewinsky.

The first excerpt is from Clinton's famous response to questions from a grand jury (August 17, 1998). When queried about the truthfulness of a statement made by his lawyer during a deposition about Clinton's relationship with Lewinsky, the then-president responded:

It depends on what the meaning of the word is is. If the—if he—if is means "is and never has been," that is not—that is one thing. If it means "there is none," that was a completely true statement…. But the—as I have testified, and like to testify again, this is—it is somewhat unusual for a client to be asked about his lawyer's statements instead of the other way around.

The next excerpt is from an official deposition of Lewinsky on February 5, 1999:

Question: *Okay. Um, tell me how you, um, began—I guess the—the—we're going to talk about a relationship with the President. Uh, when you first, uh, I guess, saw him, I think there was some indication that you didn't speak to him maybe the first few times you saw him, but you had some eye contact or sort of smiles or—*
M.L.: *I—I believe I've testified to that in the grand jury pretty extensively.*
Question: *Uh-huh.*
M.L.: *Is—is there something more specific?*
Question: *Well, again, I'm wanting to know times, you know, how soon that occurred and sort of what happened, you know, if you can—you know, there are going to be occasions where yo—obviously, you testified extensively in the grand jury, so you're going to obviously repeat things today. We're doing the deposition for the senators to view, we believe, so it's—*

These examples suggest that real-life courtroom dialogue seldom resembles the fluently scripted versions of such scenes depicted on popular television shows.

But in the other direction, moving from thought to speech, it's fairly implausible that speech precedes thought by mere milliseconds. You probably don't launch into a sentence beginning with *My stupid cat…* without having the least idea of what you're going to say about your cat. Presumably, the thought that prompted you to speak in the first place involved some complex state or event that you wanted to communicate, and not just a vague impulse to talk about your cat. Exactly how much thinking goes on before speech probably reflects how you resolve competing pressures on the language production system. On the one hand, the more you plan ahead, the more fluent you can be, and the fewer (potentially embarrassing!) errors you'll make. On the other hand, planning your entire utterance ahead of time before speaking might impose a great burden on working memory, since you'll have to store the entire thing in a memory buffer before uttering the first word. What's more, you might need to take a long time in planning your sentence. This might be a distinct disadvantage when it comes to getting a word in edgewise or holding the floor while engaging in a conversation. As you've no doubt experienced at some point, conversation can be a competitive sport!

What goes on as we prepare to speak?

If hesitations in speech reflect something about the thinking that goes on while preparing to speak, then it seems clear that more thinking happens in some parts of a sentence than in others. Instead of being spread around evenly throughout sentences, pauses and disfluencies are most likely to be found at

LANGUAGE AT LARGE 9.1

The sounds of silence:
Conversational gaps across cultures

Next time you're at a party, take note of how much time elapses between the time one person finishes speaking and another person picks up the conversational baton. Partners usually exchange conversational turns fairly briskly, minimizing pregnant pauses but avoiding jumping in and speaking over the other person. It's a truism, however, that different cultures practice different conversational pacing, and that some cultures value silent gaps in conversation while others abhor them. Lehtonen and Sajavaara (1985) report one story in which two Finnish brothers were on their way to work in the morning. One of them said, "It is here that I lost my knife." They continued in silence, but on the way back home in the evening, the other brother said, "Your knife, did you say?" On the other hand, members of a number of ethnic communities are famous for not doing anything that remotely resembles queuing up for a conversational turn, it being socially acceptable to speak simultaneously (and loudly). If it's true that different cultures expect different amounts of silence between conversational turns, it raises some interesting questions about the kinds of cognitive pressures that speakers might be subjected to across cultures—for instance, disfluency rates might be higher for those in which little time is allotted for planning.

Ethnic stereotypes aside, there are very few systematic studies that have looked at whether speakers from different cultures actually do differ that much from each other when it comes to the spaces between conversational turns. In one study, led by Tanya Stivers (2009), the findings showed a surprising amount of uniformity in the amount of time that elapsed between the end of one person's question, and the onset of the other person's answer. Stivers and colleagues looked at ten languages across five continents, studying speakers from hunter-gatherer groups, peasant societies, and post-industrial nations. For the vast majority of these languages, average response times clustered around 200 milliseconds after the end of the question—suggesting that people were *anticipating* the end of the question, and were beginning to plan their response before it had ended. Even the slowest responders—the unhurried Danes—lagged a mere syllable length behind.

So why do we have the impression that cultures vary so dramatically in the length of their conversational gaps?

One answer might be that some language groups, more than others, seem to more readily tolerate *really* long conversational gaps. For example, even though Stivers and colleagues found that the average response time for Danes was 469 milliseconds, a substantial number of gaps lingered on for 1.5 seconds or more, whereas pauses of this length hardly ever occurred for speakers of Korean or Dutch. Some cases can be much more extreme. Rod Gardner (2010), who studies the conversation of speakers of the Australian aboriginal language Garrwa, notes that in a few rare cases, speakers of this language feel under no obligation to respond directly to a question—or they may take as long as a week to do so. Here is one such example, attributed to linguist Michael Walsh (1997):

> So imagine a situation where I'm asking: "That green frog over there in the tree, have you got a name for that one?" pointing to a tree and pointing to a real frog that is right there—in front of us. What happens? Not only does the person not give me the answer. He looks away. There is no response whatsoever. There is just complete silence. Perhaps I have first asked that question on a Tuesday. When I am down at the camp again on Wednesday of the following week back comes the answer. The man says, "That one, that green one there, we call that one durket." When he says this without any kind of explicit linkage to the previous questioning session, it is already over a week. So I ask: "What is this green one?" Perhaps wondering whether I'm a little slow, he says, "You know, in the tree." And I wonder if he is referring to a leaf. "No, green one, in the tree, durket." Eventually, it dawns on me that he is referring to the green frog that I asked about over a week ago.

It's not hard to see how this kind of interaction would stick in the mind of your typical anglophone. Perhaps, when we interact with speakers from a different culture, it's precisely these infrequent but extreme outliers that we become aware of, even if the bulk of their conversation involves gaps of lengths similar to our own. It's also possible, however, that we're finely calibrated to expect conversational gaps to be of a very specific length, so even variations of mere hundreds of milliseconds lead to an impression that people are taking eons to respond, or are babbling over each other.

Continued on next page

LANGUAGE AT LARGE 9.1 (*continued*)

What is certain is that we *do* have expectations of how long people should pause before answering. When these expectations are violated, we notice. Try this just for fun: The next time someone asks you if you are single, take an excessively long time to answer. You might find that the person who asked the question finds your hesitation more significant than your actual answer. This is a pretty general reaction, as documented by Jean E. Fox Tree (2002). If the speaker takes longer than usual to respond, the hearer begins to hunt around for a *reason* for the delay. Perhaps the speaker is signaling that the question is contemptible, or potentially incriminating, or that he's carefully weighing the consequences of his response, and so on. In other words, we communicate not just with *what* we say, but with *how long* we take to say it.

It seems that there are some cultural differences in what counts as taking "longer than usual" to answer, and what hearers tend to infer from delays in responding (e.g., Roberts et al., 2011). This leaves the door open to some communicative friction: for instance, Garrwa speakers report feeling pressured by non-Aboriginals to speak before they're ready, and they are sometimes wrongly perceived as being uncooperative or disengaged in conversation.

the boundaries of clauses or long phrases, suggesting that speech might be planned in large chunks that convey fairly complex ideas. Here's an example of some speech produced by a child telling a story, with dots indicating the pauses in speech (from Hawkins, 1971):

> Well once there was a sailor and two children and a dog … and one day … the two children said … to their … the sailor … can we play with our dog and the sailor said yes … and so they did but the dog ran away … and … one day … the two children were out in the woods … and they found their dog … and they were so happy they run ran home and told the sailor … and the dog in the night … there was a window open … the sailor had forgot and the children had forgot to shut it … so … one day … the dog ran out … of the window … and then he never came back and was lost all his life.

Of course, we don't know what *kind* of thinking is going on at these pauses. In tackling the question of how far ahead we think before speaking, it makes sense to distinguish between planning *what* to say versus formulating a detailed plan for *how* to say it. Our thoughts don't spring into our minds as fully formed sentences, even if it feels that way sometimes—quite a bit of work has to be done to hammer them out into language.

First of all, lining up meanings with words is not a trivial process. Some things that we might want to talk about (like a cat) correspond conveniently to single words, but others have to be expressed by assembling groups of words (for instance, *the door handle on the front passenger side of the car*, or *the first person standing in line*). There's a certain amount of arbitrariness in whether an idea matches up with a single word, as becomes apparent when you look beyond English and notice that different languages sometimes have quite different ways of carving concepts up. In English, we have different words, *hand* and *arm*, to express these two concepts; in Hebrew, there's just one that expresses both. But Hebrew uses two words to distinguish the back of the neck and the front of the neck, whereas English is usually stuck with the single word *neck*. To complicate matters, the word *throat* is sometimes used to refer to the front of the neck, but if you say you have a sore throat, this doesn't mean the front of your neck hurts. So, part of planning for speaking clearly involves lining up our thoughts with whichever words our own language offers up as the best match. This could well take a certain amount of time *after* we've figured out what we want to say, especially if the word we're trying to retrieve happens to be a fairly unfamiliar one (it might take longer to choose the word *excoriate* compared with its synonym, *criticize*.)

We also have to make decisions about how to express the different relations among the people and things we want to talk about. For instance, the sentence *Eileen gave the money to Guy* clearly expresses the relationship between Eileen, Guy, and some money. But so do these *different* sentences:

Eileen gave Guy the money.

Guy was given the money by Eileen.

Guy received the money from Eileen.

Guy received from Eileen the money.

The money was received by Guy from Eileen.

Money passed from Eileen to Guy.

Money passed to Guy from Eileen.

Just as a listener has to decide among competing meanings for an incoming sentence, the speaker has to choose from among competing forms to express his intended meaning.

Once the words and the structure are chosen, they still need to be fleshed out in terms of their specific sounds, with a set of instructions passed down to the mouth, tongue, and lips to perform a very specific series of articulatory gestures.

In other words, at least three steps are involved in planning for speaking: (1) we have to figure out the overall meaning we want to express; (2) we need to figure out what words to use, and what order to put them in; and (3) we have to implement each word as a series of sounds that comes out of our mouths. For all we know, there might be some significant time gap between these processes. For example, think about how most people sketch a scene. They don't draw each part of the picture out in detail in sequential order from the left side of the picture to the right. Instead, they start with a rough sketch, and then go back and fill in the details later. It's entirely possible that language production works this way too. It could be that a speaker first decides on a message to express, sometime later chooses how to express it with specific words in a certain order, and then, even later, gets around to the task of figuring out how to pronounce them. Hesitations in speech tell us that some kind of mental activity is taking place in the planning process at that point. But it's hard to know exactly what.

> **WEB ACTIVITY 9.2**
>
> **Locating disfluencies** In this activity, you'll hear clips of disfluencies in recordings of spontaneous speech across various situations. Take note of the types of disfluencies that crop up, and where in the sentences they occur. Can you generate any guesses about what aspects of planning might have been going on at some of these disfluency sites?

How far in advance is language planned?

Having thought a bit about what's involved in the act of speaking, we can give some more shape to our question about thinking before speaking. Let's start by asking: What kind of *linguistic* planning do speakers normally do in advance, and how far in advance do they do it? In other words, once a speaker's already decided on the message, how far ahead does he get in choosing words and figuring out how to say them before actually starting to talk?

To answer this, we'll need some evidence that provides a bit more detail than hesitations in speech. It turns out that a useful source of data is… you guessed it, speech errors. Freud's theory of tongue slips dealt mostly with cases where a word came to be replaced by a true interloper, that is, by a word that was never *meant* to be uttered at all—for instance, *Versuchungen* ("temptations") instead of *Versuche* ("experiments"). These interloper words were supposed to give clues about the speaker's intruding thoughts. But you may have noticed that many speech errors involve words from *within* the same sentence becoming repeated or exchanged for each other. For example:

This **spring** has a **seat** in it. (*Intended:* This seat has a spring in it.)

The **tree** fell from the **apple**. (*Intended:* The apple fell from the tree.)

A stitch in **nine** saves **nine**. (*Intended:* A stitch in time saves nine.)

A **laboratory** in our own **computer**. (*Intended:* A computer in our own laboratory.)

Notice that in all of these cases, a word gets replaced by one that is supposed to occur *later on* in the sentence. Here, there's no mystery about why the intruding words would have come to mind: presumably, it's because the speaker planned to say them! But this means *the intruding words must have come to mind well before the point in the sentence where they were supposed to be spoken*, providing evidence that words, and not just concepts, are planned in advance. In the last example, for instance, the word *laboratory* must have already been selected as the speaker began the phrase, or it never would have gotten swapped for the intended word *computer*.

Most exchanges like this happen between words in the same clause, so it seems likely that not much linguistic planning takes place over a span larger than a clause. But there's experimental evidence to suggest that very detailed planning may take place on a considerably smaller scale. For example, Mark Smith and Linda Wheeldon (1999) used an interesting method to study sentence planning. They had subjects look at a computer screen displaying pictures of several objects that moved to new positions on the screen; their task was to describe which objects had moved where (see **Figure 9.1**). The researchers measured how long it took people to begin speaking depending on how complex the elements of the sentence were. They reasoned that a more complex bit of language should require longer planning time. This turned out to be true when comparing sentences like:

The dog moves up.

The dog and the foot move up.

People were faster to begin saying the first sentence than the second sentence, which has a more complex subject. This shows that they must have been preplanning at least the subject noun phrase before speaking, taking extra time to prepare the more complex subject.

But Smith and Wheeldon also showed an interesting difference between the next two sentences:

The dog and the foot move above the kite.

The dog moves above the foot and the kite.

Both sentences are equally complex. But speakers took longer to begin uttering the first sentence than the second sentence. This makes sense only if speakers weren't planning ahead all of the content of

(A)

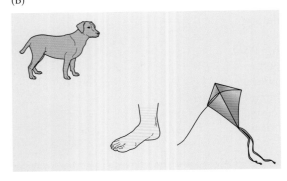

(B)

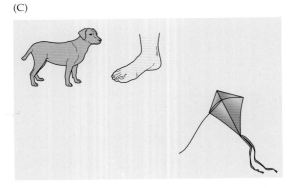

(C)

Figure 9.1 Example stimulus displays in the language production experiment by Smith and Wheeldon (1999). (A) Three target objects (dog, foot, kite) appear in their starting positions. (B) One object (dog) has moved vertically. Subjects were instructed to describe the movement of objects, and in this case, the target utterance is *the dog moves up*. (C) Two target objects (dog, foot) have moved vertically, and the target utterance is *the dog and the foot move up*.

the sentence to an equal extent. Specifically, it suggests that the subject phrase of a sentence was planned in quite a lot of detail before speech began, but an object phrase was not. Speakers paused longer before uttering a sentence with a complex subject phrase. But when the subject was simple and the object phrase was complex, they were able to begin speaking sooner, doing some of the planning of the object phrase *after* they'd begun to talk.

The experimental method used by Smith and Wheeldon is a much more refined way to make inferences about sentence planning than just using hesitations or speech errors in natural speech. It has the great advantage of allowing researchers to control the specific properties of sentences to test more precise hypotheses. But in the end, the technique is still using the presence or length of a silence to figure out how much planning is being done, without probing specifically for what *kind* of planning is being done. For example, were specific words for the subject phrase being chosen during that silence? If so, was their sound structure being fleshed out? In the next section, we look at evidence that leads us to believe that speaking consists of a number of different operations, each of which is separated in time and appears in a particular order.

9.2 Ordered Stages in Language Production

Are sound and meaning planned separately?

You'll remember that the question of ordered stages came up in chapter 8 in the discussion of language comprehension. Back then, we talked about the garden path model, which proposed that in the first stage of parsing, the language processor accesses only a limited amount of syntactic information, with more detailed semantic and contextual information playing a role only at later stages. We saw that there wasn't a lot of evidence for separate stages in parsing.. Still, the story could be quite different in language production. The requirements of the two tasks are different enough that there's no reason to suppose that production and comprehension are the same process simply run in reverse.

Let's start with the question of whether there are separate stages involved in accessing words' meanings versus their sounds. It might seem strange to think about choosing a word without automatically accessing the sounds that go into it, since the sounds of a word seem to be so inextricably tied to its meaning. But there's reason to believe that there's a stage during speaking when you might have actually selected a word, but not yet filled in its sound structure. And again, some of the first clues to this came from speech errors.

So far, we've only been talking about errors that involve entire words, like the exchanges you saw earlier, or the kinds of word substitutions that Freud talked about. But in all likelihood, your own collection from Web Activity 9.1 includes many slips that involve *parts* of words as well. You've probably heard the term *spoonerism* used to describe speech errors in which sounds get exchanged between words. This type of speech error was made famous by the Reverend William Archibald Spooner, an Oxford don who was notorious for peppering his speech with them. Some of the spoonerisms attributed to the tongue-slipping Reverend Spooner include:

The Lord is a **sh**oving **l**eopard. (*Intended:* **l**oving **sh**epherd)

We'll have the **h**ags **f**lung out. (*Intended:* **f**lags **h**ung out)

a half-**w**armed **f**ish (*Intended:* half-**f**ormed **w**ish)

Let's **gl**aze our **r**asses to the **qu**eer old **d**ean. (*Intended:* Let's **r**aise our **gl**asses to the **d**ear old **qu**een.)

BOX 9.2
Common types of speech errors

Many of these errors can be found in a seminal 1971 paper by Vicky Fromkin, which contains some of the first detailed linguistic observations of speech errors.

Errors involving word units

Substitutions, in which an intended word is replaced by one not meant to appear in the sentence:

> *nationalness* of rules (Intended: *naturalness* of rules)
>
> I have some additional proposals to *hang* out (Intended: *hand* out)
>
> chamber *maid* (Intended: chamber *music*)
>
> the *oral*—written part of the exam

Blends, in which two words, often similar in meaning, are fused together:

> I *swindged* (switched/changed)
>
> She's a real *swip* chick (swinging/hip)
>
> A tennis *athler* (athlete/player)

Exchanges, in which two words, both intended, trade places:

> examine the *horse* of the *eyes* (Intended: the *eyes* of the *horse*)
>
> *sickle* and *hammer* (Intended: *hammer* and *sickle*)

Errors involving morpheme units

Exchanges, in which morphemes are switched, rather than entire complex words:

> *nerve* of a *vergeous* breakdown (Intended: *verge* of a *nervous* breakdown)
>
> already *trunked* two *packs* (Intended: *packed* two *trunks*)

Errors involving sound units

Anticipations, in which a sound is mistakenly produced too early:

> *reek* long race (Intended: *week* long race)
>
> *alsho* share (Intended: *also* share)

Perseverations, in which an already pronounced sound is mistakenly produced again:

> John gave the *goy* (Intended: gave the *boy*)
>
> black *bloxes* (Intended: black *boxes*)

Exchanges of two sound units:

> the *n*ipper is *z*arrow (Intended: *z*ipper is *n*arrow)
>
> *f*ash and *t*ickle (Intended: *f*ish and *t*ackle)

Errors involving sound features

> *g*lear *p*lue sky (Intended: *c*lear *b*lue sky; the *unvoiced* sound /k/ in *clear* becomes *voiced* /g/, while the *voiced* sound /b/ in *blue* becomes *unvoiced* /p/)
>
> *m*ang the *m*ail (Intended: *b*ang the *n*ail; /b/ anticipates the *nasal* feature from /n/ in *nail*, the *labial* feature from /b/ in *bang* is preserved, turning /n/ to /m/)

The Reverend Spooner may have been especially susceptible to speech errors, but these anecdotal examples of sound-based errors are similar to many that have been gathered more meticulously by linguists. **Box 9.2** gives examples of some common sound-based errors. The fact that speech errors can involve *parts* of words is interesting in itself—it provides a clue that when words are chosen for the purpose of speaking, they don't come off the mental shelf as whole units. Rather, they're more like boxes that contain parts of words that still have to be assembled, the parts being the sounds that the word contains. Sound exchanges might happen because more than one selected word gets "unpacked" and assembled at the same time, and occasionally (or, if you're the Reverend Spooner, quite often) the parts from one word end up on another word that's also in the process of being assembled.

Even more interesting is the fact that exchanges of whole words seem to follow a different pattern than exchanges of sounds. When words are exchanged, the errors almost always involve words of the same syntactic category—nouns are swapped for other nouns, verbs are swapped for other verbs, and so on. The errors can take place over a number of intervening words (though typically within the same clause), which, as I mentioned, hints at advance planning.

But different rules seem to apply to sound exchanges. The span over which these errors take place is much tighter, almost always between adjacent words—for example, it would be very unusual to have a sound exchange where a sentence like *Let's raise our glasses to the dear old queen* came out as *Let's daze our glasses to the rear old queen.* Sound exchanges also don't seem to care whether the words involved come from the same category (and in fact, adjacent words hardly ever do). What they do care about is that affected sounds come from similar *parts* of words. The onsets of syllables hardly ever swap with the ends of syllables—*dear old queen* doesn't become *near old queed,* for example. Sound exchanges also involve similar types of sounds, so consonants don't exchange with vowels.

How to account for these very striking differences in the behavior of word-based versus sound-based errors? Since sound-based errors happen within a much smaller window than word-based errors, this suggests that people plan further ahead when thinking about which words to choose than they do when thinking about how to pronounce those words—which in turn suggests that during speaking, we can, at some level, identify and choose words before thinking about their sounds. That is, words can be inserted into a sentence frame as word "kits" instead of being immediately assembled into their sequences of sounds. At this earlier stage, words are tagged by their meanings and their syntactic category, since word exchanges seem to be restricted to swapping words of the same category; a later process puts all the word pieces together. Psycholinguists refer to these phonologically unassembled word kits as **lemmas**. Again, the idea is that it's a little bit like sketching: an artist might at first draw just enough to indicate that he's drawing a lion and a man, and to show the relationship between them, but only later go back to fill in the fine details.

Using experiments to study ordered stages

A close and thoughtful analysis of speech errors, then, can provide much more than an intuitively satisfying explanation for why someone blurted out the wrong word; it can provide the foundation of a theory about how speaking works. Naturally, once you have a theory, you want to test its predictions across a variety of situations, using a number of different techniques. A 1996 paper by Antje Meyer provides a good example of such a test.

Meyer's study leveraged an idea that is familiar from the study of word recognition: that words are connected to other words in complex networks, reflecting similarities of sound or meaning. On the comprehension side, we saw that these connections could often *speed up* the word recognition process as a result of spreading activation (as evident in the semantic priming paradigm). But lexical connections could also *slow down* the recognition of a word, by virtue of inhibitory links from competitors that also became activated. Since it seems unlikely that only comprehension, but not production, would involve retrieving words that are interconnected with other words, we might expect to see evidence of both facilitation and competition in speaking as well.

And we do. Some evidence of this comes from a picture-word interference task (see **Figure 9.2**). In this task, subjects see pictures of objects with words superimposed on them, and are asked to name these objects as quickly as possible while ignoring the words (or, in some variants, they hear the distractor word while viewing the picture). When the words are semantically related to the picture (for instance, the subject sees the word *cat* while preparing to name a picture of a dog), people are slower to name the picture than when the word and picture are unrelated. This suggests that semantically related words compete with each other during language production (and the effect does seem to be about *language production* rather than about accessing concepts, because

lemma An abstract mental representation of a word containing information about its meaning and syntactic category, but not about its sounds.

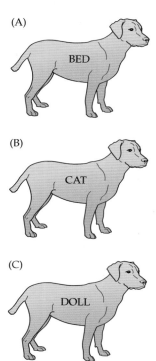

Figure 9.2 Examples of stimuli from a picture-word interference task, in which subjects name the picture (*dog*). (A) The word superimposed on the picture is unrelated in sound or meaning to the image, representing the baseline condition. (B) The word is semantically related to the picture, generally resulting in slower naming times compared with the baseline. (C) The word is phonologically related to the picture, often resulting in faster responses relative to the baseline.

you don't see this happen when people are simply asked if they recognize the objects in the picture, but don't have to name them). On the other hand, when subjects see a phonologically related word (say, *doll*, when preparing to say *dog*), they're usually *faster* to name the picture as compared with an unrelated word-picture pair. (Notice that this is the mirror image of the competition and facilitation effects you saw in Chapter 7 for word recognition, where semantic relatedness tended to yield facilitation effects, while phonological similarity often led to competition effects. In both comprehension and production, though, semantic and phonological overlap can lead to *either* facilitation or inhibition, depending in part on exactly when you probe for the accessibility of the target word.)

Meyer used these effects of semantic and phonological relatedness as a tool to test whether the window for advance planning is larger for selecting word lemmas than it is for spelling out their sounds. She showed subjects pictures of two objects side by side, and instructed them to describe the pictures using the simple sentence frame "The X is next to Y" (see **Figure 9.3A,B**). Just as the picture ap-

(A)   Visual stimulus

(B)   Target sentence

*De **kerk** staat naast de pijl.* ("The church is next to the arrow.")

(C)   Effects of semantic interference (Experiment 2 results)

Distractor word	Condition	Subjects' mean reaction time (ms)
moskee ("mosque")	1 (semantically related to Word 1)	827
broek ("pants")	2 (unrelated to Word 1)	789
speer ("spear")	3 (semantically related to Word 2)	812
wieg ("cradle")	4 (unrelated to Word 2)	786

(D)   Effects of phonological facilitation (Experiment 4 results)

Distractor word	Condition	Subjects' mean reaction time (ms)
kers ("cherry")	1 (phonologically related to Word 1)	729
beer ("bear")	2 (unrelated to Word 1)	766
pijp ("pipe")	3 (phonologically related to Word 2)	766
maan ("moon")	4 (unrelated to Word 2)	754

Figure 9.3 Summary of stimuli and results from two experiments by Meyer (1996). These studies were conducted in the Netherlands, with all instructions and linguistic stimuli in Dutch. Results showed that *semantically* related (similar in meaning) distractor words slowed down access of both the first and second targeted words. *Phonologically* related (similar in sound) distractor words, however, sped up access of the first target word, while having no effect on the second. (Adapted from Meyer, 1996.)

peared (or very slightly before or after), subjects heard the distractor word—in this case, it was either unrelated, or semantically or phonologically related to *either the first or the second word*. When the distractor was semantically related to the first word, subjects took longer to begin speaking—not surprisingly, this shows that they were in the process of retrieving the lemma for the first word before beginning to speak, and they experienced competition from the distractor. When the distractor was phonologically related to the first word, people were *faster* to begin speaking (see **Figure 9.3C,D**). This shows that they were also filling in the sounds for the first word and that they got a boost from the related distractor at this point. So far, the results provide a reassuring replication of effects found for single words.

But as Figure 9.3 shows, the results were different when the distractor was related to the *second* word. When it was semantically related, subjects again experienced a delay in launching the second, showing that they were retrieving the lemma of a word that would appear farther downstream. But there was no effect at all of the phonologically related distractor, due to either facilitation or competition. So it seems that before speaking, people had retrieved the second noun's lemma, but were not yet worrying about specifying its sounds—that would come only later, while they were already in the midst of uttering the sentence.

It's on the tip of your tongue

Meyer's study used highly precise measures to tease apart stages of production in a way that would be impossible to get at more intuitively. But just about everyone *has* had an intuitively accessible experience in which they've accessed a word's lemma, but not yet clothed it phonologically. This experience is called a **tip-of-the-tongue state**—it refers to those occasions when you *know* there's a specific word for what you're trying to express, you know exactly what it means, it's almost arrived on your tongue, it'll be there in just a moment—but it seems to be just beyond your grasp. Annoyingly, the word often pops into your head a half hour later, once the conversation is over. You might think of this experience as an enormous elongation of the usual two-step process involved in accessing a word.

There's good evidence that when people experience a tip-of-the-tongue state, they don't just have the illusion of knowing the word; they really have accessed it, although only partially. In many cases, they can remember the first letter, or can reliably guess the number of syllables it has. Often, they produce sound-alike words. One study of Italian speakers (Vigliocco et al., 1997) showed that they could reliably report the grammatical gender of the nouns that eluded them, bolstering the notion that lemmas are marked for syntactic as well as semantic information (in languages like Italian, *all* nouns are marked with grammatical gender, regardless of whether gender is semantically meaningful).

For those interested in the phenomenon for research purposes, it's actually not hard to induce a tip-of-the-tongue state in subjects, as was done by Roger Brown and David McNeill (1966). Since it reflects a state of unfinished retrieval, words that are less frequently used—and hence less entrenched in people's minds—are more vulnerable to this state than are commonly used, well-known words, whose access is usually completed quickly and easily. Brown and McNeill gave their subjects the definitions for obscure words that many people would know, but only peripherally, and asked them for the corresponding word. You can run your own version of this study by opening the nearest dictionary, pulling out some definitions of obscure words, and asking people to think of the word that matches it. For example:

tip-of-the-tongue state State of mind experienced by speakers when they have partially retrieved a word (usually its lemma, and perhaps some of its sound structure) but feel that retrieval of its full phonological form is elusive.

1. An instrument for measuring angular distances, useful for ocean navigation; commonly used in the past to "navigate by the stars."

2. A small dagger worn by orthodox Sikhs.

3. A long, flexible cable used to break up and remove clogs in sink or toilet drains.

4. To slice food into thin strips about the size of matchsticks.

5. The initial step in a criminal proceeding to confirm the identify of the accused, formally read the charges, and ask how the accused pleads.

In case you've tip-of-the-tongued yourself, the answers are: (1) *sextant*, (2) *kirpan*, (3) *auger*, (4) *julienne*, (5) *arraignment*. **Box 9.3** describes some potential consequences of lingering too long in a state of partial word retrieval.

WEB ACTIVITY 9.3

Inducing the tip-of-the-tongue state In this activity, you'll see video clips of people in a tip-of-the-tongue state. You'll also be provided with examples of materials you can use yourself to induce a tip-of-the-tongue state in others, in order to record observations about their experience of it.

BOX 9.3
Learning to fail at speaking

Practice doesn't always make perfect. Sometimes it can ingrain a bad habit, like learning to ski or play the piano with faulty technique, leading to the depressing scenario in which you actually get worse the more you work at it. It turns out that this may be true of lexical access as well: the more you rummage around for misplaced words, the more elusive they may be the next time you need them.

Amy Beth Warriner and Karin Humphreys (2008) carried out a fascinating study in which they induced tip-of-the-tongue (TOT) states in people for varying lengths of time. Adapting the classic technique, they used a computer to display definitions for obscure words, and had their subjects press a button if they found themselves in a TOT state. At this point, a computer program randomly released the subjects from their word-finding agony in either 10 seconds or 30 by displaying the correct word. (The participants were also given the option to press a button if the word leaped into their minds unaided.) The next day, the subjects came back to repeat the whole ordeal. Warriner and Humphreys were interested in finding out whether people would be more or less likely to relapse into a TOT state for the same word depending on how long they had floundered around trying to retrieve it from memory.

You might think that those who spent a long time searching for a word would feel such a strong sense of relief at *finally* getting it that this word would be firmly stamped in their memories. Apparently not. Warriner and Humphreys found exactly the opposite—those who'd been assigned to the 30-second condition for a given word were more likely to slip back into a TOT state for the same word than those who'd been assigned to the 10-second condition. A similar pattern was found even if the subjects found the words on their own before being provided the answer by the computer: those who pressed a button to show that they'd fully accessed the word in less than 10 seconds were also less likely to repeat the maddening TOT experience for that same word than subjects who'd taken more than 10 seconds to access it. Warriner and Humphreys suggest that a TOT state reflects a faulty pattern of activation of the phonological elements of a word, and that spending more time in this state somehow reinforces the bad pattern.

Karin Humphreys and colleagues (2010) followed up with another study to see whether slips of the tongue could also become ingrained in memory. The researchers used a common lab technique for inducing spoonerisms or sound exchanges (such as saying *beg pet* instead of *peg bet*—see Method 9.2 for a detailed discussion of this technique). Subjects who succumbed to the error were more than four times as likely to make the same mistake again a few minutes later than those who correctly uttered the intended words. But the danger of making the same mistake again was short-lived, and sound-exchanging subjects who were tested again 48 hours later were no more likely to make the same slip than those who'd spoken the words properly the first time around. Which suggests that if you find yourself making an embarrassing speech error, perhaps the best strategy is simply to shut up for a while.

More detailed evidence for ordered stages

We've seen some evidence that the planning and retrieval of words takes place in ordered stages, with a different scope of advance planning for each stage. Some of the clues for this came from the linguistic span over which we tend to see word exchanges versus sound-based errors. But we can squeeze even more information from speech errors. A close look reveals that different kinds of linguistic information are often accessed and assembled in a specific order. Consider, for example, the following slips:

a meeting _arathon (an eating **m**arathon)

an _istory of a **h**ideology (a **h**istory of an ideology)

In the first example, the /m/ from *marathon* has migrated to the word *eating*. But notice that this swap must have occurred *before* the indefinite article *a* was fully specified, even though the article comes before the affected noun. Why? If the sound swap had occurred *after* the assembly of the article, the resulting error would have been *an meeting arathon*. The article has adjusted its shape as a result of the tongue slip, omitting the consonant /n/ just before *meeting*. Something similar has happened with *an istory of a hideology*. What's interesting is that you don't see errors in which the shape of function words *hasn't* adapted to the surrounding sounds, which suggests that assembling the sounds of content words happens at an earlier stage than filling in the sounds for function words.

Now, think for a moment what can be deduced from the following errors (and consider very carefully how these slips would actually be pronounced):

I hate having my **pinch bum**med. (I hate having my **bum pinch**ed.)

I wouldn't give **kid**s to a **nut** I didn't know. (I wouldn't give **nut**s to a **kid** I didn't know.)

The first thing to notice is that these errors involve words exchanges, but not of complete words—for example, only the stem morpheme of *pinched* is exchanged, leaving behind the past-tense morpheme *-ed* to attach to *bum*, and similarly with *nut*, the plural morpheme is stranded. Stranding errors like these are extremely common when a noun that's inflected with a plural or past morpheme swaps places with a bare noun. In fact, you hardly ever get errors like *I hate having my bummed pinch*. This provides a clue that the selection of words (or their lemmas) happens *before* they're slotted into a syntactic frame that specifies notions like plural or tense marking. The second thing to notice is that the pronunciation of the past-tense morpheme in *bummed* adapts to the shape of the invading stem, not the original one. Remember that the past marker *-ed* can be pronounced either as a [t] or a [d] sound, depending on whether the immediately preceding sound is voiced (pronounced with vocal fold vibration) or not. *Pinched* would be pronounced with a [t] sound, but once the past-tense marker is stranded and attached to *bum*, it becomes pronounced as [d] instead. Exactly the same thing happens with the stranded plural marker; instead of being pronounced as [s] in *nuts*, it sounds like [z] in *kids*. This makes sense if the exchange has happened at a stage earlier than the spelling out of the sounds of these inflectional morphemes.

Applying the same logic, you can figure out whether the main sentence stress (bold lettering) is assigned before or after lemma selection:

He can't see the trees for the **forest**. (He can't see the forest for the **trees**.)

a laboratory in our own com**put**er (a computer in our own **lab**oratory)

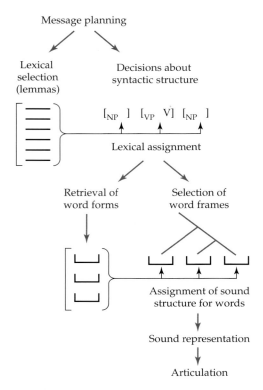

Message planning

Lexical selection (lemmas)

Decisions about syntactic structure

[_NP_] [_VP_ V] [_NP_]

Lexical assignment

Retrieval of word forms

Selection of word frames

Assignment of sound structure for words

Sound representation

Articulation

Figure 9.4 According to Garrett's model, language production occurs in successive stages. First, the conceptual content of the sentence is determined at the level of message planning. Second, syntactic structures are decided upon; lemmas are selected, and then assigned to slots in the syntactic frames. Third, word (or morpheme) forms are retrieved, frames for complex words are built, and the correct sounds for words are assigned to the word frames. This results in a fully specified sound representation, which then leads to a motor plan for articulation. (Adapted from Garrett, 1980.)

serial model of word production A model in which earlier stages of word production must be fully completed before later stages begin.

cascaded model of word production A model in which later stages of word production don't need to wait until earlier ones have been fully resolved, but can be initiated while earlier stages are still in progress.

As a result of the word exchange, *trees* is pronounced with less stress, and *forest* with more, than would have been the case if the words had stayed put in their correct slots in the sentence. This pattern is an extremely general finding with word exchanges—words tend not to carry their stress with them when they move. Again, this suggests that word exchanges, and hence the slotting of words into their sentence frames, reliably take place before stress merges with any specific words in the sentence.

Models of language production

Based on analyses like these, many of the first researchers who scrutinized speech errors concluded that speakers work their way through a sequentially ordered set of steps in which they access one specific layer of information at a time. A well-known representative example of such a model is shown in **Figure 9.4**.

To this day, psycholinguists generally agree that speaking calls for ordered stages. But there's been a good deal of discussion about whether one stage has to be neatly wrapped up before the next one can be initiated. For example, we know that the selection of a lemma starts measurably earlier than the phonological spelling out of the chosen word. But does it have to be *resolved* before sounds start being accessed? In other words, does there have to be just one winning lemma left standing, with all competitors weeded out, before specific sounds become activated? Or can competing lemmas partially activate their associated sounds? **Figure 9.5** depicts the two possibilities.

If questions like this keep you up at night, and if you get a kick out of designing experiments to answer them, you might consider setting this book aside before reading further, to see if you can figure out how you'd test the predictions of the two approaches. You should already have all the tools you'll need to come up with at least one plausible experiment.

There are a number of ways to tease apart the predictions of a fully **serial model** of word production (in which earlier stages must end before later ones begin) as opposed to a **cascaded model**, in which later stages don't need to wait until earlier ones have been fully resolved. One approach is to use a variation of the picture-word interference task you saw earlier and to leverage the effects of phonologically and semantically related words. In an elegant example of this approach, Ezequiel Morsella and Michele Miozzo (2002) had their subjects complete an unusual picture-naming task in which two pictures were presented, with one superimposed on the other, one drawn in red and the other in green (as seen in **Figure 9.6**). Subjects were told to quickly name only the object that appeared in green. Basically, this was a way to visually introduce a competitor lemma. The key ingredient to the experiment was that half of the time, the red distractor picture represented a word (*bell*) that was very similar in sound to the name for the green target picture (*bed*). The other half of the time, the name for the distractor (*hat*) was completely unrelated in either sound or meaning to the target.

A serial model predicts that there would be some competition between the two words, but only at the lemma level. Phonological activation would begin only after the lemma for the target word was selected and the competitor rejected. Hence, the sound shape of the competing distractor should have no effect whatsoever on the naming of the target. On the other hand, a cascaded model predicts that the activation of both the

(A) Serial model

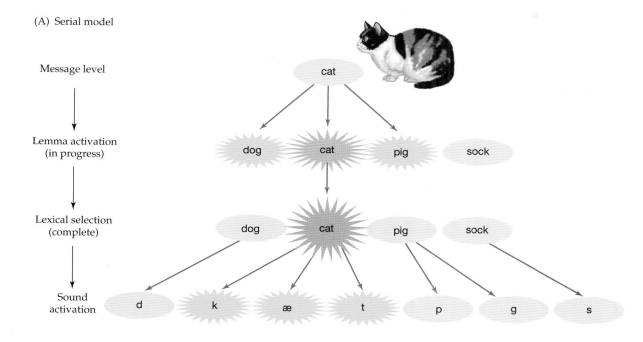

(B) Cascaded model

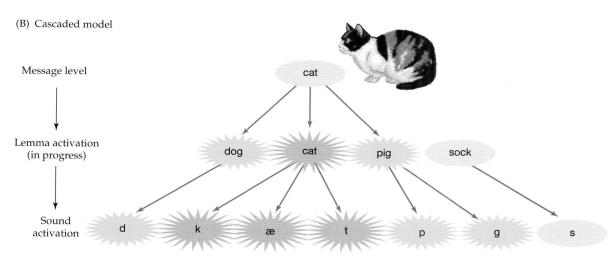

Figure 9.5 Serial and cascaded models of language production. (A) In a serial model, sound activation begins only after lexical selection is complete and a single lemma is active; hence, no sounds associated with the competitor lemmas become active. (B) In a cascaded model, sound activation begins as soon as lemmas become activated and before a single lemma is selected. As a result, sounds associated with lemma competitors become active as well. (Note: the figure doesn't show all of the sounds associated with competitor lemmas.)

target and competitor lemmas should trigger at least some phonological activation of their respective sounds. Since we know from earlier work that naming is often sped up by the activation of similar-sounding words, this theory predicts that a phonologically related distractor (*bell*) should lead to faster naming times for the target (*bed*) compared with unrelated distractors (*hat*). Morsella and Miozzo's results favored the cascaded model.

Figure 9.6 Example stimuli from a naming study by Morsella and Miozzo (2002), in which subjects were instructed to name the green target object (*bed*). (A) The name of the distractor (*bell*) was phonologically related to the target. (B) The name of the distractor (*hat*) bore no phonological similarity to the target.

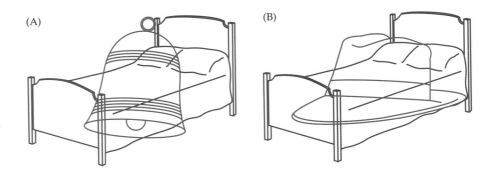

A fistful of other experiments, using a variety of designs, has also found evidence for a cascaded structure. But the results aren't uniform, and not all experiments show evidence that semantic competitors activate their sounds, as predicted by the cascaded model. Most psycholinguists are in agreement that the *general* architecture of the language production system does allow cascaded activation, but there's ongoing discussion about when and why cascaded activation can sometimes be found, and sometimes not.

Naturally, answering one question (that is, "Yes, phonological activation *can* begin before lemma selection is complete") just leads to more questions. For example, can the sound-based activation that's set off while lemma selection is still in progress *feed back* to the lemma level to influence selection? This would mean that if one semantic competitor's sounds became more activated than the sounds of another (if, for example, it shared a number of its sounds with the target word), then this would increase the likelihood of that competitor's lemma being selected over other candidates. We'll take it up in detail in Section 9.4, but in the meantime, you can go to Web Activity 9.4 to see if you can figure out what kinds of speech errors you might expect to see if it were indeed the case that the activation of sounds could bounce back up to the lemma level.

WEB ACTIVITY 9.4

Explaining and predicting speech errors In this activity, you'll consider a set of speech errors in light of what you've learned about models of language production.

9.3 Structuring Sentences

How do speakers choose the structure of a sentence?

What makes people and things worth talking about is the *relations* that exist among them. For example, we're usually not satisfied to say that some event occurred that included cheating, finding out, and killing and that this event involved Samantha, Pat, and Samantha's husband—we're eager to say who was involved in which role, and for that we need syntax. As we saw in Chapters 6 and 8, syntactic structure is crucial for conveying the relations among elements of a sentence. It also poses some thorny problems for language learning and language parsing. For instance, in language understanding, the difficulty is that at many points in the utterance of a sentence, the same string of words might map onto two or more different structures, carrying different possible meanings. Thus, even for sentences that *eventually* turn out to be unambiguous, there are points in the comprehension process where hearers have to make quick choices from among competing alternative meanings.

When speaking, you obviously *start* with an intended meaning in mind—the difficulty is that you're confronted with many choices, because the same meaning can be described in various ways. (An extreme example of choices facing a speaker is shown in **Table 9.1**.) For instance, on page 335 I noted a

TABLE 9.1 Fifty variations on a single sentence

List programmers department managers supervise.
What programmers work for department managers?
List programmers working for department managers.
List programmers who work for department managers.
List any programmers department managers supervise.
List all programmers working for department managers.
List each programmer a department manager supervises.
Which programmers work for managers of departments?
Which programmers do department managers supervise?
List all programmers who work for department managers.
List all programmers that department managers supervise.
List programmers whose supervisors manage departments.
Which of the programmers work for department managers?
Who are the programmers department managers supervise?
List every programmer any department manager supervises.
List every programmer supervised by a department manager.
List programmers with supervisors who manage departments.
Which programmers are supervised by department managers?
Who are the programmers working for department managers?
List programmers whose supervisors are department managers.
List each programmer that any department manager supervises.
List all of the programmers who work for department managers.
Who are the programmers who work for department managers?
List every programmer whom a department manager supervises.
List each programmer who is working for a department manager.
Which programmers are there working for department managers?
Which of the programmers are department managers supervising?
Which of the programmers are working for department managers?
List each of the programmers supervised by a department manager.
List the programmers who are supervised by department managers.
Which of the programmers do managers of departments supervise?
Who are all of the programmers working for department managers?
Which of the programmers are supervised by department managers?
List any programmer whose supervisor is a manager of a department.
Who are the programmers being supervised by department managers?
Who are all of the programmers that department managers supervise?
List any programmers there might be working for department managers.
List everyone who is a programmer supervised by a department manager.
List each of the programmers who is supervised by a department manager.
Which of the programmers are being supervised by department managers?
List any programmer with a supervisor who is the manager of a department.
Who are the programmers whose supervisors are managers of departments?
Which of the programmers are being supervised by managers of departments?
List any programmer who has a supervisor who is the manager of a department.
List all programmers who work for anyone who is the manager of a department.
List all programmers working for supervisors who are managers of departments.
Which of the programmers have supervisors who are managers of departments?
List each of the programmers who is supervised by anyone managing a department.
Which of the programmers have supervisors who are the managers of departments?
Who are all of the programmers who have supervisors who are department managers?

From Brennan, 1990

number of ways in which to express money changing hands between Eileen and Guy. Some of the variety among those eight sentences comes from the fact that different verbs can be used to express the relations among Eileen, Guy, and the money: Eileen *gave* Guy money, Guy *received* money from Eileen, and money *passed* from Eileen to Guy. But another part of it, which is clear when you consider Table 9.1, comes from the fact that different structures can be used to express relations within a sentence, even if the same lexical items are involved. How do speakers choose which structure to use? One answer might be that the choice is guided by very subtle shadings of meaning or emphasis, and that speakers care about making these nuanced distinctions. Consider the following pair of sentences, and try to conjure up an image of the event being described in each of them:

> The garden swarmed with bees.

> Bees swarmed in the garden.

Both of these communicate the same *relations*—in both cases, it's the bees doing the swarming, and the garden is the location where they're doing it. But many people have slightly different images for the two. The first sentence seems to suggest, more than the second one, that the garden is thick with bees, with the space in it almost entirely filled up by bees. You can see this difference even more clearly with the following sentences:

> Ben loaded the boxes onto the truck.

> Ben loaded the truck with boxes.

In the first sentence, we have the impression that whatever boxes were lying around are now all on the truck, but they haven't necessarily filled the truck. In the second, it's the opposite: the truck is probably completely full, but there might still be boxes left over that didn't fit. The syntax offers a handy way to make this subtle distinction.

Other structures offer similar opportunities for sophisticated methods of shaping meaning. Like many languages, English allows a passive structure for just about any verb, so *Monica loves Bill* can be flipped around to *Bill is loved by Monica*. Now, you might have at some point received bad writing advice, warning you that the passive is to be avoided like the plague, often on the grounds that passive sentences are "weak," or not "dynamic" enough. It does seem to be true that passives put more emphasis on the end state of an action than on the action itself. But sometimes that's exactly what you want. For example, you'd probably *want* to emphasize different aspects of the events described by the following sentences:

> The last living snow leopard was killed by a hunter yesterday.

> A werewolf killed a white-tailed deer yesterday.

What's newsworthy in the first sentence is not that a hunter carried out an action of killing; it's that the last snow leopard was the target of it, and if the passive structure emphasizes the irrevocable end state of the event, so much the better. The reverse is true for the second sentence, and we're more interested in the unusual agent who did the killing.

Speakers (and especially writers) can and do use syntax skillfully to make these kinds of distinctions, and to evoke a desired impression in the minds of hearers or readers. But, as psycholinguists have found, a speaker's choice of syntactic structure is not always driven by such masterful and nuanced language skills. Sometimes the choice comes down to whatever happens to be the *easiest* way to formulate the sentence in response to pressures of time and memory.

The importance of accessibility

As we've seen, speaking operates under certain deadlines. There's pressure to keep the length of silences between conversational turns to a minimum. More seriously, the incremental nature of language production, in which speaking is begun before planning is complete, imposes a sense of temporal urgency: having already launched into speech, the speaker hopes that she'll be ready to produce a word or phrase by the time the sentence calls for it. But this is quite a leap of faith, because planning a sentence involves some hard-core multitasking, with activity going on simultaneously at numerous stages of production. It's not surprising, then, that speakers often grab whatever word or piece of structure happens to be most accessible at the time.

If you pay attention, you'll easily see the impact of accessibility in speech errors. For example, Trevor Harley (1984) reports a speech error in which someone meant to say "Get out of the car" but instead said "Get out of the clark"—while gazing at a storefront with the name *Clark's* printed on it. You've no doubt had similar experiences, of having been distracted by a word or phrase you'd just read or heard, only to inadvertently plop it into your speech a moment later. And many errors of perseveration or anticipation (see Box 9.2), whether involving words, phrases, or sounds, can be seen as examples where certain elements were inserted into the sentence because they were more activated or accessible at that moment than the intended linguistic unit.

There's evidence that people also choose specific *structures* simply because they're more accessible than the other options that would express the same idea. For example: Want to encourage someone to use more passive sentences? Try littering your own speech with them, and watch what happens.

The tendency for people to re-use structures that are floating around in the conversational ether was first systematically studied by Kay Bock (1986a) in a now-classic study of **syntactic priming**. She designed an experimental task in which subjects heard and had to repeat specific sentences that were used as primes. After each such sentence, subjects saw pictures depicting events, and they had to convey what was happening in the picture using a single sentence. Bock varied the structure of the priming sentences, in order to be able to see whether the structure of the prime influenced the freely constructed sentences that people used to describe the picture. For example, the prime sentence might be either an active or a passive one: *One of the fans punched a referee. / The referee was punched by one of the fans.* In other cases, the structure varied between a prepositional and a double-object construction: *A rock star sold some cocaine to an undercover agent. / A rock star sold an undercover agent some cocaine.*

The results showed that the subjects' choice of syntactic structure was indeed swayed by the syntactic structure that appeared in the prime sentence (see **Figure 9.7**). The prime sentence didn't *determine* the structure—for instance, the use of a passive sentence rather than an active sentence as the prime only increased the production of passive sentences by about 8%, with the majority of sentences still appearing in the much more common active voice. But it did have a discernible effect on people's choice of syntax. Bock's original result has been repeated many times, under a number of different circumstances. The tendency for people to re-use linguistic structures has also been documented outside of the lab in large collections of real-world utterances (see **Method 9.1**).

In Bock's syntactic priming experiments, people were more likely to use passive sentences because they'd just heard and repeated an earlier passive sentence—in other words, the overall structure of the passive sentence was made more accessible. But sometimes, speakers choose to use a passive structure just because one of the participants in the event they're describing is more acces-

syntactic priming A phenomenon in which speakers are more likely to use a particular structure to express an idea if they have recently used the same structure to express a different idea.

Figure 9.7 Summary of stimuli and results from Bock's Experiment 1 (1986a). The results of this classic syntactic priming study showed that the structure of the priming sentence caused speakers to produce more sentences that have that same structure. (Adapted from Bock 1986a.)

(A) Priming sentences (heard and repeated by the participant)

Active:
One of the fans punched the referee.
or
Passive:
The referee was punched by one of the fans.

Prepositional:
A rock star sold some cocaine to an undercover agent.
or
Double object:
A rock star sold an undercover agent some cocaine.

(B) Target pictures and speaker choices

Active choice:
Lightning hit the church.
Passive choice:
The church was hit by lightning.

Prepositional choice:
The man is reading a book to the child.
Double object choice:
The man is reading the child a book.

(C) Results

Priming structure	Percent speakers responding	
	Active	Passive
Active	73	12
Passive	65	20

Priming structure	Percent speakers responding	
	Prepositional	Double object
Prepositional	48	31
Double object	25	53

 **METHOD 9.1**

Finding patterns in real-world language

As you've seen, progress in understanding the mechanics of speaking has often gone like this: First, an astute researcher notices something interesting in naturally produced speech (for example, patterns of speech errors, disfluencies, or tip-of-the-tongue states). Based on the original observation, a hypothesis is formed. The researcher then tests the hypothesis in a carefully controlled lab setting.

There's no doubt that lab experiments have accelerated our understanding of language production. They have several advantages when compared with the process of collecting a large sample, or *corpus* (Latin for "body"; the plural is *corpora*), of naturally occurring speech and analyzing it for patterns. As a case study, let's look at syntactic priming, a result that is robust and highly replicable in a lab setting. In principle, we could look for the same effect in large samples of real language by counting all the instances of two possible structures that can express the same idea:

> Chuck sent a nasty note to Victoria. (*prepositional structure*)
>
> Chuck sent Victoria a nasty note. (*double-object structure*)

We could then check to see whether either structure was more likely to be used if another one of the same type had appeared a bit earlier in the sample. Essentially, we'd be looking for *statistical evidence of syntactic priming in the wild*.

This approach comes with some challenges. In real-world language, unlike in the lab, there are many variables that can shift between one conversational setting and another. This complexity can easily obscure real phenomena, simply because it's hard to find many examples of language in natural settings that differ just on the critical dimensions we might want to examine. And if we did find evidence that syntactic structures tend to be repeated, there'd be more ambiguity about the causes of that recurrence. For example, it *could* be that the first occurrence of the structure really did prime the second occurrence, as shown in the lab studies. But it could also be that special communicative demands of the situation made a particular structure more appropriate than the other. In that case, multiple sentences might be pulled in the direction of that structure, but not because the first use had made that structure more accessible for later uses.

Despite the potential for some messiness, there are some good reasons to go diving for data in a language corpus. For starters, it would be nice to see whether the phenomena that show up in the lab extend to the real world. If we find evidence of syntactic priming in a corpus, this shows that syntactic priming plays a meaningful role in shaping sentences in everyday language use, with all its complexity and messiness, and not just in the lab when researchers have stripped away all the other influences that could possibly tug on language.

Stefan Gries (2005) made a strong case for looking at real-world data, based on his corpus analysis of syntactic priming. First, he *did* find evidence that certain structures were more likely to occur if another sentence of the same structure had occurred prior. He also replicated some important patterns that had turned up in the syntactic priming effects in the lab. Bock (1986a) found that the strength of the syntactic priming effect depended on the specific structures involved. For example, the double-object structure in the second example above exerted a stronger

influence on subsequent sentences than the prepositional structure in the first example. Gries found the same in his corpus. This provides some reassurance that similar mechanisms are responsible for the repetition of structure in both the lab experiment and the corpus data.

But most importantly, Gries was able to pull out some new information from his corpus. A sizable corpus contains a much larger and varied set of examples than your typical experiment, which usually relies on (at best) a few dozen sentences as stimuli. Gries was able to study 3,003 examples, allowing him to notice that the size of the priming effect varied dramatically depending on the specific verb that was involved in the sentence. He found that some verbs had a very strong preference for either the double-object or prepositional structure; these verbs resisted being pulled away from their preferred structure even if an earlier sentence had used the opposite structure. The priming effect was strongest for those verbs that showed no particular bias for one structure over the other. This shows that, just as you saw for comprehension in Chapter 8, verb-specific knowledge plays an important role in guiding the choices that speakers make during sentence production, interacting with other constraints.

It might have taken a while to figure this out relying only on lab experiments. First, it would have to occur to researchers to specifically design stimuli to test for this possibility. Second, without the benefit of corpus data, researchers would just be guessing (or, at best, relying on intuition) about the extent of a verb's bias toward one structure or the other. It would take quite a few experiments to test the range of verbs that are easily pulled out of an existing corpus. This study by Gries is a good reminder that the tidiness of experimental work can be supplemented in important ways by the sheer quantitative power of corpus analysis. These days, language scientists benefit from a number of large language samples that have already been collected and annotated for syntactic structure and are readily available for research purposes. You can explore some of these in Web Activity 9.5.

WEB ACTIVITY 9.5

Digging for data in a corpus
In this activity, you'll learn about some of the corpora that are available to researchers, and you'll get an idea of the hypotheses that these bodies of information can be called on to test.

sible. For example, imagine trying to describe an event similar to that drawn in Figure 9.7, in which lightning is striking a church. Suppose that in the planning process, the word *church* comes to mind more quickly than the word *lightning*. The pressure to begin speaking might lead you to simply utter whichever of these nouns is further along in the planning process, as a way to buy time for planning the other noun. This would constrain your choice of syntactic structure—uttering *church* before *lightning* commits you to using a passive structure in order to express the right meaning.

There are a number of techniques that experimentalists can use to make one entity or participant in an event more accessible than another, and to see whether the increased accessibility exerts some influence on the choice of syntax. In one study, Bock (1986b) was able to increase the accessibility of words like *church* or *lightning* by presenting semantically related primes (either *worship* or *thunder*). Making a word accessible through priming increased the likelihood that it would be uttered first, and thereby affected the syntactic structure of the spoken sentence. For example, when people received the prime *worship*, they were more likely to utter *church* first, resulting in a higher number of passive structures (*The church was hit by lightning*), as compared with having been primed with *thunder*.

This study shows that making a word linguistically or conceptually accessible has consequences for syntactic formulation. But so does simply directing attention to one particular participant. In a clever experiment, Russell Tomlin (1997) showed subjects short animated videos in which two fish of different colors swam toward each other, and one ended up swallowing the other. A marker flashed near one of the fish, luring people's eyes to it. When cued by a beep, subjects had to describe what had happened (for example, "The yellow fish ate the green fish" or "The green fish was eaten by the yellow fish"). Tomlin found that people were more likely to use the passive construction if the marker was flashed near the fish that ended up as dinner rather than near the fish that did the swallowing. In a more recent study by Leila Gleitman and colleagues (2007), similar effects were found even when attention was directed subliminally, using a marker that subjects were unaware of detecting.

WEB ACTIVITY 9.6

Object salience and syntactic choices   In this demo, you'll see the videos used by Tomlin and by Gleitman and colleagues to make one of the participants in an event more salient than the other.

Memory pressures

So far, we've seen that a good amount of syntactic choice is driven by whatever is quickest and easiest to say, whether it's an accessible structure, or a particular word that becomes available for pronunciation more quickly than others. These effects all come about because of the need to plan an utterance quickly. Maybe this is a good time to revisit the question: Why don't people simply take longer to plan? Why do speakers insist on being so incremental in planning and so eager to begin speaking early in the production process? If you planned out the entire sentence in detail before you began to speak, wouldn't you make fewer errors, have fewer disfluencies, *and* be more effective in choosing a syntactic structure that creates precisely the right effect for the hearer? So why the rush to start speaking?

One possible answer to this question is that planning more before speaking might overload your memory. If you took the time to lay out your whole sentence in detail before letting any of it past your lips, you might forget the earlier part of your sentence while you were putting the finishing touches on the end of the sentence, before getting around to saying any of it. Speaking before you've filled in all the details of a sentence allows you to dump some verbal material out of memory.

There's some interesting evidence pointing to memory load as an important factor in speaking—and once again, syntactic choice offers a way to make the act of speaking more manageable.

Earlier, I listed a number of different ways of paraphrasing the sentence *Eileen gave the money to Guy.* Here's one I didn't list: *Eileen gave to Guy the money.* To most native speakers of English, this structure, in which the prepositional phrase (*to Guy*) sits right next to the verb, seems ungrammatical, or at least very weird and awkward. But notice that it suddenly gets better if I do this:

> Eileen gave to Guy the money that he'd been pestering her to pay back for the last 3 months.

In fact, this seems not only grammatical, but actually preferable to a version in which the unwieldy direct object noun phrase (in square brackets) is nestled right next to the verb:

> Eileen gave [the money that he'd been pestering her to pay back for the last 3 months] to Guy.

The option of placing a long direct object at the end of the sentence instead of in its normal spot adjacent to the verb is an example of **heavy-NP shift**. It's only one of a few cases where the length or complexity of a phrase allows or even forces it to be moved from its more usual position. For instance, consider the following contrasts, where awkward sentences are marked with a question mark:

> He called her up.
>
> ?He called the girl who had casually dropped her phone number onto his desk in class last week up.

> ?He called up her.
>
> He called up the girl who had casually dropped her phone number onto his desk in class last week.

> Fiona considers Ben a scoundrel.
>
> ?Fiona considers anyone who'd take her out to a lavish, romantic dinner three times before finally disclosing that he's married with children a scoundrel.

> ?Fiona considers a scoundrel Ben.
>
> Fiona considers a scoundrel anyone who'd take her out to a lavish, romantic dinner three times before finally disclosing that he's married with children.

> the photo of Jill on the wall
>
> ?the photo of the lady who'd spent three years in an insane asylum even though she was perfectly sane on the wall

> ?the photo on the wall of Jill
>
> the photo on the wall of the lady who'd spent three years in an insane asylum even though she was perfectly sane

heavy-NP shift A syntactic structure in which a long noun phrase, usually a direct object, is moved toward the end of the sentence instead of in its normal spot adjacent to the verb.

This kind of shifting makes perfect sense in light of our discussion about how people tend to produce the most accessible words or phrases first. Generally, a short, simple phrase will be planned much more quickly than a long, complex one. And it's easy to see how, if you were planning to utter one of the long phrases in these examples, it might be very beneficial to not *also* be simultaneously holding a less complex phrase in memory if you had the option of dumping it.

A number of researchers (e.g., Arnold et al., 2004; Stallings & MacDonald, 2011) believe that this is exactly why speakers choose to utter shifted structures (or at least, one important reason among several). In a number of lab experiments across a variety of different speaking tasks, it's been shown that speakers are more likely to shift a phrase to the end of a sentence if it's substantially longer than other phrases that would normally follow it. This provides an interesting slant on the fact that languages often have multiple syntactic options available to express the same meaning. Perhaps instead of making the act of speaking harder by imposing a set of competing choices on the speaker, a menu of syntactic options might sometimes make it *easier* for the speaker—it allows the speaker some flexibility to use whichever structure makes the fewest demands on the process of sentence planning.

An intriguing study by Vic Ferreira (1996) confirms this view of syntactic indeterminacy as more help than hindrance to the speaker. In his study, Ferreira had subjects create sentences out of collections of words that were presented on a screen. For example, subjects saw a pair of words (such as *I gave*) that they were instructed to use at the beginning of the sentence, followed by a random collection of words they were told to use in any order they wanted (such as *toys/children*). For this particular example, subjects had the option to produce one of two sentence structures: *I gave the children the toys* or *I gave the toys to the children*. These stimuli were contrasted with ones where the verb allowed only one of the options. For example, if *I donated* was followed by *toys/children*, then only one syntactic structure was available: *I donated the toys to the children*. The verb *donate* is too finicky to allow *I donated the children the toys*.

Ferreira wanted to know: Which is easier for speakers? The prompt that restricts the options to just one, or the one that allows greater choice? He found that subjects made fewer errors and began to speak faster when they had to create a sentence using the more flexible verb *gave* rather than the rigid verb *donate*. Naturally, as a researcher, you want to know that it's the (non) availability of syntactic options that's driving this effect, and not just some other difference in how easy or difficult it is to produce a sentence with *gave* versus *donate* aside from their possible syntactic frames. To test for this, Ferreira also had a condition in which he included a preposition among the words to be used in the sentence, so that *I gave* was followed by *toys/children/to*. Despite the permissiveness of the verb *gave*, this added requirement restricted the choice to just *I gave the toys to the children* and precluded *I gave the children the toys*, since the second option would leave off the preposition *to*. Backed into a syntactic corner, subjects again made more errors and took longer to begin speaking.

So, the research on language production suggests that syntactic choice often serves a purpose that is more practical than aesthetic, and a speaker's syntactic decisions don't always reflect a judicious selection of the most appropriate shading of language. In many cases, they reveal an opportunistic speaker who manipulates syntax as a way of easing the burden of speaking. Perhaps this paints a portrait of the speaker in action as someone who is a bit harried and self-absorbed. One of the questions we haven't considered yet is

WEB ACTIVITY 9.7

(Un)natural methods for studying language production

Language production experiments hinge on getting experimental subjects to produce speech in a way that reflects normal speaking processes, while also often steering them toward using specific words or structures. In this activity, you'll get a taste for some of the different methods that researchers have used to solve this problem.

LANGUAGE AT LARGE 9.2

Language detectives track the unique "prints" of language users

Language production involves choices about how to express a message, drawn from a menu of options that include similar words, or alternative structures. As we've seen, these choices can be shaped by previous experience—for instance, a speaker who has just used a word or structure is more likely to re-use the same expression or structure than an alternative one.

But psycholinguists generally see such priming effects as more than just cognitive flickers that quickly dissipate, leaving no long-term traces. Rather, the thinking is that each instance of priming also contributes in a subtle way to long-term learning. Repeated priming reinforces particular words or structures in memory with the result that, over time, some options will reliably be chosen more than others by an individual speaker. Since each of us has a collection of somewhat different experiences, different options may become especially accessible to different people; each person is apt to sink into her own particular speaking ruts, developing a stable, personal linguistic style that reflects the cumulative effects of these experiences.

These ruts can be distinctive enough to have legal implications. Forensic linguist Gerald McMenamin (2010) discusses a case in which a woman had written a will leaving her estate to her daughter. But after the woman's death, a new will surfaced, in which her husband was named as the main beneficiary. The question was: Was this more recent will a valid one, or was it a fiendish fraud perpetrated by her husband?

An analysis of the syntax of the disputed will provided some clues. The new will contained several instances of an unusual sentence structure in which the indirect object appeared next to the verb, instead of the direct object. For example: *I give to John my estate.* As we've seen, this structure is often used when the direct object is especially long, as in the sentence *I give to John the lavish estate that I've been able to amass due to his generous love and support*—but it's rarely used otherwise. When linguists inspected the older will, which was known to be valid, they found no occurrences of this particular structure. Rather, the author of that will had used the more common structures, as in *I give John my estate* and *I give my estate to John.* The next step was to compare the questionable will to documents that the husband had written, to see if it matched his style of syntactic structure.

Indeed, these documents yielded several occurrences of the quirky structure. The jig, as they say, was up.

It's rare that an author's identity can be pinned down with any certainty based on a single linguistic variable like this one. But an individual's overall pattern of language choices can prove to be quite distinctive. For example, when expressing a causal relationship, are you more likely to use the word *since* than *because*? Well, so might a lot of other people. But do you *also* use the word *and* at the beginnings of sentences? Prefer to break up sentences into single clauses rather than use long sentences with multiple clauses? Occasionally use the word *whom*? Do you like to stack multiple adjectives in front of nouns? Are you prone to mismatching the number of the subject and verb when they're separated by some distance (as in *The **key** to the problems **are** easy to find*)? Do you use contractions when using pronouns (*I'm* versus *I am*)? Do you avoid them when using the negative (*did not* versus *didn't*)? Do you regularly insert or omit apostrophes counter to the official rules of grammar (*its mine* or *I hate you're guts*)?

By comparing two documents on *many* dimensions like these, experts can often assess whether they were likely to have been written by the same person. These kinds of techniques have proven useful in a number of practical situations, including: identifying and prosecuting the "Unabomber" terrorist, Ted Kaczynski; sleuthing out the likely authors of ransom notes; figuring out whether Shakespeare did in fact write some pieces that were attributed to him; resolving whether a work was plagiarized from someone else; and flagging the authors of anonymous comments on the Internet.

WEB ACTIVITY 9.8

Test your skills as a language detective In this activity, you'll read six short pieces of text; three different authors wrote two pieces each. Your task will be to match up each piece with the other piece written by the same author. You'll need to justify your reasoning by appealing to similarities and differences of word choice, syntactic structure, and orthography across all of the documents.

whether the speaker might tailor his syntax in a way that eases the burden on the *hearer*—for example, in many cases, the available syntactic options could also serve to increase or reduce the degree of ambiguity for the hearer. (Instead of the horrendous sentence *The horse raced past the barn fell*, one *could* say, less ambiguously, *The horse that was raced past the barn fell*.) For the time being, I'll set aside this question of the depth of the speaker's sensitivity to the hearer's needs, but we'll pick it up again in detail in Chapter 11.

9.4 Putting the Sounds in Words

As we saw in Section 9.2, word retrieval is like shopping at IKEA: once you've selected what you want, you still have a lot of assembling to do. We know this because so many speech errors involve the addition, omission, exchange, or mutilation of sounds, suggesting that words aren't retrieved along with their complete arrangement of articulatory gestures, but get "filled in" with sounds at a later stage, with fairly regular mishaps along the way.

Furniture assembly, at least for me, is also not an error-free process. And I confess that there have been times when, after putting the wrong piece in the wrong place, I've let loose a torrent of complaints blaming whoever designed the product or created the instructions—the rationale for my tantrum being that the flawed design was bound to be confusing to anyone of normal intelligence, that the error was just *waiting to happen*.

As it turns out, the same is true of sound-based speech errors: some errors are waiting to happen, more than others. Now, if I were designing furniture kits and collecting data on the mistakes people made in the assembly process, I'd start paying attention if I saw many people making the same mistake over and over again. I'd want to come up with an explanation for why this was the case, with the hope of correcting the source of the error. Needless to say, when psycholinguists see the same kinds of errors cropping up again and again, they're curious about what the underlying explanation is—not because they have the power to redesign the language production machine, but just because they want to know how the thing works. In this section, we'll explore some of the errors that are just "waiting to happen," and talk about what this reveals about the design of the language production system.

The lexical bias effect

Let's start with the errors attributed to poor Reverend Spooner, many of which induce chuckles: for instance, *queer old dean* [*dear old queen*], or *the lord is a shoving leopard* [*loving shepherd*]. The reason they're amusing, of course, is that they wind up forming incongruous or inappropriate sequences of words. But notice: the errors result in actual *words*. This could easily be otherwise. For instance, if I randomly pull sequences of two adjacent words from the preceding paragraphs, and spoonerize them, I don't necessarily get words:

deneral **g**irection (*Intended:* general direction)

pistakes **m**eeple (*Intended:* mistakes people)

enderlying **u**xplanation (*Intended:* underlying explanation)

panguage **l**roduction (*Intended:* language production)

wet **g**urds (*Intended:* get words)

If you have the gut feeling that most of these sound like rather implausible speech errors, you're right. And I'm guessing that among them, you found *wet gurds* to be the most plausible, and *panguage lroduction* the least likely. In that case, your intuitions line up with the findings of psycholinguists Gary Dell and Peter Reich (1981), who combed through a sizable pile of speech error data to conclude that, more often than you'd expect from sheer chance, speech errors tend to result in actual words rather than non-words. That is, sound-based speech errors show a **lexical bias**, and errors that result in real words are, statistically, just waiting to happen.

Before we dig into why this would be, let's devote a minute to thinking about whether we can rely on statistical patterns in a speech error corpus for evidence of the most likely errors. It should worry us a bit that the whole enterprise of recording speech errors inevitably has to be run through the cognitive machinery of a *hearer*. Could the hearer's perception of the speech errors be skewed in such a way that he notices and remembers mostly those slips that sound like real language rather than sound mash? Or might he even fall prey to a perceptual illusion—a slip of the *ear*—that the speaker has produced a real word? If so, that could lead to biases in the data that have nothing to do with the *production* of speech.

Even if this could be averted through rigorous recording and coding procedures, mining a corpus of speech errors while looking for revealing patterns promises to be an enormously time-consuming process. You'd have to wait around for people to produce enough errors so that you could make a meaningful comparison—and you'd have limited control over factors like how fast they were speaking, how complicated the language was that they were producing, which specific sounds were involved in the errors (it might matter), whether one speaker was more tired or drunk than another, and so on. It's enough to make a psycholinguist fantasize about having a technique that *induces* speech errors, and specific types of errors at that.

Inducing speech errors in the lab

Fortunately, a technique for inducing speech errors *does* exist, invented by Michael Motley and Bernard Baars (1976). It's called SLIP (spoonerisms of *laboratory-induced predisposition*), and it works a lot like this practical joke my son liked to play on his friends when he was eight:

Son: Say "You're a dork."

Friend: You're a dork.

Son: Say "You're a dork."

Friend: You're a dork.

Son: Say "You're a dork."

Friend: You're a dork!

Son: What do you use to eat soup?

Friend: A fork.

Son: You eat *soup* with a fork??!? You're weird.

You see what's happened here. The hapless friend has been primed with a set of sounds, luring him to produce a similar-sounding word even though he normally might not have been predisposed to do so in answer to that particular question.

Psycholinguists were delighted to find that using a similar strategy makes it more likely that people will generate spoonerisms. You simply give subjects

lexical bias The statistical tendency for sound-based speech errors to result in actual words rather than non-words.

 METHOD 9.2

The SLIP technique

Devising methods to study language production in the lab can be even more challenging than coming up with methods to study language comprehension. Often we want to be able to test specific hypotheses, contrasting two chunks of language that are similar in all dimensions but the ones of interest—comparing apples and apples, rather than apples with oranges or bananas. At least in comprehension tests, the experimenter has complete control over the language that serves as the hearer's input. But controlling the speaker's *output* is not so easy. In spontaneous speech, speakers rarely oblige researchers by producing sets of neatly contrasting words that align with just the variables that the researcher is hoping to test. We have to come up with a way to somehow influence what the speaker says but still allow him to engage in a fairly normal process of speaking.

The SLIP (spoonerisms of *l*aboratory-*i*nduced *p*redisposition) technique nudges the speaker to make many speech errors, while allowing the experimenter to control key aspects of the stimuli in order to be able to directly compare whether more errors are made in one condition than another. The goal is to see how often, for any given target pair of visually presented words (for example, *barn door*), speakers will produce a spoonerism, or sound exchange, yielding *darn bore*. The nudge comes from having an *interference set* of words preceding the target word pair. The interference set contains words that begin with the same sounds as the target, but in reverse order (*dark bone*). The intent is to produce phonological priming of a certain pattern, to heighten the likelihood that the speaker will fall prey to a sound exchange. For interesting reasons, some kinds of stimuli might be more vulnerable than others to the sound exchange.

In a SLIP task, the goal is usually to produce priming at the stage where speakers are *planning* to speak, rather than to prime specific motor sequences involved in actually uttering the words. For this reason, researchers usually want subjects to utter the target word pairs, but not the interference sets. This is done by showing subjects pairs of words, one pair at a time, and telling them to read each pair of words silently to themselves as they're presented. They're to read the words aloud only if they hear a buzzer as a cue. This puts them in a state where for each word pair, they have to prepare for the possibility of speaking, without actually speaking unless instructed.

Target words (which are always uttered) and their interference sets (which are never uttered) are interspersed with filler items, which are sometimes uttered. This is done so that subjects will be less likely to notice the relationship between the interference sets and target pairs, and also to increase the number of word pairs that the subject needs to read aloud, without requiring that the interference sets be spoken. So, a subject might be confronted with a sequence like the following. The specific function of each word pair is given in parentheses, and *** signals that the subjects would hear a buzzer as a cue to read the pair aloud:

SALE RECEIPT***	(filler)
VERB PHRASE***	(filler)
SHOE SOLE	(filler)
FLAT TIRE	(filler)
COMB NEAT	(interference set)
COLD NUN	(interference set)
NOSY COOKS***	(target set)

repetitions of a certain sound pattern, for example instructing them to read the following list of word pairs in their heads:

dawn boat

dark boast

dart bone

You then prompt them to read aloud the following target of interest:

barn door

Like my son's practical joke, this is a psycholinguistic ambush: the priming effect of the lure words will increase the likelihood that the subject will read the target words as *darn bore*.

METHOD 9.2 (*continued*)

Some of the resulting speech errors are full sound exchanges (*nosy cooks → cozy nooks*), but some are only partial (*nosy cooks → nosy nooks* or *cozy cooks*).

The interference sets play a critical role in inducing errors. Without them, many people are able to read long lists of word pairs like *nosy cooks* out loud without making any speech errors at all. But Motley and Baars (1976) found that by slipping in the interference sets, they were able to coax errors out of subjects on about 10% of target word pairs—and subsequently, researchers have been able to get as high as a 30% yield on speech errors.

If you're going to design SLIP studies, there are some things to keep in mind. First, you can induce more errors by using interference sets that are very similar to the target pairs—for example, if the target pair is *barn door*, a slip (*darn bore*) is more likely to occur after the interference set *dart bone* than after *deep bed*, even though these have the same initial consonants. This is because the interference set has more phonological overlap with the target pair. Subjects are also more likely to slip if they've seen quite a few interference sets than if they've seen just one. But if you're too heavy-handed in using many highly similar interference sets, your subjects might begin to notice the connection between the interference sets and the target pairs, and strategically adjust their speaking.

Second, timing matters. After some tinkering, Motley and Baars found that their optimal presentation rhythm was to show word pairs for about one second each, with less than one-tenth of a second between pair views. When word pairs flashed by too quickly, the task became so hard that people made too many different kinds of speech errors, making it hard to focus on and compare sound exchanges. But a too-slow presentation made the task too easy, and subjects were able to avoid slips almost entirely. Experimenters often do some pretesting of different timing rates, to make sure the task will give them a big enough error rate, with the right mix of errors to allow them to test their hypotheses.

Once properly calibrated, the SLIP technique is a terrific tool that can be used to nail down a variety of different questions about patterns in speech errors. These patterns then serve as important evidence in building and testing different models. Here's a sampling of just some of the questions that can be answered using the SLIP method:

- Do sounds that are similar to each other (e.g., ***b**arf **d**ope*) exchange more readily than sounds that are very different (***b**arf **l**ope*)?

- Are more very common sounds/words involved in errors more (or less) often than less frequent sounds/ words?

- Are words that are semantically related to each other more likely to exchange sounds than words that are not related to each other?

This technique creates a scenario that boosts the probability that a certain kind of speech error will occur. Using this as a base, you can then compare specific stimuli and see whether subjects make more errors with one set of stimuli over another. For instance, to test for a lexical bias, the target word pair *barn door* could be compared with *barge dope*, for which a spoonerism would result in a pair of non-words: *darge bope*. Using the SLIP technique, Baars et al. (1975) found that subjects slipped more often when the error resulted in a pair of words than when it resulted in nonsense, thereby providing experimental support for the lexical bias (see **Method 9.2**).

WEB ACTIVITY 9.9

Design your own SLIP study
In this activity, you'll identify a research question and design a miniature SLIP study to test it, incorporating your knowledge of some of the practical issues involved in using this method.

Does activation flow in both directions?

Now that we feel more confident about the sturdiness of the lexical bias effect, let's try to explain it. One explanation might have already occurred to you, based on having worked through Web Activity 9.4. In that section, we talked about the fact that lemmas, or lexical units, become activated at an earlier stage than the individual sounds that they contain. We discussed whether words can send activation down to their component parts *before* they are finally selected, while activation among several options is still building, or whether activation flows down to sounds only from the "winning" lemma. We concluded that multiple lemmas probably activate their sounds, as predicted by cascade models of production. But as shown in Figure 9.5, we only compared models in which activation flows in one direction, from lemma to sounds.

I ended that section by raising this possibility: If several words can simultaneously activate their sounds before selection occurs, then is it possible that the activated sounds can bounce some of that activation back up to the word level? In other words, we'd like to know whether our model looks more like **Figure 9.8A** or **Figure 9.8B**.

What would be the consequences of having activation flow from sounds back to the lemma level before the winning lemma is selected? Well, it would mean that the activation of sound units could boost the activation of lemmas; these boosted lexical units would in turn send activation back down to their component sounds.

If feedback does bounce back up to the lexical level, it could help explain the lexical bias effect. To see this, let's first consider how activation patterns might lead to sound exchanges, and then walk through the reasoning for why an exchange might be more likely to be triggered with *barn door* going to *darn bore* than with *barge dope* going to *darge bope*.

Why do we pronounce the wrong sound in a slot in a word, for instance, uttering /d/ instead of /b/ when planning to say *barge* followed by *dope*? Basically,

Figure 9.8 Two versions of a cascaded model. (A) This model contains unidirectional links between the lemma and sound levels, so activated sounds do not feed back to the lemma level. (B) This model incorporates bidirectional links between the lemma and sound levels, which allows activation from the sound level to flow back up to influence the activation of lemma candidates.

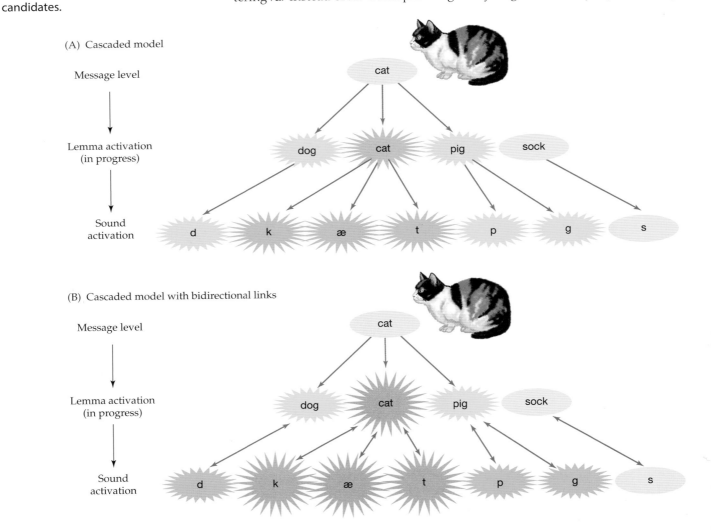

(A) Cascaded model

Message level

Lemma activation (in progress)

Sound activation

(B) Cascaded model with bidirectional links

Message level

Lemma activation (in progress)

Sound activation

this can be described as a situation in which the activation of that incorrect sound /d/ has for some reason exceeded the activation of the correct sound /b/ at the very moment that it's being slotted into a word frame. Normally, later words and their component sounds (for example, *dope*) are less activated than words that are about to be pronounced immediately (*barge*). But suppose that the lexical unit *dope* has been selected especially quickly—perhaps it's a frequent word, or is more accessible for some reason. Also relevant is the fact the *sound* /d/ is more frequent than /b/. As a result, the /d/ in *dope* might surge in activation more quickly than the actual targeted sound /b/ and get selected as the first consonant in _arge. Once the /d/ has been selected, its activation drops off, but in the meantime, the activation of the never-used /b/ has peaked, and therefore is a prime candidate when it's time to choose the first consonant of _ope.

Now, let's add to the mix the added complexity of the SLIP decoy words, and the possibility that activation flows up from sounds to lexical units as well as the reverse. Here's a sketch of what might happen with the *barge dope* stimuli when it follows the interference sets *dawn boat, dark boast*, etc.: Because of the words that act as lures, a certain phonological pattern is primed, in which /d/ occurs as the first consonant of the first word, and /b/ in the first consonant slot of the second word. When *barge dope* is read, these words activate all their component sounds, including the consonants /b/ and /d/ for the first and second word respectively. Once all the sounds are activated, their activation flows back up to the lexical level to activate all words that contain them—for instance, to varying degrees, they might also activate *large, cope, bard, dole,* and so on. But all of these competing words are receiving less activation than *barge* and *dope,* so they're unlikely to be selected, and their activation drops off. In planning to utter *barge,* the speaker is still going to have some competition between /b/ and /d/ for the first consonant slot, due to the activation that's coming from the primed pattern. A similar competition is set up for the second word, and all of this *could* result in a spoonerism, as did in fact happen on some small number of trials in the study by Baars and his colleagues. But by and large, the correct sounds are likely to receive the most activation and, hence, be pronounced in their right places.

But here's why the switcheroo is far more likely with *barn door* as the target: As in the previous example, the lure words will prime a pattern that introduces competition for the first consonant of each word. And, like before, the activated sequence of sounds from *barn* and *door* will also activate their component parts. The individual sounds will send *their* activation back up to the lexical level. Now, notice that this will activate a set of competitors including *yarn, moor, bard, dole,* etc.—but *especially* the "supercompetitors" *darn* and *bore,* because these words are receiving activation from the sounds that make up *barn* and *door, and* from the primed phonological frame. This might push their activation levels up even higher than the target words, resulting in their selection. If *darn* and *bore* are selected, then the activation of the other competing words drops off (including the actual target words), and the component sounds of *darn* and *bore* become activated, and ultimately pronounced. This complex scenario makes it quite a bit more likely that the wrong sounds will become activated.

The internal censor

The possibility that the activation of sounds spreads back up to the lexical level provides a handy explanation for the lexical bias effect, as argued by researchers such as Gary Dell (1986). But other researchers have proposed an alternative explanation for the lexical bias effect, one that doesn't rely on activation flowing from sounds to words. Instead, they claim, the tendency for speech errors to result in real words comes from a process of self-monitoring: the idea is that as we speak, we have an internal quality control manager that is inspecting the assembled words that are about to leave our mouths. A good many errors are caught this way, especially those that result in nonsense, like *darge bope*. But errors that are real words—just not the ones intended—are harder for the monitor to notice because they don't stand out as obviously flawed.

The notion that a self-monitoring process prevents us from making speech errors has some concrete experimental support. One of the most fascinating of these studies comes from Motley, Camden, and Baars (1982), who must have had the same sense of humor as my son, because they used the SLIP technique to trip people up and cause them to utter socially taboo words. For example, read the following pairs of words aloud:

> kook tin
>
> coop tilt
>
> coon tips
>
> tool kits

Making a sound exchange in that last pair of words would be somewhat embarrassing, to say the least. Most people would be pretty motivated to try to avoid awkward errors like this—and because of their taboo nature, an internal monitoring mechanism might be especially likely to censor them out. This is what Motley and his colleagues found. Their subjects were more likely to exchange sounds when such an error would lead to a nice, neutral set of words—for instance, there were more sound exchanges when the target was *tool carts* (resulting in *cool tarts*) than *tool kits*. What's more, there's evidence that something unusual was happening with the more emotionally charged *tool kits* stimuli: even though subjects pronounced them correctly more often, they took longer to do so, suggesting that on at least some of those trials, some production problem was roiling under the surface. And there's even evidence that whatever that problem was, it was causing the subjects some discomfort: while performing the task, they wore sensors measuring their galvanic skin response, which is often used as a general measure of stress. This measure revealed that the speakers were most stressed on the trials that had the potentially taboo stimuli. This suggests that, whether consciously or not, they had some inkling of the potential for embarrassment, even though they mostly managed to avert it. (Under certain circumstances, though, such awkward errors are more likely to slip out; see **Box 9.4**.)

More evidence for bidirectional activation

So, it looks like there are two plausible explanations for the lexical bias effect in speech errors: the monitoring account, and the story in which activation spreads from sounds to words. But the spreading-activation story has the advantage of being able to also explain two other patterns found in the speech error data.

You can get a feel for the first of these additional phenomena by coming back to my son's practical joke involving the word *fork*. Notice that two factors seem important in his getting his friends to reliably answer that they eat soup with a fork: The first is the phonological priming that they get from having repeatedly said *dork*. The second is that the correct answer to the question—*spoon*—is very closely semantically related to *fork*. The joke would fail if instead of asking, "What do you use to eat soup?" my son had asked, "What do you wear on your head in the winter?" Despite all that phonological priming, it seems highly unlikely that anyone would answer "fork"—or "pork" or "cork," for that mat-

BOX 9.4
Was Freud *completely* wrong about speech errors?

It's time to admit that I've been a bit unfair to Sigmund Freud. Even though Freud was most interested in how repressed thoughts might lead to slips of the tongue, he also had the insight to suggest, many decades before the birth of psycholinguistics as a thriving discipline, that speech errors probably also reflected the mechanics of speech. We've seen that a great many errors can easily be attributed to mechanical aspects of the speaking process—probably much more than Freud initially thought. But in defense of Freud's central ideas, that doesn't necessarily mean that there's absolutely no *additional* contribution from distracting thoughts or emotional states, even if it's just a small effect.

To cite one example, it's easy enough to give a psycholinguistic explanation of Dave Lenihan's error of uttering *coon* while discussing Condoleezza Rice (see p. 329). It may well have come about as a word blend, in which he combined the semantically and phonologically similar words *coup* and *boon* while trying to say that getting her into the position of NFL commissioner "would be kind of a big *coup/boon*." Fine. But it's still a fair question to ask: Wouldn't such an error be somewhat more *likely* for a racist to make than a non-racist?

As far as I know, no one's looked at whether a person's deeply held beliefs and attitudes can push up the likelihood of making a certain kind of speech error. But our intrepid inventors of the SLIP technique, Michael Motley and Bernard Baars, *have* applied their experimental know-how to see if it's possible to create a loaded situation in which certain spoonerisms are more prone to slipping out.

In one study, Motley and Baars (1979) recruited male subjects and randomly assigned some of them to a condition in which the SLIP test was administered by an attractive, provocatively dressed female experimenter. Other subjects were less lucky and were randomly assigned to a condition in which they wore fake electrodes, and were (falsely) told that mild electric shocks might be applied during the experiment. All the subjects did the same SLIP test, in which they read interference sets and target pairs that consisted of nonsense syllables (for example, they might have to read a sequence like *bood tegs, goot negs, goob leks, lood gegs,* etc.). Some of the target pairs, when spoonerized, resulted in real words along a "sexy" theme (*lood gegs → good legs*). Other target pairs might lead to real words of an "electrical" theme (*shad bock → bad shock*). Motley and Baars found that the subjects who interacted with the seductive experimenter made more "sexy" spoonerisms, while their poor counterparts who were under threat of being zapped made more "electrical" sound exchanges.

Notice that the spoonerisms were all preceded by interference sets, which provided phonological priming for the sound error. Without these, there would have been far fewer slips of the tongue, if any. What's more, sometimes the guys in the "sexy" condition made "electrical" speech errors and vice versa. So a Freudian explanation obviously can't completely account for the errors, and we'll still need all our fancy models of language production. But the experiment provides a glimmer of a suggestion that a person's anxieties or mental state might have at least some effect on speech errors.

Still, for any given error, it's impossible to tell whether it came about because the subject had a certain mindset, or whether it was simply due to a minor glitch in the activation of sounds (or to some combination of both factors). In the same way, we'll never know if Dave Lenihan's error was completely racially neutral or not. What is clear is that using a slip of the tongue to infer his racial attitudes is pretty flimsy from a scientific standpoint.

---

ter. It's the *combination* of the semantic relation to spoon *and* the phonological priming that seems to stack the odds against the victim of the joke.

This intuition is supported by certain patterns of speech errors. Consider the following tongue slips:

infini**ty** clauses (*Intended:* infini**tive** clauses)

It's at the **bottom** of the stack of books. (*Intended:* **top** of the stack)

tennis **bat** (*Intended:* tennis **racquet**)

When's my next **apart**ment? (*Intended:* **appoint**ment)

mixed errors Speech errors that involve similarities of both sound and meaning.

Similarity is implicated in all of them. In some, like *racquet → bat*, the speaker inserts a word that means something very similar to the target; in others, like *infinitive → infinity*, a similar-sounding word intrudes. But a number of studies (e.g., Dell & Reich, 1981; Martin et al., 1989) have shown that the number of **mixed errors** that involve similarities of both sound *and* meaning is especially high. That is, substituting *rat* for *cat* is more common than substituting a word that is just semantically similar (*dog*) or just phonologically similar (*vat*). Actually, this is predicted even under a model in which there's no feedback from sounds to the lexical level—such a model says that you'd expect *cat → rat* substitutions to be about as frequent as *cat → dog* substitutions *plus cat → vat* substitutions, simply because the error has the opportunity to come about either as a lemma selection error (*cat → dog*) or as a sound-based substitution (*cat → vat*). But mixed errors occur even more frequently than this, so you end up with a bonanza of slips like the following:

> Let's **start**. (*Intended:* **stop**)
>
> I miss my **rat**. (*Intended:* **cat**)
>
> Look it up in the **dictionary**. (*Intended:* **directory**)
>
> That's a **psycho**logical (*Intended:* **phono**logical) issue.
>
> Many of us were in Rome at the **president**'s (*Intended:* **pope**'s) funeral. (*uttered by U.S. Senator Joe Biden*)

LANGUAGE AT LARGE 9.3

George W. Bush: A modern-day Reverend Spooner?

Almost nothing is known as of yet about whether some people are simply more prone to making certain kinds of speech errors, or why that might be the case. But it's unlikely that a tendency to make speech errors is a sign of an overall lack of intellectual endowment. It's more likely that some disruption occurs in choosing among multiply activated representations. We know, for example, that the Reverend Spooner was a highly successful academic, but was exceedingly absentminded and susceptible to distraction.

Most of our own speech errors are evanescent. We misspeak, catch and correct ourselves, and everyone moves on. But today's public figures, who live in a spotlight where their utterances are not only preserved but widely circulated over the Internet, often suffer unwarranted consequences of their minor lapses in language production. In many cases, speech errors are held up as examples of their specific ignorance or a general lack of intelligence.

Not many recent political figures have been as broadly ridiculed for their slips of the tongue as former U.S. president George W. Bush. It does seem as if Bush was more prone than the average politician to making speech errors, many of which probably reflect a language production glitch as opposed to ignorance, lack of education, or muddled thinking. As we've seen, a great deal happens in the space between thinking and speaking. To paraphrase an old proverb, "There's many a slip twixt the thought and the lip."

Comb through these "Bushisms" and see if you can make some guesses as to where the breakdowns occurred:

"I'm going to put people in my place, so when the history of this administration is written at least there's an authoritarian voice saying exactly what happened."—on what he hopes to accomplish with his memoir, as reported by the Associated Press, Calgary, Canada, March 17, 2009

"And they have no disregard for human life."—on the brutality of Afghan fighters, Washington, DC, July 15, 2008

"Soldiers, sailors, Marines, airmen, and Coastmen—Coast Guardmen, thanks for coming, thanks for wearing the uniform."—at the Pentagon, March 19, 2008

"And so, General, I want to thank you for your service. And I appreciate the fact that you really snatched defeat out of the jaws of those who are trying to defeat us in Iraq."—to Army General Ray Odierno, Washington, DC, March 3, 2008

A disproportionate number of mixed errors is in fact predicted by a model in which activation from sounds can flow back up to words and influence lexical selection. Here's why: in a semantically based substitution, *dog* might replace *cat* because during lemma selection, related words compete for activation, and occasionally the wrong one may become more activated than the target. On the other hand, in a sound-based substitution, like *cat* → *vat*, the sound /v/ competes with /k/ as the first consonant of the word. But that's as far as it goes, in both cases. The effects of competition are restricted to the level where the competition originated, and there's no cross-talk between levels. But what happens with *cat* → *rat* is more complicated: at the lemma level, *rat* is activated because of its semantic similarity to the target, along with words like *dog, mouse,* and so on. All of these competing words send some activation down to the sound level, so along with /k/, /æ/, /t/, there's activation of the sounds /d/, /g/, /r/, /m/, and so on (from *dog, rat, mouse,* etc.) Now, since activation is allowed to bounce back up to the word level, sounds like /æ/ and /t/ will activate *cat*—but they'll *also* activate *rat*, so by virtue of its sound similarity to *cat*, *rat* will get an extra boost of activation, which will cycle back down to its component sounds. In this way, /r/ becomes much more activated than it could ever be if it weren't linked to a semantically related word (for instance, it becomes much more activated than /v/ could be). And the lemma *rat* becomes more activated than it could be based solely on its semantic relationship to *cat* (that is, it becomes much more activated than *dog* or *mouse* could be). Because of the flow back and forth between levels, activation from two separate levels becomes amplified.

LANGUAGE AT LARGE 9.3 (*continued*)

"There's a lot of people in the Middle East who are desirous to get into the Mitchell process. And—but first things first. The—these terrorist acts and, you know, the responses have got to end in order for us to get the framework—the groundwork—not framework, the groundwork to discuss a framework for peace, to lay the—all right."—referring to former senator George Mitchell's report on Middle East peace, Crawford, Texas, August 13, 2001

"I know how hard it is for you to put food on your family."—Greater Nashua, NH, January 27, 2000

"And so during these holiday seasons, we thank our blessings."—at Fort Belvoir, VA, December 10, 2004

"It's a time of sorrow and sadness when we lose a loss of life."—Washington, DC, December 21, 2004

"The enemy understands a free Iraq will be a major defeat in their ideology of hatred. That's why they're fighting so vociferously."—first presidential debate, Coral Gables, FL, September 30, 2004

"Let me put it to you bluntly. In a changing world, we want more people to have control over your own life."—Annandale, VA, August 9, 2004

"And free societies will be allies against these hateful few who have no conscience, who kill at the whim of a hat."—Washington, DC, September 17, 2004

"The illiteracy level of our children are appalling."—Washington, DC, January 23, 2004

"I am mindful not only of preserving executive powers for myself, but for predecessors as well."—Washington, DC, January 29, 2001

"The law I sign today directs new funds and new focus to the task of collecting vital intelligence on terrorist threats and on weapons of mass production."—Washington, DC, November 27, 2002

"We cannot let terrorists and rogue nations hold this nation hostile or hold our allies hostile."—Des Moines, Iowa, August 21, 2000

"Rarely is the question asked: Is our children learning?"—Florence, SC, January 11, 2000

"And there is distrust in Washington. I am surprised, frankly, at the amount of distrust that exists in this town. And I'm sorry it's the case, and I'll work hard to try to elevate it."—interview on National Public Radio, January 29, 2007

"Families is where our nation finds hope, where wings take dream."—La Crosse, WI, October 18, 2000

"You cannot lead if you send mexed missages."—September 30, 2004

A useful analogy might be to think about social "buzz" that surrounds a new product or celebrity. It's well known that such "buzz" is socially contagious—so you might think of it as a bit like spreading activation: a person who is enthusiastic about a movie star, for instance, spreads a bit of that enthusiasm when she talks to her friends about him. Now, suppose that "buzz" can only be spread from women to men, but not the other way around. There would be a limit to how popular a movie star could become. But if men's excitement could affect women's, and vice versa, a star's popularity could ascend to more dizzying heights—just as the word *rat* becomes superactivated as a result of the activation buzzing back and forth between levels when someone is trying to say *cat*.

The prevalence of mixed errors is neatly consistent with a model that involves activation in both directions. But it's consistent with other accounts as well. For example, it doesn't necessarily rule out a story that's based on a vigilant self-monitoring system. You might say, for instance, that when an impending speech error resembles the target in *both* sound and meaning, it's much harder for the monitor to detect it. Of course, this makes certain assumptions about what makes errors easier or harder to detect, which would need to be checked for their validity.

However, there's a second phenomenon that truly is hard to account for without assuming some activation from sounds to words: several studies have found that the production of words can be affected by how much a word overlaps in sound with other words.

Back in Chapter 7, we saw how some words, like *sling*, have many words that share numerous sounds with it (such words were said to live in dense phonological neighborhoods), while other words, like *stench,* occupy very sparse neighborhoods, overlapping closely with a very small number of words. Words from dense neighborhoods (like *sling*) usually take longer to recognize. This seems to be because the competing activation from similar-sounding words interferes with choosing the "winning" word as the best match. But in word production, it appears that having lots of neighbors often makes it easier to utter a word, not more difficult. For example, Trevor Harley and Helen Bown (1998) found that obscure words from dense neighborhoods were less likely than those from sparse neighborhoods to result in that frustrating tip-of-the-tongue state. In another series of experiments, Michael Vitevitch (2002) found that people were faster to produce the names for pictures when they had lots of sound-alike neighbors. He also used both the SLIP technique and a tongue-twister task to induce speech errors, and found that words from dense neighborhoods were less likely to become mangled during speech than words from sparse neighborhoods. Something about being surrounded by similar-sounding neighbors appears to make a word's phonological representation more stable when it comes to word production.

These effects make sense if you assume the model you saw in Figure 9.8B. For example, consider what happens with the high-density word *sling*. During lemma selection, *sling* becomes activated because it fits with the intended meaning of the message. As a result, it sends activation down to its component sounds. The activation of these sounds bounces back up to the word level, lighting up neighbors such as *slip, sing, bling,* and so on. In turn, activating *these* lemma representations results in the activation of *their* component sounds— many of which will be the same as those contained in *sling*. Hence, the sounds that make up the target word *sling* will get an extra jolt of activation because of its phonological neighbors. Without the extra feedback feature in the model, it's hard to see why the neighborhood density effect would show up.

Researchers always hope (and often assume!) that the results of clever lab techniques such as the SLIP method or tip-of-the-tongue task reveal something about how language is produced during normal, everyday conversation. But it doesn't hurt to try to confirm these results with more naturalistic methods, especially those in which target words are embedded within complete sentences. This was done in an elegant study by Florian Jaeger and his colleagues (2012). They had subjects describe pictures of events that involved various characters handing different objects to other characters. As in real life, these events could be described in a number of different ways—for example, you could say *Patty gave Simon the ball*, or use the verb *passed* or *handed* instead. The researchers ingeniously chose names for the characters so that some of them overlapped in sound with the possible verb choices—*Gabe* was similar to *gave*, *Patty* to *passed*, and *Hannah* to *handed*. They found that the choice of the verb depended in part on whether it was similar to the previously uttered subject of the sentence. This result is a nice addition to the collection of findings showing that phonological overlap affects the production of words in some way.

The thread of research in this section leads to a few conclusions. It shows us that some errors are undoubtedly averted by our internal monitoring. But it's unlikely that all speech error patterns can be accounted for as failures of quality control. Some of them come about because of the way activation spreads within the language production machinery—and it seems probable that some allowance needs to be made for sounds to activate lexical representations, as well as vice versa.

But a more general lesson is that it's well worth a researcher's while to think about the patterns of those speech errors that are bound to happen most often, and about why they might be so close to the surface (see **Box 9.5**). When researchers noticed the lexical bias for speech errors, this led to competing theo-

---

BOX 9.5
Patterns in speech errors

We've already seen that speech errors that result in real words are more common than ones that don't, and that speech errors involving similarities of both sound and meaning are also extremely likely to occur. Researchers have been able to make some additional generalizations, as shown below.

Think about these patterns in the context of the models of word production in Figure 9.8. What implications do the patterns have for a model of language production? For example, do they help us to choose between the models in Figure 9.8A and 9.8B? Or do they tell us that we need to build something entirely new into our model?

Pattern 1: Intended sounds are more likely to be replaced by very similar sounds than by very different sounds:

> *more likely:* sad sheep → shad seep
>
> *less likely:* bad sheep → shad beep

Pattern 2: Sounds that are embedded in similar phonological environments are more likely to be exchanged than sounds that are embedded in very different environments:

> *more likely:* beer deal → deer beal
>
> *less likely:* beer date → deer bate

Pattern 3: When speech errors result in non-words, they're very likely to result in "possible words"—that is, sequences of sounds that respect the language's *phonotactic* constraints:

> *more likely:* play bait → blay bait
>
> *less likely:* play mate → mlay mate

Pattern 4: Speech errors are more likely to replace rare sounds with common ones than vice versa:

> *more likely:* dim thistle → dim distle
>
> *less likely:* dim thistle → thim thistle

Pattern 5: Sound exchanges almost always involve sounds that appear in the same position within a syllable:

> *more likely:* beer deal → deer beal
>
> *less likely:* beer deal → leer deab

ries, each of which provided new insights about the design of the speaking apparatus. It turns out that there are quite a few other patterns in speech error data, each of which also triggers a set of possible explanations that spawn new and yet more refined questions about how speaking works. We won't trace the detailed lines of research that have come from noticing these other patterns, but you can get a sense of what some of the patterns are from Box 9.5.

On the more practical side, knowing something about the underlying production system and where it's likely to go wrong can give you some important ammunition in defending yourself if you make an embarrassing slip of the tongue. With enough knowledge, perhaps you'll be able to explain that an error was the result, not of socially abhorrent attitudes, but of activation flow between phonological and lexical levels. And maybe you'll even be able to explain why calling your spouse by the name of the person you *used* to be married to was a mistake "just waiting to happen," regardless of how you currently feel about either spouse—*especially* if both of them happen to have phonologically similar names like Carmen and Susan.

GO TO
sites.sinauer.com/languageinmind

for **web activities, further readings, research updates, new essays,** and other features

---

DIGGING DEEPER

Planning ahead

I started off this chapter with the question: How far ahead do you plan what you're going to say? You might have noticed I never gave a definite answer to that. But what you've already learned from this chapter is this: (1) people usually start speaking before they've planned their entire utterance, and (2) planning units are of a larger span for "higher" levels of language production than they are for "lower" levels. That is, you plan further ahead when choosing your words (lemmas) and formulating syntactic structure than you do when you're filling in the sound details of individual words. There's evidence for this from both speech errors and experimental studies.

Beyond these basic facts, though, researchers are still up in the air on a number of points. One of these is a very fundamental one: Is there even a *fixed* span that consistently corresponds to a planning unit, such that you must have planned that particular unit before you begin speaking? Obviously, this span would have to be different for different levels of representation. But you could imagine, for example, that people would hold off speaking until they've mapped out at least a complete syntactic phrase with words chosen and slotted into their appropriate positions. And at the phonological level, perhaps speakers fill in the details for an entire word unit before they begin uttering it. An alternative view would be that there's no fixed size at all to the units that speakers prepare and buffer in memory before beginning to talk. Maybe the size of planning units is entirely elastic and depends on the situation or the speaker's choice.

Let's first consider why it might make sense to think that planning units could be fixed, rather than flexible. The most compelling reason is that language parts often "clump" together in ways that affect the shape of the individual pieces within that clump—and sometimes the form of one word is dependent on the choice of a specific word that only appears farther downstream. This is easier to see in a language like French than it is in English. In English, suppose you were planning to say a phrase like *the very small cup*. In principle, you *could* begin to utter the phrase before you'd managed to finish retrieving the word *cup*. But in French, you'd be confronted with a decision at the very first word of the phrase, namely, whether the definite article should be expressed as *le* (masculine) or *la* (feminine)—but *that* decision depends on exactly which noun you're going to utter three words downstream! The adjective requires the same decision: Is it going to be *petit* (masculine) or *petite* (feminine)? Both of these decisions hinge on the fact that the French word for a cup (*tasse*) is feminine, but you can't know this until you've accessed its lemma. (And you really do have to have accessed the lemma for *tasse*, because grammatical gender, which is part of the lemma representation, is almost never predictable from the conceptual properties of the noun— what exactly is feminine about a cup?) So, at least in some languages, key words appear at the right edges of phrases, and often determine the form of earlier parts of the phrase. It's quite possible that the size of planning units in language production is set up to be able to be responsive to these kinds of linguistic dependencies, which turn out to be pretty common across languages.

On the other hand, there are also clear advantages to being flexible about how much planning ahead you do before you begin speaking. There are probably opposing pressures that bear on the issue of how much planning is optimal. Planning further ahead allows you to speak more fluently, because it makes it less likely that you'll reach a point in the sentence where it's time to utter a word that you haven't yet retrieved. On the other hand, if you plan too far ahead, this means you'll have to store in memory a lot of yet-to-be-uttered material, possibly more than you can reliably keep active. Also, there might be conversational pressure to begin speaking within a certain amount of time from the end of your partner's conversational turn. The smaller the planning units, the faster you can begin speaking. If planning units are fixed, then as a speaker, you have fewer options for figuring out how to respond to these sometimes conflicting pressures. And you'll be less able to adapt to changes in communicative circumstances. For example, if you're driving while talking, you might have less in the way of processing resources to spend on speaking, which would make memory demands more pressing than they might otherwise be. Shrinking the size of planning units would be handy in that situation. On the other hand, in public speaking, it might be especially important to focus on your delivery—stretching out your planning units might help you to avoid sprinkling your presentation with pauses, stammers, or the ubiquitous *um* and *er*.

Researchers have carried out dozens of experiments using a variety of ingenious methods and designs to try to pin down the planning units for language production. Overall, the harvest from all this research amounts to a resounding body of disagreement about the size of the planning units.

Let's look at just some of the studies focusing on the higher level of language production, that is, on the process of choosing words and formulating structure. The evidence from these studies hints at planning units that are as small as one word, or larger than an entire clause.

For example, Mark Smith and Linda Wheeldon (1999) presented evidence that at least some planning is done over very long stretches of language. They had subjects look at a computer screen with pictures of objects that moved into new positions on the screen. The subjects' task was to describe which objects had moved where. So, they might be prompted to produce sentences such as *The dog and the foot move up* or *The dog and the foot move up and the kite moves down*. The researchers then compared the amount of time it took people to begin talking for sentences like these that had either one clause or two clauses. The idea here is that if people usually

Figure 9.9 If you were to ask your classmates to name each of these nine objects, how much agreement would there be among them? Some objects are more definitively codable than others.

plan no further than one clause ahead, then the time before speaking should be exactly the same for one- and two-clause sentences. But that's not what Smith and Wheeldon found. Instead, people took longer to start uttering the two-clause sentences, suggesting that some planning ahead was happening even beyond the clause boundary.

At the other end of the spectrum, Zenzi Griffin has published a series of papers in which she's argued that the language production system is far more myopic, with a planning scope as small as one substantive word. In one of these papers (2001), she devised an experiment that hinged on the fact that it takes less time to choose a lemma for a concept that is highly *codable* than for a concept that is less codable. **Codability** as used here refers to whether or not there's a lot of agreement among speakers of a language about what word to use for the concept. In the domain of nouns, for example, there might be doubt about whether something should be called a "couch" or a "sofa" (see **Figure 9.9** for more examples). And describing a color might result in little in the way of naming controversy *if* everyone agrees that the color in question should be called "blue," but might also lead to a passionate debate over whether it should be called "teal," "aqua," "turquoise," "azure," or "blue-green." It shouldn't be surprising that it takes longer to retrieve the lemma for a concept that's low in codability, because that concept is linked

codability The degree of agreement among speakers of a language about what word to use for the concept.

to more than one plausible word representation. So, when you try to retrieve the lemma for *couch*, competition from *sofa* can slow down the retrieval process.

Griffin measured how long it took subjects to begin uttering complex sentences such as *The clock and the sofa are above the needle,* where the sentence frame was always *The A and the B are above/below the C.* She manipulated the codability of all three nouns, with the idea that this could provide a window into how deep into the sentence lemma selection needs to take place before speaking is initiated: If all the lemmas in the clause need to be chosen before the speaker opens her mouth, then it should take longer to speak when *any* of the three objects are low in codability, including the very last one (that is, C). But if lemmas only need to be selected for the subject noun phrase, which included the objects A and B, then the codability of the first two nouns (A and B) should affect speaking times, but it shouldn't matter whether C is high or low on codability, since its lemma doesn't need to be selected before the onset of speech. Griffin actually found that planning units were even smaller than this. It turned out that the codability of only the *first* object (A) mattered. The codability of B and C made no difference in how long people paused before speaking, which suggests that lemma selection didn't even need to extend to the entire subject noun phrase. Nevertheless, this tightly incremental approach to language production didn't cause the subjects to run into problems—for the most part, their responses were perfectly fluent even though they didn't seem to be planning much beyond the first noun.

It's hard to know how to integrate the results from Griffin's study with those of Smith and Wheeldon. And a deeper survey of the literature turns up even more in the way of conflicting results, with some researchers arguing for the phrase as the planning unit, while others argue that it's either larger or smaller than that. This lack of consensus obviously doesn't bode well for the idea that there is a single, fixed size of planning unit at each level of language production.

On the other hand, our alternative hypothesis is that the size of planning units is flexible—but presumably not *random.* So we shouldn't be content to stop at the conclusion that different sizes of planning units turn up across different experimental situations. Ideally, we'd like to know what factors can affect the amount of preplanning that takes place before speaking. Is the scope of planning affected by the nature of external communicative pressures? Personal preference and temperament? The processing demands imposed by certain especially challenging bits of language? Or by individual cognitive differences?

It seems that speakers have at least some control over the size of planning units in a way that allows them to respond to specific communicative demands. For example, Fernanda Ferreira and Benjamin Swets (2002) had people solve mental arithmetic problems and verbally report the result with sentences such as *The answer is 47,* or *47 is the answer.* Subjects were confronted with problems of varying difficulty—for instance, it's easier to mentally compute the sum for 21 + 22 than it is for 23 + 68. The difference in difficulty between problems was used as a tool to tackle the question of whether people would be running through the calculations before speaking, or simultaneously while speaking. Ferreira and Swets found that, left to their own devices, people consistently took longer to begin speaking when confronted with the harder problems, whether they reported the sum at the beginning of the sentence or at the very end. This shows that they were computing the sum before beginning to speak. What's more, there was no difference in the *duration* of the sentences for the easy problems versus the hard problems, which suggests that all of the computing was done before speaking was initiated—otherwise the difference in difficulty would have also been reflected in the degree to which speakers dawdled through the sentences while trying to figure out the answers to the tough problems.

But the picture changed a bit when subjects were told they had to respond quickly before a buzzer sounded. In this situation, they were able to begin talking before the computation was complete—they still took longer to begin speaking in reporting the hard problems than the easy ones, but now they also took longer to pronounce the sentences for hard problems compared with easy ones. This shows that at least some of the calculations were still being done after they began speaking.

You might complain that this is a very artificial experimental situation, and that conversations don't normally involve tests of one's knack for math. It's possible that subjects were unnaturally stalling before speaking, to avoid looking foolish for getting the wrong answer. Nevertheless, the fact that they were able to adjust the amount of calculation they did prior to speaking, depending on whether they had an externally imposed "deadline," does raise the interesting possibility that people can be strategic about just how incrementally they plan their utterances. In normal conversation, external deadlines might come from a number of sources—the need to jump into the conversation quickly to get a word in edgewise, or the pressure that comes from social expectations that silences between conversational turns not be overly long (as discussed in Language at Large 9.1).

Some research suggests that planning units might be stretched or shortened in very subtle and unconscious ways, partly as a technique for maintaining fluency. Zenzi Griffin (2003) noticed that on average, people take just under a second to identify a picture, find the corresponding lemma to express it, fill in its sounds, prepare an articulatory plan, and begin pronouncing its name. But the actual *pronunciation* of many words can span significantly less time than that.

This means that, if speakers are planning ahead no more than one word at a time, speech will often run ahead of planning. For example, if a long and difficult word follows on the heels of a short one, the planning of the second word might easily take more time than the uttering of the first one. In this scenario, failing to plan further ahead than a single word would inevitably result in hesitations, pauses, or disfluencies.

We've seen that speech does contain many disfluencies. But Griffin proposed that speakers aren't powerless to avoid them, and can adjust the size of planning units in just these sticky situations. She constructed an experiment in which subjects were shown two pictures side by side, and were told to name them in left-to-right sequence without pausing between words. For example, if shown a picture of a wig to the left of a carrot, subjects were to say "wig carrot" without inserting any pauses between the two words. They were able to do this fluently, which implies that some of the planning of the word *carrot* was in fact taking place before people began to utter the short word *wig*. Griffin then compared sequences like *wig carrot* to sequences in which the first word was longer, such as *windmill carrot*. Since *windmill* takes longer to say than *wig*, this leaves a bit more time to plan *carrot* while in the midst of saying *windmill*. Griffin found that when the first word was longer, people were faster to begin uttering the word sequence. At first blush, this seems strange, because if people were uttering single words in isolation, it would normally take them more time to produce a longer word like *windmill* than a shorter word like *wig*. Griffin concluded that in the two-word sequences, speakers allotted extra time to prepare *carrot* before uttering *wig* because they instinctively realized that, since *wig* is such a short word, they might not have enough time while pronouncing it in which to plan the word *carrot*. Their response to this disfluency hazard was to extend the size of the planning unit to include the second word as well. This entirely subconscious strategy on the speakers' part is a bit like what a driver might do when he spots a speed bump farther down the road: he applies the brakes early on to reduce his speed so that he won't hit the bump down the road with undue violence.

This fascinating study suggests not only that speakers have some control over the size of planning units for speaking, but that they exercise this control in quite sophisticated ways, predicting potential speed bumps and preparing a nimble response. It suggests that they can adapt not just to external communicative demands to speak more quickly or more fluently, but also to the internal demands that are imposed by the properties of the very language they are in the midst of producing. More recent evidence also suggests that speakers stretch or shrink the scope of planning as a way to manage their processing resources during language production. For example, Agnieszka Konopka (2012) has shown that when a target syntactic structure has been previously primed, thereby making it more accessible, speakers broaden the scope over which they perform syntactic planning—presumably, some resources have been freed up that allow speakers to plan further ahead. And conversely, Valentin Wagner and colleagues (2010) have shown that when cognitive pressures are dialed up (for instance, by introducing a concurrent task), speakers respond by *narrowing* the scope of their advance planning.

As we've seen throughout the chapter, the simple act of speaking is much like a three-ring circus, with a bewildering variety of complicated cognitive events taking place all at once. It shouldn't come as a surprise that in the chaos of all this activity, speech errors will unavoidably slip out and the flow of speech will inevitably be disrupted by hesitations or disfluencies. Luckily, for most of us who don't work in the media or run for public office, we're usually forgiven our speech errors, even by our spouses. Nonetheless, we have our own tools for avoiding certain speech calamities. Ongoing research suggests that perhaps we cope with the demands of speaking in part by making intelligent on-the-fly decisions about how far ahead to cast our attention, how much to think before we speak. Without this ability, we might find ourselves tongue-tied a great deal more often than we already are.

PROJECT

Design a study in which you test for cross-cultural differences in the timing between conversational turns. In Language at Large 9.1, we considered whether there are different cultural expectations about the timing between conversational turns. Do expectations of conversational turn-taking have an impact on the size of planning units that people regularly apply during speaking? You'll need to propose a method for testing conversational timing expectations, and a separate experimental task to measure planning units.

10 Discourse and Inference

By this point, you might be ready to concede that the whole business of amassing and deploying knowledge of words and language structure is more involved than you'd initially thought. But once basic language skills are in place, and words can be dependably retrieved for language production or comprehension, and once the machinery for assembling well-formed sentences and computing their meanings is running smoothly, we're home free, right?

Not exactly. Try reading the following collection of impeccably formed English sentences:

> *Frank became convinced that his brother, a handsome and witty doctor, was having an affair with his wife. The doctor warned her that it was only a matter of months until probable death. Her only hope was to undergo a disfiguring surgery. But she was afraid to do so. She lingered for some time, but eventually, Frank had to confront the fact that she was gone from his life. Then he learned the truth. Racked with sorrow, he killed himself. It was a brutal stab in the back. She thought that she should eventually tell Frank. Frank's wife was secretly being treated for a dangerous illness. He was consumed with rage over it.*

For added fun, now look away from the text and try to paraphrase what you've just read. I'll admit the passage is hard to make sense of. But there's nothing wrong with the sentences themselves. In fact, they seem to pose no problem at all when arranged in a somewhat different order, like this:

> Frank became convinced that his brother, a handsome and witty doctor, was sleeping with his wife. It was a brutal stab in the back. He was consumed with rage over it. Then he learned the truth. His wife was secretly being treated for a dangerous illness. The doctor warned her that it was only a matter of months until probable death. Her only hope was to undergo a disfiguring surgery. She thought that she should eventually tell Frank. But she was afraid to do so. In the end, she lingered for some time, but eventually, Frank had to confront the fact that she was gone from his life. Racked with sorrow, he killed himself.

Why is this version so much easier to read than the previous one? It's not just that this version is "orderly" and the first version is "disorganized." The sharp contrast between the two comes from the fact that our understanding of the passage is supplied only partially by the language itself—the rest of its meaning is actually filled in by the connections that we draw between sentences and the extra details that we throw in.

Normally, when people talk about "reading between the lines," they have in mind some especially skilled or attentive scrutiny of the message; the phrase usually refers to hunting for some underlying meaning that's been slipped in or hidden, invisible to anyone who's not carefully looking for it. But in reality, whether as hearers or readers, we read between the lines of language all the time without thinking about it. Further, as producers of language, we *rely* on our audience to be able to do it. Take the seemingly complete sentence *The doctor warned her that it was only a matter of months until probable death.* There are many pieces of information that this sentence leaves out. We know that some doctor (but we don't know exactly which one) warned someone female (but who?) that someone (but who?) would likely die (but from what?) in a matter of months (but how many?). Because this sentence is nestled among others in the two passages above, much of this information gets filled in, though the result is somewhat different in the two contexts:

> Frank became convinced that his brother, a handsome and witty doctor, was having an affair with his wife. *The doctor warned her that it was only a matter of months until probable death.*

> His wife was secretly being treated for a dangerous illness. *The doctor warned her that it was only a matter of months until probable death.*

Because a specific doctor and a specific female have already been mentioned in each version, we can easily figure out who is referred to by *the doctor* and by *her*. But only the second context leads to a clear and sensible inference about whose death is under discussion. In the first context, we're left wondering exactly who will die. The wife? Her lover, the doctor? Will they be murdered by the husband? The story only gets more mysterious with the sentence *Her only hope was to undergo a disfiguring surgery.* If you look back at the first passage, you'll see that much of its jarring effect comes from the fact that you can't help but try to make connections among the pieces of the text, sometimes with bizarre effects.

Hearers and readers can be counted on to bring this connection-making mindset to the task of language comprehension, which in turn has a powerful effect on the choices that a speaker makes about how much meaning gets packed into the language itself. If all meaning had to be encoded explicitly through language, we would end up with stories that sound like this:

Frank became convinced that Frank's brother, a handsome and witty doctor, was sleeping with Frank's wife. According to Frank's belief, the fact that Frank's brother was sleeping with Frank's wife was a horrible betrayal by Frank's brother and Frank's wife, much like the experience of Frank being brutally stabbed in the back by Frank's brother and Frank's wife. Frank was consumed with rage over Frank's belief that Frank's brother and Frank's wife were sleeping together. Then Frank learned the truth about the situation between Frank's brother and Frank's wife.

This passage is hard to read (not to mention highly annoying), even though it is meant to take the guesswork out of comprehension.

Any account of how human minds engage with language has to grapple with the fact that the meaning that's conveyed by the actual linguistic code has to be dovetailed with knowledge that comes from other sources. These "other sources" don't just represent icing on the cake of linguistic meaning. They interact with linguistic form and meaning in complex ways, and without them, it would be impossible for us to use language to communicate with each other efficiently.

The goal of this chapter is to give you a sense of the wide-ranging ways in which we all "read between the lines" of language, using the linguistic content of sentences as a starting point—and not the end point—for the construction of an enriched meaning representation. You'll see how we fill in certain details that are not provided by the language itself; we do this by mentally re-creating the real-world situations that gave rise to the sentences in question. This allows us, among other things, to infer the cause-effect relationship between sentences even when they're not explicitly stated, to have a clear sense of how things and events that are described in a text are related in real time and space, to add vivid perceptual detail to our understanding of a narrative, and to draw very precise meanings from linguistic expressions that are inherently vague, such as words like *she* or *his*.

10.1 From Linguistic Form to Mental Models of the World

Beyond linguistic content

The whole purpose of talking (or writing) to others is to implant certain thoughts in their minds (often with the goal that these thoughts will lead to specific actions). At its heart, then, language comprehension involves transforming information about linguistic form into thought structures. Knowledge of the rules or patterns of language imposes some hard constraints on what those thought structures look like—as you've seen from previous chapters, a firm understanding of the meanings of words and the syntactic patterns of a language are needed in order to be able to recover a speaker's intended meaning. But recovering the linguistically coded content of a sentence is just the first step. Let's start by taking a look at what the linguistic code does and does not contribute to meaning.

Consider a sentence like *Juanita kissed Samuel*. Your knowledge of English does not allow you to transform this sentence into a thought representation in which Samuel receives a violent wallop from Juanita or where Samuel is the one doing the kissing—the sentence itself simply doesn't map onto these meanings. Note: with a whole lot of background knowledge, you might understand that these events either *led to* Juanita kissing Samuel, or are the *consequence* of Juanita kissing Samuel. Crucially, however, these additional events hinge on the thought representation of the Juanita-kissing-Samuel event—it's this

proposition The core meaning of a sentence as expressed by its linguistic content. This core meaning captures the real-world event or the situation that would have to occur in order for that sentence to be judged to be true.

mental models Also known as **situation models**. Refers to detailed conceptual representation of the real-world situation that a sentence evokes.

latter event that is part of the core meaningful content of the sentence, which is derived entirely from knowledge of the sentence's word meanings and syntactic structure. Language researchers call this core meaning the **proposition** that corresponds to a sentence. You can think of propositions as the interface between sentences and their corresponding representations of reality.

In print, it's common to see propositions written down as logical formulas that follow specific notational conventions, so you might see the proposition that's expressed by a sentence like *Juanita kissed Samuel* as:

kiss (j, s)

This is simply shorthand for a thought structure that looks something like this: In the world we're talking about, there was a kissing event in which the person referred to as Juanita kissed the person referred to as Samuel. Propositions represent the bare bones of a sentence, capturing those things about a situation that have to be true in the world in order for the sentence to be considered true. But when you think about it, this proposition leaves a fair bit of detail unspecified. For example, the sentence *Juanita kissed Samuel* is true regardless of whether Juanita gave Samuel a brief peck on the cheek, or whether she kissed him on the mouth for an entire minute without drawing a breath; whether Juanita refers to Samuel's mother or to his lover; whether Samuel enjoyed it or was repulsed by the kiss, etc. Presumably, some details along these lines were present in the situation that caused the speaker to utter this sentence in the first place. But none of this is contained within the sentence's propositional content.

The propositional content is the end result of unpacking the words and syntactic structure of a sentence, so propositions are determined by the structural relationships of elements within the sentence. (Notice that you get a different proposition for the sentence *Samuel kissed Juanita*.) However, you might remember that in Chapter 9, I talked about the fact that speakers can often choose from a fairly wide variety of sentence structures to express the same meaning. So, a number of different linguistic forms can give rise to the same proposition: *Samuel was kissed by Juanita; It was Juanita who kissed Samuel; It was Samuel who was kissed by Juanita,* etc. All of these have the same core meaningful content. What this means is that all of these sentences are either true or false under the same set of circumstances. If you imagine any situation in the real world in which the sentence *Juanita kissed Samuel* is true, then all of the above paraphrases are true as well. Conversely, any situation in which *Juanita kissed Samuel* is false also renders the other paraphrases false.

When linguists talk about the meanings of sentences, they often have in mind their propositions. But we do much more during language comprehension than just extract the abstract propositional content of a sentence. To some extent, we also mentally encode the specific event or situation that might have triggered the utterance of the sentence. That is, we tend to build a fairly detailed conceptual representation of the real-world situation that a sentence evokes. Such representations are often called **mental models** or **situation models**. They aren't anywhere near as detailed as the real triggering events, but they're a lot richer than just the sentence's propositional content.

It seems self-evident that understanding language must involve some form of enriched mental encoding. Admittedly, if all we did with language was to recover the propositional content of sentences, language would still be useful—consider, for example, that one of your distant ancestors may well have survived long enough to reproduce solely because of the *very* useful propositional content of a statement like, "There's a sabertooth tiger behind you!" But there are some things that propositional content alone can't do. For example, it's not likely to move you to tears when embedded within a novel, or to create enough suspense to cause you to stay up all night turning the pages of a well-written thriller. It's often been suggested that fiction is as compelling as it is precisely because the reader's mental representations of the events that are described in the text are similar to the information that she'd encode if she were actually participating in those events.

But figuring out *exactly* what information is contained in that mental model is no trivial matter for psycholinguists. One challenge is that trying to probe for its contents could well change the type of information that people encode, making it hard to infer what they represent spontaneously when curled up with a book on the couch. (Think about it: How much detail do *you* think you represent in the normal course of reading sentences? As soon as you try to analyze your mental representations in response to a sentence, the very act of scrutiny probably changes them.) Even less trivial is explaining precisely how the information in the mental model got there, and what cognitive mechanisms were involved. There's a surprising amount we still don't know about the thought structures that language implants in us. But we do have a bit of a sense of what these mental models look like from an intriguing variety of experimental scenarios and results.

What information do mental models contain?

The first step in investigating mental models is to establish that thought representations for sentences do in fact look more like real-world situations than like abstract propositions. So, what do real-world situations look like?

At the most basic level, when a sentence describes a situation, certain things and people are involved. But not all things that are *mentioned* are actually present in the situation that's being described. For example, consider the following sentences:

Simon baked some cookies and some bread.

Simon baked some cookies but no bread.

Both of these sentences specifically mention bread. And the propositional content for each sentence also includes bread. (The proposition for a sentence like *Simon baked no bread* can be paraphrased as something like: it's false that there was an event of baking in which the person referred to as Simon baked bread; **Figure 10.1A**.) But things are a bit different if we look at the actual *situations* in the

(A) Sample sentences

Simon baked some cookies and some bread.	Simon baked some cookies but no bread.
bake (s, cookies) & bake (s, bread)	bake (s, cookies) &¬ [bake (s, bread)]

(B) Mental representation

Figure 10.1 Propositions versus situations for sentences with and without negation. (A) Propositions and corresponding target sentences. Note that the symbol ¬ indicates the logical concept of negation, which is understood as stating that the proposition under negation is false. (B) Drawings showing the real-world situations that are consistent with the meanings of each of the target sentences.

world that correspond to these sentences (**Figure 10.1B**). The first sentence evokes a situation in which there are cookies and bread; no bread exists in the situation evoked by the second sentence. The question is, Do our mental representations of the sentences somehow reflect this difference between the situations, as shown in Figure 10.1B? Or do they, like the propositions in Figure 10.1A, include the concept of bread to an equal degree for both example sentences?

To find out, Maryellen MacDonald and Marcel Just (1989) probed readers' mental models using a memory task. Subjects read a collection of 20 stimulus sentences describing a situation that called either for the existence of certain objects (e.g., bread) or negated that object (**Figure 10.2A**). Subjects saw only one stimulus sentence per trial, followed immediately by the probe word. The stimulus sentences came from one of three possible conditions. After reading each stimulus sentence, subjects had to respond to the probe word by pressing a "Yes" or "No" button to indicate whether that word had appeared somewhere in the stimulus sentence (**Figure 10.2B**). Subjects were faster to respond "Yes" correctly when the probe word in question (*bread* or *cookies* in our example) actually existed (that is, had not been negated) in the situation that the stimulus sentence described (**Figure 10.2C**).

One way of interpreting these results is that even when the word *bread* appeared in all the critical sentences, the concept of bread was more heavily activated when the sentence required its existence in the real-world situation it described. This suggests that readers' representations of sentences are more like encodings of real situations than like abstract propositions.

Similar probe tasks have been used to study specific aspects of mental models. A number of studies show that these mental representations aren't fixed, static recordings; rather, the degree to which entities are active in memory waxes and wanes, much as a camera might zoom in to capture something in more detail, then zoom out again, only to focus on something else. The shifts in focus can reveal interesting things about how people structure their mental representations as they interpret language.

For example, Art Glenberg and colleagues (1987) had their subjects read stories that contained a particular object of interest (here, a sweatshirt). In half the stories, the object was spatially connected with the main character of the story, like this:

> John was preparing for a marathon in August. **After doing a few warm-up exercises, he put on his sweatshirt and went jogging.** He jogged halfway along the lake without too much difficulty. Further along his route, however, John's muscles began to ache.

The other half of the stories were very similar, with one slight, but important change; in the second sentence, the critical object becomes separated from the protagonist:

> John was preparing for a marathon in August. **After doing a few warm-up exercises, he took off his sweatshirt and went jogging.** He jogged halfway along the lake without too much difficulty. Further along his route, however, John's muscles began to ache.

The researchers varied whether the memory probe appeared immediately following the critical second sentence, or after either one or two additional sentences. They found that immediately after the key sentence, subjects were quite fast to respond to the probe (*sweatshirt*) in both types of stories, suggesting that this object was highly active in memory. But for the second story, in which the sweatshirt was peeled away from the main character, the sweatshirt quickly faded in memory, and responses to the probe were considerably slower if just one sentence intervened between the mention of *sweatshirt* in the text and the

(A) Sample stimuli

Condition	Sample stimulus sentence
Noun 1 (bread) negated	Almost every weekend, Elizabeth bakes no bread but only cookies for the children.
Noun 2 (cookies) negated	Almost every weekend, Elizabeth bakes some bread but no cookies for the children.
No negation	Almost every weekend, Elizabeth bakes some bread and some cookies for the children.

(B) Experimental procedure

After each stimulus sentence was read, it was obscured by dashes and a probe word was presented. Participants had to respond to the probe by pressing one of two buttons ("Yes" or "No") to indicate whether or not that word had occurred in the sentence or not. The probe word could be either Noun 1 or Noun 2 to elicit a "Yes" response. ("Filler" trials were also included, such that 40% of probes called for a "No" response.)

(C) Results

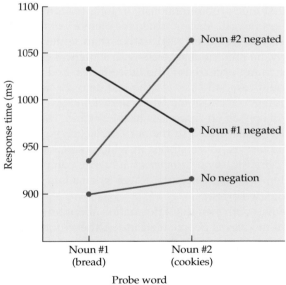

Figure 10.2 Summary of MacDonald and Just's (1989) Experiment 1 (1989). (A) Stimulus sentences were designed for three experimental conditions, with or without negation. The "Noun 1" and "Noun 2" sentences were identical except that the positions of the nouns were swapped; this was done to insure that response times reflected whether or not the noun was negated, rather than something particular about that noun, or its position in the sentence. (B) In the experimental task, a stimulus sentence was presented and then obscured. Participants then responded to a probe word, indicating whether or not the word had occurred in the stimulus sentence. (C) Response times to the memory probe word. Participants were faster to respond "Yes" correctly when the object described by the probe word had in fact been present in the situation described. (Adapted from MacDonald & Just, 1989.)

memory probe. In contrast, for the first story, in which the critical object stayed attached to the main character, responses to the *sweatshirt* probe were faster, suggesting that the sweatshirt concept stayed highly activated in memory. Despite the fact that there's no further mention of the sweatshirt in either story, subjects must have constructed some mental representation of what the protagonist was wearing as he jogged around the lake, causing them to respond more quickly to the probe when the sweatshirt was attached to his body. But by the fourth sentence of the story (two sentences after the mention of the sweatshirt), the activation of the sweatshirt concept waned to the point that responses were equally slow for both story types.

The memory-probe technique is interesting because it reveals something about how attention to various entities shifts over time and in response to the nature of the situation and the relationships between entities. In the study by Glenberg and colleagues, it's apparent that the spatial relationship between entities can affect such shifts of attention. Other work with memory probes has shown that temporal information is also coded in the mental model.

In one such study, Rolf Zwaan (1996) had people read stories that described a series of events. At some point in the story, a new event was introduced with one of the following phrases: *A moment later/an hour later/a day later.* For example, embedded within a story describing an aspiring novelist settling down to work, readers might encounter the following pair of adjacent sentences: *Jamie turned on his PC and started typing. An hour later, the telephone rang.* After reading the second of these sentences, subjects had to respond to a memory probe that tested for content that had appeared in the first sentence, just before this temporal phrase (for example, *typing*). They took longer to respond "Yes" to the probe when the temporal phrase expressed a longer interval of time (*an hour later/a day later*) than when it expressed a very short interval, suggesting that material in a mental model becomes less accessible if it has to be retrieved from beyond the conceptual barrier of a long time interval. In addition to this finding, Zwaan's study revealed that people took longer to read the sentences that introduced a long temporal shift of an hour or a day. He took this to mean that when a temporal phrase introduces some kind of discontinuity between events, it becomes harder to integrate these events in a mental model.

Moreover, the connection between events that are separated by a longer time interval seems to be coded much more tenuously in long-term memory. In a variation on the memory-probe task, Zwaan tested for memory of the stories' content after all of the stories had been read, rather than while people were reading them. Specifically, he presented subjects with sentences describing events that either had or had not occurred in the little stories, and probed to see how quickly people would respond "Yes" to the test item *the telephone rang* immediately after responding to the test item *Jamie started typing.* The idea here is that if the first test item speeds up responses to the second, this must be because the two events are tightly linked in memory. Subjects' responses to the second event were quite fast for those stories in which the two events were separated by just a very brief interval (*a moment later*); by comparison, responses to the second test item were significantly slower when a longer time interval intervened between the two events.

A large number of studies have confirmed that information about time tends to be a stable fixture of mental models as people read text. Other information is also encoded in mental models—for instance, the representation of a character's goals, as is illustrated by these two contrasting stories:

(a) Betty wanted to give her mother a present. She went to the department store. She found out that everything was too expensive. Betty decided to knit a sweater.

(b) Betty wanted to give her mother a present. She went to the department store. She bought her mother a purse. Betty decided to knit a sweater.

In (a), Betty's decision to knit a sweater is best interpreted as serving the goal of giving her mother a present. In (b), Betty has already satisfied this goal while at the department store, and the decision to knit a sweater seems unrelated. Tom Trabasso and Soyoung Suh (1993) found that content related to a character's goals became less accessible if the goal had been satisfied, but if the goal remained unfulfilled, depriving the reader of a sense of closure, the same content stayed highly active in memory. (Incidentally, this is not the only study that shows that a lack of closure leads to stronger memory for the unresolved elements—another example can be found in a 2009 paper by Richard Gerrig and colleagues. Such results may make you wonder whether cliff-hanger endings in TV episodes actually help you remember their content better. Lab studies have looked at memory over fairly short intervals of time within a single lab session, but it wouldn't be hard to design an experiment that looks to see whether cliff-hangers help people remember key events over the period of a week or so.)

Various studies have explored dimensions such as time, space, cause/effect relations, or information about a character's goals or characteristics, and all of these seem to play a part in building mental models that are triggered by linguistic content. There's still a fair bit of ongoing work to do, though, to establish whether some of these dimensions are more important than others (and if so, why), and how they might interact with each other.

There's also still a fair bit that we don't know about the amount of perceptual detail that goes into mental models. For example, we usually take it for granted that when people read novels, they conjure up a lot of perceptual detail through their own imaginations (though there may be some significant individual differences; see **Box 10.1**). When a novel gets adapted into a movie, many people have strong opinions about whether the actors in the film version look "right," suggesting that they have mentally encoded these details while reading. But how much detail, exactly, and of what kind?

One intriguing study used a nifty twist on the common memory-probe task to test whether readers actually bring to mind the *sounds* that are verbally described. Tad Brunyé and colleagues (2010) showed their participating readers sentences that contained auditory descriptions (for example, *The engine clattered as the truck driver warmed up his rig*). Subjects then had to classify certain sounds as either real sounds that could occur in the world, or computer-generated artificial sounds. This test included sounds that had been described in the previous sentences, as well as sounds that had not. People were faster to classify the sounds that had been described in the earlier sentences that they'd read, suggesting that they had to some extent mentally activated these sounds—rather than merely represented them as abstractions—so the sounds were primed, or more familiar, by the time subjects took the sound categorization test. This is consistent with a mound of work in brain imaging, which shows that when people read perceptually rich sentences, this activates those areas of the brain that are responsible for *perception* in those domains.

At the same time, not all perceptual details of an event are represented by readers of texts—or even by their writers, as sometimes becomes apparent when a novel is adapted for the movie screen. In a *New Yorker* magazine piece about the screen adaptation of David Mitchell's novel *Cloud Atlas*, Aleksandar Hemon (2012) notes some of the challenges that unexpectedly arose in creating real objects out of the novel's material:

> The scene in the control room, for example, features an "orison,"
> a kind of super-smart egg-shaped phone capable of producing
> 3-D projections, which Mitchell had dreamed up for the futuristic
> chapters. The Wachowskis [the film's directors], however, had to
> avoid the cumbersome reality of having characters running around
> with egg-shaped objects in their pockets; it had never crossed
> Mitchell's mind that that could be a problem. "Detail in the novel
> is dead wood. Excessive detail is your enemy," Mitchell told me,
> squeezing the imaginary enemy between his thumb and index finger.

BOX 10.1
Individual differences in visual imagery during reading

Are you the sort of person who savors long descriptive passages in novels, wallowing in their visual richness, or do you skip over them impatiently to get to the "good" parts? Do you get a really clear picture in your mind of what characters look like, or are you fairly indifferent to visual details when you read? People seem to engage in varying degrees of visual imagery during reading (or even just thinking about situations), and as a result, they don't all experience texts in the same ways.

In one interesting study, Michel Denis (1982) compared the reading patterns of "high imagers" with those of "low imagers." First, he sorted his test subjects into these two groups by administering the Vividness of Visual Imagery Questionnaire (VVIQ), a 16-item questionnaire that instructs participants to think about specific scenes and situations and then rate the vividness of the resulting image. Responses to this test appear to capture stable differences among individuals, and have been shown to correlate with individual differences in brain activity as measured by fMRI (see, for example, Cui et al., 2007). Subjects who scored higher than average on the VVIQ were deemed to be in the "high imager" (HI) group, while those who scored below average were considered to be in the "low imager" (LI) group.

Denis had both groups read a simple narrative text of about 2,000 words, in which descriptive language is used to tell the story of a farmer who rides in his wagon to a nearby village to sell his crops and meets with a series of incidents on his way home. The subjects were simply told to read the text carefully, at their own pace, without rereading, and to expect a short quiz at the end. The test involved simple questions such as, "In Antoine's wagon there were: (a) carrots, (b) turnips."

There were some interesting differences between the HI and LI groups. First, the HI group took about 14% longer to read the text. Denis suggested that this extra time reflected the fact that members of this group were spontaneously devoting more time and cognitive resources to visualizing the scenes and events in the story. Second, the HI group did better on the quiz, having remembered more of the details in the story. This finding meshes with results from quite a few other studies, all of which indicate that increased visualizing results in more robust memory for a text. In fact, when Denis compared the ten top scorers (out of 42 subjects) on the VVIQ with the ten lowest scorers, the differences in reading times and test performance grew even wider.

In order to confirm that visual imagery was likely responsible for the differences between the two groups, Denis ran a second experiment in which another set of HI and LI subjects read a rather dry and abstract excerpt from

"In film, if you want to show something, it has to be designed." The Wachowskis' solution: the orison is as flat as a wallet and acquires a third dimension only when spun. Mitchell, who had been kept in the loop throughout the process (and has a cameo in the film), was boyishly excited by the filmmakers' "groping toward exactitude."

WEB ACTIVITY 10.1

What's in a mental model? So far, we've covered only a small portion of the kinds of detailed information that readers could potentially represent in their mental models while reading. In this activity, you'll have the opportunity to think of a dimension we haven't discussed and sketch out an experiment using memory probes (or some other techniques; see Method 10.1) to figure out whether such information is normally present in readers' mental models.

Clearly, David Mitchell, the novel's author, had never envisioned the "orison" in enough detail to imagine it bulging in his characters' pockets, and it's doubtful that his readers had either—nor is it likely that even the most committed readers designed it in their minds to the point of giving the device the aesthetically pleasing feature of shifting from two dimensions to three.

This is not surprising, because it probably takes quite a bit of time and effort to instantiate detailed visual representations (by one estimate, it can take up to *three seconds* for people to generate a detailed image of an object; see Marschark & Cornoldi, 1991). When it comes to language processing speeds, three seconds is a thoroughly

BOX 10.1 *(continued)*

a psychology manual (Guillaume, 1963; translated by Denis, 1982), containing language like this:

> *In the issues which are studied in psychology, one has the aim, as in natural sciences, to describe facts and to determine their conditions, that is other facts whose observation points to their steady relationship with the former ones; in other words, one has the aims to set up laws.*

Such a text presents scant opportunity for visualization, even for the most visually oriented HI readers!

The results of this second experiment were quite different from the earlier version. Given this abstract text, there were no differences in reading times or test performance between the HI and LI groups—even the 10 highest and 10 lowest scorers on the VVIQ showed comparable results. This suggests that the results of the previous experiment really did involve a visualization component, rather than merely reflecting a general difference in reading ability between the two groups.

In a third experiment, Denis used the same text that was used in the first experiment (the farmer's story), but this time he instructed both groups to read as quickly as possible. The results for the LI group were no different in this experiment than in the first, suggesting that in the first experiment, LI readers had already adopted a strategy that allowed them to approach their fastest reading speed,

presumably because they were already spending minimal time on visualizing. This was later supported by their test performance in a fourth experiment (described next). On the other hand, when instructed to read quickly, the HI readers showed a significant decline in the amount of time they spent reading the passage—and a corresponding drop in performance on the memory test. This suggests that readers have some voluntary control over the amount of visualizing they do during reading.

Denis repeated the experiment a fourth time, this time instructing his subjects to be sure to visualize the scenes and events in the story. In this version of the study, reading patterns for the HI and LI subjects were statistically identical, due to the fact that the LI readers slowed down their reading pace and performed better on the test compared with the LI group in the first experiment. This suggests that just as the HI readers in the third experiment could voluntarily engage in *less* visualization, the LI readers could also strategically do *more* of it, and reap the rewards as a consequence. On the other hand, the HI subjects in this fourth experiment read at the same speed and showed the same accuracy as the HI group in the first experiment. The instructions to visualize had no measurable effect on HI readers, probably because such readers spontaneously engage in heavy visualizing regardless of whether they're instructed to do so.

glacial pace—the average word can be read as much as ten times faster than that. Presumably, slower reading would allow for more visual detail to be elaborated by the reader (so, if you want to experience a novel more vividly, stop skimming!), but there's still a great deal that's unknown about which features are most likely to be spontaneously brought to mind during ordinary recreational reading.

What information "sticks" in memory?

Let's step back for a moment, and think about the implications of mental models (see **Method 10.1**). The picture I've painted so far is one in which getting to the right *linguistic* representations is not the end result of comprehension processes, but simply the means to an end—admittedly, a highly complex and powerful means, but not the ultimate goal that drives all the work that goes into language processing.

If instead of reaching the right linguistic representation, constructing mental models is the goal of language comprehension, we might imagine that these mental models would be privileged over more abstract linguistic representations. And it seems that they are, at least when it comes to what's accessible in conscious long-term memory. In what's now considered a classic study of

METHOD 10.1

Converging techniques for studying mental models

Many of the studies you've seen so far in this chapter have tried to measure the activation of certain words (or their related concepts) as readers wound their way through a text. This is usually done by interrupting the text at critical points with a memory probe consisting of the relevant word or its control, and measuring how quickly readers are able to respond "Yes," that the word had indeed appeared earlier in the text. Variants of this technique might ask readers to make a lexical decision about the word, noting whether it's a real word or not, or to utter the target word out loud. (Naturally, for tasks requiring a yes/no response, an appropriate number of filler items call for a "No" response, to avoid making the task a no-brainer).

The probe task has the great advantage of being able to reflect shifts in activation over time, because response times to probes can be compared at different points in the text. The hope is that the data capture something real about how people would normally read the text even if they weren't taking part in a lab study involving memory probes. But it presents a pretty artificial task, so it raises some questions about whether the response times really reflect the shifts of activation that take place in normal, uninterrupted reading. For example, if response times to a probe word are very fast, does this mean that the word

or concept was already highly active in the mental model before the probe word appeared? (This is how such results are normally interpreted.) Or do response times reflect a process that was *triggered* by the probe word, and that wouldn't have happened if the probe hadn't appeared?

Other more general concerns arise: Does the strange task invite readers to lean on a strategy of tracking and mentally rehearsing certain words in the text, knowing that they might be quizzed on them at any point? Or does being tested on certain elements from the text (for example, sounds, or spatial relations) cause readers to pay more attention to them? If so, by introducing this secondary task as a way of measuring activation, experimenters might be unwittingly distorting patterns of activation, rather than simply observing those that would have happened even if subjects had been reading the text without having to respond to the memory probes.

Because of these concerns, researchers look for supporting evidence from other tasks. One approach is to present readers with uninterrupted text, and try to glean some useful information from the time it takes people to read specific portions of the text. Since reading times are affected not just by how easy it is to read individual sentences, but also by how easy it is to integrate a new

mental representations, John Bransford and his colleagues (1972) had people listen to a list of sentences. Afterward, their subjects were given a memory test in which they had to state whether they had heard that sentence earlier, *in exactly that same form*. Bransford and colleagues made various subtle changes to the original sentences from the list, so that they appeared in slightly altered form on the memory test. For example, subjects might first hear:

> Three turtles rested beside a floating log, and a fish
>   swam beneath them.

and later, might have to respond to the following:

> Three turtles rested beside a floating log, and a fish
>   swam beneath it.

Though the difference in wording is very slight, people had little trouble recognizing that the second sentence was different from the first. But they showed a whole lot more confusion if they first heard this:

> Three turtles rested on a floating log, and a fish
>   swam beneath them.

and later had to respond to this:

METHOD 10.1 (continued)

sentence with the preceding text, stimuli can be set up to manipulate interesting ways in which the sentence fits with preceding text.

For example, to test whether certain information (say, about spatial relations) has been represented in the mental model, an experimenter might later plant a sentence that is inconsistent with this information. Longer reading times would presumably reflect that the reader had encoded the spatial information and was now having some trouble integrating the new, conflicting information.

Or, the experimenter might play around with variations on a specific dimension of information to see if it affects ease of integration. For instance, Rolf Zwaan found in his 1996 study that people took longer to read sentences that were introduced by the phrase *a day later*, rather than *a moment later*. This suggests (1) that time is being represented in the mental model, and (2) that the ease of integrating events in the mental model depends in part on the time lapse between them. Later in this chapter, you'll see the same kind of logic being applied to studies of causal relations between sentences.

Reading time tasks are more natural than probe studies, but they have several downsides too. One of these is that researchers lose the ability to test for changes in the reader's mental model that might be happening on a word-by-word basis, especially if the reading times are measured over whole sentences or large sentence chunks. Another is that reading time measures are a bit of a black box—so many factors contribute to them, including the frequencies of words and their relationships to lexical competitors, as well as syntactic complexity or potential ambiguity. Even when these potential confounding variables are carefully controlled (for instance, stimuli might be pretested by having subjects read the critical sentences in isolation, to make sure that sentence-internal factors are all equivalent across experimental conditions), it might still be hard to know exactly *why* one sentence is harder to integrate with previous text than another.

Some of the shortcomings of these measures can be overcome with eye-tracking techniques or ERP measures that tap into brain activity. Both of these approaches will be discussed later on in the chapter.

WEB ACTIVITY 10.2

Investigating mental models In this activity, you'll explore how various hypotheses about mental models might be tested using converging evidence from probe techniques and reading time studies.

Three turtles rested on a floating log, and a fish swam beneath it.

In terms of the surface linguistic structure of these sentences as well as their propositional meanings, the difference between the second pair of sentences was no greater than the difference between the first pair. Yet people reacted in a way that suggested the difference in the first pair was much more striking or memorable. Naturally, the key here seems to be that the sentences in the first pair lead to dramatically different mental models—in the first sentence of this pair, the fish swims beneath the turtles, while in the second, the fish swims beneath the log and *not* the turtles. But in the second pair, the sentences result in nearly identical mental models (see **Figure 10.3**). This gives us a hint that what people remember is the mental model that is the product of the linguistic information. Having constructed a mental model, they have little use for devoting attention to the linguistic representations that gave rise to it. The language is merely the delivery device for the really valuable information.

I should add a qualifying remark to the conclusions that we can draw from this famous study. It's certainly true that linguistic form is not particularly memorable when it comes to our ability to *consciously* assess what we've previously heard. But that's not to say that

WEB ACTIVITY 10.3

What do you remember? In this activity, you'll take a memory test to get a sense of the difference between what a text says, and what you retain from it. The materials on the website will guide you through a set of stimuli and test questions.

(A)

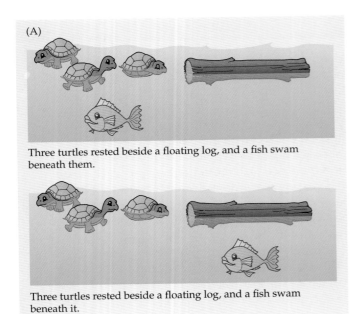

Three turtles rested beside a floating log, and a fish swam beneath them.

Three turtles rested beside a floating log, and a fish swam beneath it.

(B)

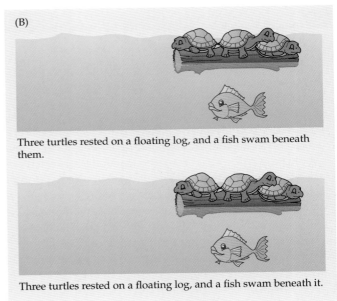

Three turtles rested on a floating log, and a fish swam beneath them.

Three turtles rested on a floating log, and a fish swam beneath it.

Figure 10.3 (A) Two sentences for which a small difference in wording leads to a large difference in their corresponding mental models. (B) Two sentences with a small wording difference but identical mental models. Study results indicate the difference between the two sentences in (A) is remembered much more accurately than the difference between the sentences in (B)—that is, people remember differences between mental models more readily than differences between sentences. (Adapted from Bransford et al., 1972.)

the details of linguistic form are entirely absent from long-term memory. In numerous chapters throughout this book, you've seen many examples where people *do* retain memory for details of linguistic form, and then make efficient use of this information. Here are just a few examples of phenomena that rely on preserving information about linguistic form in long-term memory: tracking the transitional probabilities of syllables in order to segment words, learning the most probable ways of completing a temporary syntactic ambiguity, and being primed by a previous bit of syntactic structure so that you're more likely to later reuse that same structure.

The importance of background knowledge

Readers and hearers readily build mental models that reflect the connections between neighboring sentences—as you've seen, the information conveyed by each sentence is integrated into a model that contains information from earlier sentences. But the information that fills out a mental model can also come from other information sources, including the background knowledge that we bring to a text. If this background information is missing, it can sometimes make a text extremely hard to understand. Consider the following passage (from Bransford & Johnson, 1972):

> The procedure is actually quite simple. First, you arrange things into two different groups. Of course, one pile may be sufficient depending on how much there is to do. If you have to go somewhere else due to lack of facilities, that is the next step; otherwise you are pretty well set. It is important not to overdo things. That is, it is better to do fewer things at once than too many. In the short run this might not seem important, but complications can easily arise. A mistake can be expensive as well. At first the whole procedure will seem complicated. Soon, however, it will become just another facet of life. It is difficult to foresee an end to the necessity for this task in the immediate future, but then one can never tell. After the

procedure is completed, one arranges the material into different groups again. Then they can be put into their appropriate places. Eventually they will be used once more, and the whole cycle will have to be repeated. However, that is part of life.

Raise your hand if you have a very clear image in your head of what's being described in this passage. Not likely—the passage contains a heap of extraordinarily vague words and phrases: *you arrange things* (*what* things?); *one pile* (of what?) *may be sufficient; lack of facilities* (what kind of facilities?); *It is important not to overdo things,* and so on and so on. Chances are, your mental model of this whole "procedure" is fairly scant. But let's activate some background knowledge, simply by slapping a title onto this passage: *Instructions for washing clothes.* Now, go back and reread the paragraph, and notice how your mental model suddenly sprouts many details that you had no way of supplying before. This little exercise demonstrates how skimpy the linguistic content can get, and still be perfectly comprehensible—provided we have the means to enrich our mental models either through background knowledge or by connecting the dots within a text. It also raises an important set of pedagogical implications: that the understanding of a text can be very heavily dependent on the reader's having access to a body of knowledge that is presumed by the writer of the text. Even when the ability to decode the linguistic content is there, comprehension can really suffer without that added knowledge base (see Language at Large 10.1). For example, if you've led a highly sheltered life when it comes to the mechanics of laundry, and you really *don't* know what's involved in washing clothes, the title may not have helped you that much.

WEB ACTIVITY 10.4

Activating background knowledge In this activity, you'll conduct a small language comprehension experiment, using the clothes-washing passage above from Bransford and Johnson (1972). Using the documents on the website, download two versions of the story, one with a title, and one without a title. Find a handful of willing subjects, and give half of them the titled story, and the other half the untitled story. Ask them to recall as many main ideas from the passage as they can. Compare the number and detail of the ideas that are provided by your two groups of subjects.

10.2 Pronoun Problems

Language underspecifies meaning

One of the key points to take away from the previous section is that hearers and readers are very good at mentally filling in an abundance of meaning even when the language itself isn't precise. This means that communication doesn't depend entirely on information that's made explicit in the linguistic code, a fact that has far-reaching implications for how human languages are structured.

In Chapters 7 and 8, you learned how language's startling potential for ambiguity rarely poses a serious problem for comprehension. In Box 7.2, I explored the idea that all languages are likely to contain ambiguity, not only because ambiguity rarely creates a real barrier for communication, but also because it offers some potential benefits for language production: the speaker gets to reuse easy-to-produce bits of language for multiple purposes. Under this view, ambiguity in language reflects a balance between ease of comprehension and ease of production.

If, as we've seen in this chapter, readers are able to flesh out detailed meanings when confronted with imprecise language, this too makes a speaker's job much easier. In many contexts, speakers can get away with using vague, common, and easy-to-produce words like *thing* or *stuff* rather than digging deeper into the lexicon for a less accessible word, and

WEB ACTIVITY 10.5

Titles in literary texts Many literary texts leave a lot to be filled in by the reader's imagination. One goal, though, is to make sure that the reader has enough guidance to generate some of the important information that the text leaves implicit. Often, a useful title helps set the context. In this activity, you'll see some literary examples that achieve this, and you'll be asked to find your own examples.

What does it mean to be literate?

Here's an excerpt from a 2012 *National Geographic* story by Russ Rymer about vanishing languages:

In an increasingly globalized, connected, homogenized age, languages spoken in remote places are no longer protected by national borders or natural boundaries from the languages that dominate world communication and commerce. The reach of Mandarin and English and Russian and Hindi and Spanish and Arabic extends seemingly to every hamlet, where they compete with Tuvan and Yanomami and Altaic in a house-to-house battle. Parents and tribal villages often encourage their children to move away from the insular languages of their forbears and toward languages that will permit greater education and success.

Who can blame them? The arrival of television, with its glamorized global materialism, its luxury-consumption proselytizing, is even more irresistible. Prosperity, it seems, speaks English.

Someone who has truly understood this passage should be able to answer questions like these:

- How did national borders and natural boundaries previously offer protection to remote languages? What has changed, and why do these protections no longer apply?

- Describe what a "house-to-house battle" between Russian and Tuvan might look like.

- Explain how the availability of television in remote areas promotes a language like English at the expense of more local languages.

But notice that the author himself provides very little in the way of information that would answer these questions—instead, he alludes to existing knowledge that he assumes the reader will have, and leverages this knowledge to reach certain conclusions. As a reader, you have to already know what it means to live in a globalized, connected age, and that geographic boundaries like rivers or mountains might have previously hindered different linguistic communities from interacting with one another, but no longer have the same impact. You have to know what television is, and what kinds of programs it might be broadcasting in the English language. Without such knowledge, you would find this excerpt as mystifying as the clothes-washing passage from Bransford and Johnson (1972) minus the clarifying title. This example demonstrates

they can avoid spelling out more detail than is necessary—in short, a great deal of information can be left unstated. Nothing demonstrates this as neatly as the existence of pronouns like *she* or *they*. Much like the words *thing* or *stuff*, pronouns contain very little semantic information. This becomes evident if you meet one in an out-of-the-blue sentence like *She promised to come for lunch.* Who's *she*? All we know from the pronoun itself is that it refers to someone female. Yet, when pronouns are used in text or conversation, we usually have no trouble figuring out the specific identity of the person in question.

As far as I know, all languages contain pronouns (though, as you'll see in a moment, there can be some variety across languages in the specific information that pronouns carry inside themselves). It's easy to miss just how stripped bare of meaning pronouns can be if you only consider your own familiar language. Their semantic starkness can be more visible from the outside. A revealing example can be found in a discussion of pronouns by the journalist Christie Blatchford (2011), who covered the murder trial of an Afghan-born Canadian, Mohammed Shafia. Together with his wife, Tooba Yahya, and their son, Hamed, Shafia was charged with murdering his three daughters and his first wife. Writing in the *National Post*, the journalist noted that there were some linguistic difficulties that arose in the testimony of a relative of the slain woman (Ms. Amir) because the witness spoke in Dari, a dialectal variant of the Farsi language:

LANGUAGE AT LARGE 10.1 (*continued*)

that texts that rely heavily on background knowledge are readily found "in the wild," and not just in carefully constructed, deliberately vague experimental stimuli.

This raises an interesting quandary, though: When we test children for their reading comprehension in school, what exactly are we testing for? It's been shown that children often perform badly on reading comprehension tests if they have very little background knowledge about the topic of the reading passage. It's also been noted that American children—especially those from low-income families—show a dip in scores of reading ability between the third and fourth grades, and that over time the gap between wealthier and poorer students widens. Many researchers and educators (e.g., Hirsch, 2003; Johnston, 1984) believe that these two sets of findings are connected: In the early grades, reading tests tend to focus on basic decoding and word recognition abilities, whereas later on there's an emphasis on overall comprehension of more complex texts. Since background knowledge can affect the richness of the mental model that is constructed from a text, one possibility is that the income gap in scores reflects not just a gap in reading ability, but a lag in general knowledge.

Reading tests, then, seem to be biased against students with a smaller knowledge base. One could argue that this sort of bias should be removed from reading tests, as it

leads to an unfair picture of the reading abilities of some students. On the other hand, the reality is that actual texts, even those intended for very general audiences, *do* rely heavily on readers' being able to fill in many blanks by drawing on a substantial body of knowledge. One could just as well argue, then, that since we do want all students to eventually be able to read publications like *National Geographic*, de-biasing tests to remove the effects of prior background knowledge would fail to reflect the students' readiness to understand a broad variety of texts. And, in recognition of the important connection between prior knowledge and deep reading comprehension, many educators are arguing that teaching in the early grades should focus not just on general reading skills, but also on bulking up domain knowledge.

Still, it would be valuable to be able to distinguish whether a student is having trouble understanding his science textbook because he can't fluently decode or recognize words, because he lacks a general ability to make important connections and inferences, or because he has an impoverished knowledge base—this might tell us whether he'd most benefit from reading lots of novels or from spending his time watching science programs on TV or going to the science museum. A good set of reading assessment tools should be able to make these important distinctions.

[The witness] also said in the last months of her life, Ms. Amir was unhappy, often calling to complain about her life, and that she told her she'd overheard a conversation among the parents and Hamed, during which Mr. Shafia threatened to kill Zainab, who in April of 2009 had run away to a women's shelter, and "the other one," which Ms. Amir took to mean her.

But because the Dari/Farsi languages have no separate male and female pronouns—essentially, everyone is referred to as male, it apparently being the only worthy sex—she can't be sure if it was Ms. Yahya who asked about "the other one" or Hamed.

Blatchford went on to remark that ongoing interpretation difficulties arose at the trial in part because Dari and Farsi are "imprecise languages." But she's wrong to attribute imprecision (not to mention sexism) to an entire language based on the potential ambiguity of its pronouns. Pronouns are by their very nature imprecise, as Ms. Blatchford might have concluded had she taken a moment to survey the pronominal system of *English*. English, as it turns out, doesn't bother to provide information about the gender of any of its pronouns except the third-person singular; it entirely forgoes marking number on the second person; and it blurs the subject/object distinction for several pronouns (see **Table 10.1**). In short, using the English pronoun *they* to refer to a group of

TABLE 10.1 English pronouns (subject/object forms)

	Singular	Plural
First person		
Male	I/me	we/us
Female	I/me	we/us
Neuter	I/me	we/us
Second person		
Male	you/you	you/you
Female	you/you	you/you
Neuter	you/you	you/you
Third person		
Male	he/him	they/them
Female	she/her	they/them
Neuter	it/it	they/them

women (or to a group of men) leaves an English speaker in exactly the same boat as a speaker of Dari—nothing about the linguistic form of the pronoun gives the hearer a clue about gender. **Box 10.2** describes some of the different pronomial systems found in languages other than English.

Even when gender *is* marked on pronouns, the potential for ambiguity is rife, and yet, highly skilled users of language persist in wielding them. Below are a few passages pulled from acclaimed literary works. As you'll see, pronouns are used despite the fact that there's more than one linguistic match in the discourse that precedes them. In these examples, the same color font is used for pronouns (underlined) and all their linguistically compatible matches (that is, all the nouns that agree in number and gender with the pronouns):

> In **the boxes**, **the men** heard **the water** rise in **the trench** and looked out for **cottonmouths**. <u>They</u> squatted in **muddy water**, slept above <u>it</u>, peed in <u>it</u>.
>
> *from Beloved by Toni Morrison (1987)*

> Now **the drum** took on a steady arterial pulse and **the sword** was returned to **the man**. <u>He</u> held <u>it</u> high above <u>his</u> head and glowered at the crowd. **Someone** from the crowd brought <u>him</u> the biscuit tin. <u>He</u> peered inside and shook <u>his</u> great head.
>
> *from In Between the Sheets by Ian McEwan (1978)*

> In 1880 **Benjamin Button** was twenty years old, and <u>he</u> signalized <u>his</u> birthday by going to work for <u>his</u> **father** in Roger Button & Co., Wholesale Hardware. It was in that same year that <u>he</u> began "going out socially"—that is, <u>his</u> **father** insisted on taking <u>him</u> to several fashionable dances. **Roger Button** was now fifty, and <u>he</u> and <u>his</u> **son** were more and more companionable—in fact, since **Benjamin** had ceased to dye <u>his</u> hair (which was still grayish) they appeared about the same age and could have passed for brothers.
>
> *from The Curious Case of Benjamin Button by F. Scott Fitzgerald (1922)*

Every now and then, pronouns do result in confusion, as evident in the Shafia trial testimony. Most of the time, however, they're interpreted without fuss exactly as the speaker or writer intended. How is this done?

How do we resolve the meanings of pronouns?

It's obvious that in many cases, we can call on real-world knowledge to line up pronouns with their correct referential matches, or **antecedents**. In the Toni Morrison quote above, while both the nouns *boxes* and *cottonmouths* match the *linguistic* features on the pronoun (they're both plural), practical knowledge about boxes and cottonmouths (venomous snakes) allows us to rule them out as antecedents for the pronoun in the phrase *they squatted*; only *the men* remains as a plausible antecedent for *they*.

antecedent A pronoun's referent or referential match; that is, the expression (usually a proper name or a descriptive noun or noun phrase) that refers to the same person or entity as the pronoun.

BOX 10.2
Pronoun systems across languages

Pronouns in many languages tend to have certain grammatical clues that help hearers link them to their antecedents. Usually, number and gender are marked, though not always in the same ways; for example, Standard Arabic marks dual number (specifically two referents), not just singular and plural (**Table A**), while German has neuter gender as well as masculine and feminine (**Table B**). Some languages, like Persian (Farsi) and Finnish (**Table C**), fail to mark gender at all. The tables below illustrate subject pronouns only. You'll notice that, regardless of how many dimensions a language might encode, certain pronoun forms are often recycled across dimensions, so they become inherently ambiguous. You'll notice also that more linguistic information tends to get preserved in the third-person pronouns than in the first- and second-person pronouns, presumably because the context usually makes it clear who we're referring to when we use pronouns such as *I* or *you*.

A complicating factor is that, in many languages, pronouns are often dropped entirely and are used only for special emphasis or stylistic purposes. Usually (but not always), this is allowed in languages where verbs are conjugated in such a way that they preserve at least some of the linguistic information that would appear on the missing pronoun. For example, in Spanish (**Table D**), verb marking preserves information about person and number when pronouns are dropped, but it doesn't preserve gender. Thus we get:

Yo veo una montaña. → *Veo una montaña.*
("I see a mountain.")

El ve una montaña. → *Ve una montaña.*
("He sees a mountain.")

Ella ve una montaña. → *Ve una montaña.*
("She sees a mountain.")

Ellos ven una montaña. → *Ven una montaña.*
("They see a mountain.")

Pronoun-dropping is yet another way in which languages show a subtle interplay between the inherent ambiguity of linguistic form and the information that can be recovered from context.

TABLE A Standard Arabic

Number	Person	Masculine	Feminine
Singular	1st	anaa	anaa
	2nd	anta	anti
	3rd	huwa	hiya
Dual (two persons)	1st	naHnu	naHnu
	2nd	antumaa	antumaa
	3rd	humaa	humaa
Plural	1st	naHnu	naHnu
	2nd	antum	antunna
	3rd	hum	hunna

TABLE C Finnish

Number	Person	
Singular	1st	minä
	2nd (informal)	sinä
	2nd (formal)	Te
	3rd	hän
Plural	1st	me
	2nd (informal)	te
	2nd (formal)	Te
	3rd	he

TABLE B German

Number	Person	Masculine	Feminine	Neuter
Singular	1st	ich	ich	ich
	2nd (informal)	du	du	du
	2nd (formal)	Sie	Sie	Sie
	3rd	er	sie	es
Plural	1st	wir	wir	wir
	2nd (informal)	ihr	ihr	ihr
	2nd (formal)	Sie	Sie	Sie
	3rd person	sie	sie	sie

TABLE D Spanish

Number	Person	Masculine	Feminine
Singular	1st	yo	yo
	2nd (informal)	tú	tú
	2nd (formal)	usted	usted
	3rd	él	ella
Plural	1st	nosotros	nosotros
	2nd (informal)	vosotros	vosotros
	2nd (formal)	ustedes	ustedes
	3rd	ellos	ellas

But when real-world plausibility is not enough, information in the mental model can help. For instance, in the Ian McEwan passage, by the time we get the pronoun *it* in the second sentence (*He held it high above his head*), we've seen three possible linguistic matches for the pronoun in the first sentence: the drum, a steady arterial pulse, and the sword. The pulse can be ruled out because of basic knowledge about how the world works—you can't hold a pulse—but something more is needed to decide between the drum and the sword. Here, the mental model derived from the first sentence is critical: only the sword is in the hands of the man (who is the sole possible antecedent for *he* in *He held it high above his head*), and therefore is the most likely candidate. So, just as mental models are useful for filling in all sorts of implicit material, they can also help fix the reference of ambiguous pronouns.

But even more than this is required. In the quote by F. Scott Fitzgerald on page 390, the first sentence introduced Benjamin Button and his father Roger. How should we interpret the pronoun in the second sentence: *It was in that same year that he began "going out socially"*? Either Benjamin or the father are viable antecedents, given the situation model at that point, and in fact, the text goes on to elaborate that both of these characters go out together. Yet most readers will automatically assume that *he* refers to Benjamin, and not his father. Why is that? (Go ahead and answer—the question's not purely rhetorical.)

If you did attempt an answer, you might have said something to the effect that Benjamin is the person that the passage is *about*, or the person who's being focused on in the text. If so, you were exactly on the right track. Remember that in the previous Section 10.1, I described some results by Art Glenberg and colleagues (1987) showing that when entities are entered into a mental model, they wax and wane in terms of their accessibility, depending on what's going on in the text—typically, this accessibility was measured by memory probes. Let's revisit the following two stories:

> John was preparing for a marathon in August. **After doing a few warm-up exercises, he put on his sweatshirt and went jogging.** He jogged halfway along the lake without too much difficulty. Further along his route, however, John's muscles began to ache.

> John was preparing for a marathon in August. **After doing a few warm-up exercises, he took off his sweatshirt and went jogging.** He jogged halfway along the lake without too much difficulty. Further along his route, however, John's muscles began to ache.

We saw from the Glenberg study that the *sweatshirt* entity was more accessible in a situation like the first one, where it was spatially connected with the main character, than in the second case, when it was cast aside at some point in the story. It turns out that the degree of accessibility, as measured by a memory probe, also predicted how easy it was for subjects to read sentences containing pronouns. Consider this story:

> Warren spent the afternoon shopping at the store. He set down his bag and went to look at some scarves. He had been shopping all day. He thought it was getting too heavy to carry.

Did you trip over the pronoun *it* in the last sentence, hunting around for what was being referred to? If you did, try this version:

> Warren spent the afternoon shopping at the store. He picked up his bag and went to look at some scarves. He had been shopping all day. He thought it was getting too heavy to carry.

If the the second version felt smoother, then your intuitions align with the results from the study by Glenberg and colleagues, who found that their subjects spent longer reading the last sentence in the first passage than in the second passage. Notice that the sentence itself is identical in both cases, so the difficulty must have come from trying to integrate this sentence with the preceding discourse, presumably because people had some trouble tracking down the antecedent of the pronoun. Based on the results from the memory task, a likely explanation for the difficulty is that the antecedent had already faded somewhat in memory.

Pronouns, then, seem to signal a referential connection to some entity that is highly salient and very easily located in memory; the fact that the entity is so readily accessible is probably exactly what *allows* pronouns to be as sparse as they are when it comes to their own semantic content. You might view this as one example of a much broader language phenomenon: that the easier it is for hearers to recover or infer certain information, the less the speaker relies on linguistic content to communicate that information (see **Box 10.3**). This gen-

BOX 10.3
The scientific study of mumbling

This chapter focuses on the many ways in which hearers (or readers) create rich interpretations that go beyond the specific linguistic input that they're taking in. The extra work that hearers do often means that speakers will be understood even if they don't go to the effort of specifying all the information they meant to convey, or if they utter vague or ambiguous linguistic forms, so long as the overall context provides enough support for the right interpretation. Happily, speakers seem to be most prone to slide into "lazier" language in just the right contexts. As we've seen, a good example of this is the way in which pronouns pattern; these minimalist bits of language tend to be produced on just those occasions where their antecedents are strongly focused or easy to identify.

This general pattern goes beyond speakers' decisions about what content to include in a sentence, or whether to use a vague word or a precise one. It even seems to apply to how *distinctly* speakers utter their words. Most of our conversations don't sound like elocution exercises—for example, a sentence like *How am I supposed to know what you like on your sandwich?* might come out something like, "How'my s'posta know whachu like on yer sanwich?" In running speech, we often shorten words, pronounce sounds in ways that don't clearly distinguish them from other sounds, meld adjacent sounds together instead of maintaining their separate integrity, and even drop consonants or vowels entirely—in short, the amount and quality of linguistic information can become quite degraded, putting a greater burden on the hearer when it comes to word recognition.

But there's apparently a method to mumbling. Speakers regularly produce lower-quality output when the words they're speaking are more predictable. For example, the word *nine* would typically be uttered with less care in a sentence like *A stitch in time saves nine*, where the word can be more easily guessed from the context alone, than in a sentence like *The next word is nine*, where it's totally unpredictable (Lieberman, 1963). Speakers also tend to articulate less clearly when the words they're using are very common ones, or when they've recently been uttered in the conversation. In other words, the acoustic quality of speech is usually the lowest in situations where the task of word recognition is the easiest for hearers, allowing hearers to do more interpretation with less linguistic information. This seems to pattern neatly with other phenomena in language, like the use of pronouns.

It's tempting to conclude from this that, far from being "lazy," speakers are superbly tuned to the needs and capabilities of their hearers, and adjust their speech accordingly. But this isn't the only explanation for the fortuitous alignment between hearers' needs and speakers' patterns of production. In the next chapter, we'll explore some competing ideas about why this alignment seems to exist, and whether it's the result of speakers putting themselves in the hearer's shoes, or whether it's just a side effect of the varying demands on language production.

eralization fits well with the idea that the amount of information that appears in the linguistic code reflects a balance between need for clear communication and ease of production.

What makes some discourse referents more salient than others?

There are quite a few factors that seem to affect the salience or accessibility of possible antecedents. As noted earlier, the relationship of various entities within the mental model can play a role; the spotlight tends to be on the protagonist of a story and other entities associated with or even just spatially close to that character. But a number of other generalizations can be made. Often, the syntactic choices that a speaker has made reflect the accessibility of some referents over others. For example, in Section 9.3, I pointed out that when a concept is highly salient to speakers, they tend to mention this concept first, often slotting it into the subject position of a sentence. This creates a sense that whatever is in the subject position is what the sentence "is about" or is the focus of attention, and has an effect on how ambiguous pronouns get interpreted. Consider these examples:

> Bradley beat Donald at tennis after a grueling match. He …
>
> Donald was beaten by Bradley after a grueling match. He …

There's a general preference for the subject over the object as the antecedent of a pronoun (Bradley in the first sentence, Donald in the second).

Let's look more closely at the excerpt from F. Scott Fitzgerald on page 390. In that passage, the cues guiding the reader through the various interpretations of the third-person pronoun come largely from the syntax. In the first sentence, Benjamin Button is established as the subject and, with two pronouns referring back to him, is the more heavily "lit" character; his father is mentioned more peripherally as an indirect object:

> In 1880 **Benjamin Button** was twenty years old, and **he** signalized **his** birthday by going to work for **his** father in Roger Button & Co., Wholesale Hardware.

Hence, it's easy to get that the pronoun in the next sentence refers back to Benjamin:

> It was in that same year that **he** began "going out socially"—that is, **his** father insisted on taking **him** to several fashionable dances.

But notice what happens in the next sentence:

> **Roger Button** was now fifty, and **he** and **his** son were more and more companionable—in fact, since **Benjamin** had ceased to dye **his** hair (which was still grayish) they appeared about the same age and could have passed for brothers.

Here, focus has shifted to the father, Roger Button, who now appears in subject position—and as a result, the next appearance of the pronoun *he* now refers back to Roger, not Benjamin. In fact, the next time that the author refers to Benjamin in the text, he uses his name, not a pronoun.

This last fact turns out to be quite revealing, and suggests that the Benjamin character has been demoted from his original position of prominence in the mental model. Throughout the narrative, the spotlight has moved from one character to the other, as made apparent by the occupant of the subject position of the various sentences, and by the preferred interpretation of the pronouns.

The repeated-name penalty

Psycholinguists have found that if an entity is highly salient, readers seem to expect that a subsequent reference to it will involve a pronoun rather than a name, and actually find it *harder* when the text uses a repeated name instead, even though this name should be perfectly unambiguous (e.g., Gordon, Grosz, and Gilliom, 1993). This set of expectations can be inferred from reading times. For example:

> Bruno was the bully of the neighborhood. He chased Tommy all the way home from school one day.

> Bruno was the bully of the neighborhood. Bruno chased Tommy all the way home from school one day.

Readers seem to find the repeated name in the second example somewhat jarring, as shown by longer reading times for this sentence than the corresponding one in the first passage. This has been called the **repeated-name penalty**. But if the antecedent is somewhat less salient, no such penalty arises. Consider this sentence:

> Susan gave Fred a pet hamster.

Presumably, Susan is more accessible as a referent than Fred. Hence, a repeated-name penalty should be found if Susan is later referred to by name rather than tagged by a pronoun; but no such penalty should be found if Fred is referred to by name in a later sentence.

This is precisely what Gordon and his colleagues found. That is, sequence (a) below took longer to read than sequence (b):

> (a) Susan gave Fred a pet hamster. In his opinion, Susan shouldn't have done that.

> (b) Susan gave Fred a pet hamster. In his opinion, she shouldn't have done that.

But there was no difference between sequences (c) and (d):

> (c) Susan gave Fred a pet hamster. In Fred's opinion, she shouldn't have done that.

> (d) Susan gave Fred a pet hamster. In his opinion, she shouldn't have done that.

While expressing a referent as a subject has the effect of boosting its salience, certain special syntactic structures—often called **focus constructions**—are a bit like putting a referent up on a pedestal. Observe:

> It was the bird that ate the fruit. It was already half-rotten.

This sounds odd, because the pronoun in the second sentence can only plausibly refer to the fruit; but because the bird has been elevated to such a salient status (using a construction called an **it-cleft sentence**), the inclination to interpret *it* as referring to the bird is very strong, leading to a clash with plausibility knowledge. There's no such clash, though, when the first sentence puts focus on the fruit instead, as in the following (using a construction called a **wh-cleft sentence**):

> What the bird ate was the fruit. It was already half-rotten.

Amit Almor (1999) found that, not surprisingly, when a repeated name was used to refer back to the heavily focused antecedent in constructions like these,

repeated-name penalty The finding that under some circumstances, it takes longer to read a sentence in which a highly salient referent is referred to by a full noun phrase (NP) rather than by a pronoun.

focus constructions Syntactic structures that have the effect of putting special emphasis or focus on certain elements within the sentence.

it-cleft sentence A type of focus construction in which a single clause has been split into two, typically with the form "It is/was X that/who Y." The element corresponding to X in this frame is focused. For example, in the sentence *It was Sam who left Fred*, the focus is on *Sam*.

wh-cleft sentence A type of focus construction in which one clause has been divided into two, with the first clause introduced by a *wh-* element, as in the sentences *What Ravi sold was his old car* or *Where Joan went was to Finland*. In this case, the focused element appears in the second clause (*his old car, to Finland*).

readers showed the repeated-name penalty. That is, readers took longer to read the repeated name (*the bird* or *the fruit*) in the second sentence of passages like these (antecedents that are in focus are in boldface):

    (a) It was **the bird** that ate the fruit. The bird seemed very satisfied.

    (b) What the bird ate was **the fruit**. The fruit was already half-rotten.

rather than these:

    (c) It was **the bird** that ate the fruit. The fruit was already half-rotten.

    (d) What the bird ate was **the fruit**. The bird seemed very satisfied.

Repeated names seem to do more than just cause momentary speed bumps in reading—they can actually interfere with the process of forming an accurate long-term memory representation of the text, as found by a subsequent study by Almor and Eimas (2008). When subjects were later asked to recall critical content from the sentences they'd read (for example, "Who ate the fruit?" or "What did the bird eat?"), they were less accurate if they'd read passages (a) and (b) than if they'd read passages (c) and (d).

We've seen that there are several factors that heighten the accessibility of a referent, making it a magnet for later pronominal reference: the degree to which entities are spatially linked to central characters in a text, and syntactic structure, including subject status and the use of focus constructions. In addition, the salience of a referent can be boosted by a number of other factors such as being the first entity to be mentioned in a sentence (either as the subject or not), having been recently mentioned, or having been mentioned repeatedly. Variables like these are famous for affecting the ease with which just about any stimuli can be retrieved from memory (for instance, if you're trying to remember the contents of your grocery list, it's easiest to remember items that appeared at the top of the list, or last on the list, or those you happened to write down more than once). It's interesting to see that the same variables also have an impact on the process of resolving pronouns.

Finally, some researchers have argued that the specific **thematic role** that a referent plays in an event can affect how salient it is and, hence, how likely it is to be the antecedent of a pronoun. For instance, given the following sentence, try to supply a plausible next sentence to continue the discourse:

    John passed the comic to Bill.

According to research by Rosemary Stevenson and colleagues (1994), study subjects were more likely to provide a continuation that focused on the goal or endpoint of the event—that is, they more often referred to Bill, rather than John, despite the fact that *John* appears in the subject position. This lined up neatly with how people tended to interpret an ambiguous pronoun in the following snippet:

    John passed the comic to Bill. He …

Again, study subjects were likely to supply a continuation in which Bill was the antecedent for the pronoun *he*. Similar results were found by Jennifer Arnold (2001) in an analysis of speech from Canadian parliamentary proceedings: speakers often focused on the goal or end point of an event, rather than its source or origin, and in a subsequent event, they were more likely to refer back to the goal or end point of the event.

But what comes into focus can depend on the nature of the event, as well as the relations between events that are explicitly coded in the language. Try continuing these sentences:

thematic role Information about the role of various participants in an event described by a verb. For example, in the sentence *Patrice sent the letter to Felicia*, Patrice assumes the role of "agent," or instigator of the event, while Felicia assumes the role of "goal," or the endpoint of the event.

Sally admired Miranda because she …

Sally apologized to Miranda because she …

The word *because* throws into relief a causal connection between the first event and whichever event is coming next; but the specific events of admiring or apologizing place different emphases when it comes to their typical causes. Normally, you'd apologize to someone because of something *you* did, but you'd admire someone because of something about that other person, not yourself. Hence, in the first sentence, the focus is on the subject (*Sally*), whereas in the second, it's on the object (*Miranda*). A number of researchers have noted that different verbs seem to evoke different expectations of **implicit causality** (this was first noticed by Garvey and Caramazza, 1974).

WEB ACTIVITY 10.6

Finding antecedents for ambiguous pronouns In this exercise, you'll be see a number of different examples in which a pronoun is linguistically compatible with more than one antecedent. These examples will give you a sense of whether the potential ambiguity of the pronoun translates into a real interpretive ambiguity. What are some of the factors that make it easier to feel confident about the reference of ambiguous pronouns?

10.3 Pronouns, Ambiguity, and Real-Time Processing

Are ambiguous pronouns cost-free for language comprehension?

All of the discussion in the preceding section helps to explain why pronouns are usually perfectly interpretable, despite their blatant grammatical ambiguity. It also provides additional evidence for the general fact that human languages are shot through with potential ambiguity—we've already seen this in Chapter 8, when we talked about the many different kinds of temporary ambiguities that are due to the incremental nature of language processing. But in that chapter, we also saw that, although ambiguities are almost always resolved without too much trauma for the audience, they're not cost-free, either. They very often exert a processing cost that can be detected through experimental techniques, whether or not that cost is consciously registered by a hearer or reader.

So, what kind of strain does pronoun resolution cause for the interpretive system—and if there is detectable strain, what conditions cause it? Let's dig a bit more into the moment-by-moment process of matching pronouns with their antecedents. Doing so might help us to figure out whether certain conditions are especially error-prone, and also whether there are conditions under which people don't complete the process of interpreting pronouns. For example, a hearer who isn't able to immediately find the referent for *she* upon hearing a sentence like *She promised to come for lunch* might simply treat the pronoun as a referential placeholder—knowing that *she* refers to a female, but deciding to wait and see whether the specific referent will become apparent later, rather than searching for the correct antecedent right away. This might be done for the simple reason that a fuller interpretation would consume too much in the way of processing resources.

Having a detailed sense of how pronouns are resolved under the time pressures of typical language use could well have some practical applications. Think about how good it might be to be able to predict the risk of referential failure in high-stress situations—for instance, pilots' communicating with air traffic controllers in a crisis situation, or directions from a surgeon to an assistant when things turn bad in the operating room.

At the very least, pronoun resolution involves the following three general sources of information: (1) the grammatical marking of number, gender, etc., on the pronouns themselves, where this is available; (2) the prominence of an-

implicit causality Expectations about the probable cause/effect structure of events denoted by particular verbs.

tecedents in a mental model; and (3) real-world knowledge that might constrain the matching process. How are these sources of information coordinated by hearers? One possibility is that grammatical marking acts as a filter on prospective antecedents so that only those that are linguistically compatible with the pronoun are ever considered as candidates; information about discourse prominence or real-world information might then kick in to help the reader/listener choose among the viable candidates. On the other hand, exactly the opposite is possible. It may be that the most accessible antecedent automatically rises to the top, being the most prominent item in memory, and therefore becomes automatically linked to any pronoun that later turns up; grammatical marking might then serve as a retroactive check, serving to verify that the match was an appropriate one.

A number of serviceable techniques can be used to shed light on the time course of pronoun resolution, but probably the most direct and temporally sensitive method is to track people's eye movements to a scene as they hear and interpret the pronoun. As you've seen in Chapters 7 and 8, when people establish a referential link between a word and an image, they tend to look at the object in the visual display that's linked with that word. The same is true in the case of pronouns as well. Researchers can use eye movement data to figure out how long it takes hearers to identify the correct antecedent for the pronoun, as well as whether any other entities were considered as possible referents.

Coordinating multiple sources of information

In a 2000 study, Jennifer Arnold and her colleagues had their subjects listen to miniature stories, and tracked their subjects' eye movements to pictures that depicted the various characters and objects involved in these narratives. The story introduced two characters either of the same gender or of different genders. Each story contained a key sentence with a pronoun. Depending on which characters had been introduced, this pronoun was grammatically compatible either with both of the characters, or with just one of them:

> Mr. Biggs is bringing some mail to Tom, while a violent storm is beginning. He's carrying an umbrella, and it looks like they're both going to need it.

> Mr. Biggs is bringing some mail to Maria, while a violent storm is beginning. She's carrying an umbrella, and it looks like they're both going to need it.

The above stories and their accompanying illustrations are shown in **Figure 10.4**. For participants looking at the depictions in Figures 10.4A and 10.4C, it would be obvious that *Mr. Biggs* is the correct referent for the pronoun *he*. He also happens to be the character that is mentioned first and occupies the subject position in the first sentence.

Now, if grammatical marking serves as a filter on antecedents so that only matching antecedents are considered, we'd expect that when there's only one male character, people would be very quick to locate the antecedent of the pronoun, and that they wouldn't consider Maria as a possible referent for the pronoun *he*. That is, their eye movements should quickly settle on Mr. Biggs, and not be lured by the Maria character. But in the stories with two male characters, they should briefly consider both Mr. Biggs and Tom as possibilities, and this should be reflected in their eye movements. The discourse prominence of Mr. Biggs might kick in slightly later to help disambiguate between the two possible referents.

(A) Same gender, first mention

Mr. Biggs is bringing some mail to Tom, while a violent storm is beginning. He's carrying an umbrella, and it looks like they're both going to need it.

(B) Same gender, second mention

Mr. Biggs is bringing some mail to Tom, while a violent storm is beginning. He's carrying an umbrella, and it looks like they're both going to need it.

(C) Different gender, first mention

Mr. Biggs is bringing some mail to Maria, while a violent storm is beginning. He's carrying an umbrella, and it looks like they're both going to need it.

(D) Different gender, second mention

Mr. Biggs is bringing some mail to Maria, while a violent storm is beginning. She's carrying an umbrella, and it looks like they're both going to need it.

Figure 10.4 Visual displays and critical stimuli from the eye-tracking study (Experiment 2) by Arnold et al. (2000). The character carrying the umbrella was always the referent of the critical pronoun. (Note: the pictures shown here are modified from the well-known cartoon characters that were used in the original study.)

On the other hand, if pronoun resolution is driven mainly by the accessibility of the antecedent, then grammatical marking has a more secondary role to play when it comes to processing efficiency. For the stories above, *only* Mr. Biggs should be considered as the possible antecedent, regardless of whether the pronoun is grammatically ambiguous or not. So eye movements should favor Mr. Biggs over *either* Tom or Maria as soon as the pronoun *he* is pronounced. But now let's suppose that the picture shows the less prominent discourse entity (that is, either Tom or Maria) as the umbrella holder, and hence the correct referent of the pronoun *he* in the second sentence. Now finding the referent should be slower and more fraught with error. This should be true regardless of whether the pronoun is grammatically ambiguous (Figure 10.4B) or specific (Figure 10.4D).

When Arnold and her colleagues analyzed the eye movement data from their study, they found that hearers were able to use gender marking right away to disambiguate between referents, even when the antecedent was the

(A) Same gender, first mention

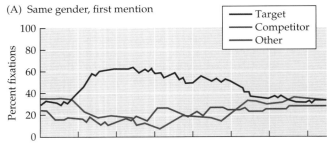

(B) Same gender, second mention

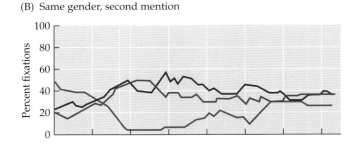

(C) Different gender, first mention

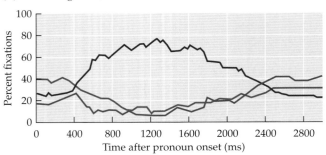

(D) Different gender, second mention

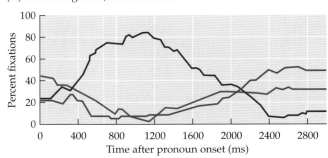

Figure 10.5 Results of Arnold et al.'s Experiment 2. The patterns of eye movements plotted against the three objects in the visual displays shown in Figure 10.4. The graph tracks the mean percentage of looks (within a 33-ms timeframe) to each of the three objects in the display. Target = correct character (with umbrella); competitor = competing character (no umbrella); other = elsewhere in the display (e.g., clouds). (Adapted from Arnold et al., 2000.)

less prominent of the discourse entities (see **Figure 10.5**). That is, as soon as participants heard the pronoun *he*, they rejected Maria as a possible antecedent. This was evident by the fact that very shortly after hearing the pronoun, their eye movements for the illustrations 10.4C and D settled on the only male referent. So, grammatical marking of gender seems to be used right away to disambiguate among referents. But *discourse prominence* had an equally privileged role in the speed of participants' pronoun resolution. That is, when the pronoun referred to the more prominent entity, hearers quickly converged on the correct antecedent, regardless of whether the pronoun was grammatically ambiguous. The only time that hearers showed any difficulty or delay in settling on the correct referent was when the pronoun was *both* grammatically ambiguous and referred to a less prominent discourse entity (see Figures 10.4B and 10.5B).

These results may have a familiar ring to them. Back in Chapter 8, we tested various theories of ambiguity resolution, focusing on temporarily ambiguous garden path sentences. For the most part, the findings from that body of work show that there don't seem to be dramatic differences in the relative timing with which various types of information are recruited in order to disambiguate the structure of the sentences. The results from the pronoun study we've just seen fit in quite nicely with the ambiguity-resolution data: people seem to be able to simultaneously juggle multiple sources of information in order to resolve the potential ambiguity inherent in pronouns.

In the eye-tracking study described in Figures 10.4 and 10,5, Arnold and her colleagues showed that people are able to immediately make use of information about grammatical gender and discourse prominence to figure out who or what pronouns refer to. But their data also revealed that, in some cases, interpreting a pronoun can cause difficulty—specifically, their hearers took a while to resolve the pronoun when it was grammatically ambiguous *and* referred to the less prominent antecedent. You don't have to dig too far in the experimental literature to find other examples where pronouns create some processing costs for readers/hearers.

For example, Bill Badecker and Kathleen Straub (2002) measured reading times for sentences like these:

(a) Kenny assured Lucy that he was prepared for the new job.

(b) Julie assured Harry that he was prepared for the new job.

(c) Kenny assured Harry that he was prepared for the new job.

The researchers found that the second clause of sentence (a) was read faster than the second clause of either sentence (b) or (c). In (a), both gender and discourse prominence converge to favor *Kenny* as the antecedent, while in (b), the pronoun *he* is grammatically consistent with a single antecedent (*Harry*), but this antecedent is not discourse prominent, and in (c) the (presumed) antecedent *Kenny* is discourse prominent but the pronoun is grammatically consistent with both *Kenny* and *Harry*. These results suggest that pronoun resolution goes most smoothly when multiple sources of information (or perhaps a single very strong one) favor a single antecedent. (Notice that Badecker and Straub's results don't align exactly with the eye-tracking data from Arnold et al., where a delay in interpreting the pronoun was only found in the situation where *neither* gender marking nor discourse prominence was helpful in finding the referent. See if you can generate ideas about why the two experiments didn't pattern exactly alike.)

The results from pronoun resolution studies offer yet more evidence that ambiguity sometimes results in some processing difficulty, but at other times poses no discernible burden for language comprehension. In fact, the repeated-name penalty shows that sometimes it can actually be *more* difficult for readers to connect a name back to that entity than a pronoun (even if the pronoun is grammatically ambiguous). This is interesting because it shows that at times a perfectly *un*ambiguous expression can wreak more processing havoc than an ambiguous one. But the repeated-name penalty seems to be limited to just those cases in which one antecedent is clearly more favored than other competing referents. If that condition isn't met, it often takes longer to resolve the pronoun than a name or an explicit descriptive phrase.

Pronoun resolution by children

Pronouns, then, however ubiquitous they may be across the world's languages, do come with some processing cost at least some of the time, and they do require hearers to efficiently coordinate the activation and inhibition of competing alternatives. But as I discussed in Chapter 8, such coordinating skill is not to be taken for granted. It requires considerable cognitive control, something that's lacking in certain populations—little kids, for example. It's possible that shakiness in cognitive control skills could have implications for the successful interpretation of pronouns.

In fact, a glance through some texts written for children makes it seem as if the authors think that pronouns might tax the abilities of their young readers. In the following passage, repeated names occur in contexts where an adult reader might expect (and prefer) a pronoun. For example:

"Jelly! Roll!" exclaimed Amelia Bedelia. "I never heard tell of jelly rolling." But Amelia Bedelia got out a jar of jelly. Amelia Bedelia tried again and again. But she just could not get that jelly to roll.

Amelia Bedelia washed her hands. She got out a mixing bowl. Amelia Bedelia began to mix a little of this and a pinch of that.

from Thank You, Amelia Bedelia *by Peggy Parish (1993)*

Is this kind of writing doing kids a favor? What information is there about how young children manage the interpretation of pronouns?

Hyun-joo Song and Cynthia Fisher (2007) discovered that even tots as young as two and a half are able to pick out one of two possible characters in a story as the referent for an ambiguous pronoun, based on the referent's prominence in the discourse. Their young participants looked at pictures while listening to stories like these:

> Look at the dog and the horse. On a sunny day, the dog walked with the horse to the park. And what did he see? Look! He saw a balloon!

By tracking the children's eye movements, Song and Fisher were able to see that their little subjects preferred to look at the more prominent character (the dog) rather than the less prominent one (the horse) upon hearing the ambiguous pronoun, much as the adults did in the study by Jennifer Arnold and colleagues (2000). But the youngsters were far slower to apply this information than the adults; where adults tended to settled on the more prominent character within 200 milliseconds of the end of the pronoun, it took the children more than 3 seconds to do the same. (Just slightly older children, above 3 years of age, were already considerably more efficient.) So, at a very young age, kids are already starting to develop the tools to interpret ambiguous pronouns, although this ability is still sluggish.

Looking at somewhat older kids, Arnold et al. (2007) found that 4-year-olds were consistently able to use gender marking to pick out the correct antecedent of a pronoun, and that by the age of five, they were as quick as adults in applying that knowledge. But their ability to use information about discourse prominence was not clearly apparent even by the age of five. Hence, there's good reason to believe that children's interpretation of grammatically ambiguous pronouns truly is somewhat vulnerable.

In fact, well after they show clear knowledge of some of the constraints on pronominal reference, kids still seem to be readily distracted by other discourse entities. Kaili Clackson and her colleagues (2011) tracked children's eye movements to narratives like these:

> (a) Peter was waiting outside the corner shop. He watched as Mr. Jones bought a huge box of popcorn for him/himself over the counter.
>
> (b) Susan was waiting outside the corner shop. She watched as Mr. Jones bought a huge box of popcorn for her/himself over the counter.

There's no real ambiguity here for either of the sentences (see **Box 10.4**). In (a), constraints on ordinary personal pronouns (*him*) and reflexive pronouns (*himself*) dictate the correct antecedents (*him* = Peter; *himself* = Mr. Jones). It's the same in (b), except that now there is information from gender marking in addition to these linguistic constraints on pronouns and reflexives.

When Clackson and her colleagues tested 6- to 9-year-olds, they found that the kids reliably picked out the correct antecedent in response to questions like, "Did Mr. Jones buy the popcorn?" Nevertheless, their eye movements hinted at lingering troubles in suppressing the competing referent when it matched the gender of the actual antecedent. That is, in the (a) sentences, kids often looked at the wrong character upon hearing the pronoun. Adults, on the other hand, were very adept at ignoring the wrong character, even when it matched the gender of the antecedent.

Despite taking some time to fully stabilize in their understanding of pronouns, kids seem to have a good sense of what pronouns, in their stripped-

BOX 10.4
Pronoun types and structural constraints

So far, we've looked only at basic pronouns like *she* or *him*. But languages make use of a variety of pronoun types, including reflexive pronouns like *myself* or *himself*, which are used in situations where the subject and the object (either direct or indirect) refer to the same person:

I washed myself.

He's really full of himself.

For the most part, ordinary pronouns and reflexive pronouns are not grammatically interchangeable. This is easy to see with more complex sentences, where the pronoun category imposes some real constraints on possible antecedents:

Harry reported that Mr. Rogers had badly injured himself.

Harry reported that Mr. Rogers had badly injured him.

Note that the first sentence *can't* mean that Mr. Rogers had injured Harry, while the second sentence can't mean that it was Mr. Rogers who sustained the injury. This means that hearers have access to grammatical information about pronouns other than just gender and person marking that can help to disambiguate possible antecedents (notice that both *him* and *himself* are marked as masculine third-person singular).

There's some disagreement among linguists about how best to capture these structural constraints, which are normally referred to as **binding constraints**. And there do seem to be some structures in which either a personal or a reflexive pronoun can be used. But to simplify things quite a bit, the general observation is that a reflexive needs to have a nearby antecedent, usually the subject in the same clause. A regular pronoun, on the other hand, *can't* refer back to the subject of the same clause.

Binding constraints, then, provide yet another source of information about potential antecedents. But languages differ in terms of the different categories of pronouns that they have to offer, and how these categories are structurally constrained. This is something that children have to learn about their language, presumably without anyone explicitly telling them the rules for interpretation. It appears that this knowledge takes some time to stabilize. For example, several studies have shown that as late as 5 or 6 years of age, kids seem to be more lax than adults in the way that they interpret sentences with pronouns. For example, they're more likely than adults to accept that a sentence like *Mama Bear is pointing to her* means the same thing as *Mama Bear is pointing to herself*, while grown-ups are adamant that *her* can't be referring to Mama Bear in the first sentence (Chien & Wexler, 1990).

---

binding constraints Structurally based constraints on the possible antecedents of personal pronouns such as *she* or *him* and on reflexive pronouns such as *himself* or *themselves*.

---

down linguistic essence, are for—that is, they serve as a practical shorthand for referring to highly salient discourse entities. Maya Hickmann and Henriëtte Hendriks (1999) found that, across various languages, children age four and above appropriately used pronouns to refer back to more prominent discourse entities rather than repeating their names. And there's some evidence that 7-year-olds show a repeated-name penalty when a proper name refers back to a highly salient entity, preferring a grammatically unambiguous pronoun in its place (Megherbi & Ehrlich, 2009).

Hence, for all their bareness, pronouns play a useful role in language, one that apparently makes up for the ambiguities they create. Like all ambiguity, the referential uncertainty that pronouns introduce does at times have a discernible processing cost for hearers and readers. Again, as with other species of ambiguity, the degree of difficulty falls on a continuum, depending on how strongly various information sources sup-

WEB ACTIVITY 10.7

Scientifically informed editing As noted earlier, even the superb writing of elite writers is riddled with grammatically ambiguous pronouns, most of which pose no difficulty for the reader. But even professional writers don't always succeed at creating a silky-smooth pronoun experience for their readers. In this activity, you'll examine samples of writing that involve a grammatically ambiguous pronoun. You'll predict which ones are most likely to create processing wrinkles for the audience, and you'll propose ways to test your predictions.

port one interpretation over another. Most of the time, the ambiguity is perfectly manageable—but in certain situations, and for hearers of certain ages, the odds of successful, effortless reference are less certain.

10.4 Drawing Inferences and Making Connections

Meaningful links between sentences

If you go back to the introduction to this chapter and read the two versions of the story about Frank, his wife, and his brother the doctor, you'll see that the well-sequenced discourse makes it easy to interpret pronouns in a smooth and sensible way, while the jumbled discourse often does not. But there are other important ways in which discourse structure affects interpretation. For example, look again at the following snippets from the two versions:

> Frank had to confront the fact that she was gone from his life. Then he learned the truth. Racked with sorrow, he killed himself.

> In the end, she lingered for some time, but eventually, Frank had to confront the fact that she was gone from his life. Racked with sorrow, he killed himself.

When we read or hear a narrative, we don't always have the luxury of having the relationships between sentences spelled out with explicit connecting words like *therefore, moreover, however, nevertheless, in spite of,* or *as a result.* In their absence, we work hard to infer these relationships—which is what makes the first of the above segments difficult to read. We struggle to fill in what "truth" Frank learned—connecting the second sentence back to the first seems to imply that his wife wasn't gone from his life after all. But then the third sentence mystifies when we try to read it in the context of the second: why would this particular turn of events cause Frank to kill himself out of sorrow? In the second, smoother passage, on the other hand, connecting the last sentence with the previous one provides us with a perfectly reasonable explanation for Frank's sorrow and ultimate suicide.

Bridging inferences

In order to understand a text as coherent, we often have to draw inferences that connect some of the content in a sentence with previous material in the text or with information encoded in the mental model. Such inferences are called **bridging inferences**. There's good evidence that people routinely and spontaneously try to generate bridging inferences as part of normal language comprehension. For instance, in one study, John Black and Hyman Bern (1981) presented readers with contrasting sentence pairs such as these:

> The cat leapt up on the kitchen table. Mike picked up the cat and put it outside.

> The cat walked past the kitchen table. Mike picked up the cat and put it outside.

The first pair of sentences offers a readily accessible causal link between the two sentences. We infer that the cat's action of leaping onto the kitchen table is likely what caused Mike to deposit it outside. But no handy causal connection is available in the second pair. Black and Bern had their subjects read through a series of such sentence pairs, and then distracted them for about 15 minutes before administering a memory test. They found that their readers were better able to

bridging inference An inference that connects some of the content in a sentence with previous material in the text, or with information encoded in the mental model.

recall the content of the second sentence when cued with the first if the two sentences were easily interpreted as cause and effect than if they were not. Moreover, in a slightly different version of the memory test, when subjects were asked to simply freely recall the content of the little discourses, they found that for the causally related sentences, there was a greater tendency to remember the two sentences as a unit: people tended to remember the content of both sentences, if they recalled either one of them, and they were more likely to roll them together into a simple complex sentence connected by an explicit linking word.

Another way to see the integration process in action is by looking at the reading times of discourses that offer strong versus weak inferential connections between sentences. Jerome Myers and colleagues (1987) measured how long it took people to read a sentence that had either a very close or a more distant causal connection to the preceding sentence. For instance:

(a) Cathy felt very dizzy and fainted at her work. She was carried away unconscious to a hospital.

(b) Cathy worked very hard and became exhausted. She was carried away unconscious to a hospital.

(c) Cathy worked overtime to finish her project. She was carried away unconscious to a hospital.

(d) Cathy had begun working on her project. She was carried away unconscious to a hospital.

Reading times for the target sentence (*She was carried away unconscious to a hospital*) got progressively longer as the causal relationship between the two sentences became more opaque, with the sentence being read fastest in passage (a) and slowest in passage (d). At the same time, memory for the content of the sentences was best when the causal connection was clearest, in line with the data from Black and Bern's study. These results suggest that during reading, people do generally invest the processing resources—even if unconsciously—to establish causal connections between sentences. (As discussed in Language at Large 10.2, similar visual inferences are at play when we watch movies.)

Causal links between sentences are just one type of bridging inference. Another common type involves linking referents across sentences, when the relationship is not linguistically explicit, as in:

Horace took the picnic supplies out of the car. The beer was warm.

The most natural way to interpret *the beer* is to assume it's among the picnic supplies that were taken out of the car. Plausible enough, but it seems some extra work needs to be done in order to make that connection; in one of the earliest studies of bridging inferences (Haviland and Clark, 1974), reading times for the target sentence *The beer was warm* were longer when the link to the preceding sentence was implicit than when it was explicit, as in:

Horace took some beer out of the car. The beer was warm.

The relationship between the two parts of the bridge can be instantiated in various ways. It can involve a set-membership relationship between the bridged element and the previous content, as in the picnic supplies example or the sentence below, in which we infer the captain is a member of the Canadian Olympic hockey team (as indicated by the matching color font):

The Canadian Olympic hockey team looks really strong this year.
The captain is brimming with confidence.

LANGUAGE AT LARGE 10.2

The Kuleshov effect: How inferences bring life to film

Film does away with a lot of the cognitive work that anyone reading a novel is forced to do on his own—especially when it comes to the details of sight and sound. Some people argue that this is exactly what makes movies less engaging than books: a reader's imagination has to be switched on in ways that movies don't require of their viewers.

Remember, however, that film was born in an era when there was no recorded sound, and hence no possibility of using language in the film (with the exception of short bursts of written text, or "subtitles," interspersed between the live scenes). Early filmgoers had to do a different kind of cognitive work, interpreting events—often highly social interactions—without the benefit of linguistic content. Some of the pioneers of film were acutely aware of the imaginative burden they were placing on their viewers, and concluded that their audience was up to the task.

In a famous unpublished experiment, Lev Kuleshov, a Russian filmmaker in the 1910s and 1920s, observed that people's interpretations of visual scenes could change dramatically depending on which other scenes they were assembled with (an account of the study can be found in Giannetti & Eyman, 1986). Kuleshov noticed that if he took a shot of a fairly expressionless actor's face and edited it so that it followed the image of a young girl in a coffin, people thought he looked sad; if it came after a shot of a bowl of soup, viewers said the actor looked hungry; if the same actor's face was preceded by the image of a beautiful young woman, viewers said he was looking at her with desire (see **Figure 10.6**).

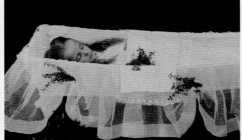

Figure 10.6 The Kuleshov effect. In film, the same shot of an actor's neutral expression is interpreted in different ways depending on the preceding shot. Kuleshov argued that viewers automatically draw connections between the objects that appeared in the preceding scene and the motivations and intentions of the actor.

The bridge can involve a part-whole relationship, like this:

> **My car** broke down on my way to work. It was **the radiator**.

> Be careful carrying **that box**! **The bottom** is about to give out.

The bridging relationship can involve an alternative (often unflattering) way of describing the referent:

LANGUAGE AT LARGE 10.2 *(continued)*

The connections that viewers make between visual scenes in a film are very similar to many of the inferences that connect sentences together. In Kuleshov's experiment, viewers had to infer that the actor was looking at whatever image was presented just before the head shot, and that the object of his attention caused some particular emotional response. This colored their perception of the actor's somewhat bland expression (in fact, a number of Kuleshov's viewers allegedly complimented the actor on his expressive talents).

Film techniques have been deeply influenced by an understanding of the inferential glue that binds seemingly unrelated visual scenes together. Some directors have argued that much of a movie's magic comes from exactly this kind of imaginative labor done by viewers, and really comes into the foreground when language plays less of a role. For example, Michel Hazanavicius, who created the award-winning 2011 silent film *The Artist*, had this to say in an interview: "Dialogue is very efficient. But to say the important things, you don't use dialogue. The sound is so important to a movie that when I leave the responsibility to the audience, people do it so much better than I could do" (LaMattina, 2012). The thought is echoed in a 2012 TED talk by Andrew Stanton, who made the acclaimed animated film *WALL-E* (which relies on very little dialogue). Remarking that humans are born problem solvers, Stanton claims that it's "the well-organized absence of information" that draws us into a story. He describes his filmmaking as being driven by "the unifying theory of 2 + 2. Make the audience put things together. Don't give them 4. Give them 2 + 2."

I can't stand **my physics professor**. I'd be happy if **the windbag** dropped dead.

My son is starting to get on my nerves. **The damn child** won't stop whining.

Or, the bridge can involve an element that's known to be associated with a particular scenario:

Timmy's birthday party was a great success. **The cake** was shaped like a triceratops.

Our final exam came to an abrupt halt when **the proctor** fell to the floor in a dead faint.

Presuppositions

The two types of bridging inferences we've discussed so far—causal and referential inferences—differ in an interesting way. Let's look again at an example of each:

Stuart was caught plagiarizing his essay. He was expelled immediately.

Horace took some beer out of the car. The beer was warm.

In the first example, which involves a causal inference, there's nothing in the second sentence to signal that the hearer needs to connect up the second sentence with previous material—the sentences are spontaneously integrated as the hearer attempts to relate the second sentence in some sensible way to the first sentence. But sometimes, the integration is guided a bit more precisely by a specific word or phrase that signals that a particular piece of new content *has* to be linked back with some older content. In the second example above, it's the definite article in the phrase *the beer* that forces the link. Notice how the connection between the two sentences seems weaker in the sequence *Horace took the picnic supplies out of the car. Some beer was warm.* Unlike an indefinite noun phrase (*some beer*), the definite description signals that the speaker is referring to something that's already been established in the discourse or, at the very least, can be presumed to exist. Consider, for instance, the difference between these two sentences:

Sandra wants to vote for an honest politician.

Sandra wants to vote for the honest politician.

The first sentence makes sense even if there's no such thing as an honest politician anywhere, but the second requires not only that one exists but that there's a *specific* one that's already familiar in the discourse. So, certain bits of language can serve as triggers that force a bridging inference because they communicate exactly what information should already be present in the mental model—such language is said to carry a specific **presupposition**. Linguistic expressions that trigger presuppositions come in a variety of forms, from definite referential phrases (*the beer, his dog*), to certain types of verbs (*regret, know, stop*), to some adverbs (*again, once more*), and even to certain kinds of syntactic constructions, like the focus constructions you say in Section 10.2.

Here are a few other examples, with the presupposition-triggering expression marked in bold type:

Daniel **regrets** that he wasted five years of his life studying geology.
(*Presupposes that Daniel wasted five years studying geology.*)

Jana has finally **stopped** illegally importing smutty comic books.
(*Presupposes that Jana has been illegally importing comic books.*)

It was her boyfriend's boss who Melinda irritated at the party.
(*Presupposes that Melinda annoyed some person at the party.*)

Ganesh escaped from jail **again**.
(*Presupposes that Ganesh has escaped from jail before.*)

Presuppositional language basically acts as an instruction to the hearer to go search for specific content in the mental model. It can greatly enhance the efficiency of communication, by serving as a pointer to already-encoded material. For example, in a certain context, you could tell your friend:

So, the problem with my car turned out to be the battery.

The definite descriptions in this sentence (*my car, the battery,* and *the problem with my car*) allow you to make certain assumptions about what your friend already knows. You don't need to say:

So, I have a car and my car has a battery. The car had a problem, and the problem turned out to be the battery.

Now, suppose you and your friend have never spoken about your car before. It's reasonable to suppose that, despite this, she knows that it's common for people to own a car, and for cars to have batteries. But she may not have known that you were having problems with your car. By using the phrase *the problem with my car*, you're essentially signaling to her that you assume this information is already in her mental model, so it would be natural for her to insert this as background knowledge through a process known as **accommodation**. This happens to be a really interesting consequence of presuppositional language, and can have powerful effects on the inferences that get added to the mental model. Imagine attending your first day of class, and having the instructor tell the students, "You need to have this form signed by your probation officer." At

presupposition An implicit assumption that is signaled by specific linguistic expressions, and whose existence or truth is taken for granted as background information.

accommodation The process of updating a mental model to include information that is presupposed by a speaker, as evident by his use of specific presupposition-triggering expressions.

LANGUAGE AT LARGE 10.3

Presuppositions and President Clinton's re-election

Political strategist Dick Morris was in charge of Bill Clinton's 1996 re-election campaign. In his 1997 book *Behind the Oval Office*, he related the following anecdote:

> [Clinton's] achievements were a problem. In strategy meetings, he often complained that he had created seven million jobs and cut the deficit but nobody seemed to notice. In speeches, he referred to the achievements awkwardly. Our polls showed audiences either already knew about them or didn't believe they were true. At one strategy session, Bob Squier suggested a better way to draw attention to what he had done. The key, Squier explained, was to cite the achievement while talking about something he was going to do. For example: "The hundred thousand extra police we put on the street can't solve the crime problem by themselves; we need to keep anti-drug funding for schools in the budget and stop Republicans from cutting it." Or: "The seven million jobs we've created won't be much use if we can't find educated people to fill them. That's why I want a tax deduction for college tuition to help kids go on to college to take those jobs."

Morris claims that this approach was much more effective with voters.

If you look closely at the new-and-improved statements, you'll notice that the reworked language is loaded with presuppositions. Here is some of the information that's being presented as presupposed: Clinton's administration put 100,000 extra police on the street; there's a crime problem; anti-drug funding is set aside in the budget; Republicans are trying to cut this funding; Clinton's administration created 7 million jobs; Clinton wants a tax deduction for college tuition.

Using presuppositional language provides an ideal solution to the problems that were highlighted in the campaign polls. Its function is to signal that the presupposed material is already presumed to be in the hearer's mental model, or at the very least, to be highly consistent with it. This aligns neatly with those viewers who were already aware of Clinton's achievements—this information is not being presented as new, but as simply referring back to something voters were already assumed to know.

But what about the other viewers, those whose mental models didn't include these achievements, and who were in fact skeptical of Clinton's boasts? By coding the accomplishments as presupposed, rather than directly asserting them as new information that should be added to the hearer's mental model, the statements were subtly sending the signal that this information was generally accepted by *other* people, that there wasn't anything especially controversial about it. And not surprisingly, information about what other people think can have a strong influence on opinion. For example, scores of social psychology studies have shown that people modulate their own opinions and responses quite strongly if they're presented with evidence of a consensus of others' opinions that collides directly with their own. Moreover, they may be less likely to critically evaluate opinions that are presented as the majority view than opinions that are claimed to be held only by a minority of people.

Presuppositions in persuasive language are discussed in detail in a book I coauthored with linguist Greg Carlson (Sedivy & Carlson, 2011). There, we use the following analogy in thinking about how Clinton's campaign team solved the problem of getting past voters' resistance to his claims: Think about how you might get into a room or building that you had no permission to enter. Your best strategy might be to saunter in casually and behave as if your presence there were the most unremarkable thing in the world, as if it had never occurred to you that anyone might question your right to be there—*that's* what presuppositions accomplish linguistically.

Clinton is not the only politician whose boasts tend to be met with resistance. His own vice president, Al Gore, met with a great deal of derision over his assertion that his policy initiatives had helped to create the Internet—in fact, people typically misremember him as claiming that he "invented" the Internet. Who knows, perhaps the claim would have been more gently and unobtrusively entered into voters' mental models if he'd slid it in as presupposed information, using it to preface some new idea, something like, "The policy initiatives I put in place to help start the Internet will provide a foundation for … ."

this, you might cast nervous glances around at your classmates. You can infer, based on the definite description *your probation officer*, that it's typical for the students in the class to have a probation officer—or at least, that the instructor thinks so!

Because presupposition can serve as a trigger to add (presumably familiar) information into a mental model, these linguistic devices have caught the attention of researchers who study the phenomenon of false memories. False memories arise much more often than people think, partly because the mental models we build as a result of communicating with others are not neatly divided from the memories we have of events that we've witnessed or experienced ourselves. Language-based memories have a way of sloshing over to other kinds of memories, and vice versa. For example, memory researchers have discovered that people sometimes come to believe that they themselves have experienced something they've only heard about. (Perhaps this has happened to you. Have you ever mistakenly absorbed as your own memory a story you've repeatedly heard a relative talk about, only to have that person later object that the event happened to *her* and not you?)

All this raises some thorny questions about the accuracy of eyewitness testimony in situations in which a person has witnessed a crime or an accident. Do their accounts really reflect the person's first-hand memories and perceptions of the event, or have their recollections become contaminated by how other people have *talked* about the event? If the latter, it becomes important to look at the kind of language used in the course of discussing the event—for example, there's a concern that the language used by police while interrogating a witness could taint the witness's reported memories.

One particularly provocative research thread involves looking at whether presuppositional language—with its *presumption* that certain information is already known—can induce hearers to falsely remember events or referents. Memory researcher Elizabeth Loftus and her colleagues (1978) carried out some classic experiments to see whether people could be nudged to misremember events as a result of leading questions that triggered presuppositions. For instance, in one scenario, subjects played the role of eyewitnesses to a traffic accident, and afterward were questioned about the series of events that led to the accident. Those who heard the question, "Did you see the stop sign?" were more likely to answer "Yes" than those who heard, "Did you see a stop sign?"—in neither case was there a stop sign in the scene. Later work by Klaus Fiedler and Eva Walthier (1996) confirmed that questions containing presuppositions led subjects to falsely remember objects in a scene at a rate of 10–40%, and that these false memories became more likely as the time gap between first hearing the presuppositional language and the memory test lengthened. This finding hints at the very real possibility of corrupting the memories of witnesses in real-life situations, given that witnesses often must wait weeks or months between first being questioned about an event and eventually testifying about it in a court.

Beyond eyewitness accounts, it's worth taking a close look at presuppositions in persuasive messages. Since presuppositional language signals that certain information should already be present in the hearer's mental model, it may well have the force of making controversial statements feel more settled and less open to debate than they would be if the same notions were overtly introduced as new information to add to the mental model. Or, it may signal something about implied social norms. For example, one married lesbian woman has told me that she makes a point of casually referring to her spouse using the definite description *my wife*, even to people who are unfamiliar with the fact that she has one. She explains that by

---

WEB ACTIVITY 10.8

The impact of presuppositions In this activity, you'll see examples from persuasive messages in which presuppositions are introduced. You'll have the opportunity to identify what information is presumed to be already known, and how this might affect the persuasive force of the message. You'll also be asked to do some fieldwork to test whether encoding some ideas as presupposed, rather than as baldly asserted, results in these ideas becoming more readily accepted.

doing so, she can communicate that it's a common, unremarkable fact for two women to be married to each other—just as a heterosexual man wouldn't feel the need to explicitly say, "So, I have a wife," before referring to his spouse as "my wife."

Elaborative inferences

So far, we've been looking at examples where inferences are required in order for a sentence to become properly integrated with *previous* discourse or material that's presumed to be already encoded in the mental model. But not all inferences have this quality of backward connection. For instance:

> The intruder stabbed the hapless homeowner three times in the chest.

> The hungry python caught the mouse.

> After years of training, the swimmer won a bronze medal at the Olympics.

Though these sentences don't say so, you may have arrived at the following conclusions: the intruder used a knife to stab the homeowner, and not an ice pick or a pair of scissors; the python ate the mouse after catching it; the swimmer didn't win any silver or gold medals at the Olympics in addition to the bronze medal. Such inferences aren't dependent on making connections between sentences. Instead, they seem to capture fairly natural assumptions about what's typical for the events that are being described, or what the speaker was likely intending to convey. Such inferences are called **elaborative inferences**.

In a sense, elaborative inferences feel less necessary than bridging inferences in that they're not needed in order for a text to stick together in a cohesive way. Rather, they feel a bit more like some of the "extra" aspects of meaning in mental models that we talked about in Section 10.1—for example, very specific sensory representations about the sounds of the events being described, or, as in the vague passage about doing laundry (see pp. 386–387), all the added details that brought the passage to life. In many cases, nothing terribly serious hinges on whether the elaborative inferences are drawn, and they often seem truly optional from the perspective of the speaker's intended message—perhaps they make the message richer or more memorable, but skipping the details doesn't necessarily impede understanding. At other times, though, speakers might feel they'd been misunderstood if the hearer failed to compute the inference; and conversely, the hearer might feel that the speaker had somehow been deceptive or uncooperative if he hadn't meant to imply a certain additional meaning. For example, a hearer would be right to complain if a speaker described the achievements of superstar swimmer Michael Phelps with the sentence *Phelps won two silver medals at the 2012 Olympics*, when in fact, the athlete had won four gold medals as well. (We'll talk more in Chapter 11 about how the kinds of expectations that hearers and speakers have about each other play out in language comprehension and production.)

Overall, the body of psycholinguistic literature suggests that while hearers or readers consistently compute bridging inferences, they don't always compute elaborative inferences. They're more likely to do so if the context sets up very strong expectations in support of the inference. For example, Tracy Linderholm (2002) created small discourses that invited varying degrees of **predictive inference**—these are inferences about the likely outcome of a described event, as illustrated above with the hungry python sentence (which led to the plausible inference that the python ate the mouse after catching it). The degree of con-

elaborative inference Refers to inferences that are not required in order to make a discourse coherent, but that enrich the meanings of sentences to include material not explicitly encoded on the linguistic content of the sentence.

predictive inference A type of elaborative inference that involves making predictions about the likely outcome of a sentence.

textual support for the inference was manipulated by varying the final sentence of the following discourse:

> Patty felt like she had been in graduate school forever. Her stipend was minimal and she was always low on cash. Some weeks, she had nothing to eat but peanut butter and jelly. Patty packed her lunch every single day to save money. She yearned for the day she could afford to eat in a restaurant. Alas, she pulled out her sack lunch and looked at its contents. Patty bit into her apple, then stared at it.

The final sentence could then read either:

> It had half a worm in it. *(high support)*
>
> *or* It had an unpleasant taste. *(moderate support)*
>
> *or* It had little flavor. *(low support)*

A plausible predictive inference is that Patty spit out her mouthful of apple—this would be far more likely in the event of finding half a worm (high support) than if the apple were merely bland (low support). Linderholm tested for the presence of this inference by using the standard tool of comparing reading

BOX 10.5
Using brain waves to study the time course of discourse processing

As you've seen, a number of reading-time studies hint at the extra work that goes into enriching meanings with inferences beyond their straightforward sentence meanings. But I haven't yet given you a good picture of the more precise timeline along which these inferences are generated. For example, do hearers or readers first compute the linguistic meaning of an entire sentence, and only then build the meanings that connect them together? Or do they compute these inferences in parallel with meaning that's derived directly from the linguistic code? Given the processing price tag that comes with many aspects of discourse-based meanings, we might expect discourse processing to lag behind the work of basic language decoding. On the other hand, in Chapter 8, you saw some examples of how people were able to predict some aspects of the linguistic code based on subtle contextual information—could inferences be rapidly used in the same way, to help constrain expectations about the upcoming linguistic content and structure?

To study these questions, we need a method that's very sensitive to the time course of processing, ideally in a language task that's as natural as possible. Eye tracking is one possible method, but it's limited to situations where the output of interpretation can be directly linked to what people look at in a visual display. Another approach is to use event-related potential (ERP) techniques to measure brain wave activity while people simply listen to recorded speech (or in some cases, read text).

ERP studies of discourse processing have focused mostly on the N400 component, which seems to reflect how easy it is to integrate words into a meaningful interpretation. For example, as you saw in Chapter 3, people show an increase in N400 activity when they're confronted with words that are implausible in context, as in *He spread the warm bread with* **socks**. Remember also that N400 activity is less pronounced with highly frequent words, with words that have been previously primed by other semantically related words, or with words that are predictable in some way.

Overall, research from ERPs shows that discourse-based meaning is more than the proverbial icing on a fully baked interpretive cake. For starters, basic word-by-word integration within a sentence seems to get easier or harder depending on whether the discourse offers a general coherent framework for interpretation. Marie St. George and her colleagues (1994) measured brain wave activity while people read paragraphs like the classic clothes-washing passage you read in Section 10.1. They found that N400 activity ramped up—showing evidence of greater processing effort—for content words throughout the passage when the readers didn't have access to an times for sentences that were either consistent or inconsistent with this inference: *Patty spit out the bite of apple* versus *Patty swallowed the bite of apple*. She found longer reading times for the inconsistent sentence than for the consistent one only in the "high support" context, suggesting that it takes a fairly loaded context before people will generate plausible predictions of events.

But there was a catch to this finding. The likelihood that her subjects computed an inference was also dependent on their working-memory capacity. Linderholm administered a reading span test to all her participants (as discussed in Section 8.6), so she was able to separate them into those with a high memory span and those with a low memory span. The low-span subjects showed no evidence of computing the inference for any of the contexts—a reliable difference in reading times for consistent versus inconsistent target sentences was limited to the high-span subjects, and even then, only in the "high support" contexts. Other studies have confirmed the role of both contextual factors and individual differences in determining whether certain inferences are likely to be drawn.

Here's an especially interesting variable: people are more likely to predict outcomes that they *want* to happen than they are to predict undesired outcomes. Have you ever read a novel and reacted with utter disbelief when you

---

BOX 10.5 *(continued)*

illuminating title that helped them understand what the passage was about. This means that the use of general information from the context seems to be sewn into the moment-by-moment interpretation of the passage. When a passage lacks overall coherence, it's not just that the final mental model is impoverished, but that the incremental interpretation of individual words gets more effortful.

More detailed evidence for the tight interplay between linguistic and contextual information comes from a Dutch study by Jos van Berkum and colleagues (2003). In their study, they manipulated the plausibility of target words so that these words were perfectly sensible within the sentences in which they appeared, but could be bizarre when considered within the events of the larger story. For example: *The dean told the lecturer there was ample reason to promote him.* On its own, there's nothing within the sentence to make the word *promote* seem odd, compared with, say, the word *fire*. And, as you'd expect, when subjects heard either of these words in the isolated sentence, there was no greater N400 activity for one versus the other. But when the sentences are part of a story in which the dean has discovered that the lecturer has committed fraud, the word *promote* becomes a misfit. In this situation, subjects showed stronger N400 activity for the implausible word. What was really striking was just how quickly this response showed up, beginning at about 150 milliseconds after the onsets of the critical words—in other words, after only the first two or three phonemes had been uttered. For

this response to have been triggered, the hearers must have connected the target sentence with the preceding events, inferred that whatever the dean was telling the lecturer was causally related to the fraudulent activity, generated a set of predictions about likely outcomes, and put this all together with the target word *promote*, all before actually hearing the entire word. In this particular study, the N400 effect that showed up for words that were implausible due to the discourse context was every bit as fast as an N400 effect for words whose weirdness was due to the sentence's meaning (for example, the researchers compared sentences like *Gloomily, the men stood around the **pencil** of the president* with ordinary sentence such as *Gloomily, the men stood around the **grave** of the president*).

Studies like these show that there don't seem to be sharply separate stages in interpretation, with linguistic meaning fully interpreted before hearers start to generate discourse-based inferences. Instead, the two types of interpretation run in parallel, and if it's fast enough, discourse-based meaning can even influence how linguistic meaning is recovered. Nevertheless, these results have to be reconciled with the fact that, at times, discourse inferences are quite costly or not even computed at all. Psycholinguists don't yet have all the answers about when enriching meanings through discourse information might be fast and easy, and when it might be slow and hard. But ERP methods are likely to provide a useful tool in those detailed investigations.

got to the part where your favorite character died? That sense of disbelief may be a reflection of your predictive processes in action.

In a well-known study of predictive inferences, Gail McKoon and Roger Ratcliff (1986) found that people rarely generated specific predictions when presented with sentences such as this:

> The director and cameraman were ready to shoot close-ups when suddenly the actress fell from the fourteenth story.

Instead of inferring, say, that the actress died as a result of the fall, they encoded something more vague, along the lines of "something bad will happen." David Rapp and Richard Gerrig (2006) probed a bit deeper, and suggested that the specificity of people's predictions might depend on how they felt about the actress. What if she was a tireless advocate for charity work? Would people be less likely to predict her death than if they thought she was presented as a dishonest and abusive person? To test this question, they created stories that varied on several dimensions. Some of the stories were written so that the final sentence represented a probable outcome of the story's events:

> Peter was hoping to win lots of money at the poker table in Vegas. He was holding a pretty lousy hand but stayed in the game. Peter bet all of his money on the current hand. Peter lost the hand and all of his money.

Stories like these were compared with ones where the final sentence described a very unlikely outcome—for example, the same story about Peter might end with the sentence *Peter won the pot of money with his hand*. Not surprisingly, when subjects were asked whether the outcome was a likely one, they were much more likely to agree that it was likely for the first version of the story, in which Peter lost his money, than for the second version. They also spent more time reading the final sentence when it described an unlikely outcome—this suggests that the sentence clashed with their expectations about the story's continuation, and is consistent with the study by Tracy Linderholm, in which strong contextual information in the story led to certain predictions.

The interesting twist in Rapp and Gerrig's study was that at the very beginning of the story, subjects were given some information that was intended to get readers to either root for Peter, or hope he would lose his money:

> Peter was trying to raise money to pay for his sister's college education. Peter was hoping to win lots of money at the poker table in Vegas. He was holding a pretty lousy hand but stayed in the game. Peter bet all of his money on the current hand.

Do you want Peter to win? Of course you do. Now consider this version:

> Peter was raising money to finance a racist organization in the United States. Peter was hoping to win lots of money at the poker table in Vegas. He was holding a pretty lousy hand but stayed in the game. Peter bet all of his money on the current hand.

Rapp and Gerrig assumed (based on ratings with a separate set of subjects) that for this story version, the majority of readers would hope Peter would lose. Moreover, they predicted that readers' *desires* about the outcome would help shape their predictive inferences. That's exactly what they found: in addition to the likelihood of the outcome in the final sentence, people also took into account the information about Peter's character and goals. When the story was biased to favor the story's conclusion *and* was consistent with readers' desires, subjects agreed 95% of the time that the outcome was very likely. However, when this probable outcome clashed with their own desires for how the story should end, the agreement rate dropped to 69%. Reading times of the final sentence also showed that people were slower to read the outcome sentences when they were mismatched with readers' preferred outcomes. To a significant degree, their predictions about the text were driven by wishful thinking.

Overall, the study of elaborative inferences reveals several findings. Detailed inferences are not always generated by readers. A number of factors determine whether they are encoded. One of these is the amount of available processing resources (in terms of working memory). This suggests that making inferences can be fairly expensive from a cognitive point of view—contextual support can reduce the cost by boosting the accessibility of some inferences, but even so, there have to be enough resources available in working memory for even fairly accessible elaborative inferences to be spontaneously generated. The likelihood of making an inference, then, seems to reflect the combination of its accessibility (which affects its processing cost) and the available processing resources.

The cognitive costs of elaborative inferences

It's worth saying a few words about the apparent costliness of many inferences. You might remember that even bridging inferences, which readers mostly do seem to spontaneously generate, showed evidence of processing cost as reflected in longer reading times. This cognitive price tag for inferences raises some interesting questions. Psycholinguists often think of language understanding as something that we do automatically and without the need for conscious deliberation. If someone is talking to you, you have to go out of your way *not* to understand what they're saying, you might have to cover your ears to block out the sounds of speech. You don't *choose* to figure out what someone is saying in the same way that you choose (or don't) to figure out a math problem, and then allocate your attention and cognitive resources to the task. But when it comes to certain inferences or elaborations of meaning, it's a bit less clear whether these are part and parcel of the automatic, reflexive aspect of language understanding.

Certainly, it seems there would have to be some limits to the depth of detail and number of inferences and elaborations that hearers typically compute for any given sentence. For example, the simple sentence *The hungry python caught the mouse* could, in theory, lead to all of the following extra meanings layered on to the sentence: the python ate the mouse; the python swallowed the mouse whole; the mouse was brown and furry; the python squeezed the mouse before eating it; the mouse wriggled while being squeezed; the python had a bulge afterward; the python wouldn't be hungry for awhile, and so on. But it's doubtful that we have the brainpower to actively generate all of these inferences in the course of everyday language use—and even if we did, it might not be adaptive to worry about all of these details in most contexts.

This brings us to an interesting paradox. On the one hand, normal communication seems to rely very heavily on the ability of hearers to read between the lines of the meaning that's provided by the linguistics code. On the other hand, hearers have to spend precious cognitive resources to do so, which might put some limits on the extra meanings they can derive. As psycholinguists, we'd like to know: Are some inferences less costly than others, or computed more automatically? If so, what accounts for the differences in processing cost among various inferences? Are they generated in different ways? And if there are inferences that aren't automatically generated, do speakers manage to predict which ones their hearers are most likely to compute, and does this drive speakers' decisions about how much needs to be said explicitly? In the upcoming Digging Deeper section, we'll look more closely at debates over which inferences

reverse cohesion effect The finding that under some circumstances, readers retain more information from a text in which the coherence relations between sentences are not made explicit and must be inferred by the reader.

are automatically generated, and what specific mechanisms are involved. The question of how well speakers anticipate what their hearers will understand will be left to Chapter 11.

It seems apt to end this section by pointing out that the hard work of generating inferences can have some interesting side effects or benefits for the hearer or reader. When the audience has to work at connecting the dots, the resulting meaning sometimes has more impact than if it had been hand-delivered in the form of more explicit language. Some researchers who study instructional texts have noted that many textbooks do a poor job of clearly connecting ideas to each other or marking the relationships between concepts. Textbook authors can make reading less strenuous by supplying overt cohesion markers in the text—for example, by replacing pronouns with noun phrases; adding descriptive content to link unfamiliar concepts with familiar ones; adding connecting words and phrases such as *in addition, nevertheless, as a result*; and so on. But, paradoxically, readers who already know a fair bit about the subject matter sometimes seem to learn and retain more from a text that leaves out these convenient linguistic markers (e.g., see McNamara & Kintsch, 1996). This **reverse cohesion effect** may arise because the more challenging texts force the readers to activate their knowledge base in order to make sense of the text. This added activation may well result in a more robust mental model of the material in the text.

WEB ACTIVITY 10.9

Pros and cons of inferential leaps Many advertisements lean heavily on readers making complex inferential leaps. This activity provides a selection of examples, and offers the opportunity to discuss potential benefits and risks of leaving so much to the imagination of the consumer.

In more artistic domains, writing instructors have long extolled the virtues of a "show, don't tell" approach to writing narratives. Writers who subscribe to this approach may lay out a specific event or patch of dialogue, but let the reader pull out the important meaning or conclusions to be drawn from it—this is supposed to be more satisfying for the reader than having the author wrap up the meaning in a bow. (See Language at Large 10.2 for the same theory expressed by filmmakers.) There isn't a vast collection of empirical studies that confirm the aesthetic virtues of the "show, don't tell" doctrine, but a couple of studies provide some glimmers that the idea holds water. For example, Marisa Bortolussi and Peter Dixon (2003) reported a study in which subjects read either an original version of a short story by Alice Munro or one that had been doctored to overtly explain a character's internal emotional state, rather than simply hint at it. The readers of the more explicit text seemed to have a harder time getting into the character's head, as evidenced by lower ratings about the extent to which the character's actions were connected to her internal motivations and emotions.

In a similar vein, in a 1999 study by Sung-il Kim, participants read versions of stories in which important information was either spelled out or left implicit, to be filled in by the reader. The enigmatic versions of the stories were judged to be more interesting than the more explicit ones. But this effect depended on readers' having the opportunity to resolve the puzzle in the first place; they found the implicit texts more interesting than the explicit ones only if they were given ample time to compute inferences; when the text flew by at a brisk 400 milliseconds a word, the difference between the two versions disappeared. Kim suggested that when language moves by at such a fast clip, readers don't have enough time to generate rich inferences. It may be, then, that whatever advantages come from letting readers connect the dots could easily evaporate if readers aren't able or motivated to invest the cognitive resources to draw inferences, or don't have the right background knowledge to bring to the task.

GO TO
sites.sinauer.com/languageinmind

for **web activities, further readings, research updates, new essays,** and other features

DIGGING DEEPER

Shallow processors or builders of rich meaning?

As I pointed out in Section 10.4, there have to be some reasonable limits on the extent to which we enrich meanings beyond the linguistic code, at least in the most typical situations of language use. When it comes to spoken language, the sheer velocity of speech puts a cap on the number and depth of inferences that we can mentally crank out before we're forced to process the next incoming sentence. Throughout this chapter, I've used the terms *hearer* and *reader* pretty much interchangeably. But in reality, things might look quite different for reading text as opposed to hearing speech; in reading, the reader and not the writer controls the pace of processing, so this opens up the possibility that readers enrich meanings to a much greater extent with written text than they normally are able to do with spoken language—perhaps filling in more details of imagery and sound, exploring alternative explanations for characters' actions, or anticipating possible upcoming events and outcomes. The experience of reading could in principle turn out to be very different from the experience of drawing meaning from spoken language.

But a good bit of research shows that much of the time, readers pass up the opportunity to engage in really deep processing of meaning. We've already seen in Section 10.4 that many plausible elaborative inferences are not computed unless the context really makes them leap out. In addition, some researchers have argued that people don't always bother to fully resolve ambiguous pronouns—or even unambiguous ones for that matter (e.g., Love & McKoon, 2011). Readers might interpret a pronoun like *she* as simply a placeholder for some female person, rather than linking it back to a specific character about whom they've already learned some specific facts. So it seems that readers are often satisfied to take linguistic content at face value, declining the extra work of filling in the skeletal meanings that language offers. But evidence for shallow processing goes beyond this, and suggests that readers even gloss over aspects of the structure or wording of language itself (for a brief review, see Ferreira et al., 2002). For instance, when reading a garden path sentence in which they have to choose between two possible interpretations of an ambiguous phrase, they might never fully suppress one of the possible readings, even after getting information in the sentence that should be enough to make it perfectly clear which of the two readings is correct. Other research has shown that readers often fail to notice the precise meanings of words. For instance—quick, answer this question: How many animals of each kind did Moses bring onto the ark? If you answered "Two," you're just one of many people who skim over the biblical fact that it was Noah and not Moses who brought animals onto the ark. Or, if asked, "Can a man marry his widow's sister?" people commonly overlook the fact that if a man has a widow, he must be dead, and therefore is ineligible to marry anyone!

Results like these suggest that some aspects of language comprehension are treated as "optional" and don't necessarily happen reflexively. They bring us back to some of the issues raised in Section 8.2. There, I talked about one of the major obsessions that has preoccupied researchers studying sentence processing, namely, whether it was possible to draw a sharp line between comprehension processes that happen quickly and automatically, and those that are more sluggish and under more deliberate control. As you might recall, this debate, which was fought largely on the battlefield of ambiguity resolution, was just one instantiation of a more general view: that human beings are equipped to solve problems through different routes, some of which are intuitive, fast, and "dumb" in that they rely on a limited amount of information, in contrast to others that involve sifting through more nuanced information in a more evaluative, goal-driven way. These overarching themes have been very much in play when it comes to research in discourse processing. Two dramatically different kinds of explanations have been offered for how links are made between discourse referents and events, as well as for how inferences are generated.

The first class of explanations can be described as memory-driven. The basic premise of the **memory-driven account** is that information from incoming text acts as a signal to automatically activate information in long-term memory—this can include information from earlier in the text, as well as information that's part of general knowledge or something that's been learned before. A successful link between incoming and previously coded information depends on two things: a strong signal from the incoming text, and the degree to which the appropriate old information can be activated.

---

memory-driven account of discourse processing Theoretical approach to discourse processing that emphasizes the role of passive, automatic memory-based processes, in which the integration of incoming discourse information is accomplished by activating existing representations in memory.

The strength of the signal from the incoming text can depend on factors like how much attention is being paid to its various elements. For example, linguistic material that sits in a heavily focused part of the sentence normally sends an especially strong signal to activate content from long-term memory (as in the bold portion of *It was the **butler** who killed the lady of the manse*). The degree to which concepts from memory will be activated—or, as researchers who work in this field like to say, the degree to which earlier-stored concepts will "resonate" in response to the incoming signal—depends on how close a match there is between these concepts and the signaling text, and on how accessible the various concepts are to begin with. Concepts that have been more recently or more frequently activated offer themselves up as stronger candidates than those loitering in memory's shadows. And concepts that overlap a great deal with the signaling text will also become more strongly activated. This general view can account for various phenomena.

For instance, it can help to explain why some causal inferences are easier and faster to get than others. Consider these examples from Myers et al. (1987):.

(a) Cathy felt very dizzy and fainted at her work. She was carried away unconscious to a hospital.

(b) Cathy worked very hard and became exhausted. She was carried away unconscious to a hospital.

The pair of sentences in (a) is much easier to integrate than the pair in (b); as we saw, this is reflected in how long people take to read the second sentence for each pair. But notice that in (a), there's some pretty strong overlap between the concepts in the first and second sentences: your knowledge of fainting lets you know that lack of consciousness and perhaps falling are typical results, and this is consistent with the concepts of being carried away and being unconscious in the second sentence. Moreover, dizziness and fainting are symptoms that often call for medical attention. So, there's a strong degree of resonance between the concepts in the first and second sentences in (a), while that's not the case in the more difficult pair of sentences in (b).

This view also helps to explain why pronouns tend to be used in just those situations where there is a specific, highly salient antecedent, and why repeating the name of an antecedent is the best strategy when a speaker is referring back to an entity that's more distant in memory. When the antecedent is highly active, the hearer or reader can readily access this in response to a pronoun, even though the degree of overlap between the name and the pronoun is quite low. But when the antecedent is less accessible to start with, then the speaker might need to rely on an anaphor that has a great deal of overlap with the antecedent (in the case of a repeated name, it'll be completely overlapping) so that the antecedent becomes active enough for the linking to take place.

A memory-based account also offers a nice story for some less obvious findings: for example, consider the difference between these sentence pairs:

(a) A robin would sometimes wander into the house. The bird was attracted by the food in the pantry.

(b) A goose would sometimes wander into the house. The bird was attracted by the food in the pantry.

Reading times for the second sentence are typically faster for sequence (a) than for sequence (b) (Garrod & Sanford, 1977). This can be explained by the fact that, as a highly typical member of the bird category, a robin has more overlapping features with the concept of bird than does a goose.

Under the memory-based view, the activation of concepts is a highly automatic and "dumb" process—no higher-level goals come into play, and salient, strongly overlapping concepts become available for discourse integration without the need for any deliberate search through memory. The whole process is seen as a fairly passive one, much like the process of semantic priming in word recognition that you saw earlier in Chapter 7; there's nothing strategic about it, and it arises "for free" simply as a by-product of the connections that exist in memory.

The second class of theories, known as the **explanation-based view**, sees discourse processing as a much more goal-driven process. This view emphasizes the role of the reader as someone who is guided by an active search for meaning. It assumes: (1) that discourse can be processed differently depending on the reader's goals; (2) that the reader searches for a coherent interpretation of the text, looking for sensible connections between sentences but also for some overarching theme or purpose; and (3) that the reader's meaning representation is driven by an attempt to explain why certain entities and actions are mentioned in the text. Causal inferences, for example, come about because the reader tries to explain why two separate events have been mentioned—the cause-effect relationship is a reasonable hypothesis for this. But readers might also generate inferences about why the author chose a particular word over another (we'll talk more about this last variety of inference in Chapter 11).

Most researchers these days agree that both memory-based and goal-driven mechanisms are needed to give a full picture of what's involved in language comprehension, especially when it comes to reading. But there's still some disagreement about exactly which aspects of meaning-

explanation-based view of discourse processing Theoretical account of discourse processing that emphasizes the active role of the reader as engaged in goal-driven processes of interpretation. The meaning that a reader constructs is assumed to be informed by her particular goals, and her attempts to construct a coherent representation that will explain why certain entities and actions are mentioned in a text.

building are driven by fast-and-dumb memory processes as opposed to the more subtle goal-driven mechanisms.

For example, when linking an incoming concept to an existing one in memory, can readers use goal-driven processes to guide their search through memory so that only the most relevant ones are activated? Or are these smarter processes reserved for a later processing stage, where they help decide *which* of the already-activated concepts are relevant or irrelevant? There's some evidence that even irrelevant concepts are activated, providing support for the view that activation in memory is driven by an automatic resonance process. For example, Edward O'Brien and colleagues (1998) built little stories in which a certain concept (being a vegetarian) was connected in the text with a particular character (Mary). The researchers were interested in seeing whether linking this concept with Mary would cause problems when subjects later read a target sentence that seemed to be at odds with this trait (for example, *Mary ordered a cheeseburger and fries*). The hitch was that in one story, the trait of vegetarianism really was inconsistent with the target sentence (that is, Mary was truly a vegetarian in the story), whereas in the other, it was a decoy (the story included an episode in which a friend deceived others into *thinking* that Mary was a vegetarian). In both cases, the concept of vegetarianism should be associated in memory with the Mary character. But it's only in the first case that it's relevant to the question of what Mary might actually order—in the second, it has no bearing on Mary's choice of food. So, if the target sentence is connected back to earlier concepts through passive resonance, then readers should detect an inconsistency in both passages, which should be reflected in longer reading times compared with a control condition. But if a search through memory is constrained by information that's relevant to the target sentence, then readers should detect an inconsistency only in the first case, in which Mary was truly a vegetarian. These studies found that readers slowed down at the target sentence in both passages (compared with control passages). The authors of the study argue that this shows that concepts can become activated as candidates for discourse links even when they're irrelevant for a particular text.

There are some very practical concerns to all this. Having a good understanding of the continuum between deep and shallow processing and its relationship to processing effort would allow us to have a better idea of how rich and stable a meaning various readers might be able to construct from a text. Rather than simply assuming that all readers can make all the connections and inferences that the author intended, we'd have a better idea of what certain readers might realistically be able to get from reading a text.

Some important research has looked at what distinguishes strong readers from poor readers who seem to understand very little from complex texts. A very useful finding is that comprehension gaps often happen because readers fail to spontaneously use goal-driven reading strategies. This seems to be at least partly a matter of habit—it's not simply that these readers try to generate inferences as much as the strong readers but then run up against built-in limitations such as working memory. It turns out that explicitly training people to ask questions about elements in a text, or to query the author's purpose in presenting material in a certain way, can have some quite dramatic effects on comprehension (for a review, see McNamara & O'Reilly, 2009). Detailed research along these lines could really help in the development of effective reading instruction programs. And a better understanding of how inferences work could be extremely useful for authors of complicated texts, allowing them to consciously manipulate the amount of inferring that readers have to do, and to prompt readers to generate the most important questions that drive the critical inferences.

Finally, it probably shouldn't surprise you that sheer enjoyment of a text and the degree to which you find it absorbing can also have an impact on how deeply you process its meaning. In one interesting study, researchers Jessica Love and Gail McKoon (2011) looked at whether readers' engagement with a text caused them to resolve pronouns more fully. In some versions of the study, readers were made to read unexciting "stories" like this one:

> Rita and Walter were writing an article for a magazine. They had to get it done before next Tuesday. Rita edited the section that Walter had written and then (probe$_1$) she smoked a cigarette to relax. (probe$_2$)

Readers saw each word in the story presented for 250 milliseconds. They also had to respond to a memory probe in one of two positions, indicating whether a specific character had appeared previously in the story. For the critical trials, the probe occurred either just before the pronoun in the last sentence (at the position marked "probe$_1$"), or at the end of the story (probe$_2$), and was either the antecedent of the target pronoun (*Rita*) or the name of the other character in the story (*Walter*). The idea here is that resolving the pronoun *she* ought to reactivate *Rita*, so responses to *Rita* should be faster than responses to *Walter* at the probe$_2$ position, but not at the probe$_1$ position, before readers had seen the pronoun.

But Love and McKoon found that when readers were fed these insipid little stories, there was no evidence from the memory-probe measure that they had connected the pronoun to the character in the story (that is, there was no difference in responses to *Walter* versus *Rita* at either probe position), despite the fact that fully resolving this unambiguous pronoun would be very easy to do. The results changed, however, when the stories were spiced up with some added details:

Rita and Walter were writing an article for a magazine. They had to get it done before next Tuesday. Rita didn't trust Walter to get the facts right. Once, he'd written a piece about aliens landing in Chicago. "I'm going to get dragged down with you," Rita said at the time. However, neither of them had been fired. Rita edited the section that Walter had written and then (probe$_1$) she smoked a cigarette to relax. (probe$_2$)

For these versions, readers responded more quickly when probed with *Rita* versus *Walter*, but only in the second probe position, after seeing the triggering pronoun. This result suggests that in these stories, the pronoun had indeed successfully reactivated the antecedent character. Love and McKoon argued that this was because the readers found these longer stories to be more engaging—a notion that was supported by the readers' ratings of the stories. (An important follow-up experiment also showed that the results were not due simply to having repeated the characters' names more often in the longer stories—the same result turned up when the stories contained extra details that did not refer to the main characters.)

In short, as human beings, we can convey so much meaning with so little language. This is largely because of our capacity for connecting ideas, reading between the lines, and making intelligent guesses about intended meanings. These skills allows us to communicate far more meaning than we pack directly into the linguistic units we use to express ourselves. But not all of this impressive mental work in comprehension happens automatically and for free. The depth of our communicative experiences depends on a variety of factors that we have yet to understand—and likely varies quite a bit depending on the specific situation, our individual traits and knowledge base, and even the amount of pleasure we're getting from the experience.

PROJECT

A common complaint (mostly from older people) is that heavy Internet use and constant multitasking have trained a generation of shallow information processors—young people who are incapable of thinking or reading deeply. Is this true? Apply some of the experimental tools you've learned about in this chapter to the exploration of this controversial idea. Design your study with the aim of tackling a specific hypothesis that you formulate. You might want to consider variables such as age, patterns of Internet use, and individual differences in working memory or reading strategies.

11 The Social Side of Language

The film *Thirteen Days* portrays the efforts of President John F. Kennedy and his staff to deal with the 1962 Cuban Missile Crisis. With the Cold War at its chilliest, the Americans have learned that Soviet missiles have been installed in Cuba, within easy striking range of many U.S. cities. Kennedy needs to apply pressure on the Soviets to force them to withdraw their missiles. But he's trying *not* to respond in an overly aggressive way that might be interpreted by the Soviets as an intent to go to war, thereby triggering a full-scale nuclear confrontation. Kennedy's first move is to declare a blockade of all Soviet ships headed to Cuba. In a later scene of the film, several Soviet ships have crossed the blockade lines, and Secretary of Defense Robert McNamara learns that one of the admirals under Kennedy's command has taken it upon himself to fire blank warning shots above one of the offending ships. McNamara yells at the admiral that he is not to fire unless directly ordered by the president. The admiral replies that he's been running blockades for decades and knows how it's done. McNamara explodes: "You don't understand a thing, do you admiral? This is not a *blockade*. This is *language*. A new vocabulary, the likes of which the world has never seen. This is President Kennedy *communicating* with Secretary Khrushchev!"

At first glance, it might seem that the mutual messages Kennedy and Khrushchev are sending here are very *unlike* what happens when people use conventional language to communicate. Most of the time, people don't communicate by relying on subtle signals encoded in the movement of ships and the presence or non-presence of gunfire. The whole point of having language would seem to be to make such mind-reading feats unnecessary. After all, isn't meaning precisely and conveniently packaged up in the language? Linguistic communication, one might argue, doesn't require mind reading, just straightforward information processing to decipher a code that maps forms fairly directly to meanings.

For the most part, this book has focused on how humans learn and process the linguistic code. We've discussed the mechanisms that allow people to transmit linguistic information, or decode it, or discover its patterns and generalizations, all under the assumption that language form and meaning are intrinsically connected. From this angle, the problem of recovering meaning from language is very similar to the problem of interpreting, say, a visual scene, or deciphering musical patterns. In all of these cases, information that hits our senses has to be processed and structured into sensible representations before we can recognize specific objects, make sense of a chord progression, or figure out what a sentence means.

Except it's a bit misleading to talk about "what a sentence means." When you really think about it, words and sentences don't convey meanings—*people* do, by *using* certain words and combining them into sentences. This might seem like a distinction without a difference until you consider just how often people bend language to their will and manage to convey messages that are very remote from the usual meanings of the words or sentences that they're using. A waitress might communicate a customer's complaint to the kitchen staff by "The steak sandwich says his meat was overcooked," using the phrase *the steak sandwich* to refer not to the food itself, but to the person who ordered it. Or, a person might ask the object of his affections, "Do you feel like having dinner sometime?" This is usually understood as an invitation to go out on a date, and not as a question about whether the other person is likely to ever be inclined to eat food in the evening. Or, a boss might describe her employee metaphorically, saying "That guy's my best worker. He's a bulldozer." And, if you've ever resorted to sarcasm ("I'm *really* looking forward to my exam this afternoon"), you probably figured that your hearer could work out that what you really meant was pretty much the exact opposite of the usual meaning of the language you used.

In all of these cases, communicating through language seems to come a lot closer to the problem that Kennedy was trying to solve. The question is not "What does this bit of language mean?" but instead, "What is the speaker trying to communicate by using this particular bit of language in this situation?" In other words, the hearer has to hoist herself into the speaker's mind and guess his intended message, using the language he's uttered as a set of clues.

It might seem that all this sophisticated social cognition is restricted to a smattering of instances of language use—those unusual cases where a speaker's intended meaning has somehow become disconnected from the inherent meanings of the language he's recruited. But the bigger point here is that there *are* no inherent meanings in language, even when we're talking about its more "fixed" aspects. The only reason there's a connection between specific sounds and specific meanings is that this connection has been socially sanctioned. In this way, language is deeply different from many other kinds of information processing that we do. When it comes to visual perception, for instance, the array of lines, shadows, and colors that we have to interpret is intrinsically related to the real-world objects that we're perceiving. But there's no intrinsic connection between the sounds in the word *dog* and the thing in the world it refers to—its meaning comes entirely from the fact that a bunch of people within a common linguistic community have tacitly agreed to use that word for that thing. That same group of people can also agree to invent new words for new meanings, like *Internet*, or *mitochondria*—and subgroups can agree to appropriate existing words for new meanings, so words like *wicked*, *sick*, and *cool* can mean completely different things, depending on who's saying them and in what context.

So for language, unlike for many kinds of perception, our interpretation of the stimuli doesn't derive from the laws of physics and biology. Instead, it's mediated by social conventions, or agreements to use certain words and structures for certain meanings. It's hard to imagine that someone could possibly be a competent user of language without having a deep grasp of these social underpinnings of language. In fact, as you'll soon see, it's common for conversational partners to spend a fair bit of time in everyday conversation negotiating the appropriate language to use.

None of the above is especially controversial among language scientists. Where the disagreements bubble up is over the question of *how much* active social cognition takes place under the time pressures of normal conversation or reading. In other words, how much of language use is straightforward decoding and how much of it looks like mind reading, *Thirteen Days* style? Once we've learned the conventional, socially sanctioned links between language and meaning, it seems that we should be able to use them as efficient shortcuts to the speaker's intended meaning, allowing us to bypass the whole business of having to put ourselves inside his mind. For instance, when someone uses the word *dog,* we should be able to activate the mental representation of a four-legged domestic canine without asking ourselves, "Now, what is the speaker trying to convey by using this word?" At the same time, there's no guarantee that the speaker's intended meaning lines up neatly with the conventional meaning of the language he's chosen to use, so some monitoring of his communicative intentions would certainly be useful. And from the speaker's perspective, having a sense of the *hearer's* knowledge or assumptions could be useful in deciding exactly how to express an idea.

For some researchers, mind-reading capabilities are absolutely central to how language works and are part of the core skills of all language users in all situations. To others, these capabilities are more like icing on the cake—extremely useful to have in many situations, handy in avoiding or clarifying miscommunications, but not always critical for bread-and-butter language use. This chapter explores some ideas about the extent to which we track one another's mental states in the course of normal language learning, production, and comprehension.

WEB ACTIVITY 11.1

Communication lapses   In this activity, you'll keep a journal log of various communication failures or misunderstandings that you observe or are involved in. You'll try to identify the origin of each misunderstanding. Was it based on a problem in deciphering the linguistic code—that is, mishearing words or misparsing sentences—or did it involve something that could be described as a failure of mind reading, either on the speaker's or the hearer's part?

11.1 Tiny Mind Readers or Young Egocentrics?

How entwined is language learning with social cognition?

Anyone who's locked eyes with a 5-month-old baby on a bus or in a grocery store checkout line has experienced the eagerness of human infants for social contact. From a very young age, babies demonstrate a potent urge to make eye contact with other humans, to imitate their facial expressions and actions, and to pay attention to objects that hold the attention of others. Long before they know any words, babies love to engage in "conversations" with adults, cooing and babbling in response to their caregivers' utterances. This remarkable degree of social attunement suggests that, right from the start, babies' learning of the linguistic code may be woven together with an appreciation of the social underpinnings of language and of speakers' goals and intentions. In previous chapters, we've discussed the close connection between social understanding and language: in Chapter 2 we explored the possibility that complex social cognition is a prerequisite for the development of language in a species, and in Chapter 5 we saw that children draw heavily on inferences about a speaker's referential intent in learning the meanings of words.

However, in spite of the strikingly social inclinations of very young babies, there's also evidence that it takes children quite a while to develop a sophisticated social understanding, and that in some ways, social cognition lags behind language development. At an age when children can speak in complex sentences and show mastery over many aspects of grammatical structure, they can still have a lot of trouble understanding the mental states of others. And when the language code collides with communicative intent, children tend to stick close to the language code for recovering meaning—metaphorical language or sarcasm are often completely lost on kids younger than seven or eight. These findings suggest that language learning may proceed somewhat independently of mind reading, and that it takes some time for the two to become well integrated.

In this section, we'll look closely at the relationship between children's emerging social cognition and language learning and use. What assumptions do young children make about speakers or hearers, and how do these assumptions shape their linguistic behavior? To what extent can children take into consideration evidence about their conversational partner's mental state?

Social interaction enhances language learning

Language exists for social purposes and arises in social contexts. But it also takes place in physical space as a series of auditory or visual signals. As amply documented in several of the previous chapters, these signals have a great deal of internal structure. In principle, it should be possible to learn something about how linguistic elements pattern without needing to project yourself into the mind of the speaker, or, for that matter, engage in social interaction at all. And in fact, there's evidence that babies can learn a great deal about language simply by being exposed to structured repetitions of a natural or artificial language, disembodied from any social communication. In Chapter 4 you saw that infants are able to learn to segment words and form phonemic categories based on the statistical regularities in prerecorded speech. In Chapter 6 I presented evidence that young children were able to use statistical information about co-occurring words to infer the grammatical categories of novel words. None of these studies involved communicative interaction—rather, the children were able to pick up on the statistical patterns present in input that was piped in through loudspeakers.

You also saw that other species of animals can pick up on regularities inherent in human speech. This too suggests that certain aspects of language learning may not require grasping that language is a socially mediated phenomenon. At some level, it's possible to treat the sounds of human language as just that—sounds whose structure can be learned with sufficient exposure.

Still, there's some intriguing evidence that even for these very basic and physically bound aspects of language learning, social interaction matters. Patricia Kuhl and her colleagues (2003) tested whether social interaction affected the ability of 9-month-olds to learn phonemic contrasts that don't occur in their native language. As you learned in Chapter 4, over the second half of their first year, babies adapt to the sound structure of their own language and "lose" the ability to easily detect contrasts between two sounds that are not phonemic in their own language (for example, English-reared babies become less responsive to the distinction between aspirated consonants like p^h and unaspirated consonants like p). Kuhl and her colleagues targeted monolingual American-raised infants at an age when they had already lost the distinction between certain contrasts that occur in Mandarin Chinese. They wanted to know: Could the American babies learn to pick up on the Mandarin sound contrasts? And would they learn better from a live speaker than from a video or audio recording?

In 12 sessions over a period of 4 to 5 weeks, a number of the babies interacted with native Mandarin speakers who read books to them and played with toys while speaking Mandarin in an unscripted, natural way. By the end of this period, they had clearly learned the Mandarin sound contrasts—in fact, their performance was indistinguishable from babies of the same age who had been raised in Taiwan and learned Mandarin as their native language.

This robust learning was all the more startling when compared with the abject failure of another experimental group of the same age to learn the Mandarin sounds. Just like the successful learners, this group was exposed to the same amount of Mandarin language, with the same books and toys, over the same period of time, uttered by the same native speakers of Mandarin. This time, however, the infants were exposed to the language through video, or just heard the same recording only on audio. There was no evidence of learning in either of these cases (see **Figure 11.1**). Mere exposure to the language was not enough. Learning only happened in the context of live interactions with a real speaker. This phenomenon, in which learning is enhanced through social interaction, is known as **social gating**.

Why was live social interaction so important for this task, when many other studies have shown that babies can learn certain sound patterns merely by

social gating The enhancement of learning through social interaction.

Figure 11.1 The effects of live interaction on speech perception. (A) Nine-month-old English-monolingual infants were exposed to Mandarin over 12 sessions either by interacting with a live speaker or via TV or audio-only exposure. A control group had live exposure to English only over 12 sessions. (B) Results from head-turn preference experiments show the babies' success in discriminating Mandarin sounds. In the left and middle panels, babies were tested after the training intervention. The right panel shows the performance of monolingual infants who did not receive any special training. (A from Kuhl, 2007; B from Kuhl et al., 2003.)

(A)

Live exposure

TV exposure

(B) Phonetic discrimination of Mandarin sounds

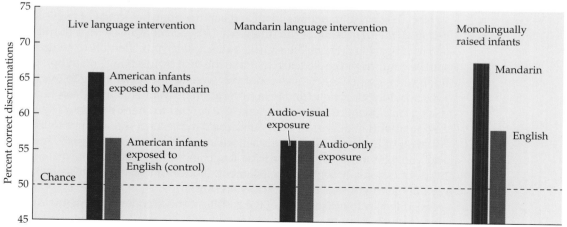

Age (10–12 months)

pedagogical stance A receptive mindset adopted by the learner in response to cues that signal that an interactive partner is intending to convey some new and relevant information.

listening to snippets of prerecorded speech? The researchers suggested that language learning in a child's natural habitat tends to be much more complex and variable than your typical artificial language experiment, which usually presents a sample of speech carefully designed to provide information about key statistical patterns. Hence, real language learning needs some additional support from social interaction. But what's the nature of this support? There are several possibilities.

One is that interacting with a live speaker simply caused the babies to pay more attention to the speaker and to be more motivated to learn from the speech input. In the experiments involving the Mandarin phonemes, there was evidence that babies were paying more attention to the speaker in the live interactions than in the videos, and they also became quite excited whenever the live speaker entered the room, more so than when the TV screen was switched on.

Another possibility is that the babies were able to pull more information out of the speech stream when interacting with a live speaker. In the live interaction, the babies had a richer set of cues about the speaker's referential intentions, which may have given them an advantage in identifying specific words. This would have helped them structure the speech stream in a more detailed way than they could without the strong referential cues, and in turn, this enriched structure would have helped them to figure out which sounds are used to make meaningful distinctions in Mandarin. Under this second interpretation, inferences about a speaker's intended meaning can indirectly shape even the most basic aspects of language learning, by providing additional information about how the speech stream should be carved up.

A third possibility is that the live interaction allowed the babies to adopt a special, highly receptive mindset because they recognized that the adult speaker was trying to *teach* them something. Researchers György Gergely and Gergely Csibra (2005) call this mindset the **pedagogical stance**. They argue that while other species of animals are capable of learning through social imitation, and even show evidence of social gating (see **Box 11.1**), only humans have evolved a special capacity to transmit information by means of focused teaching. When we slide into teaching mode, we instinctively adopt certain communication techniques that signal that we're trying to impart some knowledge that's new and relevant to our hearers. And according to Gergely and Csibra, human infants are able to instinctively recognize when someone is trying to teach them; once they see that the speaker is in teaching mode, they automatically assume that the information will be new and relevant, and focus their efforts on learning it quickly and efficiently.

Not all social interactions involve teaching. So, what kinds of cues signal a pedagogical act? Think of the difference between chatting with a friend while you're preparing a chocolate soufflé and *teaching* your friend how to make the soufflé. Your friend could learn to make the dish by imitating you in both cases, but he'd be more likely to succeed if you were deliberately trying to teach him. How would your actions and communication be different? In the teaching scenario, you'd be more inclined to make eye contact to check that your friend was paying attention at critical moments. You'd make a special attempt to monitor his level of understanding. Your actions might be exaggerated and repetitive, and you'd be more likely to provide feedback in response to your friend's actions, questions, or looks of puzzlement. Notice that many of these behaviors rely on having the learner physically present.

So, one way to make sense of the results of the Mandarin phoneme learning study, which demonstrated huge benefits of live social interaction, is that the babies were being exposed to a very particular kind of social interaction. The

BOX 11.1
Social gating is for the birds

You learned in Chapter 2 that, while non-human primates show very little talent for vocal imitation, this capacity is highly developed in songbirds. Like human speech (and unlike many primate vocalizations), birdsong has to be learned. If young birds are kept isolated from competently singing adult songbirds, they grow up to be abnormal singers. And, echoing the results of the study with human infants by Patricia Kuhl and her colleagues (2003), research with birds shows that song-learning requires more than just being able to *hear* the right sounds. Social interaction seems to be crucial.

When it comes to learning, the European starling (**Figure 11.2**) is an example of an intensely social species. If young starlings are kept separate from adult "tutors" but hear plenty of recorded adult birdsong, they fail to learn normally, even though they do pick up on some structural aspects of the birdsong (Chaiken et al., 1993). On the other hand, if provided with rich enough social interaction with human caretakers, they can even learn to imitate some human vocalizations (West & King, 1990). [Incidentally, parrots also need to interact with live humans in order to learn human speech sounds, as found by Irene Pepperberg (1997). So if your parrot swears, don't try to blame it on the TV.]

Figure 11.2 The European starling is also known as the common starling (*Sturnus vulgaris*).

Several studies highlight the influence of social relationships on song learning by European starlings, showing how social contact can be more important than hearing virtuoso singing. In a fascinating study led by Colline Poirier (2004), researchers created three different social conditions for young European starlings. In one group, young birds were housed in aviaries with adults; in a second group, young birds of the same age were housed together; and in a third group, young birds were kept isolated from any other birds. Regardless of their social circumstances, all the birds heard the same adult song, because the sounds from the first group (which included the adult birds) were picked up by microphone and piped in to the living quarters of the second and third groups.

The researchers found that birds raised together with their peers had larger song repertoires than the birds who lived alone. But the songs of these peer-group raised birds reflected less copying of structures from the adult song that was piped in, and they seemed to pay less attention to what came over the speakers. The presence of a live playmate appeared to reduce the birds' motivation to learn the well-formed adult songs that were coming over the loudspeakers.

A subsequent study (Cousillas et al., 2008) showed that even when a live adult tutor was available in the social environment, the songs of young female starlings reflected their preferred social relationships. Female starlings have a strong propensity to form same-sex bonds, and tend to copy the songs of adult females but not males. In this study, the young female starlings were raised in groups with peers and only male adults. The young females didn't establish close social bonds with the males, nor did they copy their songs, despite their presence as potential role models. Their vocal learning was restricted to the songs they shared with their inexperienced peers—a result that may strike some fathers of adolescent girls as poignantly familiar. In fact, when the scientists studied the brain responses of these birds to recordings of birdsong, they found abnormalities that resembled those of birds who were kept entirely separate from adult tutors. Voluntary social segregation had effects that were similar to physical separation.

infants probably got many cues that signaled a teaching interaction, and as a result they adopted a focused pedagogical stance to the language input that they were hearing.

Csibra and Gergely argue that the pedagogical stance doesn't require babies to make any sophisticated inferences about the speaker's state of mind or communicative intentions. Rather, they see it as an instinctive response to behaviors that human adults display when they're purposefully trying to impart their knowledge. They suggest that these behaviors automatically trigger the infant's default assumption that the adult is in possession of relevant knowledge that he's trying to share. Eventually, children may have to learn that not everyone who exhibits these behaviors actually *is* knowledgeable, or is demonstrating knowledge that is relevant or new.

Evaluating the reliability of speakers

The next stop on our tour of the social cognition of young language users is the child who's trying to learn the conventional meanings of words. As you saw in Section 5.3, children are often reluctant to map a word onto a meaning without some good evidence that the speaker meant to use that word for a particular purpose. For clues, they pay attention to the speaker's eye gaze or other behavior to identify the object of the speaker's referential intent.

But as a youngster absorbed in the task of word learning, you might be well advised to do more than just look for signs of referential intent. A speaker might be utterly purposeful in using the word *dax* to refer to a dog, and she might well display this intent for all to see. But that doesn't mean that the word she uses is going to match up with what other speakers within your linguistic community agree to call the furry creature. Maybe she speaks another language. Maybe she doesn't know the right word. Maybe she's pretending, or even lying. Or maybe she's insane. Perhaps you should approach such interactions with a grain of skepticism, in light of the fact that the speaker may not always be a reliable source of linguistic information. Naturally, knowing something about the speaker's underlying knowledge or motivations would be helpful in deciding whether to adopt this new word.

But what evidence would you look for to figure out whether the speaker can be trusted as a teacher of words in the language you're trying to acquire? Assessing the speaker's reliability seems to involve a level of social reasoning that's a notch or two more sophisticated than simply looking for clues about referential intent. Nevertheless, an impressive array of studies shows that preschoolers, and perhaps even toddlers, do carry out some sort of evaluation in deciding whether or not to file away in memory a word that's just been used by an adult in a clearly referential act.

Mark Sabbagh and Dare Baldwin (2001) created an elaborate scenario in which they established one speaker as clearly knowledgeable about the objects she was referring to, while a second speaker showed evidence of uncertainty. In this scenario, a 3- or 4-year-old child heard a message recorded on an answering machine from a character named Birdie, who asked the experimenter to send her one of her toys, which she called a "blicket." Birdie's collection of "toys" consisted of a set of weird, unfamiliar objects. Half of the children interacted with an experimenter who claimed to be very familiar with these objects. This speaker told the child, "I've seen Birdie play with these a lot. I'll show you what this does. I've seen all these toys before." This "expert" then proceeded to demonstrate how to play with Birdie's toys. In response to Birdie's request for the blicket, this experimenter confidently announced, "You know, I'd really like to help my friend Birdie, and I know just which one's her blicket. It's this one."

The experimenter asked the child to put the blicket into a "mailbox," saying, "Good, now Birdie will get her blicket."

The other half of the kids interacted with an experimenter who acted much less knowledgeable. Upon hearing Birdie's request, she said, "You know, I'd really like to help my friend Birdie, but I don't know what a blicket is. Hmm." While playing with Birdie's toys, she said, "I've never seen Birdie play with these. I wonder what this does. I've never seen these toys before." She played with the toys quite tentatively, and pretended to "discover" their function while manipulating them. Finally, she told the child, touching the same object that the "expert" speaker had, "Maybe it's this one. Maybe this one's her blicket. Could you put it in the mailbox to send to Birdie?" When the child complied, the experimenter said, "Good, now maybe Birdie will get her blicket."

In both of these experimental conditions, the children heard the experimenter use *blicket* to refer to the same object exactly the same number of times. The question was whether the preschoolers would be more willing to map the word to this object when the speaker claimed to know what she was talking about than when she was unsure. In the test phase, both the older and the younger children were more likely to produce the word *blicket* to refer to the target object if they'd heard the word from the "expert" speaker, and both groups were also more likely to identify the correct object from among the others when asked to pick out the blicket.

Since this initial study, a steady stream of experiments have looked at other cues that kids might use when sizing up the speaker's credibility. For instance, children seem to figure that a good predictor of future behavior is past behavior: they take into account whether the speaker has previously produced the right labels for familiar objects like a rubber duck or a shoe; if the speaker has offered up something other than the words *duck* and *shoe*, children are less eager to embrace her subsequent labels of unfamiliar objects (see, e.g., Koenig and Harris, 2005).

It's hard to know, though, whether children's evaluations of a speaker's credibility are truly rational, based on assessing what speakers *know*, and making predictions on that basis. Sure, it's logical to conclude that someone who expresses uncertainty about their knowledge, or someone who's behaved unreliably in the past, is more likely to be an unreliable communicator. But we want to be careful not to attribute more knowledge and sophistication to children's behavior than the data absolutely indicate. Are kids really reasoning about what speakers know (not necessarily consciously), or does their distrust of certain speakers reflect more knee-jerk responses to superficial cues? For example, preschoolers are also more reticent in accepting information from people who are simply unfamiliar, or who have a different accent or even different hair color than themselves. There are still a lot of questions about how children weight these various cues at different ages, and just how flexibly they adapt their evaluations, as one might expect of a fully rational being, in the face of new, predictive information about a speaker.

Still, there's quite strong evidence that in many communicative situations, even very young kids make accurate inferences about the mental states of others. In a 2007 study by Henrike Moll and Michael Tomasello (2007), 14- and 18-month-old children interacted with an adult, with adult–child pairs playing together with two objects. The adult then left the room while the toddler played with a third, novel object. When the adult returned, she pointed in the general direction of all of the objects and exclaimed with excitement, "Oh, look! Look there! Look at that there!" She then held out her hand and requested, "Give it to me, please!" It seems that even 14-month-olds know that excitement like this is normally reserved for something new or unexpected. More impressively, the child subjects seemed to be able to transport themselves into the adult's head and work out which object was new to the adult. All three toys were familiar to the children; nevertheless, they handed over the new-to-the-adult item more often than either of the two objects that the adult had played with earlier.

Limits to children's mind-reading abilities

Studies like those by Moll and Tomasello point to very early mind-reading abilities in children and, as discussed in Chapter 2, a number of researchers have argued that humans are innately predisposed to project themselves into each other's minds in ways that our closest primate cousins can't. But these stirring demonstrations of young tots' empathic abilities seem to contradict the claims of many researchers who have emphasized that children are strikingly *egocentric* in their interactions with others, often quite oblivious of others' mental states.

Indeed, anyone who's ever interacted with very young children can be struck by their lack of ability to appreciate another person's perspective or emotional state. It seems they constantly have to be reminded to consider another person's feelings. When they choose gifts for others, they often seem to pick them based on their own wish lists, oblivious to the preferences and needs of others. And they do sweetly clueless things like play hide-and-seek by covering their faces, assuming that if they can't see you, you can't see them, or they nod their heads to mean yes while talking on the phone, seemingly unaware that the listener can't see them.

The famous child psychologist Jean Piaget argued that it's not until at least about the age of seven that children really appreciate the difference between their own perspective and that of others. This observation was based partly on evidence from what's now known as the "three mountains study," which involved placing children in front of a model of a mountain range, while the experimenter sat himself on the opposite side of it and asked the young subjects to choose one photo from among a set that best depicted his own viewpoint rather than the child's (Piaget & Inhelder, 1956). Before the age of seven, most kids simply guess.

It seems that Piaget overestimated children's egocentrism, partly because his experiments required kids to be able to do some fairly fancy visual transformations in their heads rather than simply show awareness that another person's viewpoint could differ from theirs. Many other studies since then have found that kids can take another person's perspective or knowledge into account at a much younger age if the task is simple enough.

It's now established that well before the age of seven—in fact at around the age of four—most kids show a clear ability to reason about the mental states of others, as evident by their ability to handle a tricky setup known as a **false belief test**. There are several variants of this basic task, but a common one goes like this: A child is shown a familiar type of box that normally contains a kind of candy called "Smarties." She's asked to guess what's inside, and not surprisingly, kids usually recognize the box and say "Smarties." The experimenter then opens the box to show the child that—alas!—the box contains pencils, not candy. Then the experimenter asks the child what another person, who had not witnessed this interaction, would think was inside the box. At age three, children tend to say "pencils," seemingly unable to shift themselves back into the perspective of someone who saw only the outside of the box. But by four or five, they tend to say that the other person will be fooled into thinking it contains Smarties. To use the terminology of developmental psychologists, success on the false belief task provides solid evidence that children have

false belief test A test intended to probe for the ability to recognize that the mental state of another person can be different from one's own. In the typical false belief test, the subject learns some new information that has the effect of altering a previous belief. The subject is then asked to report on the belief state of another person who has not been privy to the new information.

acquired a **theory of mind** (**ToM**)—that is, an understanding that people have mental states that can be different from one's own.

Still, although small children show signs of early sensitivity to the intentions and even the knowledge of others, they're far from adult-like when it comes to using this knowledge to solve potential problems of communication. This can be seen by using a common type of experimental setup known as a **referential communication task** (see **Method 11.1**). In this paradigm, the subject usually plays a communication "game" with an experimenter (or, in some cases, a secret experimental confederate who the subject believes is a second subject, but who is really in cahoots with the experimenter and follows a specific script). The game involves a set of objects that are visible to the speaker and hearer, and the speaker has to refer to or describe certain target objects in a way that will be understood by the hearer. The array of objects can be manipulated to create certain communication challenges.

It turns out that children can be quite bad at communicating effectively with their partners in certain referential contexts. In one study by Werner Deutsch and Thomas Pechmann (1982), children played the speaker role, and had to tell an adult partner which toy from among a set of eight they liked best as a present for an imaginary child. The toys varied in color and size, and the set included similar items, so in order to unambiguously refer to just one of them, the child had to refer to at least two of its properties. For example, a large red ball might be included in a set that also contained a small red ball and a large blue ball, so simply saying "the ball," or "the red ball," or "the big ball" would not be enough for the partner to unambiguously pick out one of the objects. So, to successfully refer, the kids had to recognize that a hearer's attention wasn't necessarily aimed at the same object that they were thinking of, and they had to be alert to the potential ambiguity for their partner.

But preschoolers were abysmal at using descriptions that were informative enough for their hearers: at the age of three, 87% of their descriptions were inadequate, failing to provide enough information to identify a unique referent. Things improved steadily with age, but even by the age of nine, kids were still producing many more ambiguous expressions (at 22%) than adults in the same situation (6%). Their difficulty didn't seem to be in controlling the *language* needed to refer unambiguously, because when their partner pointed out the ambiguity by asking "Which ball?" they almost always produced a perfectly informative response on the second try. It's just that they didn't always seem to be spontaneously aware of the comprehension needs of the hearer.

We can get an even clearer idea of the extent to which kids are able to take their partner's perspective by looking at referential communication experiments that directly play around with the visual perspective of each partner, as discussed in Method 11.1. In these studies, the child and adult interact on opposite sides of a display case that's usually set up so that the child can see more objects than the adult can. The nature of the communication task shifts depending on which objects are in common ground (visible to both partners) versus privileged ground (visible only to the child). For instance, if there are two balls in common ground, it's not enough for the speaker to just say "the ball"; but if one of the balls is in the speaker's privileged ground, it is, because from the hearer's perspective, this phrase is perfectly unambiguous. Conversely, suppose the hearer sees two balls, but one of these is in privileged ground so that the speaker only sees one; in this case, if the speaker says "Point to the ball," this should be perfectly unambiguous to the hearer, assuming she's taking her partner's perspective into account. However, the instruction would be completely ambiguous if both balls were in common ground.

theory of mind (ToM) The ability to grasp the nature of mental states such as beliefs, knowledge, and intentions, and to recognize that different people may have different mental states under different conditions.

referential communication task An experimental task in which speakers refer to a specific target object in the context of a number of other objects. The method may be used to probe the behavior of either speakers or hearers. Speakers are faced with the task of choosing a linguistic expression that successfully distinguishes the target object from the other objects that are present. Hearers are required to successfully identify the target object based on the speakers' choice of linguistic expression. The task may vary the nature of the objects that are present, the linguistic descriptions of the objects, or various aspects of the interactive context.

METHOD 11.1

Referential communication tasks

One of the most basic aspects of communication is the ability to successfully refer to things in the world, and to understand other people when they refer. But successful reference involves more than just producing a description that fits the object in question; the description also has to single out that object from among others that might be present or relevant, so the choice of linguistic expression is very context-dependent.

In order to see whether children can adapt to the appropriate context, either in producing or in understanding referring expression, a referential communication task is often used. This involves a communication game with objects in a visual array—these objects might be real things on a tabletop or in a display case, or they might be pictures on a computer screen. The game requires the speaker to refer to a particular object in a way that allows the hearer to identify it. Sometimes, the game is set up so that the speaker has to tell the hearer to move specific objects around to new locations in order to end up with a different arrangement. Sometimes the speaker simply has the hearer pick up or point to a specific object. The complexity of the game often depends on the age of the children that are to be tested, and is chosen to be within their capabilities but not overly boring.

The purpose of this method is to allow the experimenter to manipulate the visual displays in order to see how this affects the subject's production or comprehension of referring expressions. The array of non-referent objects can be manipulated to create certain communication challenges, and for an added twist, it can be set up so that the speaker and hearer don't see exactly the same objects. The task can be reversed so that the subject is the hearer, responding to specific descriptions spoken by an experimenter or confederate—or, both the speaker and the hearer can be bona fide subjects. This method allows researchers to collect multiple measures—when the experimental subjects are in the speaker role, researchers are usually interested in which linguistic expressions they produce across various conditions. For hearers, the measures of interest can be their responses in terms of which objects they choose. In many cases, the eye movements of hearers or speakers (or even both) are monitored and analyzed.

Figure 11.3 shows an example of two visual arrays from a simple referential communication task. In this example, the child subject is the speaker, and the adult is the hearer. The two arrays are set up in a way that forces different solutions for successful reference. In Figure 11.3A, there's just one ball, so the child could effectively describe the target referent simply by saying "the ball." But in Figure 11.3B, there are two balls, so the child has to include some

Figure 11.3 A simple referential task in which the child verbally instructs the adult to pick up a particular target object (the red ball with stripes). Different amounts of information must be included for unambiguous reference. (A) The simple phrase *the ball* is sufficient to unambiguously identify the target referent. (B) The context requires the child to specify additional information, such as the color, markings, or location of the target referent.

additional information about the ball—in this case, she could choose to focus either on the color of the ball, the fact that it has stripes, or its spatial location. The specific choice of referring expression can be very revealing to researchers.

Figure 11.4 shows a more complex setup, in which the visual perspectives of the game partners are different. Here, the child subject is the hearer, and the adult is the speaker. In the visual arrangement illustrated here, the child can see two glasses, one small and one large. However, the adult can see only one. Only the larger glass is in the "common ground," which includes information shared by both partners; the smaller glass is in the child's "privileged ground." From the adult's perspective, it is sufficient to describe the target object as "the glass." But in order for the child to successfully interpret this referring expression, he has to become aware of the fact that the speaker can see only one glass, and hence only the glass visible to the speaker is a viable referent, despite the fact the "the glass" is ambiguous from the child's perspective.

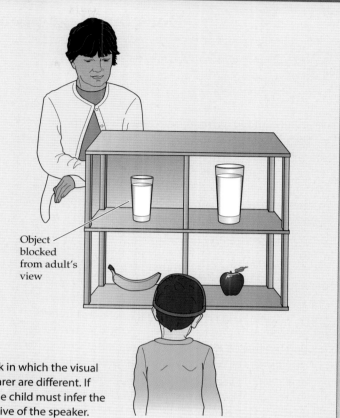

Object blocked from adult's view

Figure 11.4 A referential communication task in which the visual perspectives of the adult speaker and child hearer are different. If the adult says to the child "Pick up the glass," the child must infer the intended referent based on the visual perspective of the speaker.

Studies along these lines have shown that as early as three or four, kids show some definite sensitivity to their partner's perspective, both in the expressions they produce, and in their comprehension as hearers (Nadig & Sedivy, 2002; Nilsen & Graham, 2009). But they're not as good at it as adults are, and there are hints that when it comes to linguistic interactions like these, kids may be more egocentric than adults as late as adolescence (Dumontheil et al., 2010). So, the general conclusion seems to be that while many of the ingredients for mind reading are present at a very young age, it takes a long while for kids to fully hone this ability—longer, even, than it takes them to perfectly acquire some of the most complex aspects of syntax.

This raises the question of what it is that has to develop in order for mind-reading abilities to reach full bloom. There are likely several answers to that. One factor in kids' shortcomings is whether the task requires them to keep track of very simple representations in their partners' minds, or very complex ones. For instance, Piaget's early experiments hinged on children's being able to represent very detailed and complex aspects of visual scenes. When kids merely have to keep track of *which* objects their partner can see, rather than exactly what they look like to their partner, they're able to do this at a much earlier age. The same likely goes for tracking simple versus more complex mental states.

Another important aspect, though, is that in order to be able to shift into the perspective or knowledge state of a partner, kids often have to ignore or sup-

BOX 11.2
Does language promote mind reading?

Being able to tune in to the internal mental and motivational states of others is clearly a handy skill to have in the process of learning a language, as we've seen in this section and earlier chapters. It may help to explain why many autistic children, who have serious impairments in their mind-reading abilities, also often show delays and difficulties with language.

But the relationship between language and mind reading may also work the other way around: language may be helpful in honing an awareness of the mental states of others. Emerging evidence supports this idea. For example, Brenda Schick and her colleagues (2007) report a study of deaf children in which they compare those born to deaf parents with others born to hearing parents. Deaf children whose parents are also deaf are at a distinct linguistic advantage; their parents already know sign language, and can communicate with them using a rich and complex language right from birth. But hearing parents and their deaf children often struggle to communicate in a common language, and children from these families usually develop language more slowly than their peers. Schick and colleagues found that the two groups also differed in their mind-reading skills: the deaf kids born to deaf parents outperformed the children from hearing parents on a false belief test. Moreover, a statistical analysis showed that it was language skills that predicted success on the false belief test, rather than the other way around. This suggests that language helps children to acquire a theory of mind.

Possibly the most intriguing study of how language contributes to a developing theory of mind comes from a study of Nicaraguan Sign Language (NSL) speakers by Jennie Pyers and Ann Senghas (2009). As you read in Chapter 2, NSL sprang up when the Nicaraguan government began educating deaf children together in a special school; what began as a gesturing system among the children flowered into a more elaborate conventional language. Since the language became progressively more complex with each cohort of speakers that moved through the school, it's possible to look at subgroups of speakers from different stages of the language's evolution. The earliest speakers have a much more rudimentary version of the language, compared with the later speakers.

Pyers and Senghas had two groups (early NSL cohorts versus later ones) perform a false belief task. They also tested to see how often the NSL speakers used mental state verbs like *think*, *know*, or *believe* in describing the events in some videos. The videos were designed to try to elicit these verbs by showing characters who acted in odd ways because of some mistaken beliefs. For example, in one video, a woman sat next to a table holding a glass of water; without her being aware of it, someone came and replaced the water glass with a vase of flowers, and a moment later the woman raised the vase to her lips to drink.

The researchers found that the younger speakers who'd been immersed in the more evolved version of the language had clearly benefited from the added linguistic complexity, compared with the older speakers who'd learned a more basic version of NSL. They used a higher proportion of mental state verbs, and did better on the false belief test. But the really interesting twist to the story showed up when the researchers went back to Nicaragua to test the two groups of subjects 2 years later. In those 2 years, the older group had acquired new language skills, as made evident by the fact that they now used as many mental state verbs as the younger group. They also had caught up to the younger group on their performance in the false belief test. A closer look at the data showed that all of the subjects who'd increased their mental state vocabulary passed the false belief test, but not the other way around. This suggests that the increase in vocabulary preceded the improvement in mind reading.

So what happened in that two-year period? Pyers and Senghas speculate that the younger group graduated and began socializing within the adult deaf community, coming into more contact with the older group of NSL speakers. As a result, the older group became exposed to the more complex variety of NSL spoken by the younger group—including an enhanced vocabulary to describe mental states.

It's not clear exactly why exposure to the more developed language might have improved the mind-reading abilities of older NSL speakers. One possibility is that once they had the tools to be able to talk about people's knowledge and beliefs, they spent more time talking about these topics, which may have focused their attention more on the mental states of others. Whatever the reason, though, the study offers a fascinating window into the evolving language of NSL, and shows that even adults with limited language and mind-reading skills need not stay stuck at that stage of development.

press their *own* perspective or knowledge. And as we've seen already in Section 8.6, children are especially bad at inhibiting a competing representation or response, whether this happens to be a lexical item that stirs up competitive activation, or the lure of a misleading syntactic interpretation for an ambiguous sentence fragment. All of these examples rely on highly developed cognitive control (also referred to as "executive function")—that is, the ability to flexibly manage cognitive processes and behavior in the service of a particular goal. Unfortunately, cognitive control follows a long and slow developmental path, and it's now well known that the regions of the brain that are responsible for its operation are also among the last to mature. So, many of children's egocentric tendencies may not be due to the fact that they're neglecting to consider their partner's perspective. Instead, it may be too hard for them to suppress the information that comes in from their own perspective. (For an interesting discussion on this topic, see Nilsen & Fecica, 2011; and Nilsen & Graham, 2009.)

What conclusions can we draw about how social cognition is woven together with children's learning of language? If we look back to a baby's first year, we can already see that real-life social interaction helps kids learn language. These early social effects, though, don't necessarily involve babies doing much mind reading to augment their learning—instead they may reflect heightened motivation in social situations, or automatic responses to situations in which adults show signs of being in a teaching mode. However, very early in the process of learning new words, babies show signs that they're interpreting a speaker's referential intent against some understanding of the specific experiences and knowledge state of that speaker. By about 3 years of age, they're selective about which speakers they learn from, favoring those who show evidence of reliably producing conventional labels for words. By four or five, they perform like adults on false belief tasks (see **Box 11.2** for evidence that language learning could help kids acquire the skills needed for these tasks). However, despite their apparent mind-reading abilities, kids don't always succeed in adapting to the perspective of their partners in complex communicative situations. In the next section, we'll discuss whether adults manage to consistently integrate social inferences with linguistic information, or whether for adults, too, social inferences are fragile in some circumstances.

WEB ACTIVITY 11.3

Resolving contradictory data In this activity, you'll be asked to consider the data from two seemingly conflicting studies, both involving referential communication tasks. One of the studies argues for very fluent perspective-taking abilities in young children, and the other for much starker limitations to this ability. Based on the discussion in this section, you'll compare the details of the experimental design of the two studies, and see if you can find a way to explain the apparent conflict.

11.2 Conversational Inferences: Deciphering What the Speaker Meant

Enriching the language code through implication

As I've already suggested, one of the great benefits of language is that it should eliminate the need for constant mind reading, since the linguistic code contains meanings that the speaker and hearer presumably agree upon. But in Chapter 10, I used up a lot of ink in describing many situations in which the linguistic code by itself was not enough to deliver all of the meaning that readers and hearers routinely extract from text or speech. Hearers have a knack for filling in the cracks of meanings left by speakers, pulling out much more precise or elaborate interpretations than are made available by the linguistic expressions themselves—which, as we've seen, can sometimes be pretty sparse or vague.

It turns out that a good bit of this meaning enrichment involves puzzling out what the speaker *intended* to mean, based on his particular choice of words.

Suppose you ask me how old I am, and I produce the spectacularly vague reply "I'm probably older than you." My vagueness *could* be due to the fact that I have trouble keeping track of my precise age, but it seems rather unlikely that I wouldn't have access to this information. A more plausible way to interpret my response is that I'm intending to let you know that my age is not open for discussion (and maybe you should apologize for asking). But this message strays quite far from the conventional meaning of my reply, and clearly it *does* require you to speculate about my knowledge and motivations. So, in this case, even though you can easily access the conventional meaning of the sentence that I've produced, you still need to do some mind reading to get at my intended meaning.

The well-known philosopher H. Paul Grice argued that reasoning about a speaker's intended meaning is something that is so completely woven into daily communication that it's easy to mistake our inferences about speakers' meanings for the linguistic meanings themselves. For example, what does the word *some* mean (as in *Some liberals approve of the death penalty*)? It's tricky to pin down, and if you took a poll of your classmates' responses, you'd probably get a number of different answers. But if your definition included the notion that *some* means "not many" or "not all" of something, Grice would argue that you're confusing the conventional meaning of the word *some* with an inferred conclusion about the most likely meaning that the speaker intended. In other words, the conventional meaning of *some* doesn't include the "not all" component. Rather, the speaker has used the word *some* to communicate—or imply— "not all" in this specific instance.

To see the distinction, it helps to notice that there are contexts where *some* is used in which the "not all" aspect of meaning doesn't seem to be present at all. (The sentence I gave you above was unfairly designed to make you jump to the conclusion that *some* means "not all," because that's the most likely speaker meaning of that sentence.) Imagine instead a detective investigating the cause of a suspicious accident. She arrives at the scene of the accident, and tells one of the police officers who's already there: "I'm going to want to talk to some of the witnesses." If the police officer lined up every single witness, it's doubtful that the detective would chastise him by saying, "I said *some* of the witnesses—don't bring me *all* of them." Here, the detective seems to have used *some* to mean "at least a few, and all of them if possible." By looking closely at how the interpretation of *some* interacts with the context of a sentence, Grice concluded that the linguistic code provides a fairly vague meaning, roughly "more than one." You can think of the linguistic code as providing the "hard" part of meaning in language, the part that's stable across contexts and is impossible to undo without seeming completely contradictory. For example, it sounds nonsensical to say "Some of my best friends like banjo music—in fact, none of them do." But you can more easily undo the "not all" aspect of the interpretation of *some*: "Some of my best friends like banjo music—in fact, they all do." The "not all" component seems to be part of the "soft" meaning of *some*, coming not directly from the linguistic code, but from inferences about what the speaker probably meant to convey.

Grice used the term **conversational implicature** to refer to the extra "soft" part of meaning that reflects the speaker's intended meaning over and above what the linguistic code contributes.

Grice suggested that making inferences about speaker meaning isn't limited to exotic or exceptional situations. Even in everyday, plain-vanilla conversation, hearers are constantly guessing at the speaker's intentions as well as computing the conventional linguistic meaning of his utterances. The whole enterprise hinges on certain shared core assumptions that communication is a purpose-

conversational implicature An aspect of the speaker's intended meaning that cannot be derived directly from the linguistic code, but must be inferred by the hearer on the basis of expectations about the speaker's probable communicative goals and behavior.

ful and cooperative activity in which (1) the speaker is *trying* to get the hearer to understand a particular message, rather than simply verbalizing whatever thoughts happen to flit through his brain without caring whether he's understood, and (2) the hearer is *trying* to interpret the speaker's utterances, guided by the belief that they're cooperative and purposeful.

Sometimes it's easier to see the force of these unspoken assumptions by looking at situations where they come crashing down. Imagine getting the following letter from your grown son:

> I am writing on paper. The pen I am using is from a factory called "Perry & Co." This factory is in England. I assume this. Behind the name Perry & Co. the city of London is inscribed; but not the city. The city of London is in England. I know this from my schooldays. Then, I always liked geography. My last teacher in that subject was Professor August A. He was a man with black eyes. There are also blue eyes and gray eyes and other sorts too. I have heard it said that snakes have green eyes. All people have eyes…

Something's gone awry in this letter. The text appears to be missing the whole point of why it is that people write letters in the first place. Instead of being organized around a purposeful message, it comes across as a brain dump of irrelevant associations. As it happens, the writer of this letter is an adult patient suffering from schizophrenia, which presumably affects his ability to communicate coherently (McKenna & Tomasina, 2008; the letter itself comes from the case studies of Swiss psychiatrist Egon Bleuler).

Once you know this fact, the letter seems a bit less puzzling. It's possible to suspend the usual assumptions about how speakers behave because a pathology of some sort is clearly involved. But suppose you got a letter like this from someone who (as far as you knew) had all of his mental faculties intact. Your assumptions about the purposeful nature of communication would kick in, and you might start trying to read between the lines to figure out what oblique message the letter writer was intending to send. Unless we have clear evidence to the contrary, it seems that we can't help but interpret a message through the lens of expectations about how normal, rational communication works. (See Language at Large 11.1 for some intriguing demonstrations of what happens when absurdist writers or artists befuddle their audiences by violating communicative norms, making their intended meaning very hard to recover.)

How do rational speakers behave?

Exactly what do hearers expect of speakers? Grice proposed a set of four **maxims of cooperative conversation**, which amount to key assumptions about how cooperative, rational speakers behave in communicative situations (see **Table 11.1**). These maxims are discussed in detail below.

MAXIM 1: QUALITY   Hearers normally assume that a speaker will avoid making statements that are known to be false, or for which the speaker has no evidence at all. Obviously, speakers can and do lie, but if you think back to the last conversation you had, chances are that the truthful statements far outnumbered the false ones. In most situations, the assumption of truthfulness is a reasonable starting point. Without it, human communication would be much less useful than it is. (For example, would you really want to spend your time

maxims of cooperative conversation
A set of communicative expectations that are shared by speakers and hearers regarding how speakers typically behave in order to be understood by hearers. The four maxims of Quality, Relation, Quantity and Manner are attributed to the philosopher H. P. Grice.

TABLE 11.1 Grice's "maxims of cooperative conversation"[a]

1. **Quality** If a speaker makes an assertion, he has some evidence that it's true. Patently false statements are typically understood to be intended as metaphorical or sarcastic.

2. **Relation** Speakers' utterances are relevant in the context of a specific communicative goal, or in relation to other utterances the speaker has made.

3. **Quantity** Speakers aim to use language that provides enough information to satisfy a communicative goal, but avoid providing too much unnecessary information.

4. **Manner** Speakers try to express themselves in ways that reflect some orderly thought, and that avoid ambiguity or obscurity. If a speaker uses a convoluted way to describe a simple situation, he's probably trying to communicate that the situation was unusual in some way.

---

[a]That is, mutually shared assumptions between hearers and speakers about about how rational speakers behave.

taking a course in which you regarded each of your instructor's statements with deep suspicion?) In fact, when a speaker says something that's blatantly and obviously false, hearers often assume the speaker's intent was to communicate something other than the literal meaning of that obviously false statement—perhaps the speaker was being sarcastic, or metaphorical.

MAXIM 2: RELATION   Hearers assume that a speaker's utterances are organized around some specific communicative purpose, and that speakers make each utterance relevant in the context of their other utterances. This assumption drives many of the inferences we explored in Chapter 10. Watch how meaning gets filled in for these two sentences: *Cathy felt very dizzy and fainted at her work. She was carried away unconscious to a hospital.* It's normal to draw the inferences that Cathy was carried away from her workplace, that her fainting spell triggered a call to emergency medical services, that her unconscious state was the result of her fainting episode rather than being hit over the head, and so on. But all of these rest on the assumption that the second sentence is meaningfully connected to the first, and that the two sentences don't represent completely disjointed ideas.

Adjacent sentences often steer interpretation, but inferences can also be guided by the hearer's understanding of what the speaker is trying to accomplish. For example, in the very first episode of the TV series *Mad Men*, adman Don Draper has an epiphany about how to advertise Lucky Strike cigarettes. Given that health research has just shown cigarette smoking to be dangerous (the show is set in the early 1960s), the tobacco company has been forced to abandon its previous ad campaign, which claimed its cigarettes were healthier than other brands. Don Draper suggests the following slogan: "It's toasted." The client objects, "But *everybody's* tobacco is toasted." Don's reply? "No. Everybody else's tobacco is poisonous. Lucky Strike's is toasted."

What Don Draper understands is that the *audience* can be counted on to imbue the slogan with a deeper meaning. Consumers will assume that if the quality of being toasted has been enshrined in the company's slogan, then it must be something unique to that brand. What's more, it must be something desirable, perhaps improving taste, or making the tobacco less dangerous. These inferences are based on the audience's understanding that the whole point of an ad is to convince the buyer why this brand of cigarettes is better than other brands. Focusing on something that all brands have in common and that doesn't make the product better would be totally irrelevant. Hence, the

LANGUAGE AT LARGE 11.1
Absurdity, intent, and meaning in art

Have you ever read a surreal story, or stood in front of a strange piece of art, and wondered, "But what is it supposed to *mean*?" You may even have felt irritated—I know someone who's prone to feeling actual rage after reading an avant-garde poem.

What's this unsettled (or even angry) feeling all about? At its heart, it reflects a failure to get at the intent of the writer or artist. You assume he must have had one. But the norms you've come to expect of the genre have been violated. You begin to suspect that the true intent of the artist was to confuse you, to alienate you, or make you feel dumb for not "getting" it. Dang it, the fellow just seems so deliberately … *uncooperative*.

When confronted with a clearly intentional product like a poem or a painting, we humans seem driven to pursue its intended meaning until we reach a satisfactory conclusion. When that doesn't happen, we exhibit some interesting reactions, as discovered by several social scientists who have made a career out of studying failures to recover meaning. For example, Travis Proulx, Steven Heine, and their colleagues have published a series of studies looking at how people responded to strange and unconventional art forms, including an absurdist story by Franz Kafka, a strange Monty Python parody, and the surreal painting *Son of Man* by René Magritte, which depicts a man wearing a bowler hat, his face obscured by a hovering green apple.

The researchers found that exposing people to bewildering art has some weird lingering effects. For example, people do better at finding the statistical patterns in a set of stimuli generated by an artificial grammar; they're more likely to feel aligned with their ethnic or national identity; they're more likely to say that a prostitute should be punished in a mock courtroom scenario. What do all of these effects have in common? According to Proulx and Heine (2010), these reactions all reflect a drive to reaffirm meaning when a sense of meaning has been threatened—whether that drive is expressed by finding patterns in abstract stimuli, valuing traditional identities, or aligning with cultural norms of acceptable behavior. The researchers argue that when a sense of coherence or meaning is undermined, people reach for whatever meaning structures are readily on hand to compensate for the unsettling experience. (Notice the irony: the sociopolitical impact of avant-garde art—not normally seen as a funding priority for right-of-center political groups—seems to be to trigger responses that are normally associated with a *conservative* world view.)

Now, Proulx and Heine construe the notion of "meaning" very broadly, far beyond our discussion of conventional linguistic meaning and speakers' intended meanings. Their research program consists of showing that various "meaning threats," whether achieved by a Kafka story or by getting people to think about their own mortality, are equivalent in terms of their effects on people's need to reaffirm meaning.

But their studies on absurdist art are relevant to our discussion here about communicative purpose, because the strange responses that people have to the absurdist art seem to vanish if they're given some clues about the intent of the creator. For instance, in one study, some readers who were given an absurd story were first informed that it was meant to be a joke, a Monty Python parody of adventure stories for young boys. But other readers were led to believe that they were about to read a classic adventure story for young boys—only the latter group showed any signs of "meaning threat" (Proulx et al., 2010).

This suggests that being able to connect an author's or artist's purpose to the way in which the work is implemented is essential, and that when the audience can't easily do this, the disorienting effect can ripple out in unexpected ways.

strong underlying assumption of relevance leads the audience to embellish the meaning of the slogan in a way that's wildly advantageous for the company.

If you think advertising techniques like this only turn up in TV fiction, consider what advertisers are really claiming (and hoping you'll "buy") when they tell you that their brand of soap floats, or that their laundry detergent has special blue crystals, or that their food product contains no additives. Inferences based on assumptions of quality and relevance likely spring from the hearer's curiosity about the speaker's underlying purpose. They allow the hearer to make sense of the question, "Why are you telling me this?" The next two conversational maxims that Grice described allow the hearer to answer the question, "Why are you telling me this *in this particular way*?"

MAXIM 3: QUANTITY   Hearers assume that speakers usually try to supply as much information as is needed to fulfill the intended purpose without delving into extra, unnecessary details. Obviously, speakers are sometimes painfully redundant or withhold important information, but their tendency to strive for optimal informativeness leads to certain predictable patterns of behavior. For example, in referential communication tasks, speakers try to provide as much information as the hearer needs to unambiguously identify a referent, so an adjective such as *big* or *blue* is tacked onto the noun *ball* more often if the hearer can see more than one ball. This is evident too in expressions like *male nurse* where the word *male* presumably adds some informational value—when's the last time you heard a woman described as a "female nurse"? This asymmetry reflects the fact that the speaker probably assumes that nurses are female more often than not and figures that it doesn't add much extra information to specify female gender.

From the hearer's perspective, certain inferences result from the working assumption that the speaker is aiming for optimal informativeness. Grice argued that this is why people typically assume that *some* means "not all," or "not most," or even "not many." The argument goes as follows: The conven-

LANGUAGE AT LARGE 11.2

On lying and implying in advertising

Advertising depends very heavily on implication to get its message across. I suspect there are several reasons for this. One is that implied messages in ads sometimes take quite a bit of work to figure out, which makes the ads much more involving and memorable for the audience, like a mental puzzle that needs to be solved. Another is that there's some evidence that when people have to infer a message, rather than simply decode it, they may be somewhat less skeptical of it.

Advertisers sometimes succumb to the temptation to *suggest* a message that's not really true. In the fictional *Mad Men* example you saw earlier, the Lucky Strike ad falsely implied that there was some unique advantage to toasting the tobacco for the brand's cigarettes, even though all cigarette tobacco is toasted. Many countries have regulations that prevent ads from making false claims about their products. Do these regulations extend to implied messages, or do they apply just to what ads state outright? And *should* deceptive implications be treated just the same as blatantly false assertions?

To many people, deception through implication is sneaky all right, but it doesn't feel quite the same as lying. Somehow, it seems that Lucky Strike would have committed a greater offense if they'd advertised their cigarettes by saying: "They're the only ones that are toasted, so they taste better." Yet, this is pretty much what's implied by the company's slogan "It's toasted."

From a psychologist's perspective, implied claims that are untruthful can be every bit as misleading as flat-out lies. In Chapter 10, you read about the classic experiments of Bransford and colleagues (1972) showing that once hearers build up a mental model by means of an inference, they can easily lose track of whether that information was actually present in the linguistic code. So, when they'd heard a pair of sentences like "The turtle was sitting on a log. The fish swam under the log," subjects misremembered the exact content, and often thought that they had heard "The fish swam under the turtle."

Several studies have shown that implied advertising claims can also be misremembered in the same way and that they are treated just like directly asserted claims. In one study, Alan Searleman and Helen Carter (1988) had their research subjects listen to mock commercials like this:

Tossing and turning again? Having trouble getting to sleep? Get a good night's sleep and feel refreshed in the morning. Buy DreamOn Sleeping Pills. The ones in the purple package.

tional meaning of *some* is compatible with "all," as well as "most" and "many." (The test: you can say without contradicting yourself "Some of my friends are blonde—in fact, many/most/all of them are.") Because *some* is technically true in such a wide range of situations, it's very vague (just as the vague word *thing* can be applied to a great many, well, things). If I were to ask you "How many of your friends are blonde?" and you answered "Some of them are," I could make sense of your use of the word *some* in one of several ways, including the following:

1. You used the vague expression *some* because that was all that was called for in this communicative situation, and you assumed that all I cared about was whether you had at least one blonde friend, so there was no need to make finer distinctions (in some contexts, this might be the case, but normally, the hearer would be interested in more fine-grained distinctions).

2. You used such a vague expression because, in fact, you didn't know how many of them were blonde (this seems unlikely).

3. You used the vague word *some* because you couldn't truthfully use the more precise words *many, most,* or *all.* Hence, I could conclude that only a few of your friends, and not many, or most, or all, were blonde. This line of reasoning can be applied any time a vague expression sits in a scalar

---

LANGUAGE AT LARGE 11.2 (*continued*)

After hearing the commercials, the subjects were asked to judge the truth or falsity of statements like this:

> DreamOn Sleeping Pills will make you get a good night's sleep and feel refreshed in the morning.

Now, that's not what the commercial *said*, as you'll see if you go back and re-read it. But did the subjects behave as if they had actually heard this claim? When they were tested immediately after hearing the commercial, they were somewhat less likely to accept the statement as true if it was implied, as above, than if it was directly stated. But that difference vanished within 5 minutes; if there was a short delay between hearing the commercial and responding to the test sentences, subjects accepted the implied claims as true just as often as the directly stated claims.

A series of studies like these dating back to the 1970s robustly confirms that as far as their impact on consumers' memories and beliefs, there's no clear difference between stated versus implied claims. So where do the regulatory organizations sit on the issue? In the United States, advertising is overseen by the Federal Trade Commission (FTC). In its policy statement on deception in advertising (www.ftc.gov/bcp/policystmt/ad-decept.htm), the FTC very explicitly states that claims that are "likely to mislead" are not permitted, and this includes implied claims as well as directly stated ones. As the policy statement makes

clear, in deciding whether the message is likely to mislead, the FTC has the right to consider "an evaluation of such factors as the entire document, the juxtaposition of various phrases in the document, the nature of the claim, and the nature of the transactions"—in other words, the entire context of the communicative exchange. In defending this broad approach to defining deception in advertising, the FTC cites a decision by a court of appeals, which stated: "Without this mode of examination, the Commission would have limited recourse against crafty advertisers whose deceptive messages were conveyed by means other than, or in addition to, spoken words."

Looks like Don Draper will need to think of another slogan for Lucky Strike cigarettes.

WEB ACTIVITY 11.5

Implication in advertising In this activity, you'll have the opportunity to see a large variety of commercial ads whose main messages are conveyed through implication, rather than by claims that are directly stated. You'll discuss what's involved in understanding the intended meanings, and why this indirect approach might be more effective than a more direct one.

BOX 11.3
Examples of scalar implicature

A number of implicatures follow a common pattern. For example:

I like some kinds of pies.
Implies: I don't like all kinds of pies.

It's possible that the Red Sox will win the World Series.
Implies: It's not likely that the Red Sox will win the World Series.

Your essay was adequate.
Implies: Your essay was not excellent.

Sex between Fiona and Gary was pleasant.
Implies: Sex between Fiona and Gary wasn't fantastic.

The latest Dan Brown novel is interesting.
Implies: The latest Dan Brown novel isn't riveting.

In all of these cases, the speaker of the sentence has chosen to use a vague or weak scalar expression rather than a stronger one. Here's a useful way to think about which expression is stronger or weaker: *all* is stronger than *some* because if it's true that I like all kinds of pies, then it's automatically true that I like some kinds of pies (even though it would be incomplete to *express* the notion using the word *some*). But the reverse is not the case—if it's true that I like some pies, then it may or may not be true that I like them all. You can see a similar one-way relation between all the pairs of relevant words in the examples above: <*possible, likely*>, <*adequate, excellent*>, <*pleasant, fantastic*>, <*interesting, riveting*>.

The common structure in all of these examples of implicature is that in choosing the weaker word from each pair, the speaker is probably conveying that the stronger word of the pair is not true. In Section 11.2, I've sketched out a Gricean explanation suggesting how a hearer might understand the speaker's intended meaning by reasoning about the motivations that underlie the speaker's choice of words. But in Digging Deeper at the end of this chapter, we'll explore an alternative explanation in which hearers compute the implicature more directly from their knowledge of the word meanings of scalar expressions and the relations among them, without necessarily getting inside the speaker's head to guess at his meaning.

relation to other, more precise words, yielding what language researchers call a **scalar implicature** (see **Box 11.3**).

MAXIM 4: MANNER Hearers typically assume that speakers use reasonably straightforward, unambiguous, and orderly ways to communicate. For instance, speakers normally describe events in the order in which they happened—so the speaker is probably conveying quite different things by saying "Sam started hacking into his boss's email. He got fired" versus "Sam got fired. He started hacking into his boss's email." Speakers also generally get to the point and avoid using obscure or roundabout language. It would be strange for someone to say "I bought some frozen dairy product with small brown flecks" when referring to chocolate chip ice cream—unless, for example, she was saying this to another adult in front of small children, and meant to get across that she didn't want them to understand what she was saying. In fact, any time a speaker uses an unexpected or odd way of describing an object or a situation, this can be seen as an invitation to read extra meaning into the utterance. To see this in action, next time you're having a casual conversation with someone, try replacing simple expressions like *eat* or *go to work* with more unusual ones like *insert food into my oral cavity* or *relocate my physical self to my place of employment*, and observe the effect on your listener.

scalar implicature A type of conversational implicature that occurs when a speaker chooses a relatively vague expression rather than a stronger, more specific one. In many contexts, the speaker's choice of linguistic expression leads the hearer to infer that the speaker has used the weaker, vaguer expression because the stronger one would be inaccurate under the circumstances.

Grice argued that conversational implicatures arise whenever hearers draw on these four maxims to infer more than what the linguistic code provides. An important claim was that such inferences aren't triggered directly by the language—instead, they have to be reasoned out, or "calculated," by the hearer who assumes that the speaker is being cooperative and rational. The speaker, for his part, anticipates that the hearer is going to be able to work out his intended meaning based on the assumptions built into the four conversational maxims.

WEB ACTIVITY 11.6

Enriching meanings via conversational maxims In this activity, you'll see a number of examples in which the meaning of a sentence has been enriched by implicature. You'll identify the sources of the implicatures by explaining how the hearer might have calculated them on the basis of one of Grice's four conversational maxims.

When do children derive conversational inferences?

Grice made a convincing case that conventional linguistic meaning has to be supplemented by socially based reasoning about speakers' intentions and expected behaviors. As speakers, we tend to take it for granted that our listeners can competently do this, even when we're talking to young children. For example, a parent confronted with a small child's request for a cookie might say "We're having lunch in a few minutes" or "You didn't eat all of your dinner." To get a sensible answer out of this, the child has to assume that the parent is intending to be relevant, and then figure out *how* this reply is meant to be relevant in the context of the question. Some fairly complex inferencing has to go on. Should the parent be so confident that the message will get across? (And if the child persists in making the request, maybe the parent shouldn't impatiently burst out, "I already *told* you—the answer is no!" After all, the parent hasn't *actually* said that, but merely implied it.)

Some researchers have presented evidence that kids have slid well into middle childhood or beyond before they compute conversational implicatures as readily as adults do. For example, a number of studies have shown that children have trouble understanding indirect answers to questions like the one above until they're about 6 years old (e.g., Bucciarelli et al., 2003). Even by the age of ten, kids appear not to have fully mastered the art of implicature. In one such study, Ira Noveck (2001) asked adults and children between the ages of 7 and 11 to judge whether it was true that "some giraffes have long necks." Adults tended to say the statement was false, reflecting the common inference that *some* conveys "not all." But even at the upper end of that age range, kids mostly accepted the sentence as true. In other words, they seemed to be responding to the conventional meaning of *some*, rather than to its probable intended meaning.

But other researchers have suggested that these experiments underestimate kids' communicative skills, arguing that many of the studies that show very late mastery of conversational inferences require kids to reflect on meanings in a conscious way. This makes it hard to tell whether the trouble they're having is in generating the right inferences in the first place, or in describing or making judgments about those interpretations. Studies that use more natural interactive tasks, and probe for the inference implicitly rather than explicitly, tend to reveal more precocious abilities. Cornelia Schulze and her colleagues (2013) had 3- and 4-year-old children play a game in which the young subjects were to decide which one of two things (cereal or a breakfast roll) to give to a puppet character. When the puppet was asked "Do you want cereal or a roll?" she gave an indirect reply such as "The milk is all gone" from which the child was supposed to infer that she wanted the roll. The researchers analyzed how often the kids handed the puppet the correct object. They found that the responses of even the 3-year-olds were not random: more often than not, the kids understood what the puppet wanted. But both 3- and 4-year-olds were still not as reliable as an adult control group in generating the inferences based on assumptions of relevance.

In Section 11.1 you saw that even toddlers are often able to detect the communicative intentions of others, showing that some of the ingredients for understanding conversational implicatures are in place from a young age. Certainly, understanding that communication as a cooperative and purposeful social act is present very early in childhood. But other important skills mature over time: a complex understanding of others' mental states, the real-world knowledge that's often needed to work through the various steps of the inference, a more reliable system of cognitive control, not to mention sheer computational power.

Taking time to generate conversational inferences

Speaking of computational power, just how much of it do hearers need in order to be able to decipher the speaker's intended meaning? The emerging view is that it takes some non-trivial amount of processing effort and time to get from the linguistic code to the intended meaning when there's a significant gap between the two.

Let's go back to the scalar implicatures that come up in sentences like *Some tuna are fish*. To adults, this sentence seems odd, and is usually judged as false because it's taken to imply that not all tuna are fish. But getting to this implicature takes some work. Lew Bott and Ira Noveck (2004) devised a study in which they explained to their subjects the difference between the conventional linguistic meaning of *some* (the conventional meaning is often referred to as its **semantic meaning**) and the commonly intended meaning associated with *some*, which involves the scalar implicature (or its **pragmatic meaning**). They then instructed their subjects to push buttons to indicate whether they thought the sentence was true or false. Half of their subjects were told to respond to the semantic interpretation of the sentence (which would make it true), and the other half were told to respond to the pragmatic reading (which would make it false). Even though the pragmatic meaning seems to be the preferred one when people are left to their own devices, the researchers saw evidence that people have to work harder to get it: the subjects who were told to judge the truth or falsity of the pragmatic interpretation took more time to respond than the others, and made more errors when they had to respond under time pressure.

In a follow-up study, Wim De Neys and Walter Schaeken (2007) carried out a similar study with a twist: before subjects saw each target sentence, they were shown a visual arrangement of several dots in a grid and had to memorize them. They then responded to the target sentence by pressing a button to indicate whether it was true or false (they were given no specific instructions about how to respond), all while holding the dot pattern in memory. After their response, they saw an empty grid and had to reproduce the dot pattern. The whole sequence was repeated until the subjects had seen all the experimental trials (see **Figure 11.5**). The results showed that when the dot pattern was hard to remember (thereby putting a strain on processing resources), subjects were more likely to push the "True" button for sentences like *Some tuna are fish*, compared with trials where the dot pattern was easy to remember. This suggests that even though the reading with the scalar inference (leading subjects to say the sentence was false) is the most natural one for hearers in normal circumstances, such a reading consumes processing resources, and is vulnerable to failure when there's a limit on resources and/or time.

The results of these processing studies provide some potential insight into why even 10-year-olds often fail to generate the most plausible or useful in-

semantic meaning The aspect of meaning that can be derived directly from the linguistic code, based on the conventionally agreed-upon meanings of the linguistic expressions involved.

pragmatic meaning The aspect of meaning that is not available directly from the conventional code, but that must be inferred on the basis of contextual information or information about the speaker's likely intentions.

(A) Experiment design

1. Subjects saw a pattern of dots on a 3 × 3 grid for 850 milliseconds (0.85 seconds) and were told to memorize it. The dot pattern could be either easy or difficult to remember.

Easy   Difficult

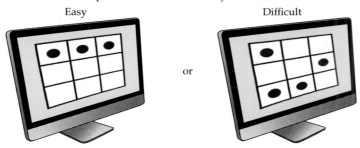

or

2. Subjects read a target (critical) sentence and pressed designated keys to show whether they thought the sentence was true or false. The sentence remained on the screen until the subject made a response.

3. Subjects saw an empty 3 × 3 grid and had to reproduce the dot pattern they had seen in Step 1.

(B) Results

Dot pattern	Pragmatic (judged false) responses	
	Pragmatic responses (%)	Mean pragmatic response times (sec)
Easy	78.9	6.031
Difficult	73.2	6.727

Figure 11.5 Summary of experimental design and results from De Neys & Schaeken, 2007. (A) Experiment design. Steps 1–3 were repeated until the subject had been exposed to all of the critical target sentences and all of the filler sentences. [Example filler sentences for this particular critical sentence might be *Some birds are eagles* (true) and *Some pigeons are insects.* (false)]. (B) Tabularized results, giving the percentage of "pragmatic" responses (that is, the statement was judged false, based on scalar inference) for the critical target sentence; and response times for the pragmatic responses, separated by whether they occurred in the easy or difficult dot pattern condition. (Adapted from De Neys & Schaeken, 2007.)

terpretations of these sentences. Indeed, all of this has important real-world implications, quite aside from the issue of whether kids are likely to understand their parents' more oblique statements. There may be times when it's best to produce sentences whose intended meanings can be read directly from the language code. In his book *Blink*, author Malcolm Gladwell describes a fascinating aviation case study in which indirect statements were both common and lethal. During the 1990s, Korean Air had an alarmingly high accident rate. An analysis of key accidents revealed that, in keeping with Korean conventions of politeness, first officers often had trouble giving their higher-ranking captains direct advice or instructions. (There's a general tendency for people to be indirect when addressing someone of higher social status—for example, to nudge

BOX 11.4
Using conversational inference to resolve ambiguity

Back in Chapter 8, you saw that hearers could draw on information from the referential context to help resolve syntactic ambiguities inherent in sentences such as "Put the apple on the towel into the box." If there were two apples present in the visual context, hearers avoided being tricked into thinking that the phrase *on the towel* indicated where the apple in question should be moved; they expected additional information to identify *which* of the two apples should be moved (see Figure 8.3). Essentially, the hearers had faith that the speaker was adhering to the maxim of Quantity, and would provide enough information to distinguish between the two apples in the display. This expectation about how speakers are likely to behave was generated quickly enough to be useful in solving the incoming ambiguity.

There's additional evidence that in similar ways, hearers can also resolve ambiguities via the expectation that speakers won't be *more* informative than necessary. Consider the visual displays in **Figure 11.6**, and the accompanying instruction "Pick up the tall glass." Imagine where you might be looking as you hear the word *tall*. In Figure 11.7A, there are two objects that could be described by that adjective (the glass and the pitcher). The pitcher is somewhat taller than the glass, so you might be tempted to take it to be the referent, but really, the phrase is ambiguous at this point.

Now consider Figure 11.7B. In this display, there are still two potentially tall objects, but there's also a short glass. This changes things, because if the speaker intended to identify the pitcher, he could easily have just said "Pick up the pitcher," as there's just one pitcher in the display. But in referring to the glass, it would be natural to use the word *tall* to distinguish between the two glasses. In these displays, do hearers expect that the adjective *tall* is being used to refer to the glass on the grounds that the adjective is more communicatively relevant for that referent?

Experimental evidence shows that hearers can use their expectations about the speaker's communicative behavior in exactly this way. Eye-tracking data have shown that when there's a contrasting object in the display (for example, a short glass in addition to the tall glass), people are faster to locate the referent (the tall glass) and less likely to look at the other tall object (the pitcher) in the display (Sedivy et al., 1999). This

suggests that their inferences about speakers' probable communicative behavior can help hearers reduce the ambiguity that's inherent in the linguistic code.

Interestingly, when subjects are told that the speaker is suffering from an impairment that affects his language and social skills, the usual expectations about how speakers typically behave are lessened, and subjects are less likely to assume that the adjective is being used with optimal efficiency to refer to the glass rather than the pitcher (Grodner & Sedivy, 2011).

(A)

(B)

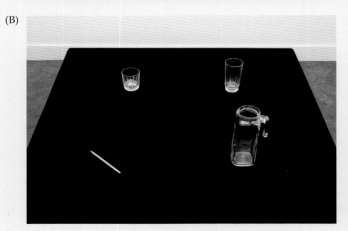

Figure 11.6 Example displays from the eye-tracking study by Sedivy et al. (1999). The accompanying instruction is "Pick up the tall glass." (A) In this display, the word *tall* is ambiguous; it can apply to the glass or the pitcher. (B) In this display, the contrasting short glass provides communicative motivation to use the adjective *tall* in referring to the taller of the two glasses.

your boss to be punctual for a meeting, you might hint, "What time was that meeting again?" even though you know full well when it is. This tendency to be indirect with social superiors is especially strong in cultures that place a lot of weight on acknowledging differences in social status.)

In a fatal crash involving extremely poor visibility due to weather conditions, the plane's recorder revealed that the first officer had tried to diffidently suggest to the captain that he switch on the weather radar by hinting, "The weather radar has helped us a lot." A very polite hint, to be sure—much more delicate than saying "Turn on the weather radar *right now!*" But the captain, who was trying to land the plane under extreme cognitive load, apparently failed to compute the critical inference. He is recorded as saying distractedly, "Yes, they have helped us a lot" moments before slamming the plane into a hillside.

Not all conversational inferences necessarily involve a lot of processing time or effort. The exact processing costs probably vary a great deal depending on how many inferential steps are involved, how much information has to be retrieved from or held in memory, how engaging the task is, and what other processing demands the hearer is coping with. At least in some cases, there do seem to be measurable costs to understanding conversational implicatures over and above the costs of computing conventional meanings. Nevertheless, there's evidence that such inferences can be computed incrementally as a sentence unfolds, just as hearers incrementally compute the conventional meanings of sentences. Once in place, inferred meanings can even be used by hearers to resolve ambiguities that are present in the incoming linguistic code (see **Box 11.4**).

Brain networks for thinking about thoughts

If you look back to Figure 3.13, which shows the brain regions thought to be involved in language, you'll notice that there are no areas in that diagram representing the mind-reading processes that I've just argued are so important for language use. Why is that?

The absence of mind-reading areas from the brain's language networks is actually perfectly consistent with Grice's view of how human communication works. Grice argued that the mental calculations involved in generating or interpreting implicatures aren't specifically tied to *language*—rather, they're part of a general cognitive system that allows people to reason about the intentions and mental states of others, whether or not language is involved. So, despite the fact that social reasoning is so commonly enlisted to understand what people mean when they use language, it shouldn't surprise us to find that it's part of a separate network.

Over the past 15 years or so, neuroscientists have made tremendous progress in finding evidence for a brain network that becomes active when people think about the thoughts of others. A variety of such tasks—both linguistic and non-linguistic—have consistently shown increased blood flow to several regions of the brain, especially the medial prefrontal cortex (mPFC) and temporoparietal junction (TPJ) (see **Figure 11.7**).

Some of the earliest evidence for brain regions devoted to mind reading came from experiments using false belief tasks like the famous "Smarties" test discussed in Section 11.1 Following the terminology used by child development researchers, neuroscientists often refer to these areas as the "theory of mind (ToM) regions." Similar patterns of brain activity have been found during many other tasks that encourage subjects to consider the mental states of others. To isolate the ToM regions, researchers try to compare two tasks that are equally complex and involve stimuli that are very similar to each other, but are designed so that thinking about mental states is emphasized in one set of

Figure 11.7 Brain regions for "theory of mind" (ToM). The medial prefrontal cortex and the temporoparietal junction have been found to be especially active in tasks that require subjects to think about the mental states of others.

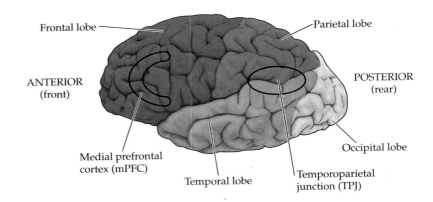

stimuli, but not in the other. For example, Rebecca Saxe and Nancy Kanwisher (2003) had their subjects read stories like this:

> A boy is making a papier-mâché project for his art class. He spends hours ripping newspaper into even strips. Then he goes out to buy flour. His mother comes home and throws all the newspaper strips away.

This story encourages readers to infer how the boy will feel about his newspaper strips being thrown out. This next story also invites an inference, but one of a physical nature rather than one involving mind reading:

> A pot of water was left on low heat yesterday in case anybody wanted tea. The pot stayed on the heat all night. Nobody did drink tea, but this morning, the water was gone.

The researchers found that activity in the TPJ was higher for the stories that involved reasoning about people's thoughts and emotions. **Figure 11.8** presents examples of various other contrasts that have been tested, all with the result that tasks or stimuli that emphasize social reasoning are associated with more activity in the ToM regions. Converging results have been found regardless of whether the tasks involve language or images, and single thoughts or complex scenarios [for a summary, see Koster-Hale & Saxe (2013)].

The discovery of a social reasoning network is a handy tool for psycholinguists. It offers a good way to test Grice's theory that certain aspects of linguistic meaning involve socially based inferences. This was precisely the goal of an fMRI study by Jana Bašnáková and her colleagues (2013). In their experiment, the researchers measured blood flow in subjects' brains as they heard the last sentence of a short narrative. In one of the experimental conditions, there was no need to go beyond the meaning provided by the linguistic code in order to make sense of the final sentence:

> John needs to earn some extra course points. One of the possibilities is to attend a student conference. He has never been to a conference before, and he has to decide whether he wants to present a poster, or give a 15-minute oral presentation. He is talking to his friend Robert, who has more experience with conferences. John knows that Robert will be realistic about how much work it takes to prepare for a conference.
>
> **John:** How is it to prepare a poster?
>
> **Robert:** A nice poster is not so easy to prepare.

"Mind reading" (social) stimuli

That morning, people sat around looking at each other, wondering if they were dreaming, because everything looked purple. Some people were shocked. Some people thought that it was funny to see everybody all purple. But even the smartest scientists didn't know what had happened.

In spite of her neighborhood, Erica has a strong dislike of violence, and believes that conflicts can usually be resolved without fists.

Sam thinks he can grow trees with fruit that tastes like pizza. How likely is it that Sam wants these trees for a treehouse too?

How likely is Queen Elizabeth to think that keeping a diary is important?

John was on a hike with his girlfriend. He had an engagement ring in his pocket and at a beautiful overlook he proposed marriage. His girlfriend said that she could not marry him and began crying. John sat on a rock and looked at the ring.

Control (non-social) stimuli

The whole world had turned purple overnight. Just about everything was purple, including the sky and the ocean and the mountains and the trees. The tallest skyscrapers and the tiniest ants were all purple. The bicycles and furniture and food were purple. Even the candy was purple.

Erica lives in Los Angeles. One night recently she was in a bar where a fight broke out between two drunk men and she was caught in between.

In the backyard are trees with fruit that tastes like pizza when ripe. How likely is it that these trees can be used for building a treehouse?

How likely is Queen Elizabeth to sneeze when a cat is nearby?

John was playing soccer with his friends. He slid in to steal the ball away, but his cleat stuck in the grass and he rolled over his ankle, breaking his ankle and tearing the ligaments. His face was flushed as he rolled over.

Figure 11.8 Activity in the TPJ (see Figure 11.7) has been shown to be higher for stimuli that involve "mind reading," or social reasoning about other people's thoughts and emotions. The examples of social stimuli increased activity in "theory of mind" areas relative to the control (non-social) stimuli at the right. (Examples from summary by Koster-Hale & Saxe, 2013.)

John: And how about a presentation?

Robert: It's hard to give a good presentation.

But in another condition, the final sentence was used to convey an implicature. Subjects had to puzzle out the speaker's intended meaning, using the linguistic meaning of the final sentence as the starting point for their inference:

> John and Robert are following a course in Philosophy. It is the last lesson of the semester, and everybody has to turn in their assignments. Some people have written a paper, and others have given a presentation about a philosopher of their choice. John has chosen the latter. When the lesson is over, he is talking to Robert.

John: I'm relieved it's over!

Robert: Yes, the lecturer was really strict.

John: Did you find my presentation convincing?

Robert: It's hard to give a good presentation.

The researchers found that the indirect replies led to increased blood flow to a number of brain regions, including the mPFC and the right TPJ, which are generally thought to be part of the ToM network (see **Figure 11.9**).

As you'll see in the upcoming sections, it's not always clear whether certain language behaviors really do involve reasoning about the minds of others or whether the meaning can be recovered by some other mechanisms. In some cases, mind-reading explanations compete with other accounts, generating vigorous debates among researchers. Cleverly designed behavioral tests can help sort out these disagreements. But over the coming decade, I'm sure that we'll also see a growing number of studies like the one by Bašnáková and colleagues, in which researchers look for activity in the ToM areas to help resolve the disputes.

Figure 11.9 These fMRI image shows brain regions in which there was increased activity for indirect responses, compared with activity for direct responses. In addition to several other areas, the subjects showed increases in the medial prefrontal cortex (mPFC) and right temporoparietal junction (TPJ), which have previously been shown to be active in "theory of mind" tasks. (From Bašnáková et al., 2013.)

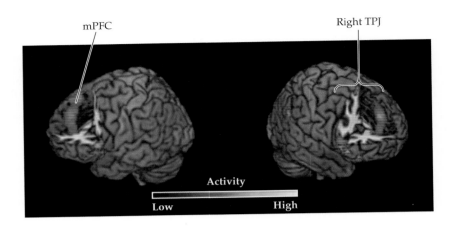

mPFC

Right TPJ

Activity

Low   High

11.3 Audience Design

Do speakers try to avoid ambiguity?

So far in this chapter, we've looked at how language users of various ages blend together mind-reading skills with their knowledge of the linguistic code. We've focused mainly on experiments dealing with language learning and comprehension. In this section, let's put the spotlight on the speaker. To what extent does mind-reading behavior show up in the task of producing language?

In Chapter 9, you saw that the act of speaking involves a constant series of choices. The speaker has to pick certain words over others that may be nearly as good, and she has to commit to building a specific syntactic structure while rejecting other options that convey much the same meaning. You learned about some of the factors that affect the speaker's choices—including the degree to which certain linguistic options happen to be more accessible than others at the precise moment of speech planning. Now let's look at whether there's also any evidence that in making their choices, speakers tailor their speech to their hearers.

The notion of **audience design**, in which speakers adapt their utterances to their listeners, can encompass many aspects of production, from speaking more slowly to foreigners, to using less formal language when hanging out with friends, to pronouncing words in a particular local accent. In this section, I'll concentrate on whether speakers take into account the comprehension challenges of their listeners, and choose linguistic options that will be as unambiguous as possible.

A Gricean view of language use, as outlined in the previous section, certainly suggests that speakers do actively consider the needs and abilities of their hearers. For example, Grice's maxims of Manner and Quantity state that speakers craft language that is unambiguous and that has as much information as is called for. Do speakers live up to these standards? The usual referential tasks show that for the most part, speakers do succeed at avoiding ambiguity in situations where there are multiple referents of the same category that have to be distinguished from each other. For example, if a speaker is trying to direct the hearer's attention to a specific pair of shoes in a visual context where there's more than one pair, she would normally use a more precise phrase like *the brown shoes* or *the loafers* rather than simply *the shoes*. Speakers can even throw themselves into the perspective of their hearers when their own visual perspective conflicts with that of their partners, adapting their language to the partners' perspective—though there's some evidence that under time pressure,

audience design The practice of adjusting aspects of one's language with the goal of communicating effectively with a particular audience or hearer. This adjustment may be conscious or unconscious, and may relate to various aspects of language production, including lexical choice, pronunciation and choice of syntactic structure.

the ability to shift perspective drops off somewhat (Horton & Keysar, 1996). Overall, speakers do quite well at averting referential ambiguity by choosing as much content as is needed to uniquely pick out the target object.

But there are many other ways in which linguistic input can be ambiguous or difficult for the hearer to understand. There might be a lexical or a syntactic ambiguity to resolve. Or the speaker might use a stripped-down expression such as a pronoun, forcing the hearer to search through a number of possible antecedents. Or the speaker might expect the hearer to make inferences that are just too demanding under the time pressures of spoken language. Or the pronunciation of a word might simply be indistinct, leading to confusion with other similar-sounding words. Once you start looking at the full range of possible comprehension pitfalls, it becomes less apparent that the hearer's needs figure very prominently in a speaker's linguistic choices.

For example, Vic Ferreira and his colleagues (2005) adapted a referential task to test whether speakers would steer clear of producing lexically ambiguous words as competently as they manage to avoid referential ambiguities. The study included visual displays that contained two objects that could be described by the same ambiguous word—for example, *bat* could refer either to a flying nocturnal animal, or to a baseball bat. Without any additional information, just saying *the bat* would be as ambiguous for the hearer as saying *the ball* in a visual display with more than one ball. If speakers are attentive to this potential problem for their listeners, they should either choose a different word, or add some disambiguating information (such as *the baseball bat, the flying bat*). For comparison, the researchers also included trials in which the display contained two objects of the same kind that differed in size (for example, two flying bats, one large and one small) as well as control trials in which all of the objects were unrelated (see **Figure 11.10**).

The results showed that when all of the objects were unrelated and therefore created no potential ambiguity, speakers tended to produce (65% of the time) a single bare noun (e.g., *the bat*). When the display had two objects of the same kind (two flying bats), speakers were almost always able to avoid referential ambiguity by including additional information, and generated ambiguous bare nouns only 1% of the time. But speakers were much less adept at producing unambiguous phrases when the visual displays created the opportunity for *lexical* ambiguity (the flying bat and baseball bat)—in this case, ambiguous bare nouns such as *the bat* were produced 40% of the time. If you compare this condition to the control display with unrelated objects (which resulted in bare

Figure 11.10 Examples of the type of displays used in the study by Ferreira and colleagues (2005). (A) The display contains a potential nonlinguistic ambiguity with regard to the word *bat*. (B) There is a potential linguistic (lexical) ambiguity with regard to the word *bat*. (C) This group displays no potential ambiguity.

(A) Nonlinguistic ambiguity

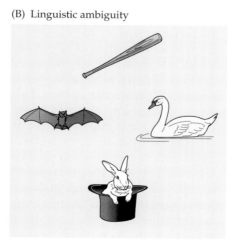

(B) Linguistic ambiguity

(C) No ambiguity (control)

nouns 65% of the time), it seems obvious that speakers were adapting their speech to avoid the potential ambiguity some of the time. But despite their efforts, an ambiguous phrase escaped their lips in a very large portion of trials.

Why are speakers so good at avoiding non-linguistic referential ambiguities, but quite bad at steering clear of lexical ambiguity? This pattern might seem very puzzling at first. But it becomes a lot less surprising if you take into account the mechanics of how language production works. As discussed in Chapter 9, speaking involves an ordered set of stages: the speaker first settles on a meaning she wants to convey, then chooses an appropriate syntactic frame, then chooses lexical items that match up with that meaning and fit into the sentence's frame, and finally assembles and executes the sounds that make up the words. Different types of ambiguities tap into different stages of production. Avoiding a non-linguistic referential ambiguity (distinguishing between two flying bats of different sizes) can be done at the very earliest step in production, when the speaker is still sketching out the meaning of the utterance. But avoiding a lexical ambiguity would have to take place at a later stage, when the specific words are being chosen. The demands on the speaker might be quite different at these two stages of production.

What's more, the process of detecting the ambiguity is very different in the two situations. In the easier case of avoiding a referential ambiguity, the speaker needs to make sure that enough *conceptual* material is present to distinguish among similar referents. But in order to avoid the lexical ambiguity, the speaker has to become aware that the same form can be linked to two different meanings. Since the intended meaning is so prominent in the speaker's mind, the competing meaning (which, after all, is irrelevant from the speaker's perspective) may never become active enough for her to register the ambiguity. You might think of the process as analogous to trying to proofread your own writing—people often can't "see" their own typos, because knowing what they intended to mean makes them blind to the forms with which they express it.

The moral of the story is that even if Grice is right and the speaker has heartily sincere intentions of avoiding ambiguity in her speech, there might still be a lot of variation in how well she succeeds in meeting that goal. The specific task of ambiguity avoidance might look very different for different types of ambiguity. And in some cases, what might look like intentional avoidance of ambiguity could simply reflect the internal mechanisms of speaking (see **Box 11.5**).

Syntactic ambiguity and audience design

When it comes to avoiding syntactic ambiguities, speakers have an abundant array of options available to them: they can choose a different unambiguous structure that has the same general meaning as a potentially ambiguous one; they can use intonation to help clarify which of the possible meanings was intended; and in many cases, they can disambiguate a structure merely by inserting a small but useful grammatical marker. Consider the ambiguous sentence fragment *The coach knew you...*. This can be read either as a simple clause in which *you* is the direct object of *knew* (as in *The coach knew you too well*) or as a more complex sentence in which *you* is the subject of an upcoming clause (for example, *The coach knew you had it in you*). If you were wanting to express the second option, you could do your hearer a great favor by splicing in the little word *that*: *The coach knew that you...*. Ambiguity problem solved!

Just as with lexical ambiguities, though, the stumbling block is whether speakers are able to realize that certain structures will be potentially ambiguous for the hearer. Again, since the intended meaning is already obvious to the speaker, becoming aware of the ambiguity means the speaker has to anticipate

BOX 11.5
Do speakers consider hearers' needs in deciding when to mumble?

In Box 10.3, we talked about how speakers appear to show some consideration for their hearers when they mumble. A person is most likely to speak indistinctly when the words are highly predictable from the context of the surrounding sentence, and more likely to speak clearly when the words are unexpected, and would be difficult for hearers to recognize. This looks very much as if speakers are anticipating potential comprehension troubles for their hearer, and adjusting the amount of effort they put into speaking as a result of this assessment.

But this isn't the only explanation for the alignment between hearers' needs and speakers' patterns of production. It could be instead that speakers put in less articulatory effort on words that are easy to produce, without necessarily considering the effect on the hearer at all. Luckily for the hearer, words that are easy to produce are often also those that are easy to recognize during language comprehensions, including common or highly predictable words. Unluckily for the researcher, this makes it tricky to figure out which explanation is the right one.

With a bit of digging, it's possible to find a situation where a variable that makes words easy to produce has exactly the opposite effect on the hearer: Back in Chapter 7, we talked about how challenging it is for hearers to recognize words that come from dense phonological "neighborhoods," that is, words that are very similar in sound to many other existing words. This is because the similar-sounding words compete for activation during the word recognition process. You've probably had the experience of mishearing one word for another from the same neighborhood (for example, "Did you say you lost your *cap*, or lost your *cat*?") If the speaker were being

considerate of your word recognition needs, he'd utter the relevant word with the utmost clarity.

But from the speaker's perspective, words that come from dense neighborhoods are often *easier* to produce. This is because, rather than identifying the meanings of words based on their sounds, as the hearer does, he has to activate the sounds of words based on their meanings. In Chapter 9, we talked about how speakers first choose words from among competing words with similar meanings, and then flesh them out in terms of their sounds. This means that for the speaker, activating words with similar *meanings* creates competition—but we reviewed some evidence showing how activating words with similar sounds can actually help speed up the sound-assembling stage of word production.

So, we have a situation that would make any language researcher happy: Exactly the same variable—the phonological density of the words that speakers produce—is predicted to lead to clearer pronunciation by the audience design theory of mumbling, while it's expected to lead to less distinct pronunciation under the ease-of-production account. So far, the evidence appears to fall on the ease-of-production side (for one detailed study, see Gahl et al., 2012).

Naturally, this doesn't rule out the possibility that in some situations, things would be reversed, and the speaker might put a greater premium on the hearer's comprehension that on his own ease of production. By the end of this chapter, you might have a sense of how different communicative situations could vary in important ways—you might even be curious enough to test out one or two of your own hypotheses.

---

the experience of the hearer while deeply engaged in the act of speaking. The research literature is riddled with studies that showcase speakers' failures to do this. For example, as you saw in Box 8.3, speakers are not particularly strategic about using intonation to disambiguate, even though this information could be quite helpful to hearers. And when it comes to picking from the menu of syntactic options, their choices are often driven more by what makes their own task of language production easier than by what makes comprehension easier for their listeners.

This last point is apparent in a detailed study by Jennifer Arnold and her colleagues (2004) looking at whether speakers take pains to avoid ambiguities in how prepositional phrases (PPs) are attached. As you saw in Chapter 8, potential "garden path" traps often lurk in sentences with prepositional phrases, causing readers or hearers to settle on an interpretation that turns out to be wrong. For example:

> The foundation gave Grant's letters to Lincoln to a museum
> in Philadelphia.

On hearing the prepositional phrase *to Lincoln*, a hearer might be fooled into thinking that the foundation gave the letters in question to Lincoln (the PP is attached to the verb phrase, or VP). But instead, the phrase is really just clarifying *which* letters the foundation gave to the museum (that is, the PP is attached to the noun phrase, or NP). Of course, the speaker could rearrange the constituents of this sentence in a way that makes the problem vanish:

> The foundation gave a museum in Philadelphia Grant's letters
> to Lincoln.

Here, the recipient of the verb *gave* is ordered first (*a museum in Philadelphia*), so by the time the hearer gets to the phrase *to Lincoln*, there's no way he can mistakenly interpret the prepositional phrase as referring to the recipient of *gave*. The researchers confirmed that hearers did indeed have less difficulty with this unambiguous version than the earlier ambiguous one. The question was: Would speakers veer away from the ambiguous structures to produce the sentences that hearers clearly prefer?

In order to test whether speakers' sentence choices were shaped by the potential ambiguity of a sentence, the experiment had to include a good baseline to measure how often speakers ordered the recipient first when the alternative choice *wouldn't* lead to an ambiguity. For example, the following sentence is very similar in meaning to the ambiguous sentence above, but poses no potential ambiguity:

> The foundation gave Grant's letters praising Lincoln to a museum
> in Philadelphia.

If speakers make syntactic choices in part by anticipating problems for the hearer, there should be little pressure to reorder the sentence to make the recipient first, as in the following sentence:

> The foundation gave a museum in Philadelphia Grant's letters
> praising Lincoln.

In other words, examples like sentence B in **Table 11.2**, for which the alternative is ambiguous, should outnumber examples like D, where the alternative is unambiguous. But that's not what the researchers found. Speakers chose the two

---

TABLE 11.2 Example stimuli and results from Arnold et al. (2004), Experiment 2

Spoken responses	Results (% of responses)
Potential ambiguity	
(A) *Ambiguous:* The foundation gave Grant's letters to Lincoln to a museum in Philadelphia.	33
(B) *Unambiguous alternative:* The foundation gave a museum in Philadelphia Grant's letters to Lincoln.	67
No potential ambiguity	
(C) *Unambiguous:* The foundation gave Grant's letters praising Lincoln to a museum in Philadelphia.	20
(D) *Unambiguous:* The foundation gave a museum in Philadelphia Grant's letters praising Lincoln.	80

types of sentences with about the same frequency, suggesting that the potential ambiguity of their sentences didn't make a dent in their syntactic choices.

What *did* affect speakers' choices were factors that relieve the pressures of *production*. One of these was the relative weight of the two NPs that follow the verb. In Chapter 9, you saw that when choosing among various options for ordering two NPs, speakers use the one that allows them to pronounce shorter phrases first—the idea is that the planning of shorter phrases is completed before the longer ones, and by dumping whichever phrase is ready first into the sentence frame, the speaker can clear some material out of working memory. So, regardless of potential ambiguity, speakers were inclined to produce the first of the following sentences rather than the second sentence. To allow you to compare their length, the main constituents after the verb are marked off in square brackets:

> The foundation gave [Grant's letters to Lincoln] [to a highly
> respected American history museum in Philadelphia].

> The foundation gave [Grant's famous recently recovered letters to
> Lincoln] [to a museum in Philadelphia].

These results suggest that in syntactic planning, speakers take the option that lightens the load for speaking, rather than the one that makes comprehension easier. Presumably, this is either because the pressures on language production are so strong, or because it's too hard to keep track of potential ambiguities from the hearer's perspective, or a combination of both.

A similar conclusion was reached by Vic Ferreira and Gary Dell (2000), in a study that looked at whether speakers strategically make use of disambiguating grammatical words to make their sentences less ambiguous. As I pointed out a little earlier, in some cases, ambiguity could easily be avoided simply by including disambiguating grammatical words. For instance, the potential garden path structure *The coach knew you* . . . could be transformed into the unambiguous *The coach knew that you*. . . . This applies to several types of ambiguous structures. For example, the troublesome reduced relative clauses that we spent so much time discussing in Chapter 8 can also be disambiguated in a similar way, as shown in the sentences below:

> The horse raced past the barn fell.

> The horse that was raced past the barn fell.

As in the Arnold et al. (2004) study, Ferreira and Dell reasoned that if speakers take into account potential ambiguities while planning to speak, then they should be especially likely to use the helpful, disambiguating word *that* in sentences where omitting it would lead to an ambiguity. In contrast, they should be less likely to include it in sentences that would be unambiguous regardless of whether *that* is included. So, compare the following two fragments, with and without the inclusion of *that*:

> The coach knew (that) you...

> The coach knew (that) I...

The second fragment is unambiguous even without *that*, simply because in the first person, the subject pronoun *I* is different from the object pronoun *me*, so there's no possibility of taking the pronoun to be the direct object of the verb. Because the second-person pronoun *you* takes the same form regardless of whether it's a subject or object, the *that*-less fragment is completely ambiguous at this point in the sentence.

To get speakers to produce sentences that would allow for a focused comparison (rather than simply waiting for speakers to spontaneously produce enough examples of exactly the right type), the study used a sentence recall task. Participants saw a set of sentences, including the critical ones revolving around potential ambiguity (*The coach knew you/I missed practice*), and then based on a two-word cue from each sentence (for example, *coach knew*), had to try to recall it as best they could from memory. In a sentence recall task like this one, subjects usually don't reproduce the sentences word for word, and typically make wording adjustments while keeping the meaning consistent. The aim was to see whether, in recalling these sentences, speakers would be more likely to utter the word *that* in situations where it would be helpful in averting ambiguity.

But like Arnold and colleagues, Ferreira and Dell found that the decision to insert *that* was not influenced by the potential ambiguity of the target sentence. Instead, it was affected by the accessibility of the pronoun that came after the main verb. What seemed to be going on was this: When the postverbal pronoun was very accessible, it got dumped into the sentence as soon as possible, so the speaker chose to forgo the option of introducing the embedded clause with *that* in favor of getting the subject pronoun out the door as quickly as possible. On the other hand, when the pronoun was less accessible, speakers took advantage of the optional *that* as a placeholder while still working on the retrieval and planning of the pronoun. So, rather than exploiting the disambiguating power of this little word for their hearers' benefit, speakers appeared to be using it as a way of smoothing out the demands of language production.

The importance of feedback from hearers

At this point, you might be objecting that verbally recalling sentences in response to an experimenter's instructions is hardly what you'd call a truly communicative task that might awaken a speaker's cooperative impulses. From the speaker's perspective, the goal of the recall task is to reproduce the sentences accurately, as opposed to being understood by the hearer. In fact, the "hearer" seems no more than an abstraction in this experiment—is the hearer the research assistant who administers the experiment? The one who codes the data? The scientist(s) who designed the study? Why should the speaker care whether she produces sentences that are easy for this nebulous hearer to understand?

This is a very valid objection. In order to test whether speakers take hearers' comprehension needs into account while planning their utterances, doesn't it make sense for the speaker to have some evidence that: (1) there *is* a hearer, and (2) the hearer actually does have needs, or is invested in understanding what the speaker says? So far, I've argued that in considering whether the speaker can get inside the head of his hearer, it's important to think about the specific production mechanisms that are in play and the processing demands on the speaker that these mechanisms impose. Perhaps it's just as important to consider whether the hearer's requirements play a part in the equation.

Not surprisingly, the answer is that it often *does* seem to matter who the hearer is and what he or she is doing. For one thing, it can make a difference if there's an actual flesh-and-blood person, rather than an "abstract" listener, or even an alleged conversational partner sitting in an adjoining room who in reality is a computer emitting a set of prerecorded utterances. It can matter whether the hearer is just a passive listener, or an active partner in an interactive task. (For example, Sarah Haywood and her colleagues reported in 2005 that speakers did show some ability to anticipate and avoid syntactic ambiguity. Their task involved a highly interactive game in which research participants alternated being in the speaker and hearer roles so that they were able to have some firsthand experience of how disruptive ambiguity could be for comprehension.) And, it might even matter whether the hearer is a confederate who is hired to follow an experimental script or a naive, off-the-street, bona fide conversational partner.

For an interesting case study that addresses this last point, let's look at a pair of experiments that showed different degrees of audience design on the part of speakers. In a classic study by Paula Brown and Gary Dell (1987), subjects read little stories and then retold the same stories to a listener. Each of the stories described an action involving some specific instrument. For example:

> The robber hid behind the door and when the man entered the kitchen he stabbed him in the back. He wiped the blood off the knife and rummaged through the drawers. Later police investigators found his fingerprints all over the knife and had no trouble catching him.

In this story, the instrument (the knife) is the typical instrument you'd expect to be used in a stabbing incident. Half of the stories contained predictable instruments like this one, while the other half involved unusual instruments—for example, an ice pick might have been used in the stabbing instead. Brown and Dell found that in retelling the stories, speakers explicitly mentioned the instruments twice as often when they were unusual ones than when they were highly predictable.

At first glance, this seems to be perfectly aligned with Grice's suggestion that speakers produce as much information for their hearers as is needed, but no more. When the instrument is highly typical, speakers might count on the fact that listeners can easily infer the instrument, so it doesn't need to be mentioned. But Brown and Dell cautioned that the results don't necessarily mean that speakers were actually calculating what their hearers might or might not be able to infer—instead, the speakers could simply be following a general strategy of not mentioning highly predictable information, perhaps based on a history of their own experiences with language. Their proposal reminds me of an experience I had while traveling on a plane from my home in Calgary, Canada. I sat next to a man who was on his way home to Florida. He told me that he and his family were just coming back from a wonderful vacation in the Rocky Mountains—evidently, they'd had a great time "snow skiing." To my Canadian ears, it struck me as odd that one would bother to specify that skiing was done on snow. It seemed a bit like saying you'd eaten a "bread sandwich" or had bought a "metal car." I asked him whether he would ever just say "skiing" instead of "snow skiing." He patiently explained that yes, he would, but then that would take place on the water. In this case, my plane-mate revealed a *lapse* in audience design. His choices of skiing terminology seemed to have more to do with his own sense of what usually takes place when you put skis on, and of what the word *skiing* generally refers to, rather than on any evaluation about the amount of information that I needed.

Much of the time, a general strategy based on the speaker's own experiences would coincide nicely with the communicative needs of the hearer, making the speaker's behavior *seem* fully cooperative (for example, if I too had been from Florida, I wouldn't have batted an eye at the speaker's choice of words). Brown and Dell argued that in order to really test whether speakers take on the hearers' perspective in designing their utterances, you'd have to create a situation in which the hearers' actual informational needs didn't line up with the usual patterns of predictability. For example, what would happen if the situation made it easy for the hearers to infer even the atypical instruments like the ice pick? To find out, the researchers designed a version of the experiment in which, while retelling the story, some of the speakers showed the hearers a picture of the event that illustrated the instrument in question. Other speakers showed the hearers either no picture at all or one that didn't reveal the instrument.

Obviously, the hearers who saw the informative picture should have no trouble figuring out the instrument even if it was never mentioned in the speakers' retelling. But speakers didn't seem to take their partners' visual perspective into account, and still mentioned the atypical instrument about twice as often as the more common one even when hearers had access to the picture that showed the instrument. Brown and Dell concluded that the predictability of certain elements in events, rather than mind-reading efforts, was the main force behind their speakers' design of utterances.

LANGUAGE AT LARGE 11.3

Why are so many professors bad at audience design?

Throughout my many years of teaching university students, I've heard (and overheard) an extremely common complaint that students have about their professors: it seems that many professors fail catastrophically at adapting their lectures to their students' level of understanding. Sometimes, the complaint goes, the lecturer treats them like high school kids, or worse. But more often, she gives convoluted explanations without unraveling them, and marches on to the next topic oblivious to the fact that her students are three steps behind her. How can so many instructors have so poor an ability to shift themselves into their students' perspective, and imagine a mental state in which someone doesn't already have a grasp of the course material?

Now, I don't want to defend bad teaching. I merely want to invite you to approach the question with scientific curiosity, and consider whether there's something about the typical college classroom that makes it so likely that instructors will exhibit spectacularly poor mind-reading skills during the course of a lecture. (For the purpose of our discussion here, let's set aside the very real possibility that in the spectrum of individual differences, professors just might have lower-than-average theory of mind capabilities).

One of the recurring themes throughout this chapter is that being able to anticipate a partner's mental state or communicative needs can take a real cognitive toll. You've also seen that *speaking* takes a cognitive toll and that in many situations, speakers choose options that make their own task of language production easier over those that make their utterances easier to understand for their hearers. On the scale of demanding situations for a speaker, giving a university lecture has to rank pretty high. The material to be talked about is very complex, and regularly strains working memory. And then there's the fact that speaking in front of a large group is inherently anxiety producing, which sucks away badly needed

mental resources. As one of my colleagues put it: "My IQ is inversely related to my distance from the blackboard; the closer I get to it, the dumber I become." So, just in terms of the performance demands on the speaker, lecturing seems to stack the deck against being able to mobilize mind-reading abilities.

I invite you to think about one more factor in the equation: the extent to which the speaker takes the hearer's perspective may be shaped by the behavior of the hearer. As you've seen, there's evidence that stronger perspective-taking effects show up when speakers are involved with their hearers in an interactive setting. I find it interesting that students' complaints about their professors' lack of mind reading are more common for large lecture classes than they are for more intimate seminars. But perhaps this distinction shouldn't be surprising, when you think about the difference in back-channel responses that are available in the two settings. In a small seminar, students are more likely to interrupt, ask for clarification, and respond when directly asked a question. In a large lecture auditorium, even the visual cues are impoverished for the instructor; the students might be so far away and the room so dimly lit that the lecturer can't see whether they're screwing up their faces in confusion or nodding in apparent understanding. And, as you undoubtedly know, many (most?) students choose not to call attention to themselves and so deliberately try to avoid showing any visible reaction. So, the next time you notice a lecturer veering off into incomprehensibility, look around you at the students that are her audience. Do they have the look of conversational participants who are invested in understanding, who might have actual comprehension needs, and who are accepting some level of responsibility in conveying those needs? Or do they have the look of an experimental confederate who's heard the same story dozens of times and who is by now just going through the motions?

But a later study by Calion Lockridge and Susan Brennan (2002) yielded different results, despite using a near identical experimental design. This time, speakers did show a sensitivity to the visual information that their hearers were privy to. That is, speakers were more likely to mention the atypical instruments when the hearers didn't see a picture than when they saw one that showed the instrument of the action. Why the different results? One of the main differences between the two studies was that Brown and Dell ran their experiment with experimental confederates in the role of the hearer. That is, two students pretended to be one-time research participants who were recruited for the study just like the speakers were, and who were completely unfamiliar with the stories—but in fact, unbeknownst to the speakers (who were the true research subjects), each of the confederates was paid to run through 40 iterations of the experiment. Lockridge and Brennan, on the other hand, actually did recruit one-time participants as both speakers and hearers, and randomly assigned their recruits to one or the other role. This means that the hearers genuinely had no knowledge of the experimental structure or the stories.

Why would this matter, especially if the speakers were successfully duped into thinking that the confederates were real subjects? Lockridge and Brennan point out that in real conversations, hearers don't just passively listen and wait for the speakers to say what they have to say, without showing any reaction. Even when they're not speaking, listeners are often busy providing the speakers with a slew of cues about whether the speakers are being effective—a furrowed brow, a quizzical look, or a slight impatience to get on with the story and stop beating around the bush. If the message is clear, hearers might nod, or make little approving sounds, or say "OK" in a decisive way. Cues like these from the hearer to the speaker are called **back-channel responses**. But experimental confederates who've already heard the same stories over and over again might not emit the kinds of cues and responses throughout the story that naive hearers would. So, even if the speakers believed at a conscious level that the confederates were hearing the stories for the first time, they still might not be exposed to continuous feedback that provided them with real evidence of the hearers' efforts to process what they were saying. And this lack of back-channel feedback could conceivably affect the speakers' motivation to consider their partners' communicative needs and perspective—after all, if your partner seems to understand you pretty well no matter how you choose your words, why bother devoting precious processing resources to tailoring your speech for her benefit?

back-channel responses Behavioral cues (e.g., nods, murmurs of agreement, etc.) produced by a hearer that provide the speaker with information about the hearer's degree of comprehension.

WEB ACTIVITY 11.7

Back-channel responses In this activity, you'll observe a pair of conversational partners. You'll be asked to note the behaviors of the listener in response to the speaker and discuss how the speaker reacts in return to these cues.

11.4 Dialogue

Conversation as a collaborative process

If you spend time listening to people talking to each other, it becomes clear that conversation is very different from written language. When you write, you do what you can to craft an understandable message, you send it out, and you hope for the best. Your reader's job is to do his best to accurately interpret what you wrote, but his actions don't shape the way you structure your message. In conversation, though, roles aren't so rigidly divided and hearers and speakers often adopt a mutual, step-by-step responsibility for successful communication. Speakers depend on hearers to provide feedback about how the interpretive effort is going, and they make their next conversational moves contingent on that feedback. Conversation isn't just about two partners taking turns being the active and passive participants in a talk exchange. In live dialogue, the actions and responses of hearers can have a profound influence on the communicative behavior of speakers.

A detailed discussion of the joint effort can be found in a paper by Herb Clark and Deanna Wilkes-Gibbs (1986). Here's an example (originally from Sacks & Schlegoff, 1979) that illustrates the hearer's contribution to shaping an utterance during a conversation:

> **A:** … well I was the only one other than the uhm tch Fords? Mrs. *Holmes* Ford? You know, uh… the cellist?
>
> **B:** Oh yes. She's she's the cellist.
>
> **A:** Yes. Well she and her husband were there.

As Clark and Wilkes-Gibbs point out, in the first conversational turn, Person A introduces the Fords into the conversation, but seems to have some question about whether B will understand who these people are, as suggested by the questioning intonation. Getting no response from B at first, A tries a slightly different expression, offering the full name *Mrs. Holmes Ford?* again as a question. The lack of a response from B elicits yet a third attempt: *the cellist?* Finally B responds, showing agreement with the description, and the conversation can move on.

Clark and Wilkes-Gibbs argue that it's misleading to say that speakers refer and hearers interpret. Instead, they see referring as a collaborative process for which both participants are responsible. Speakers propose referring expressions, sometimes tentatively, and then wait to see whether their conversational partners accept them. Sometimes, the speaker will explicitly invite feedback by posing a question, or by using rising intonation. But often the hearer takes the initiative and signals agreement even without being explicitly invited to do so, as in this example (Cohen, 1985):

> **A:** Take the spout—the little one that looks like the end of an oil can—
>
> **B:** Okay.
>
> **A:** —and put that on the opening in the other large tube. With the round top.

At other times, the partner might correct or clarify an expression, or even jump in when the speaker signals some difficulty in production:

> **A:** That tree has, uh, uh…
>
> **B:** tentworms.
>
> **A:** Yeah.
>
> **B:** Yeah.

Clark and Wilkes-Gibbs argue that when hearers take their conversational turn without questioning or correcting the speakers' choice of wording, they implicitly ratify the speakers' linguistic choices, which makes it likely that the expression will be used again in the future. In this way, the hearers' responses shape how the speakers will proceed.

Establishing common ground between conversational partners

For Clark and Wilkes-Gibbs, examples like the above reveal something profound about the very nature of conversation. The whole process is seen as a joint effort to establish common ground with a conversational partner—that is, to identify the body of mutual knowledge, mutual beliefs, and shared assumptions that serves as the basis for communicating with that partner. Both partners contribute to building up common ground, whether it's by proposing, rejecting, acknowledging, modifying, or clarifying information, and in order for new information to be entered as part of the common ground, it has to be *grounded*—that is, it has to be accepted as sufficiently well understood (whether overtly or tacitly) by both partners. Partners can also rely on reasonable predictions about what's likely to be in the common ground that they share with a partner. These predictions might be based on community membership (for example, if you're a fellow rock climber, I might reasonably assume that you know what I'm referring to when I say "What kind of belay device do you like to use?"). Information might also be assumed to be part of common ground if both partners have witnessed it or heard about it, as long as there's evidence that they were both paying attention to that information. Notice that under this worldview, tracking a conversational partner's attentional state and knowledge base is central to successful communication.

Susan Brennan and Herb Clark (1996) showed how once two partners have accepted a referring expression as part of common ground, there's momentum to re-use that expression with the same partner, even when other wording choices might seem natural. Pairs of subjects were involved in a card-matching game in which both partners got the same set of picture cards (see **Figure 11.11**). One partner (the director) had to communicate to the other partner (the matcher) how to arrange the cards in a particular order. The goal of the study was to see how the director would refer to certain target objects—for example, a dog, or to be more precise, a cocker spaniel. The identities of the other cards in the set were manipulated so that some of the time, there would be another object of the same kind (another dog, but of a different breed), while at other times, the target card would be the only object of its kind.

Figure 11.11 Examples of the type of experimental stimuli used by Brennan and Clark (1996). Pairs of subjects receive identical six-card sets. One partner verbally directs the other to arrange the cards in a specific order. (A) Card set in which the target referent (the dog) is the only one of its kind; hence reference by means of a bare, basic-level word (*dog*) is adequate to avoid ambiguity. (B) Card set in which the target referent is accompanied by another object of the same basic level; reference to *the dog* would be ambiguous, motivating the use of a more detailed expression (*the cocker spaniel*; *the dog with the spots*) in directing the cards' arrangement.

conceptual pact A tacit "agreement" that evolves over the course of a communicative exchange in which conversational partners settle on a particular linguistic expression to refer to a particular referent.

We've already seen that people tend to refer to objects by using basic-level nouns (*the dog*) unless there's some specific reason to add more information, such as the need to distinguish one dog from another—in which case, they use more detailed expressions like *the cocker spaniel,* or *the brown dog,* or *the dog with the floppy ears.* Brennan and Clark found that this was true for their conversational participants. But the real question of interest was how the directors would refer to a lone dog in a card set after they'd been forced to provide extra detail because the card set in the previous trial had included a second dog. Under the grounding view of reference, there should be some motivation to re-use the more specific expression (*the cocker spaniel*), because that wording that had been ratified earlier by both participants. In Brennan and Clark's words, the partners had entered into a **conceptual pact** to describe the object in a particular way. But would this pact prevail, even when the detailed phrase had become more informative than necessary?

In fact, conceptual pacts seemed to play an important role in shaping speakers' choices. When speakers had previously used a more specific expression, they often kept on using that same phrase or a very similar one even when the basic-level term was all that was needed for unambiguous reference. The more firmly tethered that phrase was in common ground (that is, the more times it had been used previously), the more likely it was to be re-used. Finally, the tendency to persist in using the familiar expression was linked to the original partner. When interacting with a new, unknown partner, a speaker was more likely to revert to using a bare, basic-level term.

Other researchers have also found a tendency for conversational partners to become closely aligned in the way they use language. Simon Garrod and Anthony Anderson (1987) had pairs of subjects play a computerized maze game in which one partner had to guide the other to a destination in a maze made of interconnected boxes. This game left open a number of ways you could describe the locations in the maze (see **Table 11.3**). For example, you could anchor yourself to a starting point, and describe the path you'd follow from that point to your current location (Table 11.3A). Or you could impose an abstract grid over the maze structure, and use a coordinate system to refer to locations (Table 11.3B). Or, you could focus your descriptions on saying which line you were in, and which box from the left within that line (Table 11.3C). Garrod and Anderson found that their subject pairs quickly settled on one approach, with both partners persisting in using a consistent structure for their descriptions.

How much mind reading takes place during conversation?

Clearly, conversation is a coordinated activity, with partners affecting each other's behavior and speech. But not all researchers agree that coordination is achieved by having the partners maintain a representation of common ground. To do this, people would have to track and update information about each other's mental states, knowledge, and beliefs. And they'd have to be able to keep all this information in memory while coping with the chaotic demands of real-time conversation. Is all this really computationally feasible? And more important, is it really *necessary* to assume such depth of mind-reading activity in order to explain the typical patterns of dialogue? Or, could the effects be captured instead by simpler and dumber mechanisms?

A number of researchers have argued that results like those found by Brennan and Clark don't really require partners to negotiate conceptual pacts and retain these pacts in memory. Among such researchers are Martin Pickering and Simon Garrod (2004). Pickering and Garrod agree that the mechanism that causes partners to converge on similar bits of language does have a so-

TABLE 11.3 Sample dialogues from Garrod and Anderson (1987)

(A) Sample dialogue illustrating a "path" strategy

Speaker A: Right from the bottom left-hand corner: above the wee purple thing: go along one and up one and that's where I am.

Speaker B: Right I'm the same only on the other side.

A: I'm two along, up one now: from the bottom . . . from the left.

B: I'm down one.

A: Oh down one.

A: Uh-huh.

A: What, from where?

B: One along from the right . . . I'm one along from the bottom right.

(B) Sample dialogue illustrating a "coordinates" strategy

Speaker A: O.K.? right—er Andy we've got a six by six matrix.

Speaker B: Yup.

A: A, B, C, D, E, F.

B: 1, 2, 3, 4, 5, 6.

A: Correct, I'm presently at C5 O.K.

B: E1.

A: I have to get to A, B, B, 1.

B: B1.

A: I take it you have to get to—

B: No.

A: D5, is that correct?

B: Er—A, B, C, D, E: A, B, C, D, E. yeah.

A: So you're now at D1 are you?

B: Uh-huh.

A: And I'm in B5.

(C) Sample dialogue featuring a "lines and boxes" strategy

B: I'm on the top line, fourth box along.

A: I'm on the second row, second box along.

B: So I'm fourth box on the top row now.

B: You're on the bottom line second box along, Yeah.

A: Uh-huh.

B: The fourth box on the second row.

A: Second row, first box.

B: Fifth, fifth box fifth row.

B: Fifth box fourth row.

B: Fifth box on the second row.

B: Sixth box on the fourth row.

A: I'm on the second box on the fourth row.

A: That's me on the first box on the fifth row.

cial basis. They just don't think that it involves something as sophisticated and complex as modeling a conversational partner's mental states. Instead, they think that speakers resonate to and copy each other's linguistic expressions for reasons that are a lot like why it is that yawning is contagious, or why people

interactive alignment model A theory of dialogue that minimizes the role of representing a conversational partner's perspective or mental state. Rather, much of the alignment that emerges between conversational partners is attributed to automatic mechanisms of priming in memory.

subconsciously imitate each other's body language or accent. To explain this kind of imitation, they believe that a straightforward, general-purpose priming mechanism should do the trick.

As you've already seen, hearers find it easier to access material that's been recently activated in memory—either because it's been heard a short while ago, or because it's closely associated with something recently heard. On the other side of the conversational table, speakers also seem eager to produce material that's highly activated in memory. The phenomenon of syntactic priming shows that speakers are more likely to recycle a recently used structure than generate a fresh one that conveys the same meaning. All of these basic priming results are simple by-products of the way that language is pulled out from memory. To Pickering and Garrod, conceptual pacts are cut from the same cloth. According to their **interactive alignment model**, reflexive mechanisms like priming can explain a great deal of the coordination that happens between conversational partners. When this simple mechanism fails, a handy set of interactive repair mechanisms can be called upon to fix misalignments that result in misunderstanding. Finally, more sophisticated and cognitively expensive strategies that do rely on representing the partner's mental space are available. But for Pickering and Garrod, these are fairly rarely used, occurring as a last resort when all else fails, or in unusual situations that call for strategic mind-reading efforts. This view is quite different from that of Clark and colleagues, for whom being attuned to a partner's knowledge, beliefs, and experiences is a fundamental aspect of conversation, playing a role in just about every utterance.

There are other researchers who echo Pickering and Garrod's claims that mind reading plays a secondary and not a primary role in conversation. For example, Boaz Keysar and various colleagues (Horton & Keysar, 1996; Kronmüller & Barr, 2007; Lin et al., 2010) have argued that all *automatic* processes in language take place within an egocentric frame of reference—it's not until a later and more strategic stage of monitoring that speakers and hearers take into account perspectives other than their own. Like the interactive alignment model, Keysar's assumption is that the fast and general egocentric mechanisms are fairly sharply separated from the slow process of reasoning about the mental states and beliefs of others. In contrast, those who think that socially based inferences are a primary, core aspect of linguistic ability often argue that these inferences can take place very quickly, are quite likely automatic, and possibly even have an innate basis or a specialized cognitive "module" devoted to them (e.g., Sperber & Wilson, 2002).

In the battle between collaborative accounts and egocentric ones, researchers have focused on two key areas where the two theories clash in their predictions:

1. The two accounts make different predictions about *how quickly people will make use of information about the contents of common ground relative to information that comes directly from the linguistic code.* Collaborative theorists claim that that even in the earliest moments of language production and comprehension, people show sensitivity to a partner's perspective or knowledge state. However, egocentric theorists argue that the earliest moments of language processing are limited to automatic processes that are triggered by the linguistic code, with awareness of the partner's perspective being integrated only at a later stage of processing.

2. The two accounts make different predictions about *the degree to which the repetition of previous linguistic expressions is linked to a specific partner.* Collaborative theorists claim that conceptual pacts are set up between partners who have negotiated (usually implicitly) a joint agreement to use a certain linguistic expression to fulfill some purpose. The agreement

doesn't automatically extend to a different partner, so the bias to link a previously used expression with a certain referent (or **lexical entrainment**, as it's often called) shouldn't necessarily generalize when someone interacts with a new partner. But egocentric modelers say that lexical entrainment happens because words that have been used recently or frequently are highly active in memory, making them very accessible for the production or comprehension system. This heightened accessibility holds regardless of who uttered the words, so the bias for repetition should persist even into interactions with new partners.

To test the first prediction about whether information in common ground affects the earliest moments of language processing, researchers usually rely on some version of a referential task like the one we discussed in Section 11.1, where some objects are visually blocked off from the view of one of the partners, but the other partner is able to see all of them. The question then becomes whether the partner who can see all the objects is able to immediately restrict the domain of reference to just those objects that his partner can also see, or whether he experiences some temporary interference from a possible competitor for reference in his own (privileged) perspective.

As I write this, there's a resounding lack of consensus among researchers on this point. Some studies have presented very speedy effects of perspective-taking (e.g., Hanna & Tanenhaus, 2004; Heller et al., 2008; Nadig & Sedivy, 2002), while others have shown sluggish or very weak effects (e.g., Barr, 2008; Epley et al., 2004; Keysar et al., 2000). Arguments boil over about which methods are best suited for testing the predictions. For example, different results have turned up depending on how interactive the task is, how complex the displays are, what the natures of the stimuli are, and precisely how the data are analyzed, to name a few of the experimental details. (Mucking about in the literature on this topic is highly recommended as an exercise in how to navigate through unsettled scientific issues—see if *you* think the evidence is more convincing one way or the other.)

Let's look at the second point that the egocentric versus collaborative accounts have fought over: Is lexical entrainment something that is intrinsic to interactions with a particular partner, or does it generalize more broadly as predicted by a priming account? A typical experimental setup to investigate this question involves having a research participant hear someone produce a specific phrase to refer to a certain object. There's a short break in the experiment, after which the hearer participant either resumes interacting with the original partner or continues with a different partner. The speaker—either the original one or a new one—now refers back to the familiar object, either with the same phrase or with a different phrase.

According to the collaborative theory, subjects should expect the original partner to stick to the conceptual pact and re-use the same phrase in referring to the object. So, the old phrase should be easier to understand than the new phrase when spoken by the original speaker. On the other hand, the hearer should have no special expectations for how a *new* partner would refer to that object, so in interacting with the new speaker, there shouldn't be a difference in how easy the new phrase is to understand compared with the old one. Quite a different set of results is predicted by egocentric theories, since lexical entrainment between partners is seen as the result of a general priming mechanism. The mention of a specific referring phrase in the first part of the experiment should make that same phrase more accessible in the second. Therefore, the old expression should be easier to understand than the new one, regardless of who the partner is in the second part of the study.

lexical entrainment The tendency to link a previously used expression with a particular referent.

Though the predicted patterns sound clear enough as I've just laid them out, in real-world research, things are a bit more subtle. For example, the researchers who argue for the collaborative approach don't deny that general priming mechanisms do exist, and that priming might *also* have a noticeable effect on the comprehension results, on top of any effects of conceptual pacts. So, it wouldn't be surprising to see that the old expression is somewhat easier with a new partner as well as with the original partner—it's just that in comparison, the advantage should be even greater for interactions with the original partner.

Conversely, most advocates of egocentric models assume that people *are* able to consider mutual experiences and beliefs while using language—just that this knowledge is used strategically and slowly. So, the disagreement comes down to when in the processing stage we should see partner-specific effects. Again, papers have been published arguing in favor of both the collaborative view (Brown-Schmidt, 2009) and the egocentric priming view (Barr & Keysar, 2002; Kronmüller & Barr, 2007), with much methodological discussion.

Complicating the picture even further is the objection that partner-specific effects *could* arise from pure memory-based mechanisms (for example, as argued by Horton & Gerrig, 2005). So, even if it turns out that lexical entrainment is closely linked to one partner, this doesn't necessarily show that people are actively tracking their partner's knowledge state, as claimed by the collaborative account. Instead, the partner-specific effect could be explained like this: The original speaker is connected in memory with the old expression, so the old expression becomes even more accessible when it's uttered by the original speaker in the second part of the experiment than when it's spoken by the new speaker. But this may have nothing to do with negotiating conceptual pacts or tracking the knowledge states of conversational partners. Instead, it might be a bit like the following experience: Suppose you go out for lunch with a friend and order an exotic dish. You then go for months without thinking about that specific dish, until you find yourself out once again with the same friend. Suddenly, you think about that special dish again, simply because the presence of your friend has triggered that memory. In the same way, the presence of a specific conversational partner may trigger the memory of a particular word or phrase, without there being any mind reading on your part.

A satisfying conclusion to these debates has yet to emerge. But regardless of the outcome, the sheer volume and intensity of the discussion is a testament to the importance that researchers place on the broader question: To what extent do flexible, socially attuned representations about other minds play a central role in our use of language, and to what extent can we do without them and still manage to communicate with each other?

DIGGING DEEPER

Autism research and its role in mind-reading debates

An important thread running through this chapter is: What *looks* like evidence of conversational partners getting inside each others' heads isn't necessarily so. Suppose you can tell a nice, intuitive story based on mind reading to explain a certain pattern of behavior. The behavior might actually be driven by other mechanisms that *coincidentally* look like what would happen if the partners really were anticipating and adapting to each others' mental states. We saw this in Box 11.5, which dealt with the contexts in which people mumble. Speakers tend to phonetically reduce just those words that are highly predictable in context. This ends up making life easier for their hearers a great deal of the time—but the speakers' behavior probably isn't based on a moment-by-moment assessment of how easy their pronunciation would be to understand. In that box, you saw how some finer-grained experimentation could be used to tease the competing explanations apart.

In trying to pull apart social versus non-social explanations, researchers can get a lot of information from setting up just the right experimental contrasts to study the behavior of speakers and hearers, often under carefully contrived situations. And neuroimaging studies in which scientists look for evidence that "theory of mind" networks have been activated for certain tasks promise to add valuable information as well. But there's yet another angle that researchers can explore: they can compare patterns of behavior between typical subjects and those with autism spectrum disorder (ASD).

As you've seen in earlier chapters, autism spectrum disorders are characterized by difficulty with many aspects of social interaction. People who've been diagnosed with ASD show a very wide range of cognitive and linguistic abilities. But even among the highest-functioning individuals, there are disruptions in social aspects of communication, despite the fact that control over the linguistic code itself may seem intact—for example, morphology and syntax are normal, and there are no real problems with basic language production and comprehension. For people with ASD, the trickiest aspects of language have to do with how it is used. They often have trouble with understanding ironic intent, or grasping the relevance of a remark in context, or using the appropriate degree of formality for a social situation.

As we've discussed, some researchers have argued that the syndrome essentially reflects a disturbance of mind-reading mechanisms. Children with ASD, for example, tend to do much worse on false belief tests than other children of the same age or overall language ability.

So, the communicative impairments found in ASD are generally social, and sometimes very selective. Researchers can compare the performance of autistic and typical language users to help resolve some of those controversial cases that *look* like they might involve a mind-reading component, but that could in fact rely on other mechanisms. If people with ASD have a lot of trouble with these tasks in particular, it suggests that the tasks do indeed hinge on mind-reading skills. On the other hand, if their performance looks just like that of typical subjects, then it suggests that the task can be accomplished without relying heavily on mind reading.

Now let's see this research strategy in action by looking at two very different patterns of behavior: the interpretation of scalar implicatures and the production of pronouns in context.

In Section 11.2, I sketched out a mind-reading explanation for why a sentence like *Some apples are fruit* sounds odd—it seems to convey that not all apples are fruit, possibly because it triggers an attempt to figure out why the speaker was motivated to use the vague word *some* rather than the more precise word *all*. But there are other accounts of scalar implicature that don't require much mind reading at all. It's possible that hearers use a general strategy that looks like this: When a speaker uses a linguistic expression *x* that has some overlap in meaning with, but is less informative than, another linguistic expression *y* that I know about, I should simply assume that the speaker means *x* but not *y*.

Notice, first of all, that a strategy like this would apply to the various examples in Box 11.3; for example: when the speaker says *adequate,* she means "adequate but not great"; when the speaker says *possible,* she means "possible but not probable"; when she says *interesting,* she means "interesting but not riveting." And so on. Second, notice that it doesn't involve speculating about the speaker's motivations for using the vaguer word—the inference only requires that the hearer have accurate lexical representations for the words involved so that he's represented the scalar relationships among the various words: *<adequate, good, great>*, *<possible, probable, certain>*, *<interesting, riveting>*, and so on. With the right lexical information in place, the inference can be triggered reflexively whenever the hearer encounters a word that falls into one of these scales. Since the inference for all of these examples involves exactly the same structure, there's no need to work out the analysis afresh each time.

A heated debate has taken place among researchers about exactly what goes on in hearers' minds when they interpret scalar expressions. Some claim that the scalar implicatures are calculated much as Grice argued, with hearers interpreting speakers' linguistic choices against a set of expectations about how rational speakers behave. Others claim that the inferences are more reflexive, and are pulled off without the need to get into the speaker's head. Among the sparring scientists, measures of processing times have been the most common experimental tools of choice, with different theories predicting different patterns of response times across specific experimental conditions (to get a sense of how this plays out, see Breheny et al., 2006).

But what can we learn from how people with ASD interpret scalar implicatures? If these inferences do involve a heavy component of mind reading, we would predict that they should pose a fairly serious challenge for the ASD population. This prediction is bolstered by evidence that people with ASD don't seem to have the same solid expectations as typical subjects do about how speakers normally behave. Luca Surian and colleagues (1996) created a test where their child subjects heard conversational exchanges in which three dolls "spoke" to each other by means of prerecorded speech. In each conversational snippet, one of the dolls (Lucy) asked questions of the other two dolls (Tom and Jane); either Tom or Jane replied in a way that was at odds with Grice's cooperative principles. For example, here's an exchange in which Tom has violated Grice's maxim of Quantity:

Lucy: How would you like your tea?

Tom: In a cup.

In the next example, Jane has failed to observe the maxim of Relation:

Lucy: What is your favorite program on television?

Jane: My favorite is sandwiches.

For each question, the subjects were asked to judge which of the dolls had said something silly or funny. Overall, the children with ASD picked randomly between the dolls, unable to tell which of the two was violating conversational norms. (And among this group of subjects, those who *were* able to identify the doll with the inappropriate responses also did well on a false belief task, showing a tight link between awareness of conversational norms and awareness of others' mental states.) In contrast, two control groups of participants—typically developing kids, and kids with specific language impairment—did much better at figuring out which of the two dolls had replied in an appropriate way.

Given these results, you might expect that people with ASD would have quite a bit of trouble computing scalar implicatures—certainly, that's the prediction you'd make if you believed that scalar inferences have to be run through an understanding of conversational norms. But surprisingly, in a couple of relevant studies, participants with ASD tended to interpret sentences with scalar expressions in much the same way as typical populations.

For example, Judith Pijnacker and colleagues (2009) modeled their study after the experiments invented by Bott and Noveck (2004) involving underinformative statements like *Some tuna are fish.* They tested adult subjects with ASD (specifically, people with high-functioning autism and Asperger's syndrome) as well as a control group of typical subjects. Overall, the subjects with ASD were just as good as the typical subjects at computing the scalar inferences—that is, they were as likely to say that sentences like *Some tuna are fish* were false. Within the ASD group, the participants with high-functioning autism were slightly more likely than those with Asperger's syndrome to accept these strange sentences as true, but still, their pattern of results was strikingly similar to that of the typical group. The general findings were replicated by a later and very similar study (Chevalier et al., 2010) that also found no significant differences between the ASD subjects and the typical group.

Naturally, these results don't resolve the debate about the nature of scalar inferences once and for all. But they do introduce an interesting twist to the available body of data. It seems that either scalar inferences don't always require a heavy mind-reading component after all, or some people who fall at the higher-functioning end of the autism spectrum can use the required mind-reading skills well enough to compute the inferences, at least in a task like the one used in these studies.

The same general research strategy can be used to look at other areas where there's controversy about the extent to which mind-reading skills are needed to accomplish certain linguistic tasks. For example, in Chapter 10 you saw that despite the great potential for pronouns to be ambiguous, most of the time, hearers are able to match them to fairly obvious antecedents. What is it that makes the antecedents obvious? Well, in many cases, the best antecedent is the one that's most accessible in the mental model. But whose mental model are we talking about? The hearer's or the speaker's?

In Chapter 10, we focused mostly on several factors that make it easier for hearers or readers to connect pronouns back to their antecedents. For instance, things or people that have been recently mentioned make better antecedents than ones that have been mentioned further back in the discourse. Referents that are mentioned in subject position are preferred as antecedents over ones that appear in object position. And hearers also find it easier to map pronouns back to antecedents that are in parallel grammatical positions in the preceding clause. All of these factors conspire so that in the final sentence of the mini-discourse below, it's easiest to understand *he* as referring to Simon rather than Frank or Ron, and *him* as referring to Ron:

> Frank introduced Simon to Ron at the annual neighborhood picnic. It was a terrible idea. Almost immediately, Ron and Simon got into a loud argument over their clashing political views. Simon became so enraged, he punched Ron in the face. Then he kicked him in the shins before finally coming to his senses and apologizing.

When speakers use pronouns to refer, they tend to do so in just those contexts where the pronouns will be easily understood by hearers. Does this mean that speakers are keeping track of which referents are likely to be at the center of the hearer's attention, choosing to use either pronouns or more explicit names depending on the hearer's mental model? Some researchers have argued for exactly this. For example, Jeanette Gundel and colleagues (1993) have proposed that a speaker's choice of referring expressions is guided by cooperative goals similar to Grice's maxim of Quantity: expressions that are short on linguistic information (like pronouns) are only used when the speaker believes that, in the context in which they're being used, they'll be informative enough for the hearer to make sense of them.

But other researchers have suggested that the speaker simply decides to use pronouns to encode the referents that are most prominent in his *own* attention. An egocentric strategy like this could work if the mental models of the speaker and hearer have a tendency to align, so accessibility is the same for both the hearer and speaker, shaped by one set of discourse variables.

One argument in favor of the cooperative speaker theory is the fact that speakers are more likely to use a pronoun when, in the preceding sentence, they've mentioned only one possible antecedent than when they've mentioned a second that might compete with the intended antecedent of the pronoun. So, in the following examples, they'd be more likely to repeat the name in the second sentence pair than in the first:

> Diana went to the store. She bought bananas for the cream pie she was planning to make.

> Diana went to the store with Clarice. Diana bought bananas for the cream pie she was planning to make.

One way to think about this is that the speaker is trying to avert any potential ambiguity for the hearer by avoiding using a pronoun. But Jennifer Arnold and Zenzi Griffin (2007) have argued that speakers do this because of the constraints on *production*, not out of any sensitivity to the hearer's potential difficulty. Their story goes like this: When there's more than one referent to keep track of in the mental model, this reduces the activation in memory of the target antecedent. Since speakers only use pronouns when the

activation of the target antecedent is very high *in their own mental models*, the presence of a competing referent will lower the likelihood that they'll use a pronoun. To tease apart the explanations, they showed evidence that a speaker was less likely to produce a pronoun whenever her own mental model contained a competing referent—even when the gender of the other referent was different from the antecedent of the pronoun, which meant that there'd be no possible ambiguity for the hearer. For example:

> Diana went to the store with Michael. Diana bought bananas for the cream pie she was planning to make.

Here, *Diana* is repeated even though using the pronoun *she* would not have been ambiguous for the hearer in any way.

So, here we have another situation where there are competing explanations that disagree in terms of how much the speaker has to represent the attentional state of the hearer. It would be informative to see how people with ASD fare in producing pronouns that are comprehensible to the hearer. We can follow a logic that's exactly parallel to what you just saw in the scalar implicature case: if generating pronouns does rely heavily on tracking the attentional state or mental model of the hearer, then we might expect that people with ASD would show a pattern of pronoun production that is very different from that of typical speakers.

In one study that compared patterns of pronoun use across populations (Arnold et al., 2009), researchers found that children with ASD showed very similar results to typically developing kids. Both groups were more likely to use pronouns to refer to characters that had been recently mentioned, or had previously appeared either in subject position or in the same grammatical position as the pronoun. All of these factors are known to result in easier comprehension for listeners or readers; yet, they played just as much of a role in guiding the speech of children who had a disorder that makes it difficult to track the mental states of others. Arnold and her colleagues suggested that pronoun use may not depend heavily on anticipating the needs of hearers; instead, speakers may just be producing pronouns whenever they are referring back to things or people that are highly prominent in their own minds.

Research with autistic populations can certainly add to our understanding of the role of mind reading in language—either by challenging or supporting data from creatively designed experimental studies. But a number of issues need to be kept in mind to avoid drawing exuberant, but unwarranted conclusions. For instance, the population of individuals who have been diagnosed with ASD is a large and diverse one, and it's not at all clear that there's a unifying cause to the patterns of behavior that are thought to define the disorder. This means that it can be tricky to try to generalize broadly from one small sample. Results that hold for one group of subjects may not be part of the cognitive profile of another group, even though they share a diagnosis. For example, it's quite intriguing that the group of autistic children that participated in the Surian et al. (1996) study showed an impaired understanding of Gricean conversational norms, and yet, the adults with ASD in the Pijnacker et al. (2009) study showed no difficulties with scalar implicatures. This contrasting set of results seems to point to the conclusion that an understanding of conversational norms isn't necessary to understand implicatures. But we can't be sure that Pijnacker's subjects, who showed an intact understanding of scalar implicature, were *also* impaired in their understanding of conversational norms, as this sample of subjects was a completely different one from the group that was tested by Surian and colleagues. We'd be able to draw a more confident conclusion if the Pijnacker subjects themselves had been tested on their grasp of conversational norms, and showed some difficulties.

Another (and related) concern is that mind-reading deficits may not be the only cause of the symptoms that are associated with ASD. There's evidence that difficulties with cognitive control may also play a role. This complicates our understanding of any differences in behavior between typical and ASD populations; do the differences reveal that mind reading is an important component of that particular linguistic behavior? Or does that behavior rely critically on good cognitive control? Or both? To tease this apart, it's important to compare the results of ASD populations with those of other groups who have difficulties with cognitive control, but who don't show the mind-reading deficits that come with ASD (a group of individuals with ADHD might be an appropriate comparison).

Finally, what does it mean if we test typical and ASD populations and find no differences in their performance on a specific task, as we've seen here in the case of scalar implicature and pronoun production? Does this mean that typical subjects don't engage the mind-reading system in interpreting scalar expressions or uttering pronouns? Not necessarily. It could be that the two groups are achieving the same linguistic task with different underlying machinery, and more fine-grained experimentation might be needed to pick up on the differences. For example, in Chapter 5, we saw some evidence that in learning new words, typical children often look for direct evidence of the speaker's intent to refer to a specific object; autistic kids can learn new words too, but seem to rely more on general associative learning than on trying to figure out what the speaker meant in using that word. Competing explanations could amount to more than just providing alternative explanations for the same phenomena—it could well be that both factors sometimes actually jointly contribute to explaining a phenomenon. And, it's entirely possible that in some of the disagreements between researchers who advocate for highly social mechanisms, versus those who argue for largely egocentric ones, both sides may be right—it just depends on who you're testing.

PROJECT

The last section described research with ASD populations dealing with conversational implicature and pronouns—both areas in which there are questions about the extent to which mind-reading capabilities need to be involved. Now consider another aspect of language for which these same issues might arise (either taken from discussions in this chapter, or from your own ideas and observations). Propose and design a research program that includes testing of participants diagnosed with ASD. In designing your study, take into consideration the various methodological tools and concerns that have been addressed in this chapter. Pay special attention to considerations that come up in comparing different populations, as discussed in "Digging Deeper."

12 Language Diversity

Throughout this book, I've based discussions about psycholinguistics almost entirely on English, with only the occasional dip into other languages. All along, however, I've assumed that experiments with English speakers tell us something about how *language* works in the mind, not just how *English* works. This is an assumption that's widely shared by language researchers. Since humans seem to be able to learn any language that they're immersed in as children (rather than being genetically programmed for, say, only Germanic languages), we can reasonably conclude that the basic cognitive machinery for language is the same for all humans, regardless of the language environment they happen to be born into.

Still, it's worth noting that English represents just one grain of sand on a vast beach of linguistic possibilities. There are about 7,000 living languages spoken around the world today. To put this into perspective, researcher Mark Pagel (2000) reminds us that we humans—members of a single mammalian species—speak more different languages than there are species of fellow mammals. And the number of current languages reflects just the bare remnants of an even greater *past* diversity of languages. Pagel suggests that linguistic diversity may have peaked about 10,000 years ago, just before the development and spread of agriculture. Until then, there would likely have been many languages spoken by small, geographically isolated social groups. The invention of farming caused populations to fan out into larger geographic areas, with the likely result that local indigenous languages were often replaced by the language spoken by the spreading agricultural society. (This would be similar to how languages

The great language extinction

Raise your hand if either of your parents is a native speaker of a language other than English. Raise your other hand if English is your only language. If both your hands are in the air, you may be one small example illustrating the large-scale language loss that typically afflicts families who immigrate to an English-speaking country from elsewhere. In the United States, for example, reality runs contrary to anti-immigrant rhetoric: far from becoming isolated in linguistic ghettos and failing to learn English, most immigrant families generally *lose* their heritage language within a couple of generations, as reported by Robert Lane Greene (2011). Even among Mexican immigrants, currently the slowest group in the United States to shed their ancestral language, fewer than 10% of fourth-generation immigrants speak Spanish very fluently. As Greene points out, who needs further *disincentives* to speak the heritage language when the economic and cultural imperatives to speak English are already so great?

The language loss that's experienced by immigrants is just one part of a larger phenomenon of global language loss, in which many local languages are being abandoned in favor of larger, more economically powerful languages. Currently, about half of the world's languages are considered to be endangered. Where English is spoken,

it's not uncommon to find that between 80% and 90% of the languages native to that area have been lost. To many researchers, this accelerating rate of language death parallels the mass extinction of biological species due to industrialization and habitat loss.

For biologist Mark Pagel (2000), this parallel is more than mere analogy. He's found that similar geographic conditions seem to foster biological and linguistic diversity. In North America the highest concentration of different mammals *and* different languages occurs at about 40 degrees north latitude. The most linguistically diverse place on the entire planet is Papua New Guinea, which teems with languages as well as with wildlife; more than 800 languages are currently spoken there. Pagel argues that the key factor supporting the profusion of both languages and wildlife is the wide array of different and distinctive habitats contained within this relatively limited geographic area. Among animals, habitat diversity encourages the evolution of highly specialized traits for a particular, distinctive habitat, without intrusion by invasive species. In the same way, if people are able to find sources of food without having to travel great distances, they may be more likely to develop a highly specialized culture within their habitat, and not interact a great deal with other groups. Modern society,

spoken by smaller numbers of individuals today are being gobbled up by a few of the world's dominant languages.) By calculating the rates at which new languages may have emerged and old ones become extinct, Pagel estimates that as many as half a million languages have been spoken since humans first started talking.

A glance at the world's languages shows that language diversity isn't just a matter of different languages having different words, or of languages having slight tweaks in sound inventories or the ways in which elements are ordered in a sentence. Very different *systems* emerge from among the world's languages:

- The observed number of distinct phonemes (units of sound) in a language ranges from 11 to 164 (Maddieson, 1984).

- Languages differ enormously in the number of morphemes (units of meaning) that they allow to be stuck together to form a single word. Some languages, like Mandarin and Vietnamese, are essentially limited to a single morpheme per word—you wouldn't even tack on a separate morpheme to mark past tense or plural on a word. Other languages allow so many morphemes to be attached to a verb that a single word can capture as much information as a full sentence of English.

- Languages vary dramatically in the *kind* of information that has to be present in the linguistic code. For instance, Mandarin doesn't require that

LANGUAGE AT LARGE 12.1 (*continued*)

with its rapid industrialization and globalization, poses a threat to these diverse, self-contained habitats, and to the species and languages that they harbor.

Language extinction looms large in Australia, where an estimated 80% of native languages will not survive the current generation (**Figure 12.1**). As Pagel notes, "languages are suffering a mass extinction comparable to that of biological species, and the linguistic landscape is, like parts of Australia itself, rapidly coming to resemble a desert."

Of course, not everyone would mourn the loss of language diversity—after all, idealists have long dreamed that a universal language might unite the world's peoples and promote harmony. Still, the extinction of a language is an undeniable severing of a people's ties to its cultural heritage. And for language scientists, the mass extinction of languages is devastating—it's through the sheer variety of human languages and their possible and probable shapes that we come to learn so much about what a human language is and can be.

It's unrealistic to think that language extinction can be stopped by having people retreat back into self-contained habitats—the world is likely to require increased cross-cultural interactions for the foreseeable future. But fortunately, the human capacity for language encompasses more than just one, and there's a growing awareness in many countries that nurturing multilingualism may be the way to keep languages alive.

Languages like Maori (New Zealand), Basque (Spain/France), Irish, and many native North American languages, once stigmatized, have become the focus of energetic language revitalization efforts.

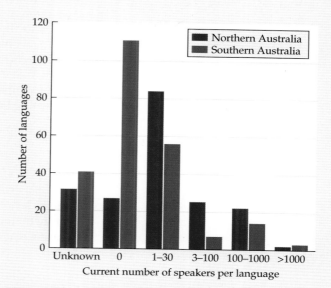

Figure 12.1 The number of speakers per language for aboriginal languages of Australia. The languages of southern Australia, which had greater numbers of European settlers, are even more endangered than languages in the north. (Adapted from Pagel, 2000.)

---

tense be encoded anywhere in a sentence—it can be left entirely up to the context to indicate whether an action is situated in the past, present, or future. On the other hand, Turkish requires a grammatical marker that encodes whether the event described by a sentence was witnessed directly by the speaker, or whether it reflects secondhand knowledge.

- Languages make use of different categories of words as their syntactic building blocks. Not all languages have adjectives or adverbs, for example, or even distinguish between nouns and verbs. On the other hand, some languages have word categories that English lacks. Japanese has a set of words called "classifiers," which you use when specifying the number of objects. The classifier captures some information about the type of object that's being counted. When expressing the concept of three pencils, you'd have to include in the phrase the classifier *hon*, which is used with long, cylindrical objects; other classifiers accompany large animals, small animals, drinks, and so on.

- Some languages, including English and French, have a very fixed word order. Some other languages, like Czech and Russian, permit a certain amount of scrambling of elements. Still others have what appears to be a completely free word order.

The tremendous variety of human languages points up a paradox: How can there be such stunning differences across languages, given that humans all share the same underlying equipment? Clearly, the human mind is able to stretch itself in various directions to accommodate a dazzling assortment of language systems. By closely examining the ways in which languages differ and the various cognitive challenges they pose, we can get an intriguing perspective on the breadth and elasticity of the human linguistic capacity.

At the same time, we also have the sense that people who speak different languages often display profound differences. To learn a new language, we're often told, is to fling open a window onto a different culture. When people make statements like this, they often mean that the language *itself* embodies important aspects of the culture of its speakers and their way of thinking—and by extension, that if you know their language, you too will be able to think like they do. For example, a web page from Bowdoin College suggests that students consider learning Japanese because:

> **Learning Japanese allows you to see the world in a different way.** The philosopher Ludwig Wittgenstein is known to have written this famous aphorism: "The limits of my language are the limits of my world." As he suggests, our ability to imagine possible worlds [is] extended by learning a new language. Companies and graduate schools are interested in cultivating talented people who can function in an increasingly diverse and interconnected world. Learning a new language is the first step towards "thinking outside the box."

Adopting a similar approach, the website of the French consulate general in Houston lists ten "good reasons to learn French," including these two:

> First and foremost, learning French is the pleasure of learning a beautiful, rich, melodious language, often called the language of love. French is also an analytical language that structures thought and develops critical thinking, which is a valuable skill for discussions and negotiations.

It's "common knowledge" that some languages are more romantic—or more orderly, harsh, delicate, simple, sloppy, nuanced, precise, or flowery—than others. (You can conduct a little experiment: survey your friends, and see how much consensus there is about which languages embody each of the above adjectives.) Like the sixteenth-century Holy Roman Emperor Charles V, one might conclude that it's best to acquire a number of different languages for different purposes. Charles is alleged to have asserted that he spoke "Spanish to God, Italian to women, French to men, and German to my horse."

If you share the intuition that languages are infused with certain cultural qualities, let me ask you this: Exactly *which* properties of, say, Italian make the language so romantic? Or what is it *exactly* about the grammar of French that helps the language to structure thought with a pristine clarity? When confronted with questions like these, many people draw a blank. But in order to evaluate the claim that learning a language will open up a different way of thinking, some serious theory-building needs to be done. In what ways could cultural values possibly be stamped into a language, and how might the resulting linguistic features shape the thinking of its new learners? In this chapter, we'll wrestle with these fascinating questions:

- How do languages differ from each other, and what do they have in common?

- Does the human mind impose limits on possible languages?
- Can a lifetime (or even a short time) of speaking a particular language in turn impose constraints on the way we think?

12.1 What Do Languages Have in Common?

How universal are language universals?

Even at a brawny half million, the set of past and present human languages represents a minuscule portion of the languages that could possibly exist. As we've discussed at various points in this book, certain basic properties seem to be critical starting points for human languages. For instance, languages combine meaningless units of sound to create an inventory of meaningful words, they combine words into complex groupings, and their grammatical patterns rely on abstract notions of structure rather than simple linear order. None of these elements are *required* by a system of communication. This becomes obvious when people deliberately set their minds to inventing an artificial language—the results aren't always constrained by even these most basic features of organic human languages (recall the example of the language invented by John Wilkins in the seventeenth century, discussed in Language at Large 2.1).

Even if you stay within the core properties of language, it's not hard to dream up highly deviant grammatical rules that are unlike anything natural languages seem to do. Here's my attempt at generating a few such weird "non-rules":

- If the subject of the sentence begins with the sound /d/, reverse the usual order of the verb and direct object.

- When nouns that refer to objects that are typically red are combined with verbs, the verb is never marked for the past tense.

- When speaking to a person of higher social rank than yourself, omit all prepositions.

- The first noun in a sentence is pronounced in such a way that its last consonant is dropped.

No one has ever compiled an exhaustive list of "outlandish rules that have yet to turn up in language" (and it would be pointless to try). But there have been serious attempts to define the boundaries of natural human languages, and to document patterns that *do* regularly crop up across many languages.

Among these attempts, the work of Joseph Greenberg (1963) has been especially influential. Like other **language typologists** who study the ways in which languages vary, rather than focusing on idiosyncratic rules or specific words, Greenberg tried to capture the broader patterns within languages, patterns that provide some insight into the "bones" of a language. Based on a survey of about 30 languages, he created a list of 45 generalizations, commonly referred to as **Greenberg's linguistic universals** (see **Table 12.1**). Greenberg's list contains some statements that were true for all of the languages that he studied. Some of these are simple, such as "All languages have categories of pronouns involving at least three persons and two numbers" (Universal 42). Others are more complex **implicational universals** of the form "If A, then B." For example, "If a language has gender categories in the noun, it has gender categories in the pronoun."

Greenberg found very few truly exceptionless patterns among the languages he sampled. And in recent years, linguists have turned up more and more cases of outlier languages that seem to violate what had been previously thought to be universal properties of language. In Box 6.3, you read about Pirahã, a language

language typologists Researchers who study the ways in which languages vary with the aim of describing and explaining crosslinguistic variation.

Greenberg's linguistic universals A set of observations about common or universal structural patterns across a sample of 30 languages by Joseph Greenberg. Published in 1963, Greenberg's observations are still used as the basis of a great deal of inquiry in language typology.

implicational universals Crosslinguistic generalizations that are formulated as conditional statements ("If a language has A, then it has B").

TABLE 12.1 Examples of Greenberg's linguistic universals[a]

Universal 1	In declarative sentences with normal subject and object, the dominant order is almost always one in which the subject precedes the object.
Universal 14	In conditional statements, the conditional clause (the *if* clause) precedes the conclusion (the *then* clause) as the normal order in all languages.
Universal 17	With overwhelmingly more than chance frequency, languages with dominant order VSO (verb-subject-object) have the adjective after the noun.
Universal 18	When the descriptive adjective precedes the noun, the demonstrative and the numeral, with overwhelmingly more than chance frequency, do so also.
Universal 19	When the general rule is that the descriptive adjective follows, there may be a minority of adjectives which usually precede, but when the general rule is that descriptive adjectives precede, there are no exceptions.
Universal 31	If either the subject or object noun agrees with the verb in gender, then the adjective always agrees with the noun in gender.
Universal 36	If a language has the category of gender, it always has the category of number.
Universal 37	A language never has more gender categories in nonsingular numbers than in the singular.
Universal 38	Where there is a case system, the only case which ever has only zero allomorphs is the one which includes among its meanings that of the subject of the intransitive verb.
Universal 42	All languages have pronoun categories involving at least three persons and two numbers.

---

[a]These are only a few of the language universals proposed by Joseph Greenberg (1963). Greenberg's original numbers are preserved here, since language researchers frequently refer to these universals by their original numbers.

that may lack syntactic recursion. And there's even a language that fails to show duality of patterning: in the emerging language known as Al-Sayyid Bedouin Sign Language (ABSL; see Figure 2.6), signs representing morphemes and words are holistic rather than being made up of decomposable parts, as is the case for all known spoken languages and other sign languages such as American Sign Language (ASL) (Sandler et al., 2011). It may be that there are very few generalizations (if any) that are true for all of the world's languages. Nevertheless, Greenberg also drew attention to patterns that were statistical rather than absolute, that is, patterns that stood out as very common across languages, but for which exceptions could be found, such as "In declarative sentences with subject and object noun phrases, the dominant word order is almost always one in which the subject precedes the object."

Greenberg's crosslinguistic studies suggested that human languages prefer to set up camp in a very small corner of the space of possible languages. Languages seem to shun not only the bizarre kinds of "non-rules" that I invented earlier, but also perfectly reasonable language choices, like ordering objects before subjects. What could explain the tendency for languages to be so like-minded? An intriguing explanation might be that the human brain imposes certain biases and limitations on what a language should look like. These could come through genetically based learning biases (that is, a universal grammar), or could result from various cognitive factors that make some linguistic forms easier to learn or to process than other forms.

How cognitively meaningful are language universals?

It's certainly tantalizing to think that we might learn something profound about the human mind by looking at the ways in which languages are alike. But as many researchers have pointed out, similarities across languages can crop up for reasons that have little to do with the inner workings of the human

BOX 12.1
Language change through language contact

While some elements are more likely to be borrowed than others, almost any aspect of one language can become folded into another as a result of language contact. Here are some examples, drawn from Thomason (2001).

Sound changes

"Click" consonants, present in the Khoisan languages of Africa, are among the most unusual sounds across languages. Rare as these sounds are, they've proven to be amenable to adoption by other languages. Several Bantu languages, such as Zulu, have integrated click consonants into their sound systems through language contact.

Before the Norman conquest of England in the eleventh century, the English sounds [f] and [v] were variants of the same phoneme; the voiced sound [v] occurred in the middles of words, while its unvoiced counterpart [f] appeared at word beginnings. However, after the Norman invasion, many French words were absorbed into the English language, including words that began with the [v] sound. Rather than conforming to the original English phonology, which would have resulted in their being pronounced with a word-initial [f] and, in many cases, sounding very similar to existing English words, these new words were uttered with word-initial [v]. Over time, this led to the two sounds splitting apart into completely separate phonemic categories /f/ and /v/.

Changes to morphology

In many languages, the pronoun for the first person plural is ambiguous between an "inclusive" meaning that includes the person(s) being addressed, and an "exclusive" meaning that does not. (Note that the English pronoun *we* contains just this kind of ambiguity. If someone tells you "We should repaint the house," does this include you or not?) The Dravidian languages spoken in southern India (including, Tamil, Kannada, and Malayalam) use distinct pronouns for these two meanings. Other Indian languages such as Marathi and Gujarati came to adopt the practice of using two separate pronouns to disambiguate the inclusive and exclusive meanings.

Mednyj Aleut, a language spoken on Bering Island, represents a blend of Russian and Aleut, and the language has imported the entire complex system of Russian verb endings.

In English, the morpheme *-able* on words like *readable* and *unstoppable* originally came into the language as an accessory on borrowed French words. Eventually, the morpheme came to be attachable to any English verb—including newly minted words like *Googleable* and *e-mailable*.

Changes to syntax

Finnish is genealogically distinct from most of the European languages, but has been shaped by close contact with its linguistic neighbors. Its basic sentence structure shifted from a subject-object-verb (SOV) word order to subject-verb-object (SVO), bringing the language more in line with nearby Indo-European languages.

Many of the languages spoken in India show evidence of having influenced each other's grammatical structures. For example, Dravidian inherited relative clauses and passive constructions from Sanskrit.

Predictors of change

Researchers who study change through language contact have noticed a few patterns. For one thing, languages that start off being quite similar to each other are more likely to borrow many elements from each other. Second, the intensity of the contact can determine the nature of the borrowing: Words are easily borrowed from one language into another even if the contact between them is very casual. But in order to mix grammatical elements together, a community usually needs to have quite a few bilingual speakers who know both languages well—after all, it takes a fairly deep knowledge of another language to incorporate its grammatical structures, as opposed to the odd word here and there.

Finally, the extent of one language's influence on another depends partly on the speakers' attitudes about incorporating linguistic changes. In some cases, speakers of a minority language may be very resistant to pressures from a dominant language. For example, current speakers of Montana Salish also know English, but the language community has resisted lexical borrowings, even when a concept has no corresponding word in Montana Salish. When speakers of Montana Salish were first acquainted with objects such as cars or televisions, they invented novel words using Montana Salish rather than importing the English words. Thus the Montana Salish word for a car is *p'ip'úyšn*—literally, "wrinkled feet," referring to the appearance of tire tracks.

mind. Recurring patterns across languages might simply reflect events of history. Many different languages can evolve out of a common ancestral tongue, and it wouldn't be surprising to find striking similarities among them merely due to their shared origins. Or, similarities could arise because speakers of two different languages came into regular contact with each other and influenced each other (see **Box 12.1** on the previous page). For instance, modern English offers a captivating record of the many imprints that other languages have left upon it. Such imprints are most obvious in the form of "borrowed" words like *lingerie* (French), *maximum* (Latin), *democracy* (Greek), *marijuana* (Spanish), *kindergarten* (German), or *futon* (Japanese). According to some estimates, as much as 75% of the vocabulary of English originated in other languages, largely Latin and French (Thomason, 2001). But language contact doesn't just affect word borrowings; more structural elements of phonology or syntax can also creep into languages from other tongues.

These historical accounts can be fascinating in their own right. But they don't necessarily tell us that much about how language works in the human mind, or where the boundaries of human language lie. To get a sense of the deeper constraints underlying language, it's important to survey a very large number of languages, placing special emphasis on those patterns that come up again and again even for languages that aren't historically related to each other, and whose speakers have not had contact with each other.

In one ambitious line of work, linguist Matthew Dryer (1992) tested Greenberg's universals against a much larger set of 625 languages, and found that, while some of Greenberg's proposed universals failed to hold up in the larger sample, others did quite well. There seemed to be particularly strong evidence for certain word order correlations. For example, if a language places the verb before the direct object in a sentence, you can bet on the fact that it also has prepositions, which occur *before* their associated noun phrases (also called prepositional objects). English is one such language (let's call it a "Type A" language):

Dimitri swept   the porch   with   a broom.

         verb   object   preposition   prepositional object

On the other hand, if a language places the verb *after* its object, as does Japanese, the chances are very good that it makes use of *post*positions, which occur *after* the associated noun phrase (let's call this a "Type B" language):

Taroo-   *waboo-*   *deinu* *-obutta*

Taroo   stick-with   dog   hit

Strong correlations like these have been taken as evidence of a deep cognitive bias. Researchers who argue for the existence of an innate universal grammar have suggested that we have inborn "settings" that constrain the possible word orders that we learn as children—we innately "know" that a language is either Type A or Type B. Other researchers have argued that the strong word order correlations reflect a general processing preference to keep word order rules consistent across different kinds of phrases.

More recently, Michael Dunn and his colleagues (2011) have argued that the word order correlations that characterize the Type A versus Type B languages don't reveal anything especially deep about the nature of human languages; instead, they simply reflect the historical development of languages. To support this argument, Dunn and his colleagues built a statistical model to take into account the lineage histories of languages. If word order correlations are indeed "true" universals that constrain the preferred word orders of human language, we'd expect them to appear independent of language lineage

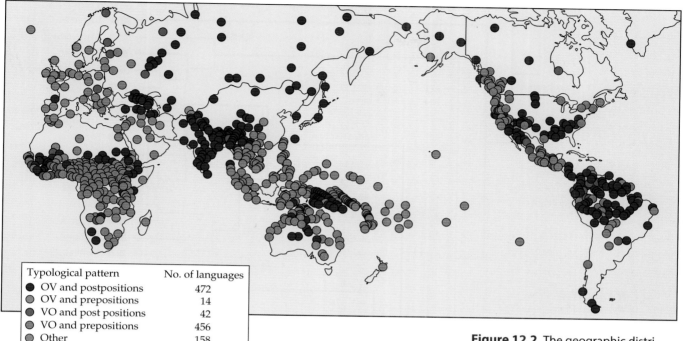

Typological pattern	No. of languages
● OV and postpositions	472
● OV and prepositions	14
● VO and post positions	42
● VO and prepositions	456
● Other	158

Figure 12.2 The geographic distribution of languages in terms of their ordering of the verb (V) and object (O) and presence of pre- and postpositions. Note how languages cluster geographically by type, suggesting that typological patterns may be due to linguistic lineage or language contact. (From Dryer, 2013c; see http://wals.info/feature/95A#2/14.9/152.8.)

or geography. But Type A and Type B languages divide up rather neatly by geography, as shown in **Figure 12.2**. Furthermore, Type A and Type B word order patterns tend to cluster in languages that are very closely related to each other, as shown in **Figure 12.3**.

The fact that word order type can be largely predicted by a language's historical roots and/or its geographic context makes it hard to rule out the possibility that either a common ancestry or contact between languages is responsible for the close connection between verb-object order and whether a language has prepositions or postpositions. Under this account, there's nothing "deep" about the fact that languages that have the verb-object order also tend to have prepositions rather than postpositions; the correlation simply reflects the fact that languages with a shared history are likely to be similar in a *number* of different ways. If you looked closely enough, you might find many other correlations, none of them particularly deep or meaningful.

Here's an analogy: Suppose you find a correlation between a language's use of tone to distinguish lexical meanings and the likelihood that its speakers use chopsticks as eating utensils. Does this point to some intrinsic connection between lexical tone and chopstick use? That seems rather unlikely. A more plausible interpretation is simply that the speakers of various tone languages share a common cultural and linguistic heritage, which included, among other things, the wielding of chopsticks during dinner.

Are there meaningful constraints on the shape of human languages, constraints that truly reflect something about the human mind? Looking at recurring crosslinguistic patterns and universals can provide some hints (and nowadays researchers can begin to explore interesting patterns with the help of research tools such as the online database of languages found in the World

WEB ACTIVITY 12.1

Variation across languages   In this activity, you'll explore the online World Atlas of Language Structures (WALS). This resource identifies many ways in which languages vary from one another, and allows you to see the geographic distributions of various linguistic features.

(A)

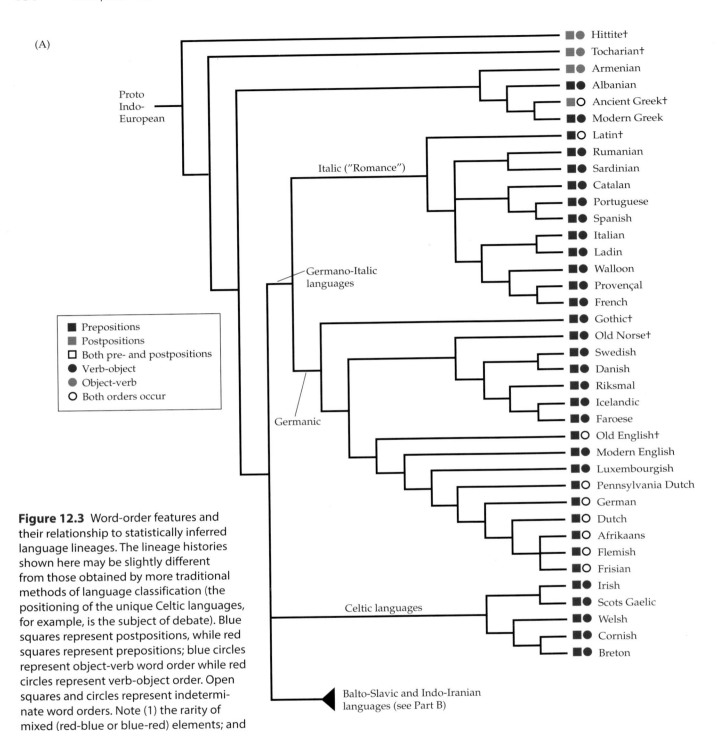

Figure 12.3 Word-order features and their relationship to statistically inferred language lineages. The lineage histories shown here may be slightly different from those obtained by more traditional methods of language classification (the positioning of the unique Celtic languages, for example, is the subject of debate). Blue squares represent postpositions, while red squares represent prepositions; blue circles represent object-verb word order while red circles represent verb-object order. Open squares and circles represent indeterminate word orders. Note (1) the rarity of mixed (red-blue or blue-red) elements; and (2) the degree to which linguistic elements are similar across closely related languages. (Adapted from Dunn et al., 2011.)

Atlas of Language Structures, or WALS). But as we've just seen, there are some remaining challenges in sorting out exactly where these similarities come from and how extensive they are. Luckily, we can work toward this question from another angle: we can start by looking at whether certain patterns are generally easier for people to learn or to produce than others, and by seeing whether there's a connection between the easy patterns and those that are commonly found across languages.

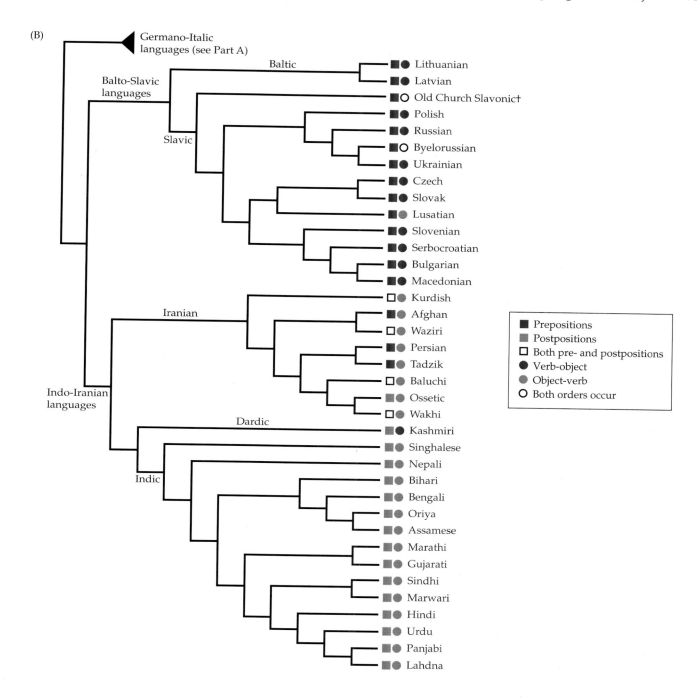

12.2 Explaining Similarities across Languages

Learning biases

Many researchers have argued that the existence of universal or recurring language patterns is evidence that the human mind plays favorites, finding some linguistic forms more "learnable" than others. But as you just saw, it's not always clear whether these crosslinguistic similarities have a cognitive basis as opposed to a historical one. Hence, a number of language scientists are finding more direct ways to search for learning biases.

If you were interested in pursuing this line of research, you'd have a few options. One strategy might be to gather detailed profiles of children's language development across a variety of languages, to see how well the learning data lined up with typological patterns. Would it take kids longer to master a weird feature that very few languages have, and would they make many mistakes on their way to learning it? This would be a perfectly logical approach, but it would come with some thorny practical and methodological challenges. For example, you could only study those "universals" for which you could find exceptions, since the whole approach would be to see whether the exceptional linguistic features were harder to learn than the common ones. This would eliminate the possibility of looking at some of the most robust—and possibly most interesting—universals. Another challenge would be that if you wanted to directly compare the learning trajectories for rare versus common structures, you'd need to make sure that the children in your studies got comparable doses of the two structures in their input. This would be a real concern, since structures that are rare across languages also tend to be rare even *within* those languages that allow them. As a result, these structures could take a long time for children to control, not because of their inherent difficulty, but simply because kids wouldn't come across them that often. None of these challenges would be insurmountable ones, but they'd constrain the questions you could ask, and make your research time-consuming and expensive.

Or, you could take the easy way out: invent a pair of miniature artificial languages with just the properties you're interested in, and compare how easily they're learned in a lab setting where you can carefully control the learners' input. This approach allows you to neatly test whether certain patterns are more readily learned than others. It even allows you to invent a language with structures that don't exist in any known human language.

We've already spent a bit of time in this book exploring the potential of experiments based on learning artificial language. In Chapter 4, you read how people (ranging from babies to adults) learned to use the statistical patterns in an artificial language to segment words from speech, even after a very short exposure to the language. In Chapter 6, you read how children learned syntactic categories based purely on statistical input, and that they showed sensitivity to statistical variation in deciding whether to generalize certain patterns. But language learners don't always faithfully reproduce the statistical patterns in the input they get, and this is where things get really interesting. For example, in a learning study with adults and 5- to 7-year-old children, Carla Hudson Kam and Elissa Newport (2005) created two versions of an artificial language. In one of these, any "noun" was always partnered with a word that functioned as a determiner (like *the* or *a* in English). In the other version, determiners showed up inconsistently, accompanying "nouns" only 60% of the time. The children and adults were later tested on their knowledge of the language (for example, by completing a partial sentence, or by judging whether certain sentences were correct). Most of the children coped with the inconsistent input by regularizing it—the majority of them produced the determiners all the time, while a few others always left them off. The adults, on the other hand, were more likely to preserve the original inconsistent patterns and produce determiners in about the same proportion as they'd heard them in the input. But a later study by the same authors showed that adults too could be nudged in the direction of over-regularization if the language was more complex or the learning task was made more difficult (Hudson Kam & Newport, 2009). So, it seems that when language learning is challenging, both children and adults are prone to changing a language by making it more systematic and regular.

TABLE 12.2 Examples of adjective/noun/numeral orders

Language	Order	Standard English order
Cherokee	*u-wo'-du a-ge-hyu'-tsa* pretty girl	pretty girl
	tso-i gu:-gu three bottles	three bottles
Yoruba	*bata titun* shoes new	new shoes
	awo meje dishes seven	seven dishes
Basque	*etxe zuri* house white	white house
	bi zuhaitz two trees	two trees
Sinhala	*loku pot* big books	big books
	geval tunak houses three	three houses

Source: Culbertson et al., 2012.

It's precisely in these gaps between the patterns in the input and the learners' output that we might find evidence of learning biases. Will certain language structures—those that are more "natural" or common for language—act as stronger magnets for generalization, causing language learners to settle into them on the basis of fairly sparse evidence in the input? If so, we might find that people are more eager to generalize patterns that are very common across languages, but don't readily generalize patterns that languages seem to avoid. This would be very compelling evidence that not all linguistic patterns have the same status in the mind.

Jennifer Culbertson and her colleagues (2012) used exactly this kind of reasoning to study a common crosslinguistic pattern known as "Greenberg's Universal 18," which states that,

> When the adjective precedes the noun, the numeral, with overwhelmingly more than chance frequency, does likewise.

The four logically possible ways of ordering adjective/noun pairs and numeral/noun pairs are:

1. adjective-noun & numeral-noun (as in English: *prickly socks & three socks*)

2. noun-adjective & noun-numeral (*socks prickly & socks three*)

3. noun-adjective & numeral-noun (*socks prickly & three socks*)

4. adjective-noun & noun-numeral (*prickly socks & socks three*)

All four word orders occur in real languages (see **Table 12.2**). But as you can see in **Table 12.3**, some of these word orders are more common across languages than others; in particular, the fourth order (adjective-noun & noun-numeral), as Greenberg originally noted, is exceedingly rare, representing just 4% of the 851 languages in the WALS sample.

Culbertson and her colleagues created an artificial learning task in which subjects had to learn the "alien" names for ten novel objects, as well as the names for five properties and five numerals. During a two-phase learning process, each

TABLE 12.3 Noun/adjective/numeral orders across 851 world languages

	Noun-adjective	Adjective-noun
Numeral-noun	149 (17%)	227 (27%)
Noun-numeral	443 (52%)	32 (4%)

Source: Culbertson et al., 2012.

(A) Learning

Phase 1: Learning nouns
Participants saw strings of single "objects" and heard and repeated made-up "nouns" that named the objects. After successfully testing on their knowledge of the nouns, they moved on to Phase 2.

"*nerka*"   "*wapoga*"

Phase 2: Learning numerals and adjectives
Participants saw novel word pairs in which adjectives designating colors or numerals combined with the previously learned nouns (nouns are in bold):

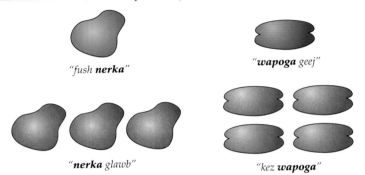

"*fush* **nerka**"   "**wapoga** *geej*"

"**nerka** *glawb*"   "*kez* **wapoga**"

Word pairs were presented in different proportions of the various possible word orders (distribution conditions). Participants were randomly assigned to one of the five distribution conditions in the table, and after 80 exposures, performed on a test (Phase 3) requiring them to correctly match each complex phrase to one of four images.

Assigned condition	Adjective-noun	Noun-adjective	Numeral-noun	Noun-numeral
0	50%	50%	50%	50%
1	70%	30%	70%	30%
2	30%	70%	30%	70%
3	30%	70%	70%	30%
4	70%	30%	30%	70%

(B) Testing

Phase 3: Subjects were required to produce a complex phrase containing adjectives or numerals as well as nouns. They were awarded 10 points for correct vocabulary, and an additional 5 points if they produced the same word order as their "alien informant." Participant responses were statistically matched to the word-order probabilities from Phase 2.

(1) Picture	(2) Participant responds	(3) Vocabulary points	(4) Informant responds	(5) Order points
	"*nerka geej*"	10	"*nerka geej*"	5

Figure 12.4 Experimental design and results from Culbertson et al. (2012). (A) Participants underwent a two-phase learning process, with evaluation for mastery at each phase. (B) The test phase was designed to assess whether participants would regularize inconsistent input in a way that lined up with the distribution of word orders across languages. (C) The graph shows the proportion of trials in which subjects produced the most common word for each input condition ("use of most common word order"). The dotted line indicates the frequency with which that order appeared in the target input. Note that participants tended to produce the most common word order with even greater regularity than it appeared in the input, except in Condition 4, which corresponded to the typologically rare distribution. (Adapted from Culbertson et al., 2012.)

(C) Results

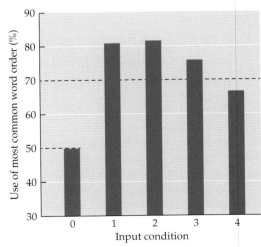

participant heard a version of the alien language in which all four of the above word orders occurred, but in varying proportions (see **Figure 12.4A**). Hence, they all received some data that was inconsistent with respect to the word order for that language. They then moved onto a test phase, in which the question of interest was whether they'd regularize the inconsistent input and (more to the point) whether they'd regularize inconsistent input in a way that lined up with the distribution of word orders across languages. If so, this would suggest it's no accident that some word orders are more common across languages than others.

In the test phase of the study (see **Figure 12.4B**), the subjects had to describe either a single alien object or a set of them, using the correct noun, adjective, and numeral words. They were awarded ten points for producing the right vocabulary items. They were given five bonus points if they generated the same word order as their computerized "alien informant." The responses of the "informant" were statistically generated in order to match the version of the language that each subject was working with—that is, if the noun-adjective order had appeared in the subject's target language 70% of the time, the "alien" was 70% likely to produce a noun-adjective order on the test items.

The researchers found that learners tended to regularize word order for some but not all of the languages (see **Figure 12.4C**). They were most likely to regularize patterns in which the noun occupied the same slot relative to both the adjective and the numeral—that is, the adjective-noun & numeral-noun pattern (Order 1 in Table 12.2), and the noun-adjective & noun-numeral word pattern (Order 2 in Table 12.2). They were *least* likely to regularize the pattern that was identified as rare by the language typologists (the adjective-noun & noun-numeral word order; Order 4 in Table 12.2). Even in a learning task that introduced some pressure to regularize, learners resisted producing a general pattern that went against the typological grain.

This study is only one of a number of experiments with artificial languages that show a close fit between learning biases and some attested crosslinguistic patterns. Findings like these make it hard to dismiss all typological universals as the results of historical forces, revealing no deeper truths about the ways in which human minds and human languages are made for each other.

Naturally, finding clear evidence of learning biases has the effect of fueling researchers' desire to explore their underlying nature. Throughout this book, we've explored two possible explanations for learning biases. One explanation, offered by researchers of a nativist bent, is that learning biases are evolutionary "gifts" that help us navigate our way through the enormous space of logically possibly languages; they are part of the innate language-specific knowledge we've inherited from our articulate ancestors. The other perspective is that learning biases reflect patterns that are especially easy to notice or remember; they come from general aspects of our cognition, and aren't necessarily language-specific.

Of course, it's possible that *both* kinds of learning biases exist, and each learning bias, as it's discovered, will need to be evaluated on a case-by-case basis. To do this, we might create non-linguistic analogues to artificial languages, and see if certain patterns are preferred over others even in non-linguistic domains. If they're found to be, that will suggest that the learning bias is grounded in general cognition. Here's one example of this approach in action, from a study by Julie Hupp and her colleagues (2009), who wanted to look at what's responsible for the fact that more languages prefer to mark inflectional information, such as plural or tense, by tagging the end of a word with a suffix (as in *cat-s*, or *walk-ed*), rather than by using a prefix at the beginning of a word (see **Table 12.4**).

TABLE 12.4 Preference for suffixes versus prefixes across 869 world languages

Preference	Number (percent) of languages
Equal prefixing and suffixing	147 (15%)
Prefer suffixing	529 (55%)
Prefer prefixing	52 (16%)
Little or no prefixing/suffixing	141 (14%)

Source: Dryer, 2013c; see http://wals.info/.

The researchers first set out to test whether this suffix-preference pattern reflects a general bias for language. They had subjects listen to a two-syllable sequence, such as *ta-tee*, and then asked them to decide whether this sequence was more similar to *bee-ta-tee*, or to *ta-tee-bee*. To make sense of this task, think about how you'd answer the question, "Is *cat* more similar to *cats* or to *scat*?" Presumably, your answer would be *cats*, because *cats* is just *cat* with an extra element attached, whereas *scat* and *cat* are two completely different words. By analogy, if people think that *ta-tee* is more similar to *ta-tee-bee* than to *bee-ta-tee*, it suggests that they find it easier to think of adding an extra piece at the end of a word (as a suffix) than at its beginning (as a prefix). When sounds are added at the beginnings of words, they might be more likely to be perceived as completely changing the identity of the original words, much as adding /s/ to the beginning of *cat* creates a completely different word. Sure enough, people generally found the sequences to be more similar if the syllable was attached to the end of the original sequence rather than to the front. The experimental results of this little study line up neatly with the crosslinguistic preference for using inflectional suffixes rather than prefixes.

The next step was to see whether this bias in similarity perceptions would extend into *non*-linguistic domains. Hupp and her colleagues concocted parallel tasks using sequences of musical notes or sequences of visual symbols as stimuli (see **Figure 12.5**). The results echoed the data for syllable strings; people thought that adding material to the front of a sequence changed it more deeply than adding material to the back end. The authors concluded that a domain-general bias nudges languages to attach inflectional information to words as suffixes rather than as prefixes.

Experiments like the ones I've just sketched represent very early explorations of learning biases in artificial languages, and more data need to be gathered. (For example, the study by Hupp and colleagues, while intriguing, was limited to English-speaking American subjects, and we'd certainly want to know how the learning task would play out for speakers of a language that handles affixes in a completely different way, or lacks them entirely.) But these studies no doubt mark the beginnings of a productive exchange between experimental psycholinguists and language typologists who meticulously pick through the languages of the world to find crosslinguistic patterns and correlations. In the lab, language scientists can test how learning biases might apply pressure on languages to settle into "friendly" grammars rather than difficult ones. They can also study how very subtle initial biases might change the shape of a language as it's transmitted from one set of users to another, mirroring historical processes of language change. And, in principle, studies of artificial language learning could also be used to address the question of whether learning biases truly *are* universal across all of the world's populations, or whether some populations might have evolved slightly different linguistic biases than others (see **Box 12.2**).

Target sequence   Prefix + target   Target + suffix

Figure 12.5 Two examples of the visual sequences devised by Hupp et al. (2009). Results of the study revealed that people judged the target strings to be more similar to the target + "suffix" sequences than they were to the "prefix" + target sequences.

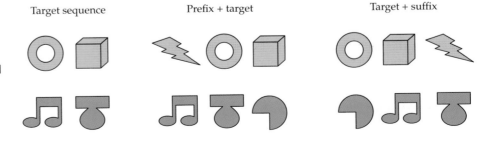

BOX 12.2
Do genes contribute to language diversity?

Throughout this book, I've adopted the common assumption that whatever genetic predisposition people have for learning language is a universal *human* predisposition. In broad strokes, this is surely right, in contrast to many more noticeable physical traits—people of, say, Japanese heritage may not usually grow to be as tall as people of Dutch heritage, but toss both of them into the same linguistic environment, and there's no noticeable difference in their mastery of that particular language, whatever it is.

At the same time, I've acknowledged that at the *individual* level, there are likely to be some genetically based differences among people. For example, disorders of language and speech (such as specific language impairment or stuttering) do tend to have a strongly heritable component. What's more, even individual differences that fall within the "typical" range of language abilities may have some genetic basis—for instance, Karin Stromswold (2001) found that heritability is a factor in the size of young children's expressive vocabularies, presumably due to a heightened capacity for word learning.

Is it possible, then, that some of the diversity found among the world's languages could be traced back to subtle genetic differences that shape the learning process of individuals within a language community? Recently, several researchers have begun to explore this possibility, as summarized by Dan Dediu (2011).

Any genetic variations that bias the learning process are likely to be very slight. This is apparent in the flexibility with which people can learn a variety of different languages, and the readiness of entire languages to absorb the traits of other languages they come into contact with. But even very slight individual differences in learning biases might be amplified within a larger population through the process of cultural transmission, as has been suggested by several computational models.

Some suggestive evidence for a possible link between genes and language structure comes from the study of tone languages, in which pitch is used to distinguish words or to convey grammatical information. Linguistic tone *is* a feature that can hop from one language to another through borrowing, suggesting that you don't need to have to be born into a specific linguistic population to be able to learn it—but Dediu has argued that the trait is more stable and less subject to language change than you'd expect if its transmission were purely culturally determined. More specifically, Dediu and his colleague Robert Ladd (2007) have argued that the geographic distribution of tone languages is connected to the prevalence of two human genes involved in brain growth and development, *ASPM* and *Microcephalin*.

It's still very, very early days for the genetic study of linguistic diversity, but in principle, the hypothesis could be systematically explored from a number of different angles. One possible approach might be to design artificial-language studies to test whether learning biases vary across geographic populations in a systematic way that is related to structural properties of the languages spoken in a geographic region.

Speakers' choices

As I've just discussed, the contours of human language may take some of their shape from learning biases that result in some structures being easier to learn than others. But this isn't the only way in which our cognitive makeup might tug language in one direction rather than another. Human language may also be influenced by factors that make some structures easier to *produce* than others.

Ultimately, the shape of a language is the result of millions of sentences uttered by its many speakers. Structures that are frequently produced are most likely to survive transmission across many generations; they are the most robustly learned, and hence the least likely to shape-shift or erode from a language over time. But what determines whether a certain structure is likely to be produced in the first place?

As you saw in Chapter 9, the act of speaking involves making constant choices from among the varied menu of linguistic options for expressing a particular idea. In that chapter, you read about how speakers' choices can be driven by cognitive pressures; in any particular instance, people will often choose a linguistic form that makes the arduous task of speaking just a little bit easier. Now, what if we zoom out and look at the production of language through the lens of linguistic universals or tendencies? Some provocative questions and predictions quickly arise.

Are some linguistic forms systematically easier to produce than others? If so, we'd expect that, wherever their language permitted, speakers would tend to use the easier forms more often than the more difficult options for expressing the same idea. This simple asymmetry could set in motion a cross-generational language shift: the input to new language learners would be riddled with the easier-to-say forms, while the harder-to-produce structures would be more sparse. We've already seen that new learners of a language have a tendency to over-regularize the input they hear; therefore, the next generation of language users would be prone to exaggerate these statistical differences. Over time, the harder structures might drop out of the language entirely, while the easier structures would be preserved. So we'd predict that if were to look across languages, we'd be more likely to find structures that ease the demands of speaking rather than corresponding structures that put more stress on cognitive resources during speaking.

Let's take a more concrete look at how production pressures could lead to common crosslinguistic patterns. I'll draw on an example from Maryellen MacDonald (2013), one researcher who has argued that production pressures are likely to play an important role in explaining crosslinguistic tendencies. In English, if we want to describe an event that involves two participants—the subject (S) and the object (O) of a verb (V)—we normally use the word order: subject-verb-object (SVO). The SVO order is just one of six possible ways in which these three linguistic units could be combined. But if we look across many of the world's languages, some of the options are wildly more popular than others. The vast majority of languages embrace the solution of placing the subject first; and languages seem to be almost allergic to ordering the object before the subject (see **Figure 12.6**).

Is it possible to tell a story about how production pressures might lead to a bias for placing the subject toward the beginning of a sentence? As discussed in Chapter 9, we know that when a word or phrase is highly accessible, speakers tend to utter it as quickly as possible. The general idea is that as soon as speakers are mentally prepared to utter a word or phrase, they spit it out in order to avoid clogging up working memory while planning the rest of the sentence. We saw that various factors could affect the accessibility of a linguistic unit. For example, shorter phrases were more likely than longer phrases to be uttered early in the sentence. Words could be made more accessible through previous mention, or through priming with a semantically related word. And in some experimental manipulations, characters or objects in a visual scene were made more visually salient through the use of flashing markers—with the result that drawing visual attention to an entity made it more likely that speakers would mention it first.

If, upon planning a sentence, speakers find that it's especially easy to bring to mind the instigators of the action they want to describe, then they should prefer to order subjects first, wherever possible. Some researchers (e.g., Bock et al., 1992) have suggested that animate concepts, such as *dentist* or *woman*, are retrieved from memory more easily than inanimate ones, such as *flower* or *car*. Animacy is very closely linked to subjecthood; notice that whenever an event involves an animate participant and an inanimate entity, the animate participant is almost always the subject—just try coming up with sentences involving the word pairs *dentist/flowers*, *steak/panther*, and *boy/book*.

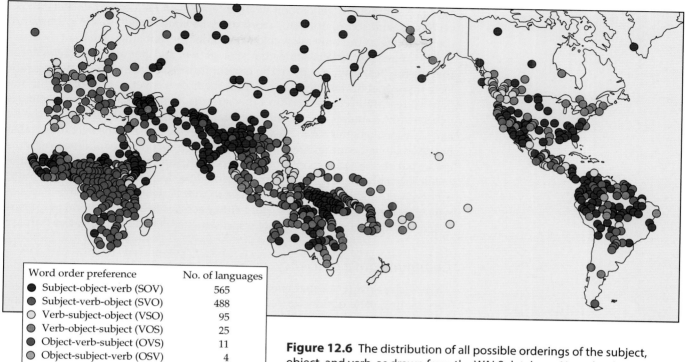

Word order preference	No. of languages
● Subject-object-verb (SOV)	565
● Subject-verb-object (SVO)	488
○ Verb-subject-object (VSO)	95
● Verb-object-subject (VOS)	25
● Object-verb-subject (OVS)	11
● Object-subject-verb (OSV)	4
● Lacking a dominant word order	189
TOTAL	1377

Figure 12.6 The distribution of all possible orderings of the subject, object, and verb, as drawn from the WALS database. Note the dramatic shortage of languages that place the object before the subject. (Adapted from Dryer, 2013a; see http://wals.info/feature/81A#2/18.0/152.8.)

Indeed, a number of studies have shown that speakers exercise their grammatical options in such a way as to order animate nouns earlier in the sentence than inanimate nouns. In the study by Kay Bock and her colleagues, subjects were more likely to use the passive voice if it resulted in the animate participant being ordered before the inanimate object in the sentence: *The boy was hit by the truck,* rather than *The truck hit the boy.*

Let's imagine that the English language evolved from a previous state in which word order was quite fluid and multiple word orders were allowed, as is the case for a number of existing languages. So, for example, all of the following sentences could have meant the same thing:

The students devoured the free pizza. (SVO)

The students the free pizza devoured. (SOV)

Devoured the students the free pizza. (VSO)

Devoured the free pizza the students. (VOS)

The free pizza the students devoured. (OSV)

The free pizza devoured the students. (OVS)

Because of the pressures on language production just described, the subject-first orders would be easier to produce than others, and hence would be the most likely to be uttered. Let's suppose that the SVO order was the most commonly produced order. (In Web Activity 12.2, you'll have the opportunity to explore why this particular order might be preferred over the other subject-first solutions.) The next generation of learners, who heard the SVO order more often than any of the others, would magnify this bias in their own language usage. The subsequent generation would see an even greater proportion of SVO sentences, and so on, until this word order became "fixed" in the grammar of the language as the only allowable word order for that language.

The above scenario is somewhat speculative, and not all researchers agree that it's the best way to explain the crosslinguistic preference for ordering subjects first—careful testing of competing theories has yet to take place. But the general research program behind this specific account is a promising one. As you saw in Chapter 9, the cognitive demands of producing language on the fly can lead speakers to systematically favor some linguistic forms over others that have the same meaning. This imbalance in the frequencies of alternative forms could put the language on a path to crystallizing the original bias with the result that only the favored alternative would be deemed acceptable. Naturally, any such production biases would have to interact with the learning biases of new learners—learning biases could either accelerate or put the brakes on language change that was triggered by speakers' tendencies to use easier forms.

Communicative efficiency

There's clear evidence that speakers often act as cognitive misers, exploiting various linguistic options to reduce their own processing costs. But avoiding extra work is obviously not the only thing that motivates speakers—after all, the whole point of talking in the first place is to get your message across. Presumably, the desire to avoid communicative breakdown also guides the linguistic choices of speakers.

One of the most common ways in which communication can break down is through ambiguity—the speaker intends one meaning, but the language he's chosen doesn't allow the hearer to figure out which one of several possible meanings he has in mind. Throughout the last few chapters, we've seen that speakers have a mixed record when it comes to detecting and avoiding possible ambiguities that could disrupt the hearer's interpretation. For instance, we've seen that speakers have a hard time noticing that words like *bat* can mean either of two very different things, or eliminating the garden path effect for sentences like *I hear you are leaving*, where the hearer might initially be lured into thinking that the word *you* is the direct object of hear (as in *I hear you loud and clear*). We've also seen that speakers don't always take into account the hearer's perspective or knowledge, showing a tendency to fall back on more egocentric strategies when cognitive resources are scarce. It's hard to make the case that avoiding processing difficulties for the hearer is uppermost in the speaker's mind as he makes rapid-fire decisions about how to linguistically encode his intended message. Still, for the most part, speakers and hearers do seem to avoid communicative meltdowns. The ambiguity that's inherent in everyday language can usually be resolved by the hearer —for instance, pronouns, which are *exceedingly* ambiguous, are usually interpreted without any angst, and only some garden path sentences cause anything more than a minor hiccup in language processing. Some balance seems to have been struck between the processing demands on the speaker, and potential for confusion by the hearer.

One intriguing idea is that speakers are freed up from having to consider potential ambiguity on a sentence-by-sentence basis because their language won't allow them to produce truly problematic ambiguities—the idea is that language quickly evolves in ways that limit the rampant possibility of gross misinterpretations. The remaining ambiguities that the language does allow can be handled quite easily by the hearer.

Many languages have flexible word orders, in which case word order doesn't provide any information about whether a noun phrase plays the role of subject, direct object, or indirect object in a sentence. Such languages often have **case markers** to do the job—these are morphemes that are attached to nouns (or some element within noun phrases) to identify who did what to whom. In English sentences like *The man bites the dog* versus *The dog bites the man*, we depend on word order to decipher meaning. But in German, you can unambiguously describe a man-bites-dog incident using either one of the following word orders:

Der Mann beißt den Hund.

Den Hund beißt der Mann.

This is because the article *der* in *der Mann* ("the man") signals that this noun phrase is a subject, while the article in the noun phrase *den Hund* ("the dog") unambiguously marks it as a direct object. If you wanted to describe a dog-bites-man occurrence, you could avail yourself of these two options, again, neither of them ambiguous:

Der Hund beißt den Mann.

Den Mann beißt der Hund.

In German, articles are always helpfully marked for case. But some languages are a bit stingier with their case markers, and use them for certain types of noun phrases but not others. What's interesting is that in such languages—referred to as languages with **differential case marking**—the case marker tends to appear in only those situations where it would be most helpful for avoiding ambiguity. For example, in Sinhalese, word order is flexible, and the case marker *-wa* often appears as a suffix on direct objects, but only if they are animate:

Amara Lalani-wa edda	or	*Lalani-wa Amara edda*
Amara Lalani pulled	or	Lalani Amara pulled

In fact, both of the above sentences would translate into English as "Amara pulled Lalani," and the case marker is crucial for letting the hearer know who did the pulling. But if the object is inanimate, the danger of ambiguity is slight, because inanimate objects rarely instigate events. In these cases, Sinhalese prohibits the object from wearing an accusative case marker, so if you want to tell someone that Amara bought a book, you can't say:

*Amara pota-wa gatta	or	**Pota-wa Amara gatta*
Amara book bought	or	Book Amara bought

Instead, the word for the inanimate object, a book, has to appear bare:

Amara pota gatta	or	*Pota Amara gatta*
Amara book bought	or	Book Amara bought

Across languages, case markers crop up where the potential for ambiguity is greatest. If other aspects of the language (such as word order) step up to take on a disambiguating function, the case system is vulnerable to erosion over time, and may eventually be wiped entirely from the language. This is what happened in the transition from Latin, which had case marking and relatively free word order, to Italian, Portuguese, and Spanish, which have more rigid word order. Although remnants of case marking stayed in the pronoun system and prepositions, most of the case markers from Latin are gone, because systematic word order is used instead. The selective presence of such markers suggests that languages settle into a "sweet spot" where the speaker is freed from unnecessary complexity, but is steered by the grammar of the language to provide enough information to avoid serious confusion in hearers.

case markers Morphemes that occur within a noun phrase to signal its grammatical function (e.g., subject, direct object, indirect object). Case markers may occur on nouns, articles, adjectives, or on any or all of these.

differential case marking A system of case marking in which case markers appear selectively on some but not all noun phrases. For example, object case marking may be limited to appearing with animate nouns.

Once again, experimenting with artificial languages provides an opportunity to test ideas about how languages might evolve to balance the demands of language production with the need for clear communication. In one such study, Maryia Fedzechkina and her colleagues (2012) created an artificial language with flexible word order, in which both subject-object-verb (SOV) and object-subject-verb (OSV) orders were allowed. This meant that speakers couldn't assume that hearers would be able to understand the meaning of a sentence based solely on its word order. The language also contained optional case markers, and hence the opportunity to disambiguate sentence meanings. But unlike languages with differential case marking, this miniature language didn't distribute its case markers in a selective way to prevent the worst ambiguities. For example, case marking appeared just as often on inanimate objects as on animate ones, despite the fact that it's much more useful for disambiguating meaning when it appears on an animate object. Adult learners of this language came into the lab for four sessions of training and testing. Even though they were exposed to input in which case markers were evenly doled out between animate and inanimate nouns, this wasn't the pattern that they reproduced in their own speech. Instead, they shifted the language toward differential case marking: they were more likely to produce case markers on animate objects than inanimate ones. In other words, case marking appeared more often in sentences whose meanings were especially hard to infer based on animacy.

This simple experiment suggests that when the grammar of a language leaves room for systematic confusion about meaning, new learners are apt to "fix" it by providing extra information where it's most likely to be needed. It's not clear exactly how this happens. For example, it could be that people are somehow biased to learn linguistic systems that maximize communicative efficiency, so informative case marking is easier to learn than less informative case marking. Or, it could be that the speakers in this study were able to anticipate the potential for serious misunderstandings, and avert communicative disaster through their judicious use of case markers. It will take some careful experimentation to tease apart the various competing explanations.

12.3 Words, Concepts, and Cultures

Different words, different thoughts?

In the previous sections, I focused on the tantalizing similarities that turn up across languages, and delved into some possible explanations for why it is that languages often look so much alike. But human nature being what it is, we're often at least as fascinated by the *differences* among groups of people as we are by the things that all humans seem to have in common. Language offers endless opportunities for creative speculation about the nature of these differences. It's worth keeping in mind, though, that while it's easy to *assert* that speakers of a different language have deeply different ways of thinking, it's much harder to come up with a plausible theory for how this might happen.

A promising place to start is with the mapping of words onto concepts. As you saw in Chapter 5 (Language at Large 5.1), languages carve up conceptual space in quite different ways. The presence or absence of specific words in a language often serves as a magnet for cultural commentary. For example, in writing about the sexual shenanigans of former Italian prime minister Silvio Berlusconi, journalist Rachel Donadio (2011) couldn't help pointing out:

> It is not always easy to translate between Italian and American sensibilities. There is no good English word for "veline," the

scantily clad Vanna White-like showgirls who smile and prance on television, doing dance numbers even in the middle of talk shows. And there is no word in Italian for accountability. The closest is "responsibilità"—responsibility—which lacks the concept that actions can carry consequences.

The Italian word *responsibilità* has a broad meaning, roughly lumping together meanings that English slices up into different words such as *responsibility, accountability, guilt,* and *liability.* In drawing attention to this fact, the writer implies that there is some connection between Berlusconi's antics and the Italian lexicon. The same connection has been drawn by other commentators in less subtle ways, as in the following from a blog post by economist Frederic Sautet (2006):

> Last week Graham Scott gave a lecture on public sector management and governance at the Mercatus Center. Dr. Scott was the Secretary of the New Zealand Treasury between 1986 and 1993, which was a very important position at the time of the NZ reform process. … During his lecture Graham Scott remarked that the word "accountability" has no translation in many languages. For instance, it has no direct translation in French and Spanish. I presume it is the same with other Latin-based languages, such as Italian or Portuguese. While the word "responsibility" is Latin in its origin (and thus has equivalents in French and Spanish and other languages), it encompasses more than just accountability and, for that reason, is much less precise. In Scott's view, the concept of accountability is at the core of the public management reforms in New Zealand. But its absence in many other languages may limit (and perhaps has already limited) the adoption of similar reforms elsewhere. Or it may lower the quality of their results. This would show the power of language in shaping institutions.

If you unpack such commentaries, you'll find that they're wrapped around at least one, and often both, of the following assumptions:

1. If a language doesn't have a word to convey a specific concept or to distinguish that concept from other similar ones, it's because its speakers don't care enough about that concept or particular distinction to devote a separate word to it.

2. If a language doesn't have a separate word for a specific concept, speakers of that language will have a hard time understanding the concept.

Let's hold these assumptions up to the bright glare of scientific sunlight, and evaluate how likely it is that they're correct.

Do words reflect culturally important concepts?

The first assumption—that the lack of a word reflects the lack of importance speakers place on the concept—is based on the premise that the relationship between concepts and the lexicon is not arbitrary. Presumably, if a concept is salient or important enough, speakers will invent a word for it. There has to be some truth to this notion. In Chapter 5, I discussed how children make reasonable guesses about the meanings of words by relying on natural ways to form categories. They have expectations about which aspects of the world are most likely to be talked about—talk about rabbits is more likely than talk about rabbit parts, or rabbit textures, or about the category that includes things that taste good in a stew.

It's likely that some conceptual distinctions are universally more salient than others, leading to some predictable ways of structuring the lexicon of any language. For example, in his book *Through the Language Glass*, linguist Guy Deutscher (2010) invites you to imagine coming across an old manuscript that describes a language called "Ziftish." In Ziftish, it turns out, there is a word *bose*, which is used to refer to white roses and all birds except those with red chests. Another word, *rird*, is used for red-chested birds and all roses except white ones. Deutscher wants to know: Do you, the discoverer of this manuscript, take it to be a factual diary of an early explorer? Or a fictional account—perhaps a long-lost sequel to *Gulliver's Travels*? The manuscript reeks of fiction, because it seems deeply implausible that a language would confer words on such unnatural categories.

This example suggests that salient or natural concepts attract words more readily than less natural ones. So what about when languages diverge in how they map concepts onto language? A reasonable hypothesis is that the divergence reflects how important these concepts are for particular communities of speakers.

It's not hard to come up with examples where certain lexical distinctions align neatly with the cultural importance of their corresponding concepts. Surely, a culture where all food is cooked on a spit over the fire or warmed up in the microwave has no need for a specialized vocabulary that distinguishes between words like *sauté, braise, grill, boil, bake, blanch, poach, broil, simmer, fricassee, flambé, steam, fry, caramelize, stew, sear*, and so on. When it comes to such words, necessity is a plausible mother of invention.

Perhaps the most striking example of how culture can drive the invention of words is in the domain of color vocabulary. Even within a single language like English, some speakers feel compelled to specify that a color is *magenta* or *chartreuse*, or to distinguish between *crimson* and *scarlet*, while others are perfectly satisfied with basic color terms like *blue, yellow*, and *red*. But if you think that all languages at least distinguish between the basic colors—much as they'd likely have separate words for general categories like birds or flowers—you'd be wrong. For example, it may surprise you to hear that color terms are virtually absent from the ancient Greek epics of Homer, as noted in 1858 by classics scholar William Gladstone (who is better known for having served four terms as the prime minister of Great Britain). This observation led Gladstone to speculate that the ancient Greeks were color-blind, and that humans have only very recently developed color vision as we have it today. This notion was taken seriously by many scientists of the time, even though some questioned whether the evolution of color vision could have developed in the short span of several thousand years of human history.

But in the twentieth century, as linguists and anthropologists began to comb through the existing languages of the world, they found many languages that didn't have separate words for green versus blue, for example, or even red versus yellow (see **Box 12.3**). The speakers of these languages weren't color-blind. They could *see* that green and blue were different colors, they just thought it would be odd to call them by different names—just as you might be able to see that two slightly different shades of red are different from each other, but wonder why anyone would need to have different words for them. Speakers of all languages, it turns out, can detect color differences that they don't bother to mark with different words. But language communities can differ widely in the number of distinct color words they feel are necessary. Many of the languages with very small color vocabularies are spoken in non-industrial societies that don't do much manufacturing of objects involving artificial color. In such a

BOX 12.3
Variations in color vocabulary

What could be more basic than color concepts like brown, green, yellow, and red? A survey of color terms across the world's languages shows surprising diversity in the number of color terms that are used in a language. In English, if we consider just those color terms that correspond to single, commonly used words, we have a total of eleven: *black, white, red, yellow, green, blue, purple, brown, orange, pink,* and *gray*. This represents the upper end of the vocabulary size for basic color terms across languages, as shown in **Figure 12.7**. Many languages make do with as few as three terms to express color.

Some languages use simple color words to make distinctions that we don't make in English. For example, Russian and Greek have separate words for dark and light shades of blue. But many other languages use a single term to name colors that English refers to by different names. For example:

Yupik (as spoken in Siberia) and Pirahã (Brazil; see Box 6.3) use a single word for green and blue.

Lele (Chad) and Javaé (Brazil) use a single word for yellow, green, and blue.

Gunu (Cameroon) and Tacana (Bolivia) refer to red and yellow with a single word.

Some researchers (most notably Brent Berlin and Paul Kay, 1969) have argued that there are certain important color-naming universals reflecting underlying perceptual constraints. As with linguistic structures, some color terms appear to be more common than others. For instance, if a language has only three color terms, the terms tend to separate into these categories: (1) white; (2) red and yellow; and (3) black, green, and blue. And, while it's common for languages to use a single word for green and blue, basic word distinctions between dark and light blue are rare.

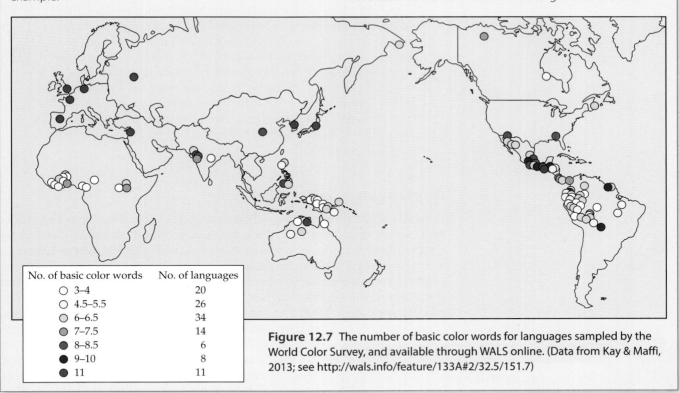

No. of basic color words	No. of languages
○ 3–4	20
○ 4.5–5.5	26
◔ 6–6.5	34
◑ 7–7.5	14
● 8–8.5	6
● 9–10	8
● 11	11

Figure 12.7 The number of basic color words for languages sampled by the World Color Survey, and available through WALS online. (Data from Kay & Maffi, 2013; see http://wals.info/feature/133A#2/32.5/151.7)

society, the color of an object is largely predictable from its inherent nature, so why would you bother to specify it?

To help you imagine what it might be like to live in a culture where a detailed color vocabulary seems unimportant, Guy Deutscher invites you to imagine a distant future in which each household has a kitchen appliance that creates food from frozen cubes. The machine can create foods that are identical to those found in nature—for instance, an avocado, or a grapefruit—but it can also be programmed to combine textures and flavors in completely new ways, allowing you to design a food with the oily consistency of an avocado, but a taste halfway between a carrot and a mango. The people who live in this world have developed a rich vocabulary to describe this space of possible flavors and food textures.

Now, imagine that this future society sends an anthropologist back to our time with a tray of 1,024 taste samples. She finds that while we "natives" can distinguish between the various tastes, when asked to provide a name for each sample, we come up with only the crudest distinctions, like "sweet" or "sour," or "it's a bit like an *X*," where *X* is the name of some natural food. The anthropologist is flummoxed; since we can obviously taste the difference between the samples, why is our language so defective? As Deutscher explains:

> Let's try to help her. Suppose you are one of those natives and she has given you a cube that tastes like nothing you've ever tried before. Still, it vaguely reminds you of something. For a while you struggle to remember, then it dawns on you that this taste is slightly similar to those wild strawberries you had in a Parisian restaurant once, only this taste is ten times more pronounced and blended with a few other things you can't identify. So finally, you say, very hesitantly, "it's a bit like wild strawberries." Since you look like a particularly intelligent and articulate native, the anthropologist can't resist posing a meta-question: doesn't it feel odd and limiting, she asks, not to have precise vocabulary to describe tastes in the region of wild strawberries? You tell her that the only things "in the region of wild strawberry" that you've ever tasted before were wild strawberries, and that it has never crossed your mind that the taste of wild strawberries should need any more general or abstract description than "the taste of wild strawberries." She smiles with baffled incomprehension.

Word-to-culture mismatches

Detailed vocabulary within a specific domain, then, might reflect something about how much a culture cares about communicating certain conceptual distinctions. On the other hand, it's also not hard to come up with examples where differences in language don't seem to be related in any obvious way to cultural values or practices. For instance, Norwegian pronouns differentiate between the masculine and feminine third-person singular (*han* versus *hun*), while Farsi, spoken in Iran, uses the same word (*u*) for both. Are we to conclude from this that distinguishing between males and females is less culturally important to speakers of Farsi than it is to Norwegians?

Other examples abound. Words that describe spatial relations are also subject to a lot of crosslinguistic variation, for no clear cultural reasons. Why, for example, does English need the different words *in* and *on*, while Spanish is content with the single word *en*? Or why does English require speakers to distinguish between the concepts of above and on (see **Figure 12.8**), while Korean does not? In some cases, a language's lexical inventory does seem to contain elements of arbitrariness.

WEB ACTIVITY 12.3

Words and culture In this activity, you'll explore some examples of crosslinguistic differences in the mapping of words to concepts. You'll be asked to generate hypotheses about which crosslinguistic differences are likely to be motivated by possible cultural differences, and which are likely to be arbitrary.

English:
The cup is **above** the table.

Korean:
cup-i thatka wi-e issta
 cup   table   top   be
              or
cup-i thatka wi-e ette issta
 cup   table   top   floating be

English:
The cup is **on** the table.

Korean:
cup-i thatka wi-e issta
 cup   table   top   be
              or
cup-i thatka wi-e putte issta
 cup   table   top   sticking be

Figure 12.8 Examples of spatial relationships that *must* be linguistically distinguished in English, but may or may not be distinguished in Korean (see Munnich et al., 2001).

There are other good reasons to doubt that the words of a language transparently reflect a culture's most important concepts. Languages tend to be a lot like houses: live in the same one long enough, and you'll accumulate piles of objects that you once bought to serve a specific need, but that now just hang around because you figure you still might use them every now and then. There may be family heirlooms that don't reflect your own tastes and values, but that seem too valuable to throw out. You may have collections of exotic objects from your various travels, chosen less for their usefulness than their novelty. Your house becomes less of a reflection of your needs and priorities right now than a historical record of your entire life.

This analogy is a reminder that the language of any existing culture reflects a linguistic code that has accumulated (usually) over a long period of time. Though it's subject to constant adjustments and tinkering, most of its elements are preserved from one generation to the next. You can see this in the way that some languages, such as English, French, or Spanish, have fanned out across very diverse cultures, and yet don't seem to have undergone dramatic reorganization in a way that reflects the scope of the cultural differences of their speakers. For the most part, English speakers in the United States make use of the same collection of words as English speakers in Australia or Singapore. Though it's true that new words are sometimes introduced to meet a culture's needs when there are glaring gaps (for example, *filibuster, outback, jackeroo, hillbilly*), most of the words in the lexicon of any English speaker are inherited from long-dead ancestors rather than invented anew to meet the needs of speakers at a particular time and place.

It's also important to keep in mind that just because a language hasn't dedicated a particular word to a concept, this doesn't mean its speakers have no way to express the concept. In English, the word *grandfather* refers to either your mother's father or your father's father, but this doesn't mean you can't use language to make the distinction—in fact, I just did. (Alternatively, you could use *maternal grandfather* or *grandfather on my mother's side*.) And while German has the handy word *schadenfreude*, which we English speakers sometimes borrow, we have no trouble using our own language to describe the feeling of glee at another person's misfortune—we just go about it in a slightly more roundabout way.

Whether a language uses a single word or a phrase to express a certain concept depends to some extent on the machinery that exists within the language for building new words. For example, the German language is unusually enthusiastic when it comes to creating complex words such as *Freundschaftsbezeigung* (meaning "demonstration of friendship") or *Unabhaengigkeitserklaerungen* ("declarations of independence"). This fact led the American humorist Mark Twain (1880) to observe: "These things are not words, they are alphabetical processions. And they are not rare; one can open a German newspaper at any time and see them marching majestically across the page—and if he has any imagination he can see the banners and hear the music, too."

In its compounding zeal, English falls somewhere between German and French; where English speakers use a word like *housecoat*, French speakers would use the expanded phrase *robe de chambre* (literally "dress for a bedroom"). All things being equal, then, a complex concept is most likely to become coined as a single word in German, and least likely to be coded as a single word in French.

It's too simple, then, to conclude that just because a particular word exists in a language, it reflects an important concept for the people who speak it, or conversely, that the absence of the word reveals that speakers are indifferent to the concept. This may be true in cases of highly specialized vocabularies, but clearly, a number of factors complicate the picture.

Do words help organize thoughts?

Let's now turn to the second common assumption about the relationship between language and culture: that a language's inventory of words has an effect on how its speakers think about or perceive the world. This notion is referred to as the **Whorf hypothesis**, after the linguist Benjamin Lee Whorf (1897–1941), or sometimes as the Sapir-Whorf hypothesis, to include Whorf's contemporary Edward Sapir (1884–1939).

In light of the previous discussion, it seems extremely unlikely that the absence of a word from a speaker's lexicon would *block* him from grasping a particular concept—after all, the concept behind *schadenfreude* is perfectly intuitive, even in its English paraphrased version, and there's nothing intrinsically difficult about the notion of a maternal grandfather, despite the fact that it requires two words to express it. Hence, we should be highly suspicious of the claim that speakers of languages that lack a single word for the notion of accountability are inevitably hampered in their efforts at public reforms. As linguist and blogger Mark Liberman (2011) notes, cheek swollen with tongue:

> In fact, it's possible that only English speakers can grasp the concept of accountability, at least if we accept that no one could possibly understand an idea that they need an expression longer than one word to name, or some context to interpret. The French, for example, would need to talk about having "comptes à rendre," requiring three or even four words. This same limitation may explain why it's so difficult for us English speakers to get our minds around things like reforming the health insurance system, since we need five or six words even to refer to the issue.

But there are more nuanced (and realistic!) ways in which to develop the idea that words leave an imprint on thought. For example, you might think of the relationship between words and concepts as analogous to the relation-

Whorf hypothesis The hypothesis that the words and structures of a language can affect how the speakers of that language conceptualize or think about the world.

ship between phonemic categories and the speech soundscape. As you saw in Chapter 4, babies are able to distinguish between a great many speech sounds very early in their lives. But experience with language soon leads them to impose phonemic categories on these speech sounds. As phonemic categories are formed, babies learn to pay more attention to the differences between sounds that fall into different categories, and less attention to sounds that fall within the same category—for example, at some level, English babies (and adults) treat aspirated [pʰ] and unaspirated [p] as equivalent, as demonstrated by classical categorical perception tests, but they're highly sensitive to the differences between /b/ and /p/. In many cases, a language will helpfully place a phonemic boundary at a "natural" juncture—that is, where the auditory system is already predisposed to detect differences between sounds. But whether these boundaries are natural or not, over time, babies' exposure to the phonemic categories that are evident in the language around them shapes their perceptual experience of the phonetic space.

Perhaps words impose category structure on conceptual space in a similar way. We don't want to say that words are *necessary* in order for concepts to be understandable, because, as we've seen, it's perfectly possible to grasp a concept even if your language doesn't have a word for it. (And, as discussed in Digging Deeper in Chapter 5, there's also some evidence that babies form certain conceptual categories well before they learn the meanings of words.) But perhaps words help to draw attention to some distinctions over others just as phonemic categories do.

WEB ACTIVITY 12.4

Testing the Whorf hypothesis
In this activity, you'll consider several examples of crosslinguistic differences in word-to-concept mappings, and you'll explore some possible ways in which you might test for the effects of language on conceptual organization.

A colorful case study

Some of the earliest questions about the relationship between language and thought arose in the domain of color. As a result, this topic has served as a magnet for crosslinguistic and experimental data.

You've already seen (in Box 12.3) some arguments that the color vocabulary of a language depends partly on universal constraints on color vision, and partly on the cultural importance of naming color as an abstract property. Regardless of whether a person's color vocabulary is large or small, though, people can usually detect many more color distinctions than they can name. Still, it's possible that a lifetime of naming colors in a particular way has made you slightly more sensitive to some color differences than others.

In 1984, Paul Kay and Willett Kempton tested whether speakers of English would have subtly different judgments about colors than speakers of Tarahumara, a language spoken in northern Mexico. Unlike English, Tarahumara has only one word, *siyo'name*, to refer to both green and blue. Are English speakers more sensitive to slight differences between colors that straddle the green/blue boundary than Tarahumara speakers? And if so, are English speakers more sensitive to small differences that cross the green/blue divide than they are to small differences between two shades of blue? An asymmetrical pattern like this would be reminiscent of the way in which English speakers "hear" the sounds [p] and [pʰ] as highly similar, while "hearing" /p/ and /b/ as clearly distinct, even if the acoustic distance between the sounds is *objectively* the same for both pairs.

To create an experiment that mirrored the categorical perception studies with sounds, Kay and Kempton needed to have a way to capture the objective differences between colors. Fortunately, one had already been developed in the early twentieth century by Albert Munsell. (The Munsell color system serves as the basis for organizing color space by categorizing colors along the

Figure 12.9 Example stimuli used by Kay and Kempton (1984) in the "odd one out" task for color perception. Subjects were asked to identify which of the color samples was more distant from the other two samples than those two were from each other. Speakers of English, but not speakers of Tarahumara, tended to exaggerate the distance between stimuli B and C, which span the English blue/green boundary.

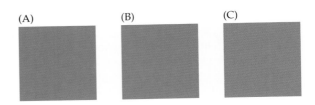

dimensions of hue, brightness, and saturation.) For each of their experimental trials, Kay and Kempton chose three closely neighboring color chips from the Munsell chart. Subjects were told that two of the colors were very similar to each other, but that one was more distant from the other two; the subjects' task was to identify the "odd one out" (**Figure 12.9**). Based on the subjects' responses over a number of trials, the researchers calculated a score of perceived distance between critical pairs of color chips, and compare these to measures of objective distance. They found that the language spoken by subjects did have an effect on the perceived distances between colors. English speakers judged the distance between a "blue" and a "green" chip to be bigger than the distance between two shades of "blue," even if the objective distances were identical. (The boundaries between the English green and blue categories were previously established on the basis of responses from English speakers who did not participate in the "odd one out" task.) On the other hand, Tarahumara speakers did not exaggerate the distance between colors across the green/blue boundary.

Is this convincing evidence that having different labels for green and blue has warped the perceptual system of English speakers? Perhaps not. It's hard to know whether the subjects' behavior on the test is truly reflecting *perception*. Possibly what's happening is something like this: The test questions are very hard to answer with any certainty, based on perceptual information alone. Maybe when confronted with a trio of very similar colors, English speakers tell themselves, "Hmm, these all look so close to each other, it's hard to tell which one of them is slightly more different from the other two. Still, two of these would probably be called 'green' and one of them would probably be called 'blue,' so I'm going to guess that the 'blue' one is the odd one out." In this case, the availability of different labels may offer a handy strategy to resolve a tricky perceptual task, rather than directly affecting how the colors themselves are perceived.

What would it take to convince you that language truly does interfere with perception? Perhaps if we design a study in which subjects are made to respond to the perceptual test as quickly as possible, this would make it hard for them to invoke a fallback strategy based on color names. In fact, we could then use the response times themselves as evidence for whether color distinctions are easier to make across word boundaries.

This was exactly the strategy used by Jonathan Winawer and his colleagues (2007) in exploiting the differences in color vocabulary between English and Russian. English speakers are able to use a single word (*blue*) to describe all the shades of blue pictured in **Figure 12.10A**, but Russian speakers are required to be more precise and distinguish between light blue (*goluboy*) and dark blue (*siniy*). (And, as it turns out, Russian speakers make the cut between *siniy* and *goluboy* at about the same place on the blue spectrum as English speakers who are forced to decide whether a color is light blue or dark blue.) Winawer and his colleagues devised a simple timed task in which English- and Russian-speaking subjects saw three squares of color, with one square on top and two on the bottom, as in **Figure 12.10B**. In each trial, one of the bottom squares was identical in color to the one on top; subjects were told to quickly press a button on

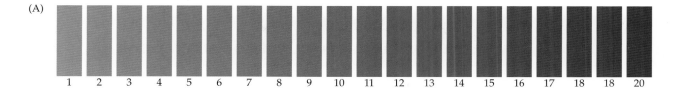

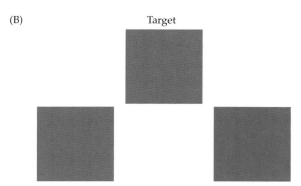

Which of these two stimuli matches the target?

Figure 12.10 (A) Stimuli from the color perception study by Winawer et al. (2007). (A) All of these stimuli can be referred to by the English label *blue*. Russian speakers, however, divide the set up into *goluboy* (light blue) and *siniy* (dark blue), with the boundary between them typically occurring between stimuli 8 and 9. (B) An example trial from the study. To respond correctly, subjects had to press a button on the left to indicate that the lower left square matched the top square in color. (Adapted from Winawer et al., 2007.)

their left if the left square matched the top square, and a button on their right if the right-hand square was the correct match.

Not surprisingly, it took both groups of subjects longer to respond if the two bottom squares were very close in color than if they were further apart. But the Russian speakers performed a bit differently than the English speakers did: if a trial contained two colors that were very similar but sat on opposite sides of the *siniy/goluboy* fence, the subjects' responses were faster than if the two colors would both be classified as either *siniy* or *goluboy*. The existence of the two distinct words appeared to sensitize them to that particular distinction in color. English speakers, on the other hand, showed no advantage for colors that straddled the *dark blue / light blue* divide.

Evidence from reaction times is a fair bit more compelling than the judgment task used by Kay and Kempton. You may still not be fully convinced, though, that people's behavior in this task reflected an involuntary, *automatic* response to perceiving color rather than the use of verbal information to make a *decision* about color. The skeptics among you are invited to work through the details of the intriguing ERP study summarized in **Box 12.4**. In this study, effects of color vocabulary for English and Greek speakers were apparent within about 100 milliseconds of the presentation of colored stimuli. Thus, it's beginning to look like perhaps language truly does influence color perception.

12.4 Adjusting the Language Dial

How to silence the Whorf effect

There's a fascinating twist to the Whorfian story. In the study by Jonathan Winawer and his colleagues, there was one condition in which the Russian speakers performed just like the English speakers in that they were no better at detecting differences between stimuli that fell into different *siniy* versus *goluboy* categories than they were at noticing within-category differences. This happened when the subjects were saddled with an extra memory task: just before seeing each color trio, they read an eight-digit number that they knew they

BOX 12.4
ERP evidence for language effects on perception

An ERP study by Guillaume Thierry and his colleagues (2009) suggests that language influences on color perception can occur quickly and automatically, even in an experimental task in which subjects are not told to focus on color at all. In this experiment, EEG recordings were taken as English- or Greek-speaking subjects saw colored shapes, most of which were circles. Following instructions, the subjects monitored for the occasional square by pressing a button when they saw one. The squares, however, were simply decoys—the true stimuli of interest were circles that deviated in color from the majority of the other circles in the trial (**Figure 12.11**). The researchers anticipated that a circle of an unexpected color

would trigger a visual mismatch negativity effect (vMMN), which is an ERP component that reflects the automatic detection of a change in the visual stimulus. It's generally assumed that the vMMN is a *preattentive* effect, that is, it occurs regardless of whether people are paying conscious attention to the aspect of the stimulus that changes, as a sort of unconscious registering of surprise.

Figure 12.11 Examples of trials in the study by Thierry et al. (2009). For each of these four trials, subjects were instructed to press a button when they saw a square (the target). EEG data were recorded and analyzed for the subjects' responses to the deviant—circles that appeared in a different color than the majority of the items in that trial.

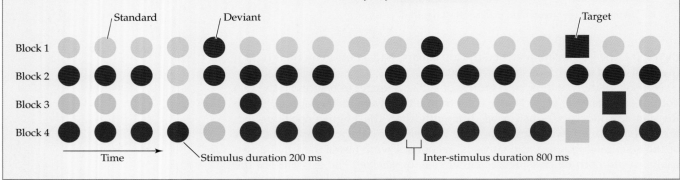

would have to correctly identify after responding to the color test. This meant that while performing the color test, they were mentally rehearsing the strings of digits and, presumably, clogging up their language system in the process. Somehow, blocking the possible activation of the color names eliminated the effects of color vocabulary on perception. And it really does seem to be that *verbal* interference was the culprit; when the Russian subjects had to remember spatial grid patterns instead of digit sequences, they once again showed heightened sensitivity to color differences across the *siniy/goluboy* boundary.

So, do color names alter the perception of color? Well, the answer seems to be yes, but apparently only if people can activate those linguistic labels while performing the perceptual task. This conclusion is supported by an inventive study carried out by Aubrey Gilbert and colleagues (2006), in which the researchers tackled the question from a very different angle.

As you'll remember from Chapter 3, words tend to be activated mainly in the left hemisphere of the brain—some evidence for this came from the classic experiments with split-brain patients that I described earlier. In those studies, patients whose hemispheres had been surgically disconnected were able to identify objects but not name them if the pictures of the objects appeared in the left visual field. Moreover, even in people whose hemispheres were properly connected, studies showed that words were recognized more efficiently when they were presented to sensory organs on the right side of the body, which are directly connected to the left hemisphere—for instance, in dichotic listening

BOX 12.4 *(continued)*

The critical question was whether the subjects' native language would affect the vMMN. As shown in Figure 12.11, the circles were either green or blue, and varied within trials as to whether they were light or dark shades of those two colors. In English, the same word *green* or *blue* can be used to apply to both light and dark versions of these colors, but Greek differentiates between light blue (*ghalazio*) and dark blue (*ble*), while using a single name (*prasino*) for light green and dark green. Hence, for Greek speakers, the perceived difference between the light and dark blues was expected to be greater than for light and dark greens, thereby eliciting a larger mismatch effect. English speakers, on the other hand, should show no difference in the size of the mismatch effect. This hypothesis is supported by the ERP results of the study (**Figure 12.12**).

Figure 12.12 ERPs elicited by the standard and deviant circles, summarized over numerous recording sites. (A) Results for native English speakers. (B) Results for native Greek speakers. As predicted, the native Greek speakers showed a larger difference in brainwave activity at around 200 ms for standard versus deviant blues as compared with the difference for standard versus deviant greens. For native English speakers, the mismatch effect was the same for greens and blues. (Adapted from Thierry et al., 2009.)

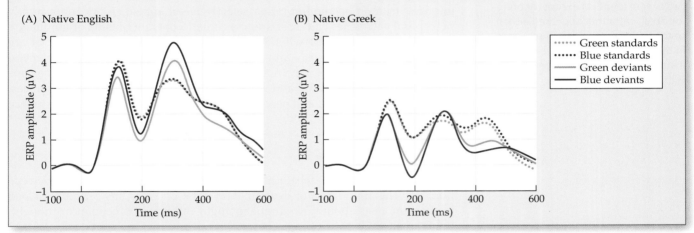

(A) Native English

(B) Native Greek

Green standards
Blue standards
Green deviants
Blue deviants

tests, where subjects heard a different word in each ear, they had an easier time recognizing the words presented to the right ear.

Given that word representations are more active in the left hemisphere, Gilbert and his colleagues wondered whether a person's color vocabulary would influence perception differently depending on whether the stimuli were presented to the left or the right visual field. They devised a study in which subjects saw a ring of colored squares, with one "oddball" square of a slightly different hue than the others. As in the previous studies, the objective differences between the color squares were kept the same for all of the trials, but the squares could represent either two different linguistic categories (green and a nearby blue) or just one (two shades of blue, or two shades of green), as shown in **Figure 12.13**. The subjects' job was to quickly press one of two buttons to indicate whether the odd-colored square appeared on the left or right side.

When the target oddball square appeared in the subjects' right visual field (with the visual information being processed in the verbal left hemisphere), people were relatively fast at distinguishing it from the other squares if it fell into a different linguistic category (for example, a blue target square among a set of green ones); they were slower to respond if the oddball bore the same label (for example, a blue among slightly different blues). This showed, once again, that language can enhance sensitivity to certain subtle color differences. But when the oddball square appeared in the *left* visual field (with the visual in-

(A)

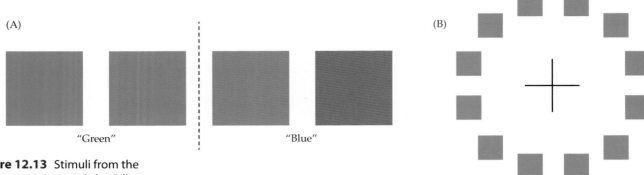

"Green"   "Blue"

(B)

Figure 12.13 Stimuli from the color perception study by Gilbert et al. (2006). (A) The four colors that were used as stimuli, and the boundary that separates the greens from the blues. (B) The arrangement of stimuli in an example trial. All color squares in the circle were identical except for one "oddball" color that appeared either to the left or to the right of the cross in the middle, where subjects were instructed to focus their eyes. (From Gilbert et al., 2006.)

formation processed in the right hemisphere), the language effect evaporated, with no heightened sensitivity for different-named colors.

Results like these argue against a version of the Whorf hypothesis in which language has permanently altered the perception of color. Instead, language imposes itself on perception rather selectively—it appears that certain purely perceptual categories can exist and continue to operate outside of language's sphere of influence. But when the corresponding linguistic categories are highly active, they can play an important role in our perceptual experiences. You might think of language not so much as the teacher or guide of perception, but as an opinionated and vocal consultant. Under some circumstances, its opinions are muffled and perception carries on alone without the influence of language.

Beyond color words

Much of the Whorfian debate has been fought in the arena of color perception, and the abundance of experimental work on color has certainly helped to sharpen ideas about how language might influence perception or thought. But how much do the findings about color tell us about the relationship of language and thought more generally? Color perception by its nature involves making subtle distinctions about gradations of hue or brightness. But in other conceptual domains, categories might be much more sharply defined—think of giraffes and elephants, for example. In these cases, language might play a less important role in influencing judgments about categories. On the flip side, in more abstract conceptual domains, some categories could be more difficult to think about at all without the help of language—for instance, try to think *non*-linguistically of concepts such as a week, democracy, theory, or a contract.

Recent research suggests that the findings from experiments with color extend to at least some other concepts. In one study, Aubrey Gilbert and colleagues (2008) applied the same methods they'd used for studying color to look at concepts involving animal categories like cats and dogs. They used the same visual search task in which subjects were asked to identify one image that differed from others arranged in a ring (**Figure 12.14**). Just as in the color study, the images could come from different categories (an image of a cat appearing in a ring of dog images) or from the same category (two different images of cats). In general, subjects were faster to identify the oddball if it came from a different category than the surrounding images. But this cross-category advantage was greater if the oddball appeared in the right visual field than if it appeared in the left. This pattern makes sense if the rapid access of the *names* for cats and dogs in the left hemisphere allowed people to be faster at detecting the visual difference between the oddball item and its neighbors. In an intriguing variant of the experiment, the researchers tested a split-brain patient, who

(A)

(B)

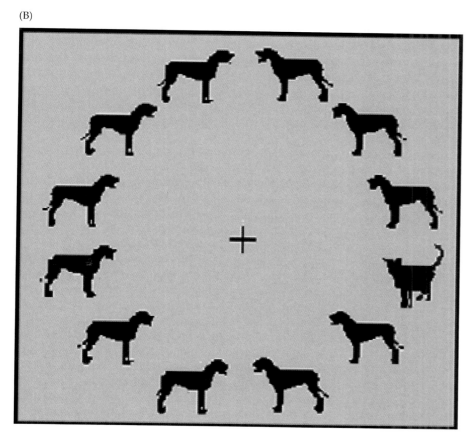

Figure 12.14 (A) The stimuli used in Gilbert's experiment (2008), including two different images in each of the cat and dog categories. (B) An example trial, illustrating an oddball that is from a different category than the surrounding images. (From Gilbert et al., 2008.)

showed an even more dramatic difference between the left-field and right-field results. In her case, the cross-category advantage disappeared entirely when the oddball images were presented in the left visual field. This suggests that when the two hemispheres weren't able to communicate with each other (that is, when language was prevented from exerting an influence on the task in the left-field condition), it was no easier to spot the difference between cat and dog images than it was to distinguish one cat image from another. So, much like the experiments with color terms, this study shows that conceptual categories can operate independently of linguistic categories, but that in some circumstances, the two become yoked to each other.

What about even more complex concepts—for instance, concepts that involve *events* rather than just objects? Not surprisingly, it's easy to find examples of languages that differ sharply in how they encode a complex event. For example, there are interesting crosslinguistic differences in the information that gets packed into verbs of motion. In English, we have a copious assortment of verbs to describe how a person might move his body from one location to another—

walk, amble, stride, trot, run, jog, saunter, and so on, all of which encode the *manner* of the motion. Now, in describing an event, it will sometimes be important to describe the *path* of the movement as well, but this dimension is usually captured not by the verb, but by a prepositional phrase that gets tagged onto the verb. For example: *Nigel jogged **up the hill**; Kim ran **into the house**; Blake ambled **down the street***. In languages like Spanish or Greek, the situation is reversed: normally the verb encodes the path, and a tagged-on adverbial phrase encodes the manner. So, in Spanish, you would typically say: *Juan entró en la casa* (literally "Juan entered the house"). If you thought it was really important to specify *how* Juan entered, you could say: *Juan entró en la casa caminando* (literally "Juan entered the house walking"). Note that there *are* Spanish verbs that do focus on manner (*caminar*—"to walk"; *correr*—"to run"), just as there are English verbs that denote path (*enter, ascend*). But the languages differ in what seems the most natural way to describe an event—for example, it's not outright ungrammatical for an English speaker to say something like "John entered the house walking," but it would strike the listener as a bit odd in most contexts. Apparently, by the age of three, English- and Spanish-speaking children already use whichever pattern is most natural for their language.

This means that English speakers normally *have* to pay attention to the manner in which a motion is executed, because this is the dimension that is usually encoded linguistically; specifying the path is more optional. On the other hand, speakers of Spanish or Greek normally pay attention to the path of the motion and, for the purpose of linguistic encoding, only occasionally focus on the manner. What happens after many years? In perceiving an event, do English speakers eventually become more automatically attuned to the manner of a motion, while Spanish or Greek speakers orient more to its path? Consider the event shown in **Figure 12.15**, which depicts a boy skateboarding into a hockey net. If you pay more attention to manner than to path, you might focus on the boy's skateboard (the manner of motion), whereas if you focus on the path, you might spend more time looking at the net (the path's end point).

To find out whether people's native language influences how they visually parse events, Anna Papafragou and her colleagues (2008) tracked the eye gaze of English and Greek speakers as they watched videos of simple events like the one in Figure 12.15. They found that the two groups did indeed show very different patterns of eye movements while watching the videos, with the Greek speakers immediately focusing on the path's endpoint, and the English speakers zeroing in on details that were relevant for identifying the manner—but

Figure 12.15 This complex event includes both a manner of locomotion (skateboarding) and an end point to the path of motion (the net). Given that English verbs of motion tend to encode the manner, whereas Greek verbs of motion tend to encode the path, will English and Greek speakers focus their attention on different components of this event? (Adapted from Trueswell & Papafragou, 2010.)

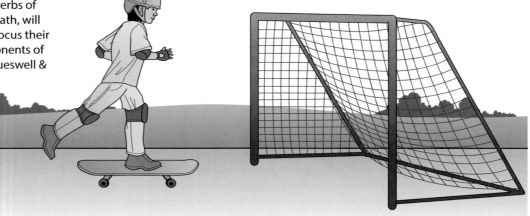

this difference only showed up when the subjects were asked to verbally describe the event right after watching the video. If their task was to remember the events in preparation for a later memory test, the eye movements of the two groups as they watched the videos were indistinguishable. Hence, thinking for speaking revealed different strategies than thinking for remembering, and it was only in the former that language strongly shaped how people were watching the unfolding events. A similar study of verbs of motion with Spanish and English speakers (Gennari et al., 2002) also found that the language spoken by the subjects had an effect on their judgments of how similar events were—but only if they had been instructed to describe the events they were seeing.

Nevertheless, the eye movement data did reveal some more subtle effects of language even in the memory task condition. It's true that in this task, the English and Greek speakers showed no differences in eye movements during the actual videos of the events—but they did show some interesting differences in the few seconds *after* the event, while watching a frozen video frame upon the event's completion: English speakers spent *more* time than the Greek speakers looking at the path's end point. Why would this be, since English linguistically encodes manner while Greek encodes the path? Exactly. The researchers suggested that in order to help them remember the details of the events, the subjects were spending extra effort committing to memory the information that wasn't already packed into the verbal content that would most naturally be tagged to the event. This interpretation assumes that, even though subjects weren't actively planning a description of the event in their minds, they were still activating verbal content in some way, and choosing a memory strategy that would complement the linguistic code. This assumption was vindicated in a later study (Trueswell & Papafragou, 2010): when subjects were asked to count aloud while watching the videos, making it harder for them to activate linguistic content related to the events, all effects of the speakers' language on eye gaze, whether during or after the videos, were eliminated.

Perceiving events of motion is quite a different mental activity than perceiving color swatches, but experiments across these domains appear to generate broadly consistent results: the language you speak can indeed influence the way you think about or interact with the world, but it doesn't permanently mold your thoughts or perception. Its influence is greatest when you're most likely to be activating the linguistic system. You can recruit linguistic knowledge—whether deliberately or unconsciously—to help you accomplish tasks that aren't overtly linguistic, and when you do so, language is likely to have some effect in organizing your thoughts.

The *selective* nature of Whorfian effects can create a methodological minefield for researchers (see **Method 12.1**). It also helps to put in some perspective some of the strong claims that people sometimes make about the relationship between language and thought—to say that we're conceptually *imprisoned* by the language we speak would be a gross overstatement. That's not to say, though, that even the subtle and selective effects of language on thought can't lead to significant consequences.

One such demonstration comes from Caitlin Fausey and Lera Boroditsky (2011). Their study focused on differences between English and Spanish speakers in how they typically describe accidental events that are caused by humans—for instance, an event in which a woman unintentionally breaks a vase. In English, it's possible to describe the event without mentioning its causal agent: *The vase broke,* or *The vase was broken.* But it's far more common to produce a sentence in which the agent appears in subject position: *The woman broke the vase.* Not so for Spanish speakers, who are more likely to describe the event by saying something like: *Se rompió el florero* (literally "The vase broke

METHOD 12.1

Language intrusion and the variable Whorf effect

As you saw in the studies of color and verbs of motion, Whorfian effects are found in some experimental situations but not in others. Variable effects that come and go demand an explanation, and in this case, the common thread underlying the variability seems to be the degree to which language itself intrudes into the task. It's true that the language that people speak can affect their performance on a cognitive or perceptual task, but this is less likely to happen when language isn't being recruited to help solve the task, or is actively prevented from participating.

Knowing that Whorfian effects depend on the degree to which linguistic representations are activated provides a useful framework for making sense of their variable nature. But it doesn't necessarily allow researchers to come up with a clear way to *predict* whether language will affect thought in any particular situation. This is simply because it's hard to know, in any given case, whether linguistic representations *will* be activated for a specific task. Obviously, at the extreme ends of the spectrum, you can either force or prevent the activation of linguistic forms— for instance, by requiring people to describe the stimuli, or by blocking access to the corresponding linguistic representations through verbal interference. But suppose you do neither of these things, and simply ask subjects to remember certain stimuli for later testing on a memory test. Or ask them to make judgments about the similarity of various stimuli. Will your subjects spontaneously enlist language to help them with the task? Surely, in order to evaluate whether people's behavior in real-world situations is likely to be affected by the language they speak, it would be good to have some solid answers to these questions.

Coming up with the answers, though, is not a simple matter. For example, in some of the studies we've reviewed, we've seen that a person's language can affect judgments of similarity when it comes to color (as found by the study by Kay and Kempton, 1984), whereas a similarity judgment task investigating verbs of motion *didn't* show any language-specific effects unless the subjects were explicitly asked to describe the events (Gennari et al., 2002). So which is it? Does a basic similarity test rely on linguistic representations or not?

A variety of factors likely determine the extent to which language is activated in a cognitive task. The linguistic representations themselves may be more accessible in some cases than in others. For example, in many of the color studies, it was easy to find language-specific effects even in tasks that didn't overtly require the use of language; these effects were then muted when linguistic access was blocked through verbal interference. This suggests that color words were activated fairly automatically. But keep in mind that in some of these tests, the researchers looked at a very small number of targeted colors—for example, just blues, or blues and greens in a very simple, repetitive task. In this case, the color words may have been highly predictable and easy to activate. Does this mean that color words would automatically be activated in, say, a more complex task that requires an interior decorator to choose from among hundreds of samples of color, involving many different objects? It's not entirely clear.

It's also more likely that language will be involved in solving a task that's hard to undertake without linguistic assistance. Non-linguistic memory for a simple event is fairly easy, but remembering the exact shade of red of your girlfriend's favorite sweater is more challenging. Applying a specific label ("cardinal red") might help. Or try remembering the exact number of geese you saw flying overhead yesterday. Being able to attach a word to this number ("nine") will increase your chances of success. In cases like these, even a nonverbal memory task may turn out to lean quite heavily on language.

All of this makes it quite complicated to compare two different populations. Tasks that might be easy and familiar for one group to solve without the benefit of language could be much more challenging for another, causing them to rely more on linguistic representation. Similarly, if the familiarity of certain concepts—or their corresponding linguistic representations—is shakier for one group than another, this could affect the degree to which language comes into the mix for a particular cognitive task.

Clearly, understanding the complex interplay between language and the rest of cognition is proving to be anything but straightforward. It would be premature to assert that Russian speakers show exceptional sensitivity in their art to different nuances of blue, based on the results we've seen so far from laboratory studies. But the ongoing accumulation of experimental work in this area promises to reveal a great deal about the range and limits of language's influence on thought and behavior.

itself"). On the other hand, when describing events that are *intentionally* caused by humans, Spanish and English speakers both encode the agent of the action.

Fausey and Boroditsky found that when English and Spanish speakers looked at videos of accidental events, they performed differently on a memory task, even if they were never asked to describe the events at any point between witnessing them and taking the test. Spanish speakers were less likely than English speakers to remember the agents of accidental events. However, when it came to remembering the agents of intentional events, both groups of speakers performed equally well. Hence, subjects' memory for the cause of the event ran in parallel with the likelihood that it would be mentioned in a sentence. Results like these raise the provocative possibility that eyewitness memory might be affected by linguistic codes that people activate at the time that they witness the event.

12.5 One Mind, Two Languages

Learn another language, expand your mind?

On page 474, I quoted from several attempts to persuade English speakers to learn a new language through the promise of an added cognitive bonus ("Learning a new language is the first step towards 'thinking outside the box'"; and "French … develops critical thinking"). Are such claims valid? Does learning another language really broaden your conceptual horizons or enhance your thinking skills?

The intuitive response would be yes, naturally. How could it not? But having now learned a great deal about psycholinguistics, you're in a position to approach the claim with some precision. First of all, it makes sense to distinguish between the benefits that might come from bilingualism itself—regardless of which languages are mastered—and the benefits that might come from knowing the particular words or grammatical devices a specific language uses.

How could the simple fact of knowing more than one language enhance cognition? As you saw in previous chapters, bilingual people don't have a firewall between their languages, and they regularly experience interference or competition between their linguistic systems. Becoming bilingual forces people to learn to manage this added competition, and this, it turns out, has some very positive side effects. There's a rapidly growing body of evidence showing that bilinguals generally achieve superior skills in cognitive control, whether it's in the form of reducing interference from irrelevant information, or switching between tasks more efficiently. These effects reach beyond the borders of language, and can have measurable effects on quality of life—for example, bilingualism slows down some of the cognitive declines that comes with age, and delays the symptoms associated with dementia (see Box 8.4). The benefits of managing two language systems can show up at the younger end of the age spectrum as well. In one study, 8-year-old bilingual kids displayed strong performance on a spatial perspective-taking task, whereas monolingual children of the same age had a harder time overcoming their own visual perspective (Greenberg et al., 2012). In another study, bilingual children in kindergarten displayed greater cognitive flexibility in their drawings than their monolingual peers (Adi-Japha et al., 2010). When asked to draw a picture of a flower that does not exist, monolingual children were fairly unadventurous, perhaps drawing a flower that was missing its leaves, or a flower with only one petal. Bilingual children, on the other hand, incorporated elements from completely different objects—producing, for instance, a flower with a tail, or a flower with teeth.

If knowing more than one language can make you more creative, better at ignoring irrelevant information, or less egocentric in your thinking, this really does seem like quite the cognitive bonanza. But there are still many open questions. In order to reap the benefits of bilingualism, how proficient do you have to become in your second language? Does the age of acquisition matter? Do you have to exercise both linguistic systems on a daily basis? Is it still beneficial if you have only a reading knowledge of a second language, and don't have the skills to chat about the weather with a stranger at the bus stop? Language research is still in the early stages of gathering the evidence to address these questions. Based on the evidence so far, however—by all means, go learn a second language!

Whorfian effects in bilinguals

Let's now turn to the question of whether there are benefits to learning a *particular* language, aside from the broader cognitive gains of becoming bilingual. Any such payoff is highly unlikely to come from the fact that a certain language is especially "logical" or "analytical"—careful comparisons of languages provide not even the slightest glimmer that some languages enjoy these general properties more than others.

But since we know that languages can tilt thinking or perception in a particular direction depending on which concepts are regularly clothed in language, a more plausible approach would be to look *specifically* at how the second language encodes information in ways that differ from the first. It's on this terrain that we might see some concrete evidence that a second language sharpens the thinking of its learners in very targeted ways. For example: In Turkish, as in many languages, if you state an assertion, you also have to linguistically mark how you came to know that information. You would have to use one linguistic tag (*di*) to mark whether you learned the information firsthand through direct observation, and another (*miş*) to mark whether you know it secondhand through hearsay or indirect evidence. So, if you had witnessed the event yourself, you'd say:

> *Ahmet gel-di.*
>
> Ahmet came. (direct evidence)

But if you heard it from a friend, you'd say:

> *Ahmet gel-miş.*
>
> Ahmet came. (indirect evidence)

In English, there are options for making the same distinction:

> I saw that Ahmet came.
>
> I heard that Ahmet came.
>
> Apparently, Ahmet came.
>
> Ahmet came, I gather.
>
> Ahmet must have come.

But English speakers aren't *forced* to make the distinction between firsthand and secondhand evidence. It's possible that being required to make the distinction between firsthand and secondhand knowledge makes Turkish speakers more attentive to the source of evidence, and maybe even allows them to remember it better. This could be very useful. Many psychology studies have shown that people are lousy at remembering the source of "known" information—for example, you may know that your childhood friend is getting married, but how do you know? Did she tell you? Did you hear it from her best friend? See it on Facebook? Perhaps speaking a language like Turkish, in which you're constantly having to categorize where your knowledge came from, would help you fix such information more firmly in your mind. And if that's true, would you get the benefit even if you started learning Turkish fairly late in life after having spent many years using English?

There's surprisingly little hard evidence for such targeted mind-expanding effects of learning a second language. But interest in the topic has heated up in recent years, so by the time you read this chapter, there will likely be many studies that shed light on it (check the book website for significant new developments). And, several studies do suggest that certain thinking patterns or mental categories can change as the result of acquiring another language (for a detailed review, see Bassetti and Cook, 2011).

It's worth noting that the data don't always point to effects in which mental categories or memory for events are *sharpened*—acquiring a second language can also lead to the blurring of information. For an illustration, let's step back into the great coliseum of color perception. In Box 12.4, I presented ERP data that showed that Greek speakers enjoyed an added sensitivity to certain shades of blue as compared with English speakers, reflecting the fact that Greek divides the color blue into a light (*ghalazio*) and a dark (*ble*) category. In that particular study, Greek speakers were found to be more sensitive than English speakers to slight differences that spanned the *ghalazio/ble* boundary. But in a later paper (Athanasopoulos et al., 2010), the researchers looked more closely at the same group of Greek speakers, dividing them into two groups depending on how long they had been living in the United Kingdom. They found that the group who had lived longer in the U.K. (an average of 42.6 months versus 7.2 months) showed signs of losing the sensitivity to the *ghalazio* and *ble* distinction.

But what does it mean to "lose" the *ghalazio/ble* distinction? We can split this notion apart into two distinct possibilities. Let's first consider the scenario in **Figure 12.16A**, which shows one way in which the linguistic labels for those bilingual in Greek and English might map onto conceptual space. In this case, the original distinctions of the Greek labels remain the same, while English labels have been added to the bilingual speakers' repertoire. So how can we explain the smearing of the *ghalazio/ble* boundary among the Greek speakers who'd spent a long time in the United Kingdom? Perhaps what's changed over time is that the Greek *labels* have become less accessible relative to the English ones. In the study by Athanasopoulos and his colleagues, the subjects were performing a task that didn't require the use of either one of their languages—they simply pressed a button if they detected an unusual shape. Since the task didn't *block* the activation of either linguistic code, it's possible that the long-stay Greek subjects were simply more likely to activate the English labels than their short-stay counterparts. Under this scenario, we might expect that if the situation turned up the dial for one set of labels over the other (for instance, by requiring subjects to name colors in a particular language), then they'd perform more like Greek monolinguals when using Greek, and like English monolinguals when using English.

On the other hand, it's possible that bilingualism changes the way in which labels map onto conceptual space, as shown in **Figure 12.16B**. In this scenario, the Greek labels *ghalazio* and *ble* still exist in the mind of the bilingual, but the distinction between them has become less crisp over time as a result of leakage from the English-

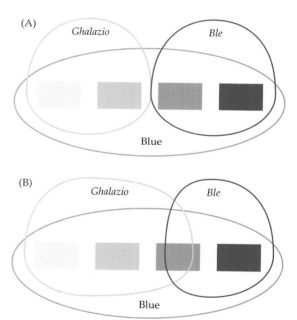

Figure 12.16 Two hypothetical ways in which color perception might change as a result of bilingualism. (A) The original Greek mapping of words to the color space remains the same for Greek speakers who have acquired English, but the relative accessibility of the Greek linguistic representations may be decreased compared with Greek monolinguals. (B) The mapping of Greek color labels to the color space has changed as a result of familiarity with the English mapping.

defined color system. By absorbing English into their cognitive system, Greek-English bilinguals would no longer think about color as their monolingual Greek compatriots did, even when speaking in Greek.

Supercharged linguistic skills

Aside from Whorfian effects, there are other ways in which a second language might reshape a person's cognitive landscape. As you've seen throughout this book, learning and using language relies on an assortment of very diverse skills. It may be that different languages demand somewhat different mixes of cognitive skills from their speakers. A language that makes use of 140 phonemes might demand finer control over the auditory and articulatory systems than one that limits itself to a dozen. A language that uses complex layers of syntactic embedding might call for a robust working-memory capacity. A language that permits free word order might require speakers to rapidly navigate a vast array of options when it comes to constructing a sentence. A language that is very sparse and resists adorning its words with morphemes that specify tense, number, person agreement, and so on might leave more work for intelligent inferring, while a language that compulsively stacks morphemes onto its words requires its learners to store all these grammatical markers in memory. It may turn out that different languages build strengths in different areas—which raises the question of whether you can become more efficient at a new language-related skill if you pick up a second language that strenuously exercises that skill. And if so, might certain buffed-up language skills spill over into other cognitive domains for which those skills are relevant?

To date, there's very little systematic research that addresses these questions—but there's just enough data to provide some assurance that the questions are worth exploring. For example, languages that use tone to distinguish word meanings have been linked to better skills at perceiving pitch. Many people can perceive *relative* pitch in order to distinguish how far apart two tones are in pitch, but people who are able to perceive *absolute* pitch, which allows them to peg the pitch of a single note produced in isolation, are in a much smaller minority. Absolute pitch is more common among speakers of tone languages, which use pitch to distinguish otherwise identical words (Deutsch et al., 2006). Moreover, it seems to be related to the level of proficiency with a tone language, providing a hint that the learning of a tone language might drive the enhanced perception of pitch (Deutsch et al., 2009). What's not yet clear is whether learning a tone language as a *second* language (especially later in life) can sharpen the perception of musical pitch.

In the domain of syntactic structure, there are entire continents of unexplored questions about the relationship between language structure and sentence-processing skills. For example, some languages have very limited recursion, so instead of nesting phrases inside each other, speakers pull them apart and form separate self-contained phrases or sentences. As you saw in Box 6.3, Pirahã appears to be such a language. Instead of saying "John's brother's house," Pirahã speakers would say something like:

Brother's house. John has a brother. It is the same one.

Or instead of saying "The man who shot the jaguar is eating pig meat," they'd express the same idea like this:

The man shot the jaguar. He is eating pig meat.

In Chapter 8, I discussed some ideas about how sentences may become very hard to interpret if they contain embedded structures that require hearers to hold in memory a number of syntactic dependencies over long stretches of time. These specific memory-taxing effects are likely to be much less of an issue for a language that doesn't have much embedding at all.

Even across languages that do enthusiastically stack phrases inside each other, there can be some striking differences in the resulting syntactic dependencies. In **Box 12.5**, humorist Mark Twain makes light of certain complex structures in German. But underneath the humor, a psycholinguist might find some serious open questions about whether different languages require the cultivation of different parsing skills.

BOX 12.5
Mark Twain on the awful
memory-taxing syntax of German

If you've ever tried to learn German as a non-native language, you may have been challenged by the fact that verbs in embedded clauses are placed at the very end, like this:

Ich glaube daß die Kinder nicht nach Berlin gefahren sind.
I   believe that the children not   to   Berlin travelled are.

"I believe that the children did not go to Berlin."

This fact, along with other features of German grammar, incited the following humorous commentary by Mark Twain in his 1880 essay "The Awful German Language":

*An average sentence, in a German newspaper, is a sublime and impressive curiosity; it occupies a quarter of a column; it contains all the ten parts of speech— not in regular order, but mixed; it is built mainly of compound words constructed by the writer on the spot, and not to be found in any dictionary—six or seven words compacted into one, without joint or seam—that is, without hyphens; it treats of fourteen or fifteen different subjects, each inclosed in a parenthesis of its own, with here and there extra parentheses which reinclose three or four of the minor parentheses, making pens within pens: finally, all the parentheses and reparentheses are massed together between a couple of king-parentheses, one of which is placed in the first line of the majestic sentence and the other in the middle of the last line of it—**after which comes the VERB**, and you find out for the first time what the man has been talking about; and after the verb—merely by way of ornament, as far as I can make out—the writer shovels in "**haben sind gewesen gehabt haben geworden sein**," or words to that effect, and the monument is finished. I suppose that this closing hurrah is in the nature of the flourish to a man's signature—not necessary, but pretty. German books are easy enough to read when you hold them before the looking-glass or stand on your head—so as to reverse the construction—but I think that to learn to read and understand a German newspaper is a thing which must always remain an impossibility to a foreigner.*

Yet even the German books are not entirely free from attacks of the Parenthesis distemper—though they are usually so mild as to cover only a few lines, and therefore when you at last get down to the verb it carries some meaning to your mind because you are able to remember a good deal of what has gone before. Now here is a sentence from a popular and excellent German novel—which [sic] a slight parenthesis in it. I will make a perfectly literal translation, and throw in the parenthesis-marks and some hyphens for the assistance of the reader—though in the original there are no parenthesis-marks or hyphens, and the reader is left to flounder through to the remote verb the best way he can:

"But when he, upon the street, the (in-satin-and-silk-covered-now-very-unconstrained-after-the-newest-fashioned-dressed) government counselor's wife met," etc., etc.

Wenn er aber auf der Strasse der in Sammt und Seide gehüllten jetzt sehr ungenirt nach der neusten Mode gekleideten Regierungsräthin begegnet.

That is from The Old Mamselle's Secret, by Mrs. Marlitt. And that sentence is constructed upon the most approved German model. You observe how far that verb is from the reader's base of operations; well, in a German newspaper they put their verb away over on the next page; and I have heard that sometimes after stringing along the exciting preliminaries and parentheses for a column or two, they get in a hurry and have to go to press without getting to the verb at all. Of course, then, the reader is left in a very exhausted and ignorant state.

Activating cultural values

Finally, I want to return to a forceful intuition for which I still owe you a satisfying explanation: Many multilinguals (myself included) have the strong subjective feeling that different languages really *are* infused with different cultural characteristics. They may feel that they think differently in their different languages—perhaps they even feel that different languages bring out different aspects of their personalities. These impressions aren't illusory. Several experiments show that bilinguals *do* exhibit different attitudes or behaviors depending on which language they're using.

In one such study, led by Dirk Akkermans (2010), Dutch subjects who also spoke English played a variant of the "prisoner's dilemma" game, intended to test whether subjects would choose a cooperative or competitive strategy. The game was set up like this: imagine that you're a business owner faced with setting the price for one of your products, and your partner in the game also sells the same product. You will reap the highest profits if both you and your partner choose a cooperative strategy of keeping prices for your products high, and the lowest profits if you play cooperatively but your partner chooses to undersell you. Since you're not able to communicate with your partner, you have to make a decision based on how you predict he or she will act.

LANGUAGE AT LARGE 12.2

Can your language make you broke and fat?

In a 2013 paper, economist Keith Chen made the startling claim that people's fiscal responsibility and lifestyle choices depend in part on the grammar of their language.

Languages differ in the devices they offer to talk about the future. For some, like Spanish and Greek, you have to tack on a verb ending that explicitly marks future time—so, in Spanish, you would say *escribo* for the present tense ("I write" or "I'm writing") and *escribir*é for the future tense ("I will write"). But other languages, like Mandarin, don't require verbs to be escorted by grammatical markers that convey future time; time is usually obvious from something else in the context. In Mandarin, you would say the equivalent of *I write tomorrow*, using the same verb form for both present and future. Chen's premise is that if you divide up a large number of the world's languages into those that require a grammatical marker for future time and those that don't, you see an interesting correlation: speakers of languages that force grammatical marking of the future have amassed a smaller retirement nest egg, smoke more, exercise less, and are more likely to be obese.

The claim is that a sharp grammatical division between the present and future encourages people to conceive of the future as somehow dramatically different from the present, making it easier to put off behaviors that benefit your future self rather than your present self.

Chen's claim is undeniably interesting—it suggests that the language you speak might have important, real-world effects, and not just subtle effects that are invisible outside of the careful probing of a lab experiment. Not surprisingly, the paper immediately generated a lot of press of the sort that's festooned with flashing lights. For example, in his popular blog, Andrew Sullivan headlined the story about Chen's paper with *Why Greeks Haven't Saved for a Rainy Day*. A facetious headline, no doubt. But before someone suggests that economic bailouts of troubled countries should be contingent on their retiring their grammatical tense markers, it's worth asking: Is the correlation between tense marking and retirement savings one that leads to the *conclusion* that grammar causes prudent behavior—or is it simply the starting point for investigating this intriguing question?

In response to Chen's paper, some researchers have emphasized that correlations between linguistic variables and cultural traits can arise quite easily even in situations where one doesn't cause the other. This often happens because speakers inherit or borrow a *number* of unrelated linguistic and cultural traits from their ancestors or from geographic neighbors—to revisit an earlier example, one language group might adopt both linguistic tone and chopstick use from another, but no one's suggesting that

Half of the subjects played the game in English, and half played the game in Dutch. The subjects who played the game in English chose a more competitive strategy (setting their prices low) than those who played it in Dutch. And the effects of language on strategy choice were especially prominent for those who'd lived in an Anglophone country for at least 3 months; among this group, those who played the game in Dutch played cooperatively 51% of the time, while those who played it in English did so only 37% of the time. In contrast, among those who *hadn't* spent more than 3 months in an Anglophone country, the rates for cooperative behavior were 48% for Dutch and 45% for English.

Does this mean English is a more "competitive" language than Dutch? I've thrown cold water on the idea that languages might *intrinsically* embody broad cultural values like rationalism or romanticism. If they don't, then what accounts for the language effect in the experiment I've just summarized? Why would speaking English cause people to behave more competitively?

A plausible account is that it's not the English language itself that is competitive. Rather, it's that the English language reminds people of the cultural practices of the people who happen to speak English. Using the English language simply serves as the trigger for priming the associated cultural norms. It's now known that cultural norms and stereotypes can be activated in any number of ways—this is not specifically a *language* effect. For example, one study showed that subjects could be induced to act more competitively if they

---

LANGUAGE AT LARGE 12.2 (*continued*)

linguistic tone leads to dexterity with chopsticks, or vice versa. We saw that this possible scenario is important in considering the significance of correlated linguistic traits, such as the word orders of two kinds of phrases. It's just as important in considering the meaningfulness of correlations between linguistic and cultural traits. And it's especially important when considering any issues that might have real-world implications for how policies are determined. [A detailed discussion of these concerns can be found in a paper by Seán Roberts and James Winters (2013).]

When carefully conducted, statistical correlations between linguistic variables and cultural traits can bring to light some interesting hypotheses. But these hypotheses need to be tested further. Experiments are especially useful in helping to determine whether one variable has a causal effect on another, and it should be possible to design one that fits the bill. The idea behind Chen's proposal is that every encounter with a distinct grammatical marker for future time creates a little mental nudge that leads to a conceptual partition between present and future time, and hence a devaluing of future benefits relative to present benefits. If that's so, then we should be able to see the effects of these little mental nudges on specific behaviors that we target experimentally.

So, we could easily set up a study that looked like this: To control for variables other than language, we might

target a group of bilingual speakers of one language that obligatorily marks future tense (for example, French) and one that does not (for example, German). This group could then be randomly split, with half of the subjects being made to describe or read about some future event in German, and the other half in French. Both groups could then be given a mock investment task that involves making decisions about how much to save versus how much to spend now. In theory, those randomly assigned to the German experimental group should be eager to save more than the French group. Just to be sure to control for any spurious differences between our random groups, we could make each group come back the following week and do the same tasks in their other language, predicting the theoretically appropriate increase or decrease in their inclination to save for the future.

Of course, there's one more thing we'd need to control for. Remember the study by Akkerman and colleagues in which the Dutch-English bilinguals played a business game more competitively when speaking English than when speaking Dutch? The lesson from that study was that language can sometimes affect behavior not by virtue of its grammar, but because of the cultural traits that have come to be associated with speakers of that language. This factor too will need to be disentangled before we can conclude that certain grammatical properties can cause your present self to be more considerate of your future self.

implicit priming A psychological phenomenon in which exposing people to certain stimuli increases the likelihood that they'll exhibit behaviors that are associated with the stimuli. For example, exposing people to words associated with the elderly may trigger behaviors that are stereotypically associated with the elderly, such as walking slowly.

sat at a table holding objects such as a briefcase and an executive portfolio, as opposed to a backpack and a cardboard box (Kay et al., 2004). In another experiment, subjects showed more conformist behavior if they'd been shown a picture of a businessman rather than a punk rocker (Pendry & Carrick, 2001). Even the subliminal presentation of the Apple logo (as contrasted with the IBM logo) resulted in higher performance on a test of creativity (Fitzsimons et al., 2008). Over the last two decades, such demonstrations of **implicit priming** have proliferated, showing that a remarkable variety of stimuli can trigger behaviors and impressions that are associated with a particular social group.

All this adds a deep wrinkle to debates about how language affects thought. To create an imaginary experimental scenario, let's suppose you run an experiment with, say, Mandarin-English bilinguals and find that when your subjects interact with someone in English, they're more likely to show egocentric patterns of language use than when they use Mandarin—to test this, you might use the referential communication task described in Chapter 11 (see Method 11.1). Does this mean that something about the Mandarin language encourages sharper mind-reading inferences? (One might hypothesize, for example, that the morphological sparseness of Mandarin puts subjects in a mode where they have to pay more attention to recovering meanings from "between the lines," requiring them to focus on the speaker's communicative intentions.) This would be a tricky conclusion, because it's also possible that speaking in Mandarin simply activates cultural expectations that one should consider the thoughts and feelings of other people. You'd need to make sure that other *non*-linguistic triggers that are connected to Chinese culture—images of Chinese people, or eating Chinese food—wouldn't lead to the same result.

Clearly, language *is* entangled with culture. To a large extent, this is what makes language so endlessly fascinating. But as I hope you've gleaned from this chapter, truly understanding the nature of the entanglement needs to go far beyond uttering some intuitive "truisms." To explore the relationship intelligently, you need to equip yourself with a good set of tools: a precise understanding of the differences among languages; some solid ideas about the skills that are needed to learn and use the structures found in language; a sense of how concepts are formed; an awareness of the social and cultural contexts of particular languages; and a good set of methodologies to study the interaction of all of these elements.

But in the end, if you apply all this knowledge to the study of language and culture, you'll be in a position to go far beyond the usual clichés about how Italian is such a romantic language, or how French helps you to precisely order your thoughts.

WEB ACTIVITY 12.5

Code-switching In this activity, you'll explore how the relationship between language and cultural associations plays out in the phenomenon of code-switching, in which bilinguals spontaneously shift between linguistic systems while speaking.

GO TO

sites.sinauer.com/languageinmind

for **web activities**, **further readings**, **research updates**, **new essays**, and other features

DIGGING DEEPER

Are all languages equally complex?

Here's a bold claim that's been around for a while in the language research community: All of the world's languages are about equal in complexity.

Now, it's pretty obvious that if you look at specific *subparts* of a language, some languages are more streamlined than others. For example, Hawaiian takes a just-the-basics approach to its phonemic inventory, with a grand total of five vowels and eight consonants, while the Khoisan language !Xóõ is a compulsive hoarder of sounds, possessing (if you count conservatively) 87 consonants, of which 43 are distinct "click" consonants. In Japanese, you have just one way of grammatically expressing the past tense:

yagio kata
I (have) bought a goat.

But Kikongo distinguishes four kinds of past tense:

nsuumbidingi nkoombo
I bought a goat (today).

yasuumbidi nkoombo
"I bought a goat (yesterday)."

yasaumba nkoombo
"I bought a goat (earlier)."

nsuumbidi nkoombo
"I have bought a goat."

Despite such examples, linguists have argued that if you were to compare the *overall* complexity of languages, you'd find that they come out about even; a miserly collection of grammatical morphemes might be balanced out by a more elaborate set of syntactic structures, as suggested by the famous linguist Charles Hockett (1958):

Impressionistically, it would seem that the total grammatical complexity of any language, counting both morphology and syntax, is about the same as any other. This is not surprising, since all languages have about equally complex jobs to do, and what is not done morphologically has to be done syntactically. Fox, with a more complex morphology than English, thus ought to have a somewhat simpler syntax; and this is the case.

The idea of such trade-offs in complexity has been widely accepted since the second half of the twentieth century. But more recently, language researchers have become quite vocal in pointing out that there's actually very little evidence for this claim.

Why then, would the notion of equal complexity hold such sway over the field despite the lack of hard data? One answer is that the rise of nativist theories of language in the late twentieth century, with their emphasis on language universals that were genetically specified, made it seem highly implausible that languages would differ wildly in their degrees of complexity. A second factor is that linguists often found themselves in the position of trying to beat back the common misconception that "primitive" cultures have less highly developed languages than "civilized" societies. This idea—which can still be found floating around on the Internet—is clearly wrong. It's not hard to find examples of small, non-industrial societies whose languages display mind-boggling grammatical nuances and ornamentation. If you'd like one for your collection, try the case of the Siberian language Ket, which, to paraphrase linguist John McWhorter (2011), has the following complications: In Ket, pronoun prefixes are routinely attached to verbs. The trick is that there are two whole sets of prefixes, with one set attaching to one class of verbs, and the second set attaching to another class—you simply have to memorize which class of verbs takes which set of pronoun prefixes. To make matters more complicated, many verbs take *two* pronoun prefixes that mean the same thing. (But many don't). For example, *digdabatsaq* means "I go to the river," with both *d* and *ba* meaning "I," much as if we'd said in English "I go to I the river."

To make matters even more complicated, the verb's meaning can change depending on whether you double the pronoun. Specifically, *digdabatsaq* means that I go to the river and come back a bit later. But *digdaddaq* (which involves the double use of the *same* pronoun prefix *d*) means something different: I go to the river and stay for the season. But the same word with just one pronoun prefix—**d**igdaksak—means I go to the river and stay some days or weeks.

Linguists often find themselves pulling out such counterexamples in weary attempts to dispel the "primitive languages" myth. But this myth, like the villain from a horror movie, seems to be unkillable. Its sheer resilience has no doubt helped to turn the claim about uniform crosslinguistic complexity into something of a mantra. Nevertheless, it's possible to avoid the trap of equating simple societies with simple languages, and yet still entertain the hypothesis that some languages might be more complex than others. John McWhorter (2001) has argued that some languages are simpler than others, not because they come from less complex societies, but because they are fairly young languages. Now, everyone agrees that newly hatched languages like Nicaraguan Sign Language, or Al-Sayyid Bedouin Sign Language (ABSL) are not as complex as more established languages like American Sign Language or English. In the spoken-language realm, we can also find simple pidgin languages, which arise when speakers of many different languages are thrown together and have to find a way to communicate. What emerges is a fairly rudimentary language that's often based on a mixture of the original languages, or on one of the more dominant languages within the group. Pidgins are less systematic or complex than more mature languages. But the general thinking has been that within the space of a few generations, as children learn the new language as their native tongue, they embellish the young language with the grammatical devices typical of a "real" language. Hence, young languages are usually thought to quickly settle into the "optimal" level of linguistic complexity. But McWhorter has argued against this prevailing view, suggesting that additional complexity grows slowly over a very long period in the life of a language.

According to McWhorter, there's a flawed assumption behind the claim of equal complexity: the notion that grammatical devices exist in a language because they serve an important communicative function. But perhaps not all grammatical devices *do* serve an urgent communicative need. Think of how some languages mark gender on all of their nouns, including forks, socks, and cabbages. Many languages survive quite nicely without having to divide the world of inanimate objects into two separate categories, so it's hard to see how this is important for communication.

McWhorter argues that in addition to acquiring genuinely useful grammatical markers over time, languages also collect ones that are less useful—or that perhaps were useful within the system at one point, but no longer are. Earlier in the chapter, in talking about a language's collection of words, I suggested that languages, like old houses, contain many not-so-useful objects that are there simply because, well, they've *always* been there, and no one has bothered to throw them out. This may apply to grammatical devices as well as words. And if it's true that some of the complexity within languages comes from the accumulation of linguistic junk, there's no reason to suppose that all languages would have hoarded exactly the same amount of it.

(If you have trouble imagining why the speakers of a language would bother to preserve bits of language that serve no pressing communicative need, I invite you to imagine what would happen if you, as a speaker of German, decided that gender marking serves no useful purpose, and

that you would henceforth simply stop distinguishing the gender of socks versus cabbages.)

In arguing for the connection between the youth of a language and its simplicity, McWhorter points to creole languages. Creole languages are the descendants of pidgin languages, and the oldest ones date back only as far as the 1600s, when colonial powers first began dislocating large numbers of people from their homes and language communities. Because creole languages were built anew by their displaced speakers, rather than simply being handed down from one generation to another, they provide the opportunity to see what languages look like when they haven't had quite as long to accumulate less useful complexities. If McWhorter is right, they may allow us to see which grammatical elements are most closely tied to communicative pressures. In a sense, studying one of these languages would be a bit like dropping in on someone who's very recently set up a new household—the things they own tells you something about what's important for their daily life.

McWhorter doesn't suggest that all old languages are doomed to carry around an ever-growing heap of grammatical knickknacks. First, there's likely an upper limit to the grammatical stuff that a language can contain and still be manageable for its speakers. Second, there may be historical events that precipitate a dramatic purging of linguistic junk, much as moving from one house to another often forces people to get rid of unnecessary things. In Chapter 2, I discussed how English lost many of its grammatical markers shortly after the influx of a large Norman population into England. McWhorter (2002) has argued that this grammatical purging took place because of the large number of *adult* learners of English in the invading population; these adult learners simplified the language because, unlike children, they were unable to learn the language in its original form.

These are provocative ideas, and they illustrate some of the field's renewed interest in taking a closer look at the assumption of equal complexity. But as scholars begin to have serious discussions about comparing the overall complexity of different languages, some challenges quickly come up. For starters, how should complexity be defined? And if we want to seriously evaluate the claim that complexities in one area of a language are balanced out by simplicity in another, how do we compare complexity across different linguistic domains? We can all agree that a language like Archi (spoken in the northeast region of the Caucasus) has a *very* complex inflectional morphology—an Archi verb can allegedly end in any one of 1.5 million forms, putting English morphology to great shame. But just how much syntactic complexity would English have to have to compensate for the intricacies of Archi verbs? (Perversely, Archi is also endowed with one of the world's largest inventories of consonants.)

Another question is whether we want to talk about the *grammatical* complexity of a language, or its *cognitive* complexity. We might propose, for example, that all languages achieve roughly equal degrees of complexity because they want to allow for a lot of expressive potential without unduly taxing the processing system. In that case, we have to think about complexity in terms of structures that are easier or harder to produce and understand, not just in terms of the number of grammatical devices that speakers of a language have to control. But this just raises another issue: sometimes there's a clash between what makes a sentence easy to produce and what makes it easy to understand. Look back at the ways in which Japanese and Kikongo mark past tense, with Japanese using one form to cover all of the four meanings that Kikongo expresses with distinct forms. On the face if it, it looks like Japanese is obviously simpler. Certainly, it would be simpler to *produce* sentences marked with past tense in Japanese. But what about the hearer's perspective?

As you saw in Chapter 10, hearers do a lot of cognitive work in *elaborating* the linguistic code through a variety of inferences. In the Kikongo examples, there's plenty of detailed information right in the linguistic code, so the hearer doesn't have to link back to the context in order to figure out exactly when the past event occurred. But in Japanese, the hearer carries a larger inferential burden.

And another question: Do we want to talk in terms of the degrees of complexity that languages *allow*, or the degrees of complexity that are regularly *produced* by speakers of that language? For example, it's been claimed that the syntax of the Pirahã language lacks any rules of recursion. This is a controversial claim, but it does appear that Pirahã speakers rarely, if ever, utter clauses that are embedded within other clauses. Now, suppose we combed through 10 million sentences uttered by Pirahã speakers and found one lone embedded clause. Of course, the proportion of embedded clauses in a random sample of English sentences would be much higher. In this imagined scenario, it looks like Pirahã *allows* recursion, it's just that its speakers almost never exercise this option. Do we want to say that in terms of syntactic embedding, English and Pirahã are equally complex?

Once you start digging into discussions about cross-linguistic complexity, it becomes apparent that not all researchers want to measure complexity in the same way, and that there are good reasons for each of the various approaches. But naturally, this makes it hard to agree on how to go about testing the hypothesis of equal complexity.

One solution offers a dose of compromise: What if we measure complexity by appealing to crosslinguistic universals? The idea would be that the rarer a phenomenon is across languages, the more "complex" that phenomenon is. As you saw earlier in the chapter, it's likely that a number of different explanations jointly contribute to the common patterns across languages, ranging from learning biases, to ease of production/comprehension, and to communicative efficiency. In that case, the implicational universals themselves might serve as a reasonable stand-in for the combined effects of all of these factors. Would we see trade-offs, so if a language proved to be an outlier in some ways, it would stick to common linguistic norms in others? [In one such study, researcher Matti Miestamo (2009) concludes "yes" for some linguistic phenomena, "no" for others.]

In the end, we may or may not find out that all human languages hit a particular "sweet zone" when it comes to complexity. But along the way, we'll no doubt have learned a lot about what human languages can look like, and why they look the way they do.

PROJECT

Conduct a comparative study of English and the fictional language Klingon (see *The Klingon Dictionary* by Marc Okrand). In Chapter 6, you were introduced to the notion that the Klingon language was deliberately designed to incorporate many highly unusual elements. Using the resources available on the WALS website, identify a number of linguistic features for which English exhibits a more common or typical pattern than Klingon. Discuss the potential implications of the differences between the two languages. If you were to measure complexity in terms of the typicality of patterns across languages, would Klingon come out as "more complex" than English? Finally, can you find a language that appears "less complex" than English, with respect to the crosslinguistic data that are available from WALS?

Glossary

A

ABX discrimination task A test procedure in which subjects hear two different stimuli followed by a third which is identical to one of the first two. The subjects must then decide whether the third stimulus is the same as the first or the second.

accommodation The process of updating a mental model to include information that is presupposed by a speaker, as evident by his use of specific presupposition-triggering expressions.

action potential An electrical pulse that travels down the axon of a neuron to a synapse, resulting in the release of neurotransmitters (signaling molecules).

affective pathway Sound production (vocalizations) arising from states of arousal, emotion, and motivation. Affective sound production is innate, doesn't require learning, and is generally inflexible.

affixes Linguistic units that can't stand on their own but have predictable meanings when attached to a *stem morpheme* such as *own*, *pink* or *cat*.

affricate A sound that is produced when you combine an oral stop and a fricative together, like the first and last consonants in *church* or *judge*.

agglutinative language A language in which words are formed by joining morphemes together. Syntax is expressed by multiple bound affixes and not by changes in position, form, stress, or tone of the root word. Each affix typically represents a single unit of meaning (such as tense or plural), and affixes do not change form in response to other affixes or different root words.

allophones Two or more similar sounds that are variants of the same phoneme; often identified by brackets; e.g., [t] and [tʰ] represent the two allophones of the phoneme /t/ (as in the words *Stan* and *tan*).

alphabetic inventory A collection of orthographic symbols that map onto individual sounds or phonemes.

alveolar Describes a sound whose place of articulation is the alveolar ridge, just behind the teeth.

amusia Loss of the capacity to make sense of music (but not of language).

analogy In regards to forming complex words, a process of comparison in which similarities between the members of pairs or sets of word forms are taken as a basis for the creation of another word form.

antecedent A pronoun's referent or referential match; that is, the expression (usually a proper name or a descriptive noun or noun phrase) that refers to the same person or entity as the pronoun.

anti-nativist view The view that the ability of humans to learn language is not the result of a genetically programmed "language template," but is an aspect (or a by-product) of our extensive cognitive abilities, including general abilities of learning and memory.

aphasia Any language disruption caused by brain damage.

argument from the poverty of the stimulus The argument that there is not enough input available to children to allow them to learn certain structures without the help of innate expectations that guide their language development.

argument structures Syntactic frames that provide information about how many objects or participants are involved in each event, and what kind of objects or participants are involved.

artificial language A "language" that is constructed to have certain specific properties for the purpose of testing an experimental hypothesis: strings of sounds correspond to "words," which may or may not have meaning, and whose combination may or may not be constrained by syntactic rules.

aspirated stop An unvoiced oral stop with a long voice onset time and a characteristic puff of air (aspiration) upon its release; an aspirated stop "pops" when you get too close to a microphone without a pop filter. Aspirated stop sounds are indicated with a superscript: pʰ, tʰ, and kʰ.

assembled phonology route According to the dual route theory, the means by which graphemes are "sounded out" against their corresponding sounds, beginning at the left edge of the word.

assimilation The process by which one sound becomes more similar to a nearby sound.

associationist theories Domain-general theories of learning that emphasize learning that takes place when items become associated in memory through experience.

associative learning Learning process by which associations between two stimuli are made as ideas and experience reinforce one another.

audience design The practice of adjusting aspects of one's language with the goal of communicating effectively with a particular audience or hearer. This adjustment may be conscious or unconscious, and may relate to various aspects of language production, including lexical choice, pronunciation and choice of syntactic structure.

auditory verbal agnosia "Pure word deafness," a condition in which people hear speech as meaningless or garbled sound but usually can speak, read, or write without any trouble; their ability to process non-speech sounds, including music, seems to be mostly intact.

autism spectrum disorder (ASD) A neurological condition that impairs the ability to coordinate attention with another person, or to make inferences about someone else's state of mind.

auxiliary verbs Often informally known as "helping verbs," a category of words that accompany a main verb. Includes *was, is, can, should, does,* and *did.*

axon Extension of a nerve cell (neuron) along which informational "output" travels to another neuron.

B

back-channel responses Behavioral cues (e.g., nods, murmurs of agreement or grunts of dissent) produced by a hearer that provide the speaker with information about the hearer's degree of comprehension.

basic-level categories The favored midlevel category of words that strike a balance between similarity among members of the category and distinctiveness from members of other categories; e.g., of the words *dog, Dalmatian,* and *animal, dog* would fall into the basic-level category.

bigrams Sequences of two words (i.e., word pairs).

bilabial Describes a sound that is produced by obstructing airflow at the lips.

binding constraints Structurally based constraints on the possible antecedents of personal pronouns such as *she* or *him* and on reflexive pronouns such as *himself* or *themselves.*

brain lateralization The specialization of the brain's right and left cerebral hemispheres for different functions.

bridging inference An inference that connect some of the content in a sentence with previous material in the text, or with information encoded in the mental model.

Broca's aphasia Aphasia characterized by halting speech and tremendous difficulty in choosing words, but fairly good speech comprehension. Also called motor aphasia or expressive aphasia.

Brodmann areas Areas of the human cerebral cortex that are distinct from each other anatomically and in cellular composition, as determined by Korbinian Brodmann.

C

cascaded model of word production A model in which later stages of word production don't need to wait until earlier ones have been fully resolved, but can be initiated while earlier stages are still in progress.

case Grammatical markers that signal the grammatical role (subject, direct object, indirect object, etc.) of a noun within a given sentence.

case markers Morphemes that occur within a noun phrase to signal its grammatical function (for example subject, direct object, indirect object). Case markers may occur on nouns, articles, adjectives, or on any or all of these.

categorical perception A pattern of perception where changes in a stimulus are perceived not as gradual, but as falling into discrete categories. Here, small differences between sounds that fall within a single phoneme category

are not perceived as readily as small differences between sounds that belong to different phoneme categories.

cerebral cortex The outer covering of the brain's cerebral hemispheres.

cognitive architecture Fundamental characteristics of the mind's structure that specify how different cognitive components interact with each other.

cognitive control Also known as executive function. The goal-directed cognitive processes responsible for directing attention and supervising behavioral responses to stimuli.

cognitive pathway Controlled, highly malleable sound production that requires extensive auditory learning and practice. Includes human language sounds and some birdsong.

cohort competitors Words with overlapping onsets (e.g., *candle, candy, candid,* etc.).

cohort model A model of word recognition in which multiple cohort competitors become active immediately after the beginning of word is detected, and are gradually winnowed down to a single candidate as additional acoustic information is taken in.

compensation for coarticulation Phenomenon in which the perception of speech automatically adjusts to take into account the tendency for sounds to be pronounced differently in different phonetic environments; thus the same ambiguous sound may be perceived differently, depending on the adjacent sounds.

complementary distribution Separation of two allophones into completely different, non-overlapping linguistic environments.

compositionality The concept that there are fixed rules for combining units of language in terms of their form that result in fixed meaning relationships between the words that are joined together.

compounding Gluing together two independent words into one unit so that the new unit acts as a single word.

conceptual pact A tacit "agreement" that evolves over the course of a communicative exchange in which conversational partners settle on a particular linguistic expression to refer to a particular referent.

connectionist framework A framework for implementing the process by which items become associated in memory, involving interconnected networks of units.

connectionist model Here this refers to a computational model of the past tense. Based on previously learned associations between verb stems and past-tense forms, the model predicts the probable shape of past-tense forms for new verb stems.

constituent A syntactic category consisting of a word or (more often) a group of words (e.g., noun phrase, prepositional phrase) that clump together and function as a single unit within a sentence.

constraint-based approach The main competitor to the garden path theory, this approach claims that multiple interpretations of an ambiguous structure are simultaneously evaluated against a broad range of information sources (or constraints) that can affect the parser's early decisions.

conversational implicature An aspect of the speaker's intended meaning that cannot be derived directly from the linguistic code, but must be inferred by the hearer on the basis of expectations about the speaker's probable communicative goals and behavior.

corpus callosum A bundle of neural fibers that connects and transfers information between the two hemispheres of the brain.

crossmodal priming task An experimental task involving both spoken and written modalities; participants typically hear prime words, which are often embedded within full sentences, and they must respond to test words displayed orthographically on a computer screen.

cultural transmission view of language change The notion that languages change over time to adapt to the human mind, with all the constraints, limitations, and abilities that human minds bring to the task of learning or using language. This view stands in contrast to the nativist view, which holds that the human mind has changed over time because it has become adapted for the requirements of language.

D

declarative memory Memory for facts and events (whether real or fictional) that can be spoken of or articulated ("declared").

dendrites Neuronal extensions that receive informational "input" from other neurons.

derivational affixes Affixes that transform a word of one category into a word of a different category or significantly change the meaning of the word; e.g., the affix -er turning the verb *own* into the noun *owner,* or the affix *pre-* changing the meaning of the word *view* (whether either *view* or *preview* is used as a noun or verb).

developmental dyslexia A common learning disability with a strong hereditary basis that leads to difficulties in learning to read, although there are no apparent spoken language or other learning problems.

dichotic listening Experimental task in which subjects listen to spoken words over headphones, with a different word spoken into each ear.

differential case marking A system of case marking in which case markers appear selectively on some but not all noun phrases. For example, object case marking may be limited to appearing with animate nouns.

diffusion magnetic resonance imaging (dMRI) Neuroimaging technique that tracks how water molecules are diffused in the brain, providing a view of the brain's "white matter highway" and insight into how information moves between various regions of the brain.

diphthong A sound made when the sound for one vowel slides into an adjacent glide in the same syllable, as in the word *ouch.*

direct route According to the dual route theory of reading, the means by which a series of orthographic symbols is directly connected with the meaning of a word, without involving sound-symbol correspondences.

distributional evidence The tendency of words or types of words to appear in certain syntactic contexts, allowing extrapolation of these tendencies to newly learned words.

ditransitive verb A verb with three participants. In English, the third participant (the indirect object) is usually introduced by a preposition.

ditransitive verbs Verbs that occur with a direct object and an indirect object (which may be introduced by a preposition).

domain-general perspective In regard to specific language impairmen (SLI), the situation in which the linguistic deficit is only one effect of more general cognitive problems that also affect non-linguistic processes.

domain-general learning Learning by mechanisms that aren't limited to learning language.

domain-specific learning Learning by mechanisms that are strictly devoted to language.

domain-specific perspective In regard to specific language impairment (SLI), the situation in which the linguistic deficit strikes at mechanisms that are particular to language rather than mechanisms that are shared with other cognitive abilities.

dorsal stream Theoretical "knowledge stream" of dorsal neural connections (i.e., located in the upper portion of the brain) that process knowledge about "how."

double dissociation In reference to language studies, the simultaneous existence of a situation in which language is impaired but other cognitive skills are normal, and a situation in which language is normal despite the impairment of other cognitive functions.

dual route model a theory of reading which proposes that there are two distinct pathways—the direct route and the assembled phonology route—that link written symbols (graphemes) with meaning.

duality of patterning The concept that language works at two general levels, with units of sound combining into meaningful units (usually words) and these meaningful units combine into a larger pattern of meaningful syntactic units.

dyslexia *See* developmental dyslexia.

E

elaborative inference Refers to inferences that are not required in order to make a discourse coherent, but that enrich the meanings of sentences to include material that's not explicitly encoded on the linguistic content of the sentence.

electroencephalography (EEG) The use of electrodes placed on the scalp to measure changes in electrical voltage over large numbers of neurons in the brain, thus obtaining information about the timing of responses in the brain.

event-related potential (ERP) The change in electrical voltage (the potential) over large numbers of brain neurons, measured with EEG and lined up with the presentation of a relevant stimulus (the event).

evolutionary adaptation A genetically transmitted trait that gives its bearers an advantage—specifically, it helps those with the trait to stay alive long enough to reproduce and/or to have many offspring.

excitatory connections Connections along which activation is passed from one unit to another, so that the more active a unit becomes, the more it increases the activation of a unit it is linked to.

executive function *See* cognitive control.

explanation-based view of discourse processing Theoretical account of discourse processing that emphasizes the active role of the reader as engaged in goal-driven processes of interpretation. The meaning that a reader constructs us assumed to be informed by her particular goals, and her attempts to construct a coherent representation that will explain why certain entities and actions are mentioned in a text.

F

facilitation Processes that make it easier for word recognition to be completed.

false belief test A test intended to probe for the ability to recognize that the mental state of another person can be different from one's own. In the typical false belief test, the subject learns some new information that has the effect of altering a previous belief. The subject is then asked to report on the belief state of another person who has not been privy to the new information.

familiarization phase A preparation period during which subjects are exposed to stimuli that will serve as the basis for the test phase to follow.

focus constructions Syntactic structures that have the effect of putting special emphasis or focus on certain elements within the sentence.

forced choice identification task An experimental task in which subjects are required to categorize stimuli as falling into one of two categories, regardless of the degree of uncertainty they may experience about the identity of a particular stimulus.

framing effect A phenomenon in which decisions or preferences regarding two identical outcomes are observed to be dramatically different, depending on the wording of the outcomes.

fricative A sound that is produced when your tongue narrows the airflow in a way that produces a turbulent sound; e.g., /s/, /f/, or /z/.

functional magnetic resonance imaging (fMRI) Neuroimaging technique that uses magnetic fields to measure hemodynamic changes in the brain while the brain is engaged in a task, on the assumption that such changes are a measure of brain activity.

G

Ganong effect An experimental result demonstrating that the identity of a word can affect the perception of individual sounds within that word. When people hear a sound that is acoustically ambiguous between two sounds, their identification of that sound can be shifted in one direction or another depending on which of the possible sounds results in an actual word.

garden path sentences Sentences that are difficult to understand because they contain a temporary ambiguity. The tendency is for hearers or readers to initially interpret the ambiguous structure incorrectly, and then experience confusion when that initial interpretation turns out to be grammatically incompatible with later material in the sentence.

garden path theory A theory of parsing that claims that an initial "first-pass" structure is built during comprehension using a restricted amount of grammatical information and guided by certain parsing principles or tendencies, such as the tendency to build the simplest structure possible. Evaluations of plausible meanings or consideration of the context only come into play at a later stage of parsing.

generative The quality of language that allows us to use whatever we know about language structure to recognize and generate new examples of never-before-encountered sentences.

glide A sound that is produced when you obstruct the airflow only mildly, allowing most of it to pass through the mouth; e.g., /w/ or /y/.

graphemes Written symbols, analogous to phonemes in spoken language;

individual graphemes may or may not correspond to individual phonemes (for example, two graphemes are used to represent the sound /k/ in *sick*).

Greenberg's linguistic universals A set of observations about common or universal structural patterns found in a sample of 30 languages by Joseph Greenberg. These observations are still used as the basis of a great deal of inquiry in language typology.

H

habituation Decreased response to a stimulus after repeated presentations of that stimulus.

head The central element of a constituent—for example, the head of a prepositional phrase is the preposition.

head-turn preference paradigm An experimental framework in which infants' speech preference or learning is measured by the length of time they turn their heads in the direction of a sound.

heavy-NP shift A syntactic structure in which a long noun phrase, usually a direct object, is moved toward the end of the sentence instead of in its normal spot adjacent to the verb.

hemodynamic changes Changes in blood oxygen levels and direction of blood flow.

heuristics Shallow but very fast information-processing shortcuts that often lead to incorrect conclusions based on superficial cues.

hierarchical Top-down (or bottom-up) arrangement of categories. With respect to language, a quality that involves how words group together into constituents, which in turn can group together with other words or constituents to form ever-larger constituents.

Hockett's design features A set of characteristics proposed by linguist Charles Hockett to be universally shared by all human languages. Some (but not all) of the features are also found in various animal communication systems.

homesign A personal communication system initiated by a deaf person to communicate through gestures with others who, like the deaf person, do not know sign language.

homographs Words that are spelled exactly the same but have separate, non-overlapping meanings (and may or may not sound the same).

homophones Two or more words that have separate, non-overlapping meanings but sound exactly the same (even though they may be spelled differently).

I

iambic stress pattern Syllable emphasis pattern in which the first syllable is unstressed, as in *reTURN*.

implicational universals Crosslinguistic generalizations that are formulated as conditional statements ("If a language has A, then it has B").

implicit causality Expectations about the probable cause/effect structure of events denoted by particular verbs.

implicit priming A psychological phenomenon in which exposing people to certain stimuli increases the likelihood that they'll exhibit behaviors that are associated with the stimuli. For example, exposing people to words associated with the elderly may trigger behaviors that are stereotypically associated with the elderly, such as walking slowly.

incremental language processing The processing of language in such a way that hearers begin to generate hypotheses about the meaning of the incoming speech on the basis of partial acoustic information, refining and revising these hypotheses on the fly rather than waiting until there is enough information in the speech stream for the hearer to be certain about what the speaker meant.

incrementality The property of synthesizing and building meaning "on the fly" as individual units of speech come in, rather than delaying processing until some amount of linguistic material has accumulated.

infixes Affixes "shoehorned" into the middle of a word (not found in English).

inflectional affixes Affixes that serve as grammatical reflexes or markers, the presence of which is dictated by the grammatical rules of a language; e.g., in English the affixes *-ed* and *-ing* change the tense of a verb. (Note that in English only suffixes are inflectional affixes.)

inhibition Processes that result in word recognition becoming more difficult.

inhibitory connections Connections that lower the activation of connected units, so that the more active a unit becomes, the more it *suppresses* the activation of a unit it is linked to.

interactive alignment model A theory of dialogue that minimizes the role of representing a conversational partner's perspective or mental state. Rather, much of the alignment that emerges between conversational partners is attributed to automatic mechanisms of priming in memory.

interactive mind design A view of the mind's structure in which higher, more abstract levels of knowledge (usually what we think of as "more intelligent" levels of knowledge) can directly inform lower-level perception.

interstimulus interval (ISI) The amount of time between the offset of the prime and the onset of the target.

intransitive verbs Verbs that take a subject but no object, such as *(Joe) sneezes* or *(Keesha) laughs*.

ions Electrically charged particles; the charge can be positive or negative. Ions that are especially important in neural signaling include sodium (Na^+), potassium (K^+) calcium (Ca^{2+}), and chloride (Cl^-).

it-cleft sentence A type of focus construction in which a single clause has been split into two, typically with the form "It is/was X that/who Y." The element corresponding to X in this frame is focused. For example, in the sentence *It was Sam who left Fred*, the focus is on *Sam*.

J

joint attention The awareness between two or more individuals that they are paying attention to the same thing.

L

lateralization *See* brain lateralization.

lemma An abstract mental representation of a word containing information about its meaning and syntactic category, but not about its sounds.

lexical bias The statistical tendency for sound-based speech errors to result in actual words rather than non-words.

lexical co-occurrence patterns Information about which words tend to appear adjacent to each other in a given data set.

lexical decision task An experimental task in which participants read strings of letters on a screen that might either be actual words (*doctor*) or nonsense words (*domter*). Subjects press one button if they think they've seen a real word, or a different button to signal that the letters formed a nonsense word. Response times for real words are taken as a general measure of the ease of recognizing those words under specific experimental conditions.

lexical entrainment The tendency to link a previously used expression with a particular referent.

language typologists Researchers who study the ways in which languages vary with the aim of describing and explaining crosslinguistic variation.

lexical representation Information that is committed to long-term memory about the sound and meaning properties of words, and certain constraints on their syntactic combination.

linguistic code The system of symbols and combinatory rules that are conventionally agreed upon by a community of language users as conveying specific meanings. Often, the linguistic code is not enough to fully convey the speaker's *intended* meaning, so that hearers must augment the linguistic code with inferences based on the context.

linguistic competence Underlying knowledge about linquistic representations and the rules for combining them.

linguistic input The linguistic forms a child is exposed to.

linguistic intake The representations a child uses as the basis for learning structure.

linguistic performance The execution of linguistic competence in speaking or comprehending.

lip rounding The amount you shape your lips into a circle; for example, your lips are very rounded when you make the sound for /w/.

liquid sound A sound that is produced when you let air escape over both sides of your tongue; e.g., /l/ or /r/.

logographic writing system Writing system in which symbols are mapped to units of meaning such as morphemes or words rather than to units of sound.

long-distance dependencies Relationships between constituents widely separated from each other in a sentence.

M

magnetoencephalography (MEG) A technique related to electroencephalography that detects changes in magnetic fields caused by the brain's electrical activity.

masked priming A priming task in which the prime word is presented subliminally, that is, too quickly to be consciously recognized.

maxims of cooperative conversation A set of communicative expectations that are shared by speakers and hearers regarding how speakers typically behave in order to be understood by hearers. The four maxims of Quality, Relation, Quantity and Manner are attributed to the philosopher H. P. Grice.

McGurk effect An illusion in which a mismatch between auditory information and visual information pertaining to a sound's articulation results in altered perception of that sound; for example, when people hear an audio recording of a person uttering the syllable *ga* while viewing a video of the speaker uttering *ba*, they often perceive the syllable as *da*.

mean length of utterance (MLU) The average number of morphemes in a child's utterances at a given point in the child's development.

mediated semantic priming The process by which a prime word (e.g., *lion*) speeds up responses to a target word (e.g., *stripes*) not because of a direct connection between *lion* and *stripes*, but due to an indirect connection via some other intervening word (e.g., *tiger*).

memory-driven account of discourse processing Theoretical approach to discourse processing that emphasizes the role of passive, automatic memory-based processes, in which the integration of incoming discourse information is accomplished by activating existing representations in memory.

mental age A person's overall level of cognitive functioning, related to the chronological age of a person with typical development.

mental models Also known as situation models. Refers to detailed conceptual representation of the real-world situation that a sentence evokes.

minimal pair A pair of words that have different meanings, but all of the same sounds with the exception of one phoneme; e.g., *tan* and *man*.

mixed errors Speech errors that involve similarities of both sound and meaning.

modular mind design View of the mind's structure in which higher levels of processing never directly influence the lower levels; instead, the higher levels integrate information based on lower-level processes, interpret it, and pass these interpretations on to even higher levels.

mondegreens "Slips of the ear" that result in errors of word segmentation.

morphemes The smallest bundles of sound that can be related to some systematic meaning.

motor theory of speech perception A theory that the perception of speech sounds involves accessing representations of the articulatory gestures that are required to make those speech sounds.

moving window paradigm A version of the self-paced reading task in which dashes initially replace each alphabetic character in a sentence, and participants press a button to successively "uncover" each portion of the sentence. This method of presentation simulates a fairly natural reading rhythm.

mutual exclusivity bias A general bias to line up object categories and linguistic labels in a one-to-one correspondence.

N

N400 An ERP in which a waveform shows a negative voltage peak about 400 ms.

nasal stop A stop consonant made by lowering the velum in a way that lets the air pass through your nose; e.g., /m/, /n/, and the ŋ sound in words like *sing* or *fang*.

nativist view The view that not only are humans genetically programmed to have a general capacity for language, particular aspects of language ability are also genetically specified.

neighborhood density effects Experimental results demonstrating that it is more difficult and time-consuming to retrieve a word from memory if the word bears a strong phonological resemblance to many other words in the vocabulary than if resembles only a few other words.

neurolinguists Scientists who study how the physical brain relates to language behavior.

neurotransmitter Molecules produced by a neuron and released across a synapse in response to an action potential. Neurotransmitters bind to receptors on a receiving cell (another neuron or a muscle cell), producing a response in the second cell.

noun phrase (NP) An abstract, higher-order syntactic category that can consist of a single word or of many words, but in which the main syntactic element is a noun, pronoun, or proper name.

O

object-relative clause An embedded clause in which the referent that is shared between the main and embedded clauses is linked to the object position of the embedded clause (e.g., I saw the cat that the dog chased).

onset The material in a syllable that precedes the vowel.

oral stop A stop consonant made by fully blocking air in the mouth and not allowing it to leak out through the nose; e.g., /p/, /t/, and /k/.

over-extension Mapping new words into categories that are too general (e.g., referring to all animals as *doggie*).

P

P600 An ERP effect in which a waveform shows a positive voltage peak about 600 ms.

paralinguistic use The use or manipulation of sounds for emphasis, clarification of meaning, or emotional color but not as an element in the composition of words or sentences.

parsing The process of assigning syntactic structure to the incoming words of a sentence during language comprehension. The structure-building mechanisms and procedures collectively are often referred to as "the parser."

particle A syntactic marker, often lacking a specific meaning, that accompanies other syntactic elements.

pedagogical stance A receptive mindset adopted by the learner in response to cues that signal that an interactive partner is intending to convey some new and relevant information.

perceptual invariance The phenomenon whereby acoustically different stimuli are perceived as examples of the same phoneme or word.

phonation Production of sound by the vibrating vocal folds.

phoneme The smallest unit of sound that changes the meaning of a word; often identified by forward slashes; e.g., /t/ is a phoneme because replacing it in the word *tan* makes a different word.

phoneme restoration effect An auditory illusion showing that when a speech sound within a word is replaced by a non-speech sound, people often report hearing both the speech and non-speech sounds.

phonemic awareness The conscious recognition of phonemes as distinct units, usually only solidly acquired by individuals who are literate in an alphabetic writing system.

phonemic inventory A list of the different phonemes in a language.

phonological awareness The ability to consciously analyze and separate strings of sounds into their subparts.

phonotactic constraints Language-specific constraints that determine how the sounds of a given language may be combined to form words or syllables.

phrase structure rules Rules that provide a set of instructions about how individual words can be clumped into higher-order categories and how these categories are combined to create well-formed sentences.

polysemous words Words that can convey a constellation of related, but different meanings, such as the various related meanings of *paper*, which can, among other meanings, refer to a specific material, or a news outlet.

positron emission tomography (PET) Neuroimaging technique that uses radioactivity to measure hemodynamic changes.

pragmatic meaning The aspect of meaning that is not available directly from the conventional code, but that must be inferred on the basis of contextual information or information about the speaker's likely intentions.

predictive inference A type of elaborative inference that involves making predictions about the likely outcome of a sentence.

prefixes Affixes attached at the front end of a word; e.g., *un-*; *pre-*.

prepositional phrase (PP) A syntactic constituent, or higher-order category, that in English, consists of a preposition (e.g., in, under, before) followed by a noun phrase (NP).

presupposition An implicit assumption that is signaled by specific linguistic expressions, and whose existence or truth is taken for granted as background information.

principles and parameters theory A theory claiming that children's language learning is dramatically constrained with the help of innate syntactic "options" or "parameter switches" that restrict the possible syntactic structures children can infer. Language learning is said to consist largely of checking the input to see which of the constrained set of options apply to the language being learned.

procedural memory Memory for physical actions and sequences of actions.

productivity In linguistics, a process that can be applied broadly to a large set of lexical items, rather than being restricted to a small set of words; the ability to use known symbols or linguistic units in new combinations to communicate different ideas.

proposition The core meaning of a sentence as expressed by its linguistic content. This core meaning captures the real-world event or the situation that would have to occur in order for that sentence to be judged to be true.

prosody The rhythm, stress, and intonation of a spoken phrase or sentence.

psycholinguistics The psychology of language; the study of the psychological and neurobiological factors involved in the perception, production, and acquisition of language.

R

reading span test A behavioral test intended to measure an individual's verbal working memory. The test involves having the individual read a sequence of sentences while holding the last word of each sentence in memory. The number of words successfully remembered corresponds to that individual's memory span.

recursion Repeated iterations. With respect to language, refers to syntactic embeddings that nest constituents (such as clauses or noun phrases) within other constituents in a potentially infinite manner.

reduced relative clause A grammatical structure in English involving a relative clause in which certain function words have been omitted (for example the reduced relative clause *raced past the barn* derives from the full relative clause *that was raced past the barn*). This structure often leads to ambiguity.

referential communication task An experimental task in which speakers refer to a specific target object in the context of a number of other objects. The method may be used to probe the behavior of either speakers or hearers. Speakers are faced with the task of choosing a linguistic expression that successfully distinguishes the target object from the other objects that are present. Hearers are required to successfully identity the target object based on the speakers' choice of linguistic expression. The task may vary the nature of the objects that are present, the linguistic descriptions of the objects, or various aspects of the interactive context.

relative clause A clause that is embedded within the main clause and shares a referent with the main clause.

repeated-name penalty The finding that under some circumstances, it takes longer to read a sentence in which a highly salient referent is referred to by a full noun phrase (NP) rather than by a pronoun.

reverse cohesion effect The finding that under some circumstances, read-

ers retain more information from a text in which the coherence relations between sentences is not made explicit and must be inferred by the reader.

rime The material in a syllable that includes the vowel and anything that follows.

S

scalar implicature A type of conversational implicature that occurs when a speaker chooses a relatively vague expression rather than a stronger, more specific one. In many contexts, the speaker's choice of linguistic expression leads the hearer to infer that the speaker has used the weaker, vaguer expression because the stronger one would be inaccurate under the circumstances.

self-paced reading task A behavioral task intended to measure processing difficulty at various points in a sentence. Subjects read through sentences on a computer screen, one word or phrase at a time, pressing a button to advance through the sentence. A program records the amount of time each subject spends reading each segment.

semantic bootstrapping hypothesis The idea that children come equipped with innate expectations of certain grammatical categories, as well as built-in mappings between key concept types and grammatical categories.

semantics The meaning of a sentence; the system of rules for interpreting the meaning of a sentence based on its structure.

semantic meaning The aspect of meaning that can be derived directly from the linguistic code, based on the conventionally agreed-upon meanings of the linguistic expressions involved.

semantic priming The phenomenon by which hearing or reading a word partially activates other words that are related in meaning to that word, making the related words easier to recognize in subsequent encounters.

sensitive period A window of time during which a specific type of learning (such as learning language) takes place more easily than at any other time.

sentential complement verbs Verbs that introduce a clause rather than a direct object noun phrase (NP).

serial model of word production A model in which earlier stages of word production must be fully completed before later stages begin.

shadowing task An experimental task in which subjects are asked to repeat the words of a speaker's sentence almost as quickly as the speaker produces them.

situation models *See* mental models.

social gating The enhancement of learning through social interaction.

specific language impairment (SLI) A disorder in which children fail to develop language normally even though there are no apparent neurological damages or disorders, no general cognitive impairment or delay, no hearing loss, and no abnormal home environment that would explain this failure.

stop consonant A sound produced when airflow is stopped completely somewhere in the vocal tract.

Stroop test Behavioral test in which subjects are required to name the color of the font that a word appears in while ignoring the (possibly conflicting) meaning of the word.

subcategorization information Verb-specific knowledge of the verb's combinatorial properties.

subcortical Refers to the internal regions of the cerebral hemispheres, lying beneath the cerebral cortex.

subject-relative clause An embedded clause in which the referent that is shared between the main and embedded clauses is linked to the subject position of the embedded clause (e.g., *I saw the cat that chased the dog*).

subordinate-level categories More specific categories comprising words that encompass a narrower range of referents than basic-level categories do; e.g., *Dalmatian* (as opposed to *dog*).

suffixes Affixes attached at the end of a word; e.g., *-able; -ed; -ing.*

superordinate-level categories The most general categories of words that encompass a wide range of referents; e.g., *animal* as opposed to *dog* (basic-level) or *Dalmation* (subordinate level).

surprisal A measure that is inversely related to the statistical predictability of an event such as a particular continuation of a sentence. Processing difficulty is thought to reflect the degree of surprisal at specific points in the sentence, so that less predictable continuations result in greater processing difficulty.

switch task A simple word-mapping test in which infants are exposed to a visual representation of an object paired with an auditory stimulus during a habituation phase. During the subsequent test phase, the infants hear either the same object–word pairing, or they hear a new word paired with the familiar object. A difference in looking times between the novel and familiar pairings is taken as evidence that the child had mapped the original auditory stimulus to the familiar object.

syllabic writing system Writing system in which characters represent different syllables.

synapse Site of connection between the axon terminal of a neuron and the receptors of another neuron or a muscle cell.

syndrome Literally, "occurring together" (Greek *syndromos*). A group of symptoms that collectively characterize a medical or psychological disorder or condition. The presence of a syndrome can lead to the identification of a genetic basis for the condition.

syntactic bootstrapping Using the syntactic properties of words to identify and narrow in on those aspects of meaning that words are likely to convey.

syntactic priming A phenomenon in which speakers are more likely to use a particular structure to express an idea

if they have recently used the same structure to express a different idea.

syntax The structure of a sentence, specifying how the words are put together, Also refers to a set of rules or constraints for how linguistic elements can be put together.

T

telegraphic speech Speech that preserves the correct order of words in sentences, but drops many of the small function words such as *the*, *did*, or *to*.

tenseness A feature of vowels distinguishing "tense" vowels such as those in *beet* and *boot* from "lax" vowels such as those in *bit* and *put*.

test phase The period in which subjects' responses to the critical experimental stimuli is tested following a familiarization phase.

thematic relations Knowledge about verbs that captures information about the events they describe, including how many and what kinds of participants are involved in the events, and the roles the various participants play.

thematic role Information about the role of various participants in an event described by a verb. For example, in the sentence *Patrice sent the letter to Felicia*, Patrice assumes the role of "agent," or instigator of the event, while Felicia assumes the role of "goal," or the endpoint of the event.

theory of mind (ToM) The ability to grasp the nature of mental states such as beliefs, knowledge, and intentions, and to recognize that different people may have different mental states under different conditions.

tip-of-the-tongue state State of mind experienced by speakers when they have partially retrieved a word (usually its lemma, and perhaps some of its sound structure) but feel that retrieval of its full phonological form is elusive.

transitional probability (TP) The probability that a particular syllable will occur, given the previous occurrence of another particular syllable.

transitive verbs Verbs that take both a subject and an object, such as *(Joe) kicks (the ball)* or *(Keesha) eats (popcorn)*.

trigrams Sequences of three words.

trochaic stress pattern Syllable emphasis pattern in which the first syllable is stressed, as in *BLACKmail*.

U

unaspirated stop An unvoiced oral stop without aspiration, produced with a relatively short voice onset time (VOT).

under-extension Mapping new words into categories that are too specific; e.g, referring to a carnation, but not a daisy, as *flower*.

uniqueness point The point at which there is enough information in the incoming speech stream to allow the hearer to differentiate a single word candidate from its cohort competitors.

universal grammar A hypothetical set of innate learning biases that guide children's learning processes and constrain the possible structures of human languages.

unvoiced (voiceless) Describes a sound that does not involve simultaneous vibration of the vocal folds; in a voiceless stop followed by a vowel, vibration happens only after a lag (say, more than 20 milliseconds).

V

velar Describes a sound whose place of articulation is the velum (the soft tissue at the back of the roof of the mouth).

ventral stream Theoretical "knowledge stream" of ventral neural connections (i.e., located in the lower portion of the brain) that process knowledge about "what."

verb islands Hypothetical syntactic frames that are particular to specific verbs, and that specify (1) whether that verb can combine with nouns to its left or right and/or (2) the roles that the co-occurring nouns can play in an event (for example, the do-er, the thing that is acted upon, and so on).

vocal folds Also known as "vocal cords," these are paired "flaps" in the larynx that vibrate as air passes over them. The vibrations are shaped into speech sounds by the other structures (tongue, alveolar ridge, velum, etc.). of the vocal tract.

voice onset time (VOT) The length of time between the point when a stop consonant is released and the point when voicing begins.

voiced Describes a sound that involves vibration of the vocal folds; in an oral stop, the vibration happens just about simultaneously with the release of the articulators (within about 20 milliseconds) as it does for /b/ in the word *ban*.

vowel backness The amount your tongue is retracted toward the back of your mouth when you say a vowel.

vowel height The height of your tongue as you say a vowel. For example, e has more vowel height than a.

W

Wernicke's aphasia Aphasia associated with fluent speech that is well articulated but often nonsensical, and enormous difficulty in understanding language. Also called sensory or receptive aphasia.

wh- island constraints Syntactic constraints that prevent wh- words (*who, what, where*) from being related to certain positions within a sentence.

wh- cleft sentence A type of focus construction in which one clause has been divided into two, with the first clause introduced by a *wh-* element, as in the sentences *What Ravi sold was his old car* or *Where Joan went was to Finland*. In this case, the focused element appears in the second clause (*his old car, to Finland*).

white matter Bundles of neural tissue (axons) that act as the brain's information networks, allowing products (signaling molecules) from one processing area to be shuttled to another area for further processing or packaging.

whole-object bias The (theoretical) assumption by babies that a new word heard in the context of a salient object refers to the whole thing and not to its parts, color, surface, substance, or the action the object is involved in.

Whorf hypothesis The hypothesis that the words and structures of a language can affect how the speakers of that language conceptualize or think about the world.

Williams syndrome (WMS) Genetic syndrome, of particular interest to language researchers, in which language function appears to be relatively preserved despite more serious impairments in other areas of cognitive function.

Literature Cited

Chapter 2

Brainard, M. S., & Doupe, A. J. (2002) What songbirds teach us about learning. *Nature, 417,* 351–358.

Bräuer, J., Call, J., & Tomasello, M. (2007) Chimpanzees really know what others can see in a competitive situation. *Animal Cognition, 10,* 439–448.

Call, J. (2004) Inferences about the location of food in the great apes. *Journal of Comparative Psychology, 118,* 232–241.

Call, J., & Tomasello, M. (2010) Does the chimpanzee have a theory of mind? 30 years later. *Trends in Cognitive Sciences, 12,* 187–192.

Catchpole, C. L., & Slater, P. L. B. (1995) *Bird song: Themes and variations.* Cambridge, UK: Cambridge University Press.

Christiansen, M. H., & Chater, N. (2008) Language as shaped by the brain. *Behavioral and Brain Sciences, 31,* 589-558.

Chomsky, N. (1986) *Knowledge of language: Its nature, origins and use.* Westport, CT: Praeger.

Colonnesi, C., Stams, G. J. J. M., Koster, I., & Noom, M J. (2010) The relation between pointing and language development: A meta-analysis. *Developmental Review, 30,* 352–366.

Corballis, M. (1999) The gestural origins of language. *American Scientist, 87,* 138–145.

Darwin, C. (1871) *The descent of man and selection in relation to sex.* London: John Murray.

De Waal, F. B. M., & Pollick, A. S. (2012) In M. Tallerman & K. R. Gibson (Ed.), *The Oxford handbook of language evolution.* Oxford, UK: Oxford University Press.

Everett, D. L. (2012) *Language: The cultural tool.* New York: Vintage.

Feher, O., Wang, H., Saar, S., Mitra, P. P., & Tchernichovski, O. (2009) De novo establishment of wild-type song culture in the zebra finch. *Nature, 459,* 564–568.

Fitch, W. T. (2010) *The evolution of language.* Cambridge, UK: Cambridge University Press.

Fitch, W. T. (2000) The evolution of speech: A comparative review. *Trends in Cognitive Science, 4,* 258–267.

Gibson, K. R. (2012) Language or protolanguage? A review of the ape literature. In M. Tallerman & K. R. Gibson (Ed.), *The Oxford handbook of language evolution.* Oxford, UK: Oxford University Press.

Goldin-Meadow, S. (2005) What language creation in the manual modality tells us about the foundations of language. *The Linguistic Review, 22,* 199–225.

Goldin-Meadow, S., McNeill, D., & Singleton, J. (1996) Silence is liberating: Removing the handcuffs on grammatical expression in the manual modality. *Psychological Review, 103,* 34–55.

Goldstein, M. H., King, A. P., & West, M. J. (2003) Social interaction shapes babbling: Testing parallels between birdsong and speech. *Proceedings of the National Academy of Sciences, 24,* 8030–8035.

Gould, J. L., & Marler, P. (1987) Learning by Instinct. *Scientific American, 255,* 74-85.

Grüter, C., Balbuena, M. S., & Farina, W. M. (2008) Informational conflicts created by the waggle dance. *Proceedings of the Royal Society B: Biological Sciences, 275,* 1321–1327.

Hare, B., Plyusnina, I., Ignacio, N., Schepina, O., Stepika, A., Wrangham, R., & Trut, L. (2005) Social cognitive evolution in captive foxes is a correlated by-product of experimental domestication. *Current Biology, 15,* 226-230.

Hare, B., & Tomasello, M. (2005) Human-like social skills in dogs? *Trends in Cognitive Science, 9,* 439–444.

Hare, B., & Tomasello, M. (2004) Chimpanzees are more skillful in competitive than cooperative cognitive tasks. *Animal Behaviour, 68,* 571–581.

Hauser, M. D., Chomsky, N., & Fitch, W. T. (2002) The faculty of language: What is it, who has it, and how did it evolve? *Science, 298,* 1569–1579.

Hayes, C. (1951) *The ape in our house.* New York: Harper.

Hermann, E., Call, J., Hernandez-Lloreda, M.V., Hare, B., & Tomasello, M. (2007) Humans have evolved specialized skills for social cognition: The cultural intelligence hypothesis. *Science, 317,* 1360–1366.

Hock, H. H. (1986) *Principles of historical linguistics.* Berlin: Mouton de Gruyter.

Hockett, C. F. (1960) The origin of speech. *Scientific American, 203,* 88–111

Hockett, C. F., & Altmann, S. (1968) A note on design features. In T. A. Sebeok, (Ed.), *Animal communication: Techniques of study and results of research.* Bloomington: Indiana University Press.

Jürgens, U., Kirzinger, A., and von Cramon, D.Y. (1982) The effects of deep-reaching lesions in the cortical face area on phonation: A combined case report and experimental monkey study. *Cortex, 18,* 125–139

Kegl, J., Senghas, A., & Coppola, M. (1999) Creation through contact: Sign language emergence and sign language change in Nicaragua. In M. DeGraff (Ed.), *Language creation and language change: Creolization, diachrony, and development.* Cambridge, MA: MIT Press.

Kirby, S., Cornish, H., & Smith, K. (2008) Cumulative cultural evolution in the laboratory: An experimental approach to the origins of structure in human language. *Proceedings of the National Academy of Sciences, 105,* 10681–10686.

Lieberman, P. H., Klatt, D. H., & Wilson, W. H. (1969) Vocal tract limitations on the vowel repertoires of rhesus monkeys and other nonhuman primates. *Science, 164*, 1185–1187.

Lipkind, D., Marcus, M. F., Bemis, D. K., Sasahara, K., Jacoby, N., Takahasi, M., Suzuki, K., Feher, O., Ravbar, P., Okanoya, K., & Tchernichovski, O. (2013) Stepwise acquisition of vocal combinatorial capacity in songbirds and human infants. *Nature, 498*, 104–108.

Lizskowski, U., Carpenter, M., & Tomasello, M. (2008) 12- and 18-month-olds point to provide information for others. *Journal of Cognition and Development, 7*, 173–187.

McWhorter, J. H. (2002) What happened to English? *Diachronica, 19*, 217–272.

Morales, M., Mundy, P., Delgado, E. F., Yale, M., Messinger, D., Neal, R., & Schwartz, H. K. (2000) Responding to joint attention across the 6- through 24-month age period and early language acquisition. *Journal of Applied Developmental Psychology, 21*, 283–298.

Mufwene, S. (2008) What do creoles and pidgins tell us about the evolution of language? In B. Laks, S. Cleziou, J. P. Demoule, & P. Encrevé (Eds.), *The origins and evolution of languages: Approaches, models, paradigms*. London: Equinox.

Okrent, A. (2010) *In the land of invented language: Esperanto rock stars, Klingon poets, Loglan lovers and the mad dreamers who tried to build a perfect language*. New York: Spiegel & Grau.

Owren, M. J., Amoss, R. T., & Rendall, D. (2011) Two organizing principles of vocal production: Implications for nonhuman and human primates. *American Journal of Primatology, 73*, 530–544.

Owren, M. J., Dieter, J. A., Seyfarth, R M., & Cheney, D. L. (1993) Vocalizations of rhesus (*Macaca mulatta*) and Japanese (*F. muscata*) macaques cross-fostered between species show evidence of only limited modification. *Developmental Psychobiology, 26*, 389–406.

Pinker, S. (1994) *The language instinct*. New York: HarperCollins.

Povinelli, D. J., & Eddy, T. J. (1996) What young chimpanzees know about seeing. *Monographs of the Society for Research in Child Development, 61*, 1–152.

Ralls, K., Fiorelli, P., & Gish, S. (1985) Vocalizations and vocal mimicry in captive harbor seals: *Phoca vitulina*. *Canadian Journal of Zoology, 63*, 1050–1056.

Ridgway, S., Carder, D., Jeffries, M., & Todd, M. (2012) Spontaneous human speech mimicry by a cetacean. *Current Biology, 22*, R860-R861.

Sandler, W., Meir, I., Padden, C., & Aronoff, M. (2005) The emergence of grammar: Systematic structure in a new language. *Proceedings of the National Academy of Sciences, 102*, 2661–2665.

Savage-Rumbaugh, E. S., Rumbaugh, D. M., & Boysen, S. (1980) Do apes use language? One research group considers the evidence for representational ability in apes. *American Scientist, 68*, 49–61.

Senghas, A. (2005) Language emergence: Clues from a new Bedouin sign language. *Current Biology, 15*, R463–R465.

Senghas, A., & Coppola, M. (2001) Children creating language: How Nicaraguan Sign Language acquired a spatial grammar. *Psychological Science, 12*, 323–328.

Senghas, A., Kita, S., & Özyürek, A. (2004) Children creating core properties of language: Evidence from an emerging sign language in Nicaragua. *Science, 305*, 1779–1782.

Seyfarth, R. M., & Cheney, D. L. (2010) Production, usage, and comprehension in animal vocalizations. *Brain and Language, 115*, 92–100.

Seyfarth, R. M., Cheney, D. L., & Marler, P. (1980) Vervet monkey alarm calls: Semantic communication in a free-ranging primate. *Animal Behaviour, 28*, 1070–1094.

Stokoe, W. C. (1960) *Sign language structure: An outline of the visual communication system of the American deaf*. Studies in Linguistics: Occasional Papers (No. 8) Buffalo, NY: Department of Anthropology & Linguistics, University of Buffalo.

Stooger, A. S., Mietchen, D., Oh, S., de Silva, S., Herbst, C. T., Kwon, S., & Fitch, W. T. (2012) An Asian elephant imitates human speech. *Current Biology, 22*, 2144–2148.

Su, S., Cai, F., Si, A., Zhang, S., Tautz, J., & Chen, S. (2008) East learns from West: Asiatic honeybees can understand dance language of European honeybees. *PLoS ONE 3(6)*: e2365. doi:10.1371/journal.pone.0002365

Theisen, C. A., Oberlander, J., & Kirby, S. (2010) Systematicity and arbitrariness in novel communication systems. *Interaction Studies, 11*, 14–32.

Tomasello, M. (2009) *Why we cooperate*. Boston: MIT Press.

Tomasello, M. (2006) Why don't apes point? In N. Enfield & S. Levinson, (Eds.), *Roots of human sociality*. New York: Wenner-Grenn.

von Frisch, K. (1967) *The dance language and orientation of bees*. Cambridge, MA: Harvard University Press.

Chapter 3

Ackerman, D. (2012) *One hundred names for love: A memoir*. New York: W. W. Norton & Co.

Bellugi, U., Lichtenberger, L., Jones, W., Lai, Z., & St. George, M. (2000) The neurocognitive profile of Williams syndrome: A complex pattern of strengths and weaknesses. *Journal of Cognitive Neuroscience, 12*, 7–29.

Bentin, S., & Deouell, L.Y. (2000) Structural encoding and identification in face processing: ERP evidence for separate mechanisms. *Cognitive Neuropsychology, 17*, 35–54.

Bentin, S., Mouchetant-Rostaing, Y., Giard, M. H., Echallier, J. F., & Pernier, J. (1999) ERP manifestations of processing printed words at different psycholinguistic levels: Time course and scalp distribution. *Journal of Cognitive Neuroscience, 11*, 235–260.

Bierce, A. (1911) *The devil's dictionary*. In *The collected works of Ambrose Bierce*, vol. 7. New York, NY: Neale Publishing Co.

Broca, P. P. (1861) Remarks on the seat of the faculty of articulated language, following an observation of aphemia (loss of speech) *Bulletin de la Société Anatomique, 6*, 330–357. Translation by Christopher D. Green, http://psychclassics.yorku.ca/Broca/aphemie-e.htm.

Brock, J. (2007) Language abilities in Williams syndrome: A critical review. *Development and Psychopathology, 19*, 97–127.

Brodmann, K. (1909) *Vergliechende Lokalisationslehre der Großhirnrinde. Localisation in the Cerebral Cortex*. Translated and edited by L. J. Garey (1994). New York, NY: Springer.

Brown, S., Martinez, M. J., & Parsons, L. M. (2006) Music and language side by side in the brain: A PET study of the generation of melodies and sentences. *European Journal of Neuroscience, 23*, 2791–2803.

Chao, L. L., Nielsen-Bohlman, L., & Knight, R. T. (1995) Auditory event-related potentials dissociate early and late memory processes. *Electroencephalography and Clinical Neurophysiology/Evoked Potentials Section, 96*, 157–168.

Chobert, J., Marie, C., Francois, C., Schon, D., & Besson, M. (2011) Enhanced passive and active processing of syllables in musician children. *Journal of Cognitive Neuroscience, 23*, 3874–3887.

De Bode, S., & Curtiss, S. (2000) Language after hemispherectomy. *Brain and Cognition, 43,* 145–148.

Dick, F., Bates, E., Wulfeck, B., Utman, J. A., Dronkers, N., & Gernsbacher, M. A. (2001) Language deficits, localization, and grammar: Evidence for a distributive model of language breakdown in aphasic patients and neurologically intact individuals. *Psychological Review, 108,* 759–788.

Dronkers, N. F., Plaisant, O. F., Iba-Zizen, M. T., & Cabanis, E. A. (2007) Paul Broca's historic cases: High resolution MR images of the brains of Leborgne and Lelong. *Brain, 130,* 1432–1441.

Emmorey, K., McCollough, S., Mehta, S., Ponto, L. L. B., & Grabowski, T J. (2011) Sign language and pantomime production differentially engage frontal and parietal cortices. *Language and Cognitive Processes, 26,* 878–901.

Garey, L. J. (1994) Brodmann's localization in the cerebral cortex. London: Smith-Gordon.

Gazzaniga, M. S., & Sperry, R. W. (1967) Language after section of the cerebral commissures. *Brain, 90,* 131–148.

Gierhan, S. M. E. (2013) Connections for auditory language in the human brain. *Brain and Language,* http://dx.doi.org/10.1016/j.bandl.2012.11.002

Gouvea, A. C., Phillips, C., Kazanina, N., & Poeppel, D. (2010) The linguistic processes underlying the P600. *Language and Cognitive Processes, 25,* 149–188.

Harlow, J. M. (1868) Recovery from the passage of an iron bar through the head. *Publications of the Massachusetts Medical Society, 2,* 327–347.

Harrison, A. H., & Connolly, J. F. (2013) Finding a way in: A review and practical evaluation of fMRI and EEG for detection and assessment in disorders of consciousness. *Neuroscience and Biobehavioral Reviews, 37,* 1403–1419.

Hauk, O., Johnsrude, I., & Pulvermüller, F. (2004) Somatotopic representation of action words in human motor and premotor cortex. *Neuron, 41,* 301–307.

Hickok, G. (2009) The functional neuroanatomy of language. *Physics of Life Reviews, 6,* 121–143.

Hickok, G., Bellugi, U., & Klima, E. S. (2001) Sign language in the brain. *Scientific American, 284,* 58–65.

Hickok, G., & Poeppel, D. (2007) The cortical organization of speech processing. *Nature Reviews Neuroscience, 8,* 393–402.

Iacoboni, M., Freedman, J., Kaplan, J., Jamieson, K. H., Freedman, T., Knapp, B., et al. (2007, November 11) This is your brain on politics. *New York Times.* Retrieved August 6, 2013, from www.nytimes.com/2007/11/11/opinion/11freedman.html?pagewanted=all

Joanisse, M. F., & Seidenberg, M. S. (1998) Specific language impairment: A deficit in grammar or processing? *Trends in Cognitive Sciences, 2,* 240–246.

Johnson, S. C., & Carey, S. (1998) Knowledge enrichment and conceptual change in folkbiology: Evidence from Williams syndrome. *Cognitive Psychology, 37,* 156–200.

Jones, J. L., Lucker, J., Zalewski, C., Brewer, C., & Drayna, D. (2009) Phonological processing in adults with deficits in musical pitch perception. *Journal of Communication Disorders, 42,* 226–234.

Koelsch, S., Gunter, T. C., von Cramon, D.Y., Zysset, S., Lohmann, G., & Friederici, A. D. (2002) Bach speaks: A cortical "language network" serves the processing of music. *NeuroImage, 17,* 956–966.

Kos, M., Vosse, T., van den Brink, D., & Hagoort, P. (2010) About edible restaurants: Conflicts between syntax and semantics as revealed by ERPs. *Frontiers in Psychology, 1,* article 222. doi: 10.3389/fpsyg.2010.00222

Kutas, M., & Federmeier, K. D. (2011) Thirty years and counting: Finding meaning in the N400 component of the event-related brain potential (ERP). *Annual Review of Psychology, 62,* 621–647.

Kutas, M., & Hillyard, S. A. (1980) Reading senseless sentences: Brain potentials reflect semantic incongruity. *Science, 207,* 203–205.

Larsen, B., Skinhøj, E., & Lassen, N. A. (1978) Variations in regional cortical blood flow in the right and left hemispheres during automatic speech. *Brain, 101,* 193–209.

Leny, R. (1793) Remarkable case of a boy, who lost a considerable portion of brain, and who recovered, without detriment to any faculty, mental or corporeal. *Medical Commentaries, 8,* 301–316.

Lopez, D. L. (2002) Snaring the fowler: Mark Twain debunks phrenology. *Skeptical Inquirer, 26.1.* Retrieved August 6, 2013, from www.csicop.org/si/show/snaring_the_fowler_mark_twain_debunks_phrenology/

Macmillan, M. (2008) Phineas Gage: Unravelling the myth. *Psychologist, 21,* 829–831.

MacSweeney, M., Capek, C. M., Campbell, R., & Woll, B. (2008) The signing brain: The neurobiology of sign language. *Trends in Cognitive Science, 12,* 432–440.

Maess, B., Koelsch, S., Gunter, T. C., & Friederici, A. D. (2001) Musical syntax is processed in Broca's area: An MEG study. *Nature Neuroscience, 4,* 540–545.

Marner, L., Nyengaard, J. R., Tang, Y., & Pakkenberg, B. (2003) Marked loss of myelinated nerve fibers in the human brain with age. *Journal of Comparative Neurology, 462,* 144–152.

Mervis, C. B. (1999) The Williams syndrome cognitive profile: Strengths, weaknesses, and interrelations among auditory short-term memory, language, and visuospatial constructive cognition. In E. Winograd, R. Fivush, & W. Hirst (Eds.) *Ecological approaches to cognition: Essays in honour of Ulrich Neisser* (pp. 193–228). Mahway, NJ: Erlbaum.

Moreno, S., Marques, C., Santos, A., Castro, S. L., & Besson, M. (2009) Musical training influences linguistic abilities in 8-year-old children: More evidence for brain plasticity. *Cerebral Cortex, 19,* 712–723.

Neville, H. J., Nicol, J. L., Barss, A., Forster, K. I., & Garrett, M. F. (1991) Syntactically based sentence processing classes: Evidence from event-related brain potentials. *Journal of Cognitive Neuroscience, 3,* 151–165.

Niedeggen, M., Roesler, F., & Jost, K. (1999) Processing of incongruous mental calculation problems: Evidence for an arithmetic N400 effect. *Psychophysiology, 36,* 302–324.

Osterhout, L., & Holcomb, P. J. (1992) Event-related brain potentials elicited by syntactic anomaly. *Journal of Memory and Language, 31,* 785–806.

Parbery-Clark, A., Skoe, E., Lam, C., & Kraus, M. (2009) Musician enhancement for speech-in-noise. *Ear & Hearing, 30,* 653–661.

Patel, A. D., Gibson, E., Ratner, J., Besson, M., & Holcomb, P. (1998) Processing syntactic relations in language and music: An event-related potential study. *Journal of Cognitive Neuroscience, 10,* 717–733.

Penfield, W., & Jasper, H. (1954) *Epilepsy and the functional anatomy of the human brain.* Boston, MA: Little Brown & Co.

Piccirilli, M, Sciarma, T, Luzzi, S. (2000) Modularity of music: Evidence from a case of pure amusia. *Journal of Neurology, Neurosurgery & Psychiatry, 69,* 541–545.

Raichle, M. E. (2000) A brief history of human functional brain mapping. In A. W. Toga & J. C. Mazziotta (Eds.) *Brain mapping: The systems* (pp. 33–77). San Diego, CA: Academic Press.

Rice, M. L., & Wexler, K. (1996) Toward tense as a clinical marker of specific language impairment in English-speaking children. *Journal of Speech and Hearing Research, 39,* 1239–1257.

Ross, E.D. (2010) Cerebral localization of functions and the neurology of language: Fact versus fiction or is it something else? *Neuroscientist, 16,* 222–243.

Ross, E. D., & Monnot, M. (2008) Neurology of affective prosody and its functional-anatomic organization in right hemisphere. *Brain & Language, 104,* 51–74.

Sadakata, M., & Sekiyama, K. (2011) Enhanced perception of various linguistic features by musicians: A cross-linguistic study. *Acta Psychologica, 138,* 1–10.

Sandrone, S., Bacigaluppi, M., Galloni, M. R., Cappa, S. F., Moro, A., Catani, M., Filippi, M., Monti, M. M., Perani, D., & Martino, G. (2013) Weighing brain activity with the balance: Angelo Mosso's original manuscripts come to light. *Brain.* doi:10.1093/brain/awt091

Schendan, H., Ganis, G., & Kutas, M. (1998) Neurophysiological evidence for visual perceptual organization of words and faces within 150 ms. *Psychophysiology, 35,* 240–251.

Schmithorst, V. J. (2005) Separate cortical networks involved in music perception: Preliminary functional MRI evidence for modularity of music processing. *NeuroImage, 25,* 444–451.

Sitnikova, T., Kuperberg, G., & Holcomb, P. J. (2003) Semantic integration in videos of real-world events: An electrophysiological investigation. *Psychophysiology, 40,* 160–164.

St. George, M., Kutas, M., Martinez, A., & Sereno, M. I. (1999) Semantic integration in reading: Engagement of the right hemisphere during discourse processing. *Brain, 122,* 1317–1325.

Thompson, C. K. (2008) Treatment of syntactic and morphologic deficits in agrammatic aphasia: Treatment of underlying forms. In R. Chapey (Ed.) *Language intervention strategies in adult aphasia* (pp. 735–753. Baltimore: Williams & Wilkins.

van der Lely, H. K., & Marshall, C. R. (2011) Grammatical-specific language impairment: A window onto domain-specificity. In J. Gouendouzi, F. Loncke, & M. J. Williams (Eds.) *The handbook of psycholinguistics and cognitive processes: Perspectives in communication disorders* (pp. 401–418). New York: Psychology Press.

Van Horn, J. D., Irimia, A., Torgerson, C. M., Chambers, M. C., Kikinis, R., & Toga, A. W. (2012) Mapping connectivity damage in the case of Phineas Gage. *PLoS ONE 7(5):* e37454. doi:10.1371/journal.pone.0037454

Wang, Y., Jongman, A., & Sereno, J. A. (2001) Dichotic perception of Mandarin tones by Chinese and American listeners. *Brain and Language, 78,* 332–348.

Wernicke, C. (1874) The symptom complex of aphasia. Reprinted in English in *Proceedings of the Boston Colloquium for the Philosophy of Science (1968)* 4, 34-97.

West, P. (2008) *The shadow factory.* Santa Fe, NM: Lumen Books.

Wright, M. (2011) On clicks in English talk-in-interaction. *Journal of the International Phonetic Association, 41,* 207–229.

Chapter 4

Bortfeld, H., Morgan, J. L., Golinkoff, R. M., & Rathbun, K. (2005) Mommy and me: Familiar names help launch babies into speech-stream segmentation. *Psychological Science, 16,* 298–304.

Curtin, S., Mintz, T. H., & Christiansen, M. H. (2005) Stress changes the representational landscape: Evidence from word segmentation. *Cognition, 96,* 233–262.

Eimas, P. D., Siqueland, E. R., Jusczyk, P. W., & Vigorito, J. (1971) Speech perception in infants. *Science, 171,* 303–306.

Fiser, J., & Aslin, R. N. (2001) Unsupervised statistical learning of higher-order spatial structures from visual scenes. *Psychological Science, 12,* 499–504.

Hauser, M. D., Newport, E. L., & Aslin, R. N. (2001) Segmentation of the speech stream in a non-human primate: Statistical learning in cotton-top tamarins. *Cognition, 78,* B53–B64.

Jusczyk, P. W., & Aslin, R. N. (1995) Infants' detection of the sound patterns of words in fluent speech. *Cognitive Psychology, 29,* 1–23.

Jusczyk, P. W., Friederici, A. D., Wessels, J. M. I., Svenkerud, V. Y. Z., & Jusczyk, A. M. (1993) Infants' sensitivity to the sound patterns of native language words. *Journal of Memory and Language, 32,* 402–420.

Jusczyk, P. W., Hohne, E. A., & Bauman, A. (1999) Infant's sensitivity to allophonic cues for word segmentation. *Perception and Psychophysics, 1999,* 61, 1465–1476.

Kudo, N., Nonaka, Y., Mizuno, N., Mizuno, K., & Okanoya, K. (2011) On-line statistical segmentation of a non-speech auditory stream as demonstrated by event-related potentials. *Developmental Science, 14,* 1100–1106.

Kuhl, P. K., & Miller, J. D. (1975) Speech perception by the chinchilla: Voiced-voiceless distinction on alveolar plosive consonants. *Science, 190,* 69–72.

Labov, W. (1972) The boundaries of words and their meanings. In C. J. N. Bailey & R. W. Shuy (Eds.), *New ways of analyzing variation in English* (pp. xxx–xxx). Washington, DC: Georgetown University Press.

Mattys, S. L., & Jusczyk, P. W. (2001) Phonotactic cues for segmentation of fluent speech by infants. *Cognition, 78,* 91–121.

Mehler, J., Jussczyk, P., Lambertz, G., Halsted, N., Bertoncini, J., & Amiel-Tison, C. (1988) A precursor of language acquisition in young infants. *Cognition, 29,* 143–178.

Nelson, D. G. K., Jusczyk, P. W., Mandel, D. R., Myers, J., Turk, A., & Gerken, L. (1995) The Head-Turn Preference Procedure for testing auditory perception. *Infant Behavior and Development, 18,* 111–116.

Pelucchi, B., Hay, J. F., & Saffran, J. R. (2009) Learning in reverse: Eight-month-old infants trace backward transitional probabilities. *Cognition, 113,* 244–247.

Pisoni, D. B. (1977) Identification and discrimination of the relative onset of two component tones: Implications for voicing perception in stops. *Journal of the Acoustical Society of America, 61,* 1352–1361.

Saffran, J. R., Aslin, R. M., & Newport, E. L. (1996) Statistical learning by 8-month-old infants. *Science, 274,* 1926–1928.

Saffran, J. R., Johnson, E., Aslin, R. N., & Newport, E. L. (1999) Statistical learning of tone sequences by human infants and adults. *Cognition, 70,* 27–52.

Saffran, J. R., Newport, E. L., Aslin, R. N., Tunick, R. A., & Barrueco, S. (1997) Incidental language learning: Listening (and learning) out of the corner of your ear. *Psychological Science, 8,* 101–195.

Saffran, J. R., & Thiessen, E. D. (2003) Pattern induction by infant language learners. *Developmental Psychology, 39,* 484–494.

Teinonen, T., Fellman, V., Näätänen, R., Alku, P., & Huotilainen, M. (2009) Statistical language learning in neonates revealed by event-related brain potentials. *BioMed Central Neuroscience, 10,* 21. doi:10.1186/1471-2202-10-21

Thiessen, E. D., & Saffran, J. R. (2003) When cues collide: Use of stress and statistical cues to word boundaries by 7- to 9-month-old infants. *Developmental Psychology, 39,* 706–716.

Toro, J. M., & Trobalon, J. B. (2005) Statistical computations over a speech stream in a rodent. *Perception & Psychophysics, 67,* 867–875.

Vitevitch, M. S., & Donoso, A. J. (2012) Phonotactic probability of brand names: I'd buy that! *Psychological Research, 76,* 693–698.

Werker, J. F., & Tees, R. C. (1984) Cross-language speech perception: Evidence for perceptual reorganization in the first year of life. *Infant Behavior and Development, 7,* 49–63.

White, K. S., Peperkamp, S., Kirk, C., & Morgan, J. L. (2008) Rapid acquisition of phonological alternations by infants. *Cognition, 107,* 238–265.

Chapter 5

Aksu-Koc, A., & Slobin, D. I. (1985) The acquisition of Turkish. In D. I. Slobin (Ed.), *The crosslinguistic study of language acquisition.* Hillsdale, NJ: Erblaum.

Baldwin, D. A. (1993) Infants' ability to consult the speaker for clues to word reference. *Journal of Child Language, 20(2),* 395–418.

Baldwin, D. A., Markman, E. M., Bill, B., Desjardins, R. N., Irwin, J. M., & Tidball, G. (1996) Infants' reliance on a social criterion for establishing word-object relations. *Child Development, 67,* 3135–3153.

Baron-Cohen, S., Baldwin, D. A., & Crowson, M. (1997) Do children with autism use the speaker's direction of gaze strategy to crack the code of language? *Child Development, 68,* 48–57.

Berko, J. (1958) The child's learning of English morphology. *Word, 14,* 150–177.

Booth, A. E., & Waxman, S. R. (2009) A horse of a different color: Specifying with precision infants' mappings of novel nouns and adjectives. *Child Development, 80,* 1, 15–22.

Callanan, M. A., Repp, A. M., McCarthy, M. G., & Latzke, M. A. (1994) Children's hypotheses about word meanings: Is there a basic level constraint? *Journal of Experimental Child Psychology, 57,* 108–138.

Casasola, M. (2008) The development of infants' spatial categories. *Current Directions in Psychological Science, 17,* 21–25.

Casasola, M., Bhagwat, J., & Burke, A. S. (2009) Learning to form a spatial category of tight-fit relations: How experience with a label can give a boost. *Developmental Psychology, 45,* 711–723.

Fennell, C. T., & Waxman, S. R. (2010) What paradox? Referential cues allow for infant use of phonetic detail in word learning. *Child Development, 81,* 1376–1383.

Fennell, C. T., & Werker, J. T. (2003) Early word-learners' ability to access phonetic detail in well-known words. *Language and Speech, 46,* 245–264.

Ferry, A. L., Hespos, S. J., & Waxman, S. R. (2010) Categorization in 3- and 4-month-old infants: An advantage of words over tones. *Child Development, 81,* 472–479.

Fodor, J. A. (1998) *Concepts: Where cognitive science went wrong.* New York: Oxford University Press.

Gelman, S. A., & Markman, E. M. (1985) Implicit contrast in adjectives vs. nouns: Implications for word-learning in pre-schoolers. *Journal of Child Language, 12,* 125–143.

Gillette, J., Gleitman, H., Gleitman, L., & Lederer, A. (1999) Human simulations of vocabulary learning. *Cognition, 73,* 135–176.

Graf Estes, K. M., Evans, J., Alibali, M. W., & Saffran, J. R. (2007) Can infants map meanings to newly-segmented words? Statistical segmentation and word learning. *Psychological Science, 18,* 254–260.

Hale, C. M., & Tager-Flusberg, H. (2003) The influence of language on theory of mind: A training study. *Developmental Science, 6,* 346–359.

Hallé, P. A., & de Boysson-Bardies, B. (1996) The format of representation of recognized words in infants' early receptive lexicon. *Infant Behavior and Development, 19(4),* 463–481.

Hart, B., & Risley, T. R. (1995) Meaningful differences in the everyday experience of young American children. Baltimore: Paul H. Brookes.

Hollich, G., Golinkoff, R. M., & Hirsh-Pasek, K. (2007) Young children associate complex words with whole objects rather than salient parts. *Developmental Psychology, 43(5),* 1051–1061.

Joanisse, M. F., & Seidenberg, M. S. (2005) Imaging the past: Neural activation in the frontal and temporal regions during regular and irregular past-tense processing. *Cognitive, Affective, and Behavioral Neuroscience, 5,* 282–296.

Kaminski, J., Call, J., & Fischer, J. (2004) Word learning in a domestic dog: Evidence for "fast mapping." *Science, 304,* 1682–1683.

Katz, N., Baker, E., & Macnamara, J. (1974) What's in a name? A study of how children learn common and proper names. *Child Development, 45,* 469–473.

Keller, H. (1909) *The story of my life.* London: Hodder & Stoughton.

Kellman, P. J., & Spelke, E. S. (1983) Perception of partly occluded objects in infancy. *Cognitive Psychology, 15,* 483–524.

Koenig, M. A., & Woodward, A. L. (2010) 24-month-olds' sensitivity to prior inaccuracy of the source: Possible mechanisms. *Developmental Psychology, 46,* 815–826.

Kundera, M. (1980) *The book of laughter and forgetting.* (M. H. Heim, Trans.). New York: Knopf.

Landau, B., Smith, L. B., & Jones, S. (1988) The importance of shape in early lexical learning. *Cognitive Development, 3,* 299–321.

Lentine, G., & Shuy, R. W. (1990) Mc-: Meaning in the marketplace. *American Speech, 65,* 349–366.

Macnamara, J. (1972) Cognitive basis of language learning in infants. *Psychological Review, 79,* 1–13.

Mandler, J. M. (2004) *The foundations of mind: Origins of conceptual thought.* New York: Oxford University Press.

McDonough, L., Choi, S., & Mandler, J. M. (2003) Understanding spatial relations: Flexible infants, lexical adults. *Cognitive Psychology, 46,* 229–259.

Moriguchi, Y., Kanda, T., Ishiguro, H., Shimada, Y., & Itakura, S. (2011) Can young children learn words from a robot? *Interaction Studies, 12,* 107–118.

Naigles, L. R. (1990) Children use syntax to learn verb meanings. *Journal of Child Language, 17,* 357–364.

O'Connell, L., Poulin-Dubois, D., Demke, T., & Guay, A. (2009) Can infants use a non-human agent's gaze direction to establish word-object relations? *Infancy, 14,* 414–438.

Orwell, G. (1946) Politics and the English language. *Horizon, 13,* 252–265.

Phillips, W., & Santos, L. R. (2007) Evidence for kind representations in the absence of language: Experiments with Rhesus monkeys (*Macaca Mulatta*). *Cognition, 102,* 445–463.

Pinker, S. (2007) *The stuff of thought.* New York: Penguin.

Pinker, S. (1999) *Words and rules.* New York: HarperCollins.

Preissler, M. A., & Carey, S. (2005) The role of inferences about referential intent in word learning: Evidence from autism. *Cognition, 97,* B13–B23.

Quinn, P. C., Eimas, P. D., & Rosenkrantz, S. L. (1993) Evidence for representations of perceptual similar natural categories by 3-month-old and 4-month-old infants. *Perception, 22,* 463–475.

Quinn, P. C., & Johnson, M. H. (2000) Global-before-basic object categorization in connectionist networks and 2-month-old infants. *Infancy, 1,* 31–46.

Rheingold, H. (2000) They have a word for it: A lighthearted lexicon of untranslatable words and phrases. Louisville, KY: Sarabande Books.

Rumelhart, D. E., & McClelland, J. L. (1986) On learning the past tense of English verbs. In D. E. Rumelhart & the PDP Research Group (Eds.), *Parallel distributed processing: Vol. 2. Psychological and biological models* (pp. 216–271). Cambridge, MA: MIT Press.

Sobel, D. M., Sedivy, J., Buchanan, D. W., & Hennessey, R. (2012) Speaker reliability in preschoolers' inferences about the meanings of novel words. *Journal of Child Language, 39,* 90-104.

Soja, N. (1992) Inferences about the meanings of nouns: The relationship between perception and syntax. *Cognitive Development, 7,* 29–46.

Stager, C. L., & Werker, J. F. (1997) Infants listen for more phonetic detail in speech perception than in word-learning tasks. *Nature, 388,* 381–382.

Tincoff, R., & Jusczyk, P. W. (2012) Six-month-olds comprehend words that refer to parts of the body. *Infancy, 17,* 432–444.

Tomasello, M., & Barton, M. (1994) Learning words in non-ostensive contexts. *Developmental Psychology, 30,* 639–650.

Ullman, M. T., Pancheva, R., Love, T., Yee, E., Swinney, D., & Hickok, G. (2005) Neural correlates of lexicon and grammar: Evidence from the production, reading and judgment of inflection in aphasia. *Brain and Language, 93,* 185–238.

van der Zee, E., Zulch, H., & Mills, D. (2012) Word generalization by a dog (*Canis familiaris*): Is shape important? *PLoS ONE, 7(11):* e49382. doi:10.1371/journal.pone.0049382

Waxman, S. R., & Markow, D. B. (1995) Words as invitations to form categories: Evidence from 12- to 13-month-old infants. *Cognitive Psychology, 29,* 257–302.

White, K. S., Yee, E., Blumstein, S. E., & Morgan, J. L. (2013) Adults show less sensitivity to phonetic detail in unfamiliar words, too. *Journal of Memory and Language, 68,* 362–378.

Whorf, B. L. (1956) Language, thought and reality: Selected writings of Benjamin Lee Whorf. Cambridge, MA: MIT Press.

Xu, F. (2002) The role of language in acquiring object kind concepts. *Cognition, 85,* 223–250.

Xu, F., & Carey, S. (1996) Infants' metaphysics: The case of numerical identity. *Cognitive Psychology, 30,* 111–153.

Xu, F., & Tenenbaum, J. B. (2007) Word learning as Bayesian inference. *Psychological Review, 114,* 245–272.

Chapter 6

Berger, K. (2006) The joys of life without God. *Salon,* August 23, 2006. http://www.salon.com/2006/08/23/shermer_2/ (accessed on December 17, 2013).

Bowerman, M. (1988) The "no negative evidence" problem: How do children avoid constructing an overly general grammar? In J. A. Hawkins (Ed.), *Explaining language universals.* Oxford, UK: Blackwell.

Bowerman, M. (1982) Evaluating competing linguistic models with language acquisition data: Implications of developmental errors with causative verbs. *Quaderni di Semantica, 3,* 5–66.

Braine, M. D. S. (1971) On two types of models of the internalization of grammars. In D. J. Slobin (Ed.), *The ontogenesis of grammar.* New York: Academic Press.

Brauer, J., Anwander, A., & Friederici, A. D. (2011) Neuroanatomical prerequisites for language function in the maturing brain. *Cerebral Cortex, 21,* 459–466.

Brooks, P., & Tomasello, M. (1999) Young children learn to produce passives with nonce verbs. *Developmental Psychology, 35,* 29–44.

Brown, R. (1973) *A first language: The early stages.* Cambridge, MA: Harvard University Press.

Crain, S., & Nakayama, M. (1987) Structure dependence in grammar formation. *Language, 63,* 522–543.

de Villiers, J. G., Roeper, T., & Vainikka, A. (1990) The acquisition of long distance rules. In L. Frazier & J. G. de Villiers (Eds.), *Language processing and acquisition.* Dordrecht: Kluwer.

Diesel, H., & Tomasello, M. (2000) The development of relative clauses in spontaneous child speech. *Cognitive Linguistics, 11,* 131–151.

Everett, D. L. (2005) Cultural constraints on grammar in Pirahã: Another look at the design features of human language. *Current Anthropology, 46,* 621–646.

Friederici, A. D., Oberecker, R., & Brauer, J. (2012) Neurophysiological preconditions of syntax acquisition. *Psychological Research, 76,* 204–211.

Gomez, R. L., & Gerken, L. (1999) Artificial grammar learning by 1-year-olds leads to specific and abstract knowledge. *Cognition, 70,* 109–135.

Gomez, R. L., & Maye, J. (2005) The developmental trajectory of nonadjacent dependency learning. *Infancy, 7,* 183–206.

Lerdahl, F. (2005) *Tonal pitch space.* Oxford, UK: Oxford University Press.

Levin, B. (1993) English verb classes and alternations: A preliminary investigation. Chicago: University of Chicago Press.

Mintz, T. H. (2003) Frequent frames as a cue for grammatical categories in child directed speech. *Cognition, 90,* 91–117.

Mintz, T. H. (2006) Finding the verbs: Distributional cues to categories available to young learners. In K. Hirsh-Pasek & R. M. Golinkoff (Eds.), *Action meets word: How children learn verbs.* New York: Oxford University Press.

Novogrodsky, R., & Friedmann, N. (2006) The production of relative clauses in SLI: A window into the nature of the impairment. *Advances in Speech-Language Pathology, 8,* 364–375.

Pearl, L., & Weinberg, A. (2007) Input filtering in syntactic acquisition: Answers from language change modeling. *Language Learning and Development, 3,* 43–72.

Pinker, S. (1987) The bootstrapping problem in language acquisition. In B. MacWhinney (Ed.). *Mechanisms of Language Acquisition.* Hillsdale, NJ: Lawrence Erlbaum Associates, pp. 399–441.

Redington, M., Chater, N., & Finch, S. (1998) Distributional information: A powerful cue for acquiring syntactic categories. *Cognitive Science, 22,* 435–469.

Rowland, C. F., Pine, J. M., Lieven, E. V. M., & Theakston, A. L. (2003) Determinants of acquisition order in wh- questions: Re-evaluating the role of caregiver speech. *Journal of Child Language, 30,* 609–635.

Rumelhart, D. E., & McClelland, J. L. (1986) On learning the past tense of English verbs. In D. E. Rumelhart & the PDP Research Group (Eds.), *Parallel distributed processing: Vol 2. Psychological and biological models* (pp. 216–271). Cambridge, MA: MIT Press.

Schuele, C. M., & Tolbert, L. (2001) Omissions of obligatory relative markers in children with specific language impairment. *Clinical Linguistics and Phonetics, 15,* 257–274.

Soderstrom, M., & Morgan, J. L. (2007) Twenty-two-month-olds discriminate fluent from disfluent adult-directed speech. *Developmental Science, 10,* 641–653.

Tomasello, M. (1992) *First verbs: A case study in early grammatical development.* Cambridge, UK: Cambridge University Press.

Tomasello, M., Akhtar, N., Dodson, K., & Rekau, L. (1997) Differential productivity in young children's use of nouns and verbs. *Journal of Child Language, 24,* 373–387.

Wonnacott, E. (2011) Balancing generalization and lexical conservatism: An artificial language study with child learners. *Journal of Memory and Language, 65,* 1–14.

Chapter 7

Allopenna, P. D., Magnuson, J. S., & Tanenhaus, M. K. (1998) Tracking the time course of spoken word recognition: Evidence for continuous mapping models. *Journal of Memory and Language, 38,* 419–439.

Bargh, J. A., Chen, M., & Burrows, L. (1996) Automaticity of social behavior: Direct effects of trait construct and stereotype activation on action. *Journal of Personality and Social Psychology, 71,* 230–244.

Barnhart, A. S., & Goldinger, S. D. (2010) Interpreting chicken-scratch: Lexical access for handwritten words. *Journal of Experimental Psychology: Human Perception and Performance, 36,* 906–923.

Berger, J., & Fitzsimons, G. (2008) Dogs on the street, Pumas on your feet: How cues in the environment influence product evaluation and choice. *Journal of Marketing Research, 45,* 1–14.

Boulenger, V., Metchouff, L., Thobois, S., Broussolle, E., Jeannerod, M., & Nazir, T. A. (2008) Word processing in Parkinson's disease is impaired for action verbs but not for concrete nouns. *Neuropsychologia, 46,* 743–756.

Coltheart, M., Curtis, B., Atkins, P., & Haller, M. (1993) Models of reading aloud: Dual route and parallel distributed processing approaches. *Psychological Review, 100,* 589–608.

Coltheart, M., Rastle, K., Perry, C., Langdon, R., & Ziegler, J. (2001) DRC: A dual route cascaded of visual word recognition and reading aloud. *Psychological Review, 108,* 204–256.

D'Ausilio, A., Pulvermuller, F., Salmas, P., Bufalari, I., Begliomini, C., & Fadiga, L. (2009) The motor somatotopy of speech perception. *Current Biology, 19,* 381–385.

Dekle, D., Fowler, C. A., & Funnell, M. (1992) Audi-visual integration in perception of real words. *Perception and Psychophysics, 51,* 355–362.

Duffy, S. A., Morris, R. K., & Rayner, K. (1988) Lexical ambiguity and fixation times in reading. *Journal of Memory and Language, 27,* 429–446.

Elman, J. L., & McClelland, J. L. (1988) Cognitive penetration of the mechanisms of perception: Compensation for coarticulation of lexically restored phonemes. *Journal of Memory and Language, 27,* 143–165.

Fodor, J. A. (1983) *Modularity of mind.* Cambridge, MA: MIT Press.

Fowler, C. A., & Dekle, D. (1991) Listening with eye and hand: Crossmodal contributions to speech perception. *Journal of Experimental Psychology: Human Perception and Performance, 17,* 816–828.

Ganong, W. F. (1980) Phonetic categorization in auditory word perception. *Journal of Experimental Psychology: Human Perception and Performance, 6,* 110–125.

Glenberg, A. M., & Kaschak, M. P. (2002) Grounding language in action. *Psychonomic Bulletin & Review, 9,* 558–565.

Goldinger, S. D., Luce, P. A., & Pisoni, D. B. (1989) Priming lexical neighbors of spoken words: Effects of competition and inhibition. *Journal of Memory and Language, 28,* 501–518.

Hockett, C. F. (1955) A Manual of Phonology. Indiana University Publications in Anthropology and Linguistics, 11. Baltimore, MD: Waverly Press.

Klatzky, R. L., Pellegrino, J. W., McCloskey, B. P., & Doherty, S. (1989) Can you squeeze a tomato? The role of motor representations in semantic sensibility judgments. *Journal of Memory & Language, 28,* 56–77.

Luntz, F. I. (2007) Words That Work: It's Not What You Say, It's What People Hear. New York: Hyperion.

Magnuson, J. S., Dixon, J. A., Tanenhaus, M. K., & Aslin, R. N. (2007) The dynamics of lexical competition during spoken word recognition. *Cognitive Science, 31,* 133–156.

Marian, V., & Spivey, M. (2003) Competing activation in bilingual language processing: Within- and between-language competition. *Bilingualism: Language and Cognition, 6,* 97–115.

Marslen-Wilson, W. D. (1987) Functional parallelism in spoken word recognition. *Cognition, 25,* 71–102.

McClelland, J. L., & Elman, J. L. (1986) The TRACE model of speech perception. *Cognitive Psychology, 18,* 1–86.

Meyer, D. A., & Schvaneveldt, R. W. (1971) Facilitation in recognizing pairs of words: Evidence of a dependence between retrieval operations. *Journal of Experimental Psychology, 90,* 227–234.

Myung, J., Blumstein, S. E., & Sedivy, J. C. (2006) Playing on the typewriter, typing on the piano: Manipulation knowledge of objects. *Cognition, 98,* 223–243.

Nelson, J. R., Liu, Y., Fiez, J., & Perfetti, C. A. (2009) Assimilation and accommodation patterns in ventral occipitotemporal cortex in learning a second writing system. *Human Brain Mapping, 30,* 810–820.

Norris, D., McQueen, J. M., & Cutler, A. (2000) Merging information in speech recognition: Feedback is never necessary. *Behavioral and Brain Sciences, 23,* 299–325.

Perfetti, C., Nelson, J., Liu, Y., Fiez, J., & Tan, L. H. (2010) The neural basis of reading: Universals and writing system variations. In P. Cornelissen, P. Hansen, M. Kringelbach, & K. Pugh (Eds.), *The neural basis of reading* (pp. 147–172). Oxford, UK: Oxford University Press.

Phillips, C. I., Sears, C. R., & Pexman, P. M. (2012) An embodied semantic processing effect on eye gaze during sentence reading. *Language and Cognition, 4,* 99–114.

Piantadosi, S. T., Tily, H., & Gibson, E. (2012) The communicative function of ambiguity in language. *Cognition, 122,* 280–291.

Pitt, M. A., & McQueen, J. M. (1998) Is compensation for coarticulation mediated by the lexicon? *Journal of Memory and Language, 39,* 347–370.

Pullum, G. K. (2012, January 15) Waterstones. Language Log. Retrieved December 10, 2013, from http://languagelog.ldc.upenn.edu/nll/?p=3705

Seidenberg, M. S., & McClelland, J. M. (1989) A distributed, developmental model of word recognition and naming. *Psychological Review, 96,* 523–568.

Slowiaczek, L. M., & Hamburger, M. (1992) Prelexical facilitation and lexical interference in auditory word recognition. *Journal of Experimental Psychology: Learning, Memory and Cognition, 18,* 1239–1250.

Spivey, M., & Marian, V. (1999) Cross talk between native and second languages: Partial activation of an irrelevant lexicon. *Psychological Science, 10,* 281–284.

Swinney, D. (1979) Lexical access during sentence comprehension: (Re)consideration of context effects. *Journal of Verbal Learning and Verbal Behavior, 18,* 645–659.

Tan, L. H., Spinks, J. A., Eden, G. F., Perfetti, C. A., & Siok, W. T. (2005) Reading depends on writing, in Chinese. *Proceedings of the National Academy of Sciences, 102,* 8781–8785.

Van Orden, G. C. (1987) A ROWS is a ROSE: Spelling, sound, and reading. *Memory and Cognition, 15,* 181–198.

Van Orden, G. C., Johnston, J. C., & Hale, B. L. (1988) Word identification in reading proceeds from spelling to sound to meaning. *Journal of Experimental Psychology: Learning, Memory and Cognition, 14,* 371–386.

Warren, R. M. (1970) Restoration of missing speech sounds. *Science, 167,* 392–393.

Warrington, E. K., & Shallice, T. (1984) Category specific semantic impairments. *Brain, 107,* 829–854.

Yee, E., & Sedivy, J. (2006) Eye movements to pictures reveal transient semantic activation during spoken word recognition. *Journal of Experimental Psychology: Learning, Memory & Cognition, 32,* 1–14.

Zwitserlood, P. (1989) The locus of the effects of sentential-semantic context in spoken-word processing. *Cognition, 32,* 25–64.

Chapter 8

Alladi, S., Bak, T. H., Duggirala, V., Surampudi, B., Shailaja, M., Shukla, A. J., Chaudhuri, J. R, & Kaul, S. (2013) Bilingualism delays age at onset of dementia, independent of education and immigrant status. *Neurology, 81,* 1938–1944.

Allbritton, D. W., McKoon, G., & Ratcliff, R. (1996) Reliability of prosodic cues for resolving syntactic ambiguity. *Journal of Experimental Psychology: Learning, Memory, and Cognition, 22,* 714–735.

Alter, A., Oppenheimer, D. M., Epley, N., & Eyre, R. (2007) Overcoming intuition: Metacognitive difficulty activates analytical thought. *Journal of Experimental Psychology: General, 136,* 569–576.

Altmann, G. T. A., & Steedman, M. (1988) Interaction with context during human sentence processing. *Cognition, 30,* 191–238.

Bekinschtein, T. A., David, M. H., Rodd, J. M., & Owen, A. M. (2011) Why clowns taste funny: The relationship between humor and semantic ambiguity. *Journal of Neuroscience, 31,* 9665–9671.

Bialystok, E., Craik, F. I. M., & Freedman, M. (2007) Bilingualism as a protection against the onset of symptoms of dementia. *Neuropsychologia, 45,* 459–464.

Bialystok, E., Craik, F. I. M., Klein, R., & Viswanathan, M. (2004) Bilingualism, aging, and cognitive control: Evidence from the Simon task. *Psychology and Aging, 19,* 290–303.

Borovsky, A., Elman, J. L., & Fernald, A. (2012) Knowing a lot for one's age: Vocabulary skill and not age is associated with anticipatory incremental sentence interpretation in children and adults. *Journal of Experimental Child Psychology, 112,* 417–436.

Brown, J. C. (1960) Loglan. *Scientific American, 202,* 43–63.

Chambers, C. G., Tanenhaus, M. K., & Magnuson, J. S. (2004) Actions and affordances in syntactic ambiguity resolution. *Journal of Experimental Psychology: Learning, Memory, and Cognition, 30,* 687–696.

Crain, S., & Steedman, M. (1985) On not being led up the garden path: The use of context by the psychological parser. In D. Dowty, L. Karttunen, & A. Zwicky (Eds.), *Natural language parsing: Psychological, computational and theoretical perspectives* (pp. 320–358). Cambridge, England: Cambridge University Press.

Daneman, M., & Carpenter, P. A. (1980) Individual differences in working memory and reading. *Journal of Verbal Learning and Verbal Behavior, 19,* 450–456.

DeLong, K. A., Urbach, T. P., & Kutas, M. (2005) Probabilistic word pre-activation during language comprehension inferred from electrical brain activity. *Nature Neuroscience, 8,* 1117–1121.

Federmeier, K. D. (2007) Thinking ahead: The role and roots of prediction in language comprehension. *Psychophysiology, 44,* 491–505.

Fodor, J. A. (1983) Modularity of mind: An essay on faculty psychology. Cambridge, MA: MIT Press.

Foster Wallace, D. (2007) The depressed person. In *Brief Interviews with Hideous Men* (pp. 37–69). New York: Little Brown and Company.

Frazier, L., & Clifton, Jr., C. (1996) *Construal.* Cambridge, MA: MIT Press.

Frazier, L., & Fodor, J. D. (1978) The sausage machine: A new two-stage model of parsing. *Cognition, 6,* 291–325.

Gibson, E. (1998) Syntactic complexity: Locality of syntactic dependencies. *Cognition, 68,* 1–76.

Gopnik, A. (2011) *Winter: Five windows on the season.* (CBC Massey Lecture.) Toronto: House of Anansi Press.

Hale, J. (2001) A probabilistic Earley parser as a psycholinguistic model. Proceedings of the Second Conference of the North American Chapter of the Association for Computational Linguistics, 2, 159–166.

Hofmeister, P., Casasanto, L .S., & Sag, I. A. (2012) Misapplying working-memory tests: A reductio ad absurdum. *Language, 88,* 408–409.

Hofmeister, P., & Sag, I. A. (2010) Cognitive constraints and island effects. *Language, 86,* 366–415.

Huang, Y. T., & Snedeker, J. (2010) Cascading activation across levels of representation in children's lexical processing. *Journal of Child Language, 38,* 644–661.

Ivanova, I., & Costa, A. (2008) Does bilingualism hamper lexical access in highly-proficient bilinguals? *Acta Psychologica, 127,* 277–288.

James, H. (1903) *The ambassadors.* Reprinted in *Henry James; Novels 1903–1911.* New York: Library of America.

Just, M. A., & Carpenter, P. A. (1992) A capacity theory of comprehension: Individual differences in working memory. *Psychological Review, 99,* 122–149.

Kamide, Y., Altmann, G. T. M., & Haywood, S. L. (2003) The time-course of prediction in incremental sentence processing: Evidence from anticipatory eye movements. *Journal of Memory and Language, 49,* 133–156.

Keysar, B., Hayakawa, S. L., & An, S. G. (2012) The foreign-language effect: Thinking in a foreign tongue reduces decision biases. *Psychological Science, 23,* 661–668.

Kluender, R., & Kutas, M. (1993) Subjacency as a processing phenomenon. *Language and Cognitive Processes, 8,* 573–633.

Kovács, A. M., & Mehler, J. (2009) Cognitive gains in 7-month-old bilingual infants. *Proceedings of the National Academy of Sciences, 106,* 6556–6560.

Kraljic, T., & Brennan, S. E. (2005) Prosodic disambiguation of syntactic structure: For the speaker or for the addressee? *Cognitive Psychology, 50,* 194–231.

MacDonald, M. C., & Christiansen, M. H. (2002) Reassessing working memory: A comment on Just and Carpenter (1992) and Waters and Caplan (1996). *Psychological Review, 109,* 35–54.

MacDonald, M. C., Pearlmutter, N. J., & Seidenberg, M. S. (1994) Lexical nature of syntactic ambiguity resolution. *Psychological Review, 101,* 676–703.

Mitchell, D. C., & Cuetos, F. (1991) The origins of parsing strategies. In C. Smith (Ed.), *Current issues in natural language processing* (pp. 1–12). Austin: University of Texas, Center for Cognitive Science.

Nieuwland, M. S., & Van Berkum, J. J. A. (2006) When peanuts fall in love: N400 evidence for the power of discourse. *Journal of Cognitive Neuroscience, 18,* 1098–1111.

Novick, J. M., Trueswell, J. C., & Thompson-Schill, S. L. (2005) Cognitive control and parsing: Re-examining the role of Broca's area in sentence comprehension. *Journal of Cognitive, Affective and Behavioral Neuroscience, 53,* 263–281.

Okrent, A. (2009) *In the land of invented languages.* New York: Random House.

Rogers, C. L., Lister, J. J., Febo, D. M., Besing, J. M., & Abrams, H. B. (2006) Effects of bilingualism, noise, and reverberation on speech perception by listeners with normal hearing. *Applied Psycholinguistics, 27,* 465–485.

Schafer, A. J., Speer, S., Warren, P., & White, S. D. (2000) Intonational disambiguation in sentence production and comprehension. *Journal of Psycholinguistic Research, 29,* 169–182.

Smith, Z. (2009) Brief interviews with hideous men: The difficult gifts of David Foster Wallace. In *Changing my mind: Occasional essays* (pp. 255–297). New York: Penguin Press.

Spivey-Knowlton, M. J., Trueswell, J. C., & Tanenhaus, M. K. (1993) Context effects in syntactic ambiguity resolution: Parsing reduced relative clauses. *Canadian Journal of Psychology, 47,* 276–309.

Sprouse, J., Wagers, M., & Philips, C. (2012) A test of the relation between working memory capacity and syntactic island effects. *Language, 87,* 274–288.

Tanenhaus, M. K., Spivey-Knowlton, M. J., Eberhard, K. M., & Sedivy, J. (1995) Integration of visual and linguistic information in spoken language comprehension. *Science, 268,* 1632–1634.

Thompson-Schill, S. L., Ramscar, M., & Chrysikou, E. G. (2009) Cognition without control: When a little frontal lobe goes a long way. *Current Directions in Psychological Science, 18,* 259–263.

Trueswell, J. C. (1996) The role of lexical frequency in syntactic ambiguity resolution. *Journal of Memory and Language, 35,* 566–585.

Trueswell, J. C., & Kim, A. E. (1998) How to prune a garden path by nipping it in the bud: Fast priming of verb argument structure. *Journal of Memory and Language, 39,* 102–123.

Trueswell, J. C., Sekerina, I., Hill, N. M., & Logrip, M. L. (1999) The kindergarten-path effect: Studying on-line sentence processing in young children. *Cognition, 73,* 89–134.

Trueswell, J. C., Tanenhaus, M. K., & Garnsey, S. M. (1994) Semantic influences on parsing: Use of thematic role information in syntactic ambiguity resolution. *Journal of Memory and Language, 33,* 285–318.

Tversky, A., & Kahneman, D. (1974) Judgment under uncertainty: Heuristics and biases. *Science, 185,* 1124–1131.

Van Berkum, J. J. A., Van den Brink, D., Tesink, C., Kos, M., & Hagoort, P. (2008) The neural integration of speaker and message. *Journal of Cognitive Neuroscience, 20,* 580–591.

Chapter 9

Arnold, J. E., Wasow, T., Asudeh, A., & Alrenga, P. (2004) Avoiding attachment ambiguities: The role of constituent ordering. *Journal of Memory and Language, 51,* 55–70.

Baars, B. J., Motley, M. J., & MacKay, D. G. (1975) Output editing for lexical status in artificially elicited slips of the tongue. *Journal of Verbal Learning and Verbal Behavior, 14,* 382–391.

Bock, J. K. (1987) An effect of the accessibility of word forms on sentence structures. *Journal of Memory and Language, 26,* 119–137.

Bock, J. K. (1986a) Syntactic persistence in language production. *Cognitive Psychology, 18,* 355–387.

Bock, J. K. (1986b) Meaning, sound, and syntax: Lexical priming in sentence production. *Journal of Experimental Psychology: Learning, Memory and Cognition, 12,* 575–586.

Brennan, S. E. (1990). Conversation as direct manipulation: An iconoclastic view. In B.K. Laurel (Ed.), *The art of human-computer interface design* (pp. 393–404). Reading, MA: Addison-Wesley.

Brown, R., & McNeill, D. (1966) The tip-of-the-tongue phenomenon. *Journal of Verbal Learning and Verbal Behavior, 5,* 325–337.

Dell, G. S. (1986) A spreading-activation theory of retrieval in sentence production. *Psychological Review, 93,* 283–321.

Dell, G. S., & Reich, P. A. (1981) Stages in sentence production: An analysis of speech error data. *Journal of Verbal Learning and Verbal Behavior, 20,* 611–629.

Ferreira, V. S. (1996) Is it better to give than to donate? Syntactic flexibility in language production. *Journal of Memory and Language, 35,* 724–755.

Ferreira, F., & Swets, B. (2002) How incremental is language production? Evidence from the production of utterances requiring the computation of arithmetic sums. *Journal of Memory and Language, 46,* 57–84.

Fox Tree, J. E. (2002) Interpreting pauses and ums at turn exchanges. *Discourse Processes, 34,* 37–55.

Fromkin, V. A. (1971) The non-anomalous nature of anomalous utterances. *Language, 47,* 27–52.

Gardner, R. (2010) Question and answer sequences in Garrwa talk. *Australian Journal of Linguistics, 30,* 423–445.

Garrett, M. F. (1980) Levels of processing in sentence production. In B. Butterworth (Ed.), *Language Production (Vol. 1)* (pp. 177–220). London: Academic Press.

Gleitman, L. R., January, D., Nappa, R., & Trueswell, J. C. (2007) On the *give* and *take* between event apprehension and utterance formulation. *Journal of Memory and Language, 57,* 544–569.

Gries, S. T. (2005) Syntactic priming: A corpus-based approach. *Journal of Psycholinguistic Research, 34,* 365–399.

Griffin, Z. M. (2003) A reversed word length effect in coordinating the preparation and articulation of words in speaking. *Psychonomic Bulletin and Review, 10,* 603–609.

Griffin, Z. M. (2001) Gaze durations during speech reflect word selection and phonological encoding. *Cognition, 82,* B1–B14.

Harley, T. A. (1984) A critique of top-down independent level models of speech production: Evidence from non-plan-internal speech errors. *Cognitive Science, 8,* 191–219.

Harley, T. A., & Bown, H. E. (1998) What causes a tip-of-the-tongue state? Evidence for lexical neighbourhood effects in speech production. *British Journal of Psychology, 89,* 151–174.

Hawkins, P. R. (1971) The syntactic location of hesitation pauses. *Language and Speech, 14,* 277–288.

Humphreys, K. R., Menzies, H., & Lake, J. K. (2010) Repeated speech errors: Evidence for learning. *Cognition, 117,* 151–165.

Jaeger, T. F., Furth, K., & Hilliard, C. (2012) Phonological overlap affects lexical selection during sentence production. *Journal of Experimental Psychology: Learning, Memory, and Cognition, 38,* 1439–1449.

Konopka, A. E. (2012) Planning ahead: How recent experience with structures and words changes the scope of linguistic planning. *Journal of Memory and Language, 66,* 143–162.

Lehtonen, J., & Sajavaara, K. (1985) The silent Finn. In D. Tannen & M. Saville-Troike (Eds.), *Perspectives on Silence.* Norwood, NJ: Ablex.

Martin, N., Weisberg, R. W., & Saffran, E. M. (1989) Variables influencing the occurrence of naming errors: Implications for models of lexical retrieval. *Journal of Memory and Language, 28,* 462–485.

McMenamin, G. R. (2010) Theory and practice of forensic stylistics. In M. Coulthard & A. Johnson (Eds.), *The Routledge Handbook of Forensic Linguistics.* New York: Routledge.

Meyer, A. S. (1996) Lexical access in phrase and sentence production: Results from picture-word interference experiments. *Journal of Memory and Language, 35,* 477–496.

Morsella, E., & Miozzo, M. (2002) Evidence for a cascade model of lexical access in speech production. *Journal of Experimental Psychology: Learning, Memory and Cognition, 28,* 555–563.

Motley, M. T., & Baars, B. J. (1979) Effects of cognitive set upon laboratory induced verbal (Freudian) slips. *Journal of Speech and Hearing Research, 22,* 21–432.

Motley, M. T., & Baars, B. J. (1976) Laboratory induction of verbal slips: A new method for psycholinguistic research. *Communication Quarterly, 24,* 28–34.

Motley, M. T., Camden, C. T., & Baars, B. J. (1982) Covert formulation and editing of anomalies in speech production: Evidence from experimentally elicited slips of the tongue. *Journal of Psycholinguistic Research, 10,* 503–522.

Roberts, F., Margutti, P., and Takano, S. (2011) Judgments concerning the valence of inter-turn silence across speakers of American English, Italian, and Japanese. *Discourse Processes, 48,* 331–354.

Smith, M., & Wheeldon, L. (1999) High-level processing scope in spoken sentence production. *Cognition, 73,* 205–246.

Stallings, L. M., & MacDonald, M. C. (2011) It's not just the "heavy NP": Relative phrase length modulates the production of heavy-NP shift. *Journal of Psycholinguistic Research, 40,* 177–187.

Stivers, T., Enfield, N. J., Brown, P., Englert, C., Hayashi, M., Heinemann, T., Hoymann, G., Rossano, F., de Ruiter, J. P., Yoon, K. E., and Levinson, S. (2009) Universals and cultural variation in turn-taking in conversation. *Proceedings of the National Academy of Sciences, 106,* 10587–10592.

Tomlin, R. (1997) Mapping conceptual representations into linguistic representations: The role of attention in grammar. In J. Nuyts & E. Pederson (Eds.), *Language and Conceptualization.* Cambridge, UK: Cambridge University Press.

Vigliocco, G., Antonini, T., & Garrett, M. F. (1997) Grammatical gender is on the tip of Italian tongues. *Psychological Science, 8,* 314–318.

Vitevitch, M. S. (2002) The influence of phonological similarity neighborhoods on speech production. *Journal of Experimental Psychology: Learning, Memory and Cognition, 28,* 735–747.

Wagner, V., Jescheniak, J. D., & Schriefers, H. (2010) On the flexibility of grammatical advance planning during sentence production: Effects of cognitive load on multiple lexical access. *Journal of Experimental Psychology: Learning, Memory and Cognition, 36,* 423–440.

Walsh, M. (1997) *Cross cultural communication problems in Aboriginal Australia.* Discussion Paper 7/1997. Darwin: North Australia Research Unit.

Warriner, A. B., & Humphreys, K. R. (2008) Learning to fail: Reoccurring tip-of-the-tongue states. *Quarterly Journal of Experimental Psychology, 61,* 535–542.

Chapter 10

Almor, A. (1999) Noun-phrase anaphora and focus: The informational load hypothesis. *Psychological Review, 106,* 748–765.

Almor, A., & Eimas, P. D. (2008) Focus and noun phrase anaphors in spoken language comprehension. *Language and Cognitive Processes, 23,* 201–225.

Arnold, J. E. (2001) The effect of thematic roles on pronoun use and frequency of reference continuation. *Discourse Processes, 31,* 137–162.

Arnold, J. E., Brown-Schmidt, S., & Trueswell, J. (2007) Children's use of gender and order-of-mention during pronoun comprehension. *Language and Cognitive Processes, 22,* 527–565.

Arnold, J., Eisenband, J., Brown-Schmidt, S., & Trueswell, J. (2000) The rapid use of gender information: Evidence of the time course of pronoun resolution from eyetracking. *Cognition, 76,* B13–B26.

Badecker, W., & Straub, K. (2002) The processing role of structural constraints on the interpretation of pronouns and anaphors. *Journal of Experimental Psychology: Learning, Memory, and Cognition, 28,* 748–769.

Black, J. B., & Bern, H. (1981) Causal coherence and memory for events in narratives. *Journal of Verbal Learning and Verbal Behavior, 20,* 267–275.

Blatchford, C. (2011, November 28) "This is Canada. Do not be afraid," relative told alleged honour killing victim. *National Post.*

Bortolussi, M., & Dixon, P. (2003) *Psychonarratology: Foundations for the Empirical Study of Literary Response.* Cambridge, UK: Cambridge University Press.

Bransford, J. D., Barclay, J. R., & Franks, J. J. (1972) Sentence memory: A constructive versus interpretive approach. *Cognitive Psychology, 3,* 193–209.

Bransford, J. D., & Johnson, M. K. (1972) Contextual prerequisites for understanding: Some investigation of comprehension and recall. *Journal of Verbal Learning and Verbal Behavior, 11,* 717–726.

Brunyé, T. T., Ditman, T., Mahoney, C. R., Walters, E. K., & Taylor, H. A. (2010) You heard it here first: Readers mentally simulate described sounds. *Acta Psychologica, 135,* 209–215.

Chien, Y. C., & Wexler, K. (1990) Children's knowledge of locality conditions in binding as evidence for the modularity of syntax and pragmatics. *Language Acquisition, 1,* 225–295.

Clackson, K., Felser, C., & Clahsen, H. (2011) Children's processing of reflexives and pronouns in English: Evidence from eye movements during listening. *Journal of Memory and Language, 65,* 128–144.

Cui, X., Jeter, C. B., Yang, D., Montague, P. R., & Eagleman, D. M. (2007) Vividness of mental imagery: Individual variation can be measured objectively. *Visual Research, 47,* 474–478.

Denis, M. (1982) Imaging while reading text: A study of individual differences. *Memory and Cognition, 10,* 540–545.

Ferreira, F., Bailey, K. G. D., & Ferraro, V. (2002) Good-enough representations in language processing. *Current Directions in Psychological Science, 11,* 11–15.

Fiedler, K., & Walthier, E. (1996) Do you *really* know what you have seen? Intrusion errors and presuppositions effects on constructive memory. *Journal of Experimental Social Psychology, 32,* 484–511.

Fitzgerald, F. S. (1922) The curious case of Benjamin Button. In *Tales of the Jazz Age.* New York: Scribner.

Garrod, S., & Sanford, A. (1977) Interpreting anaphoric relations: The integration of semantic information while reading. *Journal of Verbal Learning and Verbal Memory, 16,* 77–90.

Garvey, C., & Caramazza, A. (1974) Implicit causality in verbs. *Linguistic Inquiry, 4–5,* 459–464.

Gerrig, R. J., Love, J., & McKoon, G. (2009) Waiting for Brandon: How readers respond to small mysteries. *Journal of Memory and Language, 60,* 144–153.

Giannetti, L., & Eyman, S. (1986) *Flashback: A brief history of film.* Englewood Cliffs, NJ: Prentice-Hall.

Glenberg, A. M., Meyer, M., & Lindem, K. (1987) Mental models contribute to foregrounding during text comprehension. *Journal of Memory and Language, 26,* 69–83.

Gordon, P. C., Grosz, B. J., & Gilliom, L. A. (1993) Pronouns, names, and the centering of attention in discourse. *Cognitive Science, 17,* 311–347.

Guillaume, P. (1963) *Manuel de Psychologie.* Paris: Presses Universitaires de France.

Haviland, S. E., & Clark, H. H. (1974) What's new? Acquiring new information as a process in comprehension. *Journal of Verbal Learning and Verbal Behavior, 13,* 512–521.

Hemon, A. (2012, September 10) Beyond the matrix. *The New Yorker.*

Hickmann, M., & Hendriks, H. (1999) Cohesion and anaphora in children's narratives: A comparison of English, French, German and Mandarin Chinese. *Journal of Child Language, 26,* 419–452.

Hirsch, E. D., Jr. (2003, Spring) Reading comprehension requires knowledge of words and the world: Scientific insights into the fourth-grade slump and the nation's stagnant comprehension scores. *American Educator.*

Johnston, P. (1984) Prior knowledge and reading comprehension test bias. *Reading Research Quarterly, 19,* 219–239.

Kim, S. (1999) Causal bridging inference: A cause of story interestingness. *British Journal of Psychology, 90,* 57–71.

LaMattina., J. (2012) *The Artist: Michel Hazanavicius.* http://vimeo.com/37187304

Lieberman, P. (1963) Some effects of semantic and grammatical context on the production and perception of speech. *Language and Speech, 6,* 172–187.

Linderholm, T. (2002) Predictive inference generation as a function of working memory capacity and causal text constraints. *Discourse Processes, 34,* 259–280.

Loftus, E., Miller, D., & Burns, H. (1978) Semantic integration of verbal information into a visual memory. *Journal of Experimental Psychology: Human Learning and Memory, 4,* 19–31.

Love, J., & McKoon, G. (2011) Rules of engagement: Complete and incomplete pronoun resolution. *Journal of Experimental Psychology: Learning, Memory, and Cognition, 37,* 874–887.

MacDonald, M. C., & Just, M. A. (1989) Changes in activation levels with negation. *Journal of Experimental Psychology: Learning, Memory, and Cognition, 15,* 633–644.

Marschark, M., & Cornoldi, C. (1991) Imagery and verbal memory. In C. Cornoldi & M. A. McDaniel (Eds.), *Imagery and cognition* (pp. 133–182). New York: Springer.

McEwan, I. (1978) *In between the sheets.* London: Cape.

McKoon, G., & Ratcliff, R. (1986) Inferences about predictable events. *Journal of Experimental Psychology: Learning, Memory, and Cognition, 12,* 82–91.

McNamara, D. S., & Kintsch, W. (1996) Learning from texts: Effects of prior knowledge and text coherence. *Discourse Processes, 22,* 247-288.

McNamara, D. S., & O'Reilly, T. (2009) Theories of comprehension skill: Knowledge and strategies versus capacity and suppression. In A. M. Columbus (Ed.), *Advances in psychology research* (p. 62). Hauppauge, NY: Nova Science.

Megherbi, H., & Ehrlich, M. F. (2009) The online interpretation of pronouns and repeated names in seven-year-old children. *Current Psychology Letters, 25,* 2–11.

Morris, D. (1997) Behind the Oval Office: Selling the presidency in the nineties. New York: Random House.

Morrison, T. (1987) *Beloved.* New York: Knopf.

Myers, J. L., Shinjo, M., & Duffy, S. A. (1987) Degree of causal relatedness and memory. *Journal of Memory and Language, 26,* 453–465.

O'Brien, E. J., Rizella, M. L., Albrecht, J. E., & Halleran, J. E. (1998) Updating a situation model: A memory-based processing view. *Journal of Experimental Psychology: Learning, Memory, and Cognition, 24,* 1200–1210.

Rapp, D. N., & Gerrig, R. J. (2006) Predilections for narrative outcomes: The impact of story contexts and reader preferences. *Journal of Memory and Language, 54,* 54–67.

Rymer, R. (2012, July) Vanishing voices. *National Geographic.*

Sedivy, J., & Carlson, G. (2011) Sold on language: How advertisers talk to you and what this means about you. Chichester, UK: Wiley-Blackwell.

Song, H., & Fisher, C. (2007) Discourse prominence effects on 2.5-year-old children's interpretation of pronouns. *Lingua, 117,* 1959–1987.

St. George, M., Mannes, S., & Hoffman, J. E. (1994) Global semantic expectancy and language comprehension. *Journal of Cognitive Neuroscience, 6,* 70–83.

Stanton, A. (2012) The clues to a great story. (Talk presented at the TED conference, Long Beach California.) http://www.ted.com/talks/andrew_stanton_the_clues_to_a_great_story.html

Stevenson, R. J., Crawley, R. A., & Kleinman, D. (1994) Thematic roles, focus and the representation of events. *Language and Cognitive Processes, 9,* 519–548.

Trabasso, T., & Suh, S. (1993) Understanding text: Achieving explanatory coherence through on-line inferences and mental operations in working memory. *Discourse Processes, 16,* 3–34.

Van Berkum, J. J. A., Zwitserlood, P., Hagoort, P., & Brown, C. M. (2003) When and how do listeners relate a sentence to the wider discourse? *Cognitive Brain Research, 17,* 701–718.

Zwaan, R. A. (1996) Processing narrative time shifts. *Journal of Experimental Psychology: Learning, Memory, and Cognition, 22,* 1196–1207.

Chapter 11

Arnold, J. E., Bennetto, L., & Diehl, J. J. (2009) Reference production in young speakers with and without autism: Effects of discourse status and processing constraints. *Cognition, 110,* 131–146.

Arnold, J. E., & Griffin, Z. M. (2007) The effect of additional characters on choice of referring expressions: Everyone counts. *Journal of Memory and Language, 56,* 521–536.

Arnold, J. E., Wasow, T., Asudeh, A., & Alrenga, P. (2004) Avoiding attachment ambiguities: The role of constituent ordering. *Journal of Memory and Language, 51,* 55–70.

Barr, D. J. (2008) Pragmatic expectations at linguistic evidence: Listeners anticipate but do not integrate common ground. *Cognition, 109,* 18–40.

Barr, D. J., & Keysar, B. (2002) Anchoring comprehension in linguistic precedents. *Journal of Memory and Language, 46,* 391–418.

Bašnáková, J., Weber, K., Petersson, K. M., van Berkum, J., & Hagoort, P. (2013) Beyond the language given: Neural correlates of inferring speaker meaning. *Cerebral Cortex,* advance online publication. doi: 10.1093/cercor/bht112

Bloom, P. (2002) Mindreading, communication, and the learning of names for things. *Mind and Language, 17,* 37–54.

Bott, L., & Noveck, I. A. (2004) Some utterances are underinformative: The onset and time course of scalar inferences. *Journal of Memory and Language, 51,* 437–457.

Breheny, R., Katsos, N., & Williams, J. (2006) Are generalised scalar implicatures generated by default? An online investigation into the role of context in generating pragmatic inferences. *Cognition, 100,* 434–463.

Brennan, S. E., & Clark, H. H. (1996) Conceptual pacts and lexical choice in conversation. *Journal of Experimental Psychology: Learning, Memory, and Cognition, 6,* 1482–1493.

Brown, P. M., & Dell, G. S. (1987) Adapting production to comprehension: The explicit mention of instruments. *Cognitive Psychology, 19,* 441–472.

Brown-Schmidt, S. (2009) Partner-specific interpretation of maintained referential precedents during interactive dialog. *Journal of Memory and Language, 61,* 171–190.

Bucciarelli, M., Colle, L., & Bara, B. G. (2003) How children comprehend speech acts and communicative gestures. *Journal of Pragmatics, 35,* 207–241.

Chaiken, M., Böhner, J., & Marler, P. (1993) Song acquisition in European

starlings, *Sturnus vulgaris*: a comparison of the songs of live-tutored, tape tutored, untutored, and wild-caught males. *Animal Behaviour, 46,* 1079–1090.

Chevalier, C., Wilson, D., Happe, F., & Noveck, I. (2010) Scalar inferences in Autism Spectrum Disorders. *Journal of Autism and Developmental Disorders, 40,* 1104–1117.

Clark, H. H., & Wilkes-Gibbs, D. (1986) Referring as a collaborative process. *Cognition, 22,* 1–39.

Cohen, P. R. (1985) The pragmatics of referring and the modality of communication. *Computational Linguistics, 10,* 97–146.

Cousillas, H., George, I., Henry, L., Richard, J. P., & Hausberger, M. (2008) Linking social and vocal brains: Could social segregation prevent a proper development of a central auditory area in a female songbird? *PLoS ONE* 3: e2194. doi: 10.1371/journal. pone.0002194

De Neys, W., & Schaeken, W. (2007) When people are more logical under cognitive load: Dual task impact on scalar implicature. *Experimental Psychology, 54,* 128–133.

Deutsch, W., & Pechmann, T. (1982) Social interaction and the development of definite descriptions. *Cognition, 11,* 159–184.

Dumotheil, I., Apperly, I. A., & Blakemore, S. J. (2010) On-line usage of theory of mind continues to develop in late adolescence. *Developmental Science, 13,* 331–338.

Epley, N., Keysar, B., VanBoven, L., & Gilovich, T. (2004) Perspective taking as egocentric anchoring and adjustment. *Journal of Personality and Social Psychology, 87,* 327–339.

Ferreira, V. S., & Dell, G. S. (2000) Effect of ambiguity and lexical availability on syntactic and lexical production. *Cognitive Psychology, 40,* 296–340.

Ferreira, V. S., Slevc, L. R., & Rogers, E. S. (2005) How do speakers avoid ambiguous linguistic expressions? *Cognition, 96,* 263–284.

Gahl, S., Yao, Y., & Johnson, K. (2012) Why reduce? Phonological neighborhood density and phonetic reduction in spontaneous speech. *Journal of Memory and Language, 66,* 789–806.

Garrod, S., & Anderson, A. (1987) Saying what you mean in dialogue: A study in conceptual and semantic co-ordination. *Cognition, 27,* 181–218.

Gergely, G., & Csibra, G. (2005) The social construction of the cultural mind. *Interaction Studies, 6,* 463–481.

Gladwell, M. (2005) *Blink: The power of thinking without thinking.* New York: Little, Brown, & Co.

Grice, H. P. (1975) Logic and conversation. In P. Cole & J. Morgan (Eds.), *Syntax and semantics, Vol. 3* (pp. 41–58). New York: Academic Press.

Grodner, D. J., & Sedivy, J. (2011) The effect of speaker-specific information on pragmatic inferences. In E. Gibson and N. Pearlmutter (Eds.), *The Processing and Acquisition of Reference,* (pp. 239–272). Cambridge, MA: MIT Press.

Gundel, J. K., Hedberg, N., & Zacharski, R. (1993) Cognitive status and the form of referring expressions. *Language, 69,* 274–307.

Hanna, J. E., & Tanenhaus, M. K. (2004) Pragmatic effects on reference resolution in a collaborative task: Evidence from eye movements. *Cognitive Science, 28,* 105–115.

Haywood, S. L., Pickering, M. J., & Branigan, H. P. (2005) Do speakers avoid ambiguity during dialogue? *Psychological Science, 16,* 362–366.

Heller, D., Grodner, D., & Tanenhaus, M. K. (2008) The role of perspective in identifying domains of reference. *Cognition, 108,* 831–836.

Horton, W. S., & Gerrig, R. J. (2005) Conversational common ground and memory processes in language production. *Discourse Processes, 40,* 1–35.

Horton, W. S., & Keysar, B. (1996) When do speakers take into account common ground? *Cognition, 59,* 91–117.

Keysar, B., Barr, D. J., Balin, J. A., & Brauner, J. S. (2000) Taking perspective in conversation: The role of mutual knowledge in comprehension. *Psychological Science, 11,* 32–38.

Koenig, M. A., & Harris, P. L. (2005) Preschoolers mistrust ignorant and inaccurate speakers. *Child Development, 76,* 1261–1277.

Koster-Hale, J., & Saxe, R. (2013) Functional neuroimaging of theory of mind. In S. Baron-Cohen, M. Lombardo, & H. Tager-Flusberg (Eds.), *Understanding other minds* (3rd ed., pp. 132–163). Oxford, UK: Oxford University Press.

Kronmüller, E., & Barr, D. J. (2007) Perspective-free pragmatics: Broken precedents and the recovery-from-preemption hypotheses. *Journal of Memory and Language, 56,* 436–455.

Kuhl, P. K. (2007) Is speech learning "gated" by the social brain? *Developmental Science, 10,* 110–120.

Kuhl, P. K., Tsao, F. M., and Liu, H. M. (2003) Foreign-language experience in infancy: Effects of short-term exposure and social interaction on phonetic learning. *Proceedings of the National Academy of Sciences, 100,* 9096–9101.

Lin, S., Keysar, B., & Epley, N. (2010) Reflexively mindblind: Using theory of mind to interpret behavior requires effortful attention. *Journal of Experimental Social Psychology, 46,* 551–556.

Lockridge, C. B., & Brennan, S. E. (2002) Addressees' needs influence speakers' early syntactic choices. *Psychonomic Bulletin and Review, 9,* 550–557.

McKenna, P., & Tomasina, M. (2008) Schizophrenic speech: Making sense of bathroots and ponds that fall in doorways. Cambridge, UK: Cambridge University Press.

Moll, H., & Tomasello, M. (2007) How 14- and 18-month-olds know what others have experienced. *Developmental Psychology, 43,* 309–317.

Nadig, A. S., & Sedivy, J. (2002) Evidence of perspective-taking constraints in children's on-line reference resolution. *Psychological Science, 13,* 329–336.

Nilsen, E. S., & Fecica, A. M. (2011) A model of communicative perspective-taking for typical and atypical populations of children. *Developmental Review, 31,* 55–78.

Nilsen, E. S., & Graham, S. A. (2009) The relations between children's communicative perspective-taking and executive functioning. *Cognitive Psychology, 58,* 220–249.

Noveck, I. A. (2001) When children are more logical than adults: Investigations of scalar implicature. *Cognition, 78,* 165–188.

Pepperberg, I. M. (1997) Social influences on the acquisition of human-based codes in parrots and nonhuman primates. In C. T. Snowdon & M. Hausberger (Eds.), *Social influences on vocal development* (pp. 157–177). Cambridge, UK: Cambridge University Press.

Piaget, J., & Inhelder, B. (1956) *The child's conception of space.* London: Routledge & Kegan Paul.

Pickering, M. J., & Garrod, S. (2004) Toward a mechanistic psychology of dialogue. *Behavioral and Brain Sciences, 27,* 169–226.

Pijnacker, J., Hagoort, P., Buitelaar, J., Teunisse, J. P., & Geurts, B. (2009) Pragmatic inferences in high-functioning adults with autism and Asperger syndrome. *Journal of Autism and Developmental Disorders, 39,* 607–618.

Poirier, C., Henry, L., Mathelier, M., Lumineau, S., Cousillas, H., & Hausberger, M. (2004) Direct social contacts override auditory information in the song-learning process of starlings (*Sturnus vulgaris*). *Journal of Comparative Psychology, 118,* 179–193.

Proulx, T., & Heine, S. J. (2010) The frog in Kierkegaard's beer: Finding meaning in the threat-compensation literature. *Social and Personality Psychology Compass, 4,* 889–905.

Proulx, T., Heine, S. J., & Vohs, K. D. (2010) When is the unfamiliar the uncanny? Meaning affirmation after exposure to absurdist literature, humor, and art. *Personality and Social Psychology Bulletin, 36,* 817–829.

Pyers, J. E., & Senghas, A. (2009) Language promotes false-belief understanding: Evidence from learners of a new sign language. *Psychological Science, 20,* 805–812.

Sabbagh, M. A., & Baldwin, D. A. (2001) Learning words from knowledgeable versus ignorant speakers: Links between preschoolers' theory of mind and semantic development. *Child Development, 72,* 1054–1070.

Sacks, H., & Schlegoff, E. A. (1979) Two preferences in the organization of reference to persons in conversation and their interaction. In G. Psathas (Ed.), *Everyday language: Studies in ethnomethodology.* New York: Irvington Publishers.

Saxe, R., & Kanwisher, N. (2003) People thinking about thinking people: The role of the temporo-parietal junction in "theory of mind." *NeuroImage, 19,* 1835–1842.

Schick, B., deVillers, P., deVillers, J., & Hoffmeister, R. (2007) Language and theory of mind: A study of deaf children. *Child Development, 78,* 376–396.

Schulze, C., Grassman, S., & Tomasello, M. (2013) 3-year-old children make relevance inferences in indirect verbal communication. *Child Development, 84,* 2079–2093.

Searleman, A., & Carter, H. (1988) The effectiveness of different types of pragmatic implications found in commercials to mislead subjects. *Applied Cognitive Psychology, 2,* 265–272.

Sedivy, J., Tanenhaus, M., Chambers, C., & Carlson, G. (1999) Achieving incremental semantic interpretation through contextual representation. *Cognition, 71,* 109–147.

Sperber, D., & Wilson, D. (2002) Pragmatics, modularity and mindreading. *Mind and Language, 17,* 3–23.

Surian, L., Baron-Cohen, S., & Van der Lely, H. (1996) Are children with autism deaf to Gricean maxims? *Cognitive Neuropsychiatry, 1,* 55–71.

West, M. J., & King, A. P. (1990) Mozart's starling. *American Scientist, 78,* 106–114.

Chapter 12

Adi-Japha, E., Berberich-Artzi, J., & Libnawi, A. (2010) Cognitive flexibility in drawings of bilingual children. *Child Development, 81,* 1356–1366.

Akkermans, D., Harzing, A. W., & van Witteloostuijn, A. (2010) Cultural accommodation and language priming. *Management International Review, 50,* 559–583.

Athanasopoulos, P., Dering, B., Wiggett, A., Kuipers, J. R., & Thierry, G. (2010) Perceptual shift in bilingualism: Brain potentials reveal plasticity in pre-attentive color perception. Cognition, 116, 437–443.

Bassetti, B., & Cook, V. J. (2011) Language and cognition: The second language user. In V. J. Cook & B. Bassetti (Eds.), *Language and bilingual cognition* (pp. 143–190). Hove, UK: Psychology Press.

Berlin, B., & Kay, P. (1969) *Basic color terms: Their universality and evolution.* Berkeley: University of California Press.

Bock, J. K., Loebell, H., & Morey, R. (1992) From conceptual roles to structural relations: Bridging the syntactic cleft. *Psychological Review, 99,* 150–171.

Chen, M. K. (2013) The effect of language on economic behavior: Evidence from savings rates, health behaviors, and retirement assets. *American Economic Review, 103,* 690–731.

Culbertson, J., Smolensky, P., & Legendre, G. (2012) Learning biases predict a word order universal. *Cognition, 122,* 306–329.

Dediu, D. (2011) Are languages really independent from genes? If not, what would a genetic bias affecting language diversity look like? *Human Biology, 83,* 279–296.

Dediu, D., & Ladd., L. R. (2007) Linguistic tone is related to the population frequency of the adaptive haplogroups of two brain size genes, *ASPM* and *Microcephalin*. *Proceedings of the National Academy of Sciences, 104,* 10944–10949.

Deutsch, D., Dooley, K., Henthorn, T., & Head, B. (2009) Absolute pitch among students in an American conservatory: Association with tone language fluency. *Journal of the Acoustical Society of America, 125,* 2398–2403.

Deutsch, D., Henthorn, T., Marvin, E., & Xu, H.-S. (2006) Absolute pitch among Chinese and American conservatory students: Prevalence differences and evidence for a speech-related critical period. *Journal of the Acoustical Society of America, 119,* 719–722.

Deutscher, G. (2010) Through the language glass: Why the world looks different in other languages. New York: Henry Holt and Co.

Donadio, R. (2011, January 22) Surreal: A soap opera starring Berlusconi. *New York Times.*

Dryer, M. S. (2013a) Order of subject, object and verb. In M. S. Dryer & M. Haspelmath (Eds.), The World Atlas of Language Structures Online. Leipzig: Max Planck Institute for Evolutionary Anthropology. Retrieved January 27, 2014, from the WALS database at http://wals.info/chapter/81

Dryer, M. S. (2013b) Prefixing vs. suffixing in inflectional morphology. In M. S. Dryer & M. Haspelmath (Eds.), The World Atlas of Language Structures Online. Leipzig: Max Planck Institute for Evolutionary Anthropology. Retrieved November 25, 2013, from the WALS database at http://wals.info/chapter/26

Dryer, M. S. (2013c) Relationship between the order of object and verb and the order of adposition and noun phrase. In M. S. Dryer & M. Haspelmath (Eds.), The World Atlas of Language Structures Online. Leipzig: Max Planck Institute for Evolutionary Anthropology. Retrieved January 27, 2014, from the WALS database at http://wals.info/chapter/95

Dryer, M. S. (1992) The Greenbergian word order correlations. *Language, 68,* 81–138.

Dunn, M., Greenhill, S. J., Levinson, S. C., & Gray, R. D. (2011) Evolved structure of language shows lineage-specific trends in word-order universals. *Nature, 473,* 79–82.

Fausey, C. M., & Boroditsky, L. (2011) Who dunnit? Cross-linguistic differences in eye-witness memory. *Psychonomic Bulletin and Review, 18,* 150–157.

Fedzechkina, M., Jager, T. F., & Newport, E. L. (2012) Language learners restructure their input to facilitate efficient communication. *Proceedings of the National Academy of Sciences, 109,* 17897–17902.

Fitzsimons, G. M., Chartrand, T. L., & Fitzsimons, G. J. (2008) Automatic effects of brand exposure on motivated behavior: How Apple makes you "think different." *Journal of Consumer Research, 35*, 21–35.

Gennari, S. P., Sloman, S. A., Malt, B. C., & Fitch, W. T. (2002) Motion events in language and cognition. *Cognition, 83*, 49–79.

Gilbert, A. L., Regier, T., Kay, P., & Ivry, R. B. (2008) Support for lateralization of the Whorf effect beyond color discrimination. *Brain and Language, 105*, 91–98.

Gilbert, A. L., Regier, T., Kay, P., & Ivry, R. B. (2006) Whorf hypothesis is supported in the right visual field but not the left. *Proceedings of the National Academy of Sciences, 103*, 489–494.

Gladstone, W. E. (1858) *Studies on Homer and the Homeric Age.* Oxford, UK: Oxford University Press.

Greenberg, A., Bellana, B., & Bialystok, E. (2012) Perspective-taking ability in bilingual children: Extending advantages in executive control to spatial reasoning. *Cognitive Development, 28*, 41–50.

Greenberg, J. H. (1963) Some universals of grammar with particular reference to the order of meaningful elements. In J. H. Greenberg (Ed.), *Universals of human language* (pp. 73–113). Cambridge, MA: MIT Press.

Greene, R. L. (2011) You are what you speak: Grammar grouches, language laws and the politics of identity. New York: Delacorte Press.

Hockett, C. F. (1958) *A Course in Modern Linguistics.* New York: Macmillan.

Hudson Kam, C. L., & Newport, E. L. (2009) Getting it right by getting it wrong: When learners change languages. *Cognitive Psychology, 59*, 30–66.

Hudson Kam, C. L., & Newport, E. L. (2005) Regularizing unpredictable variation: The roles of adult and child learners in language formation and change. *Language Learning and Development, 1*, 151–195.

Hupp, J. M., Sloutsky, V. M., & Culicover, P. W. (2009) Evidence for a domain-general mechanism underlying the suffixation preference in language. *Language and Cognitive Processes, 24*, 876–909.

Kay, A. C., Wheeler, S. C., Bargh, J. A., & Ross, L. (2004) Material priming: The influence of mundane physical objects on situational construal and competitive behavioral choice. *Organizational Behavior and Human Decision Processes, 95*, 83–96.

Kay, P., & Kempton, W. (1984) What is the Sapir-Whorf hypothesis? *American Anthropologist, 86*, 65–79.

Kay, P., & Maffi, L. (2013) Number of basic colour categories. In M. S. Dryer & M. Haspelmath (Eds.), The World Atlas of Language Structures Online. Leipzig: Max Planck Institute for Evolutionary Anthropology. Retrieved November 26, 2013 from the WALS database at http://wals.info/chapter/133

Liberman, M. (2011) Annals of "No Word for X." Language Log. Retrieved November 29, 2013, from http://languagelog.ldc.upenn.edu/nll/?p=2920

MacDonald, M. C. (2013) How language production shapes language form and comprehension. *Frontiers in Psychology, 4*, 1–16.

Maddieson, I. (1984) *Patterns of sounds.* Cambridge, UK: Cambridge University Press.

McWhorter, J. (2011) What language is (and what it isn't and what it could be). New York: Gotham Books.

McWhorter, J. H. (2002) What happened to English? *Diachronica, 19*, 217–272.

McWhorter, J. H. (2001) The world's simplest grammars are creole grammars. *Linguistic Typology, 5*, 125–166.

Miestamo, M. (2009) Implicational hierarchies and grammatical complexity. In G. Sampson, D. Gil, & P. Trudgill (Eds.), *Language complexity as an evolving variable* (Studies in the Evolution of Language 13), (pp. 80–97). Oxford, UK: Oxford University Press.

Munnich, E., Landau, B., & Dosher, B. A. (2001) Spatial language and spatial representation: A cross-linguistic comparison. *Cognition, 81*, 71–207.

Okrand, M. (1992) *The Klingon Dictionary, 2nd Edition.* New York: Pocket Books.

Pagel, M. (2000) The history, rate and pattern of world linguistic evolution. In C. Knight, M. Studdert-Kennedy, & J. Hurford (Eds.), *The evolutionary emergence of language* (pp. 391–416). Cambridge, UK: Cambridge University Press.

Papafragou, A., Hulbert, J., & Trueswell, J. C. (2008) Does language guide event perception? Evidence from eye movements. *Cognition, 108*, 155–184.

Pendry, L., & Carrick, R. (2001) Doing what the mob do: Priming effects on conformity. *European Journal of Social Psychology, 31*, 83–92.

Roberts, S., & Winters, J. (2013) Linguistic diversity and traffic accidents: Lessons from statistical studies of cultural traits. *PLoS ONE 8*: e70902. doi: 10.1371/journal.pone.0070902

Sandler, W., Aronoff, M., Meir, I., & Padden, C. (2011) The gradual emergence of phonological form in a new language. *Natural Language and Linguistic Theory, 29*, 503–543.

Sautet, F. (2006) Is language a determinant of reform success? Retrieved January 26, 2014, from http://austrianeconomists.typepad.com/weblog/2006/12/is_language_a_d.html

Stromswold, K. (2001) The heritability of language: A review and metaanalysis of twin, adoption, and linkage studies. *Language, 77*, 647–723.

Thierry, G., Athanasopoulos, P., Wiggett, A., Dering, B., & Kuipers, J. R. (2009) Unconscious effects of language-specific terminology on preattentive color perception. *Proceedings of the National Academy of Sciences, 106*, 4567–4570.

Thomason, S. G. (2001) *Language contact: An introduction.* Edinburgh, UK: Edinburgh University Press.

Trueswell, J. C., & Papafragou, A. (2010) Perceiving and remembering events cross-linguistically: Evidence from dual-task paradigms. *Journal of Memory and Language, 63*, 64–82.

Twain, M. (1880) The awful German language. In *A tramp abroad.* Hartford, CT: American Publishing Company.

Winawer, J., Witthoft, N., Frank, M. C., Wu, L., Wade, A. R., & Boroditsky, L. (2007) Russian blues reveal effects of language on color discrimination. *Proceedings of the National Academy of Sciences, 104*, 7780–7785.

Photo Credits

Author Index

Subject Index

About the Book

Editor: Sydney Carroll

Project Editor: Carol Wigg

Copy Editor: Lou Doucette

Production Manager: Christopher Small

Book Design and Production: Jefferson Johnson

Illustrations: Elizabeth Morales

Photo Researcher: David McIntyre

Indexer: Sharon Hughes